FREEDOM

FREEDOM

A History

Donald W. Treadgold

NEW YORK UNIVERSITY PRESS

NEW YORK AND LONDON

Library of Congress Cataloging-in-Publication Data
Treadgold, Donald W., 1922–
    Freedom, a history / Donald W. Treadgold.
        p.   cm.
    Includes bibliographical references.
    Includes index.
    ISBN 0-8147-8190-X (alk. paper)   ISBN 0-8147-8191-8
(pbk. : alk. paper)
    1. Democracy—History.   2. Free enterprise—History.   3. Liberty—
History.   4. Pluralism (Social sciences)—History.   I. Title.
JC421.T76   1990
321.8'09—dc20   90-40671
                              CIP

New York University Press books are printed on acid-free paper,
and their binding materials are chosen for strength and durability.

Book design by Ken Venezio

Contents

Acknowledgments

To begin with, my thanks to Morris Leibman and his colleagues of the American Bar Association, who first suggested that I try something on this subject. Next, to the Rockefeller Foundation and the splendid staff, American and Italian, of the Villa Serbelloni at Bellagio, Italy, where I began this work in the fall of 1982 as Scholar in Residence, under the mistaken impression that I could produce it in a few weeks or months. Next, to my son Warren, a professor of Byzantine and Western medieval history at Florida International University, and the following colleagues at the University of Washington, who patiently read individual chapters or sections of chapters and made helpful corrections and suggestions: Dauril Alden (Latin America), A. Gerald Anderson (Scandinavia), Frank Conlon (South Asia), Jack L. Dull (China), Arther Ferrill (the ancient world), Susan Hanley (Japan), and Peter F. Sugar (East Central Europe); and to my wife Alva, who read it all, section by section, in several drafts. Finally, to my valued friend Colin Jones, director of New York University Press, who read the entire manuscript twice and made many excellent editorial suggestions which I acted upon, sometimes reluctantly, having become convinced that he was (almost always) right. All these individuals helped me remove many errors and infelicities. For those that remain, I alone am responsible.

My entrance into the computer age took place during the latter part of the seven years on which I worked (with many distractions) on this volume, a fact that both slowed down and sped up the process of writing. I owe much to Russell Carr, who introduced me to the computer and taught me how to make it do what I wished.

The footnotes contain for the most part either identification of the sources of direct quotations or close paraphrases, or explanation that might be needed by the general reader of matters referred to in the text. A full account of my sources would include virtually everything I have ever read—historical monographs and periodicals, fiction, magazines, newspapers—lectures heard, courses taken, and courses given (for, like every other teacher, I have taught myself much while lecturing), professional and recreational travels, serious as well as casual conversations. I believe it was Strindberg who somewhere penned the line for a character in one of his plays, "I have read your works; I know all your secrets." One's life may find reflection in one's writings. I hope this book is an instance of that proposition.

But the subject is not personal or private; it is a part—not the only, perhaps not the main part, but a vital and fundamental part—of the life of the human race. I would like to see the book judged as such, and not merely as one angle of vision (though of course it is also that) on the story of mankind; not just as historiography, but as history. In the year 1990 it is clear that the question of freedom, however understood, belongs to the present and future as well as the past.

Donald W. Treadgold

FREEDOM

Introduction

What This Book Is About

In 1988 Secretary of State George Shultz wrote, "Not so many years ago, democratic nations were thought to be a dwindling and embattled minority; today the idea of democracy is among the most important political forces of our time."[1] The phenomenon concerned is one for which Shultz's political party and the president whom he served claimed much credit, and no doubt both may justifiably be assigned a share. More significant, however, is surely the apparent reversal of the intellectual and territorial expansion of Marxism, seemingly unstoppable in the 1970s, and its replacement by the spread of the ideas of political democracy, free enterprise, and institutional pluralism into several hitherto inhospitable corners of the globe—above all (but by no means exclusively) into almost all Communist-ruled countries.

In the summer of 1989, Francis Fukuyama, deputy director of the State Department's policy-planning staff, published an article heavily indebted to G. W. F. Hegel in which he announced, with some reservations, the "end of history as such: that is, the end point of mankind's ideological evolution and the universalization of Western liberal democracy as the final form of human government" or, in another passage, "an unabashed victory of economic and political liberalism."[2]

Fukuyama's article provoked widespread discussion; some critics found the article too optimistic. An animated discussion of the sort often indicates that a partial truth has been stated, and so it appears in this instance. Throughout the world much has indeed been gained in respect to political democracy, free

I

enterprise, and institutional pluralism. However, much still seems to be out of reach, and much that has been gained might still be lost again in this or that country.

In this book the term *freedom* is used to refer to the situation of the individual and the body politic in the institutionally pluralistic societies of the past and present. I make an attempt to survey the historical record, from the Sumerians to the present day, of how the current extent of freedom's success (whether or not Shultz or Fukuyama has exaggerated it) came about. At the same time, the record should illuminate the difficulties of creating and preserving a free society and prepare the reader for the possibility of dramatic setbacks—such as the massacre in Tienanmen Square in Beijing on 4 June 1989.

Not many others have made the attempt. One historian who has is Herbert J. Muller, in three sizable volumes. They are very different from this work. In one of them Muller writes, "I make no apologies at all for ignoring most of the political and military history that filled the conventional histories of the past."[3] In another, he confesses, "I do not actually 'cover' modern history, decade by decade, country by country, war by war, et cetera."[4] In respect to those two issues—or are they really only one?—I take the other approach, whether it be regarded as bold or tedious; I examine political (the military only when it affects politics more or less directly) history country by country and sometimes decade by decade. Whether it is "conventional" to do so or whether what I say in substance can be so described I leave to others to judge. My judgments are my own, but if they concur with those of many of my colleagues—and, therefore, would be "conventional" perhaps—I in turn make no apologies. I give less space to social, economic, and cultural matters, not because I regard them as less interesting or important but because political and legal institutions ultimately establish the extent and shape of freedom in any given spot (even if they are regarded as economically or socially determined to some degree), and they are, therefore, my focus.

My claim is that this is the first volume to attempt the history of freedom on a world scale within a single pair of covers. I make no claim to have established the eternal truth of any of the issues I treat and invite others to improve on what I have tried to do.[5] The subject merits further study. As Gertrude Himmelfarb has recently asked, "How can we make sense of political institutions and traditions, when the history of political institutions and traditions is belittled or ignored?" She refers, incidentally, to those for whom "conventional history" is peripheral and can be dispensed with.[6]

I must add that I have tried to make clear the geographical areas in which the events in question took place. For several years the press has been filled with accounts of the hair-raising geographical ignorance of Americans—students among the worst of all. My sympathy goes to those who try to learn or teach with the aim of reducing that ignorance; political designations of particular areas are not only multitudinous but also keep changing. The historian of freedom must do his best to follow the changes. Freedom does not float in the clouds above the earth, but it develops within specific political units even if their territorial limits change.

Though I have tried to shape my analysis from a worldwide perspective, I have left out some areas important for the history of free institutions: mainly they are Canada, Australia, New Zealand, and (the white populations of) South Africa. Also omitted simply because one must stop somewhere are a few smaller countries (Belize, Guyana, Suriname) of the mainland Americas and most of the West Indies; the newly independent island groups of the Pacific and Indian oceans; the African countries that, beginning with the independence of Ghana in 1957, attempted to establish democratic systems and, with interesting exceptions such as Botswana and (for a time) Gambia, seem thus far mostly and sadly to have failed.

As for sources, they include the reading of a lifetime, plus a good deal of travel and prolonged stays in Europe and Asia. I have used some of the best recent scholarly literature, and for purposes of making sure I might be as up-to-date as possible regarding current scholarly consensus, I have found several works of synthesis and reference works to be invaluable. I can only hope that my reviewers will forgo reminding us all that no one can know all the world well enough to write a book of this sort with unvaryingly magisterial authority.

I have not sought to be original, revisionist, or to overthrow established opinion; on the contrary, I have attempted to write a history that most people can accept as recounting more or less the way things were. If the historians who scent in that aim a lamentable echo of Leopold von Ranke were just to set aside that discovery and concentrate on whether they find my account plausible in general or in particular, I should be fortunate indeed. I respect the study of historiography and believe we can learn much from it about how men and women think about the past and how they are influenced by the present in the formulation of their thoughts. But this book is not an essay in historiography but in history.

In our day we hear a good deal of relativists who brush aside the values of the West as ethnocentric and parochial and exalt other values or seek to brand Western values as hypocrisy or sham. Part of the thrust of such relativist argument—to the extent that it rises above the sheer yahooism that in the year of our Lord 1988 successfully demanded the radical revision of the course on Western culture in one of our greatest universities[7]—is driven by revulsion from self-satisfied Western attitudes of an earlier time, exemplified by the Victorian Englishman's contemplation, orally or in print, of a world outside that was assumed to be inferior to his own, past and present.

Such attitudes were first attacked by historians of the West who criticized their colleagues with the taunt "the Whig interpretation of history." Herbert Butterfield defined this as the tendency "to write on the side of Protestants and Whigs, to praise revolutions provided they have been successful, to emphasize certain principles of progress in the past and to produce a story which is the ratification if not the glorification of the present." Or, more succinctly, it is the view of the historian who is "Protestant, progressive, and whig, and the very model of the 19th century gentleman" (with no apologies to Gilbert and Sullivan).[8] Never mind that it was the great Catholic writer Lord Acton who proved to be for Butterfield the point where the Whig historian "reached his highest consciousness,"[9] and one may well overlook other possible problems with *The Whig Interpretation of History*. Its subject matter is, in fact, not Whigs and Tories (but, especially, Luther and the Roman Catholic church), so one finishes it uncertain about exactly what Butterfield thought.

However, in any case it may be argued that the Whigs of seventeenth-century England, with all their human weaknesses, did in fact take decisive steps toward the liberty that England finally secured and many other countries imitated—or, denying that they were inspired by any foreign model, duplicated. But no one today, surely, would contend that only Protestants and Whigs, or all such persons, were the leaders in the establishment of free societies, or that all successful revolutions are praiseworthy, or that all the misdeeds of the past are justified by a blameless present. I endeavor, in this volume, to avoid a "Whig" or any other interpretation that would find a single cause or an always conjoined group of causes that would account for the growth of freedom in all times and places. I am distrustful of attempts to establish such causation, whether it be in race, climate, the natural environment, or something else.

I do not seek to redefine freedom, or to discover freedom where no one else has, or to argue that freedom is the proud possession of one country or tradition or people or a happy few such places, ideas, or groups. Rather, my purpose is to show how certain elements of free society made their appearance in an amazing variety of places—from ancient Sumeria and China to medieval Japan to modern Czechoslovakia and recent Costa Rica—outside of the traditions of Western Europe and North America that are familiar to many of us. Sometimes those elements developed and flourished; sometimes they weakened and disappeared. But they may reappear in any part of the world. Recently, thousands have demonstrated for democracy—unsuccessfully in Burma, with amazing success in Poland, one million in one place at one time (though the upshot was tragic failure) in China. In another month, year, or century the place names may change, but recent events support the view that freedom is to be found imbedded as an aspiration in mankind itself.[10]

Freedom, which has matured in our time to embrace democracy and human rights, has in the past embodied various ingredients and may be defined differently in different periods. Muller has called Pericles's Funeral Oration, as reported by Thucydides, "the first manifesto of democracy" and cites Pericles's contention that "ordinary citizens, though occupied with the pursuits of industry, are still fair judges of public matters."[11] Pericles's view of the sound political sense of the citizen remains an integral part of the intellectual defense of democracy. Speaking of the eighteenth century, James Michener asserts, "Poland loved freedom; it was a restricted freedom, to be sure, and it applied only to the very rich, but nevertheless it was freedom."[12] He is here speaking mainly of individual liberties among the aristocracy of a preindustrial age.

George Shultz, speaking of 1988, writes: "Elites in the East and West recognize that advanced economic power comes from a high level of education, an openness to the world, a rational distribution of decision-making power, emphasis on individual initiative, decentralization of authority, greater freedom of information and association, and the right of the people to have a say in their own affairs and destiny."[13]

Shultz has in mind the world of the greater and lesser powers, whose military strength and political weight in international affairs rest on the size and condition of their gross national product, rate of growth, distribution of income, and the other major constituents of their economies. He argues, however, that that basic economic strength derives from making information and education available to the broadest possible populace and from securing their maximum influence on the polity of their country and their individual rights. Computers, technological innovation, and organizational mechanisms figure in Shultz's conception as they could not in that of Pericles, but the human beings concerned may still be at root the same.

Elsewhere I have contended that the major features of the pattern whose history I have tried to summarize in this book are (I have added one phrase only) (1) political pluralism: the sharing of authority by princes, in law and fact, with central and local governmental institutions, developing into constitutional government and ultimately democracy; (2) social pluralism: the existence of social classes whose property and rights were partly secured by contractual and other legal bases independent of princes; (3) strong property: possession of which is secured by contract or clear title; (4) the rule of law; (5) application of the religious doctrine of the absolute value of the individual, unevenly and intermittently but nevertheless persistently, to secular institutions.[14]

In this book I have concentrated on the first four elements; it has seemed to me that the fifth would take the reader too far afield and might best be discussed in some other context. Sometimes a plurality of political units or institutions appears to have been crucial (in Sumeria or the Holy Roman Empire), sometimes a nascent plurality of social classes (in medieval western Europe), sometimes the beginnings of genuine legal systems (in Nationalist China on the mainland). At every stage, some radicals have been heard to denounce what has been obtained because it is not everything, because the nation (whichever it is) has been asked to accept part instead of the whole of democracy. Other radicals, however, as well as liberals, may instead have tried to work with the new reforms (whatever they are), hoping to build on them toward the longer-range, broader goal. Sometimes, in their determination to do things perfectly, those who wished to defend democracy have ended by being its gravediggers, as in Russia in 1917.

The questions may be raised, What is the role of consciousness and what is the role of spontaneity in the process of the emergence of a free society? That is to say, what role may human will play? How successful can the intention to create democracy be? One of the lessons a book of this sort might teach is that there are limitations on what good intentions can do in this regard; the law of unintended consequences operates here as elsewhere.

Democracy cannot be enacted at a given moment by decree from above or mass action from below. It has prerequisites; moreover, none of them can be brought into being overnight. Without a history that includes a degree of political and social pluralism, an approach to strong property, and a rule of law, democracy will be feeble and tenuous. It will not do to expect the American government (or any other agency, Western or indigenous) to create democracy in Third World country X at 8:00 A.M. next Wednesday and then reproach it for failing to do so. On the other hand, it is unproven that because country X has never enjoyed democracy, it never can. The record of how freedom and democracy have come to parts of the world but did not succeed in coming or have been damaged or destroyed in other parts may well be of use in deciding when patience is essential and when it is simply an aid and a justification for oppression and tyranny.

How the Present Situation Came About

Summing up the achievement of the medieval West, Lord Acton wrote:

The issue of ancient politics was an absolute state planted on slavery. The political produce of the Middle Ages was a system of states in which authority was restricted by the representation of powerful classes, by privileged associations, and by the acknowledgment of duties superior to those which are imposed by man.[15]

The ancient world—that is, the Mediterranean basin—gave rise to several free institutions, beginning with Sumeria and the Near Eastern empires, as well as ideas about freedom (both "Jewish," or existential, and "Greek," or institutional, freedom), but both institutions and ideas were swallowed up in the magnificent, creative, and yet often cruel Roman Empire. The Western Middle Ages rescued or revived some remnants of the ancient creations, but the period produced a tripartite conjunction of elements that represents as close to creation *ex nihilo* as human history affords. So Acton implies, and he is right. (The Japanese creation of a genuinely pluralistic society in medieval times must be reckoned as a close competitor.)

Of course, modern times did not receive these legacies smoothly or preserve them tranquilly. The Renaissance and Reformation did not start by strengthening representative government or liberty, not even freedom of conscience. The strength of the Western church, which had done much to limit the power of the medieval states, declined markedly. In the Protestant states, Lutheran and Anglican princes seized control of the church directly; in states that remained Catholic, rulers increased their influence on ecclesiastical affairs, rejecting papal dictates, or, in the case of France, ignoring the decrees of the Council of Trent (the chief Roman Catholic answer to the Protestant Reformation).

But for the time being the most noticeable phenomenon was the way in which politics became a vehicle for religious fanaticism. High Catholic clergy, who had served their monarchs unobtrusively in earlier times, became the chief ministers of the newly powerful states—for example, Cardinals Richelieu and Mazarin. Protestant divines seemed to waffle: Calvin began by advocating abolition of popular assemblies in favor of an aristocracy of the elect, but French Calvinists responded to the Catholic monarchy's attempt to kill them all in the Massacre of St. Bartholomew by reviving the medieval doctrine of resistance to tyrants. The Dutch Calvinists deposed the Spanish Catholic king. The Scottish Calvinist John Knox advocated killing all Catholics in his country, though he was unable to do so. But the religious zealots could now operate only through their states not their churches.

A few writers still tried to think in the terms affecting all mankind (rather than particular sects), which were those of Thomas Aquinas and other medieval thinkers—for example, Richard Hooker in England and Hugo Grotius on the continent. They discussed the political verities that underlay all states and social forces and the contracts, explicit or implied, that bound society together; and Grotius, in extending such reasoning into the new "international" area that followed the Peace of Westphalia, gave us the beginnings of modern international law.

The new strength of monarchy led to an equally new political doctrine: the divine right of kings. It could draw on some New Testament support, and even the Jewish philosopher Spinoza believed that the state should control religion. But along with that doctrine its polar opposite made its appearance: the old right of resistance broadened into the right of revolution. The Dutch waged war for long years, and their final victory over their Spanish masters might be seen as a revolution. The English acted on a right of revolution, killed a king, and set up a republic—though the short-lived experiment was not adjudged successful. In the eighteenth century, control of the former English, now British (after the union with Scotland), state passed into the hands of Parliament, controlled by the landowning gentry, to which Locke's association of liberty with property seemed a secure foundation for all politics.

But the same Locke defended a right of resistance, and it was used by the American colonists to justify a finally successful rebellion, followed by the establishment of a republic. In supporting the Americans' actions, Edmund Burke declared that "if any public measure is proved mischievously to affect [the natural rights of mankind], the objection ought to be fatal to that measure, even if no charter [written law] at all could be set up against it." Thus did triumph doctrines of limited government and natural rights, rooted in medieval political teachings, and "the divine right of kings" (or parliaments) of early modern times fail.

Its failure on the European continent was accomplished, or cemented, by the French Revolution. Acting on American notions of liberty, the revolutionaries added equality, pursued by Marat on the basis of the ideas of Rousseau. "Fraternity" (a secularized version of the Christian "brotherhood of man") did less well; the radicals' zeal to kill aristocrats led to many deaths—the Terror finally claimed many more victims among the lower classes than among the highest. But equality did better; French success in breaking down legal barriers among classes—so that every Frenchman might with some justification bear the title *citoyen*—was exported eastward, partly through the tramp of French revolutionary armies and partly through eager emulation by other European peoples.

There resulted a more consistent pursuit of justice for persons of all classes and backgrounds. In the nineteenth and early twentieth centuries, English common law and the French Napoleonic codes spread into many corners of the world: in 1864 even Russia obtained a new legal system based on the goal of equal justice for all, including the newly emancipated serfs.

Equality had important political consequences. Suffrage was gradually broadened, property and other qualifications falling away bit by bit, until universal manhood suffrage was attained in many European countries as it had previously existed in many of the United States. Woman suffrage followed.

The exceptions that remained came under increasing criticism. It was agreed by all political leaders that the first and fundamental step for Russia, after the overthrow of the tsar in March 1917, was to hold elections on the basis of universal, equal, secret, and direct suffrage—the "four-tailed" formula, sacrosanct among the revolutionaries and liberals, the gift of centuries' political development in the West to the infant democracy of the Russian future. (When the elections were finally held, of course, the Bolsheviks then in power set the verdict aside.)

Liberty—"civil liberties" was the new term—of thought and expression was secured more slowly and unevenly. The basic documents existed: the English and then American Bill of Rights and the French Declaration of the Rights of Man. Once again the pursuit was launched of loopholes and shadows, and in the twentieth century all sorts of guaranteed rights were discovered by the Supreme Court of the United States to have lain unsuspected all along in the Constitution of 1787.

During the nineteenth century—or, to be precise, the hundred-year peace of 1815–1914[16]—the European countries gradually built the foundations of constitutional democracy. There were attempts to "cross the institutional divide" the wrong way, to force countries from the path of pluralism to monistic autocracy or totalitarianism (in Germany, in particular, and to a lesser degree in Italy and certain eastern European countries where democracy had never been firmly established). The boundless damage Hitler and Mussolini did to their countries, the Continent, and the world needs no recounting here. The noteworthy fact, from the standpoint of our story, is that in Germany and Italy democracy was so swiftly and successfully restored, more solidly than it had ever been, on the basis of historical experience and ideological assumptions that had been cast aside but not destroyed during the Nazi and Fascist years.

In the later twentieth century, free and pluralistic societies had come to exist in all Europe west and south of the Communist countries as well as in the former colonies or dominions of Great Britain where Anglo-Saxon majorities existed—in the United States and Canada, in Australia and New Zealand, and in South Africa, where English and Afrikaans-speaking whites together make up a small minority (a hybrid polity existed where democracy and liberty were enjoyed but by whites only), and in Japan.

There were some interesting marginal cases of the attempt to establish democracy. In India and Turkey, possibly Thailand, there was evidence that democracy might be putting down roots in mainland Asia. In Latin America only a couple of dictators remained, though countries where democratic government could be said to have been fully institutionalized were still difficult to find.

As a slogan, "civil liberties" has generally given way to "human rights." The latter has become the touchstone of public discussion, as well as intragovernmental debate in many a Western capital city, about how much to approve of the current situation in other countries. In the last years of the twentieth century, the focus of attention for men of good will, or at any rate internationally minded liberals, seems to have become the individual, not social or political systems. How badly the police behave (to be sure, often very badly) in a given country is apt to be the center of discussion instead of whether law or property rights or freedom of speech and press are institutionalized or have any prospect of becoming such. Part of the reason is doubtless the view of an increasing number of political scientists and journalists that all social and political systems, if not essentially the same, still are not fundamentally different; therefore, it remains only to try to assure the individual decent treatment everywhere.

Nevertheless, it was a remarkable phenomenon of the early 1990s to see an unmistakable, worldwide trend toward democracy—even if in many cases the direction was clear, the goal was still distant or elusive. Past history should inculcate a healthy skepticism concerning whether democracy is about to be attained everywhere in the world, as well as a preparedness for the possibility that many countries apparently close to the "institutional divide" are going to slip back rather than cross it soon. Nevertheless, the past twenty-six hundred years, or even five thousand, yield the reassuring message that during that long period freedom has improved its extent significantly, with respect both to geographical breadth and institutional depth.

The whole story, with its fits and starts and triumphs and tragedies, deserves the thoughtful reflection of everyone who, in the wish to establish and protect freedom, would avoid needless disappointment and despair and desires to act intelligently to attain the attainable. But even for the quietist, the person who has no faith in human action to improve man's lot, the story is worth pondering, for along with failure and misery it holds much that is noble and uplifting, tells of much gain for humanity through patient suffering and self-sacrifice, and catches a vision of liberty for all in the present and possible future that was inconceivable at the dawn of history.

CHAPTER I

The Ancestry of Freedom in the Mediterranean: The Jews

The earliest recorded account of an exercise of human freedom to which more than casual significance is attached may be the story of Adam as given in Genesis. Adam must have had the capacity to obey or disobey God's injunction not to eat the fruit of the tree, or his disobedience was an act without meaning. In eating it, Adam is depicted as having accomplished the Fall of Man or, more broadly interpreted, as having affected the predisposition of all subsequent members of the human race to err, to disobey, to separate themselves from the divine. Separation of oneself from God is a standard Christian definition of "sin."

Adam's act symbolically bequeathed to mankind an inheritance tending to error and misbehavior, or sin, but it did not strip man of his freedom. Moses tells the Jews, "Circumcise therefore the foreskin of your heart, and be no more stiffnecked" (Dt. 10:16)—a quality he has forcefully attributed to them. When he is close to the point of summing up the law, he declares, "See, I have set before thee this day life and good, and death and evil" (Dt. 30:15). In effect Moses is saying, now choose, for you are free to do so, but choose rightly. Indeed, law in any society has no meaning if the persons to whom it is intended to apply lack the capacity to obey it—or disobey.

Among the ancient Hebrews there was no such thing as civic equality, nor was there clear social stratification. The Greeks had both. But the Jews also had the good fortune to lack, for most of their history, something else: the governmental structures of the great Near Eastern empires in the midst of which Israel was situated. As these states rose and fell, more than once subjugating the small and weak Jewish people, it was tempting to try to imitate them. The kingdoms established under David and his successors could be independent only when the empires of Egypt and Mesopotamia suffered from periods of weakness. The Hebrew kings borrowed certain devices of their statecraft. Nevertheless, their religion did much to restrain them from institutionalizing and regularizing such devices as compulsory labor or the census.

The Old Testament chronicles much misery and oppression. There are moments of another sort, chief among them the period of the united kingdom under David and Solomon. Long subject to others, the Jews achieved their own independent state—indeed an empire, in the sense of including other peoples among those ruled—under a monarch of their own ethnic stock. For a thousand years they had lived as subjects or tributaries of oriental empires, and as far as they knew there existed nothing else in the way of political systems to choose from than Near Eastern monarchy. The reigns of David and Solomon were the apogee of success for the ancient Hebrews, the moment of brightest glory. But viewed from the standpoint of the history of freedom, the two reigns may be interpreted as Jewish contributions to the heritage of free societies precisely because they fell short of duplicating the political systems of the region; because even in its closest approximation of the despotism of its neighboring states, Israel produced monarchs whose power was incomplete, imperfect, and transitory.

Mesopotamia: Part One

Those circumstances can be fully understood only by contemplating the previous two or three millennia in the Near East. It is there, and specifically in Mesopotamia, "the land between the rivers," that civilization seems first to have appeared and history to have begun. By 3500 B.C. the Sumerians were in the area, and it is they who have left the oldest texts that survive. We know of some form of political organization among them from early in the third millennium B.C. — around 2850—by which time a network of city-states had come into existence. The names are known of about a dozen; most were quite small. In one, Lagash, the king, Uru'inimgina (earlier read as "Urukagina"), "undertook to reform the official corruption of his day and to check the oppression of the poor, thus reestablishing the "righteous laws of Nin-girsu," which had been violated by evildoers."[1] The time was the twenty-fourth century B.C.

The Sumerians were evidently conquered around 2360 B.C. by the Akkadians. They borrowed much of Sumerian culture and wrote their own Semitic language, quite different from Sumerian, in the cuneiform syllabic script the latter had developed. Though Akkadians were in the region a good deal earlier, it was then that Sargon of Akkad through conquest founded the "first true empire in world history."[2] Barbarians, known as Gutians, from the Zagros Mountains overthrew the Akkadian empire around 2180 B.C. There ensued something of a Sumerian renaissance. Part of the evidence of such a thing are lengthy inscriptions that survive of the *ensi* (god's steward), or prince of Lagash, Gudea. A sculpted representation of him, now in the British Museum, may be the oldest artistic depiction of a particular person known to us by name. When the Tigris, which the god Nin-girsu controlled, failed to rise as usual and flood the fields in the needed manner, Gudea went to the god's temple and there experienced a vision in which he understood that he must rebuild another temple of Nin-girsu—and did so.

The discharge of one's duty to family, ruler, and gods was the prime virtue of ancient Mesopotamia.[3] Our information is fragmentary, but the evidence of the existence of two such attractive figures as Uru'inimgina and Gudea within a period of three or four such remote centuries is arresting. From the earliest phase of development of the Sumerian city-states comes documentary material about a conflict between the kings Gilgamesh of Erech and Agga of Kish, which has been interpreted as showing that powerful assemblies existed then—indeed, a kind of "primitive democracy."[4] Fascinating political potentialities may well be discerned in the Mesopotamian beginnings; but whatever they were, they were not realized.

Sumerian culture survived rather better than Sumer's rough approximation of political pluralism. As late as approximately 2050 B.C., a certain Ur-nammu sponsored and encouraged much construction as well as literary activity, and he was author of the first known law code. George E. Mendenhall gives us a list of seven ancient codes of which Israel's at the time of the Exodus is the last; the previous six are all Mesopotamian. The famed Code of Hammurabi is only fourth on the list.[5] At least in the ancient world, codes are best understood as putting in writing principles generally followed by judges of the time. In several cases, codes seem to have been drawn up when significant changes in government had taken place, possibly with minor innovations or alterations reflecting the will of the new rulers.

To possess a code is not necessarily to possess law; the absence of a code is not necessarily the absence of law. And yet it is true that Mesopotamia seems to have been preoccupied with law in human affairs and order in the universe. In contrast, ancient Egypt was not. Not a single law code has ever been found by Egyptologists, and the urge to arrange even the most important things in order was so far absent that it appears impossible to place Egyptian deities in some coherent hierarchy or set of relationships.

Within a couple of centuries of the cultural flowering of the Third Dynasty of Ur (ca. 2050 B.C.), Sumerian ceased to be a spoken language and was replaced by Akkadian as the vernacular, although for several hundred years longer it continued as a language of liturgy and learning, like Latin in the medieval and early modern West. Politically, a profound change occurred. Nomadic Western Semites, called Amorites (the Babylonian name for Westerners), overwhelmed Ur, which had come to rule most of Mesopotamia, and a series of Semitic rival states appeared: Assyria (from the city of Ashur) and Mari, which were Akkadian and Amorite respectively, in the north and three Amorite principalities in the south, chief of which was Babylon.

Babylon emerged as victor under Hammurabi (d. 1686 B.C.). He crushed Ashur and Mari, drove out the ruler of another neighboring state, and presided over an impressive cultural florescence. Babylonians wrote epic poems, dictionaries, grammatical texts, and mathematical and astronomical treatises and composed the famed law code. Much of this owed its substance to Sumerian antecedents. In some respects, in fact, Sumerian culture did not die but remains with us still—the sexagesimal method, for example, of measuring the minutes of an hour, the seconds of a minute, the degrees of a circle, and so forth.

Obviously, the Sumerians had many merits and achievements to their credit. At the same time, there appeared among them a type of centralized state that was something new in human history. (More or less simultaneously a similar system emerged in other regions, apparently in a manner owing nothing to Mesopotamian example or influence.) By the time of the Third Dynasty of Ur, there were some forty provinces of the empire, each ruled by an *ensi*. That term no longer meant an independent prince; it now denoted an official appointed by the king. It seems that only occasionally could the office be transmitted from father or uncle to son or nephew. The *ensi* collected annual tribute. There was much temple land, and there existed private property of a sort (that is, not belonging to king, *ensi*, or temple). We do not know the details, or even the main features of the economic and social organization, though scholarly work under way on as yet unanalyzed documents may substantially increase what is known.

Scholars continue, however, to assume that in Ur III there was absolute rule by a monarch over a strongly centralized state, exercised through an impressively competent bureaucracy skilled in record keeping. Part of the prerequisites for the development of such a group lay in Mesopotamian mathematical achievements, but especially basic was

the idea of using soft clay not only for bricks and jars and for the jar stoppers on which a seal could be impressed as a mark of ownership but also as the vehicle for impressed signs to which established meanings were assigned—an intellectual achievement that amounted to nothing less than the invention of writing.[6]

Unfortunately, writing could be put to negative as well as positive uses, employed to distort the past as well as to record it truthfully. One of the earliest examples of that fact known to man is the so-called Sumerian king list, an account composed in the Old Babylonian period, following the one we have just been examining. It maintains the fiction that there can be only one king and one capital city in Mesopotamia at any one time. Therefore, dynasties now known to have been contemporary with one another appear in a single line of succession. Of subtler significance may be the fact that any reference is omitted to such relatively attractive elements of Sumerian history as Uru'inimgina/Urukagina (and his whole dynasty, the First Dynasty of Lagash) and the cultural flowering of ca. 3000 B.C. The motives of the compilers cannot be ascertained. In view of what happened later, however, the importance of replacing a multiplicity of states by a single one is clear. It was doubtless attractive to project the current centralization back into the past as far as possible.

How could a centralized state arise in Mesopotamia, a phenomenon unknown to mankind in the thousands of years preceding? One crucial point was that in the north agriculture based on rainfall was possible and reliable; but in the south, below a point near Samarra, only artificial irrigation could produce crops. Excavations in the village of Tall Sawwan, dating from the sixth millennium B.C., give us an indication of approximately when the penetration of irrigation agriculture into the rich lands of the south took place. The first irrigation may have been only the diversion of a bit of water from the great rivers, the Tigris and Euphrates, and their tributaries; then came possibly the collecting of flood waters in basins; finally, a system was constructed of dams, canals, dikes, and other large-scale works.

The energies and resources of more than a rich man or family—ultimately those of a great state—were needed to finance and build on such a scale. The collection of taxes, the raising of armies, and the staffing of a bureaucracy went together. Once the institutions concerned were in place, a state was capable of other things as well. In Mesopotamia, they included building a great mud-brick wall right across the country—a deed of King Shu-Sin, third successor of Ur-Nammu of Ur III, with the purpose of keeping out the nomadic tribe known as the Tidnum. In Egypt, gigantic monuments were constructed that were of no use at all to the living, though putatively they gave the dead good service.

Egypt: Part One

For Egypt, water was visibly the basis of civilized life, in that human habitation snaked narrowly along the course of the Nile while east and west of that strip uninhabitable desert stretched to the horizon. As Herodotus said, Egypt was the "gift of the Nile."

On the regular behavior of the Nile rested the prosperity, the very continuity, of the land. The three seasons of the Egyptian year were even named after the land conditions produced by the river; *akhet,* the "inundation"; *peret,* the season when the land emerged from the flood; and *shomu,* the time when water was short. When the Nile behaved as expected, which most commonly was the case, life went on as normal; when the flood failed or was excessive, disaster followed.[7]

Around 3100 B.C. it seems that two predynastic kingdoms, in Upper and Lower Egypt respectively, were united under a king known as Menes (the same as Narmer?), who established his capital near the border of the two states in a city later called Memphis. In the First Dynasty a system of writing, hieroglyphics, already existed, as did a polity in which a king ruled supreme, assisted by an extensive and efficient bureaucracy. By the time of the Third Dynasty, the Egyptian state had acquired the capacity to construct large-scale public works, starting with the Step Pyramid of Djoser (Zoser), which was planned as the king's monument and tomb. With Snefru of the Fourth Dynasty, who acceded about 2613 B.C., came the building of the first true pyramids. And under his successor, Khufu, the Great Pyramid of Giza crowned the engineering efforts made hitherto. The apogee of centralization seems also to have been reached. The king, or pharaoh, was regarded as the living god, Horus. He was able to mobilize and put to work the total resources of Egypt.

Scholars have come to believe that it was not slaves, as previously thought, who built the pyramids; it was the ordinary peasants of Egypt being employed in the time of inundation when they could not work the fields and when the great stone blocks, cut earlier by modest-sized crews, could be moved by water over the flooded land. The Great Pyramid nevertheless staggers the imagination with its 2,300,000 blocks of an average weight of two and one-half tons, and men who cut and carried stone in such quantity can scarcely be thought of as volunteers. Forced labor produced many of the world's most famous monuments.

In the Fifth Dynasty, a certain limited amount of decentralization occurred. Provincial officials secured some degree of independence from the capital, and they either were granted or successfully asserted new prerogatives and personal prominence. By the Sixth Dynasty, around 2300 B.C., the king's chief assistant, or *vizier,* had acquired considerable power; and the provincial officials, or *nomarchs* (from *nomes,* the units they administered), seemed close to warranting the name of nobles. There followed a period of turmoil and fragmentation. The nomes of Heracleopolis and Thebes vied for power. In about 2040 B.C., Mentuhotep II of Thebes reunited the country and founded what later Egyptians called the Middle Kingdom. A vizier and governor, overthrowing his king, emerged to found the Twelfth Dynasty as Amenemhet I. He built a new capital near

Memphis called Itj-towy; his successors were able to reclaim much land in the Fayyum depression by careful management of irrigation.

Amenemhet III, who ruled for forty-five peaceful and prosperous years, built his pyramid and a great, puzzling structure known as the Labyrinth in the newly reclaimed region. His father, Sesostris III, who acceded in about 1878 B.C., had carried out a sweeping and basic change: he had smashed, suddenly and in ways the historical record conceals from us, the great provincial houses and reorganized a bureaucratic regime based at Itj-towy. In the reign of the son, political stability was matched by a great cultural flowering: sculpture that is characterized by greater humanity than before, many of the classics of Egyptian literature, and a broadening of the scope of the religious cult of Osiris to include hope of salvation for all.

But the moment did not last; it never does. After the "golden age" under Sesostris III and Amenemhet III, dissolution overtook the Middle Kingdom— probably not suddenly by conquest but rather by gradual infiltration of Asiatic tribes, called Hyksos by the later Egyptian historian Manetho. Memphis was captured by their leader Salitis (who may have been known also as Mayebre Sheshi) around 1670 B.C.; he then assumed the role and trappings of an Egyptian king. The Hyksos (the name is probably from *heqau khasut,* Egyptian for "princes of foreign uplands") established a government that was not oppressive; however, like most foreign rulers, over sufficient time they came to be hated by the indigenous inhabitants. Again Thebans led the way for Egypt; their king, Ahmose, restored unity in the New Kingdom (the Eighteenth Dynasty) in 1570 B.C.

In king lists from Karnak of the Eighteenth Dynasty and from Abydos and Saqqarah of the Nineteenth Dynasty, we find history tampered with again. The names of kings thought worthy of honor are there; others are not. "Many modest and certain unpopular rulers" are omitted entirely.[8] But in earliest Egypt, as in earliest Mesopotamia, the first fifteen centuries, more or less, were quite enough to produce a phenomenon that would be repeated over and over in many parts of the world: the centralized despotism, once established, might be threatened by geographical and social fragmentation, up to the point of being undermined or apparently destroyed; but it proved capable of reconstituting itself, regaining the wayward provinces, and crushing the assertive officials or nobles. The names of some kings were suppressed, but no names were invented; and the most powerful monarchs were real enough.

Such reconstitution of the despotism also occurred in Mesopotamia after a seeming catastrophe. The Old Babylonian Empire, following the reign of Hammurabi, declined rapidly. Less than two centuries after Hammurabi's death,

Babylon had suffered invasion from the Hittites, possibly an Armenoid people coming from the west and apparently possessing a feudal state in which nobles crowned the king at first, though the monarchy later became hereditary.[9] Then, shortly after 1600 B.C., Babylonia fell under the rule of the Kassites.

Thus in the seventeenth century B.C., both Egypt and Mesopotamia succumbed to a foreign invader, but in both a subsequent revival produced centuries more of economic prosperity and military triumph.

Mesopotamia: Part Two

The Kassites were barbarians indeed, who left not a single document of inscription in their own language, though a few Kassite words have been located in Babylonian documents. But in the roughly four centuries in which they ruled Babylonia, the Kassites seem to have strongly influenced the emergence of something like a feudal system. The Kassite kings made grants, sometimes very large ones, to Kassite nobles—who were few and were rapidly Babylonized, so that no sharp ethnic lines can be easily drawn. In the words of one authority, many such grants were made to "deserving officers and civil servants"—that is to say, it was a question of turning officials into landlords.[10] (An issue we will encounter again.)

Shortly after 1500 B.C. there arose to the north, around the sources of the Khabur River, what von Soden calls simply a "feudal state," the kingdom of the Mitanni.[11] It seems that the warrior-nobility, of Indo-Iranian stock, were responsible for introducing the two-wheeled and horse-drawn war chariot into the Near East. They received their lands as inalienable fiefs; the landed properties could, therefore, not be sold in law. In fact, however, the would-be seller could "adopt" the would-be buyer in return for a certain sum. The interesting potentialities of Mitanni were not realized; the kingdom was destroyed by the Assyrians soon after 1300 B.C.

Assyria may have existed as a state several centuries earlier, but it was founded as an empire in approximately 1350 B.C. by Ashur-uballit I, who threw off dependence on Mitanni and adopted a name derived from the old capital, Ashur, since the previous name was despised by the more cultivated Babylonians. Generally, the Assyrians were weak on law and original cultural achievement (except for their impressive sculpture) but were strong on military arts and violence. The kings learned to use war-chariot troops, drawn from the landed nobles, with great effectiveness; horses were bred with great care to draw the chariots.

For a time Babylonia, reviving, surpassed Assyria in power. Such was the case under Nebuchadrezzar I (d. ca. 1103), under whom literary culture flourished and much fine poetry was composed, of which the mature version of the Gilgamesh epic, called the *Twelve-Tablet* poem, was the leading but by no means the only example. A generation later the Assyrians rallied to raid the city of Babylon, but for a considerable time they seem to have refrained from trying to destroy Babylonia out of religious motives, since the two empires shared many gods. Ashurnasirpal II and his son, Shalmaneser III, directed their conquering armies westward instead, toward Syria. It was Shalmaneser III who imposed the payment of tribute on Jehu, king of Israel, in 841 B.C.

As conquered territories were added to the Assyrian Empire, provincial governors sometimes acquired much power, often in cities that had themselves been capitals of states. Side by side with powerful officials, something like feudal landlords continued to exist in Assyria. In contrast, in Babylonia most of the estates were overrun by invading Aramaeans, and agriculture far beyond the limits of cities became nearly impossible.

After a period of decline and loss of territory in the eighth century, Assyria revived once more; the historians' term is "neo-Assyrian" empire. Tiglath-pileser III, a former general who had seized the throne, knew where the source of trouble might be; thus, he broke up many provinces to make the governors less dangerous and did much to distribute the burden of taxation more equitably. He also raised the size of the empire to its greatest extent to date by conquests in Syria and elsewhere and by taking the crown of Babylonia himself from an Aramaean who had assumed it.

At the end of the century, Sennacherib campaigned into Syria, and after a lengthy siege of Jerusalem in 701 B.C. was somehow brought to abandon it and withdraw. But he rallied his armies to conquer and utterly destroy Babylon. He built an enormous palace in Nineveh, amply adorned by sculptured representations of Assyrian military victories and practices. Along with large-scale construction, he demonstrated the power of the oriental despot to mount impressive public works. In order to provide Nineveh with water, the king had his engineers divert water by way of a canal that had to be carried across a valley. Its bottom was sealed by cement containing magnesium: two million blocks of limestone were required. Parts have lasted to this day.

Faint portents of calamity may be sensed in the reign of Esarhaddon, who had the priestesses of Ishtar call out repeatedly to him "Do not be afraid," and who was brought by omens from the heavens to designate substitute kings for three periods during his reign, during which he himself masqueraded as "Mr. Peasant"[12]— this despite the fact that he had notable successes including the conquest of Egypt. Ashurbanipal (668–627 B.C.) gave the Assyrian Empire its last years of glory, during which he quelled Egyptian rebellion, captured and heavily damaged Babylon, and destroyed Susa, capital of the old Elamite enemy. The best of Assyrian art depicts these deeds in bas-relief.

During these twilight years, Assyrian officialdom had come to number one hundred thousand, many of them men from conquered territories. Frequently, Assyrian rulers carried out large-scale deportations of the population of annexed regions and replaced them by others. No doubt such policies helped to avoid the growth of local sentiments on the basis of which rebellion might batten. The result must also have been to stifle any tendency for civic pride or loyalty to an Assyrian state to develop.

The end seems to have come rather quickly. A civil war between Ashurbanipal's sons, while he was still on the throne, weakened the empire, and it could not defend itself against invaders any longer. In 612 the Medes and Chaldeans together took Nineveh. One general, assuming the name of the founder of the empire as Ashur-uballit II, held out until 609. That was the end; Assyria passed irreversibly into history.

There was a "neo-Babylonian" as well as a neo-Assyrian empire. Nabopolassar of Chaldea on the gulf coast, encroaching on Assyria, took the title of king of Babylonia in 626 B.C. His son and successor, Nebuchadrezzar (Nabu-kudurri-usur) II, carried Babylonian arms several times into Syria. On one such excursion, on capturing Jerusalem in 597, he deported three thousand Jews to Babylonia; the episode was repeated in 587, when many thousand more followed.

In order to restore an economic base in Babylonia, Nabopolassar had begun by rebuilding the ruined canals of the region. His son added to the system of irrigation, organized a smoothly running administration, and collected enormous sums in tax and tribute moneys. Nebuchadrezzar II left behind him construction of lasting renown: the "hanging gardens" and the Tower of Babel, whose central feature and purpose was that of a temple—as well as many fortifications and religious buildings. The last Babylonian monarch was an Aramaean, Nabonidus. His reign was taken up with efforts to avoid the Persian conquest that impended.

In 529 Cyrus the Great entered Babylon without a fight; the priests of Marduk had managed to arrange surrender, leaving Nabonidus no alternative. Thus ended the era of the great Mesopotamian empires. Until Iraq gained independence in 1932 this was someone else's land, even when—as in the case of Ctesiphon and Baghdad—the capital of the rulers was in Mesopotamia.

Egypt: Part Two

In the New Kingdom the officialdom grew in size. In its early years, there was a tendency for high office to become hereditary, but it was successfully combated. Egypt's constant wars produced powerful military families; and since generals might be particularly close to the kings and yet might need to be relegated to less-demanding tasks at some point, they were often appointed to important civil posts or, also frequently, to the position of high priest—of which there were a number. There was also a trend toward the formation of high priestly families. Hereditary property or privilege of any sort is a potential danger to any absolute monarch, and the pharaohs tried to appoint outsiders high priests whenever they could. A rare document from the mid-twelfth century B.C. enables us to conclude that most of the land belonged to the state and the temples, and there is an authoritative opinion, though challenged, that the same papyrus shows that the state could tax temple property at a rate of about 10 percent.

The power of the state was certainly great. The *corvée,* or labor draft, fell on all classes except the officialdom, though the rich might purchase substitutes. The centrally managed irrigation system was thought to require such compulsory labor; and once such a body of workmen existed, it could be used, or squandered, on the construction of the royal tombs—either the great pyramids of the early dynasties or the concealed rock-cut repositories of the Valley of the Kings, which replaced pyramids starting with Amenhotep I.

The absolute primacy, indeed divinity, of the pharaohs was never placed in question. The pharaoh was god; from the late Seventeenth Dynasty, for a time the queen was the god's wife (the god at this point was Amon) and was the king's full sister. In no other ancient empire was the theology of kingship as unequivocal. (It is true that sometimes the kings were also conceded to possess human qualities, but, however that fact should be interpreted, there was no wavering on their divine character.)

Thus the ancient empires of the Near East established a pattern, imitated or duplicated by authoritarian states later and elsewhere, in which the center of the religion and the center of the polity were fused in the ruler. He (or she; there were occasional queens and empresses who did not change the pattern established by males) might be a god himself, as in the case of the Egyptian pharaoh (a claim Roman emperors imitated after conquering the country); he might be the high priest, who alone could offer sacrifices to heaven, as in China; there might be other priests, but they were clearly subordinate to him.

Thus true Caesaropapism (simply, the caesar *is* the pope) was to be found in its pure form in the Orient: the ancient Near East (and its imitator, the Roman Empire), east Asia, and the Islamic empires. In such societies, writes Karl A. Wittfogel, "the supreme representative of secular authority is also the embodiment of supreme religious authority."[13] The term *Caesaropapism* is not, incidentally, appropriate to the Byzantine Empire to which the term has frequently been applied, where the Christian church, always in theory and often in practice (as will be noted later), could challenge the state. The ancestor of the institutional relationship that developed in the medieval West between church and state was that between prophet and king in ancient Israel (at a few times a king tried to usurp the religious role, but such attempts were beaten back).

Actual pharaohs of the Eighteenth and Nineteenth dynasties in Egypt seemed a good deal less than divine, but they achieved much. Thutmose III is remembered for his crucial role in the establishment of Egypt's Asiatic empire. (During his minority his stepmother, Hatshepsut, acted as regent and then as king [not queen!]). Ahmose and Amenhotep I campaigned into Asia.

Amenhotep IV, however, produced a different sort of innovation by inaugurating what might be called a religious revolution. Taking the name of Akhenaton, the king raised the sun—interpreted as a god—to the position of sole deity or, at any rate, seemed to do so to the extent that he suppressed the worship of Amon and other gods and expunged the word "gods" from certain existing monumental inscriptions in token of his monotheism. The actual ethical or other kinds of philosophical significance of Akhenaton's innovations is far from clear. What is plain is that within a very few years his son (or such he appears to have been), Tutankhaton, reversed his father's emphasis on the Aton (the sun) and reestablished the worship of Amon-Re, taking the name Tutankhamen as symbolic of the change. That name became famous, though not because of any feature of his reign but because of the discovery of his rich, unplundered tomb in 1922.

In the Nineteenth and Twentieth dynasties, especially under the first three or four kings named Ramses and others between their reigns, the culmination of Egyptian history was reached. Huge building projects continued, relative prosperity was maintained, and intervals of peace occurred among military ventures themselves not dangerous to the state. Under Ramses II (1304–1237 B.C.), one of the longest-ruling of all monarchs, Egyptians fought inconclusively to keep their Asiatic empire. Ramses III staved off Libyan invasion and threw back attacks on land and sea by an alliance of "sea peoples" (coming from Sicily, Sardinia, and elsewhere). But after him the Asiatic possessions rapidly fell away; the influx of silver and copper stopped; and the economy declined. Under the Twenty-first Dynasty Nubia was lost, and a humbler Egypt confronting a prouder Israel sent a pharaoh's daughter to marry King Solomon.

The Libyans now managed to seize the Egyptian throne, and under the Twenty-second (Libyan) Dynasty the power to raid into Palestine was briefly regained. However, Egyptians were on the verge of losing control of Egypt for good. The Twenty-fifth Dynasty was Ethiopian or Kushite. During the dynasty's later years, the 660s, the Assyrians entered Egypt, defeated the monarch, and installed princelings loyal to them. One, Psamtik, after a time succeeded in throwing off Assyrian suzerainty and reestablishing Egyptian independence.

However, the dynasty he founded, the Twenty-sixth, was ended by the Persians. Cambyses conquered the country in 525 B.C., and Egypt's greatness was past.

Israel

In the words of John Bright:

In all the Genesis narrative no single historical figure is named who can, as yet, be otherwise identified. Nor has any mention of any Hebrew ancestor demonstrably turned up in any contemporary inscription; since they were nomads of little importance, it is unlikely that any ever will.[14]

Modern scholars are apt to agree that the Old Testament contains much historical truth but is sometimes mistaken in detail—starting, let us say, with Exodus, and assigning the previous narratives to a different order of literature. However, even if no personalities from Genesis can be given other documentary attestation, the general picture of Semites wandering from Mesopotamia to Palestine to Egypt is not at variance with what is known of the early second millennium B.C.

No support is given in Egyptian records to the story of a young Hebrew vizier to a pharaoh, the Joseph whose death concludes Genesis. But the report in the sequel of Hebrew slaves at work on the Egyptian royal cities Pithom and Raamses (Exodus 1:11) is quite plausible. The city of Raamses, or Pi-Ramesse, was the former Hyksos capital of Avaris, which was rebuilt by Nineteenth Dynasty monarchs, especially Ramses II, who seems a very strong candidate for the pharaoh from whom Moses led his escaping people. The first mention of Israel in any document comes from the reign of Merneptah, Ramses II's successor, recounting a victorious raid into Palestine in about 1231 B.C. A triumphal poem from this inscription contains the line "Israel is laid waste and has no seed." The Egyptian term refers to the people, not the country, which would be an anachronism; the implication seems to be that the Hebrews are in Palestine but are still fighting or have suffered some setback in the process of establishing themselves there.[15]

The Exodus possibly occurred about 1270 B.C. and the central thrust of the Hebrew conquest of Canaan about 1230 B.C. Perhaps there was more to both events than what could take place in a few months or even a few years. Certainly more than a single battle, at Jericho or elsewhere, under the generalship of Joshua, was involved in the Hebrew occupation of the country. Archaeological evidence cannot yet, perhaps ever, be made to square with the biblical account: a destroyed Jericho has been excavated, but the destruction is of the twenty-fourth century B.C., not the thirteenth.[16] H. T. Frank declares that it is best to interpret the entrance of the Hebrews into Canaan as a process of assimilation of Hebrew elements into Canaanite culture, though battles and sieges doubtless took place. The Book of Judges (rather than Joshua) indeed suggests a slow and difficult lodgment in the Promised Land.

The Hebrews may or may not have been related or identical to the Hapiru of the Amarna Letters, dating from roughly the fourteenth century B.C. The Israelites may or may not have been the descendants of Jacob, who took the name Israel. The Jews were evidently so named when refugees from Judah formed groups in Egypt after the disaster of 587 B.C. But Hebrews, Israelites, and Jews were all the same, and the efforts of such later writers as Eusebius of Caesarea to distinguish between good pre-Christian Hebrews and bad post-Christian Jews makes no sense. The people had achieved an identity resting on a certain number of tribes, deriving from a shared faith in Yahweh, and had acquired a political unity of sorts under a series of "judges"—that is, military and political leaders in the process of pushing back Canaanite, Philistine, and other neighbors by the end of the twelfth century B.C.

What obviously distinguishes the Jews from their neighbors in the great Near Eastern empires is the detailed record they compiled in the historical books of the Old Testament. But the basis or purpose of that account was less a love of history than a love of their God and, perhaps, fear of Him. They were clearly the first people to adopt monotheism. Many scholars discern common elements in Jewish religion and the religion of their neighbors; others firmly deny any such thing. One respected specialist declares that the religion of Israel was "absolutely different" from anything the pagan world ever knew and that it had no pagan antecedents whatever.[17] This seems an overstatement quite unnecessary to support a contention that the faith of Israel had unique aspects of great importance.

Monotheism came to be regarded by the civilizations of the West as advanced; polytheism or any compromise with monotheism as retrograde. It has been argued that monotheism may, in fact, be "no more than despotism in religion."[18] That is to say, the single god may simply be all-powerful and not good or just, or not entirely so. Another angle of examination may come from James H. Breasted's contention that "monotheism was imperialism in religion."[19] Apparently, what is meant is that monotheism was a consequence of imperialism: the Egyptian leaving his narrow valley found the same sun shining in other parts of the country or in Syria and other foreign countries, so concluded that there was but one sun and, hence, only one sun-god.

This remark may have merit but has no visible relevance to the Jews' worship of Yahweh. What Yahweh came to be regarded as being was a power that reached into every aspect of life and relations between man and the cosmos. He was not the god of anything in particular, even such a vital particular as the sun; and He was not merely supreme but moral in his actions. A measure of the newness of the kind of theism concerned was that it had political implications—and substantial ones at that.

Israel itself was, according to Martin Noth, an *amphictyony*—a term that had been used for similar organizations in Greece, Asia Minor, and Italy.[20] John Bright recommends against using the term, but his description, a "sacral league of tribes founded in covenant with Yahweh," is certainly close to the way it has been used.[21] The tribes were not all related by blood; their faith provided their unity. Israel seems very early to have had a central shrine at Shiloh, presided over by a hereditary chief priest and other clergy. To meet danger, repel an enemy, or perhaps to attack one, the tribes would be summoned and mobilized by "judges"—not monarchs, not generals, not clergy, but leaders sanctioned by, serving, even somehow speaking for God.

The Bible depicts Moses as the deliverer of the Jews from Egypt, but he dies before crossing into the Promised Land; Joshua is portrayed as the general of the conquest. After his death, Judah and Simeon served as military leaders; Othniel, however, "judged" Israel. So did the prophetess Deborah and the male she summoned to help, Barak, and thereafter Gideon.

During these stages of political development—punctuated by battles, assassinations, and all sorts of bloody deeds—the need for greater stability and continuity came to be perceived. A "judge" might gather the forces together from the tribes; when the danger had passed, the various contingents would return home. After Gideon fended off the Midianites, the men of Israel said to him, "Rule thou over us, both thou, and thy son, and thy son's son also"; but Gideon replied, "I will not rule over you, neither shall my son rule over you; the Lord shall rule over you" (Judges 8:21–22). But that did not end the pressure of sentiment for kingship. Hard-pressed by the Philistines, the Jews reluctantly adopted a different system.

The reluctance is shown in two quite different accounts, both found in 1 Samuel. In the first, Yahweh guides the election of Saul as king (chap. 9, 10:1–16, and 11); in the second, the greatest of the judges, Samuel, resists the demand of the people, lectures them at length about all the evils they will suffer under kingship, and, when it proves unavoidable to yield to their demand and make Saul king, has Yahweh produce a thunderstorm—when the wheat stands in the field ready for harvest, so that not merely momentary fright is the consequence—to show the people the wickedness of what they have done (chap. 8, 10:17–27, and 12).[22] The notion is repeatedly expressed that the acceptance of an earthly king means rejection of Yahweh, and in an amazing passage God tells Samuel to listen to the people, "for they have not rejected thee, but they have rejected me, that I should not reign over them" (1 Samuel 8:7).

Saul became king about 1020 B.C. In Egypt, the days of empire were over;

both Babylonia and Assyria were experiencing periods of relative weakness and were preoccupied with the continuing incursions of the Aramaeans. The Jews had conquered the Canaanites of the highlands, but the Philistines of the coastal areas were a more serious threat. Probably having been settled by the pharaohs as vassals in the areas concerned, they established their own control as Egyptian power declined, ruling the Canaanites, mixing with them, and adopting their culture. It seems surprising that in the eleventh century, when climactic political and military events were taking place, a cultural event of fundamental importance to the history of all mankind was somehow occurring: the invention, or perfection, of the alphabet—as distinct from pictographic, ideographic, or syllabic scripts.

It seems most credit goes to the Canaanites, whose script was converted into simple linear form by both the Phoenicians (the term may be used to mean simply Canaanites in the later period) and Hebrews. The alphabet went west to the Greeks about 800 and not long afterward to the Etruscans and then the Romans; it went east via the Aramaeans, through Syria into Mesopotamia. By the seventh century B.C., Aramaic in the alphabetic script came to be a lingua franca throughout much of the Near East and around 500 B.C. in the Achaemenian empire. The most impressive use of the alphabetic script, however, was that by the Jews, who set about composing the texts that eventuated in the Old Testament around 1000 B.C.

The Israelites were strong enough, and their previously formidable neighbors for the time being weak enough, so that they could establish firm political independence, if they could deal with the enemies immediately at hand, especially the Philistines. After initial victories, Saul encountered disaster in a battle with Philistine chariots on the plain near Mount Gilboa; his sons were killed, and he committed suicide to avoid capture. Not only was his generalship wanting. He tried to make himself head of the religious as well as the political community; this was the reason Samuel denounced him and declared, on two occasions, that his kingship should end. This happened at Gilgal and in the war against the Amalekites (1 Samuel 13:8–14 and 15:17–31). There, writes George Mendenhall, Saul "attempted to introduce the ancient oriental idea of kingship, in which the king was the chief intermediary between the gods and man."[23] It was not then acceptable for the monarch to offer the sacrifices himself; two generations later, however, it would be.

Other political and legal changes, some subtle and some not, were occurring. In the reign of Saul, outlaws came to include those who were "in debt" (1 Samuel 22:2) and thus had to flee. This was the case with the band of four hundred men who gathered around David when, escaping the jealous anger of Saul, he found refuge in the cave of Adullam. Under the old pledge system, the creditor held a piece of property, and there was no reason to flee. However, under the new system the person of the debtor was the security, so that on default he, or members of his family, were subject to seizure as slaves. This practice was identical to that followed under Babylonian and probably also Canaanite law.[24] Nevertheless, the Israelites resisted borrowing elements of Canaanite culture in important ways, a fact that is surprising given the clearly inferior and more backward state of the culture of the Hebrew conquerors.

The Canaanites had a wealthy and powerful elite, who lived in luxurious palaces; the Israelites had nothing equivalent to that class. The Canaanites had massive fortresses, which were replaced by thin walls of the new casemate type. The corvée was used in Canaan as in other Near Eastern empires; it was unknown in Israel. The word *hophshi* meant "serf" in Canaanite documents; it came to mean "freeman," presumably because the peasant (of Canaanite background or other stock under Canaan's rule) had ceased to be a serf and had become a freeborn Israelite.[25] The settlement of the Jews in Canaan was, in the view of recent scholarship, not that mainly of herdsmen or nomads but of already long-sedentary agriculturalists, a comparatively poor group leavened by a few skilled artisans.[26]

David was Saul's son-in-law and the bosom friend of his son Jonathan. Therefore, despite Saul's recurring jealousy of the popular young champion, the killer of the giant Goliath and a charismatic figure (which Saul was not), David was connected with the reign just terminated by suicide. He became established as leader of the southern tribes, and within a few years he had unified the whole of Israel under his kingship. It was about 1000 B.C.

David captured the Canaanite city of Jerusalem, defeated the attacking Philistines, and drove them to pull back to the coastal strip. He made Jerusalem his capital, since it was located near the junction of the two halves of his kingdom, and by moving the ark of the Covenant there he made it the central religious site as well. Through several military campaigns, he made Israel the leading power of Palestine and Syria, "probably as strong as any power in the contemporary world."[27]

To administer this area David assembled an officialdom that may have been partly patterned on Egypt's. He must have taxed the subject peoples and the property of the crown. He carried out a census, according to 2 Samuel 24, a deed that David himself regarded as a grievous sin and that Yahweh adjudged such a crime that he sent a plague upon the country, killing seventy thousand people. As when Saul acted as high priest, there was evidently a feeling that a census was a device alien to the Hebrews, akin to the kind of polity that existed in the neighboring empires. (Attitudes had changed, obviously, since the census of the Book of Numbers.) The census in Israel may well have been accompanied by the fiscal reorganization and pattern of conscription that went along with census taking in Egypt and Mesopotamia.

David found the succession problem difficult, finally making his son Solomon joint sovereign to head off Adonijah, whom he thought unsuitable. When David died, Solomon moved quickly to have Adonijah killed, along with others who he feared might disturb the succession. It was to be the only time the throne would pass intact and unchallenged during the Israelite monarchy.

Israel now stood at the peak of its economic and cultural development. (Not that its empire was at its maximum size, for during Solomon's reign territory was lost through rebellion in both the north and south.) Commerce and industry had grown in the formerly agrarian and pastoral society, and towns had increased in population. The powers and prerogatives of the monarchy were fully employed and extended. Solomon divided his kingdom into twelve provinces; he taxed the people heavily; he used the corvée, a device previously unknown in Israel though used by David on the conquered people of Ammon east of the Jordan (2 Samuel 12:31; for Solomon's corvée of Israelites, 1 Kings 5:13).

The king undertook ambitious construction projects, erecting new fortifications and administrative edifices, but his greatest and best-known monument was the Temple in Jerusalem. Solomon acquired a reputation for wisdom and diplomatic skill and was able to avoid long military campaigns, though he devoted attention to his standing army and introduced war-chariots into the Israelite forces. On the one hand were peace and prosperity; on the other was the burden of financial exactions, forced labor, probably military conscription—all the costs to the population that the devices of oriental monarchy impose, at last applied to Israel.

As for Solomon himself, his relations with the Almighty are not wholly clear. He offered the sacrifices himself when dedicating the Temple (1 Kings 8:62–64), a deed that brought the divine wrath (according to Samuel) down on the head of Saul a few decades earlier but had apparently become acceptable. However, Solomon had given grievous offense in another direction. He accumulated seven hundred wives and three hundred concubines (1 Kings 11:3). But polygamy per se was not the problem; it was the fact that many of Solomon's women were from foreign peoples and worshipped foreign deities. All this was part of a diplomatic pattern based on a vision of empire and a stance of cultural cosmopolitanism that belonged to the king, but the effect was to endanger Israel's religious identity. Thus on these grounds Yahweh threatened to cut the realm in half.

And so it happened. When Solomon died in 922 B.C., his son Rehoboam succeeded him in Jerusalem, but the north broke off under Jeroboam I. The united kingdom had lasted less than eighty years and would never (at least up to the time of writing) be restored. Judah in the south had Jerusalem but otherwise little but hills and desert. Israel in the north was richer, more fertile, and more exposed to the armies of foreign conquerors. The Pharaoh Shishak (Shoshenq) tried to reimpose Egyptian rule in Palestine shortly after Solomon died, but though he did much damage his expedition was a failure.

Thereafter the two kingdoms were often at odds, and each had its own foreign-policy problems. Nevertheless, in the early eighth century B.C., they were together about as large as Solomon's realm, enjoying peace and prosperity, and their aggregate population may have reached its largest total. Such achievements did not satisfy the prophet Amos, who depicts an Israel divided between rich and poor, the small farmer victimized by the moneylender, the lower strata of society deprived of redress of grievances. And, indeed, within a few years Israel would be struck down.

Among the ancient Hebrews prophecy was a religious movement or, more accurately, a cluster of religious movements; it also came to have an important political function. Prophecy was not peculiar to the Hebrews. It was found among many peoples of Egypt, Palestine, and Mesopotamia. There was a special Jewish emphasis, however, on proclamation rather than prediction (though the latter was not absent). For several centuries there were ecstatic visionaries of various sorts who were uncontrollable, were often feared, and left no record of their thoughts; thus they were called "non-writing" prophets. Nathan, at the court of David, and Elijah, regarded almost as a second Moses, belonged to the nonwriting category but were major figures in the Hebrew story.

The career of Elijah centered on a response to the royal marriage arranged by Omri, the first great ruler of the northern kingdom (d. ca. 869 B.C.), between his son Ahab and the Phoenician princess, Jezebel. She fostered the worship of the fertility god Baal in the new capital, Samaria, which Omri had built for Israel. Incensed by the queen's support of the pagan cult and reflecting also "resentment at the despotic Oriental manner of rule that Ahab, incited by Jezebel, exercised," Elijah denounced them and all their works.[28] He challenged the priests of Baal to a contest, and when he won he had them all killed. He predicted the doom of both Ahab and Jezebel, and they did indeed perish—Jezebel in a scene of horror some time after Elijah was "[taken up] into heaven by a whirlwind" (2 Kings 2:1). His heir as prophet, Elisha, inspired the killing of the whole royal family; Jezebel herself was thrown out of a window and trampled by horses, so that "they found no more of her than the skull, and the feet, and the palms of her hands" (2 Kings 9:35). The leader of the successful coup, Jehu, founded a dynasty that lasted from 842 to 745 B.C. Baal worship migrated to Judah, however, where Athaliah, daughter of Ahab and Jezebel, ruled for six years during which she supported her mother's faith before she was also overthrown and killed.

By this time the prophets had preached religious messages as well as hounded and instigated the overthrow of monarchs in the interests of religion in Israel, Judah, and other states also. But the office of prophet

was in a true sense a political office, for the prophets spoke as messengers of Yahweh's heavenly court, the appointed agents of his imperium in the world, and it was their duty to remind kings and officials of state that the real ruler of Israel is Yahweh, and to criticize and correct the state in the light of his declared will.[29]

Other Near Eastern rulers had court prophets or seers, but most of them were slow to challenge their masters or go beyond safe ambiguity in their utterances. Certainly the Hebrews had such persons too—for example, the four hundred prophets who predicted victory for Ahab but were wrong, while one, Micaiah, who foretold disaster, was right (1 Kings 22). However, courageously uncompromising types were much more prominent.

Until the eighth century B.C., the Hebrew prophets restricted themselves for the most part to advice to rulers, including reprimand or denunciation. However, beginning with the so-called classical prophets, usually reckoned from Amos, a series of figures spoke of the betrayal of the Covenant by the whole society. Amos reproached the elite and the monarchs for corruption and in so doing raised an entirely new issue. It was not necessary for the Jews to desert Yahweh for other gods in order to court condemnation; if they merely neglected the divine commands and the ethical spirit Amos discerned in them, the result would be as dire. Performance of ritual is not enough, it may be worse than nothing: "I hate, I despise your feasts, and I take no delight in your solemn assemblies" (Amos 5:21). And so ruin lay ahead.

It was soon forthcoming. As John Bright points out, for five centuries (that is, since the Exodus) no empire had existed that could trouble Israel permanently or deeply; then Assyria made its appearance.[30] In the reign of Jeroboam II (ca. 786–746 B.C.) of Israel, the state was still strong and prosperous, despite the social ills of which Amos wrote. But thereafter intrigue and confusion weakened Israel, and the Assyrians overwhelmed it in 722–721 B.C. Sargon II carried out substantial deportations of leading citizens of Samaria and importations of foreign peoples, in accordance with the usual Assyrian methods. It was the end of ancient Israel.

Judah became a vassal state of Assyria but kept its own government for more than a century longer. Its king, Hezekiah, was counseled by the prophet Isaiah, whose name is borne by one of the Bible's greatest books though its composition clearly extends over two centuries, from the late eighth to the late sixth. Under King Josiah (640–609 B.C.), a significant religious reform occurred in connection with the discovery in 621 B.C. of a book of the law, called Deuteronomy ("Second Law") from a defective Greek translation of Deuteronomy 17:18 that refers to a "copy of this law." The find occasioned or accompanied an extensive purging of alien and superstitious elements from the religion.

Though the changes were deeply felt and long remembered, military events soon edged them from the foreground. The prophet Jeremiah warned of the impending danger, called the people of Judah to repent, and advocated giving up to the oncoming Babylonians without a fight. The first king to rule in Jerusalem, Zedekiah, would not listen. Nebuchadrezzar took the city; Zedekiah was blinded and taken to Babylon, where he died; and perhaps fifty thousand were forcibly deported.[31] Of course the Babylonian Captivity was a grievous experience for the Jewish people. However, some managed to assimilate; all were permitted to associate and worship together. It appears that the institution of the synagogue is a product of the Captivity. Hundreds, perhaps thousands, fled voluntarily to Egypt and elsewhere. It seems that the term Jews, from the shattered kingdom of Judah, came to be used for these refugees and then the whole people.

Jeremiah scandalized the Hebrews by advocating submission to Nebuchadrezzar, but he also predicted a restoration of the Davidic monarchy in the future. During the following period, such promises and hopes receded into the distance. In 538 B.C. Babylon was taken by Cyrus the Great of Persia. The city surrendered, and no vengeance was wreaked on the inhabitants. Cyrus freed the Jews to return to their homeland or remain as they chose. The second part of the book of Isaiah (Deutero-Isaiah) hailed Cyrus as God's anointed, the divine instrument whereby an Israel of the future would serve as a light for all nations. Through the Suffering Servant of the Lord—whether that meant Israel collectively as a people or an individual Messiah to come—peace and justice would be brought to the Jews, or to all mankind.

Reality seldom justifies long-cherished hopes. Hostility between the first returnees and the Samaritans soon developed; the rebuilding of the destroyed Temple was slow. When a large group came back, led by Zerubbabel, hopes were raised because he belonged to the Davidic family; but we do not even know what became of him, and he was the last of the line. Nehemiah, a Jew who had become a high official at the Persian court, persuaded Artaxerxes I in about 445 B.C. to separate Jewish territory from its Samaritan overlords and to make him governor of the new province. Nehemiah soon rebuilt the walls of Jerusalem and restored morale. About the same time (some think earlier, some think later), the priest Ezra gave Judaism a more systematic form and sternly demanded that males put away non-Jewish wives and children.

Little is known of what was happening to the Jews in the subsequent period. Knowledge of Hebrew was being lost; Aramaic, the official language of the Persian empire, was becoming the common language of Palestine. Soon the Persians would be conquered by Alexander the Great; Palestine would be governed as part of the Hellenistic kingdoms that took shape after he died; Rome would replace the Seleucids as overlord; and a Roman emperor would expel all Jews from Palestine.

The Heritage of Jewish Freedom

Out of this long history of the ancient Near East came above all an experience and a tradition of sacred monarchy, or despotism. There were moments when other kinds of polity seemed on the verge of taking root: in the traces of self-government found in the Sumerian city-states or in the "feudal monarchy," in which the nobles crowned the king, of the early Hittites. But they did not; they perished utterly. There were, however, two important inheritances to the growth of free societies, both transmitted by the Jews: a conception of human freedom and ultimate success in avoiding despotism. The former has been widely discussed; the latter has not earned sufficient attention from political scientists to be given a name.

The conception of freedom comes from the Jewish religion, in a rejection of the interpretation Christians place on the Garden of Eden narrative of man's quality of Original Sin:

It is primarily within the realm of the ethical that Judaism posits freedom, recognizing the bound, or determined, quality of much of his existence (*e.g.*, his natural environment or physiological makeup). It is this ethically free creature who stands within the covenant relationship and so may choose to be obedient or disobedient . . . a creature who makes free ethical choices for which he is responsible. . . .[32]

It may be argued that the sensation of being able to choose freely is a characteristic most likely to develop in a society where an absolute ruler is not present and where life and limb are not instantly forfeit or imperiled if an imprudent choice is made. In any event, Hebrew society was unique in the ancient Near East in managing finally to avoid the techniques, devices, and institutions of despotism.

Yahweh was ruler: men were not, a man was not. In the empires of Egypt and Mesopotamia, the priest-king (or, at least in Egyptian theory, the god-king) acknowledged the primacy of the divine, of course, but he was effectively mediator and head of the cult. There was nothing whatever comparable to the Hebrew notion of covenant between God and an entire people—itself a startlingly democratic idea in the context of the ancient Near East.

Since Yahweh was ruler, there was great resistance among the Jews to the proposal that a king be chosen. Gideon rejected it utterly; Samuel agonized before allowing Saul to accept; David though king still was unable to build a temple; Solomon could and did do so. In the tenth century B.C., the borrowing of despotic methods began: the census, a sizable officialdom, large-scale construction works. And yet they did not take hold. Solomon appears to be something close to a full-fledged oriental despot. He does not seem to be restrained by strong prophets, such as those who precede and follow his time. However, Yahweh, speaking to him directly, reprimands him, promises to punish him (by splitting the realm), and proceeds to do so. The religion is still strong enough to prevent the emergence of an autocratic system; the apparent change in the polity is not to become institutionalized.

During the centuries in which there were two kingdoms, Israel and Judah, monarchical powers evidently did not regain the level of Solomon's. There may well have been further social stratification, though the invective of the eighth-century prophets of social justice—Amos, Hosea, and Micah—is scarcely conclusive evidence. The Deuteronomic reforms of the seventh century at least renewed concern for the values the classical prophets defended. William A. Irwin waxes lyrical on what Deuteronomy meant to the Hebrew legal system: "Here is the same defense of the common man against the arrogance of the monarchy and the same constitutional limitation of royal power as was voiced in [1215]."[33]

Irwin calls Deuteronomy "Israel's Magna Carta," having in mind such passages as 17:18–20: "judges and officers . . . shall judge the people with just judgment. Thou shalt not wrest judgment; thou shalt not respect persons, neither take a gift. . . ." For the comparison Irwin may be charged, or credited, with overenthusiasm. The moral equality of all men in the sight of God and legal reflection of that doctrine are, however, plainly present. Irwin declares that the Jews

stood at the crossroads of the ancient world, sensitive to all the best that was achieved within its limits. They took freely from all; their excellence is that they recognized value wherever it arose and freely appropriated it as their own. But in the process they transformed it.[34]

One might insist that the genius of the ancient Jews was that they resisted and avoided borrowing the political and social systems of their neighbors, the oriental empires. But of course they also did borrow, and transform, and transmit precious gifts to those who came after them after they were scattered to every corner of the earth.

CHAPTER 2

The Ancestry of Freedom in the Mediterranean: The Greeks

The Minoan Civilization

If the earliest high cultures, in Mesopotamia and Egypt, were connected with man's mastery of irrigation agriculture, in the course of the third millennium B.C. civilization was ready to advance into nearby regions of rainfall agriculture.[1] One such area was the southern islands of Greece. By about 2100 B.C., the Minoan civilization, named for the legendary King Minos of Knossos, had made its appearance in Crete. Its main architectural feature was a series of palaces, large and small, which possessed in each case halls used for religious ceremonies of some sort. Thus Minoan society has been thought, on the basis of archaeological evidence alone, to have been oriented to peace and the production of wealth, as contrasted with the warlike civilization that developed on the Greek mainland in the sixteenth century B.C.

Called Mycenaean after its chief center, Mycenae, this civilization experienced strong Minoan influence but still acquired its own character. Mycenae gave much greater prominence to fortifications and weapons of both land and sea warfare. The Mycenaeans may have been among the confederation of "Sea Peoples" who attacked Egypt in the twelfth century B.C., and the Trojan War, as depicted in the *Iliad* of Homer, probably is based on some actual Mycenaean seaborne expedition to the vicinity of the Dardanelles, perhaps ending in 1184 B.C., the traditional date of the fall of Troy.

In the middle of the second millennium Minoan civilization underwent several earthquakes and other disasters. Crete was invaded about 1450 B.C. by warriors from the mainland who apparently prospered for several generations before they themselves faded from the scene. Quite recently the later Minoan script, Linear B, has been deciphered to show that it is an archaic form of Greek. Thus at least Greek-speaking rulers, if not Greeks among rulers or ruled, were present in the last flourishing centuries of Cretan civilization.[2] The final destruction of the great palace of Knossos on Crete came under circumstances of which we are ignorant, though we know that the cause was fire; the same is true of the main Mycenaean centers in the Peloponnese, probably around 1200 B.C.

The Dark Ages

During the two or three centuries following, the Bronze Age yielded to the Iron Age, at the same time as the Mycenaean civilization perished and a new wave of invaders settled in the Peloponnese, Crete, and other areas. They were the Dorians, who were Greeks from the north. Others settled on the east coast of the Aegean Sea and were called Ionians; they were probably fleeing from the stronger, ruder invaders who headed for the most fertile lands.

But the refugees faced other dangers and challenges in the new lands of Asia Minor, and their response was evidently "to create the foundations of what later became the master institution of Greek civilization, the polis [plural, poleis]."[3] In the Ionian cities the Homeric epics were shaped, by talented persons working with poetic traditions derived from the Mycenaeans. And by the eighth century B.C., doubtless in areas where Greeks were in contact with Aramaic-speaking and -writing people (exactly where is unknown), Greeks learned alphabetic script and on the basis of it produced their own alphabet. Olympia in the Peloponnese had written records dating from 776 B.C.

As the Greek barbarians became civilized, the economy stabilized and the population grew. Some of the Greeks set out to locate raw materials, trading partners, and sites for new settlements or colonies. Euboeans established outposts on the north shore of the Aegean and on Sicily in the west, immediately followed by Corinthians who founded the city of Syracuse (ca. 733 B.C.); Miletus and other Ionian cities colonized on the coast of the Black Sea, centering in Olbia where contact was made with the Scythians. The Phocaeans founded Massilia about 600 B.C. and traded extensively with the people of southern France and northern Spain.

The Archaic Period

From 750 to 500 B.C., a period called "Archaic" to distinguish it from the classical period following, while the colonizing movement was spreading Greeks all over the Mediterranean, important political developments were taking place. The polis, the beginnings of which may have been Ionian, assumed clearer form. It was apt to center on a fortified hill, where defenders might repel armed assault, with homes and trading establishments surrounding it below; agricultural and pasture lands, sometimes dependent villages, were nearby. Building from the basic family unit, there were several levels of larger units defined largely by blood relationship.

The polis was not merely a city; it was a political unit in which there functioned a king, council, and assembly. Kingship derived from military leadership as it became hereditary. The council included, to begin with, leaders of the various contingents of warriors; the assembly was made up of all the warriors. As time went on, the kingship tended to weaken and become elective, while the assembly tended to get stronger. As military demands proved less pressing, adult male citizens rather than soldiers came to make up its membership. The polis was not universal. In the northwest particularly, the characteristic unit was the *ethnos,* wherein a series of unfortified villages were loosely linked, holding substantial lands—as in Phocis or Aetolia.

In the early and middle seventh century B.C., a military innovation of significance is recorded. During previous times heroic warriors who fought as individual champions were apt to decide military contests. Each had a shield, a sword, and spears to be thrown but had no armor for the head or body. The new tactic was to use armored infantrymen drawn up in close array, in what was called a phalanx. Each soldier, or hoplite, had a shield, a sword, and a spear for thrusting rather than throwing and wore ample armor on both head (helmet) and body.[4]

The social effects of this change are disputed. It was long thought that it reflected or accompanied a shift from an aristocratic to a middle-class (particularly yeoman or sturdy farmer) composition of the armies. Although that view has been challenged, it remains difficult to believe that the individual-champion style of fighting was anything other than aristocratic or that the supersession of that style by tactics using massed infantry was other than nonaristocratic in social basis.[5]

In the seventh and sixth centuries, a political innovation appeared—tyranny —especially in several cities of the Peloponnese (though not Sparta). The tyrant in ancient Greece was not necessarily cruel or oppressive; he was simply a man who had seized or assumed power with no hereditary or legal warrant to do so and usually exercised power without taking a title. In the case of the city of Sicyon, the tyrant Cleisthenes quite clearly espoused the cause of the pre-Dorian inhabitants against the Dorian *phylai,* or tribes. Some scholars have argued that tyranny was made possible by the development of the hoplite phalanx. The only indisputable common feature seems to have been the tyrants' love of displaying wealth and power, for example, in such imposing stone buildings as the treasury in Delphi built by Cypselus, tyrant of Corinth. However, many scholars believe that the chief result of the rule of tyrants was to help end the aristocratic stranglehold on government and thus to pave the way for the development of democracies.

The Classical Period

Several Greek city-states emerged by the fifth century B.C. with distinctive features. They were separated by jealousies and rivalries of various sorts, yet great external danger would force them into transitory or sporadic cooperation. The most important poleis were Sparta, Athens, Thebes, and Corinth.

It was probably during the ninth and eighth centuries that a cluster of villages forming a city called Sparta in the valley of the Eurotas expanded over the plain of Laconia to produce a sizable state. In the seventh century, the Spartans conquered Messenia to the west, and the at least formally federal polity of Lacedaemon resulting embraced the whole southern Peloponnese. Sparta was so preoccupied with taking over new lands in the peninsula that she played little part in overseas colonization. The ranking class was the citizens of Sparta; next came the free citizens of the other cities. There was a serf class called *helots;* a certain number were attached to the land allotted to each Spartan family anywhere in Lacedaemon.

In the city itself the usual pattern of king, council, and assembly was modified in the following way: the kingship was dual, with no clear division of powers between the two kings; the members of the council (other than the kings) had to be at least sixty years old; and an additional institution existed called the ephorate. Five ephors exchanged oaths every month with the kings; "the kings swore to rule according to the laws; and the ephors, on behalf of the city, swore to preserve the kingship provided that the kings kept their oaths."[6] During the seventh century, it appears that a regular process developed whereby any measure was first drawn up by the council and then had to be presented to the assembly for approval and disapproval. Perhaps other poleis imitated the process, perhaps not. In any case, Sparta may have been the earliest to work it out.

The reason "Spartan" acquired the meaning "stern and rigorously disciplined" was that in that city-state all children were taken from their parents and handed over to public institutions for education and training. At maturity girls were released, but boys moved into military units until age thirty and could be summoned to fight until age sixty. It seems that this system of state rearing of children, or *agoge,* may have been linked with the new tactics of the hoplite phalanx. Certainly Sparta was to achieve important military successes through the use of the *agoge* and phalanx. However, in the later sixth century B.C., the

Spartans greatly increased their political influence by diplomacy rather than war in the step-by-step formation, through a series of treaties, of an alliance of most of the cities of the great southern peninsula, called by later historians the Peloponnesian League.

Athens was older than Sparta, dating back well into the Bronze Age. It was the cultural center of Greek settlement by the end of the "dark ages," around 900 B.C., but it expanded politically to take control of all Attica only in the decades preceding 650 B.C. By that time, Athens had discarded its kingship and adopted instead a multiple executive of nine archons, one of whom retained the title king, though all nine had a term of only one year. All former archons made up the council, which was called the "council of the Areopagus" because it often met on the hill of that name near the Acropolis.

In the early sixth century, Athens had a lawgiver and legal reformer named Solon. His later prestige and reputation as a leader in democratization are difficult to substantiate by evidence, but he clearly did terminate the dependent, share-cropping status of a group of farmers called *hektemoroi* and doubtless furthered the legal development of Athens by consigning much customary law to written form. In 546 B.C. Athens acquired its own tyrant in Peisistratus, whose seizure of power has recently been interpreted as an expression of "the resentment toward leading families of the city [of Athens] felt by leading families of eastern Attica."[7] He and then his sons ruled until 510, when a coalition of Spartans and Athenian opponents of the Peisistratids drove them out. Peisistratus inaugurated direct taxation in Athens and undertook a certain amount of showy construction that must have been costly; yet he and his family evidently gained a good deal of popularity and won favorable evaluations from the Greek historians and Aristotle.

A clearer record of political reform was made by Cleisthenes, leader of the anti-Peisistratid party. He created a new system of organizing the citizenry: Attica was divided into more than 100 demes, each with its own assembly and annually chosen chief. Moreover, he introduced the Council of Five Hundred, the members of which were chosen for one year by lot (later a second year was allowed). Its function was to prepare measures for the assembly, by now several thousand in number. The council was itself so large, and had to include so many incompetents owing to random selection, that there must have been an inner circle that somehow actually did the job. What the council did do, most likely, was to ensure that real decisions were taken in the assembly.[8]

According to Aristotle, Cleisthenes also introduced the practice of ostracism, by which the citizens of Athens came annually to indulge their dislikes by voting formally in the assembly to exile a certain person for ten years (though he did not lose his property). Despite Aristotle's account, the origins of the practice are disputed; but in any event ostracism was definitely used by the Athenians as early as 487 B.C. The last recorded instance was in 415 B.C.[9]

The third polis was Thebes, which put together a confederation of Boeotian cities by the sixth century. Dissolved in 479, it was revived in 447 and lasted for over half a century. In the second phase, and thus possibly also the first (nothing is known about it), the Boeotian constitution provided for each city to take care of its own problems but also for a federal representative assembly of 660 men to handle the affairs of the larger entity. Corinth, whose prosperity began with the tyrant Cypselus in the mid-seventh century, extended eastward and westward its commercial and colonial ventures, which were zealously protected by an oligarchy in the sixth century. The wealth of Corinth allowed it to maneuver successfully between Sparta and Athens until the late fifth century, when it suffered losses and decline.

The Ionian cities of Asia Minor seem to have had a less vigorous political life during the period, but they were thriving economically. Culturally, a great step forward was taken: in the explorer city of Miletus, there appeared a thinker, scientist, and philosopher named Thales. We know that he predicted the solar eclipse of 585 B.C., and he was the first Greek philosopher of record—in fact, he stands at the very beginning of what the West came to call philosophy. Thales and other philosophers of the Milesian school had less knowledge than the Babylonians and the Egyptians, writes W. F. Albright, but possessed something they lacked: curiosity.[10] It was a characteristic that would have enormous consequences.

In the middle of the sixth century, a danger impended from the east: the Persians. Cyrus invaded the rich kingdom of Lydia in Asia Minor and overwhelmed it. Within a few years he had also conquered the Greek cities of the Asian mainland. For the time being, the tyrants of the island cities prevented the Persians from crossing the water, evidently benefiting from an important naval innovation—the trireme. It was a ship manned by citizen rowers, often drawn from the poor. McNeill writes:

If the phalanx was the basic school of the Greek polis, the fleet was the finishing school for its democratic version; and if the family farm was the economic basis for the limited democracy of the hoplite franchise, the merchant fleet with its necessary complement of workshops, warehouses, and markets provided the economic sinews for radical democracy.[11]

(By "hoplite franchise" is meant the provision at an earlier stage of the development of Sparta and other poleis that all citizens able to equip themselves as part of the phalanx were to have political rights.) McNeill adds the reminder that, "radical" or not, Greek democracy always excluded slaves of both sexes and all women and rarely granted resident aliens a way to obtain citizenship.

Thus just at the historical moment when the Greek cities seemed at the threshold of greatest political creativity Persian conquest threatened to engulf them.

Persia

Persis was the name for the region just north of the Persian/Arabian Gulf and was broadened by the Greeks and many Westerners ever since to refer to the whole of Iran ("land of the Aryans"). It was in the ninth century that Aryan or Indo-European, peoples appeared in the form of two groups, the Medes and the Persians. The beginnings of the Median kingdom are difficult to separate from legend, but under Cyaxares (625–585 B.C.) they were at any rate strong enough to conduct a damaging attack on Assyria and, a couple of years later in 612 B.C., to capture Nineveh. By 609, together with their Babylonian allies, they destroyed the Assyrians completely. The Persians may have been a Median vassal state to begin with. The rulers traced the origin of their dynasty to a certain Haxamanish (Achaemenes) unknown to history, but after several poorly attested monarchs Cyrus is clearly historical. In 550 B.C. he managed to throw off Median suzerainty and to sweep the Medes aside. The Achaemenid dynasty and the Persian Empire thereupon founded were to last a little over two centuries.

Among the conquests of Cyrus (later called "the Great") was Babylon, the result being to elicit the Jewish gratitude enshrined in Deutero-Isaiah. In 529 he died fighting in central Asia. His successor Cambyses conquered much of Egypt; the next ruler, Darius I, the Great, aspired to do still more. First he led armies eastward to annex substantial territories up to the Indus valley; then he turned westward, crossing the Hellespont into Europe in 516 B.C. It was the beginning of a long and fateful encounter between Persians and inhabitants of that continent.

The empire of the Achaemenids was a sudden, startling creation, subduing at a stroke ancient realms such as Egypt and Mesopotamia where states had existed almost twenty-five hundred years. Naturally it borrowed much from the conquered peoples. Darius I had a record of his deeds inscribed in the rock of Bisitun in three languages: Old Persian, Babylonian, and Elamite. The first was in a script just created for the purpose. But Aramaic soon became the most often used language of the empire. If the Persian Empire was derivative in its writing, it seems to have originated a religion: Zoroastrianism. The prophet Zoroaster, who may have flourished in the century before Cyrus (though his dating is much disputed), preached the god Ahura Mazda and his war on darkness and falsehood.

The Achaemenid rulers came to follow the Zoroastrian teaching, probably re-shaped in several respects.

Irrigation agriculture was vital to Achaemenid Persia, and the monarch him-self played an important part. In the words of Herodotus, the great Greek historian and the first historian known to us anywhere:

The king orders the floodgates to be opened toward the country whose need is greatest, and lets the soil drink until it has had enough; after which the gates on this side are shut, and others are unclosed for the nation which, of the remainder, needs it most.[12]

As in the case of other oriental empires, the ruler organized an officialdom, but it contained a new and significant element: eunuchs. Castration of humans as punishment may date to the second millennium B.C., but political eunuchs, that is, castrated males serving in high state positions, seem to be found only as early as the first millennium.[13] They could be trusted with guarding the harem of wives and concubines an Eastern monarch might possess; they were also given functions of a specially sensitive sort. They were in no danger of trying to accumulate wealth and power to pass on to their children; though they might be chief ministers, generals, or admirals, they could not aspire to be kings—who had to have, or appear to have, the capacity to be husband and father.

Some large landholdings were in the hands of some families for whom owner-ship had become hereditary, others were held by civil or military servants of the state whose tenancy was conditional on service. As elsewhere in the ancient Near East, there was continuing tension between the hereditary and appointive prin-ciples in administering the empire. It was divided into provinces each governed by a satrap appointed by the Great King or King of Kings (two of the titles used), and indeed some satraps became something like little kings, their positions hered-itary. Nevertheless, officials dispatched from the capital to report on local condi-tions helped prevent fragmentation, as did the best system of roads in history until that time, over which a speedy governmental post was carried, as well as an effective system of surveying and record keeping. Darius also wished to be remembered as a lawgiver and dispenser of justice, and carried out significant reforms in that area. The capital he founded, Persepolis, was both imposing and beautiful.

The Greco-Persian Wars and the Ascendancy of Athens

In 499 B.C. Miletus revolted against Persian rule, followed by other Ionian cities, which appealed to the mainland Greeks for support. Athens sent a fleet whose initial successes were followed by serious losses, and its remnants were brought home. The Ionian revolt was finally put down in 494. But Darius the Great sought to avenge himself on the interfering Athenians. After a miscarried naval expedition, in 490 a Persian fleet landed an army first in Eretria, whose people were shipped away as slaves, and then near Athens. On the Plain of Marathon the Athenian army, helped by a Plataean contingent, smashed a Persian force over twice as large as the Greek.

The Persian army defeated at Marathon was intended merely as a punitive expedition, but such Athenian leaders as Themistocles knew their return in force was to be expected. He therefore greatly expanded the fleet by building more triremes. But there was dissension among the Greek cities about how, or indeed whether, to resist the Persians, and the oracle at Delphi associated itself with Persian victory. After the Ionian cities had been pacified, reforms were instituted, tyrants removed, and democratic government restored—under Cyrus and Darius Persian rule had a reputation for toleration and respect for local cultures and traditions. The result in Ionia was that by 481 B.C. Persia could succeed in raising troops for the coming assault on Greece.

Darius had died in 486 and his son Xerxes I succeeded him—a monarch much less ready to make concessions or permit local ways to continue. In 480 he advanced on Greece by land and sea. King Leonidas and his Spartans held the narrow pass at Thermopylae and, after they were betrayed by a Greek traitor who showed the Persians a path around it, fought to the death. Xerxes moved south to burn Athens, but in a naval battle in the Strait of Salamis the Persian fleet was routed. Xerxes withdrew to Asia, leaving an army under Mardonius in Thessaly. The Spartan commander Pausanias defeated the Persians at Plataea, while the Greek fleet pursued the foe at Mycale near Samos in Asia Minor and dispersed them. That was the end of the Persian invasion.

The question now was how to consolidate and press home Greek victory. Athens was given leadership of the new Delian League, whose military operations against Persia were led by Cimon. He also helped the city to rebuild and produce new art and architecture. Leading an army of Athenian hoplites to assist Sparta to put down a helot rebellion, Cimon was sent away by the Spartans for uncertain reasons and then suffered ostracism in Athens in 461. His critics also managed to reduce the power of the Council of the Areopagus and extend the powers of the citizenry substantially, especially by introducing pay for the jurors of the popular courts. Thus the poorest citizens were enabled to serve. Athenian democracy approached the peak of its development.

The Greeks of Sicily and Italy had taken no part in the wars against Persia. They had fended off the Phoenicians of Carthage, and a strong and rich center grew up in Syracuse, which took the lead in extending democracy in several Sicilian cities during the 460s. Important contributions were made in philosophy and mathematics by some of the western Greeks, notably Pythagoras and Parmenides of Elea.

From 460 to 445 B.C. a war was fought between Athens and Sparta, and their respective allies, that came to be called the First Peloponnesian War. At the same time Athens sought to damage the Persians, especially by supporting an Egyptian revolt. About 450 B.C. an understanding was evidently reached between Athens and Persia in the so-called Peace of Callias. No longer with the justification of a common Persian danger, Athens imposed ever tighter controls on her allies of the Delian League. She ordered them all to use Athenian coins only, imposed on them the sort of tribute paid by colonies, and supported the cult of Athena, "queen of Athens," in the other cities of the League. In such ways the League became in effect an Athenian empire.

The chronicler of the Greek wars with Persia, Herodotus, has left a magnificent early testimonial to freedom. He attributed it to two Spartan envoys to Persia rejecting an offer of power in Greece if they would serve Xerxes, an offer made by a high Persian official:

A slave's life you understandest: but, never having tasted liberty, thou canst not tell whether it be sweet or no. Ah! hadst thou known what freedom is, thou wouldst have bidden us fight for it, not with the spear only, but with the battle-axe.[14]

And when they came into the presence of the Great King, they refused to prostrate themselves (before any man, as they put it)—and lived to tell the tale. Herodotus doubtless caught the mood of the ideologists and propagandists of the defenders when he drew a sharp distinction between Greek freedom and Persian slavery. The Greeks needed every ounce of resolution they could muster, for never did there seem a more forlorn cause than that of the scattered city-states trying to hold back the mighty hosts of the empire that embraced most of the known civilized world. Aeschylus, the great writer of tragedy, had fought at Marathon and Salamis, and came away with the conviction that the Greeks had triumphed and the Persians had been struck down, under both Darius and Xerxes, by the divine hand.

Not all Greeks fought for the Greek cause. Some served as mercenaries; others allied themselves voluntarily with the Persians; still others did the enemy's bidding for bribes. Herodotus's or Aeschylus's patriotic exaltation was not universal.

Athens had many weaknesses. After the victory over Persia it turned its strength on its fellow Greeks. Not all or most of the Athenian population participated in its democracy. And yet there was a real contrast between the institutions of the Greeks and of the Persians and also between the fighting spirit of the two.

Time after time smaller Greek forces defeated larger Persian ones. The reason was partly superior tactics and military science, based on Greek use of the hoplite phalanx and trireme. However, the tactics themselves reflected the different kinds of society and the often higher morale.

The First Peloponnesian War was concluded by the Thirty Years' Peace. The military leader of the last phases of the war became the political leader of Athens; Pericles both extended Athenian democracy and became, partly through the record left by Thucydides, its chief spokesman for all time. He rebuilt the city's temples in marble, from the Parthenon on down, using the tribute reserve from the allies. In the Athens of Pericles, writes Russell Meiggs,

public service was not confined to a minority of activists but was the natural duty of all citizens, poor as well as rich, and most offices were filled by the lot. Five hundred men had to be found each year for the Boule [council], and, as no one could serve more than twice nor be under the age of 30, a large proportion of the citizen body must have served at least once. The Boule reviewed all state business and controlled the executive; and no business could be discussed in the Assembly unless it had been put on the agenda by the Boule. A year in the Boule was an intensive political experience, and for a tenth of the year every member had to be continuously available. The sovereign body was the Assembly, in which every citizen had an equal vote. . . . anyone could address the meeting; and amendments could be proposed from the floor. Perhaps the most surprising feature of the proceedings of the Assembly was the appointment by lot of the chairman, who changed daily and was chosen from the members of the Boule. That important policies could be discussed at large open-air meetings—at some of which a quorum of 6,000 was required —and result in rational decrees is a great tribute to the tolerance of the average citizen.[15]

Even when Pericles's power and popularity were at their height, he had to answer to the institutions just described.

In 431 B.C. a minor dispute erupted into a war between Athens's Delian League and Sparta's Peloponnesian League that came to be called the Great Peloponnesian War. Neither side thought it could afford to see the other gain substantially at its expense: Sparta feared the growth of Athenian power, while Athens felt its way to be blocked by Sparta. Pericles used the strategy of committing Athens's stronger fleet, while remaining inside the city walls and declining to engage Sparta's stronger army. In 429 he died, and his successors employed more aggressive tactics, with mixed results.

The Peace of Nicias (421) brought to an end the first phase of the war. It was supposed to last for fifty years. Athens now mounted a purely expansionist venture under the brilliant Alcibiades, which aimed at the conquest of Sicily. Alcibiades was recalled on charges of sacrilege but fled to Sparta to escape punishment. The expeditionary force was finally destroyed, and Athens turned to resume the war with Sparta. The Persians tried to exploit their opportunity. Alcibiades successfully negotiated the Treaty of Miletus (412) between Sparta and Persia. In effect the two formed an alliance against Athens: Persia would pay for maintaining the large fleet Sparta had just built, overextending herself financially in the process; in return, Sparta would recognize Persian rule over all the possessions of the Great King's forebears, meaning the Greek cities of Asia Minor.

In Athens, the principle of state pay for state service had been accepted under the leadership of Pericles. However, the course of the war led many to decide that it must be modified. There was also an oligarchically minded group that wished to curb the democracy whatever the state of the treasury or the extent of the demands of war. They proposed new institutions whereby a body of Four Hundred would rule, referring periodically to a suitably qualified Five Thousand. In 410, however, democracy was restored, following a smashing victory over the Spartan fleet by Alcibiades. He had been allowed to return to the Athenian naval base at Samos, his defection to Sparta forgiven. But again he got into trouble and retired. His successors blundered into an engagement at Aegospotami in which the Athenian fleet was annihilated. Now there was no alternative but peace.

Thebes and Corinth demanded that Athens be entirely destroyed. Sparta was, however, unwilling to go that far; it did require the razing of the long walls, the surrender of all triremes but twelve, and the reorganization of Athenian government along more oligarchical lines. The latter process was begun but then disrupted when the so-called Thirty Tyrants seized power. Nevertheless within a few months they were driven out and, with the consent of new rulers in Sparta, democracy returned to Athens. It was an Athens that was now merely one of the cities of the Peloponnesian League; her empire was a thing of the past.

Many have credited Persia with a large share in Sparta's victory: "Persian gold and Spartan soldiers brought about Athens's fall in 404 B.C." [16] In any case, the Persian monarch who ruled for almost the next half century, Artaxerxes II (404–359 B.C.), found that Greek affairs would not stay settled. Near the start of his reign he had to contend with a revolt led by his brother Cyrus the Younger at the head of ten thousand Greek mercenaries. Cyrus was killed in a battle in Mesopotamia. The Greek force then retreated to Ionia in an epic action chronicled by their leader, Xenophon, in his *Anabasis*. Renewed conflicts among the Greek city-states gave Artaxerxes more opportunities to intervene. In 386 he virtually imposed a settlement, called the King's Peace, that envisaged a division of the world: Syracuse would have the west; Sparta would dominate Greece; and Persia would regain the Ionian cities. Within a few years, however, Spartan power began to falter, and Artaxerxes lost enthusiasm for his Spartan ally. Athens began to revive and to put together a new league of cities. There was more fighting between Athens and Sparta; it was ended in 371 by a broad peace settlement including all powers from Syracuse to Persia.

However, Thebes withdrew from the roster of signators at the last moment. Believing themselves ill-treated by their erstwhile Spartan allies, the Thebans had their chance for revenge when a Lacedaemonian army invaded Boeotia. They defeated the Spartan infantry decisively. For the next decade Thebes was the arbiter of Greece. Theban hegemony had been achieved suddenly; and it was lost suddenly, when Thebes's great general, Epaminondas, was killed in 362 during a battle in which he seemed about to win a great victory. It was Athens's turn to follow Sparta and Thebes into decline. The Athenian League still existed, but in 357 a revolt against Athens was instigated by Mausolus, ruler of Caria in Ionia, which spread to become the Social War (meaning "War of the Allies"). By the peace of 355, Athens had to give up most of its possessions; its military power was at an end. The great orator Demosthenes would inveigh against the rising Macedonian danger and call for strengthening Athenian arms, but it was too late.

The Genius of Athens

Both Sparta and Athens made substantial contributions to the free institutions of Greece; but it was Athens, in the fifth and fourth centuries B.C., where the greatest Greek achievements in the fine arts, literature, and thought were produced. The architectural masterpieces of Periclean Athens were matched by first-rate sculpture; most of the painting has perished, but that which has survived, mainly on pottery, is much admired. The great tragedian Aeschylus was followed by Sophocles and Euripides in the later fifth century and the writer of comedy Aristophanes, a trifle later; it would be almost two millennia before their works were equaled or surpassed.

Perhaps, however, the cultural accomplishments of longest-lasting character lay in philosophy, especially political philosophy and the philosophy of law. In the sixth century law had come to be respected as a satisfactory regulator of human relations, an alternative to the settlement of disputes by blood feud and the vengeance of the clan, a protector of weak and strong alike in a society where the lines separating the two were less hard, less hereditary than in, for example, Egypt or Mesopotamia. Beginning with Thales of Miletus and the other Ionian physicists, the speculations of Greek philosophy arrived at the view that there were laws governing nature that were independent of persons and of chance. It has been suggested that the philosophers mentally transferred the order of the polis onto the order of the universe; others have argued that cosmological conclusions hastened the development of law in Greece. Possibly both assertions are true.

From about 450 B.C., the so-called Sophists began by offering instruction in how to take part successfully in the affairs of the polis and ended—judging from our fragmentary information—with a relativism and skepticism that threatened Athenian patriotism and civic pride. Socrates, partly their contemporary, affirmed the fundamental virtues and values of the polis and human society itself but, according to Plato's portrayal, subjected virtues and values to searching and systematic inquiry. Plato (427–347 B.C.) prescribed in *The Republic* remedies for the weaknesses of the polis that he observed without taking active part in the working of its institutions.

Aristotle was less preoccupied with the polis or the city of Athens, perhaps because he came from Stagira far to the north in Thrace or perhaps because he seemed more content to study politics and all philosophy in a detached manner. In discussing the ideal state, he was quite prepared to criticize his teacher, Plato; in *The Republic* Plato wished to abolish private property and the family and to make all citizens alike. That is wrong, declares Aristotle. A differentiation of functions is natural; moreover, abolition of property would produce dissension, not remove it, and communism of wives and children would destroy the natural affection that stems from close human relationships. Aristotle notes that in *Laws* Plato abandons communism but, he says, otherwise continued to reiterate the ideas of *The Republic*.

In *Politics* Aristotle seemed unimpressed with any ideal status thus far depicted. Of existing states, he declares Sparta, Crete, and Carthage to be the best; but since Sparta is fit only for war and the Cretan cities are similar and still more primitive, it is only distant Carthage, an oligarchy with some democratic features, that carries off more than the faintest praise.[17]

He believes that the best government in general is "constitutional government," defined as "when the citizens at large administer the state for the common interest." Democracy, he thinks, is a perversion of constitutional government; by that term he means the rule of the *demos,* the poor. He argues nevertheless that when the poor meet together they "may very likely be better than the few good," even if their lack of wisdom may be dangerous and their lack of money open them to corruption when individually placed in high office. Following Plato, he declares that democracy has as its end liberty. For him those values are not axiomatic or absolute as they are for moderns in much of the world today. Aristotle's main concern is virtue—the pursuit of the good. Yet since man is a "political animal," provision needs to be made for him to take part in political discussion and decision making.[18]

The great Stagirite had no doubt that certain people had higher political capacities than others—specifically, that none surpassed the Greeks. (Here he does not as before discuss individual poleis.) He declares:

Those who live in a cold climate and in Europe are full of spirit, but wanting in intelligence and skill; and therefore they retain comparative freedom, but have no political organization, and are incapable of ruling over others. Whereas the natives of Asia are intelligent and inventive, but they are wanting in spirit, and therefore they are always in a state of subjection and slavery. But the Hellenic race, which is situated between them, is likewise intermediate in character, being high-spirited and also intelligent. Hence it continues free, and is the best-governed of any nation, and, if it could be formed into one state, would be able to rule the world.[19]

Earlier he contrasts Greek government with the despotic governments of Asiatics and "barbarians" (for example, of the north). There is no danger, he writes, that the latter will be overthrown because the regimes are "hereditary and legal" and "the people are by nature slaves."[20]

It seems that the first twelve chapters of book 7 of *Politics* (from which the just-quoted passage is drawn) date from the early 340s; the lines quoted might be a prediction of the career of the boy he began in 342 to tutor for three years, who became Alexander the Great.

Macedonia

Since about 500 B.C., the barbarian kingdom of Macedonia had taken shape and had been growing in wealth and strength. Archelaus (413–399) established a capital at Pella that was able to attract such cultural luminaries as Euripides to spend some time there. The king did much to put both government and army on a sound footing, but he was followed by four decades of dynastic disorder. They were ended when Philip, twenty-three years of age, uncle to the child-king Amyntas, was made regent. He had spent three years in Thebes as a hostage, and what he learned from Epaminondas and others there no doubt helped prepare him for the great deeds he presently undertook.

By 356 Philip had seized the throne for himself and prepared to find a pretext to invade the Greece that lay to the south. In a brilliant series of military campaigns and diplomatic maneuverings, he paved the way for his decisive victory at the battle on the plain of Chaeronea in Boeotia in 338. The peace he imposed on Athens—the leading Greek city despite its vicissitudes—was a mild one. The next year he gathered together in Corinth delegates from all cities but Sparta. They formed the Hellenic League. There was to be a league council over which the king presided in wartime but which otherwise was led by another officer. Autonomy of all members was guaranteed; no existing constitutions were to be altered; no property confiscated; no tribute required. Each member had one obligation only: to provide a portion of the federal army and fleet.

Soon Philip proposed an attack on Persia to free the Greek cities of Ionia, and a Macedonian advance guard did, in fact, cross the Hellespont. At that moment Philip was assassinated. He had unified the Greek cities of the mainland and the Aegean. His great successor was to turn east, finish what Philip had begun, and go far beyond his objectives. Only the western Greeks were left out of the Macedonian advance. Syracuse in Sicily had been developed into perhaps the world's richest and largest city by the tyrant Dionysius the Elder (405–367 B.C.), and Plato journeyed three times to Syracuse in the hope that his ideal of the philosopher-king might be realized in that setting. The hope was in vain, but the western Greeks eluded conquest for some time. By the end of the fourth century, the Romans were on the horizon; during the First Punic War (264–241), Rome annexed all of Sicily but Syracuse; during the Second Punic War (218–201), Syracuse followed.

Philip was succeeded by his son Alexander, who had learned from Aristotle to love the great Greek literature and thought and from his father to love war. Though only twenty, he moved swiftly to assume the role of monarch. A revolt flared in Thebes, on the false rumor that he had died. With incredible speed he reached the city, razed it, and killed or enslaved the entire population. He then turned east.

What Alexander intended at the outset of his invasion of Asia is not certainly known; what we do know is what he did. Crossing the Hellespont, he prepared to assault the Persians, whose throne had been shaken by repeated rebellions. At the river Granicus he won a smashing victory over the Persian army. Advancing through Ionia in triumph, he defeated Darius III at Issus in 333. Circling south to Egypt, which he captured without a fight, he had in mind depriving the Persians of their naval bases and neutralizing their fleet. He then advanced to administer a third and decisive blow to Darius at Gaugamela and burned Persepolis. Darius, the last of the Achaemenid dynasty, was murdered in 330, and the Persian Empire came to an end. Alexander entered Bactria and marched into India as far as the Hyphasis River, a tributary of the Indus. He wished to reach the Ganges—thought to mark the end of land—but the army refused to go farther.

In the course of his unprecedented expedition, Alexander conceived of his task as one of fusing Greeks and Asiatics, East and West. Certainly he wished to Hellenize the East, and in order to do so he founded thirty-four cities named Alexandria, the most important being the one in Egypt. His own marriage to Roxana, daughter of the Bactrian chief Oxyartes, and the other marriages with Asiatic girls he demanded of his followers—ten thousand at once in 324 at Susa —showed his determination to mix Hellenes and Iranians.

In such respects Alexander came to reject Aristotle's view of Greek superiority. Callisthenes, Aristotle's nephew, was in the young king's entourage as official historian; when Alexander's "half-romantic and half-political penchant for Oriental dress and behavior" led him to introduce prostration into court ceremonial,

Callisthenes's forceful protests induced him to back down. The result was that Callisthenes soon faced charges brought, probably falsely, by his enemies and was tortured and hanged. Some have said that Alexander's notions of the fusion of East and West constituted a pre-Stoic anticipation of the doctrine of the brotherhood of man. However, his program may not have had quite that breadth: it seems that though Iranians were included in his vision, Egyptians, Arabs, Phrygians, and Jews were not.[21]

Alexander came to be "gripped by the idea that he was not merely the conqueror of the Shah, but his successor as well." It is certainly true that on the map his conquests look very much like the Persian Empire. But in some ways he reached back to older Near Eastern traditions. For his capital he chose not the homeland of the Achaemenids but Babylon; it was a fateful choice, since his successors built Seleucia, Ctesiphon, and Baghdad in the vicinity over the following centuries. Finally, Alexander demanded that he be recognized as a god. The ancient conception of the god-king derived most clearly from Egypt though it had other antecedents. In such ways the conqueror sought to orientalize the Greeks.

Like all grandiose schemes, Alexander's fell short of success. He did not even live to return to Greece. He died in Babylon, worn out, in 323 b.c. He was not quite thirty-three years old.

The Greek Heritage

In the entire span of human history to date, the duration of the existence of the Greek polis was but a fleeting moment. A few decades only separate Herodotus, who celebrated the heady victories of the Persian wars, from Thucydides, who recorded the disaster of the Peloponnesian wars. The polis began before the one and lasted after the other, but only in irregular and interrupted fashion. Its star burned brightly, briefly. It was often obscured by the clouds of corruption, trickery, hysteria, and treason. And yet the brief time the polis had lasted was enough to persuade the best Greek thinkers that something of great and universal value had been produced, something so new and precious as to set off Hellas sharply from the preceding states of the Near East and its contemporary, Persia, whose empire under the Achaemenids embraced most of the civilized world, and to serve as a model for all men who would be free.

The Greek cities developed partly free societies—to put it another way: societies in which all adult male citizens were free and politically equal. Their philosophers pointed to the institutions of the polis, discussed how they had come into being and what they signified, and proclaimed their merits to mankind. For two millennia and more the ideals and realities of institutional freedom as they had been given form by the Greeks served as inspiration for political philosophers and practical politicians alike. The ideals were not always inspiring and were sometimes sordid. Even the citizenry of Periclean Athens was on occasion disorderly, stupid, and ungrateful—but also demonstrated other qualities, which were ancestral to those modern characteristics that made Winston Churchill declare that democracy was the worst of governments, except for all the others.

It is interesting, however, that the Greek political philosophers confined themselves to describing certain features of their own institutions without probing to the heart of the question, what are the essentials and prerequisites of liberty? From Herodotus to Aristotle, and earlier and later, Greek thinkers contrasted the freedom of Hellas with the despotism of Persia but without analyzing either into its basic institutional components. Even Aristotle, perhaps the most mature Greek commentator on politics, regarded the difference between Hellenic and Iranian governments as ethnic and genetic in character, and he did not try to identify and examine the instrumentalities of the Persian Empire by which the Great King maintained the power of the monarchy and from which the Hellenes were free.

But later writers could reflect on such questions. Ancient Greece created free institutions and defended them, in battle and in argument; and humanity must be grateful for those tremendous achievements. In the formula of Georg Friedrich Hegel, in the ancient Orient only one man was free (the despot); in the classical world, some were free. The amazingly difficult step from one to some was first taken by the Greeks.

CHAPTER 3

Rome and the Hellenistic Mediterranean

The Beginnings of Rome

When Alexander the Great died, his generals and officials immediately began a series of struggles that continued for decades. Ptolemy was installed in Egypt from the first; Seleucus became established in Babylonia. Antigonus the One-Eyed attempted to unify the empire left by Alexander; he failed and was killed, but his descendants came to rule Macedonia.

In Egypt the Ptolemies applied Greek management to the old Egyptian despotism. The new Greek officialdom was assiduous in keeping records of every sort: at one time the great library at Alexandria possessed seven hundred thousand rolls of papyrus.[1] The most important of the several cities founded by Alexander and given his name came to serve as the "university of the entire Mediterranean world" throughout the Hellenistic age and to retain an undiminished vitality for over a thousand years, until the Muslims founded Cairo as a rival capital.[2]

The Seleucids had the most heterogeneous of the succession states, made up of parts of Asia Minor, Mesopotamia, Syria, and Iran. Seleucus I had given up "India" to Chandragupta Maurya in exchange for a troop of five hundred war elephants, and a few decades later Greek kings had established seceding states in Bactria and adjacent areas. In the lands to the west the Seleucids tried to Hellenize without using too heavy a hand. Under the Antigonids Macedonia kept its citizen army and for that reason was able to avoid total centralization, but it did not succeed in retaining control of Greece to the south.

About 247 B.C. Arsaces, leader of the Iranian people called Parthians, founded a kingdom between Bactria and the Seleucid empire, and its rulers were Hellenizers for some time. The Parthians, having come close to restoring the power of the Achaemenid state, lasted until A.D. 226.

In the view of F. E. Peters, even before Alexander invaded Asia Hellenism had "converted" the Lydians, the Macedonians, and the Romans; after that, it was simply "yoked together" with the political systems of the Asians.[3] In the capitals of the larger succession states—Alexandria of the Ptolemies, Antioch of the Seleucids (and also Pergamum, chief city of a lesser state, in western Asia Minor), though not in Pella of Antigonid Macedonia—the pattern was one of coexistence of the brutal despotism of the Near East with fragments or remnants of Hellenic culture. Plutarch tells us, for example, that after the battle of Carrhae in 53 B.C. the head of Crassus, the Roman commander, was brought to the Parthian king, Orodes II, while he was watching a performance of Euripides's *Bacchae,* and was rolled onto the stage like a soccer ball.

Greeks performed well in the institutions of the polis; they also came to distinguish themselves as better and more efficient bureaucrats in the service of the Hellenistic courts than some of the indigenous types. From the days when Ephialtes showed the Persians how to turn the Spartan position at Thermopylae, Greeks could be found to serve despotism. Aristotle (apparently) to the contrary, there is nothing in the desire for the rule of many as against the rule of one that attaches itself to any given ethnic group.

By approximately the beginning of the Christian era, the successor kingdoms had disappeared; the conquerors were the Parthians in the east and the Romans in the west. The Romans also extended their realm in the west, and north and south as well, into regions where civilization was new. For a time they took the Greek ideals and institutions of liberty and gave them meaning and embodiment in a quite new setting.

According to the account written more than seven centuries later by Livy, Rome was founded by Romulus about 750 B.C. He was thought to be the first of seven kings and a Latin in origin (from Latium, the region of Rome). His successor was Numa Pompilius, a Sabine, whose reign was identified with law, morality, and religion. Later came the two Tarquins, said to be Etruscans, from Etruria to the north; between their reigns came "Servus Tullius," an alleged Latin but a figure many scholars regard as a patriotic invention to avoid giving credit to the Tarquins. The last king, Tarquin the Proud, was driven out by Romans who were outraged by his misconduct. They proceeded to found a republic, which at the outset was an aristocracy. The traditional date of the founding of the republic, and probably close to the correct one, is 509 B.C.

The Early Republic

The institutions of the republic were initially aristocratic. Tradition, or perhaps legend, had it that each king had been elected by the *comitia*, or Assembly, and confirmed by the *senatus*, or Senate. The Senate was made up of one hundred elders (*patres*); under the republic it was as before a consultative body but gained great power as it came to be a patrician preserve. The king's powers, political and military, came to be entrusted to two consuls, elected annually, drawn exclusively (or nearly so) from the patricians until 367 B.C. At that time a legal requirement was adopted that one consul must be from the commoners or plebeian order.

"Patricians" and "plebeians" were not mere modes of expression; they were legally defined orders of society. During the period of monarchy great patrician families took form and persisted as a small aristocratic elite. As for the overwhelming majority of Roman citizens—the plebeians—they began by having no civic obligations and being exempt from both military service and taxation. However, the Etruscan kings worked out a system of recruitment of the plebs into the army, based on the results of the census.

The Senate, in theory continuing the institution of monarchical times, was made up of the heads of the patrician clans (*gentes*), though nominally the consuls, then later the censors, selected its members—in every case for life. A second component of the membership came to be all former magistrates. The Senate came to have de facto legislative powers, supervised many other governmental functions, and sent and received ambassadors. In the late republic, it also appointed magistrates to the newly conquered provinces. These mainly patrician institutions were challenged by the plebs in the so-called Conflict of the Orders, which lasted from the fifth to the third century. Plebeians gained political equality with patricians, and some plebeian families entered the senatorial aristocracy. In a fateful confrontation of 493–492 B.C. especially, patricians were compelled to recognize officials called tribunes who would defend plebeian interests. Religious innovations—Roman religion played an important part in all political processes—provided sanctions for the retention of these changes.

During the republic three or four popular assemblies the facts concerning which are difficult to establish became significant.[4] Evidently, the oldest was the Comitia Curiata, in which the voting units were thirty curias (ten for each of three "tribes"). It passed laws confirming the power of magistrates and other officers. The Comitia Centuriata, originally a military gathering, acquired political functions; the voting units were 193 centuries and 35 tribes in which patricians dominated. It elected the (two) consuls and the (from four to eight) praetors and, every four or later five years, two censors who conducted the census, "which determined the citizen's classification according to property, and consequently the value of his vote."[5] Until 218 it was the chief legislative body, thereafter summoned only for declarations of war and confirmation of the census.

Possibly in the mid-fifth century began the Comitia Tributa, little different from the Concilium Plebis (or Council of the Plebeian Order). In both the voting units were the thirty-five tribes. After issuance of the Lex Hortensia in 287 B.C., which is regarded as terminating the Conflict of Orders and made acts of the plebs binding on the whole state, the two tribal assemblies, especially the Concilium Plebis, passed most laws.

Except for the tribal assemblies, all of them were subject to veto from tribunes of the plebs. In all the assemblies, voting was by units; but before division into units all citizens could attend a preliminary public meeting known as *conventio,* or the shortened form *contio,* at Rome. In the assemblies themselves voting at first was oral, but by 107 B.C. the written ballot had come to prevail.

The division of functions in the Roman republic was connected with the strong emphasis on law that is found in Roman annals from the earliest times. The basic document was the law of the Twelve Tables, evidently drawn up by ten officers, called decemvirs, who replaced the consuls in 450, and for that year alone. It was displayed in the Forum on twelve tablets of bronze or wood and was committed to memory by schoolchildren for centuries thereafter. It had a pervasive religious tone (to judge by the portions that survive), but the essential element was affirmation of the rights of all citizens; the right of appeal of any sentence, from any court, to the popular assembly was guaranteed.[6]

Throughout the fifth century and into the fourth, Rome was the foremost of the cities of Latium. The rest of them belonged to the Latin League, with which Rome had a treaty wherein Rome and the League treated each other as equals. In about 390 an invasion of the barbarian Gauls swept into the city and held it for a time, causing terror among the Romans; but Rome recovered, established hegemony in Latium, and in 338 dissolved the Latin League, incorporating some cities into Rome directly and granting others "Latin rights." After a prolonged struggle with the Samnites, the Gauls, and the remnants of the Etruscans, the city emerged victorious over them all. Its armies pushed south into Greek Italy, which centered on Tarentum, after finally driving off the forces of Pyrrhus, king of Epirus across the Adriatic. Thus the peninsula was conquered.

Carthage, master of the western Mediterranean, was on good terms with Rome until the latter, with its legions and a newly built navy, invaded Sicily on the appeal of a Campanian force in the city of Messana. Thus began the Punic (meaning Phoenician or Carthaginian) Wars. In the first of them Rome won most of western Sicily from Carthage (241) and constituted it as the first Roman province (227). The Carthaginian general Hamilcar Barca sought revenge. He, then his son-in-law, established a base in Spain, but Hamilcar's son Hannibal, after both the others were dead, pressed forward to attack. Crossing the Alps with the fabled elephants (probably they were few in number), he won a series of brilliant victories culminating at Cannae (216).

Rome refused to admit the defeat that many thought meant the end of the war. Recouping its fortunes slowly, it at length dispatched the gifted young P. Cornelius Scipio to invade Carthage. Hannibal was brought back from Italy to meet the invading army. Scipio crushed his great foe at Zama in 202 (gaining the name "Africanus"), ending the war.

Rome now established two more provinces, Hither Spain and Farther Spain. One other, Sardinia-and-Corsica, had been founded between the creation of the Sicilian and the Spanish provinces. By this time several slightly different forms of alliance or annexation had come to characterize Roman rule in Italy, and some of them continued to be used in the east; but annexation was the usual form of handling conquered territories in the west outside Italy.

In the first four provinces, by 197, governors were appointed annually who were also praetors. The title of praetor had been applied for more than a century to an urban magistrate who had been a colleague of the consuls, of lesser rank and power. Later in the second century B.C. it became usual to prolong the term of office of all consuls and praetors so that they moved from Rome to a province (from which practice developed the titles "proconsul" and "propraetor") with the rank of the previous year, and the extension might be for longer. The governor had an assistant who was a quaestor and in addition a substantial staff. Taxation in the provinces ballooned into exploitation of various sorts and corruption, practiced by the tax-farmers, or *publicani,* ultimately tax-farming companies, on a large scale. The result, writes M. Cary, was that "Roman rule in Italy gave general satisfaction; in the provinces it causes widespread discontent."[7]

Like others in the Hellenistic age, the Romans acknowledged Greek cultural superiority in many respects. Thus in the first phases of the four Macedonian Wars they fought, the slogan "the freedom of the Greeks" figured prominently. At the end of the Second Macedonian War, in 196 B.C., Philip V of Macedon was required to restore to liberty the Greek states he ruled and to abstain from infringing on the liberty of those he did not. The Roman army thereupon withdrew to Italy.

This settlement did not last. It became clear that cutting Philip down to size was a greater concern of Rome than Greek freedom, and in three years the troops returned. In 167 Macedonia was divided into four independent republics. One, Achaea, was forced to send one thousand hostages to Rome, of whom one was Polybius. He prospered and began to write his important history as guest of the great general Scipio Aemilianus, grandson by adoption of the victor of Zama.

An attempt was made to restore the Macedonian monarchy in 148. When it was defeated, Macedonia became a Roman province, incorporating Epirus and Thessaly. Two years later another set of disturbances led Rome to raze Corinth and enslave the inhabitants, dissolve the Achaean League, replace all democracies in the Greek cities by oligarchies, and place central and southern Greece under the supervision of the governor of Macedonia. These measures marked the end of Greek independence.

During the previous decades Carthage had enjoyed something of a revival. M. Porcius Cato made certain no one failed to notice by ending every speech in the Senate by declaring that "Carthage must be destroyed." After its army attacked the Numidian king Masinissa, who was an old ally of Rome, Scipio Aemilianus finally captured Carthage. The city was razed, abandoned, and cursed, and the surviving inhabitants were sold into slavery. The territory became the sixth province of Rome. Not long afterward, in 133, the last king of Pergamum died, leaving his realm to Rome; as "Asia" it became the seventh province.

In the course of the great conquests of the provinces in the third and second centuries, Rome often treated the conquered populations mildly, admitting many to citizenship and resettling others rather than enslaving them. Roman citizenship was highly valued, and rightly so. It originally included the right to participate in government through voting in the assemblies. One had to come to Rome to do this, and that was increasingly impracticable for most. A citizen had to pay taxes, but he enjoyed equality before the law. In Muller's words, "what had been a jealously guarded privilege in Athens, comparable to membership in an exclusive club, became the right of all free members of the community. . . . By law the citizen was a *persona:* a man with private rights to life, liberty, and property —rights declared and protected by the state."[8]

In attempting to explain the basis of Rome's success, the Greek, Polybius, "emphasized the binding force of Roman public religion as inducing in Roman public servants, through the sancrosanctity of oaths, an integrity that had no parallel in contemporary Greece."[9] Roman honor was closely linked with civic spirit that, in turn, was thought by Polybius to be related to the balance of powers existing between the principles of monarchy (the consuls), aristocracy (the Senate), and democracy (the popular assemblies)—and though consuls were scarcely kings, there had indeed been an effort to diffuse power, expressed in the official title used in legislation: SPQR, Senatus Populusque Romanus, the Senate and the People of Rome.

The wars in the eastern Mediterranean yielded a large supply of slaves. In the ancient world prisoners were regularly enslaved and sold away from their homeland, and the resulting damage to freedom foreshadowed the displacement on an immense scale of forced laborers, deportees, and refugees of all sorts that attended World War II, not to mention the extermination camps of Hitler and the massacres of suspected opponents by Stalin that occurred during the same period. Freedom and war do not go well together; it may still be argued that war has nevertheless been necessary to gain freedom (as in the American Civil War, which ended slavery) or to preserve it (as against the Nazis).

At any rate many slaves were indeed needed by the great estates, devoted to raising cattle or sheep, which grew rapidly in Italy in the wake of the Carthaginian damage done in the Second Punic War. As these *latifundia* grew, the small farmers displaced thereby flooded into Rome and a few other cities.

Through the western Greeks (that is, the Greeks of southern Italy and Sicily) and then direct contact with Greece proper, the Romans were subjected to wide and deep Greek cultural influences. Greek slaves became nurses of the babies and tutors of the children of Roman aristocrats. By the second century B.C. educated Romans spoke Greek as readily as Latin, and in some cases Greek in preference to Latin.

One school of Greek thought found a ready reception in Rome: Stoicism. The half-Greek, half-Phoenician Zeno (d. 264 B.C.), teaching in the Painted Porch (*stoa poikile*) of Athens, concentrated—as did his contemporary Epicurus—on the ethical obligations of the individual, operating in a world where universal reason guaranteed a common humanity undergirding a notion of the brotherhood of man. It

commended a life of action and encouraged participation in public affairs. Its main postulate, that the world was a theatre for the display of human will-power, and that the difficulties of human life were literally "trials," appealed directly to Roman stubbornness and self-respect; on the other hand its lack of ready sympathy with human suffering gave no shock to Roman pride.[10]

The Republic in Crisis

Greek ideas of the political and social equality of the citizenry was not congenial to Roman traditions, but some individuals may have been affected by them. So at least it was contended regarding the reform movements led by the Gracchi from 133 B.C. Tiberius Gracchus, grandson of Scipio Africanus, was concerned about the consequences of the great social changes that had occurred in the south: the danger of slave revolts (a lengthy one in Sicily had just been put down) and the shrinkage of the citizenry possessing some land and being liable for military service. As tribune, Tiberius Gracchus proposed to enforce the existing law limiting the tenure of public land to about three hundred acres and to use the land thus obtained to settle landless citizens. Through intricate legal maneuvers he pushed the measure through, but opposition to him led to his being killed in 133 along with three hundred of his followers.

In 123 Gaius Gracchus became tribune, seeking both to avenge the murder of his brother Tiberius and to resume his program. He revived Tiberius's land law and provided that the government must furnish grain at a fair price to the poor; he also proposed to extend the full franchise to Latin cities and "Latin rights" to all other Italians.

However, the Roman citizenry were not eager to share the advantages of citizenship so widely. In ensuing struggles Gaius Gracchus and his ally, Marcus Fulvius Flaccus, were killed. The land distributions of the Gracchi may have arrested for a time the decline of the rural citizenry; the measure of Gaius giving some supervisory powers over senatorial administration to eminent equestrians lasted and had benefits. During the political struggles of the Gracchan period two parties, the *optimates* (the traditional aristocrats, claiming to be the "best men") and *populares* (striving to work through the common people rather than the Senate) had sprung up and outlasted the Gracchi. If the Gracchan reforms, "in which, for the first time in Rome, Greek theoretical influences may be traced," fell short of their objective, they had some success in stabilizing Roman society.[11]

Thereafter not domestic reformers but military heroes gave direction to the republic. The first was Gaius Marius, an equestrian who had risen to become consul in 107 B.C. Mainly through the skill of his quaestor Lucius Sulla, he managed to defeat a usurper to the Numidian throne, Jugurtha, and followed this victory by destroying the forces of the barbarian Cimbri at Aquae Sextiae (Aix-les-Bains). As consul he set aside the previous system of recruitment, based on property qualifications, and accepted volunteers from the poor and rootless. These and other changes substantially improved the effectiveness of the army. As for Marius himself, he fell victim to political infighting between senators who despised him as an upstart and demagogues interested in using him for their own purposes. In consequence he left Rome in 100 B.C. for a time, and when he returned he was unable to regain his former influence.

Rome's ills resisted all kinds of effort to remedy them. The equestrian class had been given power by Gaius Gracchus to watch over senatorial administration of the provinces; its bankers and tax-farmers now demonstrated their ability to plunder the province of Asia, Rome's chief source of income. The Senate sent two of its men of greatest probity, Quintus Mucius Scaevola and Publius Rutilius Rufus, to put things in some kind of order. They did so; but on his return, Rutilius was convicted of "extortion" by a court dominated by the very group he and Scaevola had been seeking to curb. The result was that soon the governors, formerly coming from the civic-minded senatorial class and wishing good government, became corrupt as well.[12]

Dissatisfaction among the poor of Rome and the Italians outside the city led Marcus Livius Drusus, the tribune for 91, to propose a series of reforms. They envisaged granting citizenship to all Italians, admitting three hundred *equites* to the Senate, and improving the lot of the poor. The measures were blocked; Drusus was assassinated; and the Italians revolted. In the so-called Social War (or War of the Allies), Gnaeus Pompeius Strabo and Sulla, Marius's former quaestor, were mainly successful in quelling the rising.

In 88 Sulla was elected consul. A law stripping him of his military command in favor of the aging Marius aroused his ire; he managed to persuade the army that had fought under him in the Social War to follow him in a march on Rome to set the legislation aside. It was the first time a private army had acted in such a manner. The military reforms of Marius, designed to correct certain weaknesses, had by creating client armies produced a still more serious weakness. In Badian's words, "the end of the republic was foreshadowed."[13]

For several years Sulla was kept busy with sporadic civil war and conflict with Mithradates VI Eupator, king of Pontus in northern Asia Minor. While he was absent the consul Cornelius Cinna seized power, but in 82 Sulla succeeded in returning triumphantly to Rome, scattering his enemies. He was now proclaimed dictator, purportedly reviving an old legal form, for the redrafting of the constitution, and thereupon undertook systematic murder of his enemies and seizure of their property.

Nevertheless Sulla also worked at strengthening the institutions of the Republic, especially the authority of the Senate. Its membership was increased from three hundred to six hundred; the censors lost rights over admission and removal of senators; and the office of tribune was much restricted. Sulla limited legislative power to the Comitia Centuriata under senatorial control. In effect the jury reform of Gaius Gracchus was overturned; "in all the *quaestiones,* old and new, the jurors were appointed from the ranks of the Senate, and the Equites were completely excluded from the higher jurisdiction at Rome."[14]

In 79 Sulla voluntarily resigned the dictatorship and retired to a Campanian estate, where he died the following year. Cary writes, "Sulla stands in a line with Scipio Africanus and Caesar as one of the outstanding figures of the Roman Republic. . . . [However,] in the long run his own example of successful military usurpation proved more effective than the inadequate remedial measures which he devised against a recurrence of his [own] offense."[15]

At the time of Sulla's retirement the Roman republic had a half-century of life remaining, during which a series of gifted military and political leaders appeared, struggled for power, and one by one passed from the scene. The first was Pompey (Gnaeus Pompeius, the son of Gn. Pompeius Strabo), who had served as a commander for Sulla. Pompey was given the task of suppressing what may be called either the revolt or the countergovernment of Quintus Sertorius in Spain. This he finally accomplished in 72. He returned to Italy just in time to finish off the slave rebellion led by the Thracian gladiator Spartacus, though M. Licinius Crassus, a praetor, had already defeated the rebels twice.

Now Pompey and Crassus contended for the consulship. Fortunately there were two, and each man received one for the year 70. They proceeded to undo much of the Sullan reform. Censors and tribunes regained powers, and the equestrian class along with them. An ambitious beneficiary of the Sullan reforms named M. Tullius Cicero prosecuted the propraetor of Sicily, Verres, helping to bring pressure for large nonsenatorial membership on the courts.

The institutions of the republic had undergone several substantial reorganizations. By this time they were threatened by popular demagogues and ambitious commanders willing to risk using Rome's legions as their own private armies. Worst of all, however, was the weakening of the defenders of law, honest administration, and the public good; the moral fiber of the senators was not what it had been. Among other things, the Senate was no longer resistant to new annexations.

Pompey was ready to test the resistance. In 67 he was given an extraordinary command of all the Mediterranean coastline to rid the sea of pirates, and he succeeded in doing so within a few months. Sent to the east, he defeated Rome's old antagonist, Mithradates VI, drove him to suicide, and seized Pontus, his kingdom. Pompey then proceeded to reorganize Rome's possessions in the area: Asia with its riches and revenues was shielded by three provinces: Bithynia-Pontus, Cilicia, and Syria. Beyond them were client kingdoms: eastern Pontus, Cappadocia, Galatia, Lycia, and Judaea (Judah).

In Judaea, an internal crisis invited Roman intervention. Led by the Maccabees, the Jews had rebelled against the Seleucid king, Antiochus IV Epiphanes, when he banned Judaism in 168 B.C. out of Hellenizing motives. The Maccabees had gained independence, but the rulers had fallen to squabbling. In 63 Pompey invaded the country, captured Jerusalem, and imposed a settlement. He then returned to Rome, which gave him an unprecedented triumph—however, he did not obtain what he wanted most: approval of his reorganization of the East and the grant of land for his veterans.

In 60 B.C. a new figure appeared in the ranks of the leadership, Gaius Julius Caesar, descended from poor but patrician stock. In that year he returned from Spain, where he had spent a year as administrator, to seek a consulship. He got it by forging a coalition often called the First Triumvirate with Crassus, his former patron, and Pompey. Caesar obtained for Pompey his two unsatisfied demands relating to Eastern government and veteran lands, and managed comparable benefits from Crassus, using soldiers to dispose of opposition. Thereupon he secured for himself primacy in Cisalpine Gaul, Illyria, and then Transalpine Gaul. He determined to conquer the rest of Gaul to the north. In a long and tortuous war, marked by temporary forays into Britain and the territory east of the Rhine, he finally defeated the able Gallic commander, Vercingetorix, with the siege of Alesia (Alise, near Dijon) in 52 B.C.

In the meantime Crassus had been sent to Syria, became involved in a full-scale war with the Parthians, and plunged headlong into disaster. He was defeated and himself killed in the battle of Carrhae in Mesopotamia. Pompey and the Senate engaged in continual intrigues against the other triumvir. The Senate at length laid down the gauntlet to Caesar by an ultimatum to disband his army. Caesar's answer was to lead one legion across the stream named Rubicon, the southern boundary of his province, near Ravenna, in 49.

In effect the crossing opened war on Pompey. The conflict was short. Caesar caught Pompey in Greece and defeated him at Pharsalus; Pompey then fled to Egypt, where he was killed by order of a Ptolemaic official. Before learning of the murder, Caesar went in pursuit of him to Alexandria, where he was promptly besieged by Ptolemy XII, and an army of Asia had to be sent to rescue him. Caesar then proceeded to place Cleopatra VII, who had captivated him, on the Egyptian throne and continued the campaign against Pompeian forces until he finally defeated Pompey's sons at Munda in Spain in 45.

Julius Caesar brought from Egypt the knowledge needed to reform the calendar, and the "Julian" calendar, using 365¼ days per year, lasted for many centuries. But despite the virtually unlimited power he had gained, Caesar made no important structural changes in Roman government. He increased the membership of the Senate to nine hundred and also enlarged the number of quaestors and praetors; in addition, citizenship was extended to more people. He prepared to mount a campaign against Parthia to avenge Crassus, but the attendant military hazards were never to be tested. While he was planning to venture, he was assassinated in the Senate by a conspiracy in which a total of about sixty persons, partly selfless patriots and partly petty time-servers, led by M. Junius Brutus and C. Cassius Longinus, took part. It was 15 March (the Ides) 44 B.C.

Since he adopted the purple robe of Rome's kings, accepted an official cult of himself, put an image of his own head on coins, and skirted use of the title *rex,* Caesar seemed to be on the edge of restoring monarchy—whatever exactly that might have meant at the time—and also of claiming divinity. Monarchy did not necessarily mean an unpopular type of government. There were many Caesarians, headed by Marcus Antonius (Marc Antony), Caesar's fellow consul of 44, who were favorably disposed toward the prospect. But for Romans (as contrasted with Greeks or Asiatics) to be asked to accept him as a living god was another matter, even though he was formally deified after his death.

The Establishment of the Empire

Caesar's inheritance was claimed by his eighteen-year-old grandnephew and adopted son and heir, Gaius Octavius. He was initially rebuffed by Antony. However, he proceeded to raise an army and at the same time to begin a series of skillful and elusive political maneuvers. Octavian allied himself with Antony and Marcus Lepidus in a formal and legal triumvirate (*triumviri rei publicae constituendae*). The triumvirs rid themselves of several enemies by execution, Cicero heading the list. Octavian and Antony joined to defeat and drive to suicide Brutus and Cassius in Thrace. They then separated to conduct independent military campaigns or political adventures. Antony became the lover of the queen of Egypt, Cleopatra, and soon also her husband though he was already married to Octavian's sister.

His dream that the two of them would rule as Hellenistic monarchs of the East was, however, not to be realized. Octavian rallied much of the West to support him and managed to arouse much distrust in Antony's plans and projects. Securing the consulship for the year, he attacked Antony and Cleopatra in Greece. In 31 at the battle of Actium he defeated them, and they fled to Egypt. In the following year, Antony committed suicide, followed by Cleopatra. She resorted to that measure only after failing to charm Octavian—as she had done with both Caesar and Antony—when he landed in Egypt. The country was now, at last, annexed to Rome.

Octavian returned to celebrate three triumphs and to close the temple of Janus, god of war—thus signifying peace; it had been closed only twice before, by Numa Pompilius and in 235 B.C.

The End of the Republic

The victorious leader undertook a "settlement" (the decisive one of several) in January of 27 B.C. He was awarded the name "Augustus," by which he came to be known to history. He entered his seventh consulship in 27 and kept the office until 23, when he gave it up and received the powers of a tribune—not technically the office, since he had been made a patrician and only a plebeian could hold it. One or another kind of consular *imperium* provided a legal basis for his rule in the provinces. Later he received also the titles *pontifex maximus* (head of the state religion, an ancient office Caesar had also held) and *pater patriae* (father of the country), but after 23 B.C. his powers were not substantially altered.

He chose three names only, like an ordinary Roman: "Imperator Caesar Augustus," which became titles in the usage of the fifth and later successors. Unofficially he was designated *princeps*, meaning simply the first citizen of Rome;

however, the term gave rise to "principate" for his system or what came to be called the "empire," a word derived from *imperium* or *imperator*.[16]

Thus the end of the republic was not the definite, precisely datable event some historians have made it seem; nevertheless, it was a significant development in the history of Rome and the world.

Like the Greek polis, the city of Rome had never been a complete democracy. What is more, the oligarchical institution of the Senate had an importance over the whole period of the republic that far exceeded anything comparable in Greece. Aristocracy was, writes Muller, deeply embedded in Roman tradition; common men did not aspire to the dignity of their betters. "Neither was there a declared ideal of freedom, such as Pericles proclaimed in the Funeral Oration; when Livy celebrated the virtues of the ancestors he did not maintain that freedom was what had made Rome great. Yet all Romans did have a voice in their government. All were citizens with certain rights recognized by law, in a state conceived as a *res publica*—a public thing."[17]

In the early republic the balance of powers that Polybius observed and admired was not imaginary. It was sustained by a deeply ingrained reverence for law— Rome's chief cultural contribution to human history—and a religiously based conception of honor that was closely related to legality.

A vital reason for Rome's growth and continued strength lay in the sturdy Italian peasantry, which furnished a large share of the soldiery for centuries. When latifundia grew in extent and peasant proprietors were uprooted, especially during and after the Second Punic War, that anchor of stability suffered damage; the small holdings of private property in land that supported the peasantry substantially diminished. Landless rural dwellers swelled the ranks of the Roman proletariat, and continuing conquests, particularly in the East, yielded a flow of aliens and slaves that changed social patterns drastically.

Such sweeping changes would seem to be enough to disrupt any body politic. Nevertheless it may be argued that it was not alteration in the numbers and composition of the lower classes in Roman society that doomed the republic. It was rather the failure of nerve of the two upper classes: the senatorial aristocracy and the commercial equestrians. If the equestrians became especially self-serving, greedy, and dishonest, the aristocrats succumbed to the taste for expensive pleasures and luxuries that also begged endlessly for money. It was of no use, as finally became obvious, to set one of the two classes to watch the other, for corruption spread through both.

They lost faith in the gods, so lost their compunction about breaking oaths, and at last their civic pride and scruples about attaining political goals. Laws were not enforced; frantic attempts to correct these ills, incorporated in new legislation, were scorned by their authors and ignored by those whom they were intended to restrain. Thus finally there was only one way to accomplish anything: rally an army and use force. The infrastructure of the republic was eaten away; it remained to try something else.

In the words of F. E. Peters, the death of the republic came in a "veil of constitutional continuity."[18] Augustus—ostensibly and at least partly sincerely —"valued the Senate as the repository of the true Roman spirit and traditions and as the body representing public opinion."[19] But the Senate was being re-shaped. There were senators delegated to his new Council of the Principate (*Concilium Principis*), but they were changed every six months and were chosen by lot. Augustus controlled the membership of the Senate; he reduced it to about six hundred and established conditions for being a member that could be met only by those enjoying his favor. At the same time he relied extensively on the *equites* to fill official positions, both new and old, and broadened their ranks to make them into a kind of lower aristocracy, from which new recruits to the Senate also began to be drawn.

Augustus placed Italy first in his policies, but he also undertook important changes in the empire. At the time of the battle of Actium there were sixty legions. He reduced the number to twenty-eight and welded them into a standing army along with other categories of soldiers (and sailors, who constituted the manpower of an imperial fleet). The most privileged of the soldiery were the praetorians, usually Italian, while the rest rapidly became non-Italian. In newly acquired Egypt and long misgoverned Asia, important things were done. Augustus eliminated tax-farming and made cities responsible for their own accounts. For this purpose a census was introduced. Egyptian prosperity survived only among the priestly class; in the rest of the society stagnation and impoverishment prevailed. The emperor, as we may now call him, tried to invigorate the economy of Egypt by admitting private capital, but the result was mainly large absentee estates on already tilled land (though later, under Vespasian, this trend was reversed). The great city of Alexandria was different from the rest of the country. It was the center of capitalism and culture, not merely for Egypt but for much of the Mediterranean—a Greek enclave in a setting of quite another sort.[20]

Client kingdoms and new provinces were annexed or created from Mauretania in Africa through Spain and the Gauls to the Rhine, in the west; in the east from the kingdom of the Bosporus and Armenia through Asia Minor to the new province of Judaea; in the north through the alpine areas to Pannonia. An effort to push beyond the Rhine led to the great disaster of A.D. 9, when German tribes annihilated Quinctilius Varus and three legions in the Teutoburg Forest (perhaps near present-day Paderborn). Fatigued and distraught, Augustus in consequence attempted no further expansion.

Extensive public works were undertaken. Construction of many public buildings of brick and marble changed the face of Rome, formerly largely wood. An impressive network of imperial highways sprang up, as old ones were repaired after long neglect and new ones were added. Augustus established a *cursus publicus,* or state post, modeled on the Ptolemaic post of Egypt. A distinct imperial civil service took shape. Accounting and record keeping were significantly improved. More than once during his reign Augustus was able to prepare a comprehensive survey of the financial resources of the whole empire.[21]

Augustus's own private fortune came to be immense. In Rome his person was termed *divi filius* as (adopted) son of the deified Caesar; in Asia he was worshipped; in Egypt he was straightforwardly both pharaoh and god, as pharaoh had always been.[22] In the Augustan system there were tinges and overtones of the despotism of the Orient, which would become more pronounced over the following centuries. In the words of Salmon,

> while precedents can be cited for Augustus' various powers, their concentration and tenure were absolutely unparalleled. Under the republic, powers like his would have been distributed among several holders, each serving for a limited period with a colleague. Augustus wielded them all, by himself, simultaneously and without any time limit (in practice, at least).[23]

It was not simply a matter of Augustus's own power or the power he accumulated as emperor and bequeathed to his successors; it was a question of what was happening to Roman society. The ancient aristocrats and equestrians had been converted into groups subservient to the emperorship, dependent for the retention of their wealth and property and for the acquisition of power on their ability to gain and hold office through the beneficence of the ruler. Law was not dead; it had not been abolished. But it could be bent, or even broken, if the will of the *princeps* (or the needs of the state as he saw them) demanded.

All such changes had developed to a greater or lesser extent under the republic. Nevertheless Augustus carried Rome across a kind of threshold that separated a polity in which freedom was steadily growing weaker from one in which the seeds of authoritarianism were beginning to sprout. In this process the conquest of Egypt seems to have played a pivotal role. Octavian proved immune to the charms of Cleopatra, to which Caesar and Antony had succumbed, but not to the seductions of the Egyptian political order. He found it useful to imitate aspects of the pharaonic powers, but at the same time he did his best to retain what was healthy in the Roman tradition, including liberty of sorts—if the word be "understood as meaning freedom from arbitrary rule and arbitrary interference."[24]

The Empire until Its End in the West

Augustus's rule lasted forty-five years, reckoning from the battle of Actium until his death in A.D. 14. Immediately the problem of succession posed itself—a chronic problem of all nonfree and nonconstitutional polities. Hereditary monarchy provides for it in theory, not so well in practice; the Roman Empire sometimes approached hereditary monarchy, but never solved the succession problem. Augustus was succeeded by Tiberius, his stepson adopted as his son, the first of four emperors spoken of as the Julio-Claudian dynasty (Augustus the son of Julius, Tiberius descendant of the Claudii) though there was officially no dynasty and constitutionally no provision for such a thing. Tiberius was followed by Gaius, nicknamed Caligula ("Little Boot"), a cruel tyrant who was assassinated in 41.

At this point some in the Senate wished to restore the republic. However, the Praetorian Guard, the elite of the army who had been unwisely concentrated near Rome by Tiberius, blocked the move and forced the accession of Claudius. Previously regarded as a drooling imbecile, Claudius surprised the scoffers. His chief concern was the empire. He annexed client kingdoms in Mauretania, Lycia, and Thrace and began the conquest of Britain in 43. He also extended Roman citizenship widely in the provinces. In 54 his adopted son Nero acceded to the throne, by choice of the praetorians and also the Senate. His reign began well but came to be marked by misgovernment in Rome and widespread rebellion in the provinces, and the entire record was stricken by decision of the Senate upon his suicide in 68.

There ensued the "year of the four emperors"—indeed, the first, Galba, was acclaimed emperor by the legions in Spain while Nero was still alive and was then confirmed by the Praetorian Guard. A series of military intrigues and battles elevated and killed in turn Galba, Otho, and Vitellius. Order seemed to return with Vespasian, the son of an Italian tax collector, who founded the bourgeois Flavian dynasty. Apparently for the first time, a law granted him full power as emperor.

During Vespasian's reign, his son Titus completed the suppression of the Jewish rebels by capturing and destroying Jerusalem (A.D. 70). Titus succeeded his father, and his brother Domitian followed—with a reign full of arbitrary and cruel behavior that led to his assassination and an official *damnatio memoriae,* or posthumous designation as a public enemy. The Flavian period (69–96) witnessed persistent disturbances on the frontiers of the Rhine and the Danube, but peace was maintained with the dangerous eastern neighbor, Parthia, and the conquest of Britain was completed up to a point near the Scottish highlands, which were never conquered by Rome.

If the Flavians put an end to a chaos that seemed to impend, the next group of rulers continued more or less stable government. They were called "the five good emperors" (96–180), as a result of the fact that Nerva, the first, chose an able successor and adopted him; he did in fact succeed Nerva; and the precedent was emulated three more times. The five are sometimes called the Antonines, though only the last two warrant the term (along with a sixth who was an Antonine but was far from "good").

Nerva's successor, Trajan, was one of the most attractive figures to hold the emperorship; he was modest, able, and popular. In him, wrote the historian Tacitus, empire and liberty were reconciled. But he was for all that an absolute ruler, whose vigor and efficacy helped to increase the size of the bureaucracy that did his bidding, and whose powers were no less because he largely refrained from abusing them. His military adventures in the east led to severe crisis. He annexed Dacia, thereby cementing the Danubian frontier with success. But he went on to become involved in war with Parthia, and while so occupied he found his rear to be imperiled by a series of revolts. Though he had conquered territory in Mesopotamia, the cost was great and he had to abandon his gains.

The next ruler, Hadrian, was not interested in conquest and engaged in overseas fighting only to the extent of putting down the last desperate Jewish revolt under Simon Bar Kokhba and turning Jerusalem into a Roman colony from which Jews were barred except once a year. He spent much of his reign visiting the provinces, taking care to assure their defense (Hadrian's Wall in Britain and the *limes* from Mainz to Regensburg) but not attempting to enlarge them. It was a time of development of increased bureaucratization of the government and refinement of official distinctions, especially among the equestrians who held many of the positions concerned. Antoninus Pius (evidently so called because he worked hard at obtaining posthumous deification for his adoptive father) avoided the extensive travels that had evoked much criticism of Hadrian and presided over a tranquil period.

The fifth "good" emperor was of a philosophic turn of mind: Marcus Aurelius Antoninus. He was a Stoic in his views, set forth in his *Meditations*. Much of his time had to be spent dealing with dangers in the provinces, with unfortunate results. Marcus unwisely coopted Lucius Verus as coemperor. Verus was content to send his Syrian-born general, Avidius Cassius, to deal with Parthian advances. Cassius marched triumphantly east to capture the capital, Ctesiphon, but his army encountered smallpox and brought it back to Rome so that thousands died. The end of Marcus's reign was marked by wars to repel the barbarians at the Danube and repression of a revolt by Cassius. Marcus's foolish son and successor, Commodus, was assassinated after a twelve-year reign and evoked *damnatio memoriae*.

As the second century neared its end, the emperor was often being called "lord" (*dominus*). He not only had the actual power to issue decrees, as Augustus had had, but was formally acknowledged as the source of law. The phrase was *quod principi placuit legem habet vigorem* (what pleases the emperor has the force of law); increasingly legislation simply issued from the monarch in the form of *constitutiones principum*. He might indeed consult the imperial council, but he expected and received no serious opposition.

The Senate and the old urban magistracies continued to exist, but their powers were much reduced. They were increasingly overshadowed by the imperial bureaucracy, now divided into four grades and drawn ever more often from the equestrian order. In the provinces, however, the cities enjoyed a good deal of self-government, which meant government mainly by the rich and notables. Still, during the last years of the second century growing interference from the central officialdom and the mounting costs of gaining and holding local office substantially diminished eagerness to occupy such positions, and compulsion was beginning to be necessary if they were all to be staffed.

Roman citizenship was extended ever more widely (even though it meant ever less with respect to rights or privileges). In the words of M. Cary,

[The second century was] an age of general goodwill, in which the inhabitants of the empire lived together with less mutual friction than at any other time. . . . On these grounds the well-known words of Gibbon, that the human race was never happier than in the age of the five good Roman emperors, are not devoid of justification, and as a challenge to the modern world they have not yet lost their sting.[25]

The Pax Romana inaugurated by Augustus was at least partly real. Though sizable numbers of men throughout the first two centuries A.D. made the continual wars the basis for their lives, a large part of the population lived in relative security. On the other hand, the volatile and rootless Roman mob, more or less pacified by the rulers who gave it *panem et circenses* (bread and circuses, that is, the grain dole and free entertainments), was a continuing danger to public order. As for the upper classes, they were severely limited in their freedom of action. The gap between rich and poor was steadily widening in the capital as well as the provinces. Doubtless Gibbon is not talking nonsense when he suggests that the second century was the happiest (before his time), in the sense that, for many, relative security comes before relative freedom or any kind of civic rights or loyalties, and always has. However, liberty and citizenship may provide not merely a certain kind of individual satisfaction, perhaps measurable and comparable with other satisfactions; they infuse all of society with certain attitudes and impart to all of life certain qualities in short supply among second-century Romans.

After a crisis following on the assassination of Commodus, Septimius Severus emerged as emperor (193–211), though it took several years for him to dispose of challengers to his title. He inaugurated a century of what has been termed military anarchy. Creating three new legions and raising the soldiers' pay, he was a soldiers' emperor and in general an enemy of aristocracy. He relied heavily on the equestrian order and provided that simple peasants could rise into equestrian ranks, while the senatorial order was restricted and watched over, from guberna-torial positions on down.

His son and successor, known by his nickname Caracalla (from a Gallic coat he introduced into Rome), issued an edict in 212 A.D. that extended Roman citizenship to virtually all free men inhabiting the empire but whose substance simply made clear how little value that once-cherished gift retained. In the 220s a new threat in the east challenged the emperor Severus Alexander; the Parthian state collapsed and was replaced by the Sasanid dynasty. The ruler led a Roman army against the expansionist newcomers, but the campaign fell short of success. When Severus Alexander returned west to try to deal with the Germanic barbar-ians on the Rhine, he was murdered. It was the end of the Severan dynasty (235).

A wretched succession of usurpations of the imperial office followed, from the gigantic Thracian peasant Maximinus to the first of several Illyrians, Claudius II. During those thirty-five years barbarians hammered at the northern frontiers, and the Persian Sasanids captured an emperor, Valerian, who died in captivity. A partial recovery was the achievement of Aurelian, who was called *restitutor orbis* (restorer of the world); although he withdrew from untenable Dacia, he devas-tated Palmyra and shored up the northern frontiers. But even he was murdered.

At length, in 284, a man who seemed capable of reversing the decline was acclaimed emperor: Diocletian. In the words of Mason Hammond, "he desired to emulate Augustus, to revive the happy days of the early empire, but he succeeded only in creating an oriental despotism."[26] He strove to create a tetrarchy, or system of four simultaneous rulers, two emperors (Augusti) and two subemperors (Caesars) and heirs apparent. This system was imperfectly applied, but the division of the empire into two halves at a north-south line running near Sirmium at its midpoint lasted. Each ruler had a kind of oriental court, where ritual prostration was normal, access to the imperial person limited, his appearances hieratic, his head surrounded by the supernatural nimbus in portraits.[27] The title was no longer *princeps* (first citizen), but was *dominus* (lord) and had been such since Aurelian. The seats of the rulers were Trier, Milan, Sirmium, and Nico-media—Rome herself was no longer the actual capital or even one of the four. The provinces were much increased in number but then were grouped in large units called dioceses. The remnants of autonomy vanished from the cities. The military forces had grown from three hundred thousand under Augustus to five hundred thousand; the number of civil officials mounted alarmingly.

To finance all this panoply of state, ever-greater revenues were required, but the condition of the economy that had to furnish them worsened steadily. Since the death of Severus Alexander in 235, economic decline approached collapse. Inflation and successive devaluations of the currency complicated the picture. In consequence the financial exactions of the government became crushing in their weight on most of the population. Corruption spread among the members of the self-contained bureaucracy, apparently immune to the repeated efforts of emperors to prevent or punish. Along with the officialdom, the proprietors of the latifundia evaded the troubles of the rest of society. The great landlords converted many of their tenants into serfs, and they came to usurp a kind of *de facto* political authority that made the latifundia "miniature states within the state, in which we may recognize the forerunners of the medieval manor."[28]

Against these and other social ills emperors exerted themselves, with seemingly little effect. An excellent example was Diocletian's edict of 301 fixing maximum prices for food and many goods and services; it was virtually a dead letter from the moment it was issued. The decay of the Roman polity was not the fault of one emperor or all the emperors, of any single office-holder or any one social class; and neither an emperor nor any other person or group seemed able to arrest or reverse the decline.

One important objective of Diocletian's was establishing a regular method of succession. After twenty years he insisted that the other Augustus, Maximian, join him in abdicating so that the two Caesars would succeed. However, the system broke down at once. By 307–308 seven men claimed the emperorship.

Out of the resultant intrigues and civil war, Constantine, son of Constantius (one of the new Augusti of 305), emerged as victor. His defeat of one contender at the battle of the Milvian Bridge near Rome in 312 was accompanied by a miracle, dream, or vision in which a cross appeared in the sky, taken as an omen for the proximate victory of Constantine. This event was said to be associated with his conversion to Christianity. In the same year the Edict of Milan proclaimed toleration of Christianity (and all other religions—traditional Roman paganism being unaffected—but none had anything like the strength Christianity had gained by then).

Constantine's foundation of Constantinople on the site of Byzantium in 330 is often taken as the beginning of the Christian or Byzantine Empire, which lasted until 1453. Constantinople, or New Rome, became the seat of the Eastern emperors as against the Western when the division of the realm became permanent in 395. As Millar puts it:

The complex and undefinable nature of the developed monarchy was displayed most clearly of all in the foundation of Constantinople, which was many different things at once: a Christian centre with magnificent churches and its own bishop; a Greek city re-founded and re-named after himself, following a long tradition, by a Roman *Imperator;* and a reproduction of Rome, with many of its privileges, offices, and public buildings, including places of public entertainment where the emperor could appear before the people.[29]

Constantine the Great seems to have had in mind a New Rome that would be Christian in religion (free from the ingrained pagan influences of the Senate of Old Rome) and Latin in language of law and administration (since the chief achievements of the classical world in such fields—as distinguished from literature and philosophy—had been expressed in that tongue). It would seem that he entertained no concern about whether Latin would be drowned in Greek, the language spoken in the region of the new capital; he valued Greek culture and regarded it as a natural asset to the empire he envisioned, created under the aegis and protection of God himself.

The emperor, though not sacred, was "hedged" by divinity (as Shakespeare expressed it in regard to kingship in a later time). Medieval monarchy among Christians was to retain a version of Roman and also Germanic traditions connecting heaven with kingship. The emperor employed the old Roman title of *pontifex maximus,* as well as the title (to 629) of Imperator Augustus (in Greek, *Autokrator Augustos)* and thereafter *basileus,* borrowed from the Persians Heraclius had conquered. The Christian church was essential to the accession of a new ruler: the patriarch of Constantinople bestowed the diadem from the time there was a patriarch (381); a coronation rite was added after 474; the rite of anointing dated from the ninth century.[30]

In the time of Constantine it was of course uncertain how long the new capital or the old empire would last. The new religion was as yet not firmly entrenched. In 361–63 there was, briefly, a pagan emperor, Julian. Other fourth-century rulers in Constantinople at least flirted with the Arian heresy, which denied the full divinity of Christ, and connived at the conversion of the barbarian Goths to Arianism. It was only Theodosius I who made orthodox Christianity the official religion of the empire (380).

On his death (395) the empire was partitioned; soon afterward, the Western Empire was in great peril from successive waves of barbarians. The Visigoths (Western Goths) invaded Italy, driving the emperor to establish himself in Ravenna, and in 410 sacked Rome, sending shock waves to all corners of the Mediterranean world. The Huns, checked in France, entered Italy but were persuaded to withdraw, sparing Rome; the Vandals sacked Rome again (455). The end of the Roman Empire in the West has been traditionally dated in 476, with the abdication of a Romulus ("Augustulus" or "little Augustus"), so that Rome's first ruler gave his name to its last ruler.

Thus Rome died, in the sense that the city ceased to be the center of the Mediterranean world. In succeeding centuries it virtually disintegrated into a deserted and barren village before reviving to become a modern metropolis. The Byzantine Empire was a mainly Greek and Hellenizing state; Rome had never succeeded in Latinizing any part of the East, except in part Palmyra, and indeed had never tried very hard. By the third century the Roman Empire had become, in the style of its rulers and in the structure of its government, something closer to Egypt or Persia past and present than to republican Rome.

To be sure, there were important survivals of the period of the republic, including Roman law, which was bequeathed to the barbarian west and remained very much alive in Byzantium, as well as the organization of the Christian church, which owed a great deal to the empire. The transformation of the partly free Roman republic into the largely despotic Roman Empire was painful to live through, proved impossible to avert, and provoked despair in those who retained what made Rome great for centuries: her pride, her patriotism, her attachment to the ideal of justice—never fully realized, in Rome or anywhere else. Nevertheless the Roman republic deserves to be remembered for its contribution to freedom. In the words of a recent scholar, "the inner political concept of freedom in Rome was actualized in relation not to the community as a whole [as in Athens] but to the needs of the individual members of the community . . . and was above all bound up with individual rights, later given legal embodiment."[31]

But Roman civilization weakened from within, and the result was to open the way to its being overwhelmed from without. As early as the seventh century B.C. Germanic war bands had reached the lower Rhine and by 500 B.C. had arrived at the Ardennes. In 120–102 B.C. the migration of the Cimbri and their allies for the first time carried Germanic armies into the Mediterranean world and conflict with Rome. By the third century A.D. the Franks and Alemanni were overrunning Gaul; the Saxons were attacking Britain; and the Goths were assaulting the Danube frontier of the empire. Around 370 the Huns crushed the Ostrogothic state and drove them west. Finally, in the fourth and fifth centuries came the great migrations called the *Völkerwanderung,* when the Ostrogoths occupied Italy, the Visigoths southern Gaul and Spain, the Vandals (passing through the latter areas) North Africa.[32] In the fifth century the barbarians overwhelmed the Roman west.

However, the effect of that event on freedom proved not wholly of one sort. The barbarians themselves enjoyed a rough kind of freedom. The basic social unit was the clan, in turn the clans made up tribes. In war, members of the tribe elected several chiefs, who held equal powers throughout the campaign concerned. "At the season of new moon the men of each district assembled in the open air to administer justice and to make laws for themselves; and from time to time the whole nation was gathered together to discuss great questions such as those of war or peace."[33] In practice, decisions affecting the whole tribe (such as allotment of land or disputes with another tribe) were made by councils of (male) elders. By the first century A.D., there had developed councils of leading warriors and kings, "chosen by the voice of the assembled people." Slavery existed but only in rather marginal fashion, though the tribes sold slaves to Rome. Women played no part in decision making.

It was the Germanic barbarians who settled in the west, mixing with the indigenous Celtic populations and then the Romans themselves, who astonishingly managed finally to develop the most lasting and successful set of free institutions to date—or at any rate to sow the seed from which such a plant matured.

CHAPTER 4

The Beginnings of European Freedom, 350–1050

The Empire Becomes Christian

The emperor became Christian with Constantine I; the empire, officially, with Theodosius I, even though pagans remained and even gained high office long afterward. When the Western Empire came to an end, several of the Teutonic peoples were Arian Christians. The first barbarians to embrace orthodox Christianity in the West were the pagan Franks; the Arian tribes followed suit not long afterward. Other Germanic peoples remained to be converted over a vast area of northern Europe, and it was the eleventh century before they were Christianized (with a few exceptions still, the Lithuanians chief among them). Christianity was to have an effect on the politics and law of all Europe, slowly and irregularly.

In the version of the Christian message given by St. Paul, man in following the path of Jesus Christ is liberated from bondage to sin, to the flesh, to death itself, and also from the burden of Judaic legal prescriptions; he is given freedom of the spirit. Probably such areas of freedom were referred to by Jesus when he declared, "Ye shall know the truth, and the truth shall make you free." Another aspect of the matter affected by the coming of Christianity was free will. The early church Fathers fought the fatalism of heretics, and a whole host of Christian writers, from the time of the primitive church through the Middle Ages, affirmed the reality of free will. Freedom of the spirit, in the sense mentioned, and free will might be termed inner freedom.

The Christian denial of moral inequality had great potential for affecting the external freedom of the individual. In Christ, wrote St. Paul, there is "no more Jew or Gentile, no more slave or freeman, no more male and female" (Galatians 3:28). If there was to be moral equality, there was a basis for legal and civic equality.

Or, as L. A. Siedentop puts it,

the assumption that society consists of individuals, each with an ontological ground of his or her own, is a translation of the Christian premiss of the equality of souls in the eyes of God. . . . Over centuries the "individual" was gradually translated from a moral criterion into a social role, . . . which gradually undermined the caste distinctions of Western feudalism [and became the foundation for] the commitment to equality and reciprocity, as well as the postulate of individual freedom.[1]

Teachings of freedom in one form or another had been set forth in Greece and Rome, and stirring expositions of ideals of freedom were delivered even when social realities were quite different. Lord Acton, after arguing at length the magnitude of the Greeks' and Romans' contribution to the principles and practice of freedom, concludes:

But in all that I have been able to cite from classical literature, three things are wanting, —representative government, the emancipation of the slaves, and liberty of conscience.[2]

During the Middle Ages two of those elements would appear: representative government (albeit in embryo) and the emancipation of slaves in widespread fact (though only later in law). To those developments Christianity made a substantial contribution.

Representative government began with the election of leaders and the assembling of them, initially within the church. Election was practiced in Greece and Rome, but when the practice had lapsed in secular institutions it was employed in the ecclesiastical arena through the choosing of bishops. Bishops themselves might then act as representatives of their towns and the surrounding area, or "dioceses," as the term used in the Roman Empire to designate administrative districts came to be applied in the church; they served as such in regional councils, to begin with. An especially important series was the Councils of Toledo. Acton writes that they provided "the framework of the Parliamentary system in Spain, which is, by a long interval, the oldest in the world."[3]

After Constantine became the first Christian emperor, it was both safe and important to good order in the state to convene as well councils of the "whole world," that is, ecumenical councils that gathered together representatives of the entire Christian church. They continued to meet in various cities—Nicaea, Constantinople, Ephesus, Chalcedon—and their decisions were recognized as authoritative in both East and West up through the eighth century. Councils of the high clergy came to be influential in the barbarian monarchies of the West, and the clergy was everywhere termed the "first" estate among the three or sometimes four to be found on the continent, and combined with the nobles to form a single body of a total of two in England.

As slavery declined to a marginal and insignificant level within medieval society, Christianity had its effect on the change. Christians were not in those times crusading abolitionists, though a few, such as Gregory of Nyssa, expressed sentiments opposing slavery outright. Nevertheless, Christian affirmation of moral equality among all men is to be credited with steady if subliminal pressure on behalf of the economic changes that relegated slave holding to the historical trash heap. As Lynn White, Jr., puts it, a great achievement of the medieval period—he calls it the "chief glory of the later Middle Ages"—was the appearance of the first "complex civilization which rested not on the backs of sweating slaves or coolies but primarily on non-human power."[4]

From the eleventh century on three major inventions, more or less simultaneous, spread: the modern horse-collar, the tandem harness, and the horseshoe, enabling the farmer to use the horse rather than the ox. The horse "burned" more expensive fuel—grain—than the ox, which consumed hay; and for the shift to occur, the new three-field system, much more productive than the old system of two fields, was necessary.[5] Which came first, the inventions or the alteration in land use? All we can be sure of is that it all happened both gradually and at the same time.[6] But, adds White, underlying the changes was the whole motive of labor saving; and it rested on a theological assumption not common to all religions or cultures—the infinite worth of human personality.

The third of the deficiencies Lord Acton found in the classical world—liberty of conscience—would develop only in modern times, even though its roots may be traced to the very beginnings of Christianity. In the fourth and fifth centuries, in any case, all three things lay far in the future. If representative government was foreshadowed by the great councils of the church, it scarcely advanced in the functioning of the empire. To the extent that freedom—in the sense of limitations on the absolute power of the ruler—existed at all in the Eastern Roman (or Byzantine) Empire, however, Christian ideas played a part.

One legacy of Rome to Byzantium was the notion of the divine character of the office of emperor. Since the empire was ruled by God, in theory hereditary power was excluded; God had to be free to choose; *vox populi vox Dei,* and thus the people and the army must speak, their choice legitimized by the Senate.

Although the Senate of Constantinople never gained the same prestige as the Senate of Rome, it exercised several functions with greater or lesser significance over the whole duration of Byzantine history. A few days before the fall of Constantinople in 1453, the last emperor was surrounded by the Senate when he received the envoy bearing an ultimatum from Muhammad II. The body acted as city council, organ of consultation on important state matters by the emperor, and governmental assembly with an essential power:

détenteur en théorie de la souveraineté du peuple, son intervention était nécessaire à chaque avènement au trône pour légitimer le choix du peuple et de l'armée.[7]

For substantial periods such powers were empty. Diocletian devised a complex system of succession, the tetrarchy, with two Augusti and two Caesars. It was soon abandoned by Constantine, and thereafter there was a good deal of de facto hereditary succession, modified frequently by the adoption of adult sons. Yet there were times, after the Theodosian family became extinct in the fifth century and from the death of Justinian I to the accession of Heraclius, when the role of the Senate became "très important," in the words of Bréhier. In general, he contends,

le christianisme transforma la religion impériale dans son esprit, sinon dans ses rites, et l'absolutisme fut attenue par certains usages et par la puissance de l'opinion publique, représentée jusqu'au VIIe siècle par les factions du Cirque, autre legs de l'ancienne Rome, enfin dans de nombreux cas par l'intervention de l'Eglise et le respect de la loi.[8]

This is almost certainly an overstatement. The factions of the Circus, the Blues and Greens who regularly voiced their grievances to Justinian I when he appeared at the races of the Hippodrome, may have represented little but themselves and probably were more sports-fan groupings than anything else.[9] Absolute rulers have many times been restrained by custom, laws (even though they might, if pressed, ignore or rescind this or that one), and ethical and other kinds of religious precepts urged by priests; but such are not true limitations of their power.

To be sure, Christianity made a difference. Moreover, Byzantine legislation, especially Justinian's Sixth Novella, declared that church and state alike had a proper sphere pertaining to each and that both ought to function in a harmonious relationship *(symphonia)*, in which neither dictated to the other. That theoretical dualism was often overridden and violated in practice. Still, there was a legal foundation for many assertions of prerogative, sometimes successful, on the part of ecclesiastics, seeking to protect the religious area from interference or worse on the part of the state. Moreover, Christian attitudes approving marriage and disapproving infanticide may well have served to promote the increase of population and economic growth resulting therefrom and from new attitudes toward labor, as well as affecting other aspects of life outside the church.

Byzantine rulers in general have been credited with enlightened approaches to legislation and noteworthy legislative skills, exercised either personally or through wise selection of the jurists with whom the imperial office was typically surrounded. Over the ten centuries or so that Byzantium lasted, sovereigns attacked and came up with partial solutions to a series of difficult problems: they defended the frontiers of empire by uniting civil and military powers with local recruitment of soldiers in the institution of the themes; they defended small private property, menaced by the latifundia and sometimes by the church; they developed a system of effective diplomacy that was emulated by Venice and by that route the rest of Europe; and they pursued a farsighted demographic policy designed to repopulate regions wasted by war and disease and to assimilate immigrants, by Hellenizing them if their culture was not Greek, Christianizing them if they were pagans or heretics.[10] All this the emperors did by using a highly developed and well-ordered bureaucracy.

Side by side with the governmental institutions a parallel set came into existence in the ecclesiastical realm. From parishes to patriarchates, with the monasteries and convents in an auxiliary position, the church disposed of levers affecting every rank of society. From the fifth century on, the patriarch of Constantinople had to perform the ceremony of coronation that confirmed the choice of the army and Senate.

The cities ran their own affairs through city councils, or *curiae,* made up of the richer landowners of the given locality or decurions. If such men possessed property of a certain amount, they were obliged to serve on the councils. In that capacity they had to assume responsibility for providing municipal services, the post, recruitment and billeting of soldiers and the purchase of provisions for them. Such expenses often exceeded the municipal revenues allotted for the purposes concerned, and the decurions had to dig into their own pockets for the difference.

By the sixth century, however, the decurions had managed to escape their obligations, through successfully seeking exemptions in the civil service or church, to such an extent that the councils virtually disappeared. As they declined in importance, bishops took over many of their functions. Already in the fourth century the church took on the duty of providing for the poor, aliens in need, widows and orphans. By the sixth century, it was dispensing justice, managing public works, and supervising the operation of the markets.

The Christian empire was flourishing in its new core, which was the East. As the West faltered and fell in the fifth century, Constantinople was unable to aid it effectively, but by the time of Justinian in the sixth century the East had grown in wealth and strength. Justinian's domestic achievements were memorable. His legal specialists collected the decrees since Hadrian in the Code, systematized the rulings of Roman jurists in the Digest, and drew up a textbook of law in the Institutes. He spent money at home; he built a wonder of the world, the church of Hagia Sophia (the Holy Wisdom of God), and was responsible for other expenditures of less value or permanence.

However, Justinian's most ambitious undertaking, to which he devoted great energy and many resources, was the attempt to regain the West. For a time he seemed to be partly successful, taking back North Africa from the Vandals, Italy from the Ostrogoths, and part of Spain from the Visigoths; in another direction, he was able to conquer Colchis from Persia. The Vandal and Ostrogoth kingdoms were destroyed at great cost and with little result, for the Lombards invaded Italy in 568 and created a new kingdom with its capital at Pavia, extending to Benevento and Spoleto in the south. Byzantium was left with a tenuous grasp on the coasts, Rome, and the farthest south of the peninsula. Justinian's reign thus overstrained the resources of the empire to make only modest gains.

The emperor Maurice undid Constantine's separation of powers in two areas, both reconquered by Justinian: Africa and Italy. He established the exarchates of Carthage and Ravenna. A few years later Heraclius, son of the exarch of Carthage, seized power and carried the policy of Maurice further by establishing the "themes." In this new unit, civil and military authority were fused and military service was made hereditary, the eldest son serving while the rest of the family tilled the land. Ostrogorsky calls the themes "the backbone of the medieval Byzantine state."[11]

Heraclius sought to defend the empire against assaults of two powerful invaders: the Persians and the Arabs. He managed to defeat the Persians and recapture from them Egypt, Syria, Asia Minor, and Armenia. He could not match the feat in regard to the Arabs.

The armies out of the desert, having set forth on their march of conquest after Muhammad's death in 632, defeated the Byzantine forces in 636 at the Yarmuk River and occupied all of Syria. From there they were able to fan out in both easterly and westerly directions. They crushed the Persian Sasanids in two great battles in 637 and 642. Marching across North Africa, after seesaw fighting they took Carthage in 698 and advanced into Spain and France. In 751 they were driven back to the Pyrenees, mostly south of which they remained.

The world of the Roman Empire plus Iran—or, as an alternative description, the world of the ancient Near East (or the empire of Alexander the Great) plus the still uncivilized West—now consisted of three segments. Definable both politically and culturally, they would last many centuries. They were the Islamic empire of the caliphs, the Byzantine Empire and the states it converted, and the barbarian West made up of several kingdoms growing in number as they became Christianized and civilized.

In the first, the empire of Islam, freedom was to have no political expression, and legal rights for the individual were unknown despite limitations implied or demanded by the religion on what the ruler could do. In the second, the Byzantine Empire, the restraints of Christianity on the ruler plus remnants of Roman institutions and the ingrained habits of Roman judicature provided certain protections for the citizen, even though the monarchy could not be described as other than absolute. Both empires generally received and transmitted the inheritance of the ancient Near Eastern polities; both borrowed aspects of governance from the Roman Empire. In both cases the new religion made some difference — in Byzantium, in particular, some difference to the individual when confronting arbitrary power. But for free societies to develop, a new beginning seemed to be necessary. It was to be found in the exceedingly unpromising-looking kingdoms of the barbarian West.

Early States and Statelessness in Asia and Africa

By the seventh century or thereabouts, large centralized states had formed in much of the East.[12] China had a civilization and a form of statehood that rivaled the Near East in its antiquity. In Korea there were three kingdoms in the peninsula, embracing Buddhism from the fourth century on. From Korea, Buddhism was spreading to Japan in the sixth century, which developed a state about the same time. There was a great state in northern India immediately following Alexander the Great's approach; and a fairly new teaching, Buddhism, for a time aspired to reshape or supersede the ancient, amorphous religion Westerners call Hinduism. A large Burmese state with its capital at Pagan flourished in the eleventh century. A Thai state with its capital at Ayuthia took shape in the fourteenth century; it conquered the Khmer empire that had three centuries earlier built Angkor — abandoned in 1431 as a result of that conquest. The Srivishaya empire, builder in the eighth century of the great Buddhist monument at Borobudur in Java, around 1180 came to control much of what is today western Indonesia. All these states and others in Asia had much in common, along with striking differences, but free or clearly pluralistic institutions emerged in none of them before modern times, with the interesting exception of Japan.[13]

Africa deserves more space than it can be given here. Its historical beginnings lie in Egypt and then the Roman Empire. The Ethiopian state may go back to 600 B.C. Possibly around A.D. 400 there was a kingdom of Ghana; by the year 800 other West African states existed in Gao on the Niger, east of Ghana, and Kanem, east of Lake Chad.

Sacred kingship as the linchpin of statehood was to be found in many parts of Africa. One view is that it derives from Pharaonic Egypt, where (as noted previously) the pharaoh was a god, and spread south into the East African lake country or westward beyond Lake Chad, where it encountered another political model. This view is not currently popular, but the sacred attributes of typical African kingship are not in question.

Aside from the Islamic states established after the conquest of the seventh century, which reached south to approximately the tenth parallel north latitude, Africa for many centuries was a mixture of states and stateless societies. Examples of the latter include the Tiv and most of the Ibo of Nigeria (and various Berber societies, at least nominally Islamic), where conflicts between individuals were settled by representatives of their kinship groups and there was nothing describable as government. Thus the British found the Tiv "far harder to conquer than any of the large states" of Nigeria, since no authority existed capable of surrendering for all.

As for states, they ranged from tiny independent kingdoms with only a few hundred inhabitants, though they had hereditary rulers and definite boundaries, to Ethiopia, which reached a peak of influence in the fourteenth century, and the great commercial empires built by Ghana (ca. 1000) or Mali (ca. 1300), which replaced it in the same general area of West Africa. In all these formations, kinship was basic; "almost everywhere in Africa the lineage rather than the individual paid tribute or answered to the court of law."

In sum, it may be said that for many centuries African government often assumed quite different forms from those found elsewhere, and in situations approaching absence of government freedom was certainly a feature of society. Unfortunately, in the late twentieth century many African elites have concentrated on emulating one or another Western model of statehood rather than building on the heritage of Africa's own particular patterns of freedom.[14]

The West in the Dark Ages

When the Roman Empire contracted and collapsed in the West, the region was organized into Christian kingdoms ruled by Germanic dynasties.[15] In 429 the Vandals established a state in North Africa; the Ostrogoths did so in Italy in 489. In 534–54 Justinian destroyed both. Only then did the remnants of the Roman system disappear in the West: the senatorial class, the officials with Roman names, Roman attitudes. New institutions were taking their place, notably the monasteries whose basis Benedict of Nursia (d. ca. 545) borrowed from the East and which would sustain civilization through the period when urban life virtually disappeared in the West.

The Franks established a kingdom in the later fifth century. About 500 King Clovis was converted; he went straight from paganism to Catholic Christianity, thereupon securing a powerful advantage over his still-Arian neighbors.[16] With the church's backing, his dynasty, the Merovingians,[17] claimed a dominant position vis-à-vis the other West Teutonic (Germanic) peoples as far east as Thuringia and Bavaria. As a result, the Frankish kingdom was the only one on the continent to last. Living amid a Gallo-Roman majority, the Franks mixed their Germanic customary law with Roman codes in a fashion unclear to us now and possibly confusing to them at the time, but at any rate under the guidance of the Christian bishops.

After Clovis the kingdom was sometimes divided, sometimes unified. King Dagobert, who died in 639, was the last of the dynasty who really ruled. By the time of Charles nicknamed Martel ("the Hammer"), whose title was "mayor of the palace," the chief official was more powerful than the king. (It was Charles who defeated the Arabs at the battle near Tours [732] and drove them back to the Pyrenees.[18])

In 754 Pope Stephen II anointed Charles's son, Pepin the Short, as king in place of the last Merovingian. In return he received the lands that became, via the "Donation of Pepin," the Papal States—a political entity that lasted for eleven centuries. Thereby the tenant of the papal throne ceased in effect to be the Byzantine official he hitherto had been—as well as senior bishop of the church—and instead established firm ties with the Germanic barbarians or, more precisely, with the Franks, who would absorb the other Germans except for those in Britain and Scandinavia and who themselves would divide into West Franks and East Franks.

Pepin's son Charles the Great, or Charlemagne (d. 814), greatly extended the Frankish realm; he fought the Byzantines for long years and at last gained recognition from them of his emperorship—the only case in which Byzantium gave anyone else the title *basileus,* or king of kings, assumed by Heraclius after his victory over Persia.[19] On Christmas Day, 800, Pope Leo III crowned him emperor. His was, however, "a pretty poor empire," as Muller puts it, having no legal system, no civil service, no senate, lacking almost everything but "an army, a court, and a harem."[20]

The Frankish realm at that point embraced what would later be called France, Germany, and the northern half of Italy. Charles transmitted it intact to his son Louis the Pious, but after Louis died the empire was, after much fighting, divided among three sons of his. Charles the Bald received the west, Louis the German east, and Lothair a curious strip between, stretching from Antwerp to Italy, as well as the imperial crown. In the course of the struggle Charles and Louis had bound themselves as allies in the oath of Strasbourg (842), using the two tongues, proto-French and proto-German, that had become distinct from each other.

The partition of Verdun (843) did not last. Lothar died, and his successors could not prevent the division of Lotharingia between West Francia and East

Francia. Soon afterward the Carolingian empire came to an end, and the three kingdoms of France, Germany, and (northern) Italy took its place, along with three smaller states: Lorraine, Burgundy, and Provence.

In Britain, the Angles and Saxons who arrived from the early fifth century set up kingdoms in which the indigenous Celts merged with the conquerors. In the ninth century the Danes harried and mastered much of the island, leaving only Wessex in which Alfred the Great (d. 899) maintained independence. The subsequent kings of England—whose country got its name from the Angles but whose people were usually called Saxons in that period—drove out the Danes but were to succumb to other Scandinavians called Vikings. There remained a fringe of Celtic territories: the Britons in the small principalities of Wales and the large stretches of the north where chieftains from Ireland bearing the name "Scots" subdued the Celts and Germans living there and finally founded a kingdom of Scotland, which took its name from the invaders.

The Visigothic kingdom in southern France and then the Iberian peninsula lasted some 250 years (466–711). It was at first Arian, but King Recared (586–601) led his people to convert to Catholic Christianity. At the Councils of Toledo it appears that the kings described the most serious problems and then the high clergy enacted appropriate canon law and transacted secular business as well. The bishops worked out a ceremony of anointing a monarch on his enthronement in order to deter the Visigoths from the habit of assassinating their king.[21]

One Visigothic family, seeking help against a usurper, invited the Muslims to cross the Strait of Gibraltar (named after the Arab commander). They did so in 711 and immediately overran almost the whole land. As early as 722 they received their first rebuff at a battle in the far northwest; the Asturians, meanwhile striving to reconstitute the institutions of the Visigothic monarchy, thus began the *Reconquista,* a series of military operations against the Muslims that would take nearly eight centuries.

Several small Christian states sprang up: Leon, of the Asturians; Castile (from the castles built for defense), which first broke off from Leon and then conquered it; Navarre, of the Basques; Catalonia, detached from the Carolingian empire; Aragon, breaking off from Navarre.

In the ninth century three new pagan and stateless barbarian tribes attacked the Christian kingdoms of the former barbarians: they were the Vikings (Normans, Northmen, Norsemen, Varangians) in the northern seas and islands, the Saracens (a mixture of Arabs and other peoples) in the Mediterranean, and the Magyars in central Europe. Soon after 900 the Normans made a lodgment in northern France that came to be called "Normandy." From there they were successfully to invade England in 1066; they helped to organize an Eastern Slavic state called Rus in the ninth century; they appeared in southern Italy and by

1071 would overcome both Byzantines on the mainland and the Saracens in Sicily.

In Germany, signs of division appeared very early. During the reign of King Louis the Child (d. 911), the old duchies became autonomous as each region strove to set up its own defenses. There were four pre-Carolingian duchies: Saxony, Franconia, Swabia, and Bavaria; a fifth, Lorraine, was what remained of the Lotharingian state, now absorbed into the kingdom of Germany. In 919 the nobles of two of the duchies agreed to elect the Saxon duke, Henry I (the Fowler) as king of Germany. Striving to consolidate his base in the north, he also secured the submission of the other duchies. His son Otto (936–73) defeated the Magyars on the Lechfeld, and in consequence those warriors began to settle down to the task of shaping a civilized state.

In 962 Otto was crowned emperor in Rome. Thus he revived the Carolingian conception, but with two important differences: the Ottonian empire was limited to Germany, Italy, and Burgundy, leaving outside it France and other possessions of Charlemagne's; and Otto's power, unlike Charlemagne's, was limited by the new forces of the feudal nobility. He did, however, possess a power Charlemagne lacked: that of confirming the election of a pope.

The bishopric of Rome, or papacy, had been acknowledged by the whole Christian church from the first as the senior see (but not necessarily as the chief ecclesiastical power or authority). It had had an outstanding pope or two, especially Leo I the Great (d. 461), who contributed mightily both to the prestige of the papacy and the clarification of Christian doctrine achieved at the ecumenical council of Chalcedon in 451. But as the city declined so did the see, which became the plaything of Roman nobles, and fell to its lowest point in history with the ascendancy of Marozia, mistress of one pope, mother of another, who was illegitimate, and grandmother of a third, John XII. Pope John unwisely, from the standpoint of the papacy, granted the emperorship he had long sought to Otto I (who soon deposed John for his pains).

A few decades later Otto III appointed Gerbert of Aurillac pope as Sylvester II. He was perhaps the best-educated man in the West, and his selection marked a substantial step toward restoring the dignity of the papal office. Otto III made an important pilgrimage to Gnesen in Poland that led to establishment of an episcopal see there, in consequence of which the new Polish church became independent of the German ecclesiastical authorities. The same occurred in Hungary. Otto died in 1002 at the age of only twenty-one, having laid foundations for the strengthening of both empire and church in the eleventh century.

The Saxon line ended with Otto III; the Franconian, or Salian, dynasty was installed in 1024. Conrad II did his best to unite Germany and Italy more firmly by appointments and marriages across the border. His successor ·Henry III, intervened in 1046, to rescue the papacy from the power of the Roman nobles. The path of the see of Peter was now quite steadily upward with regard to both moral standing and influence.

To the west the foundations were laid of the two monarchies that would often seem to dominate later European history. In France the break-up of the Carolingian unity of West and East Franks left a kingship in the West but a weak one. The last Carolingian ruler of France was Louis V, whose short reign was followed by the election of Hugh Capet in 987. In his time the French monarchy had little power and was of little consequence; under his immediate successors, the nadir of French kingship was reached. Nevertheless, the dynasty he founded was to last for eight centuries and lead the country to greatness.

In 1066 the Norman duke, William I, successfully invaded England, defeated the Saxons, and set the English monarchy on a newly firm footing. As ruler of both Normandy and England, William the Conqueror was stronger than his contemporary, Philip I, king of France. But the latter bided his time and began a slow, painful process of increasing the extent of the royal domain and the power of the kingship. Philip had to do so at the expense of the feudal lords, who had become the real powers in France but also in much of the rest of Europe.

Feudalism

Feudalism was the system of relationships among nobles and monarchs that came to provide the framework for both law and property in the Germanic kingdoms after the collapse of the Roman Empire in the West, assuring security for individuals and countries alike and virtually for government altogether. In 1016 a German prelate wrote of the kingdom of Burgundy:

The king has now nothing save his title and his crown . . . he is not capable of defending either his bishops or the rest of his subjects against the dangers that threaten them. Therefore we see them all betaking themselves with joined hands [i.e., accepting vassalage] to serve the great. In this way they secure peace.[22]

The Roman concept of ownership and the Roman framework of government weakened and virtually disappeared; a new multiplicity of obligations and a new system of protection took their place. In the characteristic agrarian situation that came to prevail, no single owner could be readily identified: the tenant who sows and reaps, the lord to whom he owes dues, the lord of the lord—on up to the king, the village community that often recovers the use of the land once the crop is harvested, and the families of the tenant and successive lords that had to consent to certain sorts of disposition—"how many persons there are who can say, each with as much justification as the other, 'That is my field!' "[23]

The new relationship required homage and fealty. In homage one man placed his hands between the hands of another, and the two kissed each other on the mouth; the superior was called "lord," the inferior his "man," or "man of mouth and hands" *(homme de bouche et de mains),* or "vassal." Since homage evidently had a pagan German origin, from the Carolingian period onward it came to be supplemented by a Christian rite in which the vassal laid hand on the Gospels or sacred relics and swore faithfulness to the lord; its name was fealty (French, *foi;* German, *Treue).* Homage was once and forever; fealty might be renewed many times. Homage and the resultant relation of vassalage bound two men until the death of one of them. In fact the relationship usually became hereditary though in law it was not. There was legally hereditary attachment during the period, but it was serfdom among the peasantry, not a phenomenon of the privileged classes.

Vassalage was almost always accompanied by grants that in certain circumstances the lord had a right to repossess. Grants of land or property might require either payment of rent (singular, *precaria)* or services *(beneficium)* of some sort. Fief was a term meaning property granted against an obligation to do something, and came to be attached to vassals after a period in which it was used with a broader meaning. When William the Conqueror required of his chief vassals in England that they keep permanently at his disposal a certain number of knights, each noble in consequence was compelled to attach several vassals to himself. Many bishops and abbots had vassals whom they tried to keep on demesne land, but as time passed they found it unavoidable to carve out fiefs from their ecclesiastical estates.

Thus the practice of mutual dependence spread, in which more or less reliable protection was exchanged for more or less secure protection of property. Clearly it evolved out of the Germanic kingdoms, peoples, and systems of law. In theory, allodial holding was completely different. Derived from the Roman notion of ownership, it lingered after the fall of the Western Empire in such regions as northern Italy and southern France. There many holders of allods never became vassals. Nevertheless there were limits even on allodial ownership. They arose from rights of kinship and the fact that the holder might have tenants, even feudatories, whose rights severely restricted his own.[24] So it was that Maurice Keen could write, "Agricultural methods were crude and simple in this age: legal and social relations could be bewilderingly complex."[25]

The geography of feudalism was irregular. In Scandinavia, Frisia, and Ireland one finds "large blank spaces" on the map showing its extent. Or, to start the other way round, the feudal pattern was dominant in the area between the Loire and the Rhine and in the Saône valley (though it was not universal even there) for a hundred years or so before that territory was suddenly enlarged by the Norman conquests of England and southern Italy in the later eleventh century;

it then shades off in all directions until in Saxony in the north and Leon and Castile in the south feudal traces are but a light dusting, and beyond lie the just-mentioned "blank spaces." To sum up, in the words of Marc Bloch:

A subject peasantry; widespread use of the service tenement (i.e., the fief) instead of a salary, which was out of the question; the supremacy of a class of specialized warriors; ties of obedience and protection which bind man to man and, within the warrior class, assume the distinctive form called vassalage; fragmentation of authority—leading inevitably to disorder; and, in the midst of all this, the survival of other forms of association, family and State . . .—such then seem to be the fundamental features of European feudalism.[26]

Feudalism accordingly was not a system of government, or of economy, or of personal relations blessed by religion; that is to say, it was none of these alone, but all of these together. Fiefs could not be unambiguously outlined on a map, for rights were too closely and complexly interwoven, but monarchies could. "For a piece of land, as for a man, to have several lords was almost a normal thing; to have several kings was impossible."[27] Thus from the monarchs, to begin with, developed the kind of concreteness and individuation of rights and powers that characterize the modern world.

An important aspect of the emergence of the modern institution of monarchy was primogeniture. Neither the customs of Germanic kingship nor feudal law provided for the inheritance by the eldest son of the fullness of the father's power and property. The Carolingians divided their realms over and over. But gradually primogeniture was adopted in the West European monarchies, with some exceptions: Germany produced a few, as when Frederick Barbarossa chose his second son as successor. It may be, as Bloch suggests, that the German monarchy, seemingly tied to the emperorship, was affected by the Roman principle of election of the ruler—though in Rome and Byzantium there were many times when that principle was set aside.[28] For well over three hundred years the Capets were fortunate enough to have always a son to succeed to the throne in France. In England and other countries, it came to be the rule that whenever there was a son he acceded, or whenever there were two or more the eldest did.

For whatever reason, succession through the eldest son came to be the practice in the monarchies—including Germany for long periods—and among the nobility as well. The wealth and power of the dukes and counts would clearly be dissipated and would disappear altogether if there was a division among sons, or sons and daughters, every generation.

The power of the king might for some time be modest in scope and limited in territorial extent. Hugh Capet ruled a few districts close to Paris and was not much more than the senior feudal lord of West Francia in fact. The power of the vassal, sustained by primogeniture, might be imposing indeed, and enable him to match strength with the monarch. The *Sachsenspiegel* declared: "A man may resist his king and judge when he acts contrary to law and may even help make war on him. . . . Thereby, he does not violate the duty of fealty."[29] In the Oaths of Strasbourg taken by two of Charlemagne's grandsons in 843 and in the pact between Charles the Bald and his vassals in 856, a right of resistance was more or less explicitly recorded. To quote Bloch again:

Though most of these documents were inspired by reactionary tendencies among the nobility, or by the egoism of the bourgeoisie, they were of great significance for the future. They included the English Great Charter [Magna Carta] of 1215; the Hungarian "Golden Bull" of 1222; the Assizes of the kingdom of Jerusalem; the Privilege of the Brandenburg nobles; the Aragonese Act of Union of 1287; the Brabantine charter of Cortenberg; the statute of Dauphiné of 1341; the declaration of the communes of Languedoc (1356). It was assuredly no accident that the representative system, in the very aristocratic form of the English Parliament, the French "Estates," the *Stände* of Germany, and the Spanish *Cortes,* originated in states which were only just emerging from the feudal stage and still bore its imprint.[30]

Thus is comes to be clear why it may be said that feudalism is the foundation of freedom.

Byzantium, 600–1050

Heraclius (610–41) made the Greek element in the empire decisive, adopting the title *basileus* for the emperor; the hitherto official language of the empire, Latin, was discarded and soon mostly forgotten in the East.[31] He and his successors strove to meet the offensive of the Arabs, and his great-grandson, Constantine IV, met the full force of Arab attack on Constantinople itself. He managed to drive the enemy off by the use of burning naphtha ("Greek fire"), the secret of which the Byzantines had just purchased from a Syrian architect. Thus the Heraclian dynasty checked the expansion of Islam, though the still pagan Slavs poured into the Balkans while Byzantine energies were thus engaged. The dynasty faltered and ended in 695, except for a coda during which Justinian II briefly regained the throne.

In 717 order was restored by the strategos (military and civilian official in charge) of the Anatolian theme. He became emperor as Leo III and founded the Isaurian dynasty. He and then his son Constantine V launched and pursued a campaign against icons, which was also an attempt to curb the growth of monasticism and the power of the church in general. A prolonged struggle ensued, in which many iconophiles (supporters of the veneration of icons) were killed, imprisoned, and exiled. The crucial decision in the matter was rendered by the Seventh Ecumenical Council at Nicaea in 787, which upheld the iconophiles and condemned iconoclasm.

The anti-iconic policy followed by the emperors of the period as "now recognized as a symptom of the orientalization of the eastern empire in the eighth century,"[32] in the words of one writer, and may actually have been triggered by the caliph's ban of 723 on the use of icons in the Christian churches of his realm. Iconoclasm certainly served to weaken the bonds between the empire and the West. A Roman council's decision against iconoclasm provoked Leo III into transferring four dioceses from the jurisdiction of the pope to that of the patriarch of Constantinople. In turn the papacy was provoked by such measures to draw closer to the Frankish monarchy and make it another empire.

Empress Irene had been the prime mover behind the council of 787. Its judgment was challenged by several successors of hers, another string of iconoclast emperors. Theodore, archimandrite (the Eastern term for abbot of a monastery) of Studios in Constantinople, led the forces that held fast to Nicaea II, and they finally won out. In 843, under Michael III, the veneration of icons was triumphantly restored, an event commemorated in the Eastern church to this day as the Feast of Orthodoxy. Michael's reign was one of the healing of the wounds opened by the long iconoclastic controversy. It was also the time when the conversion of the Slavs began.

From the beginning of the Christian era, Slavs had evidently occupied a large area centering in what is today Poland. They made inroads into Byzantine territory in the early sixth century, often in association with the Avars. In the early seventh century, they broke through the Danubian frontier of the empire and inundated the Balkan peninsula.[33] In the words of Isidore of Seville, "the Slavs took Greece from the Romans."

The resultant demographic losses and disruption in the prefecture of Illyricum drove the empire to shift to a new recruiting ground in and around the Caucasus, especially Armenia. For a century or two the pagan barbarism of the area of present-day Macedonia made travel hazardous and deepened the gulf in communication between East and West.

In the middle of the seventh century the Great Bulgarian state on the Volga River broke up under assault from the newly arriving Khazar people. One branch of the Bulgars led by Asparuch streamed south into the Danubian delta and set up a kingdom, with its capital at Pliska, which achieved Byzantine recognition in 681. Those Bulgars were Turks, but over the next few decades their largely Slavic subjects in the new region Slavicized their rulers—whereas in contrast the Slavs to the south were Hellenized. In the early ninth century Krum, khagan (ruler) of the Bulgarian state, was strong enough to threaten the Byzantine Empire with a destruction from which only his death in 814 may have spared it.

A cultural revival in ninth-century Byzantium accompanied and may have helped produce a renewal of Byzantine society and state.[34] It was not clearly connected with any institution of higher learning; the "University of Constantinople" seems to have been the construction of recent scholars reading back into the past features of contemporary higher education. If something of the kind existed in the fifth century, it "faded out" in the seventh century.[35]

However, higher learning came to thrive again in the ninth century, especially in the church. It was the foremost scholar of the day, Photius, patriarch of Constantinople from 858, who dispatched two brothers, Constantine and Methodius, as missionaries to the Slavs of the north in 863. In Moravia, their destination,[36] they invented one new alphabet (Glagolithic) and paved the way for the invention of another (Cyrillic, after Constantine's monastic name, Cyril)—both based on Greek—for the purpose of transcribing the Slavic dialect of Thessaloniki. As "Church Slavonic" (or Church Slavic) it came to be used as the liturgical and scriptural language of all Slavs converted from Byzantium, as well as the Romanians.

Therefore Orthodox converts did not have to learn Greek, in contrast to Westerners who had to learn Latin when converted to Christianity. Classical literature was thus unfamiliar to most Christianized Romanians and Slavs of the East, and the cultural gulf that came to separate them from their cultivated southern neighbors eventually found a counterpart in social and political development. Whether those circumstances were bound to benefit or harm this or that people of eastern Europe may not be obvious. Borrowing the Byzantine system of absolutism was not necessarily the way to progress.

The Moravian state disappeared, but the Slavicized Bulgarians formed a state that lasted. The Bulgarian ruler Boris, now styled "tsar," was baptized by a bishop sent from Constantinople, and after some flirtation with Rome he accepted the way of the East.

The conversion of many Slavs came during the reign of the founder of the Macedonian dynasty, which over the next two centuries carried Byzantium to the zenith of its development. He was Basil I (867–886), an Armenian though born in Macedonia. He presided over the conversion of the Serbs and attempted to draw the Croats into the Byzantine orbit, but failed, and the fateful religious separation between the two peoples became permanent. Basil was an able ruler who rebuilt the army and navy and brought new order to the legal system.

His son Leo the Wise extended Basil's reform of Byzantine jurisprudence. At Leo's death in 912 the central government had produced an ever more complex bureaucracy that was the instrument of the emperor. The notion of "legitimate" succession, which may be credited to Basil I,[37] focused attention on male heirs born in the porphyry palace (thus *porphyrogeniti*) and helped to lend new stability to the body politic.

In four marriages, only two of which were licit, Leo managed to sire a single son, Constantine VII Porphyrogenitus, a sickly boy who nevertheless lived to reign forty-six years. His officials and generals held at bay Tsar Symeon of Bulgaria, who fought several campaigns in an effort to win the Byzantine throne, until Symeon died in 927. Thereafter Bulgaria became a "docile satellite,"[38] and soon afterward Byzantium restored its suzerainty over the Serbs, who had still not achieved statehood.

Slavs farther east, in the state of Rus with capital in Kiev, had been ruled by Varangians to begin with. They attacked Constantinople by sea in 941 and 944, and the Byzantines had to turn their attention to taming them. Princess Olga of Kiev was received and baptized in the imperial capital in 957, but the conversion of the Rus as a whole was to be delayed while her pagan son Sviatoslav ruled.

Basil I and Leo had tried to check Saracen expansion and successfully defended southern Italy, though they could not hold Sicily. In the 1970s one of the greatest of Byzantine emperors and generals, John I Tzimisces, advanced against the Muslims into Syria and was not far from Jerusalem when he judged it prudent to halt.

John was succeeded by Basil II Bulgaroktonos (the Bulgar-slayer, 976–1025). He had to contend with a variety of external dangers and the internal threat of an overweening and rebellious aristocracy. Provincial magnates *(dynatoi)* were growing steadily in number and strength as a result of taking over smallholdings, especially in Anatolia. In 971 Bardas Phocas had launched a brief rebellion based on his fellow lords and in 987 another, longer one along with Bardas Skleros, which overran Anatolia and endangered the capital. Basil II crushed this rising with the help of several thousand soldiers sent by Vladimir, prince of Kiev, who then accepted Christianity (988) and received the hand of the emperor's sister in marriage. The conversion of the Rus now proceeded steadily. Basil tried to legislate the break-up of great estates and their division among the peasantry, whom he regarded as the bulwark of Byzantine society. He had some success in doing so, but it was limited and temporary.

Basil II had greater success in war. Tsar Samuel reestablished a state in western Bulgaria with which the Byzantines fought seesaw battles for several years. In 1014, Basil finally crushed the Bulgarian army. He blinded all fourteen thousand prisoners, leaving a single eye to one in every hundred to guide his fellows, and sent them back to Samuel, who collapsed at the sight and died the next day. The Bulgarian state disappeared and its land was annexed. The king of Armenia accepted Byzantine suzerainty to avoid conquest by the newly arrived Seljuq Turks. When in the course of planning the reconquest of Sicily, the emperor died.

It was the high point of Byzantine power. The frontiers appeared secure, the peril of further aristocratic insurrection contained, the prestige of Byzantine culture unsurpassed in the Mediterranean and Near Eastern worlds. But trouble lay ahead. Basil's niece Zoe was his real successor, and through the nominal reigns of three husbands she maintained a sort of continuity. When her sister Theodora died in 1056 after a brief reign as empress, the Macedonian dynasty became extinct. Despite increasing difficulties, some achievements of the Macedonians lasted; they included the conversion of the southern and eastern Slavs. For a considerable time their relations with Constantinople were close enough to be interpreted by one scholar as making up a "Byzantine commonwealth."[39]

There was a cultural and religious pluralism in the lands of Eastern Orthodox Christianity, now dependent on Constantinople, founded on linguistic differentiation. Genuine social pluralism was another matter. The military aristocracy of the provinces faced as a rival the civilian bureaucracy of the capital, but neither seemed to have the potentiality to become a free and self-organized class. The property and influence of the clergy—both "white" (priests and bishops) and "black" (monks and nuns)—were imposing, especially after the defeat of the iconoclasts, and the ecclesiastical entity constituted a kind of limitation on the ruler; but the intermingling of church and state, in both theory and practice, impeded and ultimately prevented the emergence of the kind of independence the Western church claimed and attained.

The basileus had a status that was regarded as "the earthly reflection of God's monarchy in heaven,"[40] and yet the imperial office failed to gain stability or popular sympathy. Arbitrary and cruel methods used to seize and retain the throne inspired fear but not devotion. The Macedonians came closest to implanting the theory and practice of legitimacy, which might have come to serve as a focus of political consciousness and a basis for political unity within which some distribution of political power could have occurred. Such potentialities, if they existed, were never realized.

The Empires of Islam

On the death of Muhammad in 632 his followers, after debating whether any kind of state should survive, established an authority that would put into practice "Muhammad's solution" to the social chaos in which he had lived. It was "to provide for a central distribution of funds to those at a disadvantage and a central settlement of disputes by a divinely sanctioned moral standard."[41] The Qur'an provided directly for no government other than that of the Prophet himself.

The only position, therefore, that could be felt to be legitimate was still [that is, as before Muhammad] that of the military commander. It was the military leadership, shifting from simple raids for booty, that embarked on conquest, which soon became "the keynote of the Muslim state." But the action of government and armies was for the sake of Islam. In contrast to the Christians or the Zoroastrians of Persia, "no explicit distinction between religion and state could be made among the Muslims."

As the Arab armies fanned out over the Mediterranean world, they attracted many non-Arab recruits. Jews and Christians generally enjoyed some protection from the conquerors; Jews and Monophysite Christians, at any rate, actually assisted Muslim conquest of Egypt. In 641 'Umar, the second caliph and Muhammad's successor as leader of the new religion, drew up a register *(diwan)* of members of the newly formed elite. It ranked them by service and sacrifices made for the cause, and thus formally created an Arab meritocracy.

At first Christian monks and clergy were exempt from poll tax, but soon one *(jizyah)* was imposed on individual Christians and a land tax *(kharaj)* on the Christian community. The result, writes F. E. Peters, was about the same financial burden that the Byzantine or Sasanid empires had imposed; the difference was that the Arabs did not occupy or settle the conquered territories but instead established "purely Arab encampments where they collected their tribute and garrisoned their armies: Basrah (637) and Kufah (638) in Iraq, Fustat (642) in Egypt and Qayrawan (670) in Tunisia."[42]

Converts to Islam multiplied, and as the Muslim population of the given area grew, the amir, or military commander, might become a civil-military governor. Popular hostility to dhimmis (non-Muslims) originally insignificant, grew slowly, including denial of access to Muslim holy places.[43]

The shape of the polity took some time to develop. From 632 to 661 four caliphs succeeded one another. There were several disputes regarding the succession, and the fourth caliph, 'Ali, was murdered. Mu'awiyah, the new ruler, founded the Umayyad dynasty, which lasted until 750. His strength was centered in Syria, and Damascus came to be the capital. The 'Alid faction attempted to make Husayn ibn 'Ali ("ibn" means "son of") caliph and failed; he was murdered in Karbala', in present-day Iraq, in 680.

This event was central to the belief developed later that the representative or incarnation—there was some ambiguity—of God was the Imam, or leader of the people; the imams were 'Ali and his heirs leading to Muhammad al-Mahdi, who through a series of steps experienced final "occultation" in 941—that is, became the "hidden" Imam who will return at the Last Day.[44] This was the conviction of the Sh'ia wing of Islam, whose stronghold came to be Iran and southern Iraq but had little strength in the rest of the Muslim world.

Soon the Umayyad caliphate changed character. 'Abd al-Malik, caliph in the 690s, began to build the Dome of the Rock in Jerusalem as something like a counter-church and undertook brutal repression of Christians, hitherto often favored and accepted at court. Arabic now became the official language of government, replacing Greek, Coptic, and Persian in the western, central, and eastern regions respectively. The exemption of monks from the poll tax was rescinded. Such policies led to sharp increases in the number of converts.

Paradoxically, the model taken by the caliphs of the turn of the century was the Byzantine emperor; "the coinage, the reorganization of the *diwans,* the monumental architecture all converge on a repudiation of Constantinople and the simultaneous acceptance of the Byzantines' notion of what an emperor should be."[45]

However, a turn to the East that affected architecture, literature, and political conceptions occurred in the early eighth century. As before, Syrian military units remained the basis of the caliphs' power. But the model for the rulership shifted to the Iranian shah. The last Umayyads increased the repressive measures applied to Christians; St. John of Damascus—later often called the last Father of the Church—was a member of the Muslim civil service before 'Umar II dismissed all Christians therefrom, and he was constrained to enter a monastery.

The last ruler of the dynasty was overthrown and killed in 750, along with most Umayyad princes. One of them escaped, however, to found a new kingdom in newly conquered Spain with its capital in Cordova. The victors in the struggle for the caliphate, the 'Abbasid family, soon built for themselves a new capital, Baghdad.

In the Baghdad of the 'Abbasids several significant changes occurred. The Arab warrior aristocracy of the Umayyad period gave way to a new cosmopolitan aristocracy of service, in which Iranian and other *mawali* (non-Arab converts to Islam) took a prominent part. As Islam ceased to expand, the army could no longer be paid out of the booty of conquest, and a professional force came into being. But it was the bureaucracy that increased in size and influence.[46] A skirmish with the troops of China's T'ang dynasty in 751 brought to Samarqand Chinese prisoners who knew how to make paper; about 800 the secret reached Baghdad, and the burgeoning officialdom put it to good use at once.[47]

Baghdad turned the face of Islam increasingly eastward, though not exclusively so. Iranian intellectuals shifted from Pahlevi to Arabic, as if in response to 'Abbasid preoccupation with things Persian, while the merchant and peasant classes turned to the simpler form of the Persian language called by the Arabs Dari. Translations into Arabic from Iranian, and also Indian, writings were made with the encouragement of the chief ministers or viziers, and from Greek as well for the first time.[48]

The rough and rustic Turks, who were at that period not interested in such pursuits, had come to provide troop contingents vital to the caliphs. The palace chamberlain, a Turk, supervised the postal service, which both delivered mail (of the official variety only) and, more important, gathered intelligence from all parts of the empire that could be counted on to reach the capital rapidly.

During the early ninth century a Muslim theology was being shaped for the first time, and a more or less coherent body of Islamic law as well. The requisite spirit of rationalization and systematization owed a good deal to Hellenic influences, which along with Iranian ones were being felt in Baghdad, "Islam's Alexandria." Nevertheless, in this encounter "the Muslim accepted neither the language nor the humanistic values nor, he thought, the religion of the Greeks; his borrowings came exclusively through translation and were severely limited to a technical and scientific Hellenism."[49]

Prominent among elements of the Hellenic heritage that the Muslims did not acquire was the corpus of institutions of municipal self-government, the magistracies and councils of the polis—though it cannot be said that the caliphate destroyed them; they were moribund or dead throughout the Near East by the time of Justinian, before the Prophet was born. The cities, along with the rest of the Islamic empire, were governed by officials—military, civilian, or both—in accordance with the precepts of the newly shaped Islamic law, the Shari'ah.

The name Shari'ah meant something like "the way"—that is, the road of righteous life leading to God.[50] In the ninth century the term came to be used for law and not theology. Despite doctrinal rejection of literalism, it came to mean in fact chiefly the letter of the law. And yet it was not really a legal code; it was rather a system of moral philosophy or ethics, a list of "oughts." That law only "regulated [the Muslim's] worship of God and his contracts with his fellow Muslims; it gave him no instruction on how to rule, no model of a state, no ideal prince or ideal constitution."[51] Hodgson notes that though the Shari'ah was originally created in part to neutralize caliphal power and diffuse it among society, it never led to limiting the power of the ruler or anything like a right of resistance to him.[52]

Islam had no political theory of its own. The most that can be said is that conflicting notions about rulership grew up. Shi'ah legitimism insisted that the caliph should come from 'Ali's family; the radical Kharijite conception was that the rule might be wielded by anyone, "even an Ethiopian slave" in the Kharijite phrase; Sunnism would accept any ruler from the Prophet's tribe, the Quraysh, though at first suggesting that the ruler must "satisfy certain qualifications."[53] However, soon Sunni teaching came to demand obedience "even [to] a tyrannical ruler." Early Islam had conserved the old principles of the Arab desert: election of the ruler and exercise of authority through consultation. But in settled, postheroic Baghdad such customs were laid aside.

It was under the 'Abbasids that a religious orthodoxy was worked out in the form of Sunnism. It avoided the emotional and sectarian tendencies of the Shi'ah and the mystical paths of Sufism—ascetic, ecstatic, and intuitive by turns. "While condemning schisms and branding dissent as heretical," writes Fazlur Rahman, "Sunnism developed the opposite trend of accommodation, catholicity, and synthesis."[54] The seemingly total determinism of the Qur'an was shunted aside, and a place was found for man's responsibility as well as God's omnipotence, though some Sunni teachers stressed the former more than others did.

Under Harun-ar-Rashid (d. 809), contemporary of Charlemagne in his rough-hewn capital of Aachen, 'Abbasid Baghdad soon radiated magnificence. Politically it was not as unqualified a success. Nearly independent vassal states appeared in the remote provinces, and Baghdad was so filled with disorderly provincials that in 836 a caliph moved to a new capital at Samarra in the north.

Shadows appeared on the cultural scene. A period of religious and philosophical inquiry and experimentation was terminated by Mutawakkil, caliph from 847 to 861. He sought to return to primitive Muslim doctrine, razed the mausoleum of the martyr of Karbala', Husayn, and banned Shi'ah pilgrimages thereto. He also cruelly persecuted Christians, Jews, and nontraditionalist Muslims, notably the intellectually sophisticated Mu'tazilites who espoused the notion of free will, taught a deity of justice and reason, and had held a dominant role in the cultural world of Islam for half a century.

Mutawakkil was assassinated. What followed was short reigns and long periods of chaos. In the capital, the viziers often governed instead of the caliphs, and the Turkish guardsmen virtually controlled the army; in the provinces, hereditary potentates began to appear. In the late ninth century, the 'Abbasid caliphate lost its eastern provinces—Iran and Turkestan—to new dynasties and states.

In 909 a new family arose in Tunisia calling itself the Fatimids, since it traced descent from the Prophet's daughter Fatima and 'Ali through Isma'il, and offering a new version of religious Shi'ism called Isma'ili. In view of the fact that the Fatimids had proclaimed themselves caliphs, thus breaking the tradition of the single caliphate, the Umayyad princes of Spain sought to duplicate their feat. In 929 the Sunni religious leaders of the peninsula accorded recognition of their new title, which they kept until 1031. Thus in the tenth century there were three caliphates: 'Abbasid, Fatimid, and Umayyad.

By now the oldest caliphate was the weakest. For the Sunni 'Abbasids, there could be no such thing as an Imamate separate from the Caliphate.[55] For them, as equally for the Shi'ah, there could be no more than one caliphate, but they were willing to accept regional powers that acknowledged caliphal unity. The 'Abbasid caliphs were controlled by Shi'ite Persian warlords, the Buyids, who effectively ruled Iraq and western Iran. In Khurasan (eastern Iran and Afghanistan), the Turkish Ghaznavids held sway until in 1040 a new horde, a grouping of Oguz Turks led by the Seljuq family, struck and broke their power.

The western regions of the 'Abbasids fell to the Fatimid advance. Conquering Egypt after several unsuccessful tries, the Fatimids abandoned the city that had hitherto been the Muslim capital, Fustat, and began construction of a new one, al-Qahirah (Cairo), "the Victorious." The Fatimids pushed as far east as Syria. They claimed at various times to be headed by an imam, one who would administer the law, or a Mahdi, a divine messenger of some sort—or both or neither;—but always by a caliph, of which they (and many other Muslims) believed there could be only one legitimate exemplar at any given time, no matter what his conduct or how many claimed the title. A certainly eccentric, perhaps mad Fatimid caliph, al-Hakim, persecuted Christians and Jews, destroyed the Church of the Holy Sepulcher in Jerusalem, and in 1021 rode off into the night and disappeared forever.

Out of the welter of Turkic peoples who now ranged over much of central Asia emerged the Seljuqs. The most prominent leader among them, Tughril, entered Baghdad in 1055. He and his successors now called themselves sultans ("rulers") with the permission of the now powerless caliphs. It was Tughril's nephew, Alp Arslan, who smashed the Byzantine army at Manzikert in 1071, provoking the Crusades.

In the same year his forces dealt the Fatimids a decisive blow, though they lingered a hundred years longer. The 'Abbasid Caliphate survived to be overthrown by the Mongols in 1258 when Hulagu took Baghdad, but it had lost its significance by the middle of the eleventh century.

The Umayyad Caliphate in Cordova broke up in 1031. The wild Berber Dynasty of the Almoravids from North Africa invaded Spain in 1086 to assist the small Moorish (Muslim) successor states, beset by the Christian pressure from the north, but they soon settled down to enjoy the civilized delights of the country. The Almoravids ruled in the name of the 'Abbasid caliph in Baghdad with no fear that it would interfere with them. In general, the later eleventh century witnessed a lasting downturn in the fortunes of Islam, shown in such events as the loss of Sicily to the Normans (1060–91) and the capture of Jerusalem by the Crusaders in 1099.

For four hundred years Islam had brought to a vast area some degree of order, fluctuating levels of religious tolerance and persecution, and a concept of unity that might be honored mainly in the breach but was never forgotten. There might be one caliphate or several, and within a caliphate there might be several sultans or amirs. However, throughout Islamic society, from Morocco to India, some common features of social development may be observed. In Egypt and Syria many Byzantine institutions survived and were retained. Many landowners fled from those regions and were replaced by Arabs, who established themselves on the estates concerned, added to their holdings by purchase, and transmitted them through inheritance to the next generation.

And yet secure and strong forms of landed property did not develop. In the words of Karl Wittfogel,

In the later feudal and postfeudal societies of the West the landed nobles were able to create the one-sided system of inheritance called entail and primogeniture primarily because they were armed and because they were nationally and politically organized. In hydraulic [including Islamic] society the representatives of private property lacked the strength to establish similarly consolidated and strong forms of property, first because the governmental monopoly of armed action prevented the property holders from maintaining independent military forces, and second because the governmental network of organization (corvée, state post and intelligence, integrated army, and universal taxation) prevented the property holders from protecting their interests by means of an effective national organization.[56]

By now it should be increasingly clear that, in earlier history throughout most of the world, prevention of the fragmentation of landholding through inheritance was a key to the creation or preservation of a class strong enough to check the growth of despotism, and thus to pave the way for a wider social pluralism. As for the landlords of Muslim society, they were not able to prevent fragmentation of their holdings, with one interesting, significant exception: the *waqf,* or endowment. This Peters defines as "an inalienable bequest whose usufruct is directed toward the support of some pious purpose specified by the donor" and for such purposes is kept undivided—unlike other lands.[57] However, the state could still seize a *waqf,* and the beneficiaries of such endowments never organized effectively or emerged as a discernible class.

The most common form of landholding was service tenure, in which the land in question *(iqta')* was held conditionally upon service, which was usually military service. Private land existed, but it was a rarity in the first centuries after the Muslim conquests and never became a major factor in the society of Islam. Bureaucracy overshadowed landlordism; property did not become strong; law remained without a cutting edge for those who wished to ignore its precepts.

Of the Islamic social order that had emerged by the thirteenth century, Hodgson writes that its hallmark appeared to be "occasionalism," improvisation without reference to established position or precedence, in contrast to Western "legitimism." But if the latter sometimes led to absurdity, he adds, Islamic occasionalism "could be reduced to the arbitrary rule of violence."[58]

The subsequent story need not detain us. The Mongols conquered much Muslim territory and set up three major realms (Il-khans in Persia, Chaghatay in Central Asia, Golden Horde in Russia), which then accepted Islam and fell apart not long afterward. Islamic expansion continued even in the thirteenth century, when the still pagan Mongols were defeating all opponents (except the Mamluks of Egypt), and later, eastward into India, Indo-China, and Malaysia and westward into Europe—by Ottoman conquest.

The Ottoman Turks were delayed in their offensive westward by the crushing but transitory onslaught (1402) of Timur, who may serve as a reminder of what the "arbitrary violence" of oriental despotism might mean: he piled up mountains of severed heads, buried alive four thousand of the Ottoman armies' Christian regiments, and in one town built towers of two thousand live men who were bound and then faced with bricks and mortar.[59] But the Ottomans soon recovered; they went on to capture Constantinople and later to reach Vienna twice.

Hodgson concludes that Islam was a venture "inspired by the prophets' demand for uncompromising justice, in transforming the world's social order through the resources of prophetic vision."[60] To the extent that such transformation occurred over the centuries, it cannot be said that much space was left for pluralism or freedom.

CHAPTER 5

The High Middle Ages: The West, Byzantium, and Islam, 1050–1350

In the eleventh century, Byzantium passed in a short time from the heights of successful military and civil achievement to the depths of crisis. In 1025 the Macedonian dynasty ended with the death of Basil II; in 1071 the Seljuqs destroyed the Byzantine army at Manzikert, and during the following decade they advanced through Asia Minor to Nicaea while the Byzantines squabbled and did nothing to stop them.

In the western regions of the empire other disasters occurred. "The one great general of the post-Macedonian era," George Maniaces, was recalled from the struggle with the Normans in Sicily and executed; the Normans then advanced, captured Bari in the calamitous year 1071, and ended Byzantine rule in Italy.[1] In 1054 there took place a schism between the churches of East and West, the patriarchate of Constantinople and the papacy. The split was given theological and ritual form but was triggered by disputes about how to meet the Norman advance into Italian territory. At the time the ecclesiastical schism appeared minor and temporary; later political and military events turned it into a lasting affair.

The West was a welter of competing political and religious entities, for which the term feudalism was becoming increasingly inadequate. Empire and papacy were both imposing and rising powers. There were monarchies of varying magnitude outside them in Latin Christendom: England, Scotland, France, Castile,

Poland, Bohemia, Hungary, Norway, Sweden, and Denmark. As the monarchies grew in strength, free institutions secured a foothold in them. For the next three centuries and more, Byzantium and the Islamic empires would be no threats to the young Western states, and at times their weakness would invite or permit at least temporarily successful Western attack, notably in the Crusades.

As tender shoots of free institutions made their appearance in the West, movements in a contrary direction occurred farther east.[2] The Muslims conquered much of India, beginning from the late twelfth century, leading eventually to the foundation of the great Mughal Empire (1526–1857) that came to control much of the peninsula. In China the Sung dynasty (960–1279), brilliant in the cultural levels it achieved, still constituted a "turning point in the history of authoritarian government" in that country. By weakening the military, whereas "military forces that could readily contest the power of the state had been a prominent feature of Chinese history from the third century to the tenth," while the old aristocracy also declined, the Sungs gave the state "fiscal and military and organizational powers which it had not possessed previously." In addition, an "over-centralization of authority" occurred, marked by a paring down of the powers of local officials. In sum, writes Hsiao Kung-ch'üan, "the development of the despotic form of government during the Sung period more or less reached its completion."[3] Among Asian states great and small, only Japan seemed to move institutionally in a different direction. Especially in the eleventh and twelfth centuries, there emerged a feudalism in some ways strikingly resembling that of Europe; "the methods of mixture were quite different in Japan and in Europe, but the basic ingredients seem to have been much the same."[4]

The West, 1050–1200

Within the West, the question was whether the trend would be toward unity or plurality, a unity that would be political as in the ancient Roman Empire or theocratic as in the early Islamic entity on the one hand or, on the other, a plurality of states, which might coexist in more or less peaceful fashion while accepting a common religion.

The empire and the papacy both endeavored to attain unity, and both at least at various times postulated in theory a kind of single realm in which each could play a part. Pope Gelasius I, writing to Emperor Anastasius I just before 500, had set forth the norm: "There are two powers by which this world is governed in chief, the consecrated authority of priests and the royal power."[5] Priests must submit to royal laws pertaining to the secular realm; kings must submit to priests where salvation is concerned. Somewhat later the idea was expressed in the doctrine of *symphonia* (best translated a "harmony") embodied in Justinian's Sixth Novella.

Putting the idea into practice, in West or East, proved most difficult. Indeed the theoretical equality sometimes assumed by such statements was in other cases modified; Gelasius himself declared that the greater burden fell on the priests. St. Augustine had argued that the king must be a *justus homo,* a righteous man obeying God's commandments. Who would determine if the monarch was or was not righteous? The priest. And what if the monarch was unrighteous? The priest must depose him. So ran the papal case. Yet Augustine himself had envisaged a royal and not priestly Constantine as regularly occupying the position of headship of the earthly church, and Justinian had declared the ruler's responsibility to be enforcement of obedience to God; as the "Lord's anointed" he was no ordinary layman.[6]

And in feudal Europe the king enjoyed an extraordinary position based on religion. Marc Bloch adduces as proof that this was so the fact that, in an age of widespread violence and frequent cases of defiance, disobedience, or rebellion by vassals, who might seize and imprison their monarchs, only three were killed in the period in question: Edward the Martyr (978) in England, Robert I of France (923), and Berengar I, last of the "phantom emperors" (924).[7] It was thus the secular ruler, bearing the title "emperor" or not, who partook of the "divinity [that] doth hedge a king,"[8] and shared in the medieval conception of a unified order of social life sanctified by the church.

The papacy had not always been prepared to mount a successful defense of the ecclesiastical power, and unlike the situation in the secular sphere, there were no independent authorities in the churches of the West that could replace the Roman see. The papacy had sunk to a shameful nadir in the tenth century. However, the foundations had already been laid for its recovery.

In 910 an abbey was established at Cluny in the southern part of the duchy of Burgundy. It was exempt from any authority, lay or clerical, except papal; it strictly observed the Benedictine Rule (that is, the set of regulations laid down for monastic life by Benedict of Nursia in the sixth century). By the eleventh century Cluny was the mother house of an Order of its own, with great wealth and influence. It instituted monastic reform and supported ecclesiastical reform of all sorts; the Cluniac recipe for reform of the papacy was acceptance of the help of emperors in bringing it about.

In 1046 Emperor Henry III had given reform great impetus by wrenching the papacy from the control of the Roman nobles and then choosing to be pope four German bishops in a row who were concerned to end the abuses in the church. But a papacy controlled by the empire, however, benevolently, was not a solution the reformers could accept. Several popes in a row reflected Cluniac influence but determined to win independence for the papacy. In 1059 a papal decree enacted that the popes should henceforth be elected by the cardinal clergy alone, a measure that in turn made the College of Cardinals, at first with fifty-five members, a body with great power.

In 1073 the cardinals elected a gifted man short in height but tall in moral stature. Hildebrand, as Gregory VII, undertook to carry ecclesiastical reform through to a conclusion and also deal with the danger that the emperors, as the chief forces behind reform, would consolidate control of the church. His struggle to curb that threat came to center on the practice of lay investiture, that is, the ceremony by which a king invested or bestowed upon the bishop-elect the ring and staff that were the emblems of his clerical office. The pope prohibited the practice in 1075 and seems at first to have wished to engage the emperor's cooperation in resolving the issue.

It was not forthcoming. The empire, after a slow start following its resuscitation in the tenth century, acquired strong leadership in the Franconian (or Salian) dynasty. The century following 1024 was "the great imperial age."[9] Conrad II shrewdly gained control of most of the great dukedoms one by one; he effectively used the *ministeriales* (lay vassals on the royal domain) as officials. Henry III, "strongest of the German emperors," asserted his authority in Poland, Bohemia, and Hungary. However, one Franconian policy militated against making the empire into a unitary state: the encouragement of hereditary tenure of fiefs.[10]

After links were established and severed two or three times between the empire on the one hand and Hungary and Poland on the other, they were finally broken. In 1058 the Hungarians regained full independence and soon afterward Boleslaw II the Bold of Poland did likewise. Bohemia alone of the non-German states to the east became a permanent part of the empire.

When Henry IV began to reign, in 1067, he was caught up in conflict with the great German nobles. But the central drama of his reign was the struggle with the papacy. In its first phase, the emperor suffered excommunication, undertook the famous penance at Canossa in northern Italy, and seemed to be bound to accept the papal decree against lay investiture: "no cleric was to accept investiture of bishopric, abbey, or church from the hand of Emperor, king, or any lay person, male or female."[11]

It appeared that papal victory was complete. It was not. Gregory VII announced the deposition of the emperor. Henry led an army all the way to the Eternal City. Gregory's Norman allies drove the emperor out of Rome, but ravaged the city so brutally that the pope for safety had to withdraw to the south with his rescuers and died in 1085.

Despite his sad end, Gregory had a great and lasting achievement: it was to make papal authority effective almost everywhere in Latin Christendom with respect to the church. The exception was England, where William I the Conqueror was fervent enough in pursuit of ecclesiastical reform to make it difficult for the pope to argue that only Rome could bring it about. Gregory also found support for the position that an evil ruler violates the contract he has implicitly made with his subjects, so that the pope, who is responsible for the salvation of mankind, may depose him. A certain Manegold of Lautenbach so held. Henry's own legal advisers not surprisingly argued the contrary. That argument was not resolved, but the tradition that Christianity sanctioned the removal of an unjust ruler, forcefully enunciated by St. Augustine, was strengthened.

Gregory's policies were continued by the handsome and learned Frenchman, Urban II. Ignoring monarchs and appealing directly to the nobles and peoples, the pope summoned the whole of the West to the first of a series (as it proved) of Crusades to retake the Holy Places of Palestine from the Muslims. It was "the first great victory of the reformed Papacy," and demonstrated both the new papal prestige and the weakening of the emperors.[12]

The investiture controversy was finally compromised and terminated by the Concordat of Worms, drawn up in 1122. By its terms secular rulers could grant the temporalities but not the spiritual symbols, the ring and the staff.

The struggle of emperor and pope was, however, not over. The empire faced a recrudescence of the power of the dukes, especially in Saxony, Bavaria, and Swabia. In their challenge to imperial authority, the papacy was able to play a part. With papal aid, in 1125 the great archbishops of Mainz and Cologne prevented the election of Frederick of Swabia, of the House of Hohenstaufen, and placed on the throne as emperor instead the duke of Saxony, Lothair, of the party of Welfs.

For the next decade Welfs and Waiblingers (or Hohenstaufens; in Italy the parties were called Guelfs and Ghibellines) contested. In 1138, however, the Hohenstaufens established themselves as the imperial dynasty, and it lasted 130 years.

Emperor Frederick I Barbarossa, who began use of the term "Holy Roman Empire," came to be regarded as the ideal medieval German monarch. Though he conciliated the German magnates with some success, he failed in repeated expeditions to forge unity with Italy. In 1176, at the battle of Legnano, occurred the first major defeat of feudal cavalry by infantry and withal the victory of the townsmen from the communes of Lombardy over the imperial forces. Although the peace that followed affirmed the general suzerainty of the empire in Italy, it provided for effective autonomy for the Lombard towns.

Moreover, the south was irretrievably beyond imperial control. The boot of the peninsula and the island of Sicily were combined under a single Norman kingship conferred by the pope in 1130. Roger II established a centralized administration drawing on Norman, Greek, and Saracen elements, and art and learning flourished at his court.

Thus Frederick I failed in some ways and succeeded in others. He retained effective control of the church in Germany and rebuffed certain sorts of papal claims.

During his unusually long (1159–81) papacy, Alexander III was able to generate sufficient momentum for reform so that the Third Lateran Council in 1179 decreed that a two-thirds vote of the cardinals was needed to elect a pope—a provision that remains in force eight centuries later, at the time of writing. Alexander is remembered as a legislator and lawyer, and indeed the papacy was coming to have mountainous legal burdens as well as the disposition of substantial legal powers.

After peace in Italy was arranged, Frederick I returned to Germany to confront the great nobles. He partitioned the realm of the powerful duke of Saxony, Henry the Lion, and sliced off some of Bavaria. He then departed for the Third Crusade, and drowned in 1190 while en route to the Holy Land.

Despite his blows against the dukes, he seems to have made little sustained effort to consolidate the imperial power or to convert his office into one of lasting national rulership. The German nobles were "still nominally royal officials, and did homage to the king for the offices they held, as his subjects not his tenants." [13] But in reality they were becoming minor sovereigns in their own right.

Frederick I bore part of the responsibility for the trend in that direction, in particular by making concessions in Germany in order to assist his campaigns in Italy; he ended up weaker in both. After the brief interval of Henry VI's reign, the empire experienced a period of civil war terminated by the ascent to the throne in 1211 of a quite different sort of emperor than his predecessors, Frederick II.

During the latter half of the eleventh century the French monarchy exhibited the capacity to grow in strength and extent. A slow and painful process began to occur by which the kings annexed the holdings of feudal lords and amassed power in their office. In the reign of Philip I (1060–1108), the dukes or counts of Aquitaine, Anjou, Flanders, and above all Normandy—whose duke was king in England—were more powerful than the king. Under Louis VI and Louis VII, whose reigns stretched to 1180, the royal initiative made headway. They began to reduce the feudal holdings north of the Loire. Both depended for counsel on Suger, the lowborn abbot of St.-Denis. It was he who started construction of the first wholly Gothic building in architectural history, the abbey church of St.-Denis.

On such humble but devoted officials the rise of both the French and English monarchies partly depended—as contrasted with Germany, which lacked such assets. Louis VII gave up the lands Eleanor of Aquitaine had brought him by their marriage and Eleanor herself to Henry II, duke of Normandy and Aquitaine, count of Anjou, Maine, and Touraine, who inherited the English throne in 1154 and became immensely stronger as a result. Louis VII ruled only the royal domain, but during his reign the king's court (*curia regis*) at Paris was increasingly used for cases originating in all parts of the kingdom. His successor, Philip II, paved the streets and built the walls of Paris, very significantly extended the royal domain, and consolidated the monarchy.

In England, Norman feudalization was proceeding apace, on a much more centralized basis than had characterized Saxon feudalism. In theory, the king owned every scrap of land in England; in practice, he had about one-sixth and apportioned less than half to his followers. The church held perhaps a fourth. The Saxon shires and hundreds were continued as units for local government, under sheriffs (usually barons) who could be removed by the king but were often left alone.

The Anglo-Saxon Witan was replaced, or for the most part simply renamed, as the *curia regis,* or Great Council. It consisted of tenants-in-chief, the chancellor (an innovation of Edward the Confessor), the justiciar (a new official managing justice and finance and replacing the king when absent), and heads of the royal household staff. The Small Council, including only the tenants-in-chief who happened to be on hand (rather than the full complement of 170), tended to become the more important body.[14]

The Conqueror was a shrewd as well as powerful man. In 1085 he was able to order and carry out the great Domesday survey, described by F. W. Maitland as "an exploit which has no parallel in the history of Europe."[15] It has been suggested that the device had been borrowed by the Normans from the Byzantine and Saracen rulers of Sicily, much of which they conquered in 1072.[16] Karl Wittfogel comments that "evidently, systematic and nationwide registration was as out of place in feudal society as it was customary in the realm of Oriental despotism."[17]

The Domesday survey, at any rate, remained unique in the history of England and of western Europe. Under William I the country prospered; and after a short reign by a much-hated son of his, another son, Henry I, resumed a policy of order and growth. Anselm, archbishop of Canterbury, defended the papal position on lay investiture, and in 1107 obtained a compromise not far from what he had sought.

After an episode of feudal anarchy, Henry's grandson Henry II (1154–89) combined inherited and acquired territories in a mixed "empire." He attempted to reverse the extension of "benefit of clergy" (exemption of ecclesiastics from civil punishment of various kinds) that had been taking place. After Thomas à Becket was murdered by knights of the court who thought they were carrying out the king's orders, it was a practical impossibility for Henry II to prosecute the effort.

The king did manage, however, to advance substantially the growth of a law applying equally to the whole realm—and so termed the "common" law—and the discarding of the ordeal as a supernatural means of determining criminal guilt or civil right in favor of the jury, that is, a statement made under oath or decision taken by sworn freemen. During the reign, Wales, with no national kingship, and Ireland, with many regional but no national monarchs, were more or less reduced to English possessions; Scotland, with its own ruler, acknowledged suzerainty. In all three realms Anglo-Norman aristocracies spread.

It is not enough to establish an aristocracy; measures are needed to continue it, if continuation is desired. In England the adoption of the custom of primogeniture was a crucial step in preventing the land of the nobles from being fragmented into dwarf holdings. The eldest son inherited both title and estate; the other sons were driven to mix and marry with the lower orders of society, a process hastening the fusion of Norman and Saxon. During the reign of the mainly absent Richard I Coeur de Lion, the country was well ruled by Hubert Walter, archbishop of Canterbury and justiciar. He did much to bring the monarchy and the middle class of town and shire closer together. Charters were granted to towns; London was given the right to elect its own mayor. The knights of the shire, elected by the local gentry, were assigned local functions supplementing those of the royally appointed sheriffs.

However, the trend toward conciliation between the Norman dynasty, little more than a century old, and the Saxon people was interrupted by the reign of John. He became embroiled in a series of conflicts with the papacy, the French King, and the English barons. It was the English barons, of course, who were the chief gainers. In 1215 they extorted from the king the Great Charter (Magna Carta), whose most significant provisions are summarized by Paul Cram thus:

(1) Chapter 12: no scutage or aid (except for the traditional feudal three) to be levied without the consent of the Great Council; (2) Chapter 14: definition of the Great Council and its powers: (3) Chapter 39: "No freeman shall be arrested and imprisoned, or dispossessed, or outlawed, or banished, or in any way molested; nor will we set forth against, nor send against him, unless by the lawful judgment of his peers and by the law of the land." Even these clauses were feudal and specific in background, but centuries of experience transformed them into a generalized formula of constitutional procedure, making them the basis of the modern English constitution. At the time their chief significance lay in the assertion of the supremacy of law over the king.[18]

In this manner one of the personally most contemptible of all English monarchs became an unintentional architect of Anglo-Saxon liberty. During the previous years he had already in a curiously comparable way advanced the cause of English unity; he had been worsted in the contest with Philip Augustus through which he tried to preserve his French possessions; finally the lands north of the Loire, including Normandy, escheated to their overlord in Paris. In consequence the attention and concerns of both the Plantagenet royal house and the Norman nobles were driven to focus back on England.

In 1095 Urban II summoned all Europe to a crusade. The English and the Germans had responded, but above all the French; the pope himself was French, to be sure. With remarkably few difficulties, the Crusaders swept into Jerusalem and founded four Latin states in Syria and Palestine. Therewith feudalism, a strong church, and a none too powerful kingship were introduced into the new Latin Kingdom of Jerusalem and the three other entities over which it enjoyed nominal suzerainty. When the Muslims captured the northernmost Crusader state, Edessa, in 1144, a Second Crusade was mounted, headed by the French and German monarchs. It soon failed.

Then in 1187 the ruler of Egypt, Saladin, captured Jerusalem and unintentionally evoked a Third Crusade, led by the three outstanding rulers of the time: Emperor Frederick I Barbarossa, Richard I Coeur de Lion of England, and Philip II Augustus of France. They did not recapture the city but did succeed in arranging for Christian access to it.

By this time it was clear that the Christian West was not going to retake any large part of the Near East. In the Fourth Crusade (1204), however, the Crusaders were diverted from their goal in a dramatic and fateful way: they captured Constantinople. Driving out the Byzantines, they established a Latin Empire. That empire did not last, but Eastern memories of the conquest and pillage of their capital seemed ineffaceable.

The Christian West was more successful in the Iberian peninsula; the term "crusade" is usually not employed for the reconquest, but it is surely applicable. The Caliphate broke up in 1031. Thereafter half a dozen or more small Muslim states appeared in its place, soon absorbed by the Berber dynasty of the Almoravids, who had been summoned by one of them to help defend against the resurgent Castilians. Alfonso VI, at first king of Leon and then also of Castile, captured Toledo in 1085. His advance was briefly checked by the Almoravids. He was able to resume it with the assistance of Rodrigo de Bivar, the "Cid" (the word means "lord"), who in legend became the great Christian champion and hero of Spanish history but in fact served both sides at different times and was noted for both cruelty and vanity.

Other Christian states joined Castile in pushing back Muslim frontiers. The county of Portugal became a kingdom in 1139 and during the next decade moved its border south to the Tagus River. The Almoravids did not last; a new set of Berber invaders, the Almohads, struck them from the rear and crushed their army in 1114. The Almohads were able to restore Muslim unity in Spain and in 1195 overwhelmingly defeated Alfonso VIII of Castile.

Christian unity was not observable at this point; Leon and Navarre, not for the first time, tried to invade prostrate Castile. However, Aragon came to the rescue of the Castilians. Alfonso VIII was at length successful in rallying the Christian states and won a decisive victory against the Muslims at Las Navas de Tolosa in 1212. It was the climax of the whole *Reconquista*.

The political lineaments of Castile and Aragon were not especially unusual in the West of the day. In both states a royal council met periodically, including lay and ecclesiastical magnates. By 1150 the name Cortes had become attached to the two councils. Townsmen were growing in numbers and wealth and therefore in importance. In 1188 their representatives became the first in all Europe to sit with those from the nobility and clergy, in the Cortes of Leon. Barcelona was unique in the peninsula in having a municipal government with consuls at its head, an inheritance from the Roman Empire.

In the eleventh century, in Latin Europe to the east of Germany, Christianity and civilization were just taking hold. The Vikings had appeared in history with a raid on Lindisfarne, the Holy Island of northern England, in 793; they had subdued much of Ireland and England before 900, and after a century of peacefully exploiting their conquered lands, began a new series of raids about 1000.

By about 1050, however, they were ready to settle down, and the so-called Viking Age was at an end. Around 960 Harald Bluetooth, unifier of Denmark, converted to Christianity; Olaf Haraldsson was decisive in the conversion of Norway and was canonized only a year after his death in 1028; the convert king of Sweden, Olof Skotkonung, was a contemporary of his. During the Viking Age most Scandinavians were engaged in farming; some were freemen, equal before the law, while others were thralls or slaves with few rights. The freemen of a given area met in a *thing* to choose a king, make laws, and execute justice.[19]

About 1050 there were three Scandinavian kingdoms (Iceland was an aristocratic commonwealth with a nationwide parliament of sorts, the Althing, which was founded in 930): Norway, Denmark, and Sweden. Sometimes each had more than one king, sometimes no king. Norway expanded westward into the northern islands of Britain, Denmark southward into Germany (and experienced German expansion northward; one must remember that no clear national frontiers yet existed), Sweden eastward into Finland and the eastern shores of the Baltic. In 1262 Iceland submitted to become the personal fief of the king of Norway; after

1380 it was ruled by Denmark and regained effective independence as a republic only in 1944.

The chief organ of government in medieval Scandinavia was the assembly of the prelates of the church and landed magnates. In Denmark it was called the Hof, in Norway the Novingmote or Riksmote, in Sweden the Herredag. In each case it assisted the royal administrators but protected aristocratic interests. The beginnings are shadowy; Denmark, the most advanced state, was unified under a single king, Valdemar I, in 1157 with the capital in Copenhagen. The Hof seems to date to the reign of Valdemar II the Conqueror, which began in 1202. In the later twelfth century Uppsala became an archbishopric (1164), and Sweden was brought under one king, Erik, who died in 1196. In 1200 Norway was in turmoil but would soon emerge therefrom.

The Polish state took form in the eleventh century. Its real organizer was Boleslaw I Chrobry ("the Brave," d. 1025), who was the successor of the first Christian ruler of Poland. Despite the nominally absolute monarchical power, there were from the start sources of centrifugal pressure. The old clan system survived and was reinforced when princes strengthened local lords by bestowing land on them in return for service. The Slavic practice of dividing the royal domain instead of transmitting it intact to one successor led to much civil strife.

Part of the time Poland was tributary to the Holy Roman Empire, part not. In order to avoid such dependence, the Polish monarchy often allied itself with the papacy. In 1138 Boleslaw III divided Poland into five states for his sons, the eldest to hold the title of grand prince and reside in Cracow. This disastrous arrangement enabled the great lords (magnates) and lesser lords (gentry, or *szlachta*) to increase their power. By the time of Leszek I the White (1194–1227) the nobles, along with the clergy, virtually controlled Poland.

Bohemia was the scene of dynastic struggles whose participants might appeal either to the Empire or Poland for support. A decisive stage in conversion to Christianity had been reached before the year 1000, and the land was joined to its western neighbor by more than religion; closely associated as a vassal state with Germany, it had remained separate and elected its own duke. The duke controlled justice, taxation, and administration.

The process of administering was carried out by noble-officials who lived in castles without much land. As in Poland, the Slavic tradition prevented primogeniture in the monarchical succession, and yet the realm was not permanently divided. In 1157 the Bohemian ruler was given a hereditary crown by Frederick Barbarossa, in gratitude for support against the Lombard cities. Ottokar II (1197–1230) managed to make the new kingship a mighty force in the affairs of the Empire.

Hungary was a state much like Bohemia. Since St. Stephen (d. 1038), who received a crown from the pope in 1000, the monarchy had built up a substantial royal domain and established counties administered by counts who were royal officials. Hungary gained the status of complete independence from the Holy Roman Empire in 1058. There was a period when the Byzantines hoped to join Hungary to their empire. However, their hopes were dashed when Bela III, though he had been educated in Constantinople, turned rather in the direction of France.

His successor Andrew II lost so much power by grants of land to clergy and nobles that he was compelled, in the Golden Bull of 1222, to promise freedom from taxation and annual assembly to the magnates, knights, and clergy. By that time Hungary had definitely cast its lot with the West. Nevertheless there was a "period of two hundred and fifty years [from the mid-tenth century, when a Byzantine mission had been established east of the Tisza, to about 1200] during which Hungary, despite her formal affiliation to Latin Christendom, belonged in several respects to the Byzantine Commonwealth of nations."[20]

Byzantium and Its Neighbors, 1050–1200

In 1056 the Empress Theodora, last of the Macedonian dynasty, died. The period of Macedonian greatness was already shadowed by events darkening the horizon. Two years earlier the schism had opened between East and West in the church. Ostensibly it had been occasioned by the dispute over the single theological point of the phrase *filioque* in the Nicene Creed; more prosaically, a basic cause was the jurisdictional struggle over the south Italian church between the papacy and the patriarchate of Constantinople.

Venice, which had accepted close ties with Byzantium, and Pisa and Genoa, which had not, were fast attaining mastery of the Mediterranean at the expense of the Muslims of North Africa. The Eastern Empire did not regret the consequent discomfiture of Islam, but it was soon to suffer at the hands of the newly powerful leaders of the two Italian ports. In 1071 the Byzantines lost their last outpost in Italy—Bari—to the Normans. Added to these misfortunes was the appearance of the Seljuq Turks. Having just entered Baghdad and assumed the real power in the caliphate, they now struck westward.

The period was one of competing Comnenus and Dukas families. After a brief reign by the blunt, upright, and unpopular general Isaac Comnenus, his successor Constantine X Dukas courted popularity by allowing the size and efficiency of the army to decline. The next ruler, Romanus IV Diogenes, sought in vain to restore the Byzantine fighting forces and went down to defeat at the hands of the Seljuqs at Manzikert in 1071.

Out of the shocked confusion that ensued, there acceded to the throne Alexius

Comnenus, related to both Isaac Comnenus and Constantine Dukas. He faced mountainous problems. Much of Asia Minor was lost. A new Seljuq principality established its capital at Nicaea, 120 miles from Constantinople; thereupon the old recruiting ground of Byzantine armies for centuries disappeared. Alexius played off his enemies against one another, tried to reform the financial system, and did his best to offset his dependence on the great landlords by courting the support of the high clergy.

Alexius's weak predecessors had begged the West for help against the Seljuqs. Now the Crusaders came, not so much to help the Eastern Empire as to reconquer the Holy Land for themselves. They did recapture Nicaea for Alexius, but a complex misunderstanding led him not to appear at the siege of Antioch and led the Crusaders not to hand it over to him. Such incidents foreshadowed the more serious troubles that lay ahead for the Byzantines at the hands of the "Franks."

The emperor needed to rebuild military strength, and Alexius exerted himself mightily to do so. Great estates called *pronoiai* (singular, *pronoia*) had been granted by the monarchs of the later Macedonian dynasty and the Dukas family but were not tied to military service. The very important steps taken are described by Ostrogorsky thus:

It was under Alexius I Comnenus that this system [of the *pronoiai*] received the military service which it retained until the downfall of the Empire. The pronoiar now had the obligation of military service . . . [his] estate was not the private property of the pronoiar, but was unalienable, and to begin with it was also not heritable. Ownership . . . remained with the state, who granted it out and withheld it at discretion. But as long as it was in his possession, the pronoiar was, however, the absolute lord and master of the estate granted him and of the peasants settled on it. . . .[21]

Such developments seemed to promote the growth of feudalism, for purely internal reasons, in the Byzantine Empire. They also seemed to converge with parallel developments to the south.

As Latin principalities became established in Syria and Palestine, there "Western feudalism took root in its purest form." The relationship of vassalage, which characterized that between Alexius and the Crusader princes, "was soon applied to other princes in the Byzantine sphere and thus became a permanent feature of the late Byzantine state." Nevertheless, adds Ostrogorsky, "the two-way contract between lord and man which was characteristic of Western feudalism would have been inconceivable between Emperor and subject in Byzantium."[22] That is to say, feudalism introduced from the top by an absolute monarch was not and could not be true feudalism, in Byzantium or anywhere else.

The subsequent Comneni rulers made some headway in climbing out of the pit into which the Eastern Empire had fallen at Manzikert. John Comnenus (1118–43) administered a final defeat to the Turkic Pechenegs, regained part of southwestern Asia Minor, and took Antioch from the Crusaders. His successor Manuel I was much influenced by the ideas and customs of the West, but aspired to restore the seat of universal empire to Byzantium. In the wake of the disastrous failure of the Second Crusade, he established suzerainty over the Latin states in the Near East; increased Byzantine influence in Hungary; acquired Dalmatia, Croatia, Bosnia, and the district of Sirmium; and made the Serbian zupan, Stephen Nemanya, his vassal. Under Andronicus Comnenus in the 1180s these acquisitions were lost again, and an invading army of Normans from Sicily struck from Dyrrhachium (today Durazzo) through to Thessalonica, precipitating a revolt and the overthrow of the Comneni.

The Normans were driven back, but soon thereafter a great uprising broke out in Bulgaria that established what has been called the "second Bulgarian empire" under John and Peter Asen, whose successor and brother Kaloyan secured a crown from the pope in 1204. The new state, which had a substantial Wallachian (Romanian) as well as Bulgarian population, was to last until the Turkish conquest (1393).[23]

In between East and West for some time were the Serbs. In the first half of the eleventh century a small Serbian state, called first Dioclea and later Zeta, appeared around the bay of Kotor. For a while it was a vassal state of the papacy. By the early twelfth century, however, Zeta declined and was supplanted as the center of the Serbs by Raska (Rascia), whose princes were the Grand Zupans. Stephen Nemanya, who had been twice baptized by Latin and then Orthodox priests, regained Raskan independence. His son Stephen received a papal crown (hence he was called Stephen the First-Crowned) but was persuaded by the king's brother, St. Sava, to accept an Eastern Orthodox diadem in a new coronation held in 1222. The event may be regarded as decisive in casting the Serbian lot with Byzantine and not Roman Christianity and culture.

Byzantine civilization reached eastward as far as Russia, where a state emerged in the ninth century with a Viking ("Varangian") elite ruling a Slavic society. Such a state was first established in the north, around Novgorod. Then, after the city of Kiev was conquered from the ethnically Turkic Khazars (though they accepted Judaism as a religion, one of the very few non-Jewish peoples in history to have done so), a single realm was shaped by Oleg about 882. Several times the Russians (perhaps better described as "Rus," the ethnic result of the Slavs' gradually absorbing their Viking overlords) raided Constantinople. However, the Rus also traded with the Byzantines and served in their armies.

In 874 the Eastern Empire dispatched an archbishop for the Christians who were already to be found in Rus. The conversion of the ruler was delayed until 988. It appears that Vladimir, grand prince of Kiev and the closest thing to a single ruler the Rus possessed, aided Basil II in defeating the rebellious general

Bardas Phocas, and thereafter was rewarded by an arranged marriage with the emperor's sister Anna; at the same time Vladimir became a Christian.[24]

For a time the Christian principality of Kievan Rus flourished. By the reign of Vladimir Monomakh (d. 1125) his family was linked to north European royalty through half a dozen marriages, and trade with the West via the Kiev-Regensburg route was continuous. By the mid-twelfth century, however, Rus was no longer a unified state whose chief city was Kiev but rather a congeries of principalities, of which the most important were the two centering in Vladimir (whose not too distant neighbor, Moscow, came to overshadow it) in the north and Galich in the west.

Rus was on the exposed frontier of what was by the year 1000 Christian Europe (with minor exceptions). No geographical barriers shielded it from the successive waves of Asian nomads who crossed the Black Sea steppe from the east. In 1036 the Turkic Pechenegs were defeated and moved on westward to harass the Byzantines instead of the Rus. In the late twelfth century a new horde, the Cumans or Polovtsy, nearly severed the links between Rus and Constantinople, but by about 1200 the prince of Galich had struck them a mighty blow and reduced their power.

These two nomadic groups were able to cause much damage and disruption, but a far more dreadful invading force now made its appearance. The principalities of Rus were not strong enough to resist. The Mongols struck first through the Caucasus in a brief raid of 1223; in 1240 they returned to conquer the principalities. The Golden Horde, establishing its headquarters at Sarai (near present-day Volgograd), with only a thin upper layer of Mongols, was often referred to as the Tatars. Their rule was to last until the late fifteenth century.

During the roughly four centuries that preceded the Mongol conquest, Rus had a curious mixture of societal elements: a sizable slave population, a thriving commercial class in contact with neighboring lands on all sides, a partially free peasantry; the princes had servitors who held some lands in hereditary tenure and were linked to their overlords by ties that could well be termed semifeudal, though not identical with the relationships of the upper classes in contemporary Europe. The church soon became a powerful institution, and the high clergy in particular were a force to reckon with. All those elements, except the position of the church, changed dramatically during the period of Mongol rule.

In the eleventh century, Europe had achieved a remarkable unity. Take the case of Harold Hardrada, who is to be seen

successively fighting for his half-brother St. Olaf, king of Norway; a commander in the armies of Yaroslav, prince of Kiev; arriving in Constantinople with five hundred warriors about 1034; employed for nine years by three Byzantine emperors . . . back in Russia during the winter of 1042–3, where he married Yaroslav's daughter Elizabeth . . . proclaimed king of Norway . . . finally as prospective conqueror of England, where he met his death at the battle of Stamford Bridge in 1066. . . . The appearance of a series of strikingly accurate imitations of contemporary Byzantine coin types on Danish coins of the mid-eleventh century was almost certainly due to the arrival in Scandinavia of the vast treasure which Harold Hardrada is known to have accumulated while in imperial service.[25]

But the parts of Europe did not develop evenly. The West became civilized and grew in wealth and strength, while the civilized, even decadent East faltered— after the end of the Macedonian dynasty—and weakened. In 1000 the West was by far inferior; by 1200 the situation was reversed. As the warriors of the Fourth Crusade swept into Constantinople, the superior power of the West was all too clearly demonstrated.

The Greeks never forgot the suffering and shame of 1204. Several Byzantine rulers would subsequently try to patch up the division of the churches, which dated from 1054 but became fixed and frozen in the consciousness of the East only with the Fourth Crusade. The emperors' purpose was to obtain Western aid —in one case, the aid of the papacy against the Angevin threat, both located in the West; but in others, against the Turks. But the popular resentment in the Byzantine Empire was too great, and all such efforts came to naught.

Islam, 1050–1200

In the eleventh century the Seljuq Turks overran much of western Asia, from Khorasan through Georgia and Armenia to western Anatolia and south to Syria, in the "most nearly successful attempt" to restore Muslim unity.[26] The realm then splintered into states under various generals and notables of the original Seljuq clan or sept.

In the meantime the Fatimid caliphate in Egypt, which took shape in the tenth century, became the "most brilliant center of Moslem culture"[27] during a period when, to be sure, there was not great competition for that title. However, in the magnificence of the court, architecture, and learning, Fatimid achievements were noteworthy. In the twelfth century the Egyptian caliphate weakened and collapsed, and was replaced by the Ayyubids. The founder of the new dynasty was Salah al-Din, known to Westerners as Saladin, who overran the Latin Kingdom of Jerusalem and defeated the Western attempt to retake the area in the Third Crusade (1190–93).

During the mid-eleventh century, Muslim Spain was a "patchwork of petty states."[28] The Christians seized their opportunity; they captured Toledo in 1085 and administered the decisive blow of the *Reconquista* in 1212 at Las Navas de Tolosa.

The result was that cultural influences moved powerfully in both directions.

French culture penetrated southward; after the fall of Toledo Moorish influences streamed northward. The reception of Aristotle and other Greek writers, mediated through Islam, greatly affected the rise of Western universities and contributed mightily to the culture of the High Middle Ages in western Europe. The extent to which such writings and ideas can be said to have invigorated the culture of the Muslim countries is, however, modest and limited in the extreme.

As the power of Islam in the western Mediterranean was broken, however, advances occurred in the East. Writes Brockelmann:

> While it was the Turks who by centuries of persistent maladministration inflicted the worst damage on the once so flourishing civilization of Iran and Mesopotamia, it was reserved to the related tribe of the Tatars or Mongols, at the beginning of the thirteenth century, to bring that work of destruction to completion. In his chronicle for the year 617H (1220 A.D.), the Arab historian ibn-al-Athir, in a moving lamentation, rightly calls their breaking into the Near East the greatest misfortune to come upon the humanity he knew.[29]

The person who welded the Mongols together was Chingis Khan (the title, meaning "mighty king," of the man Temujin), who began to subdue his neighbors in 1206. At that point the Mongols were pagans, that is, adherents of no higher religion. Their conquest inflicted untold destruction on the Christian Rus and the Muslim Persians alike, whether or not they would have hesitated if they had been coreligionists of one or the other. They did become Muslim in their western territories—not in Mongolia proper—but only decades later.

The West, 1200–1350

As the twelfth century ended, it looked as if both empire and papacy were strong contenders for further growth in wealth and territory, both emperor and pope promising candidates for the augmentation in power of their offices. Following fifteen years of civil war, the puzzling figure of Frederick II became emperor. The most powerful of all popes, Innocent III, had played an important role throughout the civil war and emerged with two objectives achieved: Frederick's promise to keep the German and Sicilian crowns separate, and free election for bishops in the church in Germany.

Brilliant and complex in his mental make-up, Frederick, was both interested in and sympathetic toward Islam and the East. He managed peacefully to restore Jerusalem to Christian control for a few years. Southerner in outlook, he was much more interested in Sicily than Germany. By the Constitutions of Melfi (1231), he swept aside much of Sicilian feudalism to impose royal absolutism, partly on Arab models. He then tried to move in the direction of unifying Sicily and north-central Italy into a single kingdom as part of the empire, but he died suddenly in 1250.

Innocent III had not merely curbed Frederick's ambitions; he had aspired to theocracy in Christendom and came close to realizing it. The rulers of England, Aragon, Portugal, Hungary, Denmark, Poland, Bulgaria, and Serbia acknowledged themselves papal vassals. The Pope systematized his claims at the Fourth Lateran Council in 1215. By preaching a crusade against the Albigensian heretics, he paved the way for his successor's creation of the Inquisition in order to deal with all heresy henceforth.

Ironically, the most lasting result of his papacy from the secular point of view was that the Albigensian crusade he sanctioned came to a large extent to be a struggle between northern and southern France, in which the Capetian kings extended their effective control to the Mediterranean Sea; and it was the French monarchy that was to threaten domination of the papacy during the subsequent period. Innocent III first preached the Fourth Crusade; was horrified by its diversion to sack Constantinople; and, finally, having been persuaded (wrongly) that a by-product of that event had been the reunion of the Eastern and Western churches, was brought to accept it as justifiable.

Germany was now at the crossroads. The so-called Great Interregnum (1254–73) saw sharp struggles between the popes and the Hohenstaufens, the last legitimate heir of which family was killed in 1268. The medieval emperors virtually ceased their efforts to establish a unified German state. It was during this period that important works of political theory were composed to uphold the supremacy of the empire against papal claims: notably Marsiglio of Padua's *Defensor Pacis* (Defender of the Peace) and Dante Alighieri's *De Monarchia* (On Monarchy), but their main effect was to strengthen the party supporting general councils within the church, not to arrest the decline of the empire.

The empire's old antagonist for supremacy in Europe, the papacy, fared no better. At the beginning of the thirteenth century it had been at the peak of its power and prestige, by the middle of the century it retained a good deal of both, but by the end secular powers had gained enough to overtake the see of Peter. It was not, however, any longer the empire that was its main challenger, but France.

There was a significant difference between the class composition of Germany and its western neighbors. In England and France the social components gained rights within the same political entity. In the empire, however, there were four or five groups each of which had units in which it was dominant: the great secular tenants-in-chief (the Ascanians, dukes of Saxony; the Welfs in Brunswick; the Wittelsbachs in Bavaria; the Premyslid kings of Bohemia); the ecclesiastical princes (archbishops of Mainz, Trier, and Cologne); the knights, or *Ritterschaft;* and the imperial cities, or *Reichstädte.*

Election of the monarch was first by all tenants-in-chief, then by a small group of seven "electors"; in the thirteenth century that development was accompanied by the emergence of a two-house diet, or Reichstag, though its powers were limited and its functions undefined. The Great Interregnum was ended by the election of Rudolf of Habsburg (shortened from Habichtsburg, the family's original seat in the Rhineland). He began a long process of growth; but it was not the power of the emperorship that grew but rather that of the Habsburg family and the holdings it amassed, often through dynastic marriage.

When the last Premyslid king died in 1306, Albert I acquired the crown of Bohemia for the Habsburgs, temporarily but foreshadowing later developments. During the previous century two changes had been significant in Bohemia: substantial immigration of Germans and expansion (under Ottokar II the Great) and then contraction, in a relatively short time, of the territory of the kingdom. Germans had also been invited into Poland and entered in large numbers in the wake of the Mongol invasion of 1241, which devastated much of the country without occupying it. Along with German immigration went a growth in both Bohemian and Polish towns, which obtained much autonomy by way of the so-called Magdeburg Law enumerating urban privileges.

The Mongols had also laid waste to Hungary; there the upshot was not German settlement but rather the building of castles by feudal lords who had already secured sweeping privileges in the Golden Bull of 1222. The last king of the Arpad dynasty died in 1301, and after a few chaotic years an Angevin (member of the House of Anjou), Charles I (1308–42), restored some semblance of royal power in a state whose feudal aristocrats were by now well entrenched.

In the thirteenth and fourteenth centuries the Habsburgs acquired several territories, but because the family was not governed by the law of primogeniture repeated division of the lands among sons weakened the influence of the house within the empire (they would return to the emperorship only in 1438).

During the period of Habsburg eclipse it was under Emperor Charles IV of the House of Luxemburg that the organization of the empire was made more formal in the Golden Bull approved by the Diet in 1356. Seven electors were specified: the archbishops of Mainz, Cologne, and Trier; the elector palatine of the Rhine; the king of Bohemia; the margrave of Brandenburg; and the duke of Saxe-Wittenberg. The majority of electors were to make the decision. In addition to regulation of the mode of election, the Golden Bull introduced primogeniture into the four lay electorates (since the ecclesiastical ones could not, of course, produce heirs or at any rate acknowledge them). Greater stability thereby came to the empire, but scarcely greater unity.

Eastward from the empire Germans extended both settlement and power through the growth of two organizations. The Teutonic Knights, originating as a crusading order in the Holy Land, founded Riga in 1198 as a military and religious center. Their sway reached over a large stretch of the Baltic coast; they subdued the Estonians and Latvians and for all practical purposes exterminated the Prussians (whose very name, belonging to speakers of a Baltic not a Germanic language, they stole).

The pressure exerted by the Knights on Poland and Lithuania led to the dynastic union of the two states in 1385, resulting in the final acceptance of (Catholic) Christianity by the Lithuanians, the last pagan people in Europe. The united Polish-Lithuanian armies then inflicted a grave defeat on the Knights in the battle of Tannenberg (1410); by the Second Peace of Thorn in 1466 the Teutonic Order was confined to East Prussia and recognized as a fief of the Polish crown.

The second organization to expand eastward was the Hanseatic League, which developed out of German trading settlements of the later twelveth century on the island of Gotland and elsewhere, with an offshoot in the Russian city of Novgorod. Those settlements spread to several north European cities and founded an association called the *Hansa* at a time that cannot be precisely established, though the term was first used in a document of 1344. The league lasted effectively into the seventeenth and technically even into the nineteenth century.

The situation was quite different on the western borders of the empire. In 1291 the three Forest Cantons (Uri, Schwyz, and Unterwalden) of Switzerland revolted and henceforth maintained a common identity and effective autonomy, though independence for the Swiss confederation, by that time much larger, was granted in fact only in 1499 and formally in 1648. The provinces of the Low Countries (Nederland) started to develop their own strength and local pride; and Luxemburg, the Franche Comté, and Savoy exhibited characteristics of their own that made the whole western frontier of Germany seem spongy.

While the empire failed to demonstrate the ability to become a political unit with an effective central government, both England and France went on making slow if sometimes irregular progress in that direction. In England the repulsive King John was succeeded by Henry III. His was an important reign in English constitutional history. While he ruled (1216–72) the institution of "Parliament" got its name, about 1240, and began to take on a shape different from the Great Council that preceded it.

The process was influenced by the growth of national consciousness, stimulated by resentment against financial and other sorts of involvement in France and against papal exactions that were felt to be burdensome. Such feelings led to the Provisions of Oxford (1258), by which the barons undertook in essence to restore Magna Carta, with the support of many clergy and townsmen. However, the knights were dissatisfied, believing themselves to be left out. They managed to mobilize some of the younger barons, clergy, and townsmen to demand further reform, in a coalition whose leader was Simon de Montfort. (His father had led the crusade against the Albigensians in France.) The summoning of two knights from each shire and two townsmen from each borough, in "de Montfort's parliament" (1265), is counted an important milestone in British parliamentary evolution.

Henry's successor, Edward I (1272–1307), has been called "an able ruler and great legislator, fit to rank with Frederick II, Louis IX, and Alfonso the Wise."[30] Parliament was still an administrative and judicial organ as much as a legislative one, and its composition and powers remained uncertain. But the crown was coming to treat it with caution if not respect. Edward I consulted the knights and burgesses, as well as the nobles, in Parliament and out of it.

In 1298 he summoned the "Model Parliament," the summons to which included the famed phrase *quod omnes tangit ab omnibus approbetur* (let that which touches all be approved by all). The result was the Confirmation of Charters, which added to the provisions of Magna Carta the stipulation that no nonfeudal levy could be imposed by the king without parliamentary approval. The great common-law courts acquired much clearer identities: the courts of King's Bench, Exchequer, Common Pleas, and the higher King's Council. The common law itself came to be recorded, systematized, and transmitted in the new Inns of Court. As this process unfolded, Roman law was largely abandoned. In summary, the formation of the English "constitution" was well under way.

Edward I subdued a Welsh uprising and made his son the first Prince of Wales; he was in fact born in Caernarfon in 1284. There and elsewhere in Wales Edward I built royal castles to buttress his rule.[31] It is one of the very few cases where castles do not signify the power of feudal lords and the past presence of feudalism: castles are not to be found in Russia, China, or India. (They do exist in Japan.)

In Scotland the outcome was quite different. When three men claimed the Scottish crown, Edward was called upon to arbitrate but ended up by fighting for the possession of the country. He managed to conquer Scotland. However, after his death Robert Bruce smashed an English army at Bannockburn (1314) and thereby secured Scottish independence for three more centuries. In the thirteenth century, the Anglo-Norman colony in eastern Ireland took root, expanded, and prospered. The Irish clans in the west of the island were little affected.

Under Edward II dissatisfaction with the king and his favorite, the Gascon knight Piers Gaveston, led to baronial success in forcing on the crown the Reform Ordinances. They required consent of the "ordainers" to royal appointments, declarations of war, and even travel from the kingdom. The Ordinances did not last; they were repealed, but the king himself was deposed and then killed by a cabal organized by his queen, daughter of Philip IV of France.

During the reigns of both Edward II and III, Parliament met several times, gaining influence little by little over taxation and appointments. It was not necessarily of benefit to the common people; in the 1330s the major burden of royal taxation began to fall most heavily on the peasantry, which had previously enjoyed exemption from taxes.[32] In the 1340s, the division of Parliament into the House of Commons and the House of Lords took form. Little parliamentary hostility was shown against Edward III, in contrast to his predecessor. The king was popular, and the opening stages of the Hundred Years' War made him more so.

The French monarchy was experiencing not too dissimilar development. At the battle of Bouvines, in Flanders, Philip II Augustus (1180–1223) defeated John of England and allies of his, including several feudal lords of northern France. Then and earlier he was able to increase by threefold the royal domain. It was easier for him to do so because in France there was no custom (as there was in Germany) that escheated fiefs had to be granted to new tenants, and thus the king could lay hands on them. In this way he gained much land in the north and also in Anjou, whose great vassal family started with holdings greater than his own.

In a reign often compared with that of England's Henry III (his almost exact contemporary), St. Louis IX (1226–70), who was canonized before the end of the century, came to enjoy a reputation as the ideal medieval king. To be sure, he benefited by the fact that his predecessors had reduced a series of proud and powerful vassals and bequeathed to him a much-strengthened realm and office. But he earned widespread respect by his just and upright character. He strove to extend France's boundaries; by patient diplomacy he fixed the frontier with Aragon at the Pyrenees, though he was unable to end Henry III of England's ducal title over Guienne (around Bordeaux).

During his reign the French Curia Regis or royal court (in the judicial sense) acquired more power and specialized sections of it took form: in particular, the professional lawyers of the Parlement of Paris and the financial officials of the Chambre des Comptes (to use a couple of later designations). Louis sought peace in Europe but ardently undertook two crusades to the Holy Land; on the second he died en route, in Tunis. His successors were less noble and less saintly. Nevertheless they were able to retain an important quality he had bequeathed to them—that of serving as a focal point of loyalty: "henceforward Frenchmen looked to the king for justice, for reform, and for safety."[33]

The increase in size of the royal domain continued, and decade by decade the kingdom of France became more obviously the leading continental power. Thus when Philip IV the Fair clashed with the papacy in the person of Boniface VIII, the latter faced a formidable adversary indeed. The French monarch reduced the role of clerics and increased that of lay lawyers in his administration, but supported the high clergy of the French church as they took steps to claim ecclesiastical autonomy or "Gallican liberties" that would attract more attention later.

As the demands of royal government mounted in France (as well as other European states), Philip looked to the church for assistance. Clerical subsidies had been granted earlier ostensibly for the support of crusades. The pope now balked at approving any more. Boniface, apparently believing he still had as much power as Innocent III, flung down the gauntlet with the decretal *Clericis laicos* (1296), forbidding all levies by lay rulers on the clergy unless authorized by the pope. Philip retaliated with various financial and mercantile prohibitions, and other rulers did likewise.

Nevertheless the conflict seemed to center on the relation between France and Rome. Boniface now lifted the level of papal claim in the temporal arena to the highest point ever reached before or since with *Unam sanctam* (1302), a bull in which the old doctrine of the two swords was given a twist. Both swords were said to belong to the papacy: the spiritual sword, obviously, and the temporal sword to be exercised by monarchs but only under papal supervision.

Philip's response was to resort to force. His chief adviser invaded the papal palace and would have abducted the pope if the townsmen of Anagni had not frustrated his plan. But Boniface died shortly afterward, partly as a result of the scandalous scene. Soon a French pope was elected, Clement V, who took up residence in Avignon (in present-day France but not then in French territory) in 1309. The papacy would remain there, under the domination of the French monarchy, until 1376, in what was called by many the "Babylonian captivity" of the popes.

Philip the Fair was as ruthless with other Frenchmen as he was with the papacy. He determined to destroy the Knights Templar, whose wealth lured him and whose force of armed knights he feared, and did so largely through confessions extorted by torture and deceit. His need for money to pay for his wars with England and Flanders compelled him to turn to the Estates General. Although delegates of the nobles and clergy had been occasionally summoned in individual provinces during the thirteenth century, and townsmen had been called together by St. Louis IX, to ratify taxes or to consult on other matters, the assembly of 1302 seems to have been the first "undoubted ancestor of the later States-General."[34]

The French estates, however, did not develop the strength such bodies gained in England and several other countries. The power and prestige of the monarchy were great, defined by the king's legists and buttressed by the tradition of loyalty to the crown, and the power of the great vassals had been broken by Philip's predecessors. At the king's death, France had some thirty divisions of the royal domain, in which the royal authority was represented by appointed officials— bailiffs in the north, seneschals in the south—in turn supervised by the central bureaucracy. Philip the Fair also managed to annex Gascony, and he made an alliance (1295) with Scotland that would persist for centuries; however, he failed in his attempts to seize Guienne and to make good his annexation of Flanders.

The male line of the Capets, having produced an uninterrupted series of sons since 987, failed in 1328. Clearly no woman could have the throne; the question was raised, however, whether a woman could transmit to her son the right to the throne. An assembly of feudal lords was asked the question and answered in the negative; that rule was later termed the "Salic law" from the ancient provision among the Salian Franks that a woman could not inherit land. Application of the rule in 1328 meant conferment of the kingship on the son of Philip IV's brother, the count of Valois, and Philip VI acceded to the throne.

His realm still did not include Brittany or Burgundy, or his uncle's missed objectives, Flanders and Guienne. The English crown could count on the aid of the latter two, in case of conflict, and one soon erupted. Edward III was the son of Philip IV's daughter, who had been the wife of Edward II. On the strength of that relationship, he declared himself king of France, flouting the Salic law and renouncing his vassalage of Guienne. Philip VI thereupon declared Guienne forfeit to the French crown.

The war that now began in 1337 was the first in a series of conflicts that would earn the name of the Hundred Years' War, though it would last even longer than that, until 1453. The issue was England's possessions on the mainland territory of France, which the English kings were determined to keep and the French kings were determined to take. In the initial stages of the war the English bowmen slaughtered the French knights at the battle of Crécy (1346), and Edward III captured Calais, an important military and commercial base for over two centuries.

During these years France, after a spectacular rise in wealth and territory under royal leadership, entered a period of decline. The epidemic of bubonic plague called the Black Death, which struck in 1348 and may finally have reduced the population of northern Europe by a third, probably hit France no harder than its adversary but nevertheless seemed to many Frenchmen to portend doom.

In the Iberian peninsula the reconquest continued with certain interesting political developments. After the great victory of 1212 at Las Navas de Tolosa, the Christians had the upper hand. Under St. Ferdinand III (king and saint, like Louis IX of France), the kingdoms of Leon and Castile were finally united for good (1230). Ferdinand was strong enough to retake Cordova (1236) and Seville (1248), his conquests reaching the sea of Cadiz for the first time.

Meanwhile the kings of Portugal were clearing out the Algarve. After the Moorish state of Murcia was conquered by Aragon and annexed by Castile in 1266, only one fragment of the peninsula remained to Islam. The minor potentate, ibn-Nasr, had accepted vassalage to the Castilian king and even lent him help in the capture of Seville from his fellow Moors. As a result he had been able to establish a kingdom in Granada. It was to survive until 1492—a small state both richer and more cultured than its Christian neighbors—through the skill of the Nasrids in playing a sharp diplomatic game.

King Alfonso X the Wise (1252–84) was indeed a cultured man, codifier of law in the collection termed *Las Siete Partidas,* historian, and poet, but he was clumsy as a ruler. He disputed the Algarve with his contemporary Alfonso III of Portugal; a treaty of 1267 finally fixed the boundary with Castile that proved permanent. He wasted effort in seeking to make good his election as Holy Roman Emperor in 1257 for seventeen years thereafter, and bungled arrangements for the succession that would occur at his death. The great nobles of Castile were strong enough to begin a struggle for influence during his reign that would go on long afterward.

However, Alfonso X's years as king witnessed another sort of beginning. The idea of the state as a public institution reappeared, owing to the revival of Roman law and the rediscovery of Aristotle's *Politics;* in the *Siete Partidas* the ideal of absolute monarchy was set forth in the notion of the king as God's vicar on earth.[35] Though Alfonso the Wise was able to do little or nothing to realize the ideal, and by his concessions to a nobility that no longer feared Moors and felt strong enough to challenge monarchs actually weakened the throne, subsequent rulers built on such legal foundations. Roman law increased in influence, and when Alfonso XI promulgated the *Ordenamiento de Alcalá,* in 1348, it was securely rooted.

In the other Christian states of the peninsula the Cortes, or estates, also gained much power at the expense of the respective monarchies. The Cortes of Portugal, in which after 1254 townsmen came to join clergy and nobles, did so under Alfonso III. Catalonia, united with Aragon in 1137, was the only Iberian state in which feudalism became deeply entrenched. The Usages of Barcelona, promulgated by Count Ramon Berenguer I, 1035–76, remained the basic law for this multiple realm in the thirteenth century. In a long reign (1213–76) James I the Conqueror won the Balearic Islands in the Mediterranean and tried to establish a hold in North Africa. He also fixed a lasting frontier, at the Pyrenees, by working out what was in effect an exchange of lands with France in 1258.

There was a Cortes for each of the three lands: Aragon, Catalonia, and

Valencia (to the south); the king sometimes convened all three together. In 1283 Peter III pledged to convene the Corts (Catalan spelling) annually and to make no general law without its consent. Such promises were often broken, but could be appealed to and cited by those seeking to limit monarchical power. Around 1300 a noteworthy official, called the *Justicia Mayor,* made his appearance; he was appointed by the king from among the lesser nobles and was entrusted with the supervision of the entire system of the courts, the execution of the laws, and the preservation of the rights of all citizens. James II proclaimed the indissoluble union of Aragon, Catalonia, and Valencia in 1319, and there were now only two large states (Navarre and Granada were small) that would constitute the Spain of the future: Aragon and Castile. The Iberian legal and constitutional development was as rapid as anywhere in Europe; in particular, the assemblies of the peninsula acquired the right to approve taxes, which was the key to the growth of parliaments in the West.

In Scandinavia kings and nobles continued to struggle. Valdemar II the Conqueror (1202–41) conducted crusading expeditions into Estonia, Livonia, and the southern coast of the Baltic on behalf of Denmark but could not hold those territories. In order to engage in such adventures the kings needed warriors, and rewarded them with fiefs. The resulting nobles grew stronger; the high clergy resisted royal efforts to tax them. In consequence a charter often compared to Magna Carta was extorted in 1282 from Eric V Glipping, the Danish king, which called for the Hof to be convened yearly, enacted protections for nobles and clerics, prohibited imprisonment on suspicion only, and subordinated the monarch to the law.

The Hanseatic towns[36] that dominated Baltic trade became influential in Danish politics, and many German nobles were settled in royal fortresses. The counts of Holstein gained much power and in effect ruled Denmark in the 1330s when there was no king. The Danish nobles profited by the weakness of the monarchy. In 1340 Valdemar IV acceded and did his best to regain ascendancy over the Germans·and the Danish clergy and nobility. Unfortunately for the throne, he was forced to yield Scania (southernmost Sweden) and Estonia (to the Teutonic Knights) and in the Peace of Stralsund (1370) to accept Hanseatic predominance in the Baltic.

In Sweden as in Denmark the monarchy was not clearly hereditary during the period, retaining a substantial elective component. Although Birger Jarl of the powerful Folkung family made his son king in 1250 and curbed the magnates, his achievements did not last. In the 1280s, a hereditary nobility was created, exempt from taxation as was soon also church property. In 1318 the magnates were strong enough to seize control of Sweden and install as king the infant Magnus VII Smek. The privileges of the church and the nobility were confirmed; the monarch was forbidden to raise taxes without approval of the national council and the provincial assemblies. In about 1350 a new law code provided for election of the king, though preference was to be given to royal sons, and German merchants in the towns were guaranteed certain privileges.

In Norway Haakon IV became king in 1217 following a period of turbulence, and a Golden Age began for Norway. Haakon IV created a chancellorship and a royal council. In 1260 a new law of succession was adopted by the Hovingmote that confirmed inheritance of the crown by the king's eldest son; in 1276 Haakon IV's son Magnus VI acquired the sobriquet "Lawmender" by replacing the provincial laws with a common national code.

By this time the class of thralls had virtually disappeared. The aristocracy had lost not only their quasi-slave labor but the income from much of the commerce that had yielded them profit, for it had passed into the hands of the Hansa. Under Haakon V, who acceded to the throne in 1299, the monarchy consolidated its ascendancy over the nobility.

The Norwegian state had secured its hold on Iceland and Greenland, but Haakon's transfer of the capital from Bergen to Oslo signaled a shift of interest away from the west and toward the south. In 1300 Norway was unique among the three Scandinavian kingdoms in its strong monarchy, but its favorable position did not last long. The Black Death, which killed nearly half the population, was at least partly responsible, leaving official and ecclesiastical posts to be filled by Danes and Swedes, the more easily; because Magnus Smek was king of both Sweden and Norway from 1319 to 1355.

Byzantium and Islam, 1200–1350

From 1204 to 1261 the Franks ruled in Constantinople. However, the rest of the former Byzantine dominions were parceled out among Crusaders, Venetians, and Byzantine notables. The Greeks established themselves in the Empire of Nicaea, the Despotate of Epirus, and the Empire of Trebizond, while the Latins set up small states in other parts of the peninsula. Feudal institutions were implanted in the area around Athens, in the Peloponnesus, and elsewhere; they did not take root. From his base in Nicaea Michael Paleologus mounted an effort of reconquest that succeeded in 1261, and Constantinople was once again the Byzantine capital.

Michael's victory was partly due to an alliance with the Bulgarians. Their Second Empire reached the peak of its development under John Asen (1218–41), but in the later thirteenth century its decline was apparent. By the battle of Velbuzhd in 1330 the Serbs attained ascendancy over the Bulgars, and the ruler in the succeeding decades, Stephen Dušan, carried medieval Serbia to its zenith.

We know of national assemblies (*sabori*) among the Serbs over several centuries, but they degenerated from a genuinely consultative institution to a powerless one with brilliant ceremonial under Dušan, in close imitation of Byzantine autocracy.[37]

The Byzantine Empire was restored but with both political and geographical limitations. The rise of the nobility led to no legal curbs on the monarch but resulted in restrictions on his freedom of action. In Michael VIII's reign there began the transformation of the *pronoia* from an inalienable and conditional holding to a hereditary one. In the words of Obolensky, by the late eleventh century,

in place of the free peasant-soldier commune, two types of land holding had become prevalent in the Byzantine Empire: on the one hand the large hereditary estate of the civil or military magnate and, on the other, crown property handed out to eminent Byzantines or foreigners to administer, usually in return for military service, free of state taxation [the latter was the *pronoia* system]. The grant of *pronoia* differed from a gift of land of the first type in that it was held for a limited time, usually until the recipient's death, and was, until [c. 1250], inalienable. From the time of Michael VIII, however, *pronoiarioi* were allowed to bequeath their estates and revenues to their heirs, though they could not be otherwise alienated, and the obligation of service remained.[38]

Obolensky goes on to point out that the hereditable *pronoia* "closely resembles the West European fief," and that the double relationship of land tenure to military service and of the landlord to the peasants (*paroikoi*) was the basis for the growth in power of the landed military aristocracy that was to be so important in the ensuing period.

Comparable developments occurred in the Serbia of Dušan, which came to extend eastward as far as Macedonia in the north and the Gulf of Patras in the south, so that the Serbian monarch could describe himself with partial justification as "lord of almost the whole Roman Empire." The Byzantine emperor, Michael VIII, had to content himself with gaining a foothold in the Peloponnesus around Mistra, which became an important center of late Byzantine culture and expanded after his death.

Fearing the prospect of renewed assault from the West in the person of Charles of Anjou, king of Sicily, Michael agreed to reunion of the Eastern and Western churches under papal leadership at the Council of Lyon (1274), but few of his subjects were ready to follow his path. What saved him from the Angevin danger was the great uprising against Charles, called the Sicilian Vespers (1282), which was followed by Aragonese acquisition of the island, while Charles retained Naples with great difficulty.

Michael had achieved much by warding off threats to the restored empire, but he also strained the resources available by using large mercenary forces. He was unable to regain the lost territories north and south in the Greek peninsula, and his successors managed to do no better. Andronicus II (1282–1328), who repudiated the ecclesiastical union with Rome, faced sharp financial constraints and dealt with them by reducing the size of the army and making the decision to rely on the navy of Genoa, which had replaced Venice as Byzantine ally.

He needed all the armed forces he could muster, for a new and powerful enemy had made its appearance: the Ottoman Turks (from Osman, the founder of the dynasty), who had overrun almost all of Asia Minor. By 1300 they had seized all but a few Byzantine outposts. Andronicus hired a force of Catalans to hold off the Turks. At first they won victories but then turned to pillage among the Byzantines and had to be gotten rid of. The emperor's grandson, Andronicus III, became his rival and finally his successor. He was helpless to stop the continuing advance of the Ottomans in Asia Minor, and could do no better against the Serbs in Macedonia.

During his reign, John Cantacuzene was the chief minister and the real ruler. When Andronicus died, as John VI he became coemperor, with the support of the magnates of Thrace, and then sole emperor from 1347 to 1354. Faced with an offensive of the Serbs, he called in the Ottoman Turks to help him. They did manage to narrowly defeat the Serbs, but the main thing they accomplished was to establish themselves in Europe, near Gallipoli, in 1352, a foothold they were to expand in a fateful manner. The Serbs under Stephen Dušan now captured Adrianople and advanced toward the capital. Providentially for the Byzantines, he died suddenly, and the Serbian Empire (so proclaimed in 1345) immediately fell apart.

At almost the same moment the legitimate Paleologus emperor, John V, regained Constantinople, driving out Cantacuzene. The Paleologus dynasty would remain to the end of the empire. But the financial system and the machinery of administration of Byzantium had irretrievably collapsed. It had been reduced to a Turkish dependency. George Ostrogorsky writes:

At the height of its power Byzantine absolutism had built up a powerful bureaucratic system on the ruins of the old municipal administration and urban life had been compelled to come under the yoke of its all-embracing centralization. When the central power grew weaker, local influence had begun to gain ground once more and independent town life seemed to revive again. This revival of urban self-government was not due to the rise of new social forces, but rather to the weakening of the central power which was undermined by feudal elements; town life in Byzantium therefore produced in the late Byzantine period no flourishing class of merchants and craftsmen, as in the West, but was dominated by the local landed aristocracy.[39]

No partnership of rural lords and urban burgesses could be forged to save Byzantium.

The ties of the Byzantine Empire with its northernmost Orthodox brother state, Russia, were severely weakened by the Mongol conquest of Russia itself (1240) and by the Frankish conquest of Constantinople (1204). The prince of Novgorod (later, of Vladimir), Alexander Nevsky, submitted to the Mongols after holding the Swedes and Teutonic Knights at bay on the west. In the divided Russian principalities some plans were hatched to drive out the Mongols (or Tatars), but they came to nothing. The old center of Kiev was devastated.

Newer centers arose in the north, among which first Vladimir and then Moscow became important. Moscow's grand prince, Ivan I Kalita ("Moneybags") (d. 1341), came to be so trusted by the Tatars that he was charged with collection of the tribute from his fellow princes, and his successors took care to continue the same policy. In this way the principality of Moscow came to dominate central Russia and assert religious and political continuity with Kiev, not least because the head of the Orthodox church of Russia, the metropolitan, had come to reside in Moscow city. Meanwhile the small state of Lithuania had expanded from its center, Wilno, into the Dnieper valley and, by 1362, all the way to the Black Sea.

Islam had absorbed its Mongol conquerors. As they swept across Asia into Europe and the moribund Caliphate, they were not Muslims but pagans. But the western Mongols soon accepted the Islamic religion. Berke (d. 1266), khan of the Golden Horde, converted, and his Turkicized subjects either preceded or followed him. Hülegü, the Mongol conqueror of Baghdad and final destroyer of the Caliphate (1258), was married to a Christian and had many Nestorians in his entourage, but only under Ghazan Khan (d. 1304) did the Mongol dynasty of Persia, the so-called Il-Khans, adopt Islam in its Sunni variant. His brother and successor, Uljaitu Khodabanda, however, switched to Shi'ite teaching, and Iran would remain the chief center of Shi'a Islam. The Chaghatay khanate, third of the major states to be established in Muslim territory, was also chronologically third to accept Islam; but at the same time (around 1350) all three began to disintegrate, and soon (1368) the Mongols were overthrown in China as well.[40]

In 1260 the Mongol armies attacked the Mamluks near Mount Gilboa in Palestine; for the very first time, the Mongols were defeated. The core of the Mamluks consisted of fugitive Cumans (or Polovtsy) from the European steppe, first having served as bodyguards of the Ayyubids and then in 1250 having taken over direct rule in Egypt. They proceeded nominally to revive the Caliphate in Cairo in the person of a descendant of the 'Abbasids. It was they who captured the last of the Crusader states on the Near Eastern mainland; the island of Cyprus was still a feudal monarchy, where the "most feudal of legal codes," the so-called Assizes of Jerusalem, was composed.[41] The last Christian city of the whole region, Acre, fell to the Mamluks in 1291. They remained in power until 1517, when the Ottoman Turks took Cairo.

The Heritage of the High Middle Ages

Islam continued to be capable of high cultural achievement, but the successor states to the defunct (though ostensibly revived) Caliphate were minor despotisms unrelieved by any nascent plurality of institutions. The Crusades, leaving aside the unquestionable sincerity of the religious motives of many of their leaders as well as followers, were early colonial ventures of the burgeoning West. To the extent that they resulted from worldly ambitions and greed, they were marked by self-serving, fratricidal actions. And yet they partially and temporarily implanted in the world of mainland Asia feudal institutions that might have had important consequences and nurtured the beginnings of freedom.

By 1300 all that was but a memory. By 1350, in contrast, the feudal institutions of western Europe were weakening but were giving way not to despotism but to an early state of parliamentary development, accompanied by the systematization of law—customary, Roman, or mixed—and the codification of privileges. From Norway to Castile, France to Hungary, monarchs and landed aristocrats pulled and tugged and sometimes killed each other but more characteristically clustered, threw down gauntlets, and issued demands before settling on some new legal arrangement. Townsmen increasingly took a hand. Social classes were taking shape that could act collectively (more or less, at least at times) and produce a balance of political forces.

During the High Middle Ages the contrast between the institutions of Occident and Orient (having in mind western Asia and North Africa) became much clearer than before. In learning, Islam was the superior of Christendom in, say, the twelfth century. Ibn-Rushd, or Averroes (d. 1198), deserves the chief credit for transmitting Greek philosophy to the West and is only one of many Muslim writers, thinkers, and students of the natural world who registered great achievements during the period.

There were a number of outstanding personalities: Saladin (Salah-ad-Din, d. 1193), for example, was in nobility of character at least the equal of the Crusaders before and after him. And yet none of the Muslim empires or estates developed the political and social systems that would permit the full development of human personality and free association, and before long the institutional arrangements of Islam would seem repulsive indeed. The early Ottoman sultans revived the practice of the ancient Persian Empire; when one ascended the throne, he had his brothers executed. (Selim the Grim extended the practice to include his nephews.)[42] The Ottomans also used eunuchs in responsible civil and military positions (though slaves and former slaves played a more important part in what Barnette Miller calls a "government by a slave class").[43]

In the Byzantine Empire eunuchs were not so simply an instrument of the ruler as in the despotisms of the Near East. Steven Runciman writes, with irony not very visible, that for a boy to be really successful, it might be wise to castrate him. He was then ineligible to be emperor and physically unable to transmit anything by inheritance but otherwise could rise to high office in state or church. It was "employ[ment] of eunuchs, of a strong bureaucracy controlled by eunuchs, that was Byzantium's great weapon against the feudal tendency for power to be concentrated in the hands of a hereditary nobility, which provided so much trouble for the West. The significance of eunuchs in Byzantine life was that they gave the Emperor a governing class that he could trust."[44] Karl Wittfogel finds fault with this contention, on the grounds that eunuchism was "already fully institutionalized" in fourth-century Byzantium, when there were no feudal tendencies about.[45] That fact does not prove that eunuchs were less than a vitally important tool of the imperial office in resisting partial or nascent aspects of feudalism from developing into the full-blown phenomenon of the West.

In the words of Herbert J. Muller, "in some basic respects the feudal system was the antithesis of Oriental despotism."[46] An important part of that characteristic of feudalism was what it prevented from happening: it produced a "military stalemate," owing to the fact that mounted knights could not take a castle, but the castle could not overcome the knights. Neither lord nor vassal was supreme; the lord's rights were limited, and the vassal was of honorable estate, in contrast to what the moderns have made of the term.

As for the monarch, he was able to benefit from ancient traditions that stressed his authority but also was constrained by other conflicting or not very compatible legal elements. The notion that the king was the anointed of God and that it was generally incumbent on his subjects to obey and not resist him was derived from the memory of David and other examples of Jewish kingship, from the Oriental view of the ruler as partly or wholly divine that dated to early Egypt and Mesopotamia but was brought into the Roman Empire only with the annexation of Egypt, and from the portions of Roman law that made him supreme and gave legal status to his wish or even whim. Such tendencies in the jurisprudence of pre-Christian times were reinforced by St. Paul's letter to the *Romans* and Gregory the Great's reflections on the Christian duty of obedience, though there were other notes sounded in early medieval Christian literature—notably, Augustine's ideas about the justifiability of resisting an unjust ruler.

However, the theoretical bases for later limitation on monarchical power are to be chiefly found in feudalism. Specifically, by replacing earlier notions of decision by the ruler according to his own will with the Western belief that he must also respect the rights of others, the feudal court was the institution of greatest importance. The court was a council of the lord and his men for the settlement of disputes. . . . The striking fact is that both the lord and the vassal had precisely the same remedy in case either believed that his right had been invaded: he could appeal the decision of the other members of the court. . . . The court's decision was enforceable by the united power of its members, and in the extreme case enforcement was conceived to run even against the king. . . . Under a typical feudal organization the king was *primus inter pares,* and the court itself, or the king and the court together, exercised a joint rule, which included all that, in a modern state, would be distinguished as legislative, executive, and judicial functions of government. At the same time the essentially contractual relation between the members of the court, including the king, tended to prevent the concentration of authority anywhere.[47]

The right and the power of the nobles to curb the arbitrary power of the monarch were not, to be sure, unalloyed blessings in the history of free societies. The monarch, whatever his personal shortcomings, stood for public authority and potentially embodied the commonwealth as against the particularism of the nobility. To such men as the Comte de Boulainvilliers and Montesquieu, writing in the age of eighteenth-century absolutism, "the most striking characteristic of the Middle Ages was the parceling out of sovereignty among a host of petty princes, or even lords of villages."[48]

The princes and lords, however, had not always been the same. The medieval mobility might claim descent from the Roman senatorial order or, more rarely, from the few *edelinge,* or noble families, among Germanic tribes. From the ninth to the eleventh century the word *noble* (Latin, *nobilis*) is to be found in documents but lacked precise legal meaning. The ritual of knighting dates from around 1050, and a century or more later the right to be knighted becomes a hereditary privilege.

A noble class begins to emerge in the twelfth century. When the institutions of the fief and vassalage were moving toward full decline, in the thirteenth century, the nobility took definite shape: in England and France, barons, dukes, and marquises (the latter two, heads of several counties) along with counts, who had existed all along since Roman times. In the fourteenth century, however, kings began to create more counts. A hereditary and titled nobility thus evolved, not in an instant.

It seemed in the early Middle Ages as if hereditary clergy might also emerge. Gregory VII, as part of a zealous effort to reform the church, did much to enforce celibacy or at any rate prevent priests' wives from being recognized as legal; and if property or power was to pass from generation to generation, it had increasingly to find its way through nephews, real or alleged, or other alternatives to direct inheritance.[49] Thus a strong hereditary nobility but no comparable ecclesiastical class was in existence by the end of the period under discussion.

Perhaps it was because medieval society was still fluid that John of Salisbury, author of "the first elaborate medieval treatise on politics,"[50] completely ignores the conflicting claims of "the different political powers, feudal, royal, imperial, which were at the moment so hotly contending with one another for a demarcation of their respective jurisdictions."[51] In the *Policraticus* (1159), John, secretary of two successive archbishops of Canterbury, the second of whom, Thomas Becket, would be murdered eleven years later, was rather concerned with the "higher law" that was fundamental to medieval political thought and that was associated with Christianity and its church. Comparing the body politic with a human body, John declared that though the prince was the head, the priesthood was the soul.[52] His book is full of contradictions, but against his praise of the good and law-obeying prince must be set his defense of resistance to a tyrant, going as far as tyrannicide.

St. Thomas Aquinas, whose teachings about the state were only part of his attempt to embrace all knowledge in a seamless web, rejected John's defense of tyrannicide but nevertheless justified resistance to tyrants. Those resisting must assure themselves, however, that their action is less injurious to the general good than the abuses they object to. Aquinas regards the ruler as bound to make the positive law, or the human law, conform to natural law. Thus "he may not take private property beyond what public need requires, though strictly speaking property is an institution of Human rather than Natural Law."[53]

Rulership must above all leave intact the free moral agency of the subject. Therefore the tyrant, who fails to do so, brings upon himself resistance that is not merely a right but a duty. As for the sacerdotium, the authority of the church, it represents something of course higher than the imperium; nevertheless, Sabine describes Aquinas plausibly as a "moderate papalist" who was unimpressed by the arguments of canon lawyers that the spiritual superiority of the church could be translated into legal supremacy of the papacy or other ecclesiastical powers. Thomas died in 1274, leaving important works on political matters unfinished.

A half-century later Dante Alighieri (d. 1321) and Marsiglio of Padua (his book, *Defensor Pacis,* was written in 1324) took the case for law as supreme over the prince as proven, but in the relation between papacy and empire associated themselves with the latter. The doctrine of the two swords, formulated particularly by Pope Gelasius I seven centuries before, held that "the two powers are united only in God and consequently that the emperor has no human superior."[54] It was possible, to be sure, to stress the special ultimate responsibility of the spiritual power—that is, the papacy—in interpreting or even enforcing God's will. Dante and Marsiglio, however, emphasized the prerogatives of the emperorship; they were Ghibellines not Guelphs.

Marsiglio's work was perhaps the most influential of the genre, though possibly

William of Occam (d. 1349) had more effect in his own time. Pope John XXII had tried to intervene from Avignon in an election to the emperorship; the arguments made by the two men resounded through the whole debate that went on from 1323 to 1347. They supported the candidacy of Lewis the Bavarian, but they both showed more concern with limitations on papal power than with what happened in Germany, and Marsiglio bases his observations clearly on the theory and practice of government in the Italian city-states. He writes of the church, regarding it as the entire body of believers lay and clerical, and defends the view that only an ecumenical council (or general council, to use the late medieval term) could make decisions for the institution. But the clergy is one social class among others, in his view, and must submit to civil control.

William of Occam was at pains to deny that the imperial elections needed papal confirmation or that the emperor's authority depended in any way on the pope. The power of the emperor stemmed from the College of Electors, who spoke for the "people." In Sabine's words, "in this general sense he conceived of the imperial power—indeed any royal power—as arising from the consent of a corporate body of subjects, expressed through their magnates."[55] But above all such human institutions stood the law, human law depending at root on natural law with less distinction made between the two than Aquinas had done.

Occam argued similarly with respect to the church. It was the general council, not the papacy, that could make determinations. The papal claim of *plenitudo potestatis,* set forth by Innocent IV and carried to its most uncompromising extent by Boniface VII in *Unam sanctam* (1302), was rebutted and rejected. Boniface asserted that the papacy was supreme within the church; moreover, the Gelasian doctrine of two swords was interpreted in such a manner as to make the church in effect custodian of both, even if it did not wield the temporal sword. For the temporal sword was, Boniface declared, to be employed by kings "at the command and with the permission of priests." For William of Occam, such claims had led to the scandalous situation of the papacy at Avignon and were an intolerable infringement of Christian freedom.

Within the context of the development of political theory in the West, the differences between Aquinas and Marsiglio, Guelphs and Ghibellines, supporters of the pope and supporters of the emperor, seem significant, and one or another view may be thought to foreshadow this or that later theorist or rationalization of actions taken by a monarch, cleric, or noble. In the setting of world history, the perspective is somewhat different. All the theorists mentioned, as well as the chief ecclesiastical and political figures of the period, professed to share a belief in law in general, in the distinction between natural and positive law (even though slightly different terms might be used) and the need for the latter to conform to the former, in the distinction between the sacred and secular powers and the inadmissibility of efforts to reduce one to the other. Even Boniface VIII, in his claims imperiling the notion of separable secular power, did not dare attack it outright.

Theoretical excursuses into the desirability of representative government in the church were paralleled by references to the fact that it already existed in the government of the empire. The electors chose the emperor and thereafter his powers were exercised in conjunction with the Diet (limited by it would be too strong an expression). The councils, representing the bishops or at least the senior bishops or patriarch of the whole church, had once governed the church and ought to again. No one then spoke of direct participation of all citizens in government, but there again was wide acceptance of the claim that the justification of the state was the welfare of the citizenry. Dante put it thus: the aim of the rightful commonwealth is

liberty, to wit that men may live for their own sake. For citizens are not for the sake of the Consuls, nor a nation for the King; but contrariwise the Consuls are for the sake of the nation.[56]

By 1350 the main outlines of several of the monarchies had been shaped, though none of the national boundaries on the continent would stay exactly the same. The organization of society depended on one church (even if in 1350 it was in two ecclesiastical pieces dependent on Rome and Avignon respectively) in Europe up to the eastern border of Livonia, Poland, Transylvania, and Croatia— but on not just one empire but several states outside it as well.

In fact there had never been a single empire in the Mediterranean world since Rome accepted permanent division in 395, nor had there been in western Europe, at any rate since 476. There were important states outside Charlemagne's empire and Otto's and his successors'. But there had been in the West development in the direction of a single church; and by 1054 it was unified in the West in a way not true of the East, and by 1200 it approached reality.

By 1350, however things had changed. Political theory might still center on the papacy, which had lost much strength in the previous century or so, and the empire, whose chances of achieving real unity even within its own territories were fast disappearing; however, the increasingly clear existence of a multiplicity of states kept intruding itself on political thought. As for the themes of the importance of the citizenry and the denial of absolute power to any individual or institution, however, they remained pertinent to the changing situation, and served without difficulty to resist excessive claims by national monarchs when they were made in succeeding centuries.

CHAPTER 6

The Renaissance and the Reformation, 1350–1650

In 1350 Byzantium had still a century of tenuous and truncated existence ahead, but the Ottoman Turks were poised to cross into Europe and might have taken the New Rome then if it had not been for the appearance behind them of a threat in the shape of the army of Tamerlane. When the Turks at length ended Byzantine history, a new Eastern Orthodox state was just gaining effective independence in the north: Muscovy.

In the West the promising political developments of the High Middle Ages seemed temporarily interrupted or diverted: France and England fought a long if sporadic war; empire and papacy conducted an inconclusive struggle, as a result of which neither Germany nor Italy could achieve political unity; the smaller states had other adventures, notably in the Age of Discovery. The mixed political picture tended to be overshadowed by the art and letters of the Renaissance and the religious renewal and conflict of the Reformation.

From about 1300 one may speak of a Renaissance, not in the literal sense of the rebirth of something that was dead (Greek and Roman classical art, literature, and spirit were what those coining the term had in mind), but in an accelerated spread of learning and an outburst of artistic creation, first in northern Italy, then the Low Countries, France, England, and elsewhere as far east as Poland, with faint echoes in Russia. These developments were accompanied by greater stress, in thought and action, on the role of the individual and by the emergence of princes or princelings who gloried in and were glorified by the new art and literature. Earlier generations of historians were more inclined to regard the

Renaissance as a thrilling break with the dismal medieval past; recent scholars have stressed the way in which it marked a culmination and fulfillment of trends increasingly visible in the High Middle Ages.

The West, 1350–1450

England and France. War requires money; money means taxes; and, in the emergent states of the West (not in the oriental empires), the monarch needed the consent of representative bodies to levy taxes so that he could pay for his wars. From the need for such consent came the growth of parliaments.

The so-called Hundred Years' War (1338–1453), a dynastic conflict between England and France that produced a few overtones of protonationalism, imposed heavy burdens. The French Estates General, unwisely meeting in two separate bodies for Languedoïl and Languedoc (the areas where the word for "yes" were pronounced "oïl" and "oc" respectively in the north and in the south), were led by Etienne Marcel, the richest man in Paris. The Estates General took advantage of the situation arising when Edward, the Black Prince, defeated the French king and took him prisoner at the battle of Poitiers. The power and prestige of the French monarchy fell to a low ebb; the power of the Estates General reached its apogee: the Great Ordinance of 1357 provided for the supervision, by a standing committee, of taxation and of expenditure of the funds raised.

Tormented by taxes imposed by their own king and the pillaging of enemy soldiers, the peasants wreaked vengeance on the nobles who would not or could not protect them in the revolt called the *Jacquerie.*[1] Marcel was discredited by intrigues with the English and the peasants; the nobles now turned on him. He was murdered, and the so-called constitutional movement, spearheaded by Marcel's townsmen, ended for the time being.

Charles V the Wise now ascended to the throne. He managed to elude the constraints imposed by the Estates General by obtaining their consent to the principle that only new levies needed their approval. He introduced a new hearth tax (particularly onerous for the poor), entrusted the collection of indirect taxes to tax-farmers, thereby creating a lasting source of corruption, and in general strengthened royal powers over taxation. W. T. Waugh declares that the French Estates General ought to have insisted that their consent be obtained for all extraordinary taxation; "that demand, steadily and wisely pressed, might have given the Estates-General the stability which was being acquired by the English Parliament."[2] But they did not insist and were repeatedly outsmarted by the French monarchy.

Charles V even had luck with matters outside his control. After the pope had been persuaded to return from Avignon to Rome in 1376, another scandalous dispute kept one papacy in Rome and sent another one back. Charles V welcomed the return, having found a papacy in Avignon a political asset.

In 1377 the English king, Edward III, died after a reign of fifty years. He was popular, and though Parliament gained in power through manipulating the needs of war, it was not through direct clash with the monarch that it did so. As the war progressed, anti-French feelings prompted hostility to the French-influenced popes of Avignon. Several measures were passed reducing papal influence on the English church: in particular, the Statutes of Provisors, limiting the importation of foreign clergy, and of Praemunire, prohibiting appeals to foreign courts.

National pride was both cause and effect of such developments. At the same time, however, the nation was disturbed by social cleavage. As the Black Death wiped out a sizable proportion of the population, the Statute of Labourers sought to fix wages and prices. It could not, to be sure, remedy the real shortage of labor or stop the change now under way from servile to free tenures in land.

During the minority of Richard II, landlords tried to reestablish servile tenures; the result was the great Peasants' Revolt (Wat Tyler's rebellion) of 1381. It was put down through trickery; like the French *Jacquerie* of a quarter-century earlier, it yielded the participants no visible benefits. The king got into a squabble with Parliament, with which he had been on good terms at the start. In a dispute over finances, he resorted to packing the membership of Commons, provoking Henry of Bolingbroke, of the House of Lancaster, to lead an uprising against him. Richard was forced to abdicate and died, or was killed, in the Tower of London in 1399. He was the last Plantagenet to rule. Henry IV, the first of three Lancastrian kings, had a dubious title to the throne and was therefore compelled to conciliate Parliament.

In 1380, when Charles VI acceded, the French monarchy was in a strong position. The reign was, however, a long and unhappy one. The new king was plagued by increasing periods of insanity; uncles of his produced gross misgovernment. In a civil war between the noble-oriented Armagnacs of the south and the Burgundians, including many of the lower classes of the north, the Burgundians enjoyed a temporary triumph.

Led by the skinner Simon Caboche and his "Cabochian" followers, the Burgundians forced the king to issue an ordinance reforming the central administration. It set forth the obligation of the king and certain officials to consult the royal Council, the Parlement of Paris, or the Chambre des Comptes (note the absence of the Estates General from this plan) to obtain approval before undertaking important actions of several kinds. In Waugh's words, the authors of the ordinance "had great faith in 'election.' Most public offices were to have an electoral committee attached to them."[3] In any event, most of the provisions of the law were stillborn. The Cabochians inaugurated a minor reign of terror; the

Armagnacs swept into Paris, putting an end to it, and began to behave badly in their turn.

Meanwhile Henry V of England landed at the head of an army and smashed a French force three times the size of his own at the battle of Agincourt (1415) in Artois. For some time he continued, in fragile alliance with the Burgundians, to conquer region after region. But in 1422 Henry V died, followed only days later by Charles VI of France.

The infant Henry VI of England was acknowledged as king of France by much of the north; the holder of the French crown, Charles VII, was physically and morally weak and no very likely challenger of the ascendant English. Nevertheless he was persuaded by the peasant girl with visions, Jeanne Darc (listed in a later patent of nobility as d'Arc, whence "Joan of Arc"—or so one version has it), to rouse himself from lethargy. After she herself led an army to relieve the siege of Orléans, she persuaded Charles to be crowned at Reims. But when the Maid fell into English hands, Charles would not lift a finger to save her from the stake where she was burned in 1431.

Falling back for a time in confused incompetence, once again the king experienced good fortune. As a consequence of having advisors so capable as to yield him the appellation Charles the Well-Served, he registered significant successes.

As there were no longer Francophile popes either in Avignon or Rome, his reign saw the first of several assertions of the autonomy of the French church. In 1438 an assembly of clerical and lay notables drew up, and the king adopted, the Pragmatic Sanction of Bourges. It affirmed the superiority of general councils to the papacy, forbade appeals to Rome except when all French judicature had been exhausted, and so forth. The monarch also established the first royal standing army and carried out other military reforms. The result was that from 1449 French forces drove the English out of Normandy, Guienne, and the southwest generally. In 1453 the only bit of the French mainland to remain in English hands was the port of Calais.

Charles VII either permitted or undertook the creation of provincial *parlements,* which were mainly judicial institutions and quite unlike the English Parliament. As the reign wore on, the estates—of Languedoïl, Languedoc, and the provinces—met with decreasing frequency. The monarchy grew in power and prestige, and the end of the Hundred Years' War enhanced both. Though there was no formal treaty, and even a few skirmishes occurred after 1453, contemporaries recognized that the war was over and bestowed the title Charles the Victorious. In the words of one writer, "seldom has so inglorious a king had so glorious a reign."[4]

While the Lancastrian kings of England had been conducting the war against France, they first sparred with Parliament and then, during the long reign of

Henry VI, who was incapable of ruling, the monarchy lost control. The feudal lords of the country battled with one another with small private armies, with chaos the result. When Englishmen gave up the struggle in France, the ingredients of civil war were present, and soon there erupted the Wars of the Roses (1455–85) between the families of Lancaster and York.

Italy.   Culturally, Italy was beginning a flowering unmatched before or since; politically, it was in a sad state. In the north there had been free communes, which by the first half of the fourteenth century had disappeared. They were replaced by tyrants: for example, the Viscontis in Milan from the 1270s and the Medicis in Florence from the 1430s. In the south the Aragonese monarch Alfonso reunited the kingdoms of Naples and Sicily, though they were soon separated again.

During the absence of the popes in Avignon, the papal states of central Italy were in turmoil. In 1378 a pope was elected in Rome. Another, however, was also chosen by cardinals alarmed by the Roman prelate's promises of reform, and he returned to Avignon. There ensued the double papacy of the period of the Great Schism, which brought grievous scandal to the whole Western church and anguished debates about how to end it.

The device employed to reunite the church was the general council. The theories of Marsiglio of Padua found application in the councils of Pisa (1409) and Constance (1414–17). First the two popes were both deposed and a third was elected, but since the deposed prelates defied the council, there were now three popes. But the Council of Constance finally got rid of two, ignored the third, and elected still another: Martin V (1417–31). The councils of Basel and Ferrara-Florence continued the effort to regularize the revived institution of representative government within the church, but it was a failure. By 1449 the conciliar movement was at an end. Nicholas V inaugurated the "Renaissance papacy"—a historian's term for the century in which the popes patronized art and culture, to their eternal credit, and neglected the problems of the character and quality of the clergy and the morality of the church in general, in a nearly suicidal fashion.

Central and Eastern Europe, 1350–1450

The Empire.   In the German north a noteworthy transmutation was taking place. The struggle to produce a unified Holy Roman Empire and an emperorship capable of challenging the papacy was on the way to being lost, but a new state was taking shape in the southeast. After the Golden Bull of 1356 the method of electing the emperor was fixed, but the power of the office was almost negligible. In theory the emperor could issue laws for all the people. But even if laws were promulgated, the emperor had no way of enforcing them, and thus the whole process was nugatory.

In consequence emperors often occupied themselves elsewhere. Charles IV of the House of Luxemburg spent his energy on Bohemia, of which he was king. When his successor, Wenceslas IV, was deposed by the electors and by a great assembly at Frankfurt, the monarch refused to accept the decision, and there were soon three rival emperors "to correspond to the three rival popes."[5] It was a far cry from the days when an Innocent III could overawe kings or a Frederick Barbarossa could aspire to be a new Charlemagne; both papacy and empire had fallen to a low estate. The papacy would revive; the old empire, in its earlier guise, would not.

For the moment, indeed, there emerged from among the conflicting claims a single emperor: Sigismund of Luxemburg, in 1410. The emperorship retained one significant prerogative—that of nominating to vacant fiefs. Sigismund exercised it, for example, by conferring the mark of Brandenburg on his closest confidant, Frederick of Hohenzollern—an act of great importance for later times, since it was a step in the rise of Prussia. But Sigismund was able to do little else within the empire. He let the electors govern while he fought the Turks, and he failed either to conciliate or conquer the Hussites. His chief accomplishment may have been the extent to which he played a part in ending the Great Schism within the church.

When Sigismund died he was succeeded by Albert II of the House of Habsburg, who also took his place on the thrones of Bohemia and Hungary. Two Habsburgs had been emperor in the thirteenth century, from 1308 to 1438, the imperial dignity resided in other hands; it then returned to the Habsburgs.

Bohemia had a period of glory under the Luxemburgs and especially Charles I (the Bohemian title of the Emperor Charles IV, 1347–78). Its brightest light was its new university, founded in 1348, the first university in central and eastern Europe. There John Hus, a professor and then rector, attracted a group of radical supporters who adhered to the teachings of the Englishman John Wycliffe. Lured to the Council of Constance by a safe-conduct that was then violated, Hus was burned in 1415. His death set off a series of wars (1420–34) in which the zealous Hussites both attacked and resisted with startling success their Catholic neighbors. At length Rome came to terms with the moderate Hussite party, and one of them, George of Podiebrad, became king (1459–71). The radical Taborites were suppressed, though some aspects of their movement were continued by the Moravian Brethren.

Poland, Lithuania, and Hungary.   Casimir III the Great of Poland was in some respects comparable to Charles I of Bohemia; he led a thriving country under an efficient administration. Poland enjoyed also a cultural flowering that centered in Cracow, where a higher school founded by Casimir in 1364 was raised to university status in 1400 and became the most important intellectual center in eastern Europe.

During Casimir's reign, however, the nobility solidified its position. The king appointed a *starosta capitaneus* for each region; for almost half a millennium the position remained decisive in Polish political life. The starostas were basically aristocrats, not courtiers—their own men, not creatures of the monarchy. The nobles were governed by their own law, called the *jus Polonicum,* as distinguished from the *jus Teutonicum* that governed the burghers and the peasants.

Under Casimir III's chosen successor, Louis II of Hungary, however, the Polish monarchy began its decline. In order to try to assure the succession to his descendants, the king granted sweeping concessions to the nobles, or *szlachta.* By the provisions of the Charter of Koszyce (1374), the Polish nobility won unprecedented privileges. Numbering in the thousands, they were "exempted from almost every duty or obligation to the State."[6] However, they were not tranquil in consequence; they continued to badger the throne and to fight one another.

In 1386 Louis's daughter Jadwiga, recently elected queen of Poland, married Jagiello (Yagailo), grand prince of Lithuania. At the same time he embraced the faith of his wife, a Roman Catholic, and carried with him his people, the last pagans of Europe. The resulting personal union lasted 187 years before being replaced by virtual amalgamation of the two states.

In previous decades, the Lithuanians under Gedymin (1316–41) and Olgerd (1341–77) had expanded to rule the entire Dnieper basin and reached the Black Sea at Oczaków. In Norman Davies's words, "where Casimir the Great had merely nibbled, the sons of Gedymin gorged."[7] As a result the population of the great sprawling state was mainly Orthodox Eastern Slav, its ruling class Slavic boyars, its official language Old Belorussian (to use today's term).

The armies of Poland and Lithuania joined together to challenge and administer a crushing defeat to the Teutonic Knights at Grunwald (Tannenberg, 1410), with the support of Russians and Tatars and the help of Bohemian mercenaries, sending the Knights into a prolonged decline. The Jagellonian dynasty for a time furnished kings to Bohemia and Hungary, and by the end of the reign of Casimir IV Jagiellonczyk in 1492, the king ruled some 336,000 square miles, while his son Wladyslaw ruled 174,000 square miles more: Bohemia, Moravia, Silesia, and Hungary.[8]

In the Union of Horodlo (1413), it was enacted that both the king of Poland and the grand prince of Lithuania, regarded as equal in importance, were to be elected by the joint diets of both states. "The newly-created Lithuanian nobles, provided that they were Catholic Christians, were to enjoy all the privileges of the Polish nobles."[9]

But the royal power was limited. In the thirteenth century, the kings consulted only their small council of high officials, whose advice they were not bound to accept. But the situation gradually changed. The nobles' consent was required for taxes for "any major enterprise." As a result, the fifteenth century "saw the rise rapidly to the position of partner with the king in the conduct of the state's affairs."[10]

Jews, under the jurisdiction of the king since 1334, were the beneficiaries of greater toleration in Poland than elsewhere. When Casimir IV became king in 1447, a half-century of prosperity opened in this multiethnic realm, and once again Poland and Lithuania were ruled by a single sovereign.

If the Polish nobles thwarted attempts by the monarchy to subdue them, the same was true in Hungary. The Angevin dynasty, established in Hungary in 1308, attempted to gain control over the proud and independent-minded Hungarian nobility, exempt from taxation and casual about their supposed responsibility for defense. Louis the Great, who established his court in Buda, limited the rights of the great magnates to dispose of their property, reaffirmed the rights of the lesser nobility, and regularized the obligations of the peasantry.

Louis intended that his oldest daughter, Maria, succeed him on the thrones of both Poland and Hungary; the Poles frustrated his plan by accepting instead his younger daughter Hedwig, or Jadwiga, and marrying her to the pagan grand prince of Lithuania. Maria married Sigismund of Luxemburg. He ruled Hungary for a full half-century (1387–1437); he was also emperor, as discussed previously.

Sigismund belongs to the list of European monarchs who, by their spendthrift and oppressive rule, courted resistance that wrested from them constitutional concessions and thereby unintentionally furthered the growth of freedom in their countries. In his reign the principle became established that the Diet, representing the upper classes, must approve any additional grant of revenue and later any legislation whatever, if it were to be valid.

Iberia.   In the southwestern corner of Europe Christians were advancing in triumph. In 1340 Alfonso XI of Castile defeated a combined army of Spanish and Moroccan Muslims at the battle of Rio Salado, after which no African threat to Christian Iberia existed any longer. Castile enjoyed a plethora of charters (*fueros*) applying to the whole state, to individual regions, and to towns.

A feature peculiar to Castilian society was the brotherhoods (*hermandades*), committed to the defense of law and of the property and lives of their members. They often supported the monarchy and were also associated with the strength of the Castilian towns. In the fourteenth century both the brotherhoods and the towns entered a period of decline. Alfonso XI appointed new officials, the *corregidores,* who somewhat limited municipal autonomy, and imposed a new sales tax, the *alcabala,* which injured the towns' economy.

But the monarchy lacked the power to end the exemption from taxes and the other special privileges of the nobles and the clergy. Henry II (1369–79) made extensive grants of land and revenue to the nobility. The Cortes of Castile had to consent to any extraordinary direct tax and to the repeal of any law, and petition by one or another of the three estates often led to new legislation from the crown. Around 1400, writes Waugh, "the powers of the Castilian Cortes were much like those of the contemporary English Parliament."[11]

Why were those powers not retained and expanded? Perhaps partly because the "mutual obligations characteristic of medieval feudalism" to be found in England, as well as France and Germany, were rarely to be encountered in Spain, except for Catalonia. The Castilian monarchy seemed to weaken in the reign of Henry IV (1454–74), but his stepsister, Isabella, rescued it. She married Ferdinand of Aragon in 1469, and the two *reyes catolicos* (Catholic kings) were to bring about the unity of Spain.

The kingdom of Aragon remained a pastiche of three realms: Aragon, Catalonia, and Valencia. Each long retained its own political institutions. Its estates were four in number, including lesser nobles along with greater nobles, clergy, and townsmen. The Corts was more powerful than that of Castile, and the post of *Justicia* of Aragon was termed by an occupant around 1400 "the greatest lay office that existed anywhere in the world."[12] A famous oath was attributed to the nobles of the kingdom:

We who are as good as you swear to you who are no better than we, to accept you as our king and sovereign lord, provided you accept all our liberties and laws; but if not, not.

The wording seems to be a forgery of about 1550.[13] Nevertheless, a recent writer declares that it does "summarize very well the relations between the kings of Aragon and the Aragonese nobility [in the fifteenth century].[14] But if kingship in Aragon was less than all-powerful, its possessions made the state an imposing one. It still held Sicily and Sardinia, and Alfonso V the Magnificent added Naples to the empire in 1435. As a result of the exploits of Catalan mercenaries called in by the Byzantines, for much of the fourteenth century Aragon's sway extended to the Duchy of Athens.

Portugal had gained its later shape in 1297 under the well-loved King Diniz the Worker. It won its more or less permanent independence by dint of its victory over Castile at the battle of Aljubarrota in 1385. This was immediately followed by the long-lasting alliance with England and not long afterward by the immensely significant expeditions sent out by Prince Henry the Navigator. Never king and not himself a navigator, he launched the Age of Discovery that was to bring the Europeans into contact with all the rest of the globe. Beginning with the capture of Ceuta in 1415, Portuguese sailors ventured ever farther south until they rounded the Cape of Good Hope and reached India in 1498. The first law code of the Portuguese was adopted in 1446.

Scandinavia.   Scandinavian problems were not unlike those of the countries to the south and west. Slavery had died out by 1350. A dependent peasantry was subject to a nobility exempt from taxes for roughly a century in Denmark, Norway, and Sweden alike. The Norwegian monarchy was hereditary and wielded more power, but the Swedish and Danish kingships were a blend of elective and hereditary elements. The earlier councils of magnates (alone) had been superseded in each country by national councils, consisting of bishops and aristocratic leaders, which became powerful in Sweden and Denmark. Waldemar IV of Denmark wrestled with the power of the nobles and the church and with the waxing influence of Germans—traders as well as nobles. He fought two wars with the Hanseatic League and was beaten; the Peace of Stralsund gave the Hansa a veto over succession to the throne.

After his reign Margaret, mother of the boy-king, became regent of Denmark and then also of Norway. In 1387 she was chosen queen, and in 1397 assembled representatives of all three states agreed upon the so-called Union of Kalmar. It was never given legal force, but its basic principles, retention by each country of its own laws but a common kingship and foreign policy, were effective for a considerable period.

At the time of the Union Margaret's grandnephew Erik of Pomerania was crowned king of all three realms. Margaret was skillful in placing her supporters in "the highest local administrative positions, tied to the possession of the royal castles."[15] She had tried to conciliate the powerful Count of Holstein by granting him Slesvig as a fief. When he died, the queen sought to recover it, with the result of a prolonged war between Holstein and Denmark.

At the same time trouble erupted in Sweden. King Erik had ridden roughshod over indigenous sensibilities in appointing Danes to the castle posts. Now Engelbrekt Engelbrektsson led a rising with much peasant support, and a Diet that included representatives of the peasantry elected him regent in 1435. But the revolt spread from Sweden to Norway and forced Erik to flee from Denmark. Christopher of Wittelsbach was then called to rule all three countries for a few years, promising to appoint only native aristocrats as bailiffs in the royal castles.

Part of the motivation for the union of 1397 was to make common cause against the Germans. It was therefore ironic that Christopher, a German, was nearly powerless at the hands of the German Hansa as well as the Scandinavian nobles. In 1450 the Norwegian assembly decreed perpetual union with Denmark, and the combination lasted until 1814. If "perpetuity" in a legal document lasts over three hundred years in fact, rare success has been achieved.

In 1450 it looked as if the Danish council, which had just elected Christian of Oldenburg king but reserved real power to itself, and the nobles who were the decisive element in all three countries, had mastered the monarchy, though the Hansa towns still threatened to dominate all Scandinavia.

Byzantium, Russia, and Islam.   In the middle of the fourteenth century, the Mongols ruled Russia, and the shadow of the Ottoman Turks was looming large over the Byzantine Greeks. In 1353 the Ottomans became established on the European side of the Dardanelles; in 1357 they captured Adrianople, which soon became the chief city for their European possessions and remained so for nearly a century. John V Paleologus, restored to power at the time of the expulsion of John VI Cantacuzene in 1355, tried to obtain help from the West. His efforts were in vain, and he proceeded to acknowledge the sultan, Murad I, as his suzerain. John actually campaigned with him in Asia Minor. Such an emperor was in no position to rally Christians to resist Muslims.

Byzantium had other dangerous neighbors, to be sure. Stephen Dušan had claimed the emperorship himself a few years before he died, in 1355. His Serbian state promptly fell apart. The two major pieces were a northern principality between the Morava and the Danube and the state of Serres in eastern Macedonia. The realm of the Bulgarians lay to the east.

To its north the two principalities of Wallachia and Moldavia now carry Romanians clearly into history for the first time. For both, "the beginnings of an organized political life seem to have been linked with the successful struggle of their princes to shake off Hungarian rule."[16] Sultan Murad ended the independence of Serres by a victory in 1371; at the fabled battle of Kosovo Polje in 1389, northern Serbia was overwhelmed. In the late twentieth century, the battle remains the most memorable event of Serbian antiquity (and immensely complicates the question of what to do about an area with a large population of ethnic Albanians). In 1393 Murad's successor Bayezid I crushed Bulgaria. It looked as if the turn of Byzantium would come next.

However, a reprieve arrived from an unexpected quarter, in the advance of Timur (Tamerlane), a Mongol who had overthrown the emir of Khorasan and built a brilliant capital at Samarqand. His forces attacked and routed the Ottomans at Angora in 1402 and captured Bayezid, but he did not try to remain in Asia Minor. In a confused series of disputes and wars, Greeks and Turks, Christians and Muslims, marched and countermarched. Muhammad I the Restorer emerged triumphant and prepared the way for the two sultans who followed his death (1421) to win final victory over the Eastern Roman Empire.

The Byzantine ruler Manuel II (1391–1425) ruled only Constantinople, Thessalonica, and the Morea. Thessalonica was sold to Venice, but the Frankish part of Morea was added to the Byzantine province and remained thus for a quarter-century. A last desperate attempt was made by John VIII to obtain western help at the Council of Florence in 1439. Again reunion of the churches was the Byzantine offer; again it was accepted by Rome but repudiated in the East. A western crusade, led by the great Transylvanian general John Hunyadi, was smashed at the battle of Varna in 1444, though other western troops under Venetian and Genoese command took part in the final defense of the imperial city.

In 1453 Constantine XI, the last Byzantine emperor, died fighting on the battlements of Constantinople. The last holdings in Greece fell by 1461, Wallachia immediately afterward. Moldavia, under its prince Stephen the Great, retained independence, and Stephen resisted the Turks successfully until his death in 1504. That was the end of Christian-ruled southeastern Europe for more than four centuries, unless virtually independent though tiny Montenegro be counted an exception.

Muhammad II the Conqueror made Constantinople his capital and renamed it Istanbul. He entrusted his Christian subjects to the mercies of their ecclesiastical authorities, who were permitted, or required, to wield civil power as well. The high clergy of the Orthodox church were as a result compelled to conform to the Ottoman system or even participate in it, with its concomitants: influence, bribery, corruption, and murder. All this they had to do if they were to gain and hold the positions in which they could hope to protect their flocks and avoid worse fates for them. It was an anticipation of the dilemmas that the Orthodox would face under Communist rule five centuries later.

The Slavs, Romanians, and Greeks of the Balkan peninsula did not suffer greater oppression than the Turkish subjects of the sultan; Jews might be better off than they were in countries ruled by Christians. And yet despite what one Byzantine noble was heard to say—that he would rather see a Turkish turban in the imperial city than a cardinal's hat— [17] there were many Christians who found Muslim rule degrading, unpleasant, and oppressive. In the twentieth century, a Balkan statesman asked rhetorically, "What can one do with people who for five hundred years never ceased to regard Turkish rule as anything but a stopgap?" And doubtless many so regarded it.

In 1350 the Eastern Slavs were divided between the grand principality of Lithuania and the principality of Moscow. Lithuania was soon (1385–86) to join Poland in dynastic union; the pagan Lithuanian elite became Roman Catholic, and in neither incarnation did they share the religion of their Ruthenian subjects in the vast eastern reaches of the realm.

By the second half of the fourteenth century, Novgorod was in effect an independent republic. At the time of the conquest the Mongols had not reached the city, although it nominally had become tributary to the Golden Horde like the other Russian principalities. Actually Novgorod developed as a trading center linked with the Hanseatic towns. It also maintained direct ecclesiastical connections with the Byzantine Empire, which brought along with them artistic influences brilliantly developed and adapted by Novgorodian painters.

The political shape of the Russian principalities was not fixed by their Mongol overlords, though it has been suggested that Muscovy nevertheless ended up with a societal pattern closer to that of the Mongols than that of the West, in ways not easy to understand or describe. Legal enactments, partly indigenous in origin and partly borrowed, yield some tantalizing clues. The first Russian law code, the *Pravda Russkaia,* was issued by Yaroslav, prince of Kiev, in the eleventh century. It "shows little evidence of being based on a Byzantine model"[18] but exhibits much similarity with the law of the Franks and Anglo-Saxons. Only one Byzantium-derived legal document may be found in old Russia: the Church Statute of St. Vladimir, the ruler under whom Kievan Rus was converted to Eastern Orthodox Christianity. Even that statute contains a provision assigning one-tenth of all revenue to the church, and since the tithe was unknown in Byzantium it is thought to be a Western borrowing. But the apparent leaning to the West of the law, and perhaps the societal pattern, of early Rus was, if real for a time, at any rate abortive.

At the time of the death (1015) of Yaroslav the Wise, the vast realm of the Rus was divided into five linked principalities. His will prescribed a seniority system, with Kiev at the top, the princely office to pass from brother to brother not father to son (a system akin to that followed in Poland during the same period). The unity of the realm was clearly intended to take precedence over any single prince or his heirs, which ought to have been an impediment to any would-be autocrat.

However, the system did not last. Vladimir Monomakh (d. 1125) strove to preserve the unity of Rus, but a quarter-century later uncles and nephews were fighting over seniority in Kiev, and in 1169 the city was sacked. By 1200 there were twelve principalities, no longer subject to Kiev in any sense and not prepared to acknowledge any authority in the grand princes of Vladimir.[19] In any case they were soon overshadowed by their neighbors, the princes of Moscow.

Moscow slowly and painfully absorbed her Russian neighbors, aided by two facts: her princes managed to gain and keep the trust of the Mongol khans who ruled Russia from 1240 to about 1450, and the metropolitan and primate of the

Russian Orthodox church moved from Kiev first to Vladimir (1300) and finally to Moscow (1328), though "Kiev and all Russia" remained the formal designation of his see. Still later, in 1408, the dioceses in Lithuania were placed under Moscow's jurisdiction.

The governmental structure of the principalities centered on the assembly (*veche*) of townsmen, on the prince, and on his officials. The *veche* withered and disappeared altogether in Moscow. The prince was of little moment in the two northern trading republics but became all-important in the Muscovite state. By the middle of the fifteenth century, the princes of Moscow were only nominally subject to the Mongols (or Tatars, as they came to be called as the ethnic composition of the Golden Horde shifted). Ivan III, who ascended in 1462, was in effect independent at the start of his reign, as he was formally by the time it ended in 1505.

Thus almost at the same moment as the Byzantine Empire passed into history through conquest by the Ottomans, Russia ended its dependence on Muslim rulers. Russia was by now the largest of the Eastern Orthodox countries, independent or not. Within Russia the principality of Moscow was fast becoming master of its neighbors. Unfortunately for the history of freedom in Russia, Muscovy surpassed its neighbor states in two respects: the power of the prince was stronger; the institutions of government outside the principate were weaker. The state that stood at the opposite pole—weak princely power, strong *veche*—was Novgorod, which would fall to Muscovy in 1471.

In 1453 the Ottomans still had to extend their conquests to the south and east. The Mamluks still ruled in Egypt and also Syria. There were other Muslim states to the east. The Il-Khans of Persia died out in 1349 and their realm fell to pieces. By the mid-fifteenth century the most imposing fragment of the Persian state was Turcoman. But Muslim glories were past except for the still-growing power of the Ottoman Turks, and neither in their empire nor east of it could any wisp of pluralism be detected.

The Reformation

Dissatisfaction with the popes or the higher or lower clergy, with respect to morality, financial probity, or political claims, had been periodically expressed in the West for centuries. The West had produced little theological heresy—nothing like the great heretical movements of Arianism, Nestorianism, or Monophysitism that had earlier arisen in the East and agitated large territories and populations for centuries but only, and for a short time, a few scattered individuals and groups, chiefly the Albigensians, who revived the ancient Manichean doctrines, and the Waldensians, whose identification as heretics was more a misunderstanding than anything else.

The teachings of John Wycliffe and John Hus had had the potential of challenging the fundamentals of Christian belief but had not developed to the point of doing so despite the Hussite controversy and wars, finally more or less compromised. However, by the early sixteenth century the convergence of stronger secular princes with deeper religious discontent produced outright challenge to the church as it had existed hitherto and an organizational as well as doctrinal breach with Rome.

The Reformation had two branches. The first was the so-called Magisterial Reformation, in three subdivisions: the following of Martin Luther in the German states, taking shape from the Protest (whence "Protestant") offered at the imperial Diet of 1529; that of John Calvin (Jean Cauvin), who introduced the Reformation in Geneva in 1541, spreading then west and east; and those who followed the English king, Henry VIII (Act of Supremacy, 1534, making him head of the English church).

The second branch was the Radical Reformation, beginning with Anabaptist defection from Luther in Germany and ending with Antitrinitarianism (of which Unitarianism in Transylvania and Poland was the chief variant). What determined the extent of success of the various religious dissenters was the power and steadfastness of the princes, beginning with the support given Luther by Frederick the Wise of Saxony, without which the Reformation might have been stifled at birth.

The West, 1450–1650

England.   After the Hundred Years' War ended in 1453, England underwent the additional torment of the Wars of the Roses (1455–85). They were lengthy but not very destructive, being mainly engagements of the feudal forces of York (which wore a white rose) and Lancaster (a red rose). In the early fifteenth century Parliament had profited from the shakiness of the royal title from which the Lancasters suffered; it asserted its right to redress of grievances and began to insist on initiating financial legislation. However, the Royal council managed to relegate to the background of decision making first the feckless King Henry VI and then the Parliament. A victory of Edward of York in 1461 carried him to the throne. It was, however, a turbulent reign followed by intrigue and murder, ending in the defeat and death of Richard III on the field of Bosworth in 1485.

The victor at Bosworth was Henry Tudor, who now became Henry VII. The works of Sir John Fortescue, contrasting the constitutional spirit of the Common Law of England with the absolutist spirit of the Roman Law of France and in general praising the English monarchy as against that of France, seemed to anticipate the political stance taken by this, the first of the Tudor kings.

However, the political realities of his reign were somewhat different. The new king suppressed the feudal armies that had brought about such prolonged disorder, developed an effective system of managing royal finances, and expended the jurisdiction of the court of the Star Chamber to quell disorder. He increased the centralization of the realm by reversing the degree of autonomy Ireland had gained in the 1450s and, in "Poynings' laws," enacted that no Irish Parliament should be held nor any bill be brought forward in it without the consent of the English king.

The next Tudor, Henry VIII, won fame from his procession through six wives, in search not of pleasure (which was easily enough available to him in whatever form he chose) but of a male heir. A staunch Catholic in belief, he was awarded the title of Defender of the Faith by a pope grateful for his attacks on Lutheranism.

Nevertheless, in one of history's more notable ironies, he emerged as architect and executor of the English Reformation. After the Act of Supremacy (1534) made the monarch head of the Church instead of the pope, Henry promptly took advantage of his new position to seize a great deal of ecclesiastical property, especially the monasteries the ruins of which dot England still. Parliament cooperated with the kingship in carrying out the Reformation, and Henry rewarded it by granting its members the right of freedom from arrest.[20] Aside from the award to Ireland of the not very meaningful title of kingdom (1542), little else of moment from the constitutional standpoint occurred in his reign.

Several ironies now supervened. The male heir achieved at the cost of such turmoil, Edward VI, died after a short undistinguished reign. Soon Mary acceded to the throne; she was the girl to whom Henry VIII had been at such pains to provide a male alternative. She, too, had only a brief and troubled few years as monarch. Finally Henry's other daughter, Elizabeth, became queen and presided over possibly the most glorious half-century (to be precise, forty-five years: 1558–1603) in all English history.

The religious question remained in the forefront of public and governmental concern during the reigns of Edward VI and Mary I. The advisers of Edward moved the Church of England a bit closer to Calvinist Geneva; Mary attempted outright to restore Catholicism. Elizabeth strove to conciliate parties pulling in both directions by overseeing the so-called Anglican Compromise. A Protestant-tinged catalogue of beliefs was thereupon joined to a mostly Catholic liturgy and ecclesiastical organization, and religious conflict was postponed to the next century.

England's energies were freed to seek other objectives. Elizabeth sent Sir

Francis Drake to explore the New World, chartered the East India company that would serve as advance guard of British penetration of Asia, and built the fleet that destroyed the Spanish Armada (1588), setting England on the path to world power. Her generals put down an Irish revolt and after a tortuous series of intrigues vis-à-vis Scotland her rival and cousin Mary Queen of Scots was executed (1587).

The domestic political scene in England exhibited a mixture of royal power and parliamentary potentiality. Elizabeth arrested Peter Wentworth for speaking in support of free speech, but pretended it was for other reasons (though the arrest violated a right her father had granted). The secretary of state, Thomas Smith, declared resoundingly: "For every Englishman is intended to be there [in Parliament] present . . . and the consent of the Parliament is intended to be every man's consent."[21] The arrest of Wentworth was more representative of the realities of the reign than the declaration of Smith, and yet the latter was not nonsense.

It may be said of the Tudors, from Henry VII to Elizabeth, that they strengthened royal authority, infringing the law especially in collecting revenues but for the most part staying within its bounds. From Henry VII onwards, the crown cultivated the middle class, and Henry VIII faced no opposition from that quarter when he carried out many executions of members of the old nobility and created new nobles obligated to him. Those executions, according to one writer, "constitute as flagrant examples of tyranny as can be found in the sixteenth century [in England], but the definition of treason was expanded by act of parliament, and the executions rarely took place until arrest had been authorized by warrant and guilt had been pronounced by a jury or by the peers of the accused."[22]

The Royal Council, so powerful in the days of the Lancastrian kings, was converted into an instrument of the Tudors; there continued to be nobles among its members, but men of the middle class were more prominent. Under Henry VIII a small group of the Council was chosen to attend the monarch wherever he was, whereas the rest remained occupied at Westminster. The former came to be called the privy council.

In 1539 Parliament enacted the *lex regia,* which "gave to proclamations made by the king in council the force of law, provided they did not destroy the force of existing law or impose punishment extending to forfeiture or loss of life or limb."[23] It is explicit in its language, but it spelled out a medieval right of the monarch and did not create a new one. In the same year another statute deprived councilors of a vote in Parliament unless they were peers (and as such could vote in the House of Lords) or had been elected to the House of Commons. As a result the councilors now sought election to Commons, usually with success, and the tie between the kingship and Commons was made firmer.

The Tudors used the Council, and through the Council created or extended the sphere of activity of a series of local councils and special courts. The latter took their point of departure to some extent from Roman law. There is dispute about how restrained the dynasty was in employing the courts in question arbitrarily against real or imagined enemies of the public weal, but none about how easy it was for later rulers to misuse them. The Tudors used threats and bribes to bring about the election of members of Commons they chose.

However, they also did much to make the House of Commons more powerful and to enable its members to claim certain privileges, notably freedom from arrest and freedom of speech in their parliamentary capacities. Such privileges were sometimes denied and yet were persistently and often successfully sustained.[24] Finally, royal influence was extended downward into the localities through assigning new importance to the parish (in essence, an ecclesiastical unit) and new powers to the appointed justices of the peace. The latter might appear to be mere tools of the ruler; in fact, they did dispense justice as often as the royal will.

Elizabeth died without issue. In another great irony, the son of her dangerous rival, Mary Queen of Scots, succeeded them both. As James VI of Scotland and James I of England (1603–25), he was the first of the Stuart dynasty. James tried repeatedly but in vain to convert the personal union of England and Scotland that his reign had brought about into an organic union. He was firm, even truculent, in his insistence on the episcopacy in a church now possessing a large and growing number of Puritans (not a denomination, and not many of them were breaking off from the Church of England to form new denominations until later). He affirmed a religious basis for his position; it was he who first made public play of "the divine right of kings." A king, he declared, is responsible to God alone and is the sole legitimate fount of power on earth. Such claims led Parliament, meeting several times during his reign, to tangle with him. The climax was the Great Protestation (1621):

> That the liberties, franchises, privileges, and jurisdictions of Parliament are the ancient and undoubted birthright and inheritance of the subjects of England, and that the arduous and urgent affairs concerning the king, state, and defense of the realm . . . are proper subjects and matter of council and debate in Parliament.

In a fury James dissolved that parliament, summoned another, and died soon afterward.

Within days of his accession, Charles I (1625–49) was moving toward collision with his first parliament. The king's demands for revenue or "supply," counterdemands from the Commons for enforcement of anti-Catholic laws and Puritan-sponsored morals, and foreign adventures produced a formidable mixture leading to dissolution of two parliaments. When Charles opened the Third Parliament in

1628 with curt insistence on more revenue, Commons replied with the Petition of Right.

The document affirmed: "no man hereafter [should] be compelled to make or yield any gift, loan, benevolence, tax or such like charge, without common consent by Act of Parliament." Soldiers were not to be billeted in homes; no martial law was to be declared in peacetime; and imprisonment was to be possible only on specified charges. It was to be a milestone in English constitutional history, spelling out rights that indeed had their antecedents and precedents but had lacked explicit and systematic exposition.

Charles agreed to the Petition of Right. Nevertheless there promptly ensued a dispute between king and Commons over a form of previously existing taxation, called tonnage and poundage, which were customs duties granted as every reign began since Edward III's. There was a legal case to be made for the king's position, but the Commons' trust in him was fast disappearing. After a scene of open defiance of the king, Parliament was dissolved in 1629 and Charles undertook to rule without one.

He persisted for eleven years, skating on the margin of illegality to produce financial expedients sufficient to run the government. In 1634 a tax on seaports, called ship-money, was extended to the whole country. A country squire from Buckinghamshire named John Hampden refused to pay and was convicted in court—but was acquitted, so to speak, by public opinion. Meanwhile the High Church and anti-Puritan policies and practices of the archbishop of Canterbury, William Laud, aroused growing antagonism in England. When the king attempted to impose the Anglican form of worship on Scotland, however, he provoked resistance from a whole people.

To obtain support in subduing the Scots, he summoned a body whose leaders had been waiting for this moment: the Short Parliament of April–May 1641. Deadlock was immediate. The king now had to call the Long Parliament (1641–60). Led by Hampden, the hero of ship-money, and financier John Pym, it passed a bill of attainder for Charles's chief lay assistant, the earl of Strafford; it proceeded to require triennial convoking of Parliament, abolished the special courts, and compelled the king to accept what it had done. Meanwhile Puritans were overthrowing accepted forms of worship, and conservative-minded people recoiled into support of the king in both religious and political respects; the Irish also preferred Charles to the Protestant zealots.

The die was cast. The king himself tried to arrest five leaders of Commons within the walls of the House; Parliament submitted to Charles nineteen propositions that would have conveyed sovereignty into its hands. The monarch took refuge in the north with about one hundred members of Lords and Commons and raised his standard at Nottingham in August 1642.

The Civil War was to last four years. By and large the gentry, clergy, and peasants stood by the king; the middle classes and many nobles took the side of Parliament. In 1644, at Marston Moor, the royalist cavalry was decisively defeated by Oliver Cromwell, a country gentleman, and his newly trained troops termed the Ironsides. About a year later, at Naseby, the main royalist army was wiped out, and by early 1646 Charles was a king without an armed force.

But the victors now had fallen out. Parliament had committed itself to a Presbyterian state church; the army was by this time heavily influenced by Independents, who were radical Protestants separating from the Church of England but also opposed a religious establishment of "presbyters." One section of the Independents in the army formed something close to a political party determined on radical change: the Levellers. Their leader, John Lilburne, was a thoroughgoing democrat in a pre-democratic age. The Levellers produced a document termed the Agreement of the People; they demanded that it be submitted to popular referendum. It provided for a unicameral parliament elected by universal manhood suffrage and a bill of rights that parliament could not abridge.

The Levellers' proposed constitution (for that is what the Agreement was) had been drawn up only when the king had rejected an offer made by Cromwell for a compromise settlement. Cromwell had great difficulty maintaining a middle way between the Levellers and Parliament, which tried for its own peace with Charles while the army was busy defeating a combination of Scots and royalists in the so-called Second Civil War of 1648.

Now the army purged Parliament; a small Rump of fifty or sixty remained. The king was beheaded in 1649—the only British monarch ever to be executed. The Rump Parliament abolished the monarchy and the House of Lords and proclaimed England to be a "commonwealth" controlled by the single remaining chamber; thus the Agreement of the People was roughly put into effect, without having been adopted. Or rather, its principles were proclaimed; for the reality of the revolutionary government was military despotism presided over by Cromwell.

The Levellers were challenged from the far left by a small group of "True Levellers," or Diggers, whose spokesman was Gerard Winstanley. In 1649 they attempted to seize and cultivate unenclosed common land and to give what they grew to the poor. They preached agrarian communism, denounced private property as the chief root of evil, and declared that "Jesus Christ is the head Leveller" —that is, "True Leveller" or Digger. They were forerunners only and had no significant impact on their time.

The main thrust of the English Revolution lay just ahead. It was a revolution in the sense of overthrowing (temporarily) a government and not merely a person or persons in authority; it was also one of the four great religious wars of the period.

France. Charles VII was succeeded by a talented statesman of repulsive character. Louis XI did much, perhaps more than any other king, to create a formally unlimited monarchy. He revoked the Pragmatic Sanction of Bourges, but when it became clear that the papacy would do little by way of compensation for that concession, he reasserted royal power with regard to the church. Louis's hatred of his father led him to reverse Charles's policies wherever he could; he often deprived nobles of official positions or pensions simply because they had served Charles VII faithfully.

Louis XI made every effort to reduce the power of the feudal lords. He managed to annex both the duchy and county of Burgundy, and in rapid succession acquired Anjou, Bar, Maine, and Provence. Brittany was to lose its autonomy during the next reign when King Charles VIII married its duchess. The royal domain had come to be nearly identical with France.

In 1484 Charles VIII was still a minor. During that year's meeting of the Estates General, Philippe Pot, seigneur de La Roche, declared that when a king is incapable of ruling "government and guardianship" are temporarily transferred to "all subjects of the crown, of what rank soever they be." [25] One writer declares that such contentions, "startling though they may sound to those unfamiliar with the Middle Ages, have been aptly described as 'commonplaces of the schools' [that is, of the learned men of the great universities]," and this particular statement may be related to the interests of the noble house of the Beaujeus, who were powerful advisers to the throne. [26]

Nevertheless such declarations paved the way for legal and actual limitations on the power of the ruler and guarantees of the rights of his subjects, not only in France. On the occasion in question, a number of statements of grievances and desires were presented, but after heated argument the Estates General adjourned with minimal result.

For the time being the current ran in the direction of a strengthened, not weakened, monarchy. The Beaujeus were bolstering royal officialdom by appointment of men well trained in administration and finance. The King's Council, consisting of a few high officials, several nobles, and many lawyers, at this stage usually operated in three parts: a High Council concerned with policy matters, a treasury, and the Parlement of Paris. The Parlement, originally consisting of royal princes and great nobles, through the infusion of lawyers had been turned into a virtual instrument of the crown; over and over it had successfully combated the claims of nobles and clergy and relegated them to royal jurisdiction. On the territorial and political foundations laid by Louis XI, the crown was steadily growing in power.

Charles VIII, attracted by the "wealth and splendour and weakness of Italy" as it approached the era of the High Renaissance, invaded it in 1494 [27]—but to little profit. Francis I did better, and his Italian successes led to the Concordat of Bologna (1516), by which the king chose the bishops and abbots although the pope was to receive the annates (the first year's revenue of churchly holdings subject to the king).

Francis inaugurated two policies of the French monarchy that seemed paradoxical but were to be pursued for centuries; he put out tentative feelers to the Protestants of Germany, and he formed an entente with Suleiman the Magnificent, sultan of Turkey. Both had in view the curbing of the Habsburgs, whose domains encircled France under Charles I and V, Francis's contemporary, and remained strong in both Austria and Spain when Charles's heirs divided his inheritance.

Henry II undertook to pursue the contacts with the Protestants, whose envoys offered the French king the "three bishoprics" (Metz, Toul, and Verdun—that is, much of Lorraine) in return for his assistance; he occupied them for good. He also seized Calais from the English, who were supporting his Habsburg adversaries at that point. The peace made at Cateau-Cambrèsis in 1559 then terminated the wars between the Habsburgs and Valois.

In the preceding decades there had been several wars in which the religious issues between Protestants and Catholics, and sometimes between Protestants and Protestants, had been present; but the peace of 1559 is usually considered the point after which dynastic motives pass to the background and the "wars of religion" ensue for a century. In fact, the phrase wars of religion is used specifically to refer to the conflicts in France (1562–98), though it may also designate the broader category including the Revolt of the Netherlands, the Thirty Years' War, and the Civil War in England.

Herbert J. Muller has plausibly asserted that what worked the English middle classes up to fighting pitch was not economic factors but their Puritan religion.[28] There were also people in those days who seemed the incarnation of religious zeal and at root were anything but. Of Catherine de' Medici, the dominant personality of what was now the most centralized state in western Europe, it has been said that "it is the greatest mistake to imagine that any confessional fanaticism lay at the bottom of her political action. . . . Her chief motive was the desire to govern, and her husband's death gave her the opportunity at last."[29] She was the mother of three kings in a row and was the real ruler during their reigns.

The monarchy had gained ascendancy over the nobles of the previous, feudal times; but they were not ready to knuckle under. Many nobles joined the Huguenots (the French Calvinists) and thereby turned a ragtag band of burgesses and lawyers into a power in France. In the 1550s the king and Huguenots sparred with each other, and noble and Third Estate demands for a continuing role in government were voiced in the Estates General, summoned in 1560. Soon afterward civil war broke out.

The war troubled the country intermittently for thirty-odd years. In the infamous Massacre of St. Bartholomew (1572), Catherine tried to wipe out the Huguenot leaders. In 1576 the last of her sons, Henry III, accepted the so-called Peace of Monsieur (such was the official title of the duke of Alençon, the king's brother), which granted religious liberty in a sweeping manner, exempting only Paris and the court from the right of the Huguenots to worship as they chose. It was the product of a new and growing body of Catholics called *politiques* who wished religious peace. But a group of intransigent Catholics opposed the Peace; in 1589 a monk murdered the king, and the house of Valois came to an end.[30]

The crown went to Henry of Navarre, who had been king of the fragment of Navarre north of the Pyrenees that remained after Spain seized the rest. His house, the Bourbons, were to be kings throughout most of the remaining years of monarchy in France. At that point he was the leader of the Huguenots. He still had to fight for his throne, abjuring the Protestant faith in 1593 before being crowned. However, he sought and obtained religious peace at last by granting in 1598 toleration in the Edict of Nantes—a very successful measure, though less extensive in its provisions than had been the Peace of Monsieur.

Henry IV had much success in restoring an effective kingship over a united country. There were still a few provinces, in particular Languedoc and Brittany, which as *pays d' états* retained self-government by their old Estates, but most of France was *pays d' élection,* where royal officials held sway. Henry differentiated the clerical and lay dignitaries on the Royal Council from the twelve real administrators appointed by himself, and he had a secret council of four, chief among them the Huguenot duke of Sully, who advised him most intimately. He undermined the liberties of the cities; and let the Estates General wither. In contrast, he unwisely strengthened the Parlements when, in 1604, he introduced a system that made membership hereditary and independent of the monarch. Thereby he secured the *paulette*—a sixtieth part of the value of the offices each year—which aggregated a sizable sum but left to Henry's successors a growing problem.

Sully restored solvency to the French state, but he did not alter the burdensome system of taxation whereby the *taille* (direct tax on the land or houses of the lower classes) and *gabelle* (salt tax, again affecting the unprivileged only) made up the chief sources of revenue. The feudal lords were reduced to a shadow, but the Huguenots, possessing almost 100 towns and nobles so powerful that they could raise an army of twenty-five thousand as compared with the peacetime royal force of ten thousand, offered a new threat to the power of the monarch.

From the standpoint of high culture, there is little doubt: the seventeenth century was France's greatest. It was a striking example of how toleration benefits all parties. The Huguenots thrived; "nor was the air of freedom less favorable to the Roman Church in France, which now entered on its most glorious period, and the end of Protestant liberties was the end also of Gallican [French Catholic] brilliance."[31]

Henry IV was assassinated in 1610, and fourteen years of confusion followed. The States General were summoned in 1614 to quell an incipient revolt of Huguenot nobles, who objected to the *paulette* and were suspicious of the rapprochement with Spain that the boy-king's advisers had arranged. (The Estates General would not meet again until 1789—or, more precisely, they would never meet again, for at that time they instantly turned into something else.)

Louis XIII was not a nonentity, but he was overshadowed by the Cardinal-Duke of Richelieu, a man "of surpassing ability devoid of all engaging human weakness," who became his chief minister in 1624.[32] As a cleric he was not memorable; as a statesman he has had few equals in all modern history.

The Thirty Years' War began in 1618 and was not concluded for six years after Richelieu's death in 1642. However, it was his victory, rather than anyone else's, over his chosen enemy, the Habsburgs, rather than any religious group, that shaped the outcome. Domestically Richelieu had to deal with the Huguenots as an armed force, which he overcame by the capture of La Rochelle in 1628, but he was careful to leave them their freedom of religion. When he died, leaving affairs in the hands of Cardinal Mazarin as regent for the five-year-old Louis XIV, he bequeathed to them a much-consolidated royal power. He had employed a category of officials known as *intendants* effectively, and he had prevented the nobles, Huguenot and Catholic, from getting out of hand.

In 1648 the Peace of Westphalia codified the French triumph and yielded France much territory; yet the old nobles rose against the crown in the adventure termed the Fronde, in a curious show of indifference to the settlement. The old "nobility of the sword" was soon mastered; the "nobility of the robe" to be found in the Parlements, who sought "to substitute government by law for government by royal or any other irresponsible will,"[33] lasted longer, and both rebellions were not put down until 1653. Mazarin was back in power, and Louis XIV, in the longest of all reigns in the annals of recorded history, was about to put his stamp on a whole Age.

Italy and Iberia. The French successes in northern Italy at the turn of the sixteenth century had repercussions in other parts of the peninsula. Girolamo Savonarola, the Dominican prior in Florence, predicted doom for a wicked city, and Charles VIII obliged by making his appearance. The result was the expulsion of the Medici rulers and the purification of the republican institutions that the

Medicis had flanked and used for their own purposes rather than abolished. The reform drew partially on Venetian models. About three thousand citizens of Florence, men who had certain qualifications based on age and officeholding, were to govern. Unlike in Venice, however, appointment by lot was abolished, and no head of state comparable to the Doge was to be named. Savonarola helped bring about his own ruin and execution, and the Medicis returned in 1512.

As for Venice itself, it boasted institutions retaining some Greco-Roman characteristics and was, in the view of A. J. Grant, "the most perfect specimen of an oligarchy known to history."[34] Its Senate and Council of Ten managed a trading empire whose diplomats were inferior to none on the planet and whose commercial location was perhaps superior to all others—until the Turks blocked the eastern Mediterranean and the Portuguese and Spaniards discovered other routes to the Orient.

The papal states were brought under some degree of real control by Rome, in part owing to the exploits of the notorious Cesare Borgia, son of Pope Alexander VI. He was one of the so-called "Renaissance popes," on whose shoulders moral considerations sat lightly and who spent much of their energy as well as money on embellishing the Eternal City with art. They were also drawn into the war and diplomacy of the French invasions of the Italian peninsula. The attention of Pope Leo X (son of Lorenzo the Magnificent, who was the best known of the Medicis) was thus fixed in almost every direction except Wittenberg, where Martin Luther would in 1517 nail up his theses and thereby inaugurate the Reformation.

In the south there were two institutional features virtually absent elsewhere in Italy: monarchy and feudalism. At the end of the fifteenth century two Spanish dynasties ruled: the illegitimate branch of the House of Aragon in Naples, and the legitimate branch of the same house, whose scion was now the king of united Spain, in Sicily and Sardinia. In Naples the great nobles, so alien to culture and politics as to convince Machiavelli that nothing could be done to improve things unless it was decided to "wipe them out entirely," had assisted some unpleasant monarchs to stifle the liberties of the towns. In the early 1500s, the Spanish royal house acquired Naples; they would rule there until 1713.

Finally, an obscure state in the western Alps, Savoy, under heavy French influence at the outset of the sixteenth century, began a rise to prominence; its duke, Emanuel Philibert (1553–80), made headway in curbing the power of the nobles and establishing an effective ducal authority of his own.

Italy lacked unity, was the plaything of foreign rulers and armies, and remained for centuries longer, in Metternich's words, only a "geographical expression." Yet in the cities of the north free men raised painting and sculpture to the greatest heights to date, practiced self-government with impressive success, and demonstrated a capacity for living happy lives—skills also shared to some degree in the center and south of the peninsula.

After a lengthy period of preparation during which the Iberian peninsula had been in fragments, Spain rocketed into the first rank of European powers and became the metropolis of the first empire to be built across the oceans—along with that of Portugal, whose overseas possessions were on a smaller scale.

Portugal's achievement was the most astonishing of the Age of Discovery, epoch-making as it was for much of Europe. This tiny state sent out expeditions that crept along the African coast to round the Cape of Good Hope (1497) and reached India, where Goa soon became headquarters for the Portuguese in Asia, and finally China at Macau. The expedition (though not the person) of Ferdinand Magellan circumnavigated the globe in 1519–22. Wealth flowed into the country during the reign of Manoel I, who inherited the strengthened royal power his father had gained through harsh measures against the nobility.

However, at that point Portuguese luck seemed to fail. The refusal of John II to support Columbus's proposal for a voyage westward appears symbolic; the expulsion of the Jews in 1496 was a grave self-inflicted wound on Portuguese society. The sixteenth century saw a pause and then a decline. In 1580 Portugal passed under the rule of Philip II of Spain, and was to regain its independence only in 1640 by way of revolt supported by Richelieu's France. John IV, first king of the House of Braganza, inaugurated a period in which the power of the monarchy waxed, that of the nobility waned, and the overall prosperity of the country slid downhill.

For the first time since the Visigoths Spain became a reality as a result of the marriage in 1469 of Isabella, at the time the uncertain heiress of Castile, and Ferdinand of Aragon, carried out in secrecy in a modest house in Valladolid. She succeeded to the throne of Castile, then he to the throne of Aragon (1479), including the Balearic Islands, Sicily, and a claim to Naples. In 1492 a campaign against Granada, unwisely provoked by the Moorish ruler, ended after several years by conquest of that state. In 1512 Navarre was annexed. Only Portugal remained outside the new entity called Spain. In 1492 the first voyage of Columbus, financed by Ferdinand and Isabella (though they too had initially refused, as had the Portuguese king), began the great Spanish empire, mainly in the New World but extending as far as the Philippines, whose very name was taken from Philip II.

Spain under one pair of rulers retained the separate institutions of Castile, Aragon, and Navarre, but the *reyes catolicos* sought to construct a unified and absolute monarchy. Faced with the strength of feudalism in Aragon, Ferdinand and Isabella concentrated on increasing the power of the crown in Castile. They removed all but three of the nobles who had dominated the Royal Council, and it now contained in addition one cleric and eight lawyers. It had both judicial and administrative functions and exerted some influence in legislation, actually though not legally throughout Spain, not merely in Castile.

The rulers appointed officials called *corregidores* to control the cities, and they in turn had a decisive say regarding which burgesses were sent to the Cortes of Castile—which still had three separate chambers of clergy, nobles, and commons (representing many peasants in the capacity of citizens of towns they lived near, as well as the townsmen themselves). Ferdinand was elected grand master of the great orders of knighthood—Santiago, Calatrava, and Alcántara—and was able to draw on their great wealth in distributing patronage.

The great nobles had often placed younger sons in the richer appointments of the church, but the *reyes* gained control over many of them. Nevertheless, the property of the nobles was little affected. Exempt from taxation and enjoying many legal privileges, the nobles comprised an array that ranged from the twenty-five grandees through the rest of the titled nobility to sixty-thousand hidalgos, or knights, and a comparable number of urban nobles. The lineaments of this hierarchy, all sharply distinguished from the common people, were spelled out by Charles I in 1520. The distinction would be long lasting.

In Aragon there were four chambers in the Corts, habituated to act rather more independently of the monarch than was the case in Castile and entitled to join in the approval of legislation. But the Aragonese Corts was also brought to heel by Ferdinand and Isabella. Ecclesiastical instruments were important too: foremost, the Spanish Inquisition (different from the papal or Roman Inquisition, a less fearsome agency). Its zeal to discover hidden Jewish beliefs backfired and provoked a cessation in conversions and even reversion of converted Jews to Judaism. The upshot was expulsion of the Jews and, as in Portugal, loss of much wealth and ability. The Moors of Granada, at first treated gently and fairly, were the victims of a drastic turnabout in policy. It must be said that what Ferdinand and Isabella did to the Jews and Moors reversed the tradition of the medieval Spaniards. Some of Spain's most notable figures of the period were *conversos* or their descendants: St. Teresa of Avila, the great jurist Francisco de Vitoria, the defender of Latin American Indians Bartolomé de Las Casas, the humanist Luis Vivès.[35]

The device of royal marriage had united Spain permanently; it was now to produce yet more spectacular, though transitory, results. Mary of Burgundy, daughter of Charles the Bold, held the loyalty of Flanders after her father fell at Nancy in 1477, and thereupon it "was lost to France forever."[36] She hastened to marry Maximilian, prince of the Habsburgs—who at this point were far from what they would become. Their son Philip married Joanna, Ferdinand and Isabella's daughter, younger than both a brother and a sister but nevertheless finally heiress of Spain.

The son of Philip and Joanna, after his grandfather hesitated between him and his younger brother as the more suitable heir, at last became king of Spain as Charles I and Holy Roman Emperor as Charles V. He was master of more than half of western Europe and most of the New World. There was much luck in that amazing outcome, though whose was the luck may be debated, since Spain was drawn into many burdensome affairs it might otherwise have escaped.

From the first Charles was clumsily disrespectful of the rights of the Cortes and the privileges of the regions and citizens of Spain. Soon a rising (1520) of the northern towns *(comuneros)*, led by Toledo, took place that appeared dangerous to the throne; it was suppressed as its leaders fell out with one another and the nobles tardily combined to resist. The monarchy was not well entrenched. The towns retained some autonomy but were watched over by the *corregidores;* the Cortes continued but only eighteen "royal towns" now sent deputies, who were mainly urban nobles exempt from the taxes they were willing to vote.

Charles proposed to infringe the nobility's exemption from taxation in 1538, but the reaction brought him to execute a hasty retreat. The Spanish nobility remained free of obligations and an ever-heavier burden on the common people. Unable to restore the religious peace Luther had broken, Charles fought several wars with France, often over Italy. The last one was concluded by peace in 1559; by that time the king-emperor had abdicated in an access of weariness and ill health to enter a monastery.

His successor, Philip II, zealously pursued not religious peace but victory in the struggle with Protestantism. Succeeding to all his father's possessions except Germany, he added Portugal, winning the crown partly by Spanish arms. But other extra-Iberian involvements were failures. Even the memorable naval victory over the Turks in 1571 at Lepanto had little result because it was not followed up. He sent a Spanish army into the Netherlands to put down the Dutch revolt in 1567. It finally proved impossible to do. To cut off English help to the Dutch, Philip dispatched the great Armada in 1588, which was destroyed. In 1609, after his death, a truce in effect would yield acceptance of Dutch independence, while the south, Flanders, was to remain under Spanish rule, though only the Peace of Westphalia in 1648 recognized the "United Provinces" as independent in law.

At home, however, Philip's power reached new heights. The Cortes of Castile and Aragon still met, but the royal bureaucracy became increasingly formidable; Philip ruled through the Royal Council and other councils that were founded during his reign, with little challenge.

Reddaway asserts that "Spain had owed her amazing rise to the emergence of exceptional public servants"—Ferdinand and Isabella, Columbus, and Charles I, among others.[37] In the "Golden Century"—a slight misnomer for 150 years, the whole sixteenth century and the first half of the seventeenth—Spaniards attained the first rank in religion, law, art, and literature.

In contrast, the political scene was less inspiring. Philip III (1598–1621) was a religious recluse whose chief minister, the Duke of Lerma, presided over a system of court-centered corruption. Noble estates grew to gigantic proportions; high nobles were given a share in government. The royal administration, leaning heavily on lawyers, was reasonably efficient but was hampered by a decline in agriculture, industry, and trade, and specifically by the vast debts the state had accumulated. Lerma expelled the Moriscos (converted Muslims suspected of retaining faith in Islam), inflicting thereby further economic damage on the country.

Before Philip III's death, Spain was plunged into the Thirty Years' War. Before that war ended, Philip IV's reign had brought Spain new troubles. He chose an able minister, the Count-Duke Olivares. The minister could not reverse the introduction of high nobles into the central administrative picture, but he had plans of broad scope for governmental reform that he could not bring to fruition. By endeavoring to make the laws of the non-Castilian lands uniform with those of Castile, he provoked the great revolt in Catalonia that lasted thirteen years (1639–52). He finally managed to put it down, but he lost Portugal for good (1640). The splendid army of the Spaniards, the envy of Europe for over a century, was defeated by the French in a crucial battle at Rocroi in 1643. Spain had passed the crest of its greatness.

Central and Eastern Europe, 1450–1650

The Empire. Frederick III, "a handsome, placid fainéant," is memorable for five things, none representing any particular achievement of his own: he was the first Habsburg to succeed a Habsburg as emperor (thereby beginning a series nearly unbroken until 1806, the end of the empire); he married his son Maximilian, the real founder of the family's fortunes, to Mary of Burgundy and thereby can claim much credit for the creation of Charles V's world-empire; he adopted the five-vowel motto, *AEIOU* (*Austriae est imperare orbi universo,* or, *Alles Erdreich ist Osterreich unterthan*), which he did next to nothing to make reality; he was the last emperor to be crowned in Rome (1452), a distinction that had little effect on anything but symbolized the empire's retreat, geographically and otherwise; and since the last Byzantine emperor died along with the fall of Constantinople, he was the first emperor to have no rival in the East. Of greater importance than these points was his conclusion of the Concordat of Vienna in 1448, whereby he supported papal defiance of the last phase of the conciliar movement and in return gained a degree of control over the church in Habsburg lands that lasted for centuries.

His son Maximilian attempted once again to reform the empire. The Diet at Worms (1495) set up an Imperial Chamber Court *(Reichskammergericht)*. The main significance of this body was to bring about the full reception of Roman law in Germany, since doctors of Roman law were to make up half the membership initially and as time went on it was necessary for the other half as well to be learned in the subject. In 1498 the Court acquired a competing body in the Aulic Council *(Reichshofrat)*, which later took over much of its jurisdiction.

In 1500 and 1512 a total of ten imperial circles *(Reichskreise)* were set up to preserve the public peace. They included most of the 240 states of the empire, though not the tiny domains of the multitudinous imperial knights or Bohemia, Prussia, and effectively independent Switzerland. The Estates of the various principalities survived and in several cases grew in strength, but that process did not necessarily mean significantly limiting princely power. "In general," writes Waugh,

the Estates of fifteenth-century Germany were opposed to the partition of principalities; they were eager for peace, internal and external; and they encouraged sound administration and the employment of capable officials. Thus, while apparently placing limitations on a prince's authority, they were often really helping to increase it.[38]

The principalities' Estates were as indifferent, however, as their princes were (both lay and ecclesiastical) to the concerns of Germany as a whole. Many cities were experiencing a marked decline in their power and considerable restriction on their liberties; whether they tried to act individually or in groupings seemed to make no difference. Even the Hansa could not bestir itself. The power of the princes grew steadily; the power of the emperor did not.

Thus within the empire the shape of the future began to be perceptible. In 1417 the Hohenzollern family had established itself in Brandenburg. By the *dispositio Achillea* of 1473 it was enacted that the German custom of division of inheritance among sons should not apply to this state. A junior branch of the family headed the Teutonic Knights, whose lands were just to the east. To the west of Brandenburg lay Saxony, divided between the two brothers Ernest and Albert by a compact of 1486, the Ernestine portion retaining the electorship; for many years it was held by Frederick the Wise, soon to become the patron of Martin Luther and the guarantor of Lutheran survival. In the south, Bavaria under the Wittelsbachs had great strength and a related family held the Palatinate, located close to France, where the elector Palatine was the most important of all German lay princes. Bavaria seemed capable of absorbing the Swabian lands to its west, and the Habsburgs tried to prevent any such thing by encouraging a buffer to form around the count of Württemberg.

It seemed that the imperial election of 1519 offered a chance—perhaps the last chance—of making the empire once again into some kind of unified entity. Charles V emerged as emperor from a welter of bribery and intrigue, combining Spanish and Austrian lands with his new crown—but before final acceptance he had to promise to levy no new tax, make no war or treaty, convoke no Diet, without approval of the seven electors.[39] But his failure to unify the empire was not chiefly caused by such promises.

The most important obstacle to genuine unification had already come into view: Luther's criticism of Rome, which became defiance and finally led to schism (or, as Roman Catholics believed, heresy) in the church. Some princes became Protestant, some remained Catholic, and there was for years no room for religious minorities: the prince determined the religion of the state. There could be no political unity while religious disunity persisted.

When Luther made good his safe departure from the Diet of Worms (1521), the potentiality of lasting ecclesiastical division was apparent. A rising of imperial knights claimed affinity with the reformers, but was put down by the princes, without help from the imperial authorities. A great Peasant Revolt also seemed to associate itself with the movement. The Twelve Articles of the peasants (1525) demanded redress of their grievances against the excessive exactions of their lords and the power of the princes, appealing at every step to the Bible and Christian teaching for support. Again the princes joined to crush the revolt; Luther, after hesitating, called for the harshest measures—"strike, throttle, stab"; later he acknowledged that he had "commanded them to be slaughtered."[40] Luther broke not only with the peasants but with the gentler humanists and the more intransigent and radical Anabaptists.

And thus the Magisterial Reformation was thrust back on the protection of the princes. Frederick the Wise, elector of Saxony, having preserved the Lutheran movement through the crucial years, died in 1525. But other princes took up the cause: Philip, landgrave of Hesse; Albert, margrave of Brandenburg and grand master of the Teutonic Order, now secularized, so that he became the first "duke of Prussia"; and others. Several imperial cities followed suit, among them Nürnberg and Augsburg.

The Habsburgs stood firm as Catholics. In 1526 they were bolstered in an ironic way by quite different events. After the capture of Constantinople, the Ottoman Turks had paused for a time, then renewed their march of conquest. In 1517 they took Cairo and installed in Egypt a Turkish governor who left ruling to the Mamluks; in 1526 the greatest of the sultans, Suleiman the Magnificent, advancing to the north, defeated and killed King Louis of Hungary and Bohemia at the battle of Mohács.

Now Ferdinand, Charles V's brother, was chosen to succeed him as king in both realms (though only a small fraction of Hungary remained outside Turkish rule for the next 170-odd years), and he managed to hold Vienna against Ottoman siege. However, neither Ferdinand nor Charles could turn his energies fully toward crushing Protestantism, because Francis I of France waged several wars against the Habsburgs in cooperation with Suleiman, and from 1536 in formal alliance with the Turks.

In 1531 the majority of Protestant principalities and cities joined in the Schmalkaldic League (from the town of Schmalkalden in Thuringia). In the face of the Ottoman danger it was agreed that intra-German quarrels should be laid aside; in the meantime several more cities and states, notably Württemberg and ducal Saxony, went over to Lutheranism.

Charles V wished mightily to heal the religious breach, and a general council was summoned to try. But war could no longer be postponed among the Germans; for nine years, off and on, the two sides fought before concluding the Religious Peace of Augsburg (1555). Formally it was a "recess" (legislative act) of the Imperial Diet; in effect, it gave princes (but not the imperial government) the choice of Catholic or Lutheran ("the Augsburg Confession") religions and their subjects no choice at all.

Protestantism had won something of a victory. But by now the Roman Catholic church was mobilizing for counterattack. The new Society of Jesus served as spearhead; the Council of Trent (concluded in 1563) inspired the resistance by its decrees. The Counter-Reformation made remarkable progress in several areas. Bavaria was reclaimed for Rome; Cologne was narrowly held; Bohemia was superficially scoured clean of Protestantism, with the expulsion of the Bohemian Brethren; the Habsburgs imposed severe restrictions on the Protestants of Hungary and stopped their growth. The small imperial city of Donauwörth was forcibly wrenched away from Protestantism; the response was formation of the Union of Evangelical Estates and then the Roman retort in the Catholic League.

The Lutherans had been joined in their break with Rome by the Calvinists, whose "hostility to Rome was much keener; their ideas on theology and church government more definite; their organization much better."[41] The followers of John Calvin, the greatest figure of the Reformation, had made palpable gains in France, Switzerland, Poland, Hungary, and Transylvania before the Counter-Reformation rolled them back in the last three named. In Scotland they captured the country—their only permanent conquest of the sort. The two Protestant groups were sharply at odds with each other, and as time went on divisions within Protestantism were not reduced but multiplied.

On Charles V's abdication in 1556 his domains were divided into two parts: the Spanish Habsburgs were to last until 1700; the Austrian Habsburgs would survive in power into World War I. Powerless to revive the institutions of the weakening empire, for the second half of the sixteenth century they concentrated on their family holdings. By the recess of the Diet of Augsburg in 1555 the "imperial circles" were given greater administrative authority; the result was to diminish the power of the emperor.

Since religious antagonisms had prevented election of a president of the Imperial Chamber Court in 1608, that body was suspended. It was replaced by the Aulic Council, a change that might have been expected to buttress the emperor's authority. The effect was negligible. The circles were too strong.

The Circles embodied a permanent arrangement, comprising both strong and weak states, with a Diet for each Circle and a president chosen by themselves. The disturber of one Circle found himself faced by one, three or five of them, according to his estimated strength. If necessary, the five might appeal to the senior Elector, the Archbishop of Mainz (Mayence) to summon representatives of the Imperial Diet to Frankfort. Only if all this proved insufficient, was the Emperor petitioned to convoke a full Diet. Autonomy could hardly be more amply affirmed.[42]

The German nobility proliferated in number, since the noble transmitted his title to all his sons, and in numerous cases his property was divided among them, so that the class could not grow in strength. The principalities and princely houses were separated by old rivalries. As religious antagonisms were added to and compounded with them, the doom was sealed of any further attempts to unify the empire.

Religious antagonisms were important in the Thirty Years' War (1618–48), which administered the *coup de grâce* to imperial unity; some feared it would destroy all of Germany. But from the start political considerations were also present and became more significant as the war continued.

The grievances of the Bohemian Protestants provoked the "defenestration of Prague," in which two Catholic governors were thrown out the window of Hradčany castle but survived. The result was war. Ferdinand, duke of Styria, the most uncompromising Catholic of the Habsburg line, was elected emperor (as well as king) in 1619. He smashed the Bohemians in the battle of the White Mountain in 1620, virtually destroying Protestantism among the Czechs, greatly damaging their national pride, and left bitter feelings still unforgotten in the twentieth century.

Three successive champions kept the Protestant cause alive: Christian IV of

Denmark, Gustavus II Adolphus of Sweden, and none other than France's Cardinal Richelieu, who had been providing subsidies to the foes of his church. Finally he intervened with French troops.

The Peace of Westphalia[43] (1648) brought to an end the dreadful conflict that reduced the German population by perhaps one-half. It marked a crucial legal and political watershed. In Reddaway's words:

> For the medieval theory of Pope and Emperor, the Peace substituted a family of equal independent territorial states. It was henceforward to be assumed, indeed, that these states were born to be friends. Wherever and whenever necessary, diplomatic representatives were exchanged between them, and were regarded as sacrosanct. To imprison one of them on the outbreak of war marked the barbarism of the Turks, a power lying outside Europe and fundamentally hostile. Europeans traded with one another, except for good cause, and likewise admitted each other's subjects to their realms. But their religion henceforth admitted of no outside interference, unless such was desired by the individual state. The Pope influenced only those countries which welcomed his intervention, and the Emperor was merely the senior among the sovereigns of Europe.[44]

The territorial results of the peace may be summarized thus: Sweden received part of the southern coast of the Baltic; Brandenburg was awarded adjoining lands in compensation for the rights to Pomerania it gave up; France received title to most of Alsace-Lorraine; the independence of Switzerland and the Netherlands was recognized.

An eighth elector was designated for Bavaria. But who elected the emperor and ruled the empire henceforth mattered little. Each state within it could make alliances (if not directed against the empire) and the prince could conduct his own affairs, including the choice of religion (either Catholic, Lutheran, or, now also, Calvinist), although subjects who did not accept the choice he made had the right to emigrate. The *Reichskammergericht* was re-created, but it had little power. Germany was both devastated and reduced to political fragments.

Scandinavia.   To the north, the union of three Scandinavian kingdoms agreed upon at Kalmar (1397) was sporadically effective for some decades. Christian I (d. 1481) was king of Denmark, Norway, and Sweden, but his powers were severely limited. John (d. 1513) was the last to reign in all three. Christian did his best to impose effective Danish control on Sweden, to make the hereditary character of the monarchy secure in Denmark, and to assert the authority of the ruler. In an attempt to do so he called the four estates together for the first time (1468), the peasantry being the fourth estate. His aim was to circumvent the national council, where the clergy and nobility were strong. But Christian roused domestic rebellion and foreign attack, and failed in all his aims.

Efforts to renew the Union of Kalmar got nowhere. Gustavus Vasa, a young nobleman, led a Nationalist party (one of the earliest modern uses of the term) to Swedish independence, and he himself was elected king in 1523. Another person, the duke of Holstein, was invited by the Danish bishops and nobles to become king of Denmark and Norway. The Union thus came to an end. (A smaller union, however, continued; Norway remained united with Denmark until 1814.) Gustavus also broke the ecclesiastical tie with Rome and secured control over the Swedish church. The crown now became hereditary in the house of Vasa.

Meanwhile Christian III, a contemporary of England's Henry VIII, presided over the triumph of the Reformation in Denmark and secularized church properties. He began to support the Protestants in the empire. Norway followed the religious path of its Danish masters. In contrast, Sweden under the Vasas rose to become the chief power in the Baltic and, for a time, a European and even a world power. Its rise was perhaps due to the stronger monarchy, weaker nobles, and the less-dependent peasantry that the Vasas had inherited, in comparison with the more aristocratic system in Denmark. In a sixty-year reign, Christian IV (1588–1648) was powerless to arrest the decline of Danish strength. His withdrawal from the Thirty Years' War was followed by Gustavus II Adolphus's spectacular intervention with Swedish forces. He also managed to annex Ingria (1617) through war with Russia, and, through war with Poland, he added Livonia (1629) to the Estonia his predecessors had won in 1561.

Gustavus Adolphus conciliated his domestic opponents so that they would not impede his foreign adventures, crowned by the event (the battle of Lützen, 1632) to which the epitaph on his tomb in Stockholm refers: *Moriens triumphavit*, "he was victorious at the moment of death." But his chief contribution to his native land was the Form of Government approved by the Estates in 1634, which "placed Sweden at the head of Europe as a well-ordered constitutional country."[45] The departments of justice, army, navy, diplomacy, and finance were each given a single official assisted by a group termed "college," and these five plus fifteen other members made up a council that had much influence and in the minority of Queen Christina (1632–54) more or less ruled the nation. The chief figure during that period was Gustavus's chancellor, Axel Oxenstierna, whose wisdom enabled Sweden to continue its rise to world power.

Poland, Hungary, and Transylvania.   If the Germans of the Holy Roman Empire were having their troubles, the Germans to the east were also. Casimir IV of Poland-Lithuania (from 1440 to 1492 the grand prince of Lithuania, from 1446 the king of Poland as well) had still to deal with the Teutonic Knights, who had escaped apparently inevitable destruction after suffering defeat at Tannenberg in 1410. He was called in by dissident nobles who had leagued together against the grand master of the Order; but the Poles were worsted again and again, until

Bohemian mercenaries overcame the Knights. By the Second Peace of Thorn (1466), Poland annexed West Prussia and permitted the Teutonic Order to retain East Prussia only as a vassal state of the Polish crown. The proud and independent-minded Polish nobles unintentionally prevented the demise of the Knights by the way in which they hampered Casimir's freedom of action.

During the Teutonic wars Casimir IV had to concede "the principle that he would neither summon the army nor raise taxes without prior consultation with the nobility" (1454).[46] The result was the formation of "the basic unit of constitutional life in Poland-Lithuania," the *sejmik,* or dietine (that is, "little diet"), in which the nobles of each province met regularly to consult, though there had been earlier less formal means of such forgathering. Several particular types of *sejmik* came in time to discharge particular functions in regard to the Sejm, or Diet, for all Poland and the royal tribunals.

The nationwide Sejm may have been inspired by the Estates of West Prussia after 1466. It seems that the king first summoned it in Cracow in 1493 and that it was extended to include Lithuania after the union of 1569, shortly to be mentioned. The Sejm had an upper house called the Senate and a lower house called Izba Poselska (Chamber of Envoys—that is, from the dietines to the capital—a not inapt term).

Poland was on its way to an emasculation of the central government not unlike that occurring in the Holy Roman Empire, of which Lord Bryce had observed, apropos of the confirmation of the Golden Bull of 1356 by Charles IV, "he legalized anarchy, and called it a constitution."[47] Norman Davies implies agreement with the view that the Polish constitution was "a derivative, if not a copy, of the German system."[48] The difference was that German disintegration was chiefly based on territory, Polish on class.

The nobility, or *szlachta,* increased its power steadily from the late fifteenth century. In 1496, at Piotrków, the king granted the class a monopoly of landholding. Moreover, henceforth appointment to the highest ecclesiastical positions was limited to nobles. Alexander, first ruler of Lithuania and then also of Poland, endeavored to use the Senate, composed of senior clerics and royal officials, to curb the nobles; instead, he had to accept the statute *Nihil novi* at Radom in 1505, which required of any new law the approval of both chambers. The principle *Nic o nas bez nas,* "nothing concerning us without us," was in effect made law, the basis for the "noble democracy" that Poland was fast becoming.[49]

In the sixteenth century, the rise of the Polish nobility—moving in the direction of 9% as compared with Spain or Hungary's 5%, France's 1%, and England's 2%—was accompanied by measure after measure that tightened the reins of serfdom on the peasantry. Did all this amount to feudalism? It seems that there were elements akin to the system of the West for part of the fourteenth and fifteenth centuries, along with significant differences.

The system taking form in Poland was extended to Lithuania under the reign of Sigismund II Augustus with the Union of Lublin (1569). The amalgamation of Poland and Lithuania was made firm and lasting; the Lithuanian nobles were made equal legally to those of Poland and brought into the Chamber of Envoys. In the interregnum following the king's death, the non-Catholics secured religious liberty in sweeping terms most unusual for the period via the Confederation of Warsaw (1573).

By this time the Counter-Reformation was achieving dramatic successes in Poland, not slowed and possibly even hastened by the Confederation of Warsaw, and affected Lithuania as well. Catholic zeal and educational excellence began to exert an impact on the Eastern Orthodox who made up much of the population of the grand principate, finally resulting in the Union of Brest (1596) by which a large share of the Orthodox of the *Rzeczpospolita*—the Republic, the official title of the post-1569 state—accepted the authority of the Roman pope but retained their liturgy and ritual. The Lublin Union, by transferring the Ukraine from Lithuania to Poland, bolstered the tie of the new "Uniat" church with Rome.[50]

A "confederation" in Polish law was a recognized device from at least the early fourteenth century. It was a league of armed men who swore to persist in their cause "until justice was obtained."[51] The confederation was a device ever more frequently used up to the last years of the eighteenth century, when Poland was torn to pieces. Another oddity of the Polish system was the *liberum veto,* which meant that any member of the Sejm could stop its deliberations simply by saying "I do not agree." Usually the stoppage was temporary in the early years, but beginning in 1652 it was employed with mounting frequency. The result of such practices was to paralyze central government.

The dynasty itself—the Jagellonians, who had ruled since 1386—perished with Sigismund II. Henry of Valois was elected on condition that he accept the right of the nobles to elect the monarch and consent to severe restrictions on the ruler's power, but within a few months he threw it up as a bad job and returned to France to become Henry III. A capable successor, Stephen Bathóry, prince of Transylvania, concluded peace with Russia after the long Livonian War with Ivan the Terrible of Muscovy, but could do little with the Polish nobility.

A Swedish prince of the house of Vasa now succeeded as Sigismund III, "the Jesuit King." He was twice able to place Roman Catholic rulers—the second, his own son—on the throne of Moscow. It was the highest point of Polish political influence on Russia (though the peak of cultural impact would come only in the late seventeenth century).

With the loss of Livonia (taken from the Teutonic Knights in 1561) to Sweden in the 1620s and the ending of the adventure in Muscovy, the Polish tide receded from foreign parts. Ladislas IV (1632–48), who had been tsar of Russia briefly in his youth, tried to restore the religious toleration that his father Sigismund had infringed. He avoided entanglement in the Thirty Years' War; but John II Casimir, who acceded in 1648, began a reign during which the country almost fell apart in a series of complex events called the "Deluge"—a great Cossack insurrection, leading to the Muscovite annexation of the Ukraine, a Polish war with Muscovy, and Swedish and Turkish intervention—but ultimately survived.

The fortunes of Hungary during this period were often linked with those of Poland and also of Bohemia (which was part of the empire). In the crusade of Varna (1444), the last serious Western attempt to save Constantinople from the Turks, Ladislas III of Poland and Hungary had died fighting. The great soldier John Hunyadi had sought to avoid that calamitous defeat and had won other victories for which he was made regent; but both he and the boy-king died within a few months of each other.

Hunyadi's son, Matthias Corvinus (1458–90), became perhaps the most notable of all Hungarian kings: statesman, soldier, and patron of Renaissance culture. With doubtful wisdom he fixed his attention on Bohemia, which he thought of being a step toward the imperial throne from which he could lead a crusade against the Turks. However, he was compelled to yield the Bohemian throne to Ladislas, son of Casimir IV of Poland, and turned to a struggle with the Habsburgs, in which he conquered Moravia, Silesia, and Lower Austria. Establishing his capital at Vienna (1485), he dazzled Europe with its splendor.

Matthias Corvinus was succeeded in Hungary by the king of Bohemia, Ladislas. He was nicknamed "King Dobre" (O.K.) because he was reputed to say that to every paper laid before him, and was a "helpless prisoner" of the Magyar magnates, as Macartney puts it.[52] The Diet, which was nothing but a "mass meeting of the nobles, brave but undisciplined, exempt from taxation and contemptuous of the peasants,"[53] hamstrung Ladislas's efforts to rule. In 1514, just after a peasant revolt had been suppressed, the Diet solemnly bound the class to the soil. The measure was repealed a few years later, but the condition of the peasantry in much of eastern Europe had deteriorated into what has been called a "second serfdom," while the serfs in the west were moving out of their dependent state. Ladislas fared no better in Bohemia, which he neglected for Hungary, and where the aristocracy grew in property and influence as the townsmen and peasants lost proportionately.

Ladislas's son Louis II (1516–26) replaced him on both thrones. Weak and profligate, he fought Lutheranism with scant success in Bohemia as well as Hungary; and led a poorly disciplined army against the Turks. They killed him and smashed his soldiery at the battle of Mohács (1526), then advanced to besiege Vienna before withdrawing. Hungary was partitioned between the western strip, which went to the Habsburgs, and the eastern portion over which John Zapolya, leader of the Hungarian nobility, was king—until he died and Suleiman the Magnificent annexed central and southern Hungary directly.

When that occurred, the Turks left Ferdinand of Habsburg in his own fragment, for which he paid the sultan tribute, and John II (Sigismund) Zapolya as prince of the nominally vassal state of Transylvania but actually head of an autonomous entity. Three "nations"—the Magyars, Szeklers (Magyarized indigenous inhabitants), and "Saxons" (Germans)—met in a *Landtag*, elected the prince, and enacted legislation. The mass of the Romanian peasantry, who made up the basic population of the region, had no part in these constitutional arrangements.

For a time Transylvania flourished. Calvinism swept the country, followed by Unitarianism, which was perhaps born there. The nobles were strong enough to frustrate the plans of Prince Sigismund Báthory (1581–1602) to join the Habsburgs in a crusade to roll back the Turks. But Bethlen Gábor (1613–29), who made Transylvania "the center of Hungarian culture and national feeling,"[54] opposed the Habsburgs as the Thirty Years' War broke out. And George Rákóczi I skillfully carried Transylvania through the conflict.

In 1650 the Peace of Westphalia had just ended the tribulations of war for the sorely tried empire; the territories to the east had not suffered in the same way but were having difficulty in preserving independence, unity, or prosperity in the face of external dangers. In the previous two centuries Poland, Bohemia, and Hungary had often had monarchs who ruled two or even all three of the realms, because the proud nobles tried to avoid raising one of their own number to kingly dignity and because foreign newcomers had small chance of taming the native aristocracies. Poland seemed to move steadily toward a weakening of the central government. Hungary proper was a part of the Ottoman Empire, which would soon show itself to be strong enough to march on Vienna again. Bohemia's religious and political aspirations had been tamed by the Habsburgs. The promise of Transylvania was to prove transitory.

The Balkans and Russia.   After the Ottoman conquest Byzantine and Christian traditions of a sort survived in Serbia, which enjoyed autonomy for its Orthodox church from 1557 to 1766, and the Romanian principalities of Wallachia and Moldavia, whose rulers were vassals of the sultan but retained considerable independence in fact. Basil Lupu, prince of Moldavia from 1534 to 1653, presided over a council of Orthodox churches, held in Iasi, his capital, and including representatives of Constantinople and Kiev; he also patronized Greek culture in a striking "neo-byzantine" fashion.[55]

In the sixteenth century, the sultans, in particular Suleiman the Magnificent, systematized the so-called feudal system that had been taken over from Byzantium by the early sultans. The *timar* (the Persian equivalent of *pronoia*) was a small fief conferred on soldiers for meritorious service. Personal service might carry one to a larger estate, the *ziamet,* "but his son unqualifiedly had to begin with a *timar.*"[56] The fief holder (*sipahi*) had to furnish a certain number of horseman for the army or sailors for the navy (as did European vassals).

But the differences were crucial between the feudalism of the West and the Ottoman institutions that seemed to correspond to it. First, the tenure of the lands of the Ottoman fief holders was not fully hereditary. Second, the *timar* and *ziamet* (though not the *khass,* a larger fief given to provincial governors) were subject to inspection by special officials. These men were agents of the sultan, yet they gained for themselves the right of arbitrary enfeoffment and deprivation of fiefs, and used it liberally. Many fief holders managed to evade their obligations to furnish armed men.

Suleiman and successors of his tried to curb such abuses but had only limited success. As the "feudal" troops became less dependable, mercenaries took a more prominent role in the army. The core remained, however, as before the Janissaries, the product of the levy of Christian boys ten to fifteen years old that continued until about 1700. The army was well disciplined; the officialdom was not. It was ridden with corruption, venality, and cruelty. The great forays into central Europe were followed by campaigns to the east as well.

But the Ottoman Empire acquired a formidable eastern rival when a homogeneous Iranian state was restored by Ismail. He was proclaimed shah and decreed the Shi'a to be the official faith in 1501, founding the Safavid dynasty. As for the Ottomans, they seemed to have exhausted their energies. From the last years of the sixteenth century they fell into a rapid decline, from which they would be partially and temporarily rescued by an Albanian grand vizier. For the outside world, it seemed that "the imposing outward strength of the Ottoman Empire concealed the deep weaknesses of a military autocracy with a decaying social order. The moral bond of religious unity was of diminishing effectiveness. Corruption and disorder in government and a decline in standards were aggravated by economic backwardness."[57] Nevertheless, the Muslims in the Balkans, western Asia, and North Africa held on for decades and even centuries after it appeared that their empire was near collapse.

The Muslims in Russia—for such the Tatars had become—were another story. Ivan III the Great of Muscovy faced them off in a bloodless confrontation in 1480, subsequently called "the end of the Tatar yoke." He had more powerful enemies than the flimsy shred of the once-great Mongol Empire to which he now refused tribute. He fought Lithuania, annexed the merchant republic of Novgorod (1478) and the principality of Tver (1485), the most formidable rival of Moscow remaining in Russia.

Ivan III buttressed his claims and pretensions as a newly independent ruler by marrying the niece of the last Byzantine emperor, though she brought into Muscovy the influences of the Italy where she was reared rather than those of Greece. Notions of *translatio imperii,* earlier mooted in connection with Constantine, Charlemagne, and others, were now given the form "Moscow, the Third Rome."

This ideological tag should not be taken too seriously. It was an ecclesiastical not a political or national claim; in any case, it amounted to a repudiation of the Byzantine heritage, since the "Second Rome" (Constantinople) had perished for its sins and deservedly so, according to the monks who worked all this out. Russia sought acceptance rather in the "family of European nations whose sovereigns were equal in status," a notion that "resembled neither the Christian universalism of Byzantium nor Philotheus' [the cleric who first used the "Third Rome" phrase] notion of a world supremacy exercised by the Muscovite tsardom."[58]

Ivan III informally styled himself "tsar" (from "Caesar"); Ivan IV did so formally. Thereby they desired to assert the independence of their state; that was the reason for the term "autocrat" ("the one who himself rules") when adopted. But over time the term took on additional meaning, as the elements of pluralism in Muscovite society diminished under assault from the power of the monarch.

The causes of the process by which Russia became an autocracy, or despotism, are in dispute; the nature of the end result, much less so. The Russian nobility was a curiously amorphous and weak group, never approaching the strength enjoyed by the powerful class that led the way to Britain's limited monarchy, much less the oligarchy constituted by the Polish nobles. Before the Table of Ranks in 1722 there was not even a generic name for the nobility; there were simply the tsar's "service people of various degrees." Over several centuries two main groups may be discerned: those who held land by hereditary tenure (boyars) and those the tenure of whose land was conditional on service (*pomeshchiki,* who came to be the same as *dvoriane,* or gentry) on the model of the Ottoman and Byzantine empires.[59]

The core of the Muscovite boyars was the nontitled families who entered the service of the Moscow prince in the fourteenth century. However, many were later taken into his service from the lesser princes, though cautiously, on what was in effect a probationary status. They continued to hold high positions right down to the reign of Peter I. It was the landholding gentry, however, on whom the tsars came to rely most, and they in turn were dependent on the rulers.

Ivan IV the Terrible (the English term is not an exact translation but renders the character of the monarch accurately enough; 1533–84) killed and plundered many real or imagined enemies. The pressure he exerted on the peasantry drove them into increasing dependence and in the direction of serfdom and provoked much flight to the south of Muscovite borders. In killing his only strong son, the tsar destroyed the dynasty that had ruled since Kievan times.

Despite all this, there seems to be little evidence that he changed very much the nature of the nobility or the autocracy that dominated it. Beginning in 1549 he several times summoned an Assembly of the Land (*Zemskii Sobor*), which had similarities with the estates of West European countries, but neither in Ivan's reign nor subsequently was it effective in claiming comparable prerogatives. Soon after 1662, when townsmen demanded in vain that one be called, it withered and died.

Ivan IV conquered two fragments of the Mongol Empire, Kazan and Astrakhan; and the newly forming freebooter bands, called Cossacks, overcame a third, Sibir, which gave its name to the whole vast expanse stretching beyond it to the Pacific. But the tsar became trapped in a long and inconclusive Livonian War with Poland and Sweden and in the course of it lost the tenuous foothold on the Baltic he had earlier gained.

There followed the brief reigns of Ivan's surviving son, a weakling, and the ill-fated Boris Godunov. Then came the "Time of Troubles" (1604–13), when Polish armies captured Moscow twice and a series of shadowy figures claimed the throne for short periods. At least twice interesting constitutional experiments were undertaken, when the "boyar tsar" Vasily Shuisky and a little later Ladislas, prince of Poland, on acceding to the Muscovite throne, promised to consult the realm and accept limitations on the power of the tsar. But they were abortive, and they needed more than a piece of paper to prevail in the face of the "state stronger than society" (according to Paul Miliukov) that had existed before the "Troubles" and was restored in 1613 when Michael Romanov was elevated to the throne, the first ruler of Russia's last dynasty.

The Swedes withdrew from Novgorod, which they had occupied, but still blocked access to the Baltic for another century. Several Russian towns were handed over to the Poles when peace was made with them. In 1639 Cossacks reached the Pacific Ocean after a rapid crossing of Siberia. Other Cossacks took Azov, a Turkish fortress on the Black Sea, but could not hold it.

In 1645 Alexis succeeded Michael, and in 1649 a new code of laws (the *Ulozhenie*) was issued. Since the code finally reduced the Russian peasantry to serfdom and provided no secure protection of anyone's rights or privileges, it did not seem to harmonize well with the gentle and unworldly personality of the young tsar. But both Michael and Alexis, mild as they were personally, still presided over a state where the autocrat was supreme, the gentry dependent on him, the commercial classes servants of state needs, and the peasantry enserfed (or nearly so). All Peter I needed to do was to turn the screws a bit to produce a despotism that was, if not tidy, at any rate tidier than before.[60]

Conclusion

By the early sixteenth century, writes George H. Sabine,

absolute monarchy either had become, or was rapidly becoming, the prevailing type of government in western Europe. Everywhere there was an enormous wreckage of medieval institutions, for the absolute monarchy was a thing of blood and iron which rested in large part quite frankly on force.[61]

It is true that during the period 1350–1650 the national monarchies of the West took great strides toward territorial unity and royal supremacy. What Sabine calls "the most characteristic of all medieval institutions"—the church—suffered tremendous losses. The great wealth of the monasteries was seized by both Protestant and Catholic rulers; the secular power of clerics was much curtailed, the ability of popes to claim equality (or even superiority) for the *sacerdotium* in relation to the *imperium* had vanished, and the ecclesiastical legal system was decisively limited to the church itself. Much clerical property was either handed over or fell into the hands of the rising middle class. At the same time the excesses of feudal warfare were curbed and the nobles brought to heel.

All this was so, and yet it is wise to guard against the historians' temptation to draw sharp lines that would puzzle most of the people who lived in the neat periods that the textbooks distinguish. For one thing, the new "absolute" monarchs inherited not merely their crowns and properties but their legitimacy: they could profit from the feudal tradition of personal loyalty to the lord and the medieval Christian conception of sacred kingship. But by the same token they could not throw off the limitations on what they could do that were the heritage of feudalism and medieval Chrisitianity. If they tried, they might still provoke protest—as, for example, the English Petition of Right—or revolt—as in the case of the Fronde in France and the English Revolution.

The absolute monarchs did not rely mainly on "blood and iron." Muller declares, "by and large the kings were a progressive force, the leaders in more rational government. Ideally representing all classes in the nation, to a reputable extent they did in fact serve the interests of all but the most ambitious nobles." And to this plausible position Muller adds an assertion not quite so convincing: the nobles had "no ideal of constitutional government, only a selfish interest in recovering their feudal privileges."[62] No doubt that was so in many instances:

Muller cites the Wars of the Roses, the Fronde, and the Polish reduction of the kingship to impotence.

The Polish case is the clearest one. The nobles of Poland reduced the monarchy to a nullity, and went on to emasculate their own assembly, the Sejm. The result was to court partition by neighboring powers, which totally removed Poland from the map for a century and a quarter. And yet even that dismal record had another side. In the words of the novelist James Michener:

Poland loved freedom; it was a restricted freedom, to be sure, and it applied only to the very rich, but nevertheless it was freedom. Specifically, every incident in Polish history testified to the nation's determination to avoid autocracy and dictatorship.[63]

The peasant majority had too little freedom, and the noble minority far too much. Perhaps what was of still greater importance was the weakness of the monarchy —the institution that in other countries enfranchised and set free the peasantry, curbed the ambition of the nobles, and contributed to the rise of the middle class. But the absence or presence of rights and privileges in one social group may still affect the consciousness of the nation as a whole, and so it was in Poland. Moreover, its record in regard to the several ethnic groups within the borders of, say, 1772 (Jews, Ukrainians, Germans, and others), was far from perfect but was much better than that of a number of other European countries.

Thus Poland, though it was soon to perish, made its contribution to the history of free societies, as did Hungary, Bohemia, and even Russia (that is, Muscovy) in the period in question to a less striking extent. The Scandinavian countries and Spain and Portugal took part also. Spain often has been credited with originating the absolute monarchy of early modern Europe, and by the seventeenth century the kingship was powerful indeed—and yet the nobles and the church were by no means securely in royal control.

In fact, European "absolute monarchy" is something of a misnomer. The claims of "divine right" made by and on behalf of James I may in retrospect be regarded as having paved the way for revolution and civil war, and never were turned into reality. Such absolutism as there was had its chief exemplar in France, and later than 1650.

In any event it was during the period concerned here that political theory came to be most developed in England, France, and North America. Building on clear medieval foundations of a polarity or plurality of powers, duties, and functions as described and defended by a series of clergymen, the theorists undertook to defend as well as write critically of the role of monarchs. From Niccolo Machiavelli (1513) through Jean Bodin (1576) and the anonymous *Vindiciae contra tyrannos* (1579) to Richard Hooker (1594–97) and Thomas Hobbes (1640–51), the new (or at least significantly transformed) role of the ruler was examined from every angle.

Machiavelli admired what he considered the free and self-governing Roman republic, but it had been gone for sixteen centuries, whereas before him stood the Renaissance princes—the intelligent and ruthless rulers of the Italian states of his day and also the kings of Spain, France and England: Ferdinand, Louis XI, Henry VII. The latter, he said, were justified in founding a state or setting one in order; but once that was done, the people should participate in government.

Bodin found a lack of morals and indeed philosophy in general in Machiavelli. The latter sometimes in fact got carried away with his admiration for such possessors of *virtú* as Cesare Borgia. Bodin did seek to indicate limitations on the power of the monarch, which he believed lay in both divine and natural law; however, he also maintained that the sovereign was the source of law. The family was basic to society, and the rights of property were essential to the family; therefore the ruler could not take property without consent of the owner, and the king could tax only with the consent of the estates. The contradictions are evident (and Bodin has more than the ones just mentioned).

Machiavelli antedated the Reformation; Bodin sought to heal its wounds on the *politique* assumption that Catholics and Protestants would exist side by side in France and elsewhere and must do so in civil peace. Both writers came from Catholic countries.

The Protestant legacies were complex. They included both the duty of strict obedience to rulers and the justifiability of resistance to them, and ultimately, through the law of unintended consequences, the growth of freedom. Luther declared, "I wish to be free," and refused "to become the slave of any authority" (even though he insisted upon the authority of the Bible, as he interpreted it). He argued for "spiritual liberty" but not at all necessarily for political liberty. In his mature political position, he set forth the absolute necessity of obedience to "established authority" (not, of course, popes), however tyrannical or unjust it might appear.

As for Calvin, he was even less a defender of freedom. The regime of Calvin's Geneva, Muller writes, demonstrated that "freedom was the least concern of the Reformers, except as a menace to the monopoly they claimed on the true faith." He believed man to be utterly depraved, a creature "wholly unfit for freedom of any sort," and sternly adjured obedience even to the "most iniquitous kings."

Nevertheless, having challenged authority, asserting the right of men to think for themselves, the Protestants were apt to be open to new thought and, writes Muller, "thence to ideals of freedom of thought, speech, and press." A further step led to a right of resistance. Even in Calvin's Geneva, Christopher Goodman held that even the common people had such a right if the magistrates tried to take away all their "power and liberty." The position was then expanded and generalized by the *Vindiciae contra tyrannos,* and was acted upon by the Puritans, in the English Revolution and in New England.[64]

The author of the *Vindiciae*[65] was a French Huguenot who held religion to be the determining factor in the life of the state. Government is justified by a double contract, the first between God on the one hand and the ruler and people on the other, and the second between ruler and people. The king's power derived from God, yet if he violated God's law—that is, became a heretic and adopted false doctrine—it was justified to resist him; in fact, it was the duty of the people to do so. But it was not lawful for an individual to resist (unless the king was an usurper, and then regicide was warranted); it was for the corporate bodies of the realm, led by nobles and other "principal persons of the kingdom"[66] to represent the people in any legitimate resistance. Thus went a French Calvinist argument for a right of resistance.

In contrast, from English Anglicanism came one challenge to any right of rebellion and another ringing defense of absolutism. Richard Hooker's book *The Laws of Ecclesiastical Polity* (1594 and later) was intended to refute England's Calvinists—that is, the Puritans. In "the last great statement of what might be called the medieval tradition," Hooker affirms that civil society rests on common consent, that the law of the community ultimately derives from divine law, and that church and state are (in many respects) one. The Puritans, he argues, would separate them and perhaps make the church dominant. "Laws they are not which public approbation have not made so," he declares. Moreover, to govern without consent is tyranny. Nevertheless, there is no justification offered for resistance or rebellion. Government and church are indissolubly linked, and they are, for Hooker, English—that is, national; and here the medieval view is compromised.

Finally, with Thomas Hobbes's *Leviathan* (1651) the medieval conception is transformed beyond recognition. True, the church and state are identical as far as government is concerned, but the state, and in particular the monarch, is supreme. There had been a disorderly condition of mankind wherein the life of man was "solitary, poor, nasty, brutish, and short," and it had been terminated by a social contract. But the contract conferred such power on the sovereign that it was virtually unlimited—a subject could not be forced to injure himself or confess to his crimes, but practically in every other way he was at the king's mercy—and could not be withdrawn. Even if people considered him a tyrant, they had no right to resist him. In Hobbes's system there is no room for intermediate bodies, corporations, or associations. There is a monarch and individual human beings, each motivated by self-interest; there is nothing significant in between.

Hobbes tried to make all this part of an integrated and systematized view of the world resting on geometry and mechanics—materialism, as it may be called today. He has much to say, indeed, on religion and the church, but none of it touches him. He is the spokesman of absolute monarchy par excellence. And yet he would not have been a suitable servant of an oriental despot because of his individualism—which is, writes Sabine, the "thoroughly modern element in Hobbes and the respect in which he caught most clearly the note of the coming age."[67]

Not only religion but also sentiment, culture, and history had no place in Hobbes's scheme. Already one perceives another "modern" element in his writing: the conviction that politics must be assimilated to physical science. He wrote much about "power" and little about "justice" or "freedom." In such respects he has many imitators in the late twentieth century, and seemingly few challengers.

Nevertheless, as Muller points out, he was not "a reliable guide to the history of his own age. [For] under a limited monarchy with guaranteed rights his own country would become the stablest, strongest nation in Europe."[68] Hobbes had taken up his pen in defense of his king. Charles I had perished, but his kinsman Charles II, a rather less able and attractive figure, would set England on the path Muller indicates.

In the century ending in 1650 the religious wars, which were the upshot of the Reformation, did a good deal of damage to the cause of freedom while they were in progress. Many suffered for their beliefs in the course of the Wars of Religion in France, the Thirty Years' War, and the English Civil War and the period of the republic (Commonwealth and Protectorate) that it inaugurated, and no pluralistic political institutions were introduced while they raged. However, the aftermath was more promising. In France the peace-making king, Henry IV, issued the Edict of Nantes. In the empire, the Peace of Westphalia accepted a wider religious and political diversity than preceded the Thirty Years' War. After the Restoration of the Stuarts in Britain, free institutions resumed their growth.

In some respects the clearest gain to freedom came in the religious war that lasted the longest: the revolt of the Netherlands, which erupted in 1568 and was formally ended only by the peace of 1648. The seventeen provinces had been brought under the rule of Spain by Mary of Burgundy's marriage to the Habsburg Maximilian and division of Charles V's domains at his abdication in 1556. It had no real institutional unity, despite the introduction of an Estates General in 1463 based on French models, whose meetings were "conferences of ambassadors rather than a real instrument of central government."[69] The individual provinces were the significant political units, each with its governor (*stadhouder*) and its estates, the cities having their own institutions in addition.

Sentiments for church reform owed their beginnings in the Netherlands to

Erasmus of Rotterdam and were deepened by the spread of the ideas of Martin Luther. However, the newly established Netherlands Inquisition in 1529 prescribed death for those who even discussed such notions (unless they were theologians). After Philip II became king of Spain in 1556, he reorganized the bishoprics in a manner placing appointment to them in royal hands. The immediate result was resistance, in the form of both words and violence. First Philip withdrew the Inquisition and peace was restored; then he sent an army under the Duke of Alva, who imposed a harsh regime.

William, Prince of Orange, inaccurately called "the Silent," took the leadership of the seventeen provinces but was unable to keep them together. In 1579 the southern provinces made peace with Spain; the seven northern provinces replied in the Union of Utrecht, which led to the Republic of the United Provinces (and later the Kingdom of the Netherlands). It was the first federal government of modern times.[70] To begin with, each province remained nominally independent, and unanimity of the seven was required for any important decision.

However, the Estates General of the seven provinces proceeded in 1581 to formal abjuration of the authority of Philip II: when a king fails in his duty to cherish his people as a shepherd does his flock, "he is no prince but a tyrant. Then may the Estates of the land legally remove him and put another in his place."[71] And thus what moderns would call the right of revolution, the assertion of which could be traced back in the Christian tradition as far as Augustine at least, was finally acted upon, or at any rate used as justification of a step that scandalized many contemporaries. William the Silent was assassinated in 1584 and had no single successor of his political ability. But the provinces stuck together; in 1609 Spain conceded a Twelve Years' Truce.

Although Dutch independence was acknowledged only by the Peace of Westphalia in 1648, the seven provinces from the beginning of the century extended their commerce round the world, established colonies in both hemispheres, and registered astonishing achievements in culture. They pioneered religious freedom by reluctantly accepting the formal toleration of Arminians (who followed the path of Erasmus in asserting free will against the Calvinist view of predestination) and Roman Catholics.

In Hugo Grotius the Dutch produced the founder of modern international law in his *On the Law of War and Peace* (*De jure belli ac pacis,* 1625). Like Erasmus defending the reality of human freedom, Grotius sought to establish in the natural law that he drew from the ancients a basis for relations among states. In a world where the assumptions of a universal state (the Empire) and church were vanishing, he sought to chart rules and limits that all might accept. Their acceptability was maintained on the grounds that they were as certain as geometry.

As a Christianity that could bind—or serve—both Protestants and Catholics fell out of reach, the natural sciences of the seventeenth century seemed to replace it as a basis of certainty. Thomas Hobbes, Baruch Spinoza, Samuel Pufendorf, and others adopted the language and methods of mathematics to buttress their views on politics and ethics. It would become clear later that physics and mathematics could be used either to support freedom or attack it; moreover, as a basis for certainty in religion, philosophy, or politics the natural sciences proved unreliable. In one respect the Renaissance and Reformation, however, bequeathed a gift, or burden, of lasting character: the idea that individual conscience and judgment must take precedence over collective, corporative, and institutional determinations. The idea would take centuries to work itself out and to clarify its implications for freedom.

CHAPTER 7

The Birth of Constitutional Government, 1650–1800

Sometimes it is difficult to see in which directions ideas may lead. John Calvin declared that men had no right to rebel against even the "most iniquitous kings," and yet the Dutch, led by their Calvinist majority, carried out the first modern revolution against the Spanish monarchs. In England the seventeenth century saw every variety of political doctrine thus far expressed. The unprecedentedly egalitarian Levelers and the communist Diggers passed from the scene without a trace; the temporarily ascendant Puritan and republican dictatorship vanished; and the relaxed, often corrupt, unsystematic monarchy of the restored Stuarts was the institution from which democracy evolved, in Britain and, it may be argued, indirectly in America. Or, as Herbert Muller puts it, out of the English revolution came

the triumph of parliamentary government, with a bill of rights—the triumph of the main principles asserted by the men who had started the struggle against James I. This outcome, which set England squarely in opposition to the tendencies prevailing in all the monarchies on the continent, was certainly its pre-eminent contribution to the history of Western freedom.

The unplanned, unintended, and "mostly unwanted" revolution became, Muller declares, "the prototype of the great political revolutions that have made Western civilization so radically different from all the Eastern civilizations."[1]

All of this is certainly so, with one important exception: what made Western civilization different from the civilizations of the rest of the world in respect to polity, society, and economy was not political revolution on any model, that of the

English or any other. It is not at all necessary to denigrate the importance—positive and negative—of the English, American, or French revolutions or to argue that they had no significant effect in order to perceive that the ingredients for the social and political order of the modern West were to be found in embryo in medieval times.

By the fifteenth century—often thought to be a particularly miserable period—the West had a pluralistic society with a strong tradition of both law and private property and an accepted doctrine that the individual was of value in the sight of God. This was true of Britain, especially in England, the most centralized of any of the larger nation-states of the West, which had a Parliament counterpoised to the monarchy, a strong legal tradition, and property at the disposition of lords and merchants; France, where the Estates General, *parlements,* and various local bodies might challenge the king, and great lords still had much to say along with a rising middle class; of Spain, where the estates of the component parts of the new unified state survived; of Germany, where there was still an imperial struggle to produce national unity but the real balance of social forces was to be found within the smaller and even tiny political components of the empire; of Italy, fractured between the states of a freer and progressive north and of a poor and retrograde south; of Poland-Lithuania, just having forged a dynastic union with central and local representative bodies; of Hungary and Bohemia, enjoying fluctuating connections with the empire and a plurality of social forces; and of the one, two, three, or four Scandinavian states uniting and dividing, isolated except when they wished not to be (as in the Thirty Years' War) from many of the conflicts to their south, enjoying growing representative institutions with peasants possessing separate representation. (Japan had a number of the same features but requires different terminology.)[2]

Britain, 1650–1801

After the execution of Charles I, England proclaimed the republic that it called the Commonwealth, and Scotland and Ireland proclaimed Charles II as king. Cromwell massacred the Irish and defeated the Scots, and Charles fled to France. Soon the Instrument of Government, a written constitution, gave Cromwell the title of Lord Protector of the Commonwealth and established a one-house Parliament replacing the remnant of Commons that existed on the eve of creation of the Protectorate. The Humble Petition and Advice of 1657 restored a second house and deprived the Protector of the power to exclude members of Parliament, which he had used liberally; it also enacted toleration of all Trinitarian Christians except Anglicans and Roman Catholics. A few months after he had been offered and had rejected the title of king, Cromwell died. Since the office had been made hereditary, his son Richard became Protector, but after eight months was persuaded to resign. The Rump Parliament followed; Charles II was now summoned by a newly elected Convention Parliament to be king.

In the previous twenty years, England had lived through perhaps the period of greatest social upheaval and turmoil in her history. Recent demographic studies (made difficult by the fact that the first national census was conducted only in 1801) suggest that population growth had something to do with the turmoil, but that for a hundred years or so following the mid-seventeenth century the population was stable, which made for political stability as well.[3]

The Restoration (of the Stuarts) did inaugurate a period of stability, despite the brief episode of the "Glorious Revolution." It called back into being the limited monarchy desired by Pym and Hampden, since the Convention Parliament affirmed the validity of all reforms passed by the Long Parliament and ratified by Charles I before September 1641. The courts of Star Chamber and High Commission existed no longer; taxes required the consent of Parliament; the king still had a veto over legislation but could not legislate by decree. Nevertheless, he retained much power over which Parliament had no control. King and Parliament were now close to being evenly balanced.

As for nongovernmental matters, Puritan prohibitions were resoundingly shelved so that dancing, the theater, and games returned, but Anglican prohibitions were enacted in the so-called Clarendon Code (named for the Earl of Clarendon, the chancellor, who actually opposed many of the acts concerned). They required magistrates to take Anglican communion, clergymen and teachers to accept the Anglican book of Common Prayer, and those unwilling to do so ("Nonconformists") to hold religious meetings only in private homes if more than five persons took part.

But the growth of freedom in England is well illustrated by the fact that the Code was partly unenforceable, and its most repressive measure totally so: that was the Five-Mile Act, which required all Nonconformist ministers and teachers to swear never to attempt to change church or state or to resist the king, and forbade those who refused that oath to come within five miles of any place where they had formerly preached or taught.

Charles II tried to achieve greater toleration for Catholics and Dissenters than Parliament was willing to grant, but for the most part he left Parliament to do as it wished and allowed his advisers to conduct the affairs of government. What is more, his was a tolerant reign; on his accession there were only "a dozen or so" executions,[4] and the regicide of 1649 went largely unpunished.

The chief significance of Charles II's reign for the history of freedom lay, however, in the beginnings of the two-party system and cabinets. Clarendon, the chancellor and chief minister, was dismissed in 1667; he was largely the scapegoat for popular opposition to the repressive measures adopted by Parliament after the Restoration. No one official but rather a group of five, called the cabal, now advised the king. The word antedated this moment as a common noun, but it was also by coincidence an acronym for Clifford, Arlington, Buckingham, Ashley, and Lauderdale. They all agreed with the royal policy of religious toleration for differing reasons—two were Catholic, and three were Protestant—and opposed the parliamentary support for Anglican persecution of Dissenters. The cabal did not last long. In puzzling fashion Charles now chose the earl of Danby as his chief minister. Danby was the head of the intolerant-Anglican party in Parliament, but also advocated broad powers for the crown. His opposition was led by the earl of Shaftesbury, a defender of parliamentary supremacy but toleration for Dissenters.

Soon those two groupings acquired nicknames, in both cases at first hostile ones. Danby's people, the Tories, were so called first by Titus Oates, appropriating a term used for Catholic bandits who preyed on Saxon settlers in Ireland; Shaftesbury's followers in retaliation were dubbed Whigs, meaning Scottish Covenanters who were—sometimes accurately—charged with murdering Anglican bishops.[5] Tories included many gentry, their tenants, and clergy, while Whigs combined the larger share of the nobility, the urban commercial classes, and Dissenters.

Titus Oates, an irresponsible rumor-monger, managed to whip up anti-Catholic sentiment by inventing a series of plots attributed to adherents of the Roman faith, climaxed by the affair of the so-called Popish Plot of 1678. Much of this furor battened off popular concern at the likelihood of the succession to the throne (since the king had no legitimate children) of James, duke of York, the king's brother and a Catholic. It led to the Test Act (1673), requiring all officeholders to abjure the Catholic doctrine of transubstantiation and take communion in the Anglican church, thereby excluding Catholics and most Dissenters from office, and the Papists' Disabling Act, which from 1678 to 1829 kept Catholics out of Parliament.

But the passions that triggered public excitement over the issue later cooled, especially as the light-minded duke of Monmouth, the king's illegitimate son, was the alternative the Whigs backed. Parliament passed the Habeas Corpus Act in 1679, which obliged judges to respond to requests to produce the living body of any prisoner and show cause why he was held and forbade reimprisonment of a prisoner for the same offense once he was set free.

The Whigs were for the time being unpopular and weak. Charles brought *quo warranto* proceedings against first London and then several other cities ("boroughs"), a complex legal action that resulted in transfer of power over municipal governments from Whigs to Tories in case after case.

Charles was succeeded by his brother, as he had labored mightily to permit. Though Catholic, James II had as heirs two Protestant daughters, Mary and Anne, by his first wife. The parliament he summoned had a loyal Tory majority but soon balked when he sought to suspend the Test Act, and he prorogued the body. Now he resorted to bloody repressive measures against minor Scottish and English risings, and aroused Protestant fears by appointing Catholic officials in large numbers and asserting his power to dispense with the penalties of the Test Act.

The king attempted to rally the Dissenters to support his policy of toleration for all religions as expressed in the Declaration of Indulgence (1687), but they resisted it strongly. A second version was draw up and ordered to be read in the churches; the archbishop of Canterbury and six other bishops petitioned the king to rescind the order, and most clergy defied it on the Sunday concerned. James had the seven bishops tried for seditious libel; they were acquitted, and scenes of wild rejoicing followed. A few weeks before a son had been born to the king, who had to be expected to be raised a Catholic. The Whigs declared he had been introduced in a warming-pan, but that he was the legitimate son of his father was accepted by most Englishmen, and became a reason for revolt.

A group of "seven eminent persons" now invited William of Orange, ruler of the Netherlands, and his wife Mary (daughter of James II) to liberate the country. William landed in the west of England. James's forces disintegrated, and he fled. William summoned all veterans of any parliament of Charles II and asked their advice. They urged him to assume the headship of government temporarily and to call a "convention" (not formally a parliament since summoned by a person not yet a king), and he did.

Though Tories and Whigs agreed that James II had given up the throne, the succession was debated. The Whigs declared the throne vacant as a result of James's having broken the contract between throne and people, and carried a resolution to that effect in Commons. In Lords, where there was a Tory majority, the principle of hereditary right prevented accepting any such resolution, and Mary was declared the rightful queen. But William refused to be regent or consort. At this, most Tories gave way and joined the Whigs in offering the crown to the Dutch ruler and his wife; they became William III and Mary II. A small group of recalcitrants, the Jacobites (from *Jacobus*, Latin for James), objected in vain.

Thus was consummated the "Glorious Revolution." The events that determined the succession, once James II was driven out, were partly revolutionary—the selection of William III—and partly nonrevolutionary and traditional—the choice of Mary II. More important were the measures that accompanied regulation of the succession. Chief among them was the Bill of Rights, which accompanied the offer of the throne to William and Mary and asserted:

(1) laws could be enacted or suspended only by consent of Parliament,
(2) the dispensing power (asserted by James in relation to the Test Act) was illegal,
(3) the Court of Ecclesiastical Commission and other such courts were illegal,
(4) taxation required parliamentary consent,
(5) any subject had the right to petition the king,
(6) maintaining a standing army without consent of Parliament was illegal,
(7) it was lawful to keep arms,
(8) elections of members of Parliament must be free,
(9) there must be freedom of debate in Parliament,
(10) excessive bail was forbidden,
(11) juries should be empaneled and returned in every trial,
(12) grants of estates as forfeited before the offender was convicted were illegal,
(13) Parliament should be summoned frequently.[6]

It has been pointed out that despite the constitutional importance of this document, only one of the thirteen items was entirely new—that was the ban on standing armies. All the others had formed part of the unwritten English constitution and were here only reiterated for the sake of clarity and certainty.

Additional laws rounded out the Revolution. The Mutiny Act gave the king power to raise an army and rule it by martial law for six months; it was thereafter renewed frequently. The Toleration Act permitted all religious groups to worship freely except Catholics and Unitarians, though civil disabilities for religious belief remained and the Test Act was not repealed. Thus Dissenters obtained freedom of worship; the act has been called "William's answer to the Revocation [by Louis XIV] of the Edict of Nantes."[7] As for the Catholics, a number of petty restrictions remained, but the principle of toleration came to be accepted to such an extent that before long they could in fact worship publicly.

The act licensing printed books and papers was allowed to expire, so that Milton's prescription of freedom of the press was realized. A Triennial Act limited a given parliament to three years. A Treasons Act made the distinction between treason and mere political opposition sharper and gave protection to the accused in treason trials. All the measures mentioned were passed between 1689 and 1696.

Five years later the Act of Settlement dealt with the succession problem that loomed in the future—Anne's son having died. (Anne was the second Protestant daughter of James II and sister to the queen.) The crown was to go to Sophia, electress of Hanover and niece of Charles I, and her heirs. Inserted into this act was the prohibition of the removal of judges except by action of both Lords and Commons.

The succession of William and Mary in Scotland required entirely separate proceedings. Despite Scottish attachment to the Stuarts, the anti-Catholic feeling especially of the Protestant lowlanders led to a convention in Scotland similar to that which had been summoned in England. It offered the crown to William and Mary. A minor rising of highlanders was settled without difficulty except for the hideous massacre of the MacDonald clan at Glencoe, an event due to misunderstanding and failure of communication. William made several important concessions. Although the established church had been declared Episcopalian (Anglican in Scotland, that is to say) at the time of the restoration of Charles II, it was now made Presbyterian once again and remained so. The new king left the Scots their own parliament, and it promptly got into a series of disputes with that of England over foreign commerce.

In Ireland the overwhelmingly Catholic population had preferred Charles I to (the hated) Cromwell, James II to Charles II. When James from France, where he had fled, exhorted them to rise in support of his effort to regain the throne, they did so. However, William challenged him at the battle of the Boyne (1690) and defeated him. His army then went on to capture the last Catholic stronghold, Limerick, and promised the Irish free transportation to France for those wishing to enter French service (though William was then fighting France!), free exercise of the Catholic religion as under Charles II if the Irish Parliament agreed, and restoration of most rebel estates.

William's leniency was, however, not to prevail. The English Parliament now legislated a prohibition of Catholics in the Irish Parliament, and a series of laws providing for discrimination and outright persecution of Catholics in Ireland ensued. Political, religious, and economic measures combined to make the Irish wretched. In the words of W. E. Lunt, the Glorious Revolution "brought to England political liberty and to Scotland prosperity, [but] to Ireland it brought political and religious tyranny, moral degradation, and economic depression."[8] Nowhere in Europe was a people of different religion from its overlords so badly treated.

In England and Scotland, nevertheless, the way was charted for limitation of the power of rulers that would stand for the next three centuries as the fundamental desideratum for building a free society in all corners of the earth. Even unfree societies for the most part felt compelled to pretend that the principle was observed within their borders. The Glorious Revolution had much to boast of; its chief authors, the Whigs, it could be argued, "did more for freedom than any body of men who ever appeared on earth" (Lord Acton).

But William deserves credit too. He developed much political skill. Not yielding any of the theoretical power he had to choose any ministers he desired, he started to select them on the basis of their ability to win the backing of Parliament. By comparable adroitness he managed to establish a Bank of England and a regular national debt, and thereby succeeded in financing the wars that proved ruinous to the treasury of his opponent, Louis XIV. Thus under the constitutional government based on the cooperation of monarch and parliament, "supposedly weak, fractious, and inefficient" England emerged the victor over the despotism of France, three times as populous as her island neighbor.[9]

It was John Locke who drew theoretical conclusions from the Glorious Revolution, systematized them, and voiced them in a form that others could adopt. His historical role was to challenge Hobbes, theorist of the royalist side in the Civil War. Hobbes, the absolutist, individualist, materialist, and ultimately pessimist ("the war of all against all" as the vision of man's natural state), was confronted by Locke, the constitutionalist, Christian, and optimist (the state of nature as "peace, good will, mutual assistance").

More than that, Hobbes rested his analysis of the state on its usefulness alone; Locke declared that it was founded on natural law. In so doing he traced his descent to the medieval notion of contract, mutual dependence, and the right of revolution if rulers betrayed their side of the bargain, as set forth in the writings of Thomas Aquinas in the thirteenth century and Richard Hooker in the sixteenth century and acknowledged or at any rate constantly appealed to in the history of kings and estates in the Middle Ages. Natural law was the foundation of natural rights, which were life, liberty, and property. All of this, laid down in the *Two Treatises of Government* (1690), carried the day in political theory in Britain and vaulted the channel to France, with significant consequences.

Under Anne (1702–14) the shift in popularity back and forth between Whigs and Tories that characterized William III's reign and often perplexed him became regularized. The queen leaned to the Tories, though her ministers, the duke of Marlborough and the earl of Godolphin, were not at all fanatical in their adherence to that party. They were, however, determined to prosecute the War of the Spanish Succession, the culmination of the wars of Louis XIV, to a successful conclusion. They were thus willing to drop the Tories and ally themselves with Whigs after the latter won the election of 1705, though the queen resisted for some time.

Since the Act of Settlement (1701) had dealt only with England, it remained to solve the question of Scotland. In 1707 union of the two kingdoms was proclaimed; the motivation of the English was in large part to reduce Scottish support for the cause of the Jacobites, having in mind substantial concessions to the Scots by way of opening English trade, military service, and industrial and professional employment to them. Actually England benefited enormously as a result, but that was not known in advance. The succession was to be the same in Scotland as in England: the Protestant descendants of Sophia, Electress of Hanover. There was to be a single parliament for the united kingdom; Scotland was to send sixteen elected peers and forty-five members of Commons. No more peers of Scotland were to be created; Scottish law and religion (the Presbyterian church) were to remain; the Union Jack, fusing the crosses of St. George and St. Andrew, was to be the flag of what now became known as Great Britain.

On the issues of succession and union there was no significant difference between the two parties, but on the war there was. The Tories, who regained popularity in part because of the trial of Dr. Sacheverell (1710), were bent on making peace. The clergyman concerned was impeached by the Whig-dominated Commons, but public opinion tilted in his favor to such an extent that the Whigs let him off with a light sentence—not light enough, however, to save them from a popular backlash. The queen dismissed Godolphin and the Whigs from the cabinet. An election confirmed the Tories in their new control of the cabinet and matched it with a Tory majority in Commons. They proceeded to make peace with France in the Treaty of Utrecht (1713). Already they had sought to make things difficult for the Whigs by several legislative measures directed against Dissenters and merchants—both apt to be Whigs. The queen's death in 1714 was followed by the accession of the pro-Whig George I, and the Tories' vindictiveness was soon rendered ineffective.

In the eighteenth century, "by degrees constitutional monarchy grew to be what was afterwards called responsible government. The machinery by which it did so was the cabinet system. . . . After the first ministry of Queen Anne there was none which could be regarded as freely chosen by the unguided will of the monarch."[10] For much of the century the monarch's ministers were peers; as late as 1783 only one minister was in Commons. But already beginning in the reign of William III a relationship developed between the cabinet and Commons. William's first cabinet was drawn from both Tories and Whigs in order to assure broad national support; instead, they squabbled with one another and accomplished nothing. Thus one adviser suggested that the cabinet be made up of the party with a majority in Commons, and the king thereupon, though not at once, built up a Whig cabinet to go with the Whig Commons. However, he did not yet realize what a discovery he had made or pursue consistently the principle he had acted on once. Both king and Commons still tended to regard the cabinet as a gathering of the king's servants.

Under Anne the principle of seeking harmony between the party in the cabinet and the party with a Commons majority was observed twice—the shift from Tories to Whigs after 1705 and back again in 1710—but not very smoothly, and the first time despite the queen's great reluctance. She was in general unpredictable and difficult to deal with; thus the cabinet fell into the habit of discussing matters among themselves before she had a chance to consult any of them individually, as she had the right to do and often did, in order to present a front of unanimity to her that she was seldom prepared to challenge. Finally, the queen used the royal veto in 1708, but it proved to be the last time; she was also brought to create twelve Tory peers in 1711 in order to make the majority party of Lords the same as that of Commons, and thus make the new Tory cabinet able to avoid the previous frustration of legislation that the Lords had offered,[11] notably the making of peace.

Sir George Clark sums up the British government in the eighteenth century: "Great Britain was the first modern state in which the government had to carry out its tasks with the general consent of a governing class."[12] If the exact relation between the cabinet and Parliament was still to be worked out fully, by that time only Commons and not Lords could initiate money bills, and only the cabinet could introduce them into Commons. There had to be a general election no less often than every three years, before 1716, and under the Septennial Act, from 1716 to 1911, at least every seven years.

The increased power of Parliament had consequences for extrapolitical affairs. Parliamentary votes were reported daily. In 1702 the first daily newspaper in world history began publication in London, and by the end of Anne's reign there were journals in at least nine other towns, read by patrons of the coffeehouses and, from 1709, the members of the hundreds of voluntary societies of all sorts that came to characterize the British. Local government was strong and the interference of the national government in local affairs weak. The eighteenth century was a rather sleepy era in British history, perhaps, but it was also a peaceful and happy one in comparison to the previous hundred years.

Under George I another accident assisted constitutional government: the king did not speak English, so rarely attended cabinet meetings, and his English-speaking successor observed the same habit. The first of the Hanovers restored the Whigs to favor, and some frustrated Tories supported the Jacobite rising of 1715, in favor of James the Old Pretender. The rising was easily put down and had as its main effect to turn the Whig predominance of the moment into a hegemony of forty-five years.

It was threatened in 1721 by the bursting of the South Sea Bubble, perhaps the biggest financial crisis of capitalism thus far. Rescue was forthcoming, however, in the emergence of Sir Robert Walpole as chief figure of the cabinet, often considered the first true prime minister—of Britain or any other country. Untainted by the financial scandal, he got rid of those who had accepted bribes and reorganized the government. He remained its head for twenty-one years; George II tried for a few days to operate with a substitute and wisely gave up. Walpole, however, recognized the power of the king and cultivated the queen as a way of avoiding a test of strength.

During his long tenure Walpole succeeded in establishing the principle of unanimity of the cabinet, so that any public disagreement by a minister in the minority had to lead to resignation. Two Whig ministers dropped in this fashion joined the Tories to bring Walpole down, using the issue of foreign policy with regard to the War of Austrian Succession. He had not wanted the war, and the king's concern for Hanover placed him in an unpopular position. He resigned in 1742. However, the cabinet remained Whig, without a strong leader but nevertheless showing itself, in a parliamentary crisis of 1746, strong enough to compel George II to desist from an attempt to name a prime minister at odds with the cabinet supported by a Commons majority.

The Jacobites had just tried again, in 1745, to restore the Old Pretender with a force led by Charles Edward the Young Pretender. The attempt was a sideshow to British participation in the War of Austrian Succession against France and Prussia and helped to prolong the Whigs' power, though they continued to quarrel with one another. In 1756 the Hanoverian king led Britain into an alliance with Frederick II of Prussia, leaving Austria to complete the "diplomatic revolution" by allying itself with the old enemy, France. A war followed (the Seven Years' War) or in some ways continued, since England had been fighting France off and on since 1666 with changed allies and thus some historians speak of a Second Hundred Years' War (the first of which also had intervals of peace).[13]

After severe British defeats, the king felt compelled to turn in 1757 to William Pitt, whom he detested for his disparagement of England's sacrifices to the Hanoverian connection. Pitt became the real leader of the cabinet, nominally headed by the duke of Newcastle. The Great Commoner, as Pitt was called, rallied the nation, reorganized the army, and led a nation enthralled by his oratorical magic to victory. But the old king died, George III sought to regain the monarchical power that had been weakened under his two predecessors, and Pitt found his colleagues tiring of his popularity and position. He resigned in 1761, and the Earl of Bute as prime minister concluded peace, one which netted Britain predominance in North America and India and paved the way for British world hegemony.

Bute, a Tory, had to resign because the peace was extremely unpopular (so much for popular evaluations of current events), and for the time being the Whigs remained dominant in the cabinet. Soon disharmony with the king led George to turn again to Pitt, who now formed a cabinet combining in a coalition one Whig faction, Tories, and a new group known as King's Friends. Popular at first, George III lost credit by his prosecution of John Wilkes for insulting remarks construed as directed against the monarch, and worse, his engineering of the expulsion of Wilkes from Commons four times in a row after he was legally elected thereto. But the king succeeded in reestablishing much of the royal power by the time Lord North had put together a cabinet (1770), and for the time being the system that the previous eight decades had built fell apart.

The 1763 Treaty of Paris put into the spotlight the needs of the American colonies and imperial administration and defense. Successive attempts to make the colonists pay their fair share of those costs provoked antipathy, partly because of constant changes of ministers owing to the king's persistent parliamentary intrigues but also because of a lack of understanding of the American situation by British statesman. Finally resistance became revolution, and despite all the handicaps suffered by the American leaders, they finally encompassed the surrender of the main British army under Lord Cornwallis at Yorktown in 1781. North resigned a few months later, and it appeared that the king's system had collapsed.

George III was still able to maneuver amidst Whig factions and rivals, but to terminate the coalition cabinet formed by Lord North and Charles James Fox he had to dismiss it, in an unconstitutional manner that evoked a resolution in effect of reprimand. Nevertheless the king's choice for the next prime minister, William Pitt ("the Younger," then only twenty-five, son of the leader of a quarter-century earlier), after a prolonged political struggle, emerged as the country's choice in the 1784 election. But the young commoner, not the king, proved to be in charge, and no one would challenge the cabinet system again. It was as if John Dunning's motion of 1780 had been put into effect: "that the influence of the Crown has increased, is increasing, and ought to be diminished."

Pitt headed the government for eighteen years. He was a better administrator than his father, though an orator inferior to him. His reform of state finances was exemplary, he introduced a bill to abolish many rotten boroughs, he put an end to the system of bribery that was so blatant in the eighteenth century, and he sponsored the legislative union of Great Britain and Ireland under the name of United Kingdom. Ireland was to send 4 lords spiritual and 28 lords temporal (the latter elected for life by the Irish peers) to the upper house and 100 commoners to the lower house in London.

This act diluted the power of the proud Protestants who had made up the Parliament in Dublin (now abolished) and prepared the way for a possible genuinely representative, therefore largely Catholic, representation in London of the Irish people without threatening the Protestants with Catholic domination (since they would be only a modest minority in the British Parliament). Pitt intended to follow up the Act of Union by partially emancipating Irish Catholics from their civil disabilities and enabling them to hold seats in Parliament. The king balked, and Pitt resigned. It was an honorable exit following on a career that on balance advanced the growth of a free society, despite the fact that he had, just before and during the war with France that broke out in 1793, repressed all opposition and sponsored legislation defining treason in a sweeping manner.

The eighteenth century in England—or Britain, from 1707—was one of drastic economic change, centering in the Industrial Revolution but including substantial changes in agriculture as well. It was not a time of religious upheaval or great cultural creativity. Politically it seemed on the surface far from attractive: corruption was open, widespread, and apparently built into the whole parliamentary system; Britain's greatest leaders, Walpole and the two Pitts, were in various ways embroiled in the practices of preferment, pension, and sinecure, or in certain instances outright bribery. The Commons was elected but was scarcely representative, and seemed to defy reformers who wished to make it such.

As for the monarchy, the keystone in the arch, it failed in the reign of James II, leading to the overthrow of the king in an extralegal manner. The monarchy showed few signs of earning popular approval as the dynasty petered out and was replaced by another, and by the end of the century it lay in the hands of a king who was considered mad—intermittently from 1788, steadily from 1810 until he died in 1820. (Since the English title "protector" had been ruined by Cromwell's use thereof, the French "regent" was borrowed for the purpose by the crown prince, who acted for the incompetent king during his last decade.)[14] And yet the century saw the foundations laid of British representative government, which became the model for the whole world and compelled the vilest and cruelest tryants to pretend that they actually presided over an analogous system.

France, 1650–1800

It has long been observed that Britain and France, the two great antagonists, developed politically in diametrically opposite ways during the period. As constitutional government, with fits and starts, took hold in Britain, France slid toward absolute monarchy. And so it was, except that at the end of the slide waited revolution.

The contrast between English and French freedom, however, was not quite so stark. Machiavelli's praise of the French constitution, which bound the king to obey the laws of the land, resounded in France still during the period. In the age of Louis XIV, Bishop Bossuet obligingly dwelt on the authority of the king; Cardinal Fénelon recalled his obligations. In *Télémaque*, he wrote that the king "has all power over the people, but the laws have all power over him." There was no national parliament in France; the Parlement of Paris could not claim to be such. There were local *parlements* as well as the provincial estates with which Lois XIV often clashed; they "opposed the royal will, generally in a selfish or reactionary spirit, with an eye to aristocratic privileges rather than popular rights;

but they were nonetheless helping to maintain the tradition of constitutional government, a measure of political liberty."[15]

By the eighteenth century, the estates still met only in Languedoc, Brittany, Burgundy, Artois, and Béarn, "and only in the first two were the Provincial Estates of any importance"; there they had the power to consent to taxation,[16] and all to some degree managed to defend, or at least affirm, the liberties the crown had promised to preserve when the provinces had passed to it. In Languedoc the First Estate, the clergy (in this case simply the bishops) were dominant; the Second Estate, the nobility, were "represented" by nobles appointed by the king; the Third Estate was made up of town magistrates. As Palmer points out, "with double representation for the Third Estate, and with voting by head, the Estates of Languedoc before the Revolution enjoyed the two formal advantages demanded by the Third Estate on a national scale for the Estates General of 1789."[17]

But the bishops were too strong for the lay estates. In Brittany the clergy were less important than in Languedoc, the nobles dominant, voting by chamber and not by head. In addition to the provincial estates, there was a *parlement,* in fact a court of law supreme in its area, for every region of France. The seats in the *parlements* were usually the property of the persons occupying them. Often they had been sold by the monarch originally, but by the eighteenth century they were apt to be inherited or if purchased, from the owner not the king. The *parlement* in Grenoble had ten *présidents,* fifty-four councilors, and three royal prosecuting attorneys and was largely noble—the distinction between the *noblesse de robe* and *noblesse d'épée* having been blurred by intermarriage and social intercourse.

In summary, the "constituted bodies"—that is, the estates, *parlements,* and associations, local or national, or quite a number of different social groups— offered formidable obstacles to whoever would erect an edifice of absolutism. Aristocracy was putting down roots; rough burghers were producing sons and grandsons with fastidious manners. Even the king's officials were increasingly the product of birth; "the bureaucracy had already become and was to remain a hereditary caste whose members could no more be removed from their offices without compensation than nobles could be deprived of their fiefs."[18] This was the result of the *paulette,* the provision of payment for converting an office into something inherited, which Mazarin threatened to end in 1648 but—having helped thereby to rouse the Fronde against the monarchy—felt compelled to restore in 1657.

Mazarin died in 1661, and Louis XIV's personal rule began. His conception of his task was that of sweeping reform of government. He believed that the will of the ruler should always be obeyed and that the monarch should have "free and full disposition of all the goods possessed by clergymen as well as by laymen, in order to use them . . . according to the general need of the state."[19] Kings, he thought, were brought up to be virtuous and selfless in their pursuit of the common good, whereas nobles, clergy, and other men were selfish.

Nevertheless Louis XIV did not follow the logic of such sentiments. As Russell Major puts it, one would expect him to "crush the provincial estates and other popular organs of government for the benefit of his subjects, but at heart he was too much of a conservative traditionalist to do so." He did not even try. Like those who held the throne before him, he swore to respect the privileges of the provinces with estates and—still in the eighteenth century it was common—felt bound by his oath, at least failing some compelling reason for doing otherwise.

Louis tried to control the estates, the *parlements,* and other bodies that might obstruct his will, but not to destroy them. True, the estates more and more frequently failed to obtain the consent of the royal intendants to meet and therefore did not meet. This was the case in the *pays d'états,* by now the western and southeastern fringes of France; in the *pays d'élections,* the greater part of the country, stretching from Boulogne to Bayonne, such institutions were moribund and could be allowed to disappear without royal initiative. Still, the estates in former sections were not dead and saw a vigorous revival in the succeeding reign.

Louis XIV did much to increase royal prestige, via censorship, the patronage of literature and the arts, and the creation of a palace (Versailles) that attracted nobles to the vicinity of the capital where they could not make mischief. He also vigorously exercised royal power and increased the extent to which France was centralized. Nevertheless absolutism seems an exaggerated term to use for a king who left the same "constituted bodies" to his successor as he faced at the beginning of his reign. The society of "orders" continued and was not even the object of attack. Pomponne de Bellièvre, the chancellor, urged the king to carry France back to the reign of Louis XII; the Estates General and the provincial estates would have many responsibilities and royal officials few; towns would be semiautonomous.[20] Of course he did no such thing.

Louis XIV expended vast energies, sums of money, and numbers of men in wars of conquest, from 1667 to 1713. In doing so he created an enormous army for the time, which in turn increased monarchical power. But it was employed to little advantage, either domestically or financially in extending French borders, despite the annexation of most of Alsace-Lorraine. He left to his great-grandson —since he had outlived both son and grandson—a country that groaned under heavy taxes and had suffered heavy casualties, but was not under the control of a despotism. Perhaps his worst mistake in internal policy was the revocation of the Edict of Nantes in 1685, which action resulted in the prohibition of Huguenot worship, the requirement that children be educated in the Catholic faith, and the forbidding of emigration. Nine-tenths of the Huguenots submitted and accepted conversion; nevertheless some fifty thousand families did leave France, carrying with them skills and abilities that the country could ill afford to lose.

Such policies were lightened considerably by the regency that ruled in Louis XV's minority. Not long after he came of age, the king made his tutor his chief minister: Cardinal Fleury, whose administration lasted from 1726 to 1743. Before he died, France became involved again in war with England, which she fought first with Prussia as ally (the War of Austrian Succession) and then with Austria (the Seven Years' War).

The monarchy was continually challenged by the *parlements,* especially the Parlement of Paris, which attempted to convert the custom of registration of royal edicts into something akin to judicial review. The *parlements* were actually abolished by Chancellor Maupeou, but opposition to this action was so strong that it was reversed in the next reign. Louis XV was, for something like thirty years, influenced by a succession of mistresses. He became steadily more unpopular as they and he wasted public funds on conspicuous consumption and imposed heavy taxes.

His grandson, Louis XVI, was quite different—neither a spendthrift nor a sybarite—but his Austrian-born wife, Marie Antoinette, was careless about such things and interfered in government constantly, with disastrous results. France's already burdensome debt was greatly increased by joining the American colonists in the American Revolution. The king had earlier chosen some able ministers, among them Turgot the Physiocrat, but seemed unable to pursue any consistent policy or to retain any minister long. The financial situation became urgent and then desperate.

A body with only shadowy ancestry, the Assembly of Notables, was summoned in February 1787 and after a few weeks was dissolved without perceptible effect. The *parlements* (restored by Louis XIV at the outset of his reign) blocked several proposed remedies. The king finally turned to the Estates General, last convened in 1614. It met in May 1789: six hundred representatives of the Third Estate joined three hundred clergy and three hundred nobles. After argument, it was decided that all three, with approval of the king, should meet together. The resulting body was called the Constituent Assembly.

The notion that the royal power was not unlimited had both theoretical and practical expression in the previous decades. Montesquieu's *The Spirit of Laws* (1748) argued that the legislative power should be entrusted to both a "body of nobles, and to that which represents the [non-noble] people, each having their assemblies and deliberations apart, each their separate views and interests."[21] King, nobles, and commons must all have a part in government; the English had their Parliament to give voice to the last two, and the French also had "intermediate bodies" to fulfill that function, in the form of *parlements,* estates, and all sorts of smaller corporate entities. In the mid-1760s, the *parlements* seemed to attempt to put such ideas into effect. There were about a dozen of them:

> They now claimed that they were parts of a general or super-parlement, a parlement of all France, of which the several actual parlements were simply subdivisions. . . . This parlement-in-general, they held, represented the "nation," by which they meant the people or the governed, whether of France as a whole or of Brittany and such sub-nations in particular. No law could be valid, or tax properly authorized, they asserted, without the consent of the nation as shown by its representative, the parlement.[22]

This was new; kings had sometimes accepted the right of the *parlements* to register laws or protest against them, but an actual share in legislation had not even been claimed by the *parlements* in earlier times. The claim was thus revolutionary, having no foundation in the constitutional history of France.[23] In 1766 Louis XV publicly rejected such a position, and in 1771 his chancellor abolished the *parlements* entirely, replacing them by a much-improved judicial system and enacting a significant tax reform. The measures had much merit; but the time was past when even good laws could be enacted without consulting substantial sections of the body politic.

Jean-Jacques Rousseau's *Social Contract* (1762) seemed to go much further than the *parlements.* He postulated a "General Will" of the community that was different from the "Will of All," a collective and abstract notion that might supersede the mere sum of individual attitude. Any member of the community might be compelled to conform to the "General Will," "which is to say nothing else than that he will be forced to be free." The author added to the text an exposition of Deist theology, accompanied by a condemnation of relgious intolerance. However, he declared that any person who accepted these teachings and then went against them "should be punished with death," which is certainly not a position of consistent toleration.

Rousseau has been credited with "the rediscovery of the community," not only abstractly, for he proclaimed the special importance of the "common people." Rousseau declared:

> What is not the people is hardly worth taking into account. Man is the same in all ranks; that being so, the ranks which are most numerous deserve most respect. Study people of this humble condition; you will perceive that . . . they have as much intelligence as you, and more good sense. . . . if every king and every philosopher were cut off from among them, they would scarcely be missed, and the world would go none the worse.[24]

Man is also naturally good, and at the outset free; "man is born free and is everywhere in chains." Yet he was not interested in removing the accretions civilization had provided nature; he stood for faith, patriotism, and religion and defended them against the *philosophes* whose unlimited attachment to reason and science had undermined all three.

The Constituent Assembly proceeded to try to draw up a constitution (on the model of the American Constitution; there was no other to imitate). Within a few weeks the nobility had surrendered its feudal rights and privileges, and the Assembly had adopted the Declaration of the Rights of Man. It owed much to the American Declaration of Independence (1776), the English Bill of Rights (1689), and the ideas of the *philosophes,* notably Rousseau (who had been by no means always in agreement with the others): for example, "men are born and remain free and equal in rights." "Imprescriptible rights" included provisions that no man should be arrested or detained except by law, every man was presumed innocent until judged guilty, and so forth.

The Assembly produced a constitution for a limited monarchy with a unicameral legislature, an arrangement which did not last; it also abolished the provinces and the *parlements* and divided France into *départements,* a measure that survived all subsequent political changes. Though there had been virtually universal suffrage exercised for the choice of the deputies of the Third Estates, suffrage was now both limited and indirect. The king accepted the constitution.

However, there now appeared the first fissure in the body politic: the Civil Constitution of the Clergy provided for election of priests and bishops, dissolution of religious orders, state control of the church, and the requirement that all clergy take an oath submitting; less than half did so. A lasting form of disunity afflicted the country thereafter, separating conservatives and Catholics from the religiously indifferent and political revolutionaries.

The new system was inaugurated in October 1791 with the Legislative Assembly. It could scarcely be pretended that everything was normal; the king and his family had tried to flee from Paris and had been intercepted; the groups that stood for the constitution were steadily losing strength and were outnumbered by the Left, consisting of the Mountain (highest up on the left side of the hall), Girondins (from the Gironde around Bordeaux), and the Plain, centrist literally and figuratively. The Mountain, or Montagnards, combined the Jacobin clubs (who met in a monastery formerly occupied by the Dominicans and named for St. James [Jacobus in Latin]), led by Robespierre, with the Cordelier clubs, led by Danton and Marat.

At first a constitutionalist ministry had been formed, but within months it yielded to a Girondin ministry in response to the Prussian and Austrian rulers' cautious statement regarding possible intervention in France, misinterpreted by the war party in France as promising immediate attack. The Girondins in turn did not last. In August 1792 the Paris mob stormed the Tuileries, the palace where the king and family were kept, and in consequence the monarchy was suspended. The republicans now in the saddle planned an assembly that would be elected by manhood suffrage and would draw up a new constitution.

The new assembly was called the Convention. It met in September 1792 and proclaimed what became the First Republic. As French armies advanced eastward, the Montagnards, who were ascendant in the Convention (itself a tribunal), tried and executed Louis XVI; the queen was to follow a few months later. The executive power, as it may be loosely called, was shared by the Committee of General Security, the Committee of Public Safety, and the Commune's committee of twenty (the city council of Paris).

The Revolution entered its most radical phase when the Montagnards arrested the Girondin deputies in June 1793. Robespierre became the leader of the government, though he still had to deal with rivals within the Montagnard camp. A Constitution of 1793 would have produced democracy but was never put into effect. The Girondin deputies were executed in October, two weeks after the queen; there followed the so-called Reign of Terror. About twenty thousand were guillotined. Probably twenty thousand more were killed without trial or any kind of formal execution, and hundreds of thousands were jailed.[25] The upper classes provided only the minority of these casualties.

The assault of the Deists and atheists on Christianity was a less-noticed feature of these events. In November 1793 the worship of God was declared abolished, and the cult of Reason was proclaimed, a particular interest of the Hébertistes—a faction of the Mountain. This was followed by other cults: of the Martyrs of Liberty, of the Supreme Being, and the *culte décadaire*. Some were created by the state, others spontaneously, each having its own rituals, catechisms, and hymns, some of which lasted until the time of the Consulate.[26]

But Hébert and his chief followers were seized and executed by Robespierre with the help of the followers of Danton; the latter were then executed a few weeks later. Robespierre became high priest of the cult of the Supreme Being, as the cult of Reason had been abolished. But these gropings toward a new atheist or Deist kind of church-state relationship came to nothing.

Robespierre was not a single dictator, but he presided for much of the year and a quarter from April 1793 to July 1794 over a Jacobin oligarchy that was partly inspired by, partly sought to justify itself by the ideas of Rousseau. "Our [the Jacobins'] will is the general will," declared Robespierre to the Convention on February 5, 1794. "Is our government . . . like despotism? Yes, as the sword that flashes in the hand of the hero of liberty is like that with which the satellites of tyranny are armed. . . . The government of the Revolution is the despotism of liberty against tyranny."[27] It was the argument that there is good terror and bad terror, good lawlessness and bad lawlessness. It would be made again many times by men convinced of the justice of their cause, bent on erecting a "republic of virtue" as Robespierre wished to do and insisting on the principle that the end justifies the means.

In July (9th Thermidor, by the new revolutionary calendar) Robespierre was overthrown and executed by a conspiracy of various enemies of his, who were then driven by public opinion to limit and then break the power of the Jacobin clubs and their instruments. The so-called Thermidorean reaction overtook the Convention, which adopted a new Constitution of 1795 that established the executive power in a directory of five and a two-house legislature. Placing itself under the protection of troops commanded by General Napoleon Bonaparte, the Convention fended off royalist opposition and yielded to the new system.

French armies had already overrun the Rhineland and the Low countries; Napoleon now invaded Italy, then Switzerland, setting up new republics as he went. After a colorful but finally unproductive adventure in Egypt and Syria, he returned to France. He overthrew the Directory by the coup d'état of the 18th *Brumaire* (November 1799) and established a new form of government called the Consulate, with himself as first consul (with two other consuls). A Constitution of the Year VIII was then approved by plebiscite. Its three-headed executive was accompanied by a Senate, a Tribunate, a Legislative Chamber, and a Council of State. None of them lasted. But a reform of administration and tax collection was also enacted, and survived.

North America, to 1800

Sir Walter Raleigh landed on the Atlantic coast in 1584 in an area he named Virginia, but the first colony that lasted dated from Jamestown in 1607. Already in 1619, under James I, the new governor brought instructions for every plantation to elect two burgesses, and all those elected formed the first representative assembly in the hemisphere.

In 1620 in what became Massachusetts there arrived a group of Separatists, called Pilgrims, from the Anglican church. On reaching Cape Cod they drew up the Mayflower Compact, by which they agreed to form a government resting on their own attitudes and desires. A group of Puritans followed in 1630. The legislative body, or "general court," of Massachusetts Bay was created in 1630 but from 1634 came to include not all freemen, as before, but only their representatives, because the numbers had grown too large. A similar body appeared in Connecticut in 1639.

Thus free institutions in the British colonies of North America were pioneered by the Massachusetts General Court and the Virginia House of Burgesses. Massachusetts tangled with the crown from very early. In 1684 the colony's charter was annulled, but three years later Boston rebelled and it was restored, to be superseded by a new charter in 1691.

Freedom of religion was guaranteed to all (except Catholics), but at that time this was an innovation. Massachusetts Bay Colony had been conceived as a "City of God on earth"; though founded by Puritans who still regarded themselves as part of the Church of England, they became in effect separatist from that ecclesiastical body. More important, the charter assumed the propriety of union between church and state, and it was the General Court that legislated against heretics. Some of the latter were actually executed, though such harshness was a rarity.

Against Puritan intolerance in Massachusetts Roger Williams protested and to avoid it founded Rhode Island, where separation of church and state prevailed. The reason for it was very different from that usually given in the twentieth century: it was to keep the church pure and free from contamination owing to the presence of non-Separatists in the colony—that is, the "state." Rhode Island came to exemplify what was called "soul liberty" (freedom of belief and worship), even though it made the colony a haven for cranks of all sorts. Maryland had instituted toleration in 1649, though it discriminated against Jews and Unitarians; Pennsylvania some thirty years later proclaimed toleration for all who acknowledged one God. Toleration was practiced in both North and South Carolina (except for Catholics) as well as Georgia.

If the basis of the Puritan commonwealth in Massachusetts was the Calvinist views of the political elite, religion also played a crucial role in the government of the southern colonies, including Virginia. The parish was apt to be the basic political as well as ecclesiastical unit, several parishes forming a county. In Virginia each county sent two representatives to the House of Burgesses, elected every two years. As in Massachusetts, the political elite was small, the great planters usually making up the House. The small farmers of the south, and the farmers and tradesmen of the north, took part in electing representatives but generally suffered their betters to govern. As for the increasing numbers of Negroes arriving to work the plantations of the south as slaves and occasionally to reach free status in the north, the former had no rights at all and the latter had only an uneasy civic position; in 1860 only three states gave blacks and whites equal suffrage.

By the eighteenth century, the North American colonies had taken form in three more or less distinct categories. First was the corporate colonies, each functioning under a sort of miniconstitution providing for election of the governor: they were Massachusetts, Connecticut, and Rhode Island. At first the members of both houses of the legislative bodies were elected, but after the new charter of 1691 in Massachusetts the upper house was all appointed, as well as the governor. The second type consisted of proprietary colonies, confided to the hands of the proprietors who had received charters, for example, Maryland. The British crown supervised the third, "royal" type directly.

Following the Glorious Revolution the naming of governors was usually in fact in the hands of the English Parliament rather than the king. The colonies were given no more power than before, and the mother country was no less determined to exert its control over the trade of the colonies. In the era of Walpole and the duke of Newcastle, whose influence survived Walpole's fall, the habit of encouraging rather than regulating the colonies' trade became ingrained. However, the habit could and would be broken.

On the eve of the French and Indian War (the name given the Seven Years' War in America) the colonists made their first effort to achieve unity. Delegates from all colonies north of Virginia met at Albany in 1754 in order to deal with Indian chiefs unhappy at the state of relations with the whites. Fumbling that problem, they nevertheless adopted a plan put forward by Benjamin Franklin, from Pennsylvania, to set up an intercolonial assembly along with a new official, president-general for all the colonies together. The colonial legislatures promptly rejected the plan.

By the Treaty of Paris (1763) that ended the war, Canada went to the British; no longer did the French danger from the north or west threaten the English colonists. Already the previous year France had ceded the great expanse of Louisiana to Spain; mainland French America thereupon disappeared. (Spain also ceded Florida to England.)

George Grenville, who headed the British government in 1763, was dissatisfied with colonial behavior during the war and resolved that the colonists must pay a share of the cost of defending the western frontier against the Indians (now that the French were gone). Thus began a series of squabbles between the British and the American colonists about particular taxes levied for that purpose and finally about the right to tax.

The argument that taxation without representation was illegal was taken up by several Americans. Samuel Adams, leader of the popular party in Massachusetts, argued that what was at issue was the British constitution, which, like the constitutions of all free peoples (which did he have in mind?), was "fixed in the law of Nature and of God." Virginia echoed the claim that only the governor and legislature of the colony could tax it.

Samuel Adams had organized eighty committees of correspondence in Massachusetts, and the same device had spread to the other colonies. They now went into action, and sent out copies of the Virginia burgesses' resolution that invited all colonies to elect delegates to a congress in Philadelphia. It met in 1774,

208 Freedom: A History

consisting of men chosen by the committees of correspondence, mass meetings, or legislatures of the respective colonies.

The First Continental Congress adopted a Declaration of Rights expatiating on the indefensibility of taxation without representation. Thomas Jefferson and John Adams argued that the colonies owed allegiance only to the king and that the British Parliament had no power over them. Even if Jefferson and Adams were right, the Congress had no legal authority when it declared a boycott of British goods, threatened termination of exports to Britain and the West Indies, and inaugurated a continuing Association of the colonies for such purposes. Therefore the American Revolution may be said to have begun when the Congress thus acted.

When the governor of Massachusetts sent troops from Boston to seize munitions the militants had stockpiled at Concord, firing began between the British and American militia at Lexington, and the fighting lasted from April 1775 to 1783. Plenty of military mistakes were made on both sides. Politically sentiment moved toward the goal of independence, helped by Thomas Paine's pamphlet *Common Sense* and consecrated by Jefferson's Declaration of Independence (4 July 1776). Based on natural-right doctrines drawn from John Locke's *Second Essay of Government,* it seemed to reverse Jefferson's earlier position that the colonies depended on the king, but from another viewpoint carried it further: the king was now found at fault, and thus the only bond with the motherland was to be severed.

In November 1777 the Articles of Confederation established a makeshift government for the colonies together (a document ratified only in 1781), but the Americans won in spite of it rather than because of it. In October General Gates had compelled the British army led by General Burgoyne to surrender. That gave the French the encouragement they needed to make an alliance with the United States of America, as the latter now called themselves. Together they defeated Lord Cornwallis at Yorktown in October 1781, and peace was made by the Treaty of Paris of September 1783.

The boundary of the new United States ran along the Great Lakes and just beyond to the Mississippi River and south to the Gulf, except for New Orleans and Florida. It remained to decide how the nation would be governed.

In some ways "nation" was not accurate. There were thirteen states, each having adopted a constitution. Rhode Island and Connecticut had charters of self-government that required only to be renamed "constitution." Beginning with New Hampshire and South Carolina, the others first enacted temporary constitutions and then, following the lead of Virginia and New Jersey, permanent ones. Sometimes legislative bodies simply passed constitutions as they would, or did, ordinary laws; in Massachusetts a directly elected constitutional convention drew up a document and submitted it to the towns, two-thirds of which needed to approve and did so.

All the constitutions were "amazingly similar," in the words of a standard treatment, and several contained bills of rights; "such notions came not merely from the teachings of political philosophers like Richard Hooker and John Locke, who argued strongly in favor of the 'natural rights' of men, and were well known in America, but owed something also to colonial experience."[28] In theory and practice there was reason for the colonists' determination to continue and make more secure what they believed had been theirs for some time, if illegitimately infringed by the London government—namely freedom.

To be sure, if government was bound by certain limitations under the state constitutions, so was freedom limited. Negroes had no rights if they were slaves, and lacked full rights if they were freemen. The states possessed "established" churches, that is, churches closely bound up with the governments concerned, and some beliefs, notably those of Catholics, were the object of severe discrimination. Women had no vote. Indians were not part of the body politic. But class barriers were absent from legal prescriptions, and the freedom to speak, believe as one wished, be protected against arbitrary arrest and be assured a jury trial, and many other rights were firmer than anywhere else—except possibly Britain, whose exactions had appeared so unreasonable to the revolutionaries.

The constituent parts of the governments of the respective states were not identical but overlapped a great deal. Each had an executive, known as the governor, but his powers were strictly limited. He was to be elected, by the legislature (one or both houses thereof) except in New England where popular vote was to make the choice. His term would be short, in most states only one year; seldom could he stand for reelection, veto a measure passed by the legislature, adjourn or dissolve the legislature. For several years Pennsylvania had no governor at all, but a kind of executive council instead.

Legislatures usually had two houses, because of both British and colonial tradition and also because John Adams wanted to restrain possible legislative arbitrariness, since the checks on the executive were so stringent. Pennsylvania was again the exception in having a unicameral legislature, along with Georgia; but both soon acquired second houses. Only Nebraska (and Guam), much later, would return to the single-house pattern. Suffrage was limited, in some states to taxpayers or landowners or those holding a certain amount of property. Still, in New England over half of adult white males seem to have voted, and in Vermont all men over twenty-one were given the vote. Vermont, organized by its own people when New Hampshire and New York squabbled over which should have it, became the fourteenth state in the Union in 1791.

The period of the Articles of Confederation was one in which the confederated government demonstrated impotence and incompetence in many respects, but the Land Ordinance of 1785, creating the public domain of the United States, and the Northwest Ordinance of 1787 were legislative masterpieces. They charted the route for the seaboard colonies to become a nation stretching all the way to the Pacific. Colonization and development of a colony were to be followed by admission as a state coordinate and on the same footing with the original states. Finally, the court system (or lack of system) was built on colonial experience and was staffed by judges usually chosen by the legislatures. Already the practice of judicial review was inaugurated by Trevett v. Weeden, in which a Rhode Island court nullified a law passed by the state's legislature.

The shortcomings of the Articles of Confederation led to consideration of a closer union, and part of the evolving consciousness of such a need rested on the Massachusetts Constitution of 1780. John Adams wrote that the body politic is "a social compact, by which the whole people covenants with each citizen, and each citizen with the whole people." The covenant-compact notion goes back, in America, to the *Mayflower,* but the terms "social" and "citizen" probably derive from Rousseau, whom Adams read carefully. However, he wrote in the enacting clause of the preamble, "We, therefore, the delegates of the people. . . . ," which the state constitutional convention changed to "We, therefore, the people. . . ." R. R. Palmer writes:

> The formula, *We the people ordain and establish,* expressing the developed theory of the people as constituent power, was used for the first time in the Massachusetts constitution of 1780, whence it passed into the preamble of the United States constitution of 1787 and the new Pennsylvania constitution of 1790, after which it became common in the constitutions of the new states, and in new constitutions of the old states.[29]

Palmer compares the United States with the Dutch and Swiss federations, which were merely "close permanent alliances between disparate corporate members"— until the Dutch revolution of 1795 and the Swiss revolution of 1798. In the United States, however, a man had citizenship, both in the new federal union and in the old state that continued to exist. That citizenship, shared by the "people" (with the exceptions noted), was the mainspring of sovereignty.

First Virginia and Maryland addressed some issues of navigation; next Virginia sought to broaden discussion and invited all thirteen states to send delegates to Annapolis; then the delegates of the five states that did actually dispatch them followed Alexander Hamilton's lead and called a meeting to consider defects of the articles. It met in Philadelphia in May 1787 and elected as chairman George Washington, the leading general of the Revolution.

The basic problem was how to work out an acceptable form of representation for both citizens and states. A Virginia Plan was shaped by James Madison, giving weight to the larger states; a New Jersey Plan was drawn up in response by the smaller-state delegates. A compromise was reached providing for a two-house legislature, the lower house to be based on population and the upper house to represent all states equally. The former was to be elected every two years, the latter every six in staggered terms and by state legislatures, not popular vote. Slaves were to be counted as the equivalent of three-fifths of whites in both apportioning representatives and levying direct taxes. Attempts to safeguard the predominance of the seaboard states in the future were turned back.

Congress was to have certain specified powers, some possessed by the Congress of the Articles, some new; among the latter was the power to tax. Moreover, the states were to lose certain powers, such as coinage and foreign relations. The misinterpretation of the British Constitution popularized by Montesquieu and the traditions of the American colonies may be assigned roughly equal shares of responsibility for the efforts of the Philadelphia convention at separation of powers.

Thus the president (an office then unknown anywhere else in the world) was to be elected, not by the Congress but by "electors" themselves chosen as each state desired and assembling in an electoral college. He was to be commander in chief of the army and navy, have power to make treaties with "the advice and consent of the Senate," name envoys to foreign countries and many domestic officials, especially judges of all federal courts, and veto bills passed by Congress (though a two-thirds vote of both houses could override). Little attention was paid by the constitution-makers to the court system. Its best-known power, that of declaring laws unconstitutional, was not provided for in the Constitution but assumed by the Supreme Court; it is true, however, that Madison and others took for granted that precisely that would occur.

A method of amending the document was described; it was provided that the constitution would take effect when nine states ratified it. Delaware acted first, in December 1787; Massachusetts ratified by a narrow margin; on 21 June 1788, New Hampshire was the ninth state to approve. Nevertheless neither New York nor Virginia had been among that number, and it was widely agreed that they had effective power to block the whole scheme. They did finally ratify, New York by the slimmest margin of all on 26 July 1788. During the debate the supporters of the Constitution had become known as the Federalists and their opponents the Anti-Federalists. The new nation had a government; it would very soon have a Bill of Rights (the first ten amendments, adopted by Congress and ratified by three-fourths of the states by December 1791); like Britain, it had a two-party system and would keep it, despite periods of transition.

The First Amendment provided that Congress should not "establish" a religion, but left untouched the established churches of the states. At the time of the Revolution nine out of the thirteen colonies united church and state. Disestablishment of the Church of England accompanied revolution in the South, but the Congregational Church in New England was supported by the state everywhere except in Rhode Island. In Massachusetts "establishment" lasted until 1833. "Separation of church and state" is a phrase that may be found in the writings of Thomas Jefferson, a Deist, but nowhere in the Constitution or its amendments.

In March 1789 Congress, the first under the new government, convened; in April Washington was inaugurated as the first president. The new Secretary of the Treasury, Alexander Hamilton, gave the country a fiscal system; when Jefferson and others organized the opposition to him as the Republican (later Democratic) party, Hamilton and John Adams gave the Federalists a clearer party identity. Adams succeeded Washington as president in 1797. Jefferson succeeded Adams in 1801, the first president to be inaugurated in the new capital, Washington. There were seventeen states (after Vermont had come Kentucky, Tennessee, and Ohio) by 1802; in 1803 the vast Louisiana Territory was bought from France, to which Spain had retroceded it in 1800. The United States of America had greatly enlarged its share of the map and written golden pages in history, as attested by the individuals, groups, and countries that imitated it, envied it, were inspired by it in the ensuing two centuries.

Palmer declares that the American Revolution "was very conservative because the colonies had never known oppression, excepting always for slavery—because, as human institutions go, America had always been free." The Revolution was also radical—in the same sense that the Glorious Revolution in England was radical, violating the previously accepted legal system; in the sense that it offered a new theory of popular sovereignty carried into constitutional documents and governmental practice based thereupon; and in the sense that aristocracy for all practical purposes vanished. "Never again," adds Palmer, "would deference for social rank be a characteristic American attitude. Elites, for better or for worse, would henceforth be on the defensive against popular values."[30]

Elsewhere in the hemisphere events were less dramatic. Many people loyal to Britain fled northward during the American Revolution, increasing the ethnic Britishers' ratio to the ethnic French who were the original settlers. As a result the Canada Act of 1791, passed by the British Parliament, divided chiefly English "Upper Canada" from chiefly French "Lower Canada" at the Ottawa River. Both had governors and elected assemblies able to legislate, subject to a veto from London.

Iberia and Italy

The seventeenth century saw an actual decrease of some proportions in the Spanish population, owing to the casualties of war and disease; and the state of the central government was correspondingly dismal under intriguing priests and ministers, especially during the reign of Charles II. The war between France and Spain was concluded by the Peace of the Pyrenees in 1659. It is usually taken to mark the point at which the preeminent place of France on the continent was established and the power of Spain in Europe began to decline. The Spanish had lost Portugal in 1640 and recognized her independence at length in 1668; her losses in 1659 were more psychological than territorial, a symbol of the damage being the accompanying marriage of Louis XIV to the Spanish *infanta* (crown princess). The marriage in turn laid the groundwork for the Bourbon dynasty, in the person of Louis's grandson, to succeed as Philip V the last, hapless Habsburg king of Spain, Charles II.

It was first necessary for the War of the Spanish Succession to confirm Philip's title. The Austrians seeking to place their branch of the Habsburgs on the throne of Madrid seized Barcelona during the war. However, Philip V captured the city, by the Decree of Nueva Planta (1716) ended the local privileges, and integrated Catalonia into Spain. The area thereupon lost most official use of its language and suffered harm to its traditions and pride, but experienced considerable economic growth and prosperity.

The change in Catalonia must be counted as Spanish expansion, but there was significant contraction in the same period. By the Treaties of Utrecht and Rastadt (1713–14) Spain lost its mainland European possessions: Belgium (which now became the Austrian Netherlands), Luxembourg, much of Italy (Milan, Sardinia, and Naples), and even Gibraltar. Within the borders of Spain, the Bourbons fought the privileges of the proud and independent churchmen and nobles, established a bureaucracy that reorganized finances and reconstructed the army and navy, and made a sizable contribution to the economic development of the country. Despite conflicting parties at court—one of which wished to recover the Italian possessions, the other to concentrate on Spanish America—a series of reforming ministers made some headway in the peninsula itself. But during the wars that bear his name Napoleon intervened to force the Bourbons to yield to his brother Joseph, precipitating the long Peninsular War and dramatic political developments.

In Portugal the monarchy was also strengthened. The last Cortes met in 1697. The nobles were increasingly brought under the royal thumb, the Church to a lesser extent. The chief minister during the entire reign of Joseph I, the Marquis de Pombal, pursued the objectives of enlightened despotism—to weaken the clergy and nobility and strengthen the throne—with more success than several of the monarchs whom the *philosophes* nominated as "enlightened despots." As a symbol of his commitment to the ideas of the Enlightenment, he pushed through the expulsion of the Society of Jesus. Other Catholic countries followed, and Pombal helped persuade the pope to abolish the Society. Joseph's daughter, Maria I (1777–1816), curbed the power of Pombal and allowed nobles and clerics to regain part of what they had lost. During the Napoleonic Wars France and Spain agreed to partition Portugal, but the arrival of a British army prevented any such action.

By 1650 the energies of the Counter-Reformation in Italy had seemingly been exhausted, along with the animosities that fueled the religious wars of the northern countries. In the late seventeenth century the papacy was occupied by a series of blameless men paralyzed into inaction by the need to avoid siding with either the Bourbons or Habsburgs in their endless conflicts, to escape the ideological perils resulting from the arguments of Jansenists with Jesuits, and then, in the eighteenth century, the threat of Deism and the Enlightenment to Catholicism and the Catholic church itself. Anticlericalism grew in strength even in strongly Catholic countries. It drove Clement XIV to dissolve the Society of Jesus (1773), harassed the church in Austria, attacked the church in the French Revolution, and shook its foundations in both hemispheres.

After Utrecht (1713), the papacy—an Italian principality as well as the Catholics' seat of ecclesiastical authority—was lodged uncomfortably between two possessions the Spanish had just lost to the Austrians: Milan and Naples. The Holy Roman Emperor in Vienna also acquired Sicily in 1720. That island had gone to Savoy, whose ruler, Victor Amadeus II (1675–1730), had nimbly scrambled from side to side during the War of the Spanish Succession and emerged with a royal title as well as Sicily. But in 1720 the island was exchanged for Sardinia, and thereafter the ruler was "king of Sardinia."

Reddaway writes, "endowed with matchless artistic wealth and talent, the millions of Italians [during the eighteenth century] might be regarded as content to enjoy life without much political ambition."[31] But that was mainly true of the rest of the peninsula. Savoy, "the Prussia of Italy," boasted military achievements rather than artistic ones. The Savoyard army had its limitations, as the French would show after 1796, but its strength was sufficient to make the Kingdom of Sardinia the nucleus of the united nation of the next century.

At the end of the War of the Polish Succession, in 1735, Austria ceded Naples and Sicily to the Spanish Bourbons but barred union with Spain. The first ruler of what was to become the Kingdom of the Two Sicilies was Charles IV (1735–59), a reforming king with a reforming minister, Bernardo Tanucci; later the region fell behind. Venice retained enough of its medieval strength to take much of southern Greece from the Turks, but could not hold it, and after the Treaty of Passarowitz (1718) its empire consisted only of the Ionian Islands and the coast of Dalmatia. Genoa too preserved its independence but lost its chief possession, Corsica, to France in 1768.

The chief remaining state was Tuscany, whose capital, Florence, had been the center of the Italian Renaissance. The last Medicis were decadent and ineffective. The line died out in 1737, and the throne passed to Francis of Lorraine. Eight years later he was elected as Holy Roman Emperor; he turned over the grand duchy to his second son, Leopold I, under whom Tuscany became perhaps the most prosperous and best governed of all Italian states. Leopold reformed the administration and promoted economic stability, but above all he abolished serfdom. Serfdom was not then a single, uniform condition in all parts of Europe; it represented a partial survival of several aspects of the legal status of the medieval peasant, others having eroded with time. But the end of the eighteenth and early nineteenth centuries brought the institutions concerned to an end in much of western Europe, not only because the French and their armies proclaimed liberty.

Iberia reduced the number of effective states; Italy did not during the period in question. In neither was royal absolutism actually absolute—despite what is said or implied in many historical treatments of the period. In the two Iberian states the clergy and nobility retained much power and wealth; of the Italian statelets it may be said that their multiplicity prevented any despot from working his will unhindered on large numbers of people or vast areas.

In the eighteenth century many Iberians and Italians doubtless sighed and recalled better days or tales of such. Under effective Austrian domination, as they had earlier been under Spanish, the Italian people were not their own masters and could not count on the law, Italian or Austrian, to protect them for a certainty. Yet even in the judicial area an important step was taken when Cesare Beccaria, in his *Dei delitti e delle pene* (Crimes and punishments, 1764), charted the main lines of the modern science of penology for the world.

Germany

The Peace of Westphalia marks a watershed. The central government of the Holy Roman Empire was neither strong before 1648 nor totally without power after it, but the peace condemned it to "protracted invalidism during which its pulse beat ever more feebly." By about 1750, it "was to slip into a long coma from which it never emerged."[32] The emperor could make laws or levy taxes only with the consent of the Reichstag (the Imperial Diet), but the result was that neither emperor nor Diet had any real power, since there was no real central government.

The individual states had diets, but everywhere except Mecklenburg and Würt-temberg their strength was reduced to a nullity by the rise of the princes.

After 1648 there were about three hundred *Reichsstandschaften* (states repre-sented in the Reichstag) plus nearly fifteen hundred other entities with no lord other than the emperor. Naturally, therefore, the secular princes tried to make up in the size of their bureaucracies and the splendor of their courts what they lacked in area, wealth, and possessions, and constantly hunted for new ways to tax and new sources of revenue. The bishops and abbots did no better, "since their lack of legitimate issue made them sometimes careless of the future well-being of their [states or territories]."[33] This problem, to be sure, was common to all ecclesiastically ruled lands and agencies in the Roman Catholic church, from the papacy on down, over many centuries. The relative indifference mentioned did not prevent the clergymen in question from trying to improve the lot of members of their families.

Only a small number of princely houses were able to grow significantly. The most important were the Habsburgs. Since 1493 the hereditary lord of the Austrian lands and the elected Holy Roman Emperor had been members of that family. Usually one person held both positions. After the end of the War of the Spanish Succession, in addition to Austria proper, those lands were Silesia, Bohemia, Hungary (with Transylvania), Moravia, Tyrol, Carinthia, Styria, parts of Slavonia and Croatia. To those contiguous regions were now added the for-merly Spanish Netherlands (Belgium), Sardinia, Milan, and Naples.

Over this ethnically heterogeneous conglomerate of territories, each replete with diplomatic and military involvements—actual and potential—reigned Charles VI (1711–40). In 1713 he enacted the Pragmatic Sanction that declared the indivisibility of the Austrian lands and established an order of succession that would guarantee the throne to his eldest daughter, Maria Theresa, if he should continue to be without a son at his death. Considering that the Habsburg lands had at various times been distributed among various members of the family, were reunited only in 1665, and what held them together was only family ties, supple-mented by a near uniformity of religion in Roman Catholicism, the unity of the realm must be regarded as a remarkable achievement. There are few analogues in history for the widespread existence of *Kaisertreue* (loyalty to the emperor) in Habsburg-ruled domains for centuries and the nostalgia for rule by the dynasty to be found in much of that heterogeneous territory in the late twentieth century.

The second state in importance was Brandenburg, which became Prussia. In the aftermath of the Thirty Years' War Frederick William Hohenzollern, "the Great Elector," did his best to rebuild devastated Brandenburg; secured the end of Polish suzerainty over ducal Prussia in 1660, which he had inherited in 1618 as a fief outside the Empire; settled a contested title in 1666 to the western fragment lands of Cleves, Mark, and Ravensberg, provisionally awarded to Brandenburg in 1614; and created a standing army that would become the foundation of the country's power. In order to finance this force, Frederick William introduced new taxes, extracted consent to them from the Brandenburg Diet in 1652, and then relegated it to obscurity. The Prussian Diet was tackled directly in 1661–63, and its powers in regard to taxation were ended. The Great Elector was succeeded by Frederick III, who obtained a crown with the emperor's consent; his title became Frederick I as king *in* Prussia (since that was the part of the realm outside the Empire) in 1701. His successors continued to build up the Prussian army.

Other houses that managed to raise their lands above the level of statelets were the Wettins in Saxony, the Wittelsbachs in Bavaria, the Welfs in Brunswick and Hanover, the House of Hesse, the Zähringens in Baden, and the House of Württemberg. The elector of Saxony was chosen king by the Poles in 1697, and the descendants of the electress of Hanover were given the crown of Britain in 1714. The Wittelsbachs of Bavaria obtained the status of an eighth elector of the Empire in 1648 but aspired to the imperial crown itself. In 1742 the duke was in fact elected the first non-Habsburg emperor in centuries, but Charles VII was soon defeated by his enemies and died. There would be no other Wittelsbach emperor, but the duke successfully assumed the title of king of Bavaria in 1805.

In 1740 Charles VI had died, and Maria Theresa became queen and archduchess but not empress; at length her husband (after the Bavarian interlude) was elected emperor as Francis I. But it took the War of the Austrian Succession before the couple were secure; indeed, it looked for a time as if a second, the Seven Years' War, also threatened their crowns.

Frederick II of Prussia ("the Great") took an excellent army and made it the best army in Europe; he also made his state into a major power. He was gifted in many ways and improved the economy, the government, and the cultural level, but he did not change essentially the sociopolitical system he inherited. Prussia gained Silesia by treaty in 1742 and kept it through the Seven Years' War (1756–63). Frederick the Great sought to bring about recovery in the kingdom, and spent his last quarter-century (he died in 1786) making the Prussian bureaucracy, and government generally, a byword throughout Europe. In Maehl's words, "the king's versatility, industry, marvelous abilities, and incredible luck simply overawed everybody."[34] Moreover, Frederick's spies and his powers as monarch anchored a formidable degree of absolutism.

Once again, however, the limitations of "absolute monarchy" in the West need to be clearly perceived. Strong social corporations protected by customary law, considerable self-government in the towns, rights and immunities of the nobles coupled with administrative and judicial functions they were required to exercise, a high court—the *Kammergericht*—that the king himself exhorted to obey the law of the land and the judges' consciences at all costs—these and other institutions limited the royal power.

Maehl sums up: "Frederick's Prussia may not have been exactly a *Rechtsstaat,* but in it customary and natural law circumscribed monarchical caprice."[35] Even the peasantry had ancient and imprescriptible rights. To be sure, the nobles were able to elect rural councilors *(Landräte)* that supervised the agrarian sector. Indeed, Frederick's great domestic achievement was to keep the nobles "usefully employed" and to prevent them from coalescing into opposition by such methods rather than by the "Versailles device," by which the French kings attracted nobles to a luxurious court and away from political mischief.

In the Habsburg Empire the aristocrats retained much more strength. The regional estates survived; in order to safeguard the accession of Maria Theresa, the crown confirmed noble privileges and liberties of the regions right and left. The minister from 1746, Count von Haugwitz, managed to fuse the administrative machinery of Austria and Bohemia and suppress their estates. In 1762 a seven-member Council of State *(Staatsrat)* was created to decide the questions of policy under the leadership of Prince von Kaunitz and the monarch.

Kaunitz and Joseph II, especially after his mother died in 1780, pushed through a number of reforms. Joseph emancipated the serfs in 1781 and made them tenant farmers (rather than smallholders); he introduced a much more merciful penal code, in accordance with the doctrines of Beccaria; he did much to replace the cameralist, state-directed economic methods then prevailing (as also in Prussia) by free enterprise; he enacted religious toleration (1781) and pared down the privileges and property of the Roman Catholic church. He tried to restrict the liberties of Hungary, Lombardy (the area of Milan), and the Austrian Netherlands (Belgium); in this respect he largely failed. In general his reforms attempted too much and did not survive him.

English rationalism and in particular Deism led to the so-called Enlightenment. It was a movement of ideas that promoted, within limits, freedom of thought and scientific inquiry, religious tolerance, and opposition to oppressive feudal privilege. To the extent that it had a political embodiment, it was to be found in the ideas of "enlightened despotism," as preached by Voltaire and Diderot. The assumption was that the removal of irrationalities (chiefly clerical, noble, and military) from the body politic would enable the natural laws of social behavior to bring happiness to mankind. The *philosophes* who taught such notions were not democrats and did not trust the common people (the "rabble," Voltaire called them) and placed their faith in change from above, by the rulers— preferably instructed and advised by the *philosophes* themselves.

The closest such teachings came to being implemented was in the German lands—Prussia and Austria, in the persons of Frederick II and Joseph II. The two monarchies did not merely fight each other; they began to move into a period of rivalry for the leadership of the German lands, which was not decided until after the middle of the nineteenth century.

In 1791 Frederick William II of Prussia and Leopold II of Austria met at Pillnitz and issued a declaration threatening intervention in France under certain conditions; the French responded by declaring war. It would last twenty-three years and involve the whole of Europe.

When the brilliant young general of the French Revolutionary armies, Napoleon Bonaparte, defeated the Austrians and imposed the Treaty of Campo Formio (1797), Austria had to give up Belgium and agree to advance of the French frontier to the Rhine. Following the War of the Second Coalition, when an even more crushing defeat was administered to Austria, those arrangements were confirmed and extended (1801–2). The Holy Roman Empire was thereupon drastically affected by the end of almost all ecclesiastical principalities, which were annexed by their neighbors as a result of an Imperial Recess (*Reichsdeputationshauptschluss*). In 1806 the Empire was finally given formal burial. No longer Holy Roman Emperor, Francis I had already assumed the title, which he kept, of Emperor of Austria. A few weeks earlier a large part of Germany (except Austria, Prussia, and two other states) had been reshaped by Napoleon into the Confederation of the Rhine.

In reply Prussia decided to fight. Her army was smashed at Jena and Auerstädt (1806). In 1809 Austria did likewise; her army was defeated at Wagram. Out of ruin was to come regeneration in both states.

Scandinavia

Sweden had been carried into the rank of first-rate powers by Gustavus Adolphus, but Queen Christina could not and did not wish to play the role of such a monarch as her father. She abdicated in order to go to Rome, in the sense of becoming a Catholic as well as literally. Her cousin and successor, Charles X, fought several countries. During the Thirty Years' War the Swedish nobles had come to possess some two-thirds of Sweden's and Finland's territory through transfer of crown properties. Charles undertook to reduce the nobles' wealth through an extensive capital levy. However, his chief aim was conquest. He did expel Denmark from the southern part of the peninsula and annexed Livonia.

His successor Charles XI struck the Swedish nobles hard by a confiscation of large fiefs legislated by the non-noble part of the Estates in 1680. In consequence, the rest of the reign is known as "Carolingian absolutism."[36] The property regained was allotted to civil officials and military officers as well as soldiers on a basis of rental, which made the crown less dependent on the Estates. But the resentment this action aroused in the Baltic provinces in particular, among the German barons who ruled there, created part of the problems of Charles XII. Acceding at the age of fifteen, that remarkable young man was soon attacked by Peter I of Russia, and the war lasted from 1700 to 1721. However, he was shot to death in 1718, and the peace of Nystad yielded to Peter the Baltic provinces and marked the end of Swedish domination of the Baltic.

The constitutional laws of 1720–23 vested much power in the Riksdag, which it kept for half a century. During the period a kind of two-party system came into existence: the Caps were the doves and the Hats the hawks of the time. They were the closest analogues of Tories and Whigs to be found anywhere outside England, until the United States produced Federalists and Anti-Federalists. The Swedish case was one in which foreign policy played a determining role. The Caps wished good relations with Russia and also England, and managed to keep their distance from France. In 1738, however, the Hats displaced them. Their leader, Count Gyllenborg, made an alliance with France and sought to recover Sweden's preeminent position in the Baltic. The result was war with Russia, in which the Swedes lost a fair amount of Finnish territory (1743). In 1765 the Hats lost their power.

In 1772 Gustavus III, believing that parliamentary strength and royal weakness accounted for many of the country's troubles, restored absolutism. The power of the council was terminated, and the Riksdag could no longer take the lead in legislating as before. Gustavus sought to follow the principles of enlightened despotism: he reformed the penal laws, decreed religious toleration and a free press, and encouraged commerce. In 1789 he reconvened the Riksdag, which proceeded against his wishes to abolish most privileges of the nobility. Sweden now became involved in the web of European wars and intrigues. Russia wrested Finland from her in 1808 and the Åland Islands as well.

The last Vasa king, Charles XIII, was compelled to accept a new constitution by which the nobles regained much power, and the Riksdag chose as heir Napoleon's Marshal Bernadotte, who would sire the dynasty still ruling Sweden in the 1990s. In 1809, as Charles's reign began, Sweden was a constitutional monarchy of sorts, with a plurality of political institutions and social classes able to take part in government. In particular most of the peasantry had come to own their farms during the eighteenth century, though many tenant farmers remained.

Shortly after making peace with Sweden in 1660, Denmark witnessed a coup d'état on the part of King Frederick III, supported by the clergy and the bourgeoisie. The kingship became hereditary and nearly absolute; the council was now merely advisory; noble privileges were ended. The Treaty of Copenhagen in 1660 fixed the boundaries of Denmark, Norway, and Sweden as of the 1990s. The constitution of 1660, defended and systematized by Peter Schumacher, later chief minister as Count Griffenfeld, in a treatise called the *Kongelov* (King's law) of 1665, lasted virtually unchanged until 1848. The doctrines embodied in the 1665 work were "said to be most absolutist of all European theories of absolutism."[37]

But doctrine was one thing, practice another. A reasonably efficient bureaucracy was established, so that the kings could leave many things to the men who staffed it. The actual political leaders were large landowners, either nobles or bourgeois creditors to whom the crown sold much of the land seized from the church at the time of the Reformation. The kings might be absolute but were in fact feeble and shadowy figures from 1730 on.

Enlightened despotism came to Denmark in the shape of the administration of John Frederick Struensee (1770–72), who attempted to limit noble privilege, abolished torture, and proclaimed freedom of the press; he was overthrown and executed. A more successful reform minister was Count Andreas Bernstorff (1784–88), who carried out the virtual abolition of serfdom in Denmark, coupled with land reform, and in effect terminated the period of government by a few large landlords. As in Sweden, the majority (perhaps 60%) of the Danish peasants became landowners. Most Norwegian peasants were free and were smallholders already. Norway saw the beginning of cultural awakening among Norwegian students in Copenhagen and then at the University of Christiania, founded in 1811, but remained under Danish rule until 1814.

In 1794 Denmark and Sweden joined in an armed-neutrality treaty later adhered to by Russia and Prussia. In retaliation, the British sank much of the Danish fleet, and Denmark was drawn into alliance with France in consequence. At the end of the fighting she had to hand Norway over to Sweden, where her former dependency remained for another century.

Kings and nobles, clergy and burghers, and (more visibly than anywhere else in Europe) peasants squabbled and fought but also debated, drew up new constitutions, and then scrapped them for still newer ones. In Sweden the monarchy was notably stronger, in Denmark the aristocrats were better entrenched; but there were ups and downs for kings and nobles in both countries. In the meantime law had obtained a secure position in Scandinavian life, and property was becoming distributed among a larger number of people. The descendants of the barbarous Vikings were scarcely recognizable.

Poland and Hungary

Montesquieu wrote in the *Persian Letters* (1721) that "Poland makes such poor use of her liberty and of her royal elections that she gives thereby no satisfaction but to her neighbors, who have lost both."[38] Part of her troubles were geographical; she had no natural frontiers, and faced powerful neighbors which were sometimes also enemies: the Habsburg Empire, Sweden, Muscovy, the Ottoman Empire. However, the political system certainly did not contribute to Polish security or stability. John II Casimir, the elected Vasa king, was quite unable to handle the unrest among the serfs and the Cossacks of the Ukraine. Bohdan Khmelnitsky, hetman of the Cossacks, opted for the protection of Moscow (the exact meaning of the decision is still debated) in 1654, and after lengthy struggle Poland gave up all territory east of the Dnieper and the city of Kiev west of it. Domestically the *liberum veto* imposed paralysis on the Sejm, which might otherwise have paralyzed the monarch. The king, who made a long-remembered promise to see that justice was done to the serfs, abdicated without acting on it.

At length an outstanding soldier was chosen king: John III Sobieski. He won lasting fame from his leadership in relieving the Turkish siege of Vienna (1683), the last time the Ottomans managed to reach so far west. In the upshot they were driven back a good distance; by the Treaty of Karlowitz (1699) the Habsburgs obtained all of Hungary except the Banat of Temesvár, as well as Transylvania, eastern Croatia, and Slavonia; Venice made gains, and Poland acquired Podolia. However, the domestic anarchy remained unrepaired. By the time of Karlowitz Sobieski was dead. Another non-Polish king, Augustus II, elector of Saxony, was on the throne of Warsaw, but he managed to keep it only part of the time up to his death in 1733. The War of the Polish Succession at length placed one of his three hundred–odd children, Augustus III, on the throne.

During his reign reform sentiment coalesced around two families: the Potockis, who sought an aristocratic constitution that would actually function and were allied with France, and the Czartoryskis, who wished a strong monarchy and relied on Russian support. From that noble family to the throne came Stanislas Poniatowski, a discarded lover of Catherine II of Russia. To everyone's surprise he proved a serious reformer and ardent patriot. But he could not prevent the rulers of the three adjoining states—Prussia, Austria, and Russia—from making designs on Polish territory. In three gulps (1772, 1793, and 1795) they swallowed the whole country (Austria did not participate in the Second Partition.) As Reddaway describes the First Partition, "Austria gained the richest and most populous region; Prussia, that which she could make the most important, and Russia, the most easily digested."[39] But no part of Poland was very rich.

Poland showed its mettle in its death struggles. In May 1791 a new constitution was adopted, making the anarchically elective monarchy hereditary and ending the most egregious noble privileges, including the *liberum veto*. Russia now led the slicing of the remaining Polish state in half, of which she annexed four-fifths. What was left became a Russian protectorate. A final desperate uprising led by Tadeusz Kosciuszko was crushed, and Poland disappeared from the map.

From 1795 to 1918 there was no state named Poland. in 1772 the Austrians created something they called the Kingdom of Galicia and Lodomeria, with the emperor as distant king. Economically it was a sad area; some bitterly called it the Kingdom of Golicia and Glodomeria (*goly* means bare, *glód* means hunger).[40] However, culturally and politically it became the focus of attention of those who never lost hope of a restored Poland and was regarded as the "Piedmont" of the future nation.

In 1807 Napoleon carved a Grand Duchy of Warsaw out of Prussian Poland and enlarged it at Austria's expense in 1809. The king of Saxony was made hereditary grand duke; there was to be a bicameral parliament—the upper house appointed, the lower house elected. A constitution proclaimed equality before the law and the abolition of serfdom. The Poles loved Napoleon. Polish cavalry with great losses forced the way into Madrid for him, and Polish soldiers may have been the most enthusiastic contingent of the Grand Army that took Moscow. But the retreat from Moscow was the beginning of the end for Napoleon and for the prospect of a restored Poland under his aegis which few historians take seriously in retrospect.

As Galicia under Austria was the center of Polish self-consciousness, a somewhat similar role for Hungary was played by Transylvania, only nominally a vassal state of the Turks, through the reign of George II Rákóczi, which ended in 1660. The strip of western and northern Hungary under Habsburg rule saw a tightening of the reins that provoked uprisings. Then the Turks advanced to Vienna and were driven back, and the Treaty of Karlowitz, as noted, gave all Hungary except Temesvár to the Habsburgs; they acquired Temesvár in 1718.

The succession to the Hungarian throne had been fixed in the male line of the Habsburgs by the Magyar Diet in 1687. Leopold I (1658–1705) and his successors introduced Serbian and German immigrants into the devastated portions of the reconquered land and assigned much territory to Austrian officers and soldiers. The great magnates gravitated to the Habsburg court in Vienna, and the gentry, though they strove to defend their ancient liberties, were generally ineffective; the *jus resistendi,* secured by the Golden Bull of 1222, was abolished.[41] A revolt led by Francis II Rákóczi erupted in 1703 and achieved spectacular successes before being put down.

Charles VI (Charles III in Hungary) finally ended the worst abuses and by 1715 accepted Hungarian liberties, including freedom of religion. As a result the Diet accepted the Pragmatic Sanction, and Maria Theresa succeeded to the throne without Magyar objection. In 1741 she guaranteed immunity from taxation to the Hungarian nobles. Little more was heard from Hungary until Joseph

II. He avoided coronation so that he would not have to swear to uphold the "Hungarian Constitution," and he foolishly brought the crown of St. Stephen (symbol of Hungarian nationhood) to Vienna—and had to send it back. But, as already noted, he had to retreat on other fronts as well.

The Balkans and Russia

The Ottoman Empire experienced an apparent revival under the leadership of the Köprülü viziers, of Albanian extraction. Mehmed Köprülü, already past eighty, took over the high office in 1656 and combined reform with ruthlessness in wiping out opposition. His son and then his grandson-in-law followed him in office. The latter, Kara Mustafa, in cooperation with the Hungarian rebels assaulted Vienna. The Turks were then forced back, and some at the court of Vienna contemplated expulsion of the Ottomans from Europe.[42] For the time being the Habsburgs had to be satisfied with Hungary. Belgrade went back and forth between Turkey and Austria.

Then Russia, gradually gaining in strength, took over the role of chief antagonist of the Sublime Porte. By the Treaty of Küchük Kainarji, near Silistria on the Danube, in 1774 Catherine II acquired the right to protect the Romanian principalities, Moldavia and Wallachia, and annexed the chief Turkish fortresses on the Black Sea. From then on it was relatively easy to make additional gains at Turkish expense.

By the end of the eighteenth century the Ottoman Empire was wholly on the defensive. It was "the sick man of Europe," whose existence was prolonged only because the powers either found it convenient or could not settle among themselves on how to terminate it. In 1804 an uprising of the Serbs occurred, led by a well-off trader in pork named Kara Djordje. It was the beginning of the movement for independence among the Balkan Christians, though the uprising was not necessarily aimed at ending Turkish rule but rather sought to end the oppression by the Janissaries in Belgrade.

The chief alteration in power relations in Eastern Europe during the seventeenth and eighteenth centuries was the result of the rise of Russia. It had a great effect on the Ottoman Empire; within a little over half a century the positions of Moscow and Constantinople were reversed—from the Treaty of the Pruth (1711), in which the Turks had the upper hand, to Küchük Kainarji (1774), where the Russians could do as they liked.

Internally Russia lost some shreds of freedom that persisted into the seventeenth century. The Assembly of the Land (*Zemskii Sobor*), which had been summoned irregularly from the mid-sixteenth century onward, was called upon to elect as tsar Michael Romanov—the first of the line that ruled until 1917—

and met several times in the early years of his reign, but disappeared by the end of the century. The legal code of 1649 may be considered the nodal point at which serfdom became fixed on the landlords' peasants. They made up roughly half of the perhaps 85% of the Russian population who lived on the land; the other half were state peasants who had no landlord but the central government.

At the end of the century Peter I gained first the throne (1682) and then the real power (1694) at the death of his mother. He defeated the Swedes in the Great Northern War, and by the peace of 1721 annexed Estonia, Livonia, and the area south of Finland on which St. Petersburg, his "window on the West," had already been built. He was unable to subdue the Turks or the Persians, though he took over some territory south of the Caspian from the latter that did not remain Russian.

But Peter's central effort was to build a strong army, and he also laid the foundations for a navy. His financial, governmental, and legal measures were all intended to serve the aim of military strength. His actual governmental changes did not last in the form he gave them, but he did much to make the central administration more powerful and more effective. He did away with most of the privileges of the hereditary nobles and made the so-called gentry (*dvorianstvo*) a class that had to contribute its males for all of their adult lives to either military or civil service (with minor exceptions).

On the one hand Peter may be assigned the blame for fixing a despotism on Russia, building on the weak class structure, flimsy legal system, and absence of strong property that he inherited, and on the other hand he should be given the credit for beginning the process of dismantling absolutism by encouraging borrowing from the West, in which he himself extensively engaged.

In the eighteenth century, following Peter's death in 1725, the leading segment of the gentry, the Guards regiments, made and unmade monarchs. However, they did not seek to acquire corporate organization or rights or to limit the power of the monarchy that seemed to have become their plaything. An attempt to fetter the autocracy Peter had created was made in 1730 by the remnants of the hereditary aristocracy when they brought Anna, daughter of Peter's half-brother and co-tsar Ivan V, from Courland, where she was duchess, to Moscow as empress, subject to certain "conditions." But she tore them up, with the support of the Guards, as soon as she reached the capital.

The first serious step in the direction of modern Russian freedom may be traced to 1762, when Peter III announced the end of compulsory state service for the gentry. That measure was confirmed and codified in 1785 by Catherine II, his wife, who connived at his murder and then ruled alone from 1762 to 1796. The emancipation of the gentry meant also the first private property on any sizeable scale for the country, since the landowners now received title to the estates they had previously held only on condition they served the state. However, they still had no corporate bodies of significance, though they were permitted by the law of 1785 to elect their own local "marshals" and to meet periodically. But under Catherine the peasants' lot perceptibly worsened; serfdom became in effect slavery, with the buying and selling of human beings.

The paladins of the West European Enlightenment admired and praised the empress's professed devotion to the principles they preached. In summoning a Legislative Commission (1767–68), she seemed poised to put such principles into effect. It has to be said that even if she were in earnest about her agreement with the *philosophes,* she would have had great difficulty in acting upon it. It was not that there were limits on her power; there were none. Nevertheless her position was precarious; she had no legal title whatever to rule. The oppression from which the serfs suffered erupted in the largest peasant revolt in Russian history, Pugachev's rising on 1773–74, and gave her a real fright. From 1789 on she kept a wary eye on the French Revolution and its possible impact on Russia.

Catherine had her chief successes in war and diplomacy. Küchük Kainarji was only the first of her triumphs vis-à-vis the Turks. She proceeded to annex the Crimea in 1783, and by a second war with the Ottomans Russia moved its boundary to the Dniester River (1792). She took part in the partitions of Poland, and her territorial gains from Turkey and Poland together netted her the Ukraine and Belorussia. Catherine considered partitioning the Ottoman Empire, but the plan never got off the ground. She remained aloof from the fighting that began between the French and their neighbors in 1792. Her successor, Paul I, did not; first he fought against Napoleon, then made peace and allied with him in 1800. The tsar was killed a few months later and was succeeded by Alexander I. That ruler would lead the anti-Napoleonic coalition to final victory.

Conclusion

In the words of R. R. Palmer, during the last four decades of the eighteenth century there was a "single movement" that was different in different countries but

was everywhere aimed against closed elites, self-selecting power groups, hereditary castes, and forms of special advantage or discrimination that no longer served any useful purpose. These were summed up in such terms as feudalism, aristocracy, and privilege, against which the idea of common citizenship in a more centralized state, or of common membership in a free political nation, was offered as a more satisfactory basis for the human community.[43]

For this movement Palmer offers the term "democratic" as "appropriate and enlightening." He stresses the assertion of equality by 1800 across the continent, "an equality that meant a wider diffusion of liberty." No one can doubt the importance of the proclamation of equality and liberty as slogans, and of the extent to which they were given some practical application.

Nevertheless I hesitate to use the term "democracy": it means "the rule of the people," and such had not come about. Of course the people cannot rule, in any important sense, in any community larger than that which can be crammed into an Athenian agora in ancient times or, say, a football stadium in our day, and one may doubt whether a few decisions taken by such "direct democracy" can be said to constitute real rule by the people. It is safest to measure democracy by universal suffrage (which began with universal male suffrage of freemen) for some significant governmental office or body with the availability of genuine choice. In that sense, democracy lay ahead, by many decades even in the most progressive nations.

A free society is something less than democracy, and also more. A free society may consist of a plurality of political institutions, sharing power to some degree, and of social classes, in which no single class has a monopoly of power, property, or privilege. It may boast a legal and judicial system—an acceptance of law as a basis for regulating human relations and of courts as the device through which that occurs, both systematized in theory and practice, not necessarily proof against bribery, influence, or favoritism but resilient enough to regain dependability when an unjust law is repealed or a corrupt judge removed. It may rest on a foundation of the acceptance of private property as the natural accompaniment of the labors of civilized man, secured by law and also by the distribution of strength among social groups to prevent one group from assaulting the law with full success. All those elements may be present, and yet democracy may not have arrived.

As for the best phrase to describe what happened in Europe and North America during the period 1650–1800, it may be the arrival of constitutional government. The British have never had a written constitution, and thus it is necessary to look beyond the documents in order to date the arrival of such in the United Kingdom. Written constitutions, so characteristic of the eighteenth-century approach to the affairs of government, came into being in the United States, France, and Poland and in the 1990s retain their hold on the popular mind. Not, to be sure, the same constitutions—not even in the United States, where duly adopted amendments have made some difference (especially the first ten, in effect part of the original) and judicial interpretations and extensions of the original meaning have produced great changes.

But the idea of a constitution, the view that a government is not stable and legitimate unless and until it has one, came to embrace the whole planet. A constitution might be flouted or ignored, and the actions of a government might make a mockery of it every hour of every day; but even a people oppressed by the most brutal of tyrannies might often cling to the knowledge that the country in some sense had a constitution, which might one day be actually put into force.

Constitutional government in the literal sense, then, dates from the late eighteenth century. Nevertheless fundamental aspects of what we mean by that phrase are a good deal older, and stem from the seventeenth century in Britain. The English Revolution (or Civil War, Commonwealth, and Protectorate, to take the terms that appear in many histories instead) produced interesting innovations and daring experiments, but few of them had lasting effect.

The start of continuous development of mid-twentieth-century political patterns is to be found in the period of the Restoration of the Stuarts. It continued through the Glorious Revolution, the settlement of governmental affairs that took place in the reign of William and Mary, and the trial-and-error period of the eighteenth century, from Anne to George III. New institutions were created: the cabinet, the Bank of England, the national debt, the single parliament for England and Scotland together. New habits were formed: the monarchy ceased to use its veto, money bills had to originate in Commons, the king stayed away from cabinet meetings, the cabinet must operate on the basis of unanimity, and above all the cabinet must be able to work with the majority of Commons (and, later, must be responsible to it).

A two-party system came into being, a novelty in world history though more or less duplicated in Sweden and the United States within a century and admired rather than successfully imitated almost everywhere else. Religious toleration did not originate in Britain, but gradually took root there. Britain in the late eighteenth century was not a democracy; it has been called an "aristocracy" in the sense that the privileged class, the gentry above all, actually bore the burdens and responsibilities of governing, in the localities as well as in the central administration. Commons was more powerful than the monarchy, but it was elective only in a restricted sense and would become representative only as the nineteenth century wore on.

Britain blazed a trail for the rest of the world to follow. Yet in 1800 it seemed to have been overtaken by the United States, whose already partly self-governing inhabitants had won independence by persuading themselves that they were ruled by tyrants across the sea in London. Moreover, a claim to be in the forefront of the advance of freedom might be made by France, where the age of the citizen inferior to no one else was proclaimed, and England was feared as the most powerful enemy of the new dispensation. The French Revolution, however, was demonstrating that there could be tyranny exercised in the name of the people, perhaps even with the approval of many of them. It was a new lesson for mankind to learn. Many still more painful lessons lay ahead.

What seems remarkable, in retrospect, is that the changes of the period led toward greater freedom. Wordsworth wrote, "bliss was it in that dawn to be alive," placing his hopes at that stage in France rather than his own country, yet having in mind the progress of liberty in the world. It was a dawn indeed, despite all the disappointments. And not only in America, Britain, and France, for Napoleon brought awakening to central Europe and even hastened the fluttering of the eyelids that was observable in Russia.

Of course there were many casualties in the wars that accompanied all this. But they were not as devastating as the Thirty Years' War and not as bloody as World War I, and their scars were rather soon healed. When the Napoleonic Wars began, independent Poland had disappeared, and after the short life of the grand duchy it would disappear again. Most of Hungary having thrown off Ottoman rule, the country started to develop as an oligarchy of nobles. The beginning of the modern independence of the Balkan states lay just ahead. During his complex confrontation with Napoleon, the tsar raised hopes for freedom that achieved partial realization outside of his own country but inside Russia were to be dashed.

And yet the memory of the freer societies of France and Germany that soldiers from Russia had seen, the writings of the Western defenders and proponents of freedom that young Chinese began to read, the reports of travelers from Japan who visited Europe and America, and all the various consequences that flowed from the presence of Britain in India made their mark on the consciousness of many young people outside the West, and the resultant seeds of liberty would sprout in the two centuries that lay ahead.

CHAPTER 8

The Coming of Democracy, 1800–1990: Part One

The Restoration on the European Continent

The French Constitution of the Year VIII (the revolutionaries' calendar started from the fall of the monarchy) was replaced in 1802 by the Constitution of the Year X, on the heels of the plebiscite that was declared to have given virtual unanimous consent of Frenchmen to Napoleon as Consul for life. The powers of the Senate were increased, but Napoleon was given the right to nominate the majority of senators, to summon the body and preside over it. He became in effect the head of a limited monarchy. A longish list of republics sprang up at his bidding in nearby countries, but they were in fact of similar structure to the Consulate in France. In 1804 a genuine conspiracy of supporters of the House of Bourbon was quashed, and the clearly innocent prince of the house, the duc d'Enghien, was executed along with a few of those actually guilty.

In May the Empire was proclaimed, as if in answer to the demand for a monarch, and still another constitution was approved by plebiscite. But the constitutional change threatened France with one of the lesser Bonapartes, since the rule was now hereditary. Napoleon's divorce of Josephine, whom he loved, and marriage to Maria Luisa, daughter of the Habsburg emperor, gave him a son, but events were to deny him a Bonaparte successor. In the Battle of Leipzig he was defeated and sent to Elba, still as emperor; at Waterloo he was defeated finally and sent to St. Helena, now as an exile.

It fell to the brother of the dead Louis XVI "to uphold the social system introduced by the Revolution and the laws and institutions which Napoleon had devised."[1] Louis XVIII resumed the throne under restrictions imposed by a *charte constitutionnelle* (June 1814); a parliamentary system boasted a Chamber of Peers nominated by the king, a Chamber of Deputies elected by limited suffrage, and written guarantees of civil and religious freedom. The restored monarch was a moderate, but extremist relatives and friends wreaked vengeance on supporters of the regimes of the past two decades, and reactionaries swept the first elections in August 1815. The duc de Richelieu as prime minister did his best to check the excesses of this group in the new Chamber, and after new elections that the king called in September 1816 the deputies were as moderate as Richelieu.

Thus went the Restoration in France—not really a restoration of 1789 but not a lasting new system either. Closer to a real restoration was what happened in Spain. Ferdinand VII, promising to maintain the Constitution of 1812, returned to the throne. The constitution had been worked out by an assembly elected by the area around Cadiz, the only part of the country free of foreign troops. It provided for a single-chamber parliament and universal suffrage, and its supporters, becoming known as *liberal,* gave not only Spanish but also a host of other languages a new word of great subsequent currency. But in 1814 Ferdinand had no wish to keep the constitution and simply broke his promise, with the backing of the Church and the army but also with the acceptance of many others who were glad of the end of French tutelage. Spain had lost its Latin American colonies during the period preceding, and with them a major source of income; the king determined to reconquer them but failed.

In Italy Napoleonic rule had shattered much antique inertia and legal particularism. The reconstituted political map showed nine states, the two major ones being the Kingdom of Sardinia (whose chief region was Piedmont) under the House of Savoy and the Kingdom of Naples under the Bourbons. However, the chief political actor on the peninsula, replacing the France of Napoleon, was Austria, whose chief minister, Count Metternich, was the chief international symbol of restoration. And attempts at restoration were made in all nine states. Pius VII, who had no limits whatever on his secular power to worry about, helped by restoring the Society of Jesus, abolished in 1773 (except for Russia, where it survived throughout the period, and briefly Prussia), which thereupon returned to several of the Italian states. But young men in all of the states remembered the Napoleonic reforms (many of whose effects could not be undone), longed to throw off Austrian domination, and set as their goal the unification of Italy, which Metternich had termed only "a geographical expression."

In order to create barriers against a renewal of French expansion, the Austrian Netherlands were united with Holland to create a Kingdom of the Netherlands. Though he granted a constitution, the former prince of Orange, now King

William I, was unable to bridge the gap between north and south. The union lasted only until 1830. In Scandinavia a cartographic rearrangement had an unexpectedly successful outcome. Finland had been annexed by Russia in 1809 or, more precisely, became a grand duchy under the Russian tsar, retaining its Swedish laws. The maturing of national self-consciousness in Norway led to its readiness to break away from Denmark, and it seemed amenable to joining the realm of Marshal Bernadotte, Napoleon's gift to the Swedish throne. To be sure, this occurred only after an abortive Norwegian rising, but at length Bernadotte (first chosen crown prince, in 1810) became in 1818 Charles XIV, king of Sweden and Norway. "All the Danish fetters—monopolies, privileges, censorship of the press—had thus been abolished without sacrifice, and a constitution gained," writes Reddaway.[2] The Norwegians did not at first welcome the new order, but before long many came to accept it. Denmark, which had remained too long Napoleon's ally, lost not only Norway but Pomerania (to Prussia), but received some compensation to the south in the Duchy of Lauenburg.

The Holy Roman Empire had been formally abolished in 1806, and what was to succeed it remained a question for the country west of what was now called the Austrian Empire. Francis II, Holy Roman Emperor, had become Francis I, Austrian Emperor. By act of the Congress of Vienna the emperor became also president of a new entity called the German Confederation (*Deutscher Bund*). It was made up of thirty-nine units instead of the three-hundred-plus sovereign entities existing earlier; the rulers concerned included the kings of England (for Hannover), the Netherlands (for Luxemburg), and Denmark (for Holstein).

The confederation had no central administration and until 1821 no army. It had a representative assembly (Diet) of sorts; the lower house, or *Bundestag,* was made up of deputies appointed by the member states; the upper house, or *Bundesrat,* had a system of voting by states, each of the eleven largest having one vote, the others being placed into six groups each having a vote. The power of the Diet was negligible.

Defenders of the system have argued that it postponed violent rivalry between Austria and Prussia for half a century and that in doing so it saved Germany for that period from Prussian repressiveness. During the next five or six years quite a number of the states adopted some sort of constitution, notably in the southern regions: Bavaria, Württemberg, Baden, Nassau, and Hesse-Darmstadt, "states that had been integrated within the Napoleonic order or in which the middle class was most numerous."[3] But others retained the old system based on the medieval estates.

Austria under Metternich resisted the chief minister's efforts to modernize the bureaucracy and strengthen the State Council (*Staatsrat*) as an agency for modest change. Political opposition of any sort was severely repressed, though during the period Austria enjoyed much cultural and economic growth. Prussia under Hardenberg as chief minister for Frederick William III had been the hope of German liberals. In May 1815 the king had authorized the drafting of a constitution, but the appearance of liberal and radical youth movements in 1819 frightened the Prussian government into drawing back from reform—not the last time such a thing would occur in nineteenth-century Europe.

Napoleon had never induced political change in Russia, and it had never experienced a military defeat at his hands comparable to Jena for Prussia or Wagram for Austria. Therefore, there was not the sort of restoration to be found in other European countries. Alexander I emerged from the Congress of Vienna as grand duke of Finland, constitutional king of Poland, and absolute monarch of Russia. (There were also constitutional arrangements made in 1818 for Bessarabia.)

Perhaps the ablest of all the officials of imperial Russia, Michael Speransky, encouraged the emperor to lead the country into a constitutional system. Two fragments of such a plan were enacted: creation of a State Council (1810) to draft laws and supervise the legality of administration, and replacement of old collegia or "colleges" established by Peter the Great by new ministries comparable to those of the other European powers. As late as 1818 Alexander was considering constitutional plans, though Speransky had been dismissed as his chief adviser in 1812. However, nothing more came of them. Part of the reason had to do with the appearance of liberal secret societies, modeled on those of the German lands, which made Alexander hesitate.

France, 1816–1990.   In 1814 Napoleon was defeated and sent to Elba, still with the title of emperor, but after the Hundred Days in which he attempted a comeback (ended at Waterloo) he went to St. Helena with no title. In the previous two decades, however, successively as general of the army of the Convention and then of the Directory, as First Consul, and as Emperor, he had done more than any individual before him to change the map (in a way that did not last) and the social and political systems (in a way that did) of Europe.

The moderate restoration over which Louis XVIII wished to preside was infringed by a series of measures beginning in 1820 with the so-called Law of the Double Vote, which instituted a complex electoral system increasing the influence of the landlord class that supported the extreme rightists, or Ultras. In 1821 Jean-Baptiste de Villèle became minister. During the six years he occupied the post, several laws were enacted that had as their aim compensation to the nobility for loss of land during the Revolution, punishment for religious offenses so considered by the Catholic church, and lowering of the influence of the bourgeoisie—such as the abolition of the National Guard, where it was strong.

Charles X, king from 1824 to 1830, now called an election that went against the Ultras. After a brief gesture in a moderate direction, the monarch returned to the extremists by naming the Prince de Polignac as chief minister. He lacked the support of the majority of the Chamber of Deputies, which was not required by the constitution but had come to be customary. The Chamber and the king now were at a stand-off. Charles issued five "July" Ordinances enacting strict control of the press and a new electoral system. These provoked immediate violence: the so-called Revolution of 1830.

Radical Paris drove out the last Bourbon king, but the moderates, or Liberals, managed the solution to the problem of who or what would follow. It was Louis Philippe, duke of Orleans, from the cadet line of the Bourbons, proclaimed King of the French by a rump of the Chamber of Deputies under a somewhat revised constitution of 1814. Though the radicals, whose hero-leader was the Marquis de Lafayette, had been persuaded to accept the "July Monarchy," they soon returned to attempted revolution. The most prominent figures in the governments of "le roi bourgeois" were the duc de Broglie, the journalist Adolphe Thiers (who had led the opposition to the July Ordinances), and the historian François Guizot, author of a law entrusting control of elementary education to the Catholic church. In 1835 the so-called September Laws were effective in bringing the radicals under control. However, beneath the surface of events simmered agitation that erupted, under the stimulus of economic depression and unemployment, first into open opposition, in a "banquet campaign" and then into violent demonstrations in February 1848. The king abdicated, a republic was proclaimed, but from the start it was divided between moderates from the Chamber of Deputies, led by the poet Alphonse de Lamartine, and the radicals of Paris, led by the socialist writer Louis Blanc.

The elections of April yielded about five hundred deputies for the Lamartine group, twohundred for the supporters of the Orleans house, one hundred for the Legitimists, who supported the Bourbons, and fewer than one hundred for the Blanc group. The system of work relief called the "national workshops" came to be regarded as the center of revolutionary danger to the new government, and was abolished; the result was the bloody insurrection of June. General Louis Cavaignac, who managed to suppress it, was a candidate for the presidency, a position with much power created by a constitution finished in November, running against Prince Louis Napoleon. The nephew of Napoleon I, he swamped the opposition and became president in December.

In the spring a conservative coalition won a huge majority of seats in the new Legislative Assembly, but the Radical Republicans also made not a bad showing. Louis Napoleon avoided identifying himself with either. He pleased the church by accepting the Falloux Law, a measure that permitted lower standards for

Catholic school teachers than state ones and allowed localities to substitute Catholic schools for state schools (with the motive of saving money). He acted to repress republican agitation and undercut worker suffrage by a strengthened residence requirement.

Facing a constitutional prohibition of a second (consecutive) four-year term, Louis Napoleon first tried to repeal it. Having failed, he carried out a coup d'état in December 1851. He proclaimed universal suffrage and a plebiscite on a proposal to allow the president to draw up a new constitution; opponents were arrested and revolutionaries were shot on Parisian barricades. The constitution of January 1852 provided for three bodies: a Council of State, a Senate (both of these were appointed by the president), and a Legislative Assembly "by means of [which]" the chief of state was to govern. But with a little prodding, public opinion soon appeared to countenance—by plebiscite in November—the restoration of the empire.

Napoleon III, as he called himself (leaving the number II for the king of Rome, who never ruled, as Louis XVIII had done for the dauphin who had died in the Temple at the age of ten), promoted the expansion and reconstruction of Paris, improvement of the lot of the workers, and the growth of industry and trade. The emperor continued to favor the church and its schools. That policy also had important foreign ramifications, as when Napoleon sent French troops to Rome to protect the pope against revolutionaries in 1849, when he was still president of the Second Republic, and when he declared what came to be called the Crimean War on Russia in 1854 in a dispute over who should care for the Holy Places of Palestine. But he was no religious zealot; he wished, as the first Napoleon had, to remove religion from the area of political controversy as much as possible.

Napoleon III had been called the "first modern dictator."[4] He managed to attract what was probably real majority support for a regime in which the people exercised no power, but much of that support slipped away as the years passed. He may have been a precursor of later leaders who in a few years or decades went from widespread popularity to universal detestation; several changed over time from being constitutional executives with the approval of their people to autocrats who trampled on the law, the rights, and the welfare of those ruled. Louis Napoleon's career did not undergo that dramatic a transformation.

Certainly he succeeded in consigning to the discard the pre-1851 liberal and parliamentary institutions of France. The Legislative Assembly was elected by universal suffrage; but the government designated only one candidate for each seat, and any opposing candidate faced formidable obstacles. In any case it had no power to initiate laws or any other significant power. Political life virtually came to an end, but public opinion seems to have approved the order and tranquillity, along with prosperity and visible public improvements, that the empire had brought about.

After some foreign misadventures, however, Napoleon's popularity was affected, and he chose to permit a certain revival of political parties and parliamentary powers. Foreign affairs continued to go badly as the attempt to establish a Mexican Empire as a French client-state foundered. The emperor found it wise to permit greater freedom of the press and of assembly, and the elections of May 1869 yielded 3,300,000 oppositional votes as against 4,400,000 for the government. An eleventh-hour attempt to save a fast-weakening empire was made in a constitutional reform of April 1870, at once ratified by a heavy majority in a plebiscite.

But Napoleon III was swept away by the Prussian victory at Sedan in September 1870, and a republican government was proclaimed under Leon Gambetta. While Paris seethed with revolution, national elections produced an assembly in which republicans were only a small minority. A Paris Commune, presided over by a heterogeneous council ranging from moderate republicans to socialists, lasted from March to May 1871 before the national government, now headed by Adolphe Thiers, overwhelmed it by force. Giving up Alsace-Lorraine to newly united Germany, France was monarchically minded (as in 1797 and 1848), but the monarchists' candidate for king, the Comte de Chambord, threw away a throne by insisting on the Bourbons' fleur-de-lis as his flag (instead of the tricolor). By 1875 the Third Republic had come to be a reality. There was no new constitution, but a set of laws that established a presidency, an indirectly elected Senate, a Chamber of Deputies elected by universal and direct manhood suffrage, and a cabinet headed by a premier. The real executive was to be the premier, who in turn had to be acceptable to a majority of the legislative body, especially to its lower house.

This new system would prevail throughout the life of the Third Republic and, in essence, the Fourth as well. In Palmer's words, "under the Third Republic the substantial machinery of state-ministries, prefectures, law courts, police, army, all under highly centralized control—was carried over virtually untouched as in all upheavals since the time of Napoleon I."[5] The amount of freedom enjoyed by the individual who wished to express himself politically or exercise religious choice varied a good deal throughout the nineteenth and early twentieth centuries, and minorities were harshly treated more than once: in the Reign of Terror in 1793–94, about forty thousand of those opposed or unsympathetic to the revolution were executed; after the Paris Commune was crushed, twenty thousand accused of supporting its form of revolutionism were put to death. But most Frenchmen by the nineteenth century felt that they had some civic relation to the national government and held little fear of what it might do to their everyday activities.

In 1879 republicans won control of the Republic's government, but they introduced few changes except for the creation of a free and compulsory public school system from which clerical influence would be absent, the restoration of divorce (for the first time since 1816), and the legalization of labor unions (which had been tolerated anyway for some time). In the 1880s a variety of dissatisfied groups coalesced temporarily around General Georges Boulanger, who challenged the Republic with quite unclear goals but who botched his chances to establish personal rule in 1889 and fled into exile. Charles Cardinal Lavigerie at a banquet in Algiers summoned all to a *ralliement* (support) for the Third Republic in 1890. It appeared as if a movement for reconciliation was well under way.

However, it was disrupted once again by the Dreyfus affair. In 1894 Captain Alfred Dreyfus of the general staff of the army was accused of treason, found guilty, and deported to French Guiana. He had been framed, and the effort to exculpate him became the special cause of the defenders of the Republic. In contrast, the anti-Dreyfusards were apt to be royalist and militantly Catholic. The affair dragged on for twelve years, but in 1899 Dreyfus's most recent conviction was overturned, and he was promoted and decorated. The victory of the republicans was carried into matters affecting the church and schools. An Associations Law, passed in 1901, regulated religious congregations and schools. In 1905 a law separated church and state, overturning the Napoleonic Concordat (1801), ending the participation of the state in choosing and paying Catholic clerics, and transferring church property to private corporations formed for that purpose. (Protestants and Jews had also been linked with the state throughout the nineteenth century.) After 1906, however, the Right made a modest come-back, mobilizing around the newspaper *Action Française,* though winning no dramatic political victories. On the eve of 1914, French governments were headed by radicals or socialists, such as Georges Clemenceau and Aristide Briand, but put down strikes by the use of troops.

Although Belgium is thought to have suffered the most from World War I, France experienced great losses in men and property. The most noteworthy leader she had during the war was Clemenceau, the single-minded apostle of victory, who was premier from November 1917 to January 1920 (he had also held the office in 1906–9) and carried through France's part in the peace settlement. An electoral law passed in July 1919 gave enough proportional representation to France's voters so that frequent changes of government were assured.

The Third Republic continued with a good many political changes. The Catholic Church was allowed to resume occupancy of its former property through the device of "diocesan associations." A moderate rightist bloc won the elections of 1919. Popular desire to be tough with Germany was acted upon by Premier Raymond Poincaré, but his policy failed and brought a moderate leftist bloc into control of the Chamber of Deputies. The country remained divided: in 1933 the scandal involving the promoter Stavisky threatened to reopen the political struggles of the Dreyfus case, but this time royalists (and extreme rightist forces close to fascism) were the attackers; the fuss was, however, short-lived.

French communism had come out of the Socialist party, and in 1935 the Communists and various leftist forces, including the not-very-radical Radical Socialists (more properly: Socialist Radicals) formed a Popular Front. It was the trial run for a worldwide policy of Communist collaboration with non-Communist forces against Nazis and Fascists. In June 1936 the Popular Front formed a government under Léon Blum, the leader of the Socialist party. It proceeded to establish a forty-hour work week, to move toward nationalization of the Bank of France and the arms industry, and to legislate to better the situation of the workers. The economic results were bad and then nearly catastrophic. Although efforts were made to repair the damage, World War II overtook France when it was still militarily unprepared and economically in poor shape, and Hitler crushed it swiftly in the spring of 1940.

The man who organized French resistance to the Nazis and led the nation to establish a Fourth Republic was General Charles de Gaulle. It was much like the Third, but not by de Gaulle's wish. His provisional government—recognized as the legitimate government of France by the United States, Britain, and the USSR, in October 1944, took over the country at the end of hostilities, but he resigned suddenly in January 1946 as provisional president. A Constituent Assembly went on to draw up a constitution, ratified by the voters only on the second try in October 1946.

During the 1950s an executive responsible to a National Assembly that toppled coalition after coalition provided an air of déjà vu at the political level; but despite, or perhaps because of, the political *immobilisme* that prevailed, great economic progress was made. The unresolved problem for France was her overseas colonies, unlike Britain which had accepted the desirability of dismantling the Empire. First Indo-China (1946–54), then Algeria (1954–62) were the scenes of prolonged, searing conflict that tore the metropolitan area apart, aside from the damage done in the Asian and African regions concerned.

The Algerian War destroyed the Fourth Republic in 1958, but a stronger Fifth Republic emerged in its place. De Gaulle was recalled, and a new constitution gave greater power to the president, who presided over an effective French government from the Elysée palace. The (Gaullist) UNR (Union pour la Nouvelle République) won majorities in the National Assembly in 1962 and 1968 ("the most impressive majority ever returned in republican France"),[6] the latter saving France from domestic near-chaos begun by student demonstrations of that spring.

However, de Gaulle soon toppled from that peak of popularity. He proposed new constitutional changes, failed to win the "substantial majority" he demanded, and resigned in April 1969. Since then Georges Pompidou, Valéry Giscard d'Estaing, and François Mitterand (reelected in June 1988) have held the presidency. Party strife is much less in the forefront of public life. The Communists, once France's strongest party, have been much weakened; the Socialists (Mitterand's party) did try a Socialist economic policy but early recognized its failure and adopted a successful austerity and free-enterprise program.

The wounds of the Revolution, the struggle between monarchists of three different kinds (Legitimists supporting the Bourbons, Orleanists, and Bonapartists) and republicans, the believers in the unrealized promises of the Revolutionary tricolor who wished a Socialist or Communist France—all could be detected in aspects of French political life. But the Fifth Republic offered greater political stability, prosperity, and freedom than any polity had done for a long time.

Germany, Austria, and Hungary, 1819–1990. The unification of Germany was an unrealized dream when the German Confederation came into existence in 1815. Clearly, it would come through either Prussian or Austrian leadership. The students and professors of the numerous German universities adopted ideas of nationality—*Volksgeist* and *Deutschtum*—that pushed the smaller principalities toward the goal of unification. Prince Metternich summoned a conference of the major states that met in Karlsbad (in Bohemia) in 1819 and successfully pressed on the Confederation's Diet a series of decrees aimed at dissolving the organizations through which the universities' more impatient spirits had sought to act. Thereby he managed to put the damper on the spread of nationalism and liberalism.

Such ideas were usually generated and propagated by and within the middle classes of Europe. Altogether the German middle classes found themselves in a quandary. Such statesmen as Baron Heinrich vom Stein, chief minister of Prussia in 1807–8, and Karl August von Hardenberg, whose ministries both preceded and followed vom Stein's, had been able to carry through the emancipation of the Prussian serfs (though other ministers later led the monarchy to abandon its policy of *Bauernschutz*, or protection of the peasantry, and allowed the nobles to convert the class mostly into landless tenants performing wage labor on their newly acquired lands). Stein and Hardenberg also restored self-government to the cities and reorganized the bureaucracy. Stein perceived much in the English constitutional system that he believed Prussia should imitate; Hardenberg wished to borrow aspects of Napoleon's legal and administrative reforms. Not all their aims were achieved.

Especially in Baden and other southern states, liberal professors and progressive bureaucrats worked for a unified and limited German monarchy. Several of the states had a *Landtag*, though severely limited in power and sometimes top-heavy with nobles. As for the Diet of the German Confederation, it had become by the 1820s "the shame of Germany and the contempt of Europe" (H. von Gagern), able neither to exercise power nor to exert intellectual leadership. The middle class was divided by the continuation of the long particularist tradition of the German lands. The south adopted constitutions patterned after the French Charte Constitutionelle of 1814: Bavaria in 1817, Baden and Nassau in 1818, Württemberg in 1819. They were cautious documents retaining much power in the princes and the upper chambers of two-house legislatures and maintaining silence on the question of civil liberties. After 1830 the new grand duke of Baden sought to work for a genuine parliament, a free press, and an emancipated peasantry.

But it was Prussia and Austria that dominated the patchwork of states, from moderate sized to minuscule, between them. Austria remained the largest and strongest of the German states but was less German than before: she had lost the Netherlands and other territories across the Rhine and gained much of northern Italy, so that her non-German possessions exceeded her German ones. For the time being the ascendancy of the Austrians was accepted by their fellow Catholics in the south and their Protestant kinsmen farther north, who were distrustful of a Prussia threateningly on the make.

Prussia had been fortified by gains in 1815 of lands west and east of the Rhine, to guard against any renewed eruption of French aggression (the "watch on the Rhine," in the words of the song). It lost about half of its Polish territory—the result being to shift its attention, as well as the direction of possible future expansion, westward toward other German lands. From 1819 on Prussia took the initiative in constructing a customs union *(Zollverein)* with other German states; the first tariff treaty was signed with the insignificant state of Schwarzburg-Sondershausen, but a series of larger ones followed suit. By 1834 most of Germany outside Austria was included. Frederick William III, who had made a promise in 1815 to create a representative body based on the provincial estates, ruled until 1840 without acting on it.

But during the last decade or so of his reign, a German liberalism started to set forth aims that would realize the king's promise and go further still. Three varieties developed: First, the "dualism" of Karl von Rotteck and Karl Theodor Welcker, which envisaged a popular representative body side by side with a crown in which the powers of government would reside, in other words, democracy and monarchy in an uneasy equilibrium and indeed often in conflict. Second came the moderate school with F. C. Dahlmann at its head, much readier to accept the product of history than the rationalist "dualists," and inclined nearly to divinize the state and the princes who incarnated the state idea. Third were the radicals belonging to the group called Young Germany; they derived inspiration from the writer and polemicist Heinrich Heine, who, from a safe place in Paris, trumpeted the superiority of the French system to what was to be found in Germany. (The radicals verged on being democrats.) All demanded a constitution, civil liberties, and the rule of law; the slogan *Rechtsstaat* (meaning a government based on law) became popular on the eve of the revolution of 1848.

In 1845 a brief civil war in Switzerland made the Confederation into a federal state; in 1846 unrest in Austrian Poland led to Austrian annexation of the Free City of Cracow. These events were only curtain raisers for the Revolutions of 1848, beginning in Sicily and Naples and then jumping to Paris, the cities of Baden and other German states, Vienna, Berlin, and Budapest.[7] A national assembly, demanded first in the Baden chamber, was elected by direct manhood suffrage and convened in Frankfurt-am-Main in May; at length it produced a constitution for a German Empire and elected Frederick William IV of Prussia as emperor. He waffled and finally declined. The Frankfurt Assembly collapsed. A scheme for a Prussian Union was tried instead: Saxony, Hanover, and the smaller governments outside the Habsburg Empire accepted, but Austria forced Prussia to abandon the idea through the diplomatic surrender known as the Punctation of Olmütz (November 1850). The Germanic Confederation of 1814 was reestablished.

Popular disappointment was widespread and deep. The Revolution of 1848 was, however, not wholly in vain. A new Prussian constitution, adopted in December 1848 and given a new form in January 1850, provided for a two-house legislature, the lower house chosen by all males over twenty-five but under a system of three-class voting based on taxpaying, so that 83 percent of the voters were able to fill only one-third of the seats. This *Landtag* had the power to enact new laws and taxes, but ministers were not responsible to it and the king could issue what were in effect laws between sessions. The upper chamber (*Herrenhaus*) was, from 1854, elected by the old agrarian nobles (ninety members), the larger cities (thirty members), and the six Prussian universities (one member from each). The result was a landlord-dominated government right down to November 1918.

Austrian efforts to enter the *Zollverein* failed, as did her attempt to break it up. In 1853 the last non-Austrian German states joined the customs union: they were Hanover, Brunswick, and Oldenburg. Within Prussia a conflict erupted between the Liberals in the *Landtag* and the king, William I, over the affairs of the army. Driven by frustration to the verge of abdication, the king was brought to call the ambassador to Paris, Otto von Bismarck-Schönhausen, to become minister-president. In Holborn's words, "he [the king] himself and Germany had found their master."[8]

Bismarck was a conservative, a noble, a *Junker,* and a Prussian. As chief minister of Prussia from 1862 to 1871, he coolly put together a German Empire by way of three successive small wars (with Denmark, Austria, and France respectively), and then from 1871 to 1890 he did his best to defend the new status quo internationally and domestically. When the *Zollverein* treaty was renewed in 1865, Austria was excluded for good from the possibility of joining the customs union. After Bismarck's Seven Weeks' War with Austria (actually won in a few afternoon hours on the day of the battle of Königgrätz) ended in victory, he was able to construct—as a way station to his real goal—a North German Confederation, whose southern boundaries dipped below the Moselle and nearly reached the Main.

The new entity had a two-house legislature: a *Bundesrat·* representing the member states of the confederation, in which Prussia had seventeen out of forty-three votes and in effect controlled several others; and a *Reichstag* elected by single-member constituencies on the basis of suffrage of all males twenty-five and older. Each state retained its own government, but the king of Prussia was commander-in-chief of the armed forces and his representative, the federal chancellor (Bismarck, who remained also prime minister of Prussia), was to hold the presidium (presidency) of the confederation.

The confederation did not last long; the most important laws it enacted removed all sorts of restrictions on industry, provided for uniform legal codes, and encouraged the founding of new manufacturing and trading companies. Bismarck carried through a reorganization of the *Zollverein* wherein representatives of the south as well as the north sat in a two-house legislature (*Zollbundesrat* and *Zollparlament),* parallel to that of the confederation except in the territory it covered. He hoped that political unity would soon follow economic or at any rate commercial unity; and he was right. But what brought unity about was not rational reflection on the desirability of national unification, but the Franco-Prussian War—again a short one, lasting forty-three days until Napoleon III surrendered the army at Sedan, a few more months until peace was negotiated.

By its terms Alsace-Lorraine was annexed to the new united Germany, plainly against the will of the inhabitants. The opinion that Bismarck was pushed into reluctant acceptance of this acquisition by public opinion or whipped it up to demand the same has not fared well. In the words of Gordon Craig, "an objective view of the evidence would seem to indicate that neither public opinion nor Bismarck needed inducement."[9] Bismarck had success in reconciling Germany with her defeated opponent in the case of Austria, with which he made the Dual Alliance of 1879. With France, he did not even try.

Königgrätz (or Sadowa) had precipitated a resolution of the question of Austria's non-German territories that lasted more or less successfully until 1914. The measure referred to was the *Ausgleich* or Compromise of 1867, which divided the empire in two except for their monarch, the Habsburg king-emperor, and three ministries—foreign affairs, war, and finance (which ministry merely administered funds contributed by the two states for common purposes). In addition, instituted annual gatherings of sixty members of each of the two parliaments were to consider common problems, and a treaty was concluded covering the armed forces, tariffs, currency, and so forth, which Austria and Hungary shared in common. Austria, with a suffrage favoring the German middle class, was to dominate the peoples in seventeen provinces; in Hungary not merely were the Magyars to dominate but there was to be "a single nation, the indivisible, unitary Hungarian nation," with no differentiation among the nationalities except in official use of the vernaculars concerned.

The laws that made up the so-called "December constitution" of Austria (1867) granted civil liberties and equal rights to all the nationalities but restricted the suffrage, binding it to property holding until 1907. Though there was a parliament, the emperor was able to govern if that body could not function. The Poles were the most satisfied group among the non-Germans; they were given a good deal of self-government, and there was a special ministry for Galician affairs after 1871. There were roughly two political factions: the liberals, centralizing, anticlerical and the Conservatives, sympathetic to the Roman Catholic church, federalist, thus often allied with the Slavic minorities. The most persistent ethnic problem involved the Czechs. In 1871 Prime Minister Karl Siegmund, Count von Hohenwart, reached an agreement to grant them certain rights but then had to renounce it under Hungarian and other pressures.

During the decade of the 1880s the moderates' strength declined in several directions. The so-called Old Czechs lost support to the Young Czechs; the political Right lost support to the German nationalists under Georg Schönerer, who was the first to introduce anti-Semitism into German nationalist doctrine. The workers' associations formed a party, the Social Democrats, organized in 1889 at a conference at Hainfeld. Finally, from lower-middle-class ranks came Karl Lueger's new Christian Socialist party. Hitherto the Germans had kept ascendancy in Austria, but it now slipped away. In 1895 a Pole, Kazimierz Felix, Count Badeni, became prime minister, and managed to get through parliament a law introducing qualified universal suffrage, though the system of curias was kept and even a new one added.

At length, in 1907, came universal and equal suffrage (the curias were abolished) for all males twenty-four or older. The effect was to lessen the strength of the radicals at both ends of the spectrum: both Young Czechs and Pan-Germans suffered. The most numerous representatives in parliament came from the Christian Socialists and the Social Democrats. This situation foreshadowed Austrian politics after World War II, but it did not last at the time. In 1911 a new grouping of nationalists called the Deutscher Nationalverband won in elections the position of the strongest single party, but international affairs now took the spotlight. World War I brought forward other issues, and when the old emperor, Franz Josef, died in November 1916, his successor Charles tried to hold the empire together by conciliating the nationalities. The Germans were stubborn enough to block anything of significance. Seeing that an impasse existed on the issue, the Allies from early 1918 threw their support to the non-Germans,[10] and the Habsburg monarchy was doomed. In October 1918 Emperor Charles proclaimed the transformation of Austria (Hungary was not affected) into a federal union of four parts: German, Czech, South Slav, and Ukrainian. The Poles were to be free to join a Polish state, which they proceeded to do.

After the war ended, Austria (barred from *Anschluss* with Germany by Allied fiat) became a republic. Social Democrats dominated Vienna, the Christian Socialists the countryside. Austrian democracy was set aside by the authoritarian regime established by the Christian Socialist Engelbert Dollfuss in 1934, which made the Social Democrats illegal. But after only a few months Nazis overthrew Dollfuss and killed him in an abortive coup. His successor, Kurt von Schuschnigg, presided over the same sort of regime (though more gently than Dollfuss) until 1938, when Hitler annexed the country.

At the end of World War II, a Second Republic was formed, with two major parties: the People's party (heir of the Christian Socialists) and the Socialist party (heir of the Social Democrats). It was a democratic country. By the Austrian State Treaty (1955) it became officially neutral—the price of bringing about Soviet evacuation of its occupation zone.

Hungary was not so fortunate. The *Ausgleich* of 1867 was not seriously challenged, but despite Hungary's total control of its own internal affairs (except for extremely modest powers of the monarch) there remained opposition either in general or in detail to the compromise. From 1875 to 1890 power was in the hands of a Liberal party of the Manchester stripe, until 1890 under Kálmán Tisza. In the late 1890s "the gradual split-up of the huge government party began"; the left Liberals broke off, a new Catholic People's party began to grow, and industrial workers adopted a political platform.[11] In 1903 Count István Tisza (Kálmán's son) was named prime minister, but the opposition won the elections of 1905.

The king-emperor was prepared to appoint a coalition if it would abandon the demand for a Hungarian national army; the monarch insisted on unified command. The crown had a potent weapon: it had introduced a bill for universal and equal suffrage, which would have had a revolutionary effect on the Hungarian polity, but the bill did not have to be enacted to have effects, and was not. The coalition gave way and held office from 1906–1910. Some social legislation was passed, but labor unrest mounted. Tisza, having reorganized his Liberals as a National Labor party, returned as prime minister from 1913 to 1917; he was totally honest, strong-willed, and purblind to the wishes of the non-Magyar peoples, to which he would brook no concessions. At the end of World War I Hungary's minorities destroyed her as Austria's did. Prewar Hungary (1910) had 20,800,000 people; the state created by the Treaty of Trianon (1919) had 7,600,000. Out of 10,000,000 Magyar speakers, 3,200,000 were assigned to neighboring states.[12]

In the postarmistice confusion Béla Kun, the Communist leader, came to power. His regime, whose "Red Terror" rapidly brought on itself the widespread hatred on the populace, lasted from March to August 1919, when it was overthrown with Romanian help. The monarchy was nominally restored, with a regent, Admiral Miklós Horthy, acting for the Habsburg monarch (whom the Allies forbade to take the throne, and Hungary remained thus into World War II. Dissatisfaction was rife, but Count István Bethlen, the conservative prime minister, managed to persuade the Social Democrats to follow his lead and the peasant leaders to consent to postponing the extension of the very modest land reform that had taken place, and proceeded to attempt to win friends for Hungary as a prelude to treaty revision.

The result was to reduce the "White Terror" of the Right Radicals, whose influence was thus kept at bay until 1931. Thereafter Gyula Gömbös brought them to power, and tried (in vain) to transform Hungary into a corporate state on the model of Mussolini's ideas. After Gömbös died in 1936, the Right Radicals continued influential though not dominant.

Unlike Austria, Hungary escaped annexation by Hitler. Horthy joined Germany in attacking the USSR, but after Stalingrad he came to count on Western victory, which was at length forthcoming. However, bad diplomacy led to German occupation of the country, turning it into a battlefield, and Horthy did not foresee that victory of the West would fail to save Hungarian independence. In 1944 a democratic government was proclaimed, but Soviet troops, not the popular will, determined the outcome. By 1947 the Communists, though lacking any substantial popular support, were in the saddle. By 1949 Hungary was a fully Communist "people's republic."

In the fall of 1956, however, during the period of post-Stalin thaw, Hungary was the scene of a revolution, one which evoked far broader support and even participation than several nineteenth-century events so labeled; it was put down by Soviet tanks. Nevertheless modest economic reform, begun quietly in 1965, was in the era after Mikhail Gorbachev became Soviet leader followed by astonishing political reforms, climaxing in the official name change to "Republic of Hungary" in 1989 and the effective end of the Communist political monopoly. How far Hungary would be able to travel on the road to democracy remained unclear.[13]

In 1871 the German empire over which Bismarck presided as chancellor and William II as emperor was inaugurated in a mood of rhapsodic self-congratulation, though one writer sought to remind his countrymen that "a victory can sometimes be more dangerous than a defeat and that no victory can be more ruinous than one that is misconstrued by those who win it."[14] The annexation of Alsace-Lorraine prevented any possibility of Franco-German reconciliation and was a powerful impetus to the formation of the alliance system, beginning with Bismarck's treaty with Austria in 1879 to guard against French revenge ending with the Triple Entente of Britain, France, and Russia in 1907. The system of alliances was a keg of gunpowder ready for any tiny fuse that would blow it up, and the assassination of the Archduke Franz Ferdinand served as such.

The immediate result of the Franco-Prussian War was a Germany unified in an effective manner for the first time, since the Holy Roman Empire had never achieved unification even in a sense applicable to her medieval neighbors. It was the power predominant in central Europe, and potentially in the whole continent. And since it was the result of the prowess of the Prussian army (to be sure, with southern contingents) and the political skill of the Prussian prime minister, this Germany was one in which the monarchy and the military had the leading roles from the first, despite the universal manhood suffrage that was new in 1867. True, certain concessions to the south had been required: Bavaria, Württemberg, and Baden received certain rights; and although William I wished to be Emperor of Germany he became German Emperor, a title supposed to be easier for the south to accept. But the concessions amounted to very little.

Bismarck and the masses—this was to be the partnership. Bismarck had written, "In a country with monarchical traditions . . . the general suffrage, by eliminating the influences of the liberal bourgeois classes, will also lead to monarchical elections."[15] However, the lower classes were not to compose the parliament, for members of the Reichstag would receive no salaries; moreover, the powers of parliament were limited, and the deputies did not even press their legal authority to the limit. During the period 1871 to 1879, Bismarck used the slogan of *Kulturkampf*—that is, resistance to the newly enunciated papal claims that most German Catholics had accepted while fearing the pretensions of Protestant Prussia. Such fears were confirmed by the May Laws of 1873, invading in several respects what the Catholic Church regarded as its own territory, concerning the appointment and discipline of clergy and so forth. As a result, many bishops and priests were imprisoned, exiled, or driven from their sees and parishes.

But in 1879 two disparate phenomena—a new pope, Leo XIII, and a relatively new (1875) political party, the Social Democrats—combined to lead Bismarck in reaction to change his policy, though it took four years before the *Kulturkampf* was wholly abandoned. The new policy had a negative aspect in the Anti-Socialist Law of 1878; the newly protectionist tariff of the following year represented the other side of the coin. Bismarck's allies now ceased to be National Liberals and became instead the Conservatives and the Catholic Center. Industrialization proceeded at a rapid rate, railways bound the new nation together, the Ruhr and to a lesser extent other areas polluted the sky and made the nation rich.

The Socialists were banned, and Bismarck thought he could destroy their support by introducing a program of sickness, accident, and old-age and disability insurance enacted into law from 1883 to 1889. Having been forced to resort to publishing a party newspaper and holding party conferences in Switzerland or Denmark, the Social Democrats still had deputies in parliament and offered, not without irony, their votes in favor of Bismarck's social legislation, though seeking to amend or extend each law as it was introduced. Bismarck also tried to remove even mildly progressive elements from the Civil Service, which had earlier been famed for its liberal spirit, and the officer corps of the army, which had been earlier uniformly conservative but had recently incorporated a range of opinions as it expanded.

Bismarck's last years in office combined success and failure. In the elections of 1887 a coalition of three parties—Conservatives, Free Conservatives, and National Liberals—forming the so-called Kartell won a large majority of seats (220 out of 375) in the Reichstag, and the chancellor reached the peak of his popularity. But with the change of monarch in 1888 he showed himself mean, petty, and maladroit. The new monarch, Frederick III, was repeatedly humiliated by Bismarck and the part of the press friendly to him. After the emperor died—in only two months—Bismarck faced the young William II, determined to be his own man and to become known as a progressive in a manner Bismarck would not support. The elections of February 1890 smashed the Kartell and strengthened both the Center and Social Democratic parties. The Anti-Socialist Law came up for renewal and failed. In March Bismarck, abandoned by even the army high command, resigned.

The thankless assignment of being Bismarck's successor fell to General Georg Leo von Caprivi, and his two years were followed by six from Prince Chlodwig zu Hohenlohe-Schillingsfürst. Disappointed in his hopes of winning the workers away from socialism, the emperor turned toward foreign affairs. He boasted that he had never read Germany's constitution, since the guidance he needed came from God. Whether or not by divine direction, the government now expanded its navy and thereupon courted rivalry and finally a break with England. In 1900 Count Bernhard von Bülow became chancellor; five years earlier Wilhelm had rapturously written, he "shall become my Bismarck."[16] He was not quite that, but for nine years he held his post.

In a Germany that had become predominantly urban in a decade, the Social Democrats made gains: they won thirty-five seats in the Reichstag elections of 1890. The moderates in the party were consequently strengthened. The anti-socialist legislation having lapsed, at the Erfurt congress of 1891 the party affirmed its Marxism, relegating its Lassallean beginnings to the archives, but took care not to act on its *profession de foi*. The trade unions grew, and insisted that mass strikes were not the way to improve the workers' condition. Georg von Vollmar set forth principles of "revisionism," postponing the socialist apocalypse, and they were elaborated by Eduard Bernstein. In 1903 the Social Democrats gained, but in 1907 lost much ground, while the so-called Bülow bloc of agrarian and industrial parties swept the field after a shocking attack on the Center (which the chancellor had treated as an ally).

In 1909 Bülow was replaced by Dr. Theobald von Bethmann-Hollweg. Despite the fact that both chancellors had continued and embellished Bismarck's social-insurance program for the workers, the Social Democrats carried 110 seats in the elections of 1912 and became the largest single party in the Reichstag (though no coalition having a majority could be put together by anyone).[17] The revisionists in consequence benefited and set the party on the path that led to a vote for war credits in 1914 as entailing defense against autocratic Russia. But Germany was scarcely a parliamentary state: in November 1913, over the clumsily handled Zabern affair, the Reichstag voted no confidence, 293 to 54. The majority did nothing to follow it up, and the chancellor ignored the vote.[18]

The Great War, or World War I, killed the flower of German youth (as it did the youth of Britain, France, and to a lesser degree Austria-Hungary and Russia). It also destroyed the German Empire. Institutionally, it opened up some possibilities. In October 1917, Count Georg von Hertling became chancellor. In Craig's words, "he owed his position to the pressure exerted by the Reichstag majority . . . and was, in this sense, the first parliamentary Chancellor in the history of the Empire."[19] But he lacked power and authority, and the Empire itself lasted only a year longer.

The emperor, whose blunders had become proverbial, was at length deprived of any influence on events by successive ultimatums of the military Dioscuri, Field Marshal Paul von Beneckendorff und Hindenburg and General Erich Ludendorff. In spring 1917 an Independent Socialist party broke off from what came to be called the Majority Socialists, and both groups would survive the collapse. Ludendorff's final offensive failed in summer 1918, and during the autumn months the end came swiftly. The emperor abdicated; a republic was proclaimed.

Germany was in the throes of some kind of revolution; the question was, what kind would it be? The chancellorship fell into the hands of Friedrich Ebert, leader of the Majority Socialists. Ebert made a "telephonic pact" with General Wilhelm Groener, who had replaced Ludendorff as Supreme Commander, to prevent chaos. A Congress of Workers' and Soldiers' Councils, imitating the Russian pattern of early 1917, assembled in Berlin and declined to accept the lead of the far Left—the Spartakists under Karl Liebknecht and the gifted Polish revolutionary Rosa Luxemburg. The Independent Socialists first joined with the Majority Socialists in a coalition ministry. However, they withdrew when Ebert seemed to comply with an ultimatum from Groener to reject a seven-point resolution from the Congress of Councils demanding an abandonment of the old army for a militia with elected officers.

In January 1919 the Spartakists (now the Communist party) led a revolt, seizing several buildings in central Berlin. The army put it down; Liebknecht and Luxemburg were captured and then, separately, shot while under arrest. In the eyes of many workers and leftists it was a lasting black mark on the Socialists' record that they seemed to condone these murders. There were other Communist uprisings, culminating in the establishment of a Bavarian Soviet Republic in Munich; it lasted less than a month before it was suppressed in early May.

A National Constituent Assembly was elected in January and chose Ebert as first president of the German Republic, but the Weimar Constitution was not adopted until July 31. The president, elected for a term of seven years, would select a chancellor who in turn would choose a cabinet supported by a majority of deputies in the Reichstag; its members were to be elected on a basis of proportional representation by party lists for the whole country. An upper house, the Reichsrat, represented the eighteen states—the maximum for any one state to be two-fifths of the delegates—and could only delay legislation. The initiative and referendum were introduced, and made all too easy to use, placing the ordinary conduct of government in peril. It was a constitution formally reeking of the latest democratic theories, but unsuited to a functioning two-party system (a majority for a single party was made virtually impossible to achieve) and guaranteeing political instability. Thomas Mann had declared in 1918, "I don't want the trafficking of Parliament and parties that leads to the infection of the whole body of the nation with the virus of politics. . . . I don't want politics. I want impartiality, order, and propriety."[20]

It was easier to voice such a wish than to achieve it. The Weimar Constitution provided for a surfeit of politics on the one hand and a possible rough termination of political activity on the other, for in order to prevent the chaos of early 1919 from recurring, the president was given emergency powers, in case "public order and safety were seriously disturbed or threatened," to use armed force and to set aside the rights guaranteed to the citizen in the constitution—a power that even the emperors had not possessed.

But failing such emergency, the new basic law guaranteed political instability. The civil servants (mostly inherited from the empire) often displayed their contempt for the short-lived ministers; many judges threw the book at leftists while treating rightists gently; the professors at the universities resisted academic reform and attacked the republic in the classroom. The Allies, by compelling acceptance of the hated Versailles Treaty, had saddled the Weimar Republic with a heavy psychological handicap. They were responsible for excluding any reunion with the new and tiny German Austria, the holding of a plebiscite that handed northern Schleswig over to Denmark, the occupation of Upper Silesia (however, a plebiscite in March 1921 restored it to Germany), Germany's giving up of Danzig to become a free city, and the loss of the "Polish corridor" separating East Prussia from the rest of Germany. Finally, the Allies stripped the country of its entire colonial empire and wrote its alleged "war guilt" into the treaty as justification for imposing an enormous burden of reparations.

In March of 1920 first the Right, then the Left struck the Republic. The antirepublican forces, led by the East Prussian politico Wolfgang Kapp, were sufficiently enraged by the disbandment of troops to seize Berlin; but Ebert outsmarted them by summoning the workers to conduct a general strike. The Kapp Putsch thereupon collapsed. The Communists, cheered by the success of the strike, promptly seized much of the Ruhr; the army, which had refused to act against the mutineers of the previous week, was swift in repressing this revolt, and penalties for its previous disobedience were forgotten. An election of June 1920 showed the swing to the Right: the Democratic and Center parties lost much strength, the Socialists even more. Disheartened, the latter withdrew from the government and returned only twice and briefly before the end of the Weimar Republic.

The Communists undertook a quixotic revolt in March 1921 in Saxony at the order of the Comintern, whose only result was to halve party membership. Their memory of this failure did not last, and in October 1923 the Berlin government had once again to act. The new chancellor, Gustav Stresemann, compelled dismissal of Communist ministers in Saxony and Thuringia and put down an attempted coup in Hamburg. Such decisive action calmed down most of the restless Right, but Adolf Hitler and a small new group of Nazi (National Socialist) fanatics tried to overthrow the Bavarian government in the so-called Beer Hall

Putsch of November. They failed, and Hitler went to prison, where he wrote *Mein Kampf.*

In the meantime the worst inflation in the modern history of the world took place in the Ruhr as a result of financial stresses insuing upon the French and Belgian occupation of the Ruhr to collect reparations. After the middle classes had been nearly ruined and everyone's savings destroyed, Hjalmar Schacht ended the crisis by the curious expedient of simply introducing a new mark (each redeeming one trillion of the old marks), declaring it was "secured" by a "mortgage" on all land and industry in the country. The crisis did much to split the country into Right and Left.

Although there were fifteen governments in Germany between February 1919 and June 1928, for the last half of the decade of the 1920s President Hindenburg, doing his best to make the system work, and Stresemann as foreign minister managed to provide some continuity and hope for the republic. Moreover, the Dawes Plan and the Young Plan (1929), apparently settling the reparations problem, seemed to secure economic recovery.

All such hopes were soon dashed. In March 1930 a coalition government was formed under Heinrich Brüning, a Center chancellor with rightist support. A budget with much to commend it was blocked by the Reichstag. He enacted it by a (constitutional but impolitic) emergency decree; the Reichstag majority nullified it; Brüning dissolved the Reichstag, and enacted the budget again by decree. Both the last two acts contravened the constitution, even if not unambiguously so. The elections of September 1930 jumped the Nazis from 12 to 107 seats; the Communists won 77.

The Great Depression, already upon the United States, spread to Europe, and both political extremes benefited from the economic distress of the Germans and their disillusionment with the political system of Weimar. In July 1932 the Nazis took 230 seats. In November they lost 34 seats, dipping to 196, but regained momentum, chiefly by "subjecting the mini-state of Lippe to a propaganda blitzkrieg and then exaggerating their minor gains in the local election there." In March 1933 they won 288 seats (44%), and their Nationalist allies 52 (8%).

It can be said that the Nationalists "bore the major responsibility for undermining the republic and bringing the Nazis to power" by influencing the senile Hindenburg and supporting Hitler. Ralph Flenley singles out the Rhenish industrialist Alfred Hugenberg, the Westphalian former diplomat Franz von Papen, and General Kurt von Schleicher as the main villains.[21] Hugenberg helped to finance the Nazis, Papen and Schleicher were the last two pre-Hitler heads of government, and it was Papen who persuaded Hindenburg to name as chancellor Hitler, whom the aged president had despised as the "Bohemian corporal."

In August 1932 Hitler defended the murder of a Communist worker by five storm troopers who had just been sentenced to death, attacking the "bloody objectivity" that had led to that sentence and promising to free Germany from it. "Everybody in Germany at this moment," writes Holborn, "could see what a Hitler government held in store for the people. But the sense of law and justice had already been dangerously undermined. . . ."[22] Nevertheless, in a longer perspective Hitler is to be understood as "a force without a real historical past"; "both the grandiose barbarism of his political vision and the moral emptiness of his character make it impossible to compare him in any meaningful way with any [previous] German leader."[23]

Germany was a free society still when Hitler became chancellor on 30 January 1933. It ceased to be such in a very short time. The Communist party was banned after the mysterious fire in the Reichstag on 27 February; they played an important part in undermining the republic and had occasionally engaged in outright collaboration with the Nazis against Weimar institutions. Of course they were not banned for that, but for allegedly being the chief internal danger to the nation. But all other parties soon followed them into oblivion. By July the Nazis were the only legal party.

The Reichsrat was abolished in January 1934, and the states, deprived of any real power, continued only a purely nominal existence. All Jewish ("non-Aryan") officials, teachers, and notaries were to be retired. The court system became merely an instrument for protecting the interests of the Nazi-controlled state. Nazi Storm Troopers might engage in what violence they wished (or were ordered) to commit; opponents of the Nazis were herded into concentration camps or fled the country. By the Nürnberg laws of September 1935, all who were of one quarter or more Jewish extraction were stripped of citizenship and the right to marry non-Jews. That was only the first step to the murder of six million Jews during World War II. The Catholic and Protestant churches, at first ready to adapt themselves to the new regime, soon found themselves under heavy pressure.

Hitler made military service compulsory and universal in March 1935, rearmed the country, and proceeded to a program of systematic aggression: first in order to annex all German-speaking territories beyond Weimar borders, beginning with the Saar, won by plebiscite in January 1935, and continuing up to Austria and the Sudetenland of Czechoslovakia in 1938. Finally, abandoning pretense, Hitler began to seize non-German lands as well, beginning with the Czech lands in March 1939. The result was World War II, precipitated by the Nazi invasion of Poland in September 1939.

The horrors of the next six years, which may be laid almost exclusively at the door of the Nazis and their Japanese allies in Asia (other allies of Hitler's in Europe may be assigned rather lesser discredit), need not be summarized here.

By the spring of 1945 Hitler committed suicide, the tiny residue of territory and armed forces not already in enemy hands surrendered to the Allies, and the country was partitioned into occupation zones that later became the German Federal Republic (West Germany), the German Democratic Republic ("East" though really central Germany), and the Regained Territories of Poland.

One of the most heartening and astonishing developments of the later twentieth century has been the emergence of a prosperous, rebuilt, and democratic West Germany. How could that have happened in so short a time? Gordon Craig provides part of an explanation: Hitler, along with the immense harm he did to Germany (not to speak of other countries),

also eliminated much that was bad. And this included the conservative-militarist concern that had dominated politics in the Wilhelmine period, done everything possible to shorten the life of the Weimar Republic, and elevated him to power in 1933. [After Hitler's purges and the disappearance of the values and traditions of that group] . . . in the course of the brutal intellectual *Gleichschaltung* of the Nazi period, the most important of the obstacles that had stood in the way of progress towards a free political system had been removed.[24]

It was of course only in West Germany that such progress could occur, and did. The successful fusion of the British and American zones of occupation on 1 January 1947 was followed by French agreement in June 1948 to contribute their zone to a new free state; the Soviet response was the Berlin blockade, which was frustrated by the amazing Allied airlift but led to a virtual partition of the city of Berlin as well. The blockade ended in failure in May 1949.

In the meantime a drastic currency reform had led speedily to economic recovery, trizonal fusion occurred, and in September the Federal Republic was proclaimed. In the 1950s the economy grew at an amazing 7% after inflation (which remained lower than in any other industrialized country), in what was called the *Wirtschaftswunder* (economic miracle). Although the figure fell in the 70s and 80s, West Germans kept a high standard of living.

A "provisional" (but lasting) Basic Law (1949) created a weak presidency and a strong chancellorship—first held by the impeccably anti-Nazi Konrad Adenauer—responsible to a majority of a lower house or Bundestag, while the eleven states or Länder elected an upper house or Bundesrat. What could not be legislated but serendipitously made its appearance was something close to a two-party system: the Social Democrats (SPD) and the Christian Democrats (CDU—in Bavaria, the Christian Social Union or CSU). In 1959 the SPD adopted, at Bad Godesberg, a program discarding many socialist dogmas and accepting a market economy as well as closeness to the West. Notable among the smaller parties were the Free Democrats, who would enter coalitions with both CDU/CSU and SPD, and, from the 1970s, the Greens, who took uncompromising stands on the environment and nuclear arms. (The Greens entered the Bundestag in 1983.)

Despite the unified party system, the federal government was recently said to control only about 45 percent of public spending, the rest coming from the Länder and Gemeinden (local authorities). Bonn does operate a welfare state, including mandate government health insurance, unemployment and accident insurance, and old-age pensions.[25]

Adenauer remained—a trifle too long—as chancellor until 1963, when he was close to eighty-eight. He achieved reconciliation with both Israel (thus partially overcoming feelings left by the Holocaust in which six million Jews died) and France, established relations with the USSR, shaped the early stages of German democracy, and justified Churchill's description of him as "the greatest German statesman since Bismarck." After the Federal Republic was admitted into several international organizations in 1950–52, one German noted; "Germany's sick-leave from world history was over."[26]

After Adenauer resigned in October 1963, he was succeeded by Ludwig Erhard, architect of the *Wirtschaftswunder.* In 1966 the two large parties (and the Free Democrats) formed a "grand coalition" under Kurt Georg Kiesinger, former minister-president of Baden-Württemberg. The first SPD chancellor, Willy Brandt, former mayor of West Berlin, held office from October 1969 to May 1974, when a spy scandal led to his replacement by Helmut Schmidt, the SPD former defense and finance minister. In late 1982 Helmut Kohl, former minister-president of the Rhineland-Palatinate, brought in another CDU/CSU government, which remained in office in early 1990.

In the fall of 1989 sensational developments, clearly triggered by Gorbachev's policies in the USSR, occurred in the German Democratic Republic. In 1946 the Communist party was too weak to be able to constitute a plausible popular regime in East Germany, and therefore a merger was forced with the larger Social Democrats to produce a Socialist Unity party (SED). Walter Ulbricht was chairman until 1971; he was succeeded by Erich Honecker. Under his rule, East Germany came to enjoy the highest standard of living in the Soviet bloc, but politically was a model of totalitarian immobility. Abruptly, following a visit by Mikhail Gorbachev to East Berlin in October 1989, Honecker was toppled from power, the Berlin wall (erected in 1961) was breached so free movement to the west could occur, and the whole structure of Communist control in the GDR was called into question in a manner still rapidly changing in early 1990.

Thus Germany, having experienced the most brutal totalitarian regime in history next to Stalin's USSR, had by 1990 gone some distance toward freedom. If one writes off the former German territories east of the Oder-Neisse line as having become Poland or Russia (the north of East Prussia), there were two

Germanies: the Federal Republic, where in forty-five years post-Nazi freedom had evidently taken deep root, and the Democratic Republic, in which the effects of forty-five years of repression seemed on the verge of being cast off with dazzling speed. But a single federated or even unified free Germany appeared to be a possibility for the foreseeable future.

Spain and Portugal. The government of the Spanish Bourbons, never an unalloyed success, in effect broke down in 1808. Napoleon imposed his brother Joseph (José I) as king. A rebellion supported by all classes broke out "to save national independence and also to save the primacy of traditional religion. The whole experience was incomprehensible to Napoleon, for nothing of the sort had happened in any other area occupied by French troops."[27] Even the middle classes, elsewhere apt to welcome Napoleonic reforms, solidly backed the struggle, seemingly swept up in a fervor of national unity.

The British sent an army under Sir Arthur Wellesley, later duke of Wellington, which kept the French occupied in the Peninsular War until 1814. In 1810 the territory around Cadiz elected a "national assembly" which in May 1812 promulgated a constitution providing for a one-house parliament elected by indirect but universal male suffrage. Its supporters, using the term *liberal,* gave the world a new word and a new political doctrine. Meanwhile a regency, established by British initiative in 1807 to rule while João VI took refuge in Brazil, held sway in Portugal, but was driven out by a revolt in 1820. The insurgents adopted a constitution much like that of 1812 in Spain and arranged the return of the king from Brazil; thereupon Brazil declared its independence, but accepted the king's son, Dom Pedro, as emperor.

In April 1814 the Bourbon prince returned from exile in France as Ferdinand (Fernando) VII, perhaps "the basest king in Spanish history."[28] Immediately he approved direct intervention of the army to overthrow the constitutional system, and resumed a regime of absolutism, inefficiency, and misrule. The colonies of Spanish America won their independence during these years, and the loss of income and prestige resulting therefrom led him to prepare an army for dispatch there with the aim of reconquest. Instead the troops, concentrated in the liberal stronghold of Cadiz, mutinied (1820), and the king was forced to restore the constitution. Young officers spearheaded the revolt, which was led by Major Rafael del Riego; Russian and Italian officers were inspired to emulate them in their own countries.

Though the king was unwilling to try to make the constitutional system work, from 1820 to 1823 reforms were nevertheless resumed. Seigneurial and church landownership was curbed and the right of entail was abolished, as had been done in 1812–13, and other measures were undertaken or proposed. But radicals gained the upper hand; the French intervened—though embarrassed by Fernando's intransigence—and the king reversed almost all the progressive legislation since 1820. Under the rule of the regent, Maria Christina, who succeeded her husband in 1833, a succession of constitutions (1834, 1837, 1845) hewed a compromise path between absolutism and the fundamental law of 1812, based on a two-house legislature elected by limited suffrage. In the 1840s voters made up around 4% of the population, "the broadest European suffrage of the period."[29]

In 1834–40 and 1846–49 the militant traditionalists of northern Spain rose in revolt on behalf of Don Carlos, brother of Fernando VII, after the Salic Law was set aside so that the daughter of the king could succeed. These Carlist revolts were suppressed, but rightist forces found a parliamentary voice in the so-called Moderados. The liberal Progresistas alternated with them in heading governments, but the changes occurred through military intervention and force, not peaceful elections. French and British pressures were sporadically significant as well. From 1843 to 1851 (with brief interruptions) General Ramon Narvaez was virtual dictator.

Spain avoided any full-blown uprising in the revolutionary year 1848. During that period the Moderados established "the legal and institutional framework of a modern, centralized, parliamentary state in Spain,"[30] following in part the ideas of Juan Donoso Cortes. In 1851 Narvaez was replaced by ultraconservative elements; in 1864 and then again in 1866 he was back; he died in office in April 1868. During an interval, 1854–56, Progresistas produced a new constitution broadening the scope of Spanish liberalism and encouraging business enterprise. The leader of the group, Don Juan Prim, was both popular and politically gifted, "the only effective liberal leader" in Spain thus far.[31] (He was to be assassinated in December 1870, probably by republican radicals.)

The political system, however, continued to be unstable. The unpopular queen was overthrown in 1868. A constituent Cortes decided for a continuation of monarchy; at length a prince of the House of Savoy was chosen king, but he lasted only two years before abdicating. Now the (first) Spanish Republic was proclaimed (1873); it lasted less than two years. The Restoration brought the son of the unlamented queen to the throne as Alfonso XII. Admirable in his loyalty to constitutional monarchy, he benefited from a reshaping of the political scene that yielded two parties, the Conservatives under Antonio Canovas del Castillo and the Liberals under Praxedes Sagasta, which alternated in power peacefully with each other. A sweeping law on freedom of the press was passed in 1883 and lasted until 1936. A law of 1882 inaugurated virtually universal male suffrage in municipal and provincial elections, and in 1890 it was restored at the national level. In the 1880s, three new law codes were completed—civil, criminal, and commercial. Trade unions were legalized; trial by jury was restored.

But there were still too many illiterate peasants and the middle class was not large enough to make Spanish democracy a reality. Anarchist terrorism grew and regional sentiment burgeoned, especially in Catalonia. A revolt in Cuba simmered for three years until 1898, when the Spanish-American War took away both Cuba and the Philippines.

The king, Alfonso XIII, was declared of age at sixteen in 1902. The nation bestirred itself somewhat to pursue "regeneration" from the humiliation of 1898. The alternation of parties continued; its maximum of effectiveness was shown by the Liberal prime minister José Canalejas (1910–12). Literacy and economic development edged upward, and Spanish culture produced a Silver Age, in which the "men of '98"—philosophers (Miguel de Unamuno), painters (Pablo Picasso, Joan Miró), sculptors (Antoni Gaudí), and writers (Federico Garcia Lorca)—reached a new plateau.

But after 1913 the old parliamentary and party system fell apart. In World War I Spain was the most important neutral country, and the consequent prosperity increased the strength of organized labor. Socialism, anarchism, and autonomism (in Catalonia chiefly but also in Basque territory) grew in magnitude as problems for a liberal government and the long-simmering problem of colonial Morocco erupted dramatically in 1921 when Abd el-Krim defeated a Spanish army at Anual in the central Riff; within a few days nine thousand Spanish soldiers were killed or taken prisoner.

The Moroccan situation remained unresolved, while the Catalonian movement continued. In September 1923, a *pronunciamento* (a repeatedly used nineteenth-century device whereby a leader simply announced publicly his intention to take over the reins of government; this was the last time it was used) by General Miguel Primo de Rivera led to his assuming power. Much of the public welcomed the strong man, who at first denied he was a dictator but soon became one, as the only way to escape from political paralysis. He proclaimed martial law, dissolved the Cortes, and silenced opponents, but he also strove for constitutional reform —except that he had no notion how to go about it.

In 1926 the dictatorship weakened into a largely civilian government, still headed by Primo. It created new hydroelectric power, built highways and rehabilitated railroads, and even began a limited land reform. Yet one social group after another went into opposition. Primo was weary and ill, and in January 1930 he resigned. Republicanism had made substantial gains, and in February 1931 the king tried in vain to escape the opprobrium of association with the Primo dictatorship by restoring the constitution. It was too late; in the new municipal elections, the republicans swept the polls in the larger cities (though monarchist voters were still in the majority nationality). Less than two days later the king left Spain.

A constituent assembly now established a Second Republic with a single-chamber parliament (Cortes) elected by universal suffrage, to which a cabinet was responsible. The constitution separated church and state, secularized the schools, and nationalized church property. Further anticlerical legislation followed. Catalonia was given autonomy, but a year later its president proclaimed independence, provoking suppression of the revolt and suspension of the autonomy statute. There were short-lived risings from both Right and Left.

In February 1936 a newly formed Popular Front, grouping four leftist parties, won by a very narrow margin over a conservative coalition.[32] A new leftist cabinet took office in time to cook the election results, producing a contingent of 271 for the Popular Front, 137 for the Right, and 40 for the Center. The fraud led the Socialist chairman of the credentials committee, Indalecio Prieto, to resign in protest. A series of extralegal and illegal measures ensued in the areas of amnesty for leftist prisoners, seizure of land, and political strikes. The Communists grew from a very small number to wield much influence and take over a united Socialist-Communist youth movement. The political murder of José Calvo Sotelo, a leader of the opposition in parliament—an action "without precedent in the history of west European parliamentary regimes"—by leftist police and Communist militiamen, triggered a rightist revolt.

The Spanish Civil War began with an uprising of the military in Spanish Morocco and spread through garrison towns of Spain. It lasted from July 1936 to March 1939. In October 1936 General Francisco Franco became chief of state and obtained recognition from Nazi Germany and Fascist Italy; the Republic received extensive aid from the USSR, while the British and French attempted to follow a policy of nonintervention. The Spanish Communists were instructed by Stalin to change the line that prevailed before the Civil War broke out of replacing the Republic with a worker-peasant dictatorship to one of moderation and defense of the "bourgeois" republic. Moscow wished to avoid alienating the middle classes and public opinion in Britain and France.

But the Communists took over many crucial positions in the Republic, leading the Socialist prime minister, Francisco Largo Caballero, to try to curb their influence. They forced him out, and a new government was formed in May 1937 under Juan Negrin, who was willing to follow the Communist lead. Thereafter the Communists "exercised general hegemony in the politics, military affairs, and propaganda of the leftist zone," though leaving some non-Communists in office. The Communist line was to postpone, not press, further social revolution, but meanwhile to consolidate influence in the Republican government.

Stanley Payne sums up: "One of the great ironies of the Spanish Civil War was that it ended almost the same way it began, with a rebellion by a minority of the nominally Republican army against the Republican government on the grounds that it was in the process of becoming a Communist dictatorship."[33] A military coup in Madrid resulted in the flight of Negrin and his associates and the formation of a government that, having tried and failed to secure terms, had to surrender to the rebels.

The victorious Franco kept Spain neutral in the great war that was about to break out. After dealing severely with those who had been leaders of the republic, he rigidly repressed opposition until the 1950s, when in varying degrees toleration increased. In 1969 Franco selected the grandson of Alfonso XIII, Juan Carlos de Borbon, as his successor, and on his death in 1975 Juan Carlos became king (actually Franco handed over power to him in summer 1974). During the next decade Spain astonished the world by becoming a successful constitutional monarchy. Not all of the old antagonisms were gone, but under the skillful and widely respected leadership of the king there seemed a willingness to accept differences that exceeded anything to be seen in Spain for many decades.

Portugal had in certain respects been more fortunate in its political history (since Napoleonic times, at least) than Spain. The constitution of 1822, adopted by the first representative assembly to meet in the country since 1689, was the most democratic it would have for the next century and a half.[34] There was to be a unicameral legislature, elected by direct universal male suffrage, to which the cabinet would be responsible. However, that constitution was soon superseded by the charter of 1826, which provided for two chambers—the lower house chosen by indirect suffrage and the upper a house of peers composed of lifetime and hereditary members selected by the monarch, who appointed ministers and had the power of absolute veto over laws passed by parliament. This system with minor changes lasted until 1910.

Dom Pedro, emperor of Brazil, abdicated that position in 1831 to try to remove his brother Don Miguel, who had become king of Portugal and abolished the constitution. Making his base the Azores, Dom Pedro IV succeeded in 1834 with help from Britain—Portugal's oldest ally—and also Spain. However, he died almost at once and was followed by his daughter as queen. For twenty years she ruled under the restored charter, with an interval of a slightly more democratic regime (1838–42). After her death in 1853 Pedro V took the throne. Payne calls him "a dedicated progressive and probably the most brilliant European prince of his generation," but he died young. His brother, "a model constitutional monarch," achieved some tranquillity. In general the House of Braganza was shrewder and more discreet than the Bourbons of Spain, and the Portuguese had an ethnic homogeneity and lack of regional tension that Spain could have envied.

Portugal was a poor country, and though industry and agriculture grew and modernized to a modest extent after mid-century, the state budget was a serious and continuing problem. But the political scene was more or less stable from the

1850s to 1890, and in 1856 a system of alternation between the two parties, the Regenerators and the Historical, or Progressive party, was established that lasted for most of that time. Republicanism was a doctrine in the 1850s and 1860s. It became a party from 1880 (stimulated by the new Third Republic in France) and also a secret society (Carbonaria) after 1896. João Franco sought to restore stability by turning the government into a near dictatorship. When the king identified himself with that regime, he provoked his own assassination (and that of the crown prince) in 1908. The monarchy lasted only two years longer.

Since 1910 Portugal has been a republic. The republican government started by opposing monarchy and the church but lacked any clear positive aims. It entered World War I (Germany declared war on it in March 1916) without much result for good or ill. Although republicans of one sort or another dominated the government for sixteen years, one writer calls this period in Portugal "the most turbulent and unstable in modern European history."[35]

Nevertheless some advances were registered: women received new rights (but not the suffrage), workers obtained the right to strike and improved working conditions through legislation (organized labor was mainly anarcho-syndicalist, as in Spain), education was extended and literacy increased (though not by much). Financial insolvency and corruption, however, precipitated a coup in 1926 that established first a loose military dictatorship and then, in 1932, the long-lasting authoritarian regime of Antonio de Oliveira Salazar. (He became premier in that year but actually had become the chief figure in the government in 1930.) He set up a corporate state in which there was a president elected by limited suffrage of both sexes, a national assembly, and a corporate chamber representing occupations. Such was the Estado Novo.

At every stage of Portugal's nineteenth- and twentieth-century history it seemed to mimic or parallel events in Spain, even though with less dramatic sharpness. Now a less-radical, less-divisive leftist regime was replaced by a less-repressive rightist regime—and with next to no bloodshed, in contrast to the long agony of the Spanish Civil War. Salazar supported Franco from the start of the Moroccan revolt, and like Franco he kept neutral in World War II (no Portuguese contingent fought on Hitler's side in Russia, though a Spanish Blue Division did); and Salazar let the Allies use the Azores as a base, so that Portugal was admitted both to the grouping created by the Marshall Plan and North Atlantic Treaty Organization after the war. In 1968 Salazar suffered a freak accident and a stroke.

His successor, Marcello Caetano, lasted only until April 1974. His government was overthrown by a "Captains' Revolution," led by officers convinced that the prolonged wars to keep the African colonies should be ended. After a brief period in which it appeared that the Portuguese Communist party had nearly attained power, it was decisively defeated in the April 1976 elections. Mário Soares, the

Socialist leader, formed a government, but it did not last. Only in 1988 did a convincing victory for Aníbal Cavaço Silva's Social Democratic party appear to end a decade of instability on behalf of a working democracy, leaning toward a free-market economy. The Portuguese outcome was as heartening for democracy as what happened in Spain about the same time.

Italy. Italy could not "be called a nation any more than a stack of timber can be called a ship"—at any time from the founding of Rome to the proclamation of the united kingdom in 1861.[36] The peninsula had been the location of great achievements, unsurpassed in military, legal, literary, and artistic respects by any other region or country, but the geography had been different; it had been either smaller or larger political units in which those accomplishments had taken place. Much of the territory had fallen under the rule of two great foreign dynasties— the Habsburgs and the Bourbons—and the rest of it was in fragments.

Napoleon I entered Italy as an ethnic Italian, in a day when such a fact had much less significance than ours, but he still had a special concern for the cultural unity that, in the future, he declared, "ought to unite all its inhabitants under one sole government. . . . " Under his rule the number of political divisions fell from a dozen to three; he did much to wipe out the inheritance of feudalism, he introduced the French codes of law. It was all too much for the Bourbons in Naples, too little for the radicals.

In 1794 Filippo Buonarroti, attached to the French army, was allowed to set up a "republic" in Oneglia in the Ligurian region, where he abolished seigneurial rights and established the cult of the Supreme Being, following the doctrines of Robespierre. The minirepublic lasted less than a year, and Buonarroti (descended from Michelangelo's brother) was recalled to France and jailed—but some of the local inhabitants did not forget.[37]

In 1815 Francis I ruled in Lombardy-Venetia, Vittorio Emanuele I of Sardinia had acquired Liguria, Ferdinand IV had obtained the new title Ferdinand I of the Two Sicilies, and in the center various small states existed. Despite promises of liberty, most of these governments represented restoration indeed-restoration, that is, of absolutism, repression, and misgovernment. But the state of mind of the Italians, and even the class structure, of 1789 could not be restored. There was a widespread determination to go back to the legal order Napoleon had given the land a taste of and to throw off the Austrian hegemony that had replaced that of France.

The year 1820 saw a successful revolution in Spain, which was promptly emulated by the Carbonari in the army of Naples. Ferdinand I (who had promised to respect the constitution granted in Sicily by the British in 1812 and then annulled it a year later under Metternich's pressure) conceded a constitution comparable to the one just promulgated in Spain and begged God to strike him with lightning if he intended to break his oath. He then proceeded to attend the Congress of Laibach (today Ljubljana) on Austrian territory, where he promptly called for Austrian intervention; God did not provide any lightning strike.

While Austrian troops responded, a plan for a revolt in Piedmont (part of Sardinia) miscarried. Harsh repression by Austrians in Lombardy ensued—but not for long. In 1830 the revolution in France stimulated an uprising in the Papal States and again in Parma, Modena, and Piedmont. It was also put down with mainly Austrian troops. Giuseppe Mazzini from exile in Marseille now founded a new revolutionary society called Young Italy and conducted republican propaganda that led to a series of unsuccessful uprisings. Liberals, inspired by the books of Vincenzo Gioberti and Count Cesare Balbo, agitated for a federated Italy with a constitution based on limited suffrage. Gioberti wished the pope to head it, while Balbo looked to the House of Savoy (a view Gioberti came to share after the "liberal pope," Pius IX, disappointed liberal hopes in 1848).

Again revolution broke out in 1848, starting from Palermo in January. Ferdinand (King Bomba) granted a constitution; the same occurred in Tuscany, Piedmont, and the Papal States; revolution erupted in Milan and Venice. Once more the armies of Austria triumphed. It took time, but by the end of August 1849 the last of the revolutionaries (in Venice) had been crushed.

Piedmont had been defeated but retained its constitution and had become the hope of liberal Italians for unity. Its new prime minister, Count Camillo di Cavour, had founded a newspaper called *Il Risorgimento* in 1847 and taken the lead in demanding a constitution. One was granted that gave the state a two-house parliament: a Senate composed of life-members, appointed by the king, and a Chamber of Deputies elected by limited suffrage. The cabinet, though first serving at the pleasure of the king, by 1861 had been made by Cavour's shrewdness effectively responsible to the lower house.[38]

Like Bismarck, Cavour concluded that only armies would accomplish the unification of his country, but unlike Bismarck he could not hope that the army of his state could do the job. So he conspired with Napoleon III to fight Austria if war could be provoked in such a manner as to make it acceptable to public opinion abroad. (He had already managed to arouse the favorable notice of Britain and France by sending troops into the Crimean War and then delivering a temperate plea for the Italian cause at the Congress of Paris.)

In the war of 1859 the French and Piedmontese defeated Austria, but then Napoleon III abruptly pulled out. All again appeared lost; but this time it was not. Lombardy was ceded to France and then to Piedmont. The small central states adhered to Piedmont, Napoleon consenting at the price of annexing Nice and Savoy. A leader of freebooters, Giuseppe Garibaldi, planned to sail from

Genoa to Nice to prevent the French from taking it over; Cavour persuaded him to go south to Sicily instead. His forces overthrew the king of the Two Sicilies and headed north. The Piedmontese moved south. On 26 October 1860, Garibaldi and Vittorio Emmanuele met, and Italy was united. In February a parliament representing all Italy but Rome and Venice met and proclaimed on 17 March 1861 the kingdom of Italy, with a constitution quite similar to the Sardinian constitution of 1848. Cavour died a few weeks later, his work nearly done.

The issues of Rome and Venice were not long in being solved, but dominated the decade nevertheless. The French had had a garrison in Rome since 1849 (sent to prevent the Austrians from doing the same thing but chiefly to please French Catholics whom Louis Napoleon—not yet emperor—was courting); Garibaldi had first achieved prominence by defending the short-lived Roman republic against the arriving French force. In order to obtain Venice, in 1866 Italy first proposed to Austria an alliance against Prussia, and when Austria refused made the same offer to Prussia. It was accepted; the Italian army and fleet suffered defeat in the Seven Weeks' War, but Bismarck still saw that Venice was handed over. After the Franco-Prussian War broke out, Napoleon withdrew the last of the French troops from Rome; in September 1870 the Italian army entered the city. It was annexed and became the capital. The pope was offered financial and diplomatic privileges not so different from those he previously enjoyed, but he refused, and became a voluntary "prisoner of the Vatican" (until 1929). Except for minor changes in the north and northeast in 1919, 1947, and 1954 (the Trieste settlement), the boundaries have been the same ever since. The Risorgimento had achieved its aims.

United Italy had the same sort of liberal government Piedmont had had for the preceding generation. Property qualifications kept the electorate at about 2%; liberal, anticlerical parliaments and cabinets were the rule; largely illiterate Catholic peasants were quiescent, but workers in the industrializing areas were beginning to feel the effects of socialist agitation. In the thirty years after 1870 the output of industry reached only 20% of the gross national product. Italian conditions appeared not unlike Spanish and Portuguese; though cabinets fell not quite so frequently, they still exemplified a sort of nineteenth-century liberalism that left most of the populace alone.

Left and Right were not very far apart. The Left came to power in 1876 under a former follower of Mazzini, Agostino Depretis, and he remained premier most of the time until 1887. In 1881 the franchise was extended so that two million rather than six hundred thousand voted; the results were not startling. In 1887 Francesco Crispi, who had been Depretis's minister of interior, took over until 1891 and was back by 1893–96. Giovanni Giolitti proved even more durable: he headed four ministries over the period 1892 to 1914 and a fifth from 1920 to 1921. For much of that period the budget was a problem, corruption a widely used device, and the search for international recognition as a power and overseas glory was pursued. In 1911 the electorate was almost tripled and made almost universal (that is, for males). The first elections under the new law resulted in a loss of strength by the liberals and gains by the Socialists on the left and the Catholics on the right.

Though part of the Triple Alliance with Germany and Austria-Hungary, Italy judged the Austrian attack on Serbia an "offensive action" and declared neutrality in World War I, then in May 1915 entered on the side of the Allies. Italy suffered losses in the northern fighting, especially in the agonizingly inconclusive eleven or twelve (depending on how one counts) battles of the Isonzo (a river near Trieste). Italy's reward was a modest piece of Austrian territory. Emerging from the war with no military successes of note, sizable casualties, little benefit from the peace, economic disarray, and political gains by the far Left and the far Right, Italian liberalism was not strong enough to survive.

At first things looked hopeful: a new electoral law in September 1919 introduced universal suffrage and proportional representation. In elections held in November, the Socialist party (which had just joined the Moscow-led Third International) won 156 seats in the lower house, the new Partito Popolare Italiano, led by Don Luigi Sturzo, won 100, and Liberals and Radicals less. Under the last Giolitti ministry, the new Communist party broke off from the Socialists, and the former Socialist Benito Mussolini founded the Fascio di Combattimento. He had shared many of Vladimir Lenin's views, but World War I had sent them in opposite directions.[39] Offering order to a nation weary of disorder and the seduction of myth to a people cynical about liberal parliamentarism, he mounted a "march on Rome" that brought him to power. Boarding the train at Milan to heed the king's call to take over the government, he declared that the train must leave exactly on time: "from now on, everything has got to function perfectly."[40]

Of course it did not. The constitution remained in force for a time. In November 1923 Mussolini, using dictatorial powers given him temporarily by the king, promulgated a new electoral law providing that the party receiving the most votes (if they were one-fourth or more of the total) would be allotted two-thirds of the seats in parliament. A few months later the Fascists secured their two-thirds, partly by threat of violence. The murder of the Socialist deputy Giacomo Matteotti in June 1924 signaled a shift of policy: the opposition was now jailed or silenced. A shadowy system called the corporate state was introduced, or at least proclaimed. The long-festering problem of the papacy was solved by creating a tiny Vatican City via the Lateran treaties of 1929.

Fascism's corporate state was supposed to be based on the uniting of employers and employees in national "corporations," one for each of twenty-two branches of economic activity; but the bureaucracy had more to do with economic decision making than that system. Mussolini proclaimed: "everything within the state, nothing outside the state, nothing against the state." It was the recipe for totalitarianism, but he did not follow it exactly. He was much gentler than Hitler or either Lenin or Stalin in practice. Nevertheless Italy was no longer free from, say, 1923.

In 1943 Mussolini was overthrown. (He was captured and hanged upside down in 1945.) A "co-belligerent" Italian government functioned in the south, where Allied armies bogged down, and made contact with the largely leftist resistance in the north, behind German lines. But with the help of British and American commanders, workers' councils were ejected from factories, and resistance authorities were removed from the local level.

The Christian Democrats (DC) emerged as the strongest party in the first postwar government (December 1945). A constituent assembly chosen in the first postwar election in June 1946 ended the monarchy—never very popular, tainted by cooperation with Mussolini—and a cabinet headed by Alcide de Gasperi was formed of the three parties: Christian Democrats, Socialists, and Communists (PCI). In the wake of the issuance of the Truman Doctrine in March 1947, de Gasperi executed a maneuver that freed him from the need for Communist support and that of the Socialists who followed Pietro Nenni's lead in making common cause with the PCI. The resultant cabinet consisted of DC, Socialists who followed Giuseppe Saragat and now used the term Social Democrats, and Republicans. De Gasperi was born in the Trentino under Austrian rule and attended the University of Vienna. He debated Mussolini as early as 1909, was imprisoned by the Duce in 1927, was extracted by Pope Pius XI from jail and sheltered in the Vatican after the treaties of 1929.

On the heels of the "de Gasperi era" (1945–53) came a period of prosperity: in 1952–62, national income doubled and per capita income increased by 62%. Manufacturing had grown to a point where industrial employment exceeded agricultural employment, though in the northern "industrial triangle" of Milan, Turin, and Genoa there were problems characteristic of urbanization. The DC remained in power. The PCI proposed a "historic compromise" by which it would join the DC in governing, and finally some Communist participation in government was arranged in July 1977.

Extreme leftists, partly in objection to the "compromise," carried out a number of terrorist killings and kidnappings, capped by the murder of the DC former premier Aldo Moro. (His body was found in May 1978.) The reaction of the public was an increase in sympathy, and votes, for the DC. In local elections of

May 1988, the DC won 29%, the Communists 22%, the Socialists 18%. Under honest, intelligent, and colorless Premier Ciriaco de Mita, Italy had achieved relative political stability (despite the changing composition of cabinets), economic growth, and freedom.

Scandinavia.   Denmark sided with Napoleon in resentment at British treatment —two bombardments of Copenhagen and the theft of the entire Danish fleet (1807) so it could not be used in place of the French fleet, sunk at Trafalgar, to invade Britain. Sweden had joined the Third Coalition (1805) against Napoleon, largely because the king thought the French Revolution and all its works evil. As a result Denmark had to hand Norway over to Sweden and also Pomerania to Prussia, but Sweden was compelled to accept a constitution by which the Norwegians had their own single-chamber national assembly, or Storting. Gustav IV had the misfortune to lose Finland to Alexander I of Russia. The tsar had arranged a sort of partition of Europe with Napoleon at Tilsit (more accurately, on a raft in the middle of the Niemen River) in 1807, and one result was the Russian conquest of the long-time Swedish possession. The Russian emperors became grand dukes of Finland, which retained much of its previous constitutional system and, in comparison to the rest of the Russian Empire, its freedom. It became independent only in 1917 and remained a free country despite the Soviet-Finnish "Winter War" of 1940 and formal alliance with the Nazis in World War II.

Gustav IV had no heir. In order to find a new monarch, a Swedish officer made a pilgrimage to France seeking one of Napoleon's marshals for the purpose, and his eye fell on Jean-Baptiste Bernadotte. The upshot was that the latter became crown prince in 1810 and king as Charles XIV John in 1818. The new king chose conservative ministers, and the opposition to them grew, in the press and in the streets, until it achieved a majority in the parliament of 1840. A series of reforms begun in his reign, including compulsory education, were allowed to continue into the next. Under Oscar I (1844–59) the guilds were abolished, free enterprise and commerce were introduced or secured by several laws, equal inheritance rights were assured women, religious freedom was granted, local self-government created.

Minor disturbances in 1848 interrupted this process by alarming the king, but under his son the march of reform was resumed. The old Riksdag was replaced by a two-chamber parliament, the upper one chosen by indirect vote of the rural and urban rich, the lower by direct vote, still with property qualifications yielding the farmers ("peasants" seem no longer the word for them) an advantage. After that was done (1865–66), significant changes almost ceased until the end of the century. One important development did take place. The Social Democrats were organized in 1889, the liberal factions united in 1900, and conservatives did likewise in 1904.

The union of Sweden and Norway was never complete or very successful in its partial form. The crown prince and Danish governor, Christian Frederick, summoned a constituent assembly which, meeting at Eidsvoll (just north of Christiania), drew up the constitution of May 1814, elected Christian Frederick king, and entrusted to the Norwegian parliament more power than any legislative body in the world had outside of the United States. It could initiate legislation, and the king had only a suspensive veto. Charles XIV John as king of Norway sought to replace it with an absolute veto and failed. The new Venstre (Liberal Democratic) party, having secured control of the Storting, managed to pass a bill three times; the Conservative government rejected it but was compelled to resign after a trial in 1884 before a judicial body called the Riksretten. Thereby Norway became the first Scandinavian country to acquire a fully parliamentary system.

Norway's continual demand for more independent foreign relations finally led to its withdrawal from the Swedish union in 1905. At first refusing, Sweden at length yielded peacefully. Norwegians first offered the throne of an independent nation to a Swedish prince, but at length Prince Charles of Denmark became Haakon VII. The vote was extended before and after the rupture. The Labor party (founded in 1887) and the Venstre together had pushed through universal male suffrage in 1898 (which was extended to women in local elections in 1907 and national elections in 1913), and the royal suspensive veto was abolished. Social reforms were enacted rapidly: a factory act protecting women and children, accident and health insurance, and in 1915 a ten-hour workday.

It seems that during the whole century of union, Norway tended to draw Sweden leftward, or perhaps in a direction away from aristocracy and toward democracy. Whether it confirms or contravenes that tendency, the first real parliamentary government in Sweden followed hard on the heels of the dissolution of the union in 1905. In 1907 universal suffrage was introduced for the Second Chamber (the lower house of parliament). There was some democratization of the First Chamber, and proportional representation was adopted for elections to both. In 1911 the Liberals won the elections, and Gustav V (1907–50) asked Karl Staaff to form a Liberal government.

Sweden was neutral in World War I. In 1917 the Social Democrats and Liberals increased their majority, and a new government under Nils Eden introduced woman suffrage and universal equal franchise for the First Chamber. From 1920 to 1932 the Socialist parties on one side alternated in power with Liberals and Conservatives on the other. In 1932 Per Albin Hansson became premier of a Socialist government and led a recovery from the Great Depression that was more rapid in Sweden than in many other Western countries.

In World War II the nation was once again neutral. After 1945 the Swedish welfare state, including pensions, child allowances, rent allowances, health insurance, and educational assistance, was created but not the nationalization many expected. The Social Democrats dominated a series of governments, the chief exception being the non-Socialist cabinet of 1976–82. Tage Erlander was premier from 1946 to 1969, followed by Olof Palme, whose assassination in 1986 shook a nation not used to political violence. A new constitution took effect in 1975; the new (1971) single-chamber Riksdag was now elected by all citizens over the age of eighteen via proportional representation. The king's role was reduced to ceremonial duties. In 1988 another Social Democratic victory was accompanied by the election of twenty Greens, the first new party to enter the Riksdag in seventy years. The SD Prime Minister Ingvar Carlsson resigned in February 1990, however, in the face of a severe crisis affecting the entire Swedish democratic socialist system.

In Norway, the furthest leftward point was reached when the dominant wing of the Labor party led it into the Comintern (1919), but four years later it was disillusioned by Moscow's control and withdrew. The Conservatives, Liberals (Venstre), and Farmers' parties alternated in power up to 1935, after which a Labor-Farmers coalition pushed through additional reforms in the shape of social-security legislation. Norway sought neutrality in World War II but defended itself, unsuccessfully, when the Nazis invaded the country. After five years of being occupied, it regained independence in 1945. Labor was in power most of the time after 1930, the chief exception being the non-socialist government of 1965–71. A right-wing Progress party gained in the 1986 elections, because of its tough line on third-world immigration.

By the peace settlement of 1814–15, Denmark had lost Norway and Pomerania; in 1813 the Danish state had had to declare bankruptcy. From this parlous condition the country recovered slowly, under the popular king Frederick VI (1806–39), who for much of his reign presided over a "patriarchal autocracy."[41] After the revolutionary disturbances of 1830, however, he found it prudent to create consultative diets—two for Denmark proper and one each for the duchies of Schleswig and Holstein. A later monarch, shaken by the disturbances of 1848 in other countries, summoned a constituent assembly, which ended Danish absolutism.

The Constitution of June 1849 provided that the king should share legislative power with a two-house assembly, both chambers elected by popular vote. The upper house (Landsting) had a property qualification for suffrage that the lower house (Folketing) did not. The constitution also guaranteed civil liberties. In 1864 Schleswig and Holstein were lost to Prussia and Austria in the first of Bismarck's short wars. (The northern part of Slesvig was returned to Denmark by plebiscite in 1920.) The shock brought a conservative government into power that was able to modify the constitution in a less democratic direction: the upper house was strengthened so that the ministry could govern with its support even though the lower house was opposed, and the Landsting was now to be in part appointed by the king, in part elected by indirect voting. Thus when a Folketing majority fell to a newly formed United Left in 1872, nothing happened.

Under the Conservative ministry of Jacob B. S. Estrup (1875–94), demands to return to the 1849 Constitution got nowhere. Nevertheless old-age pension and health-insurance laws were passed in 1891–92, peasant holdings were mostly converted from leasehold to full ownership, cooperatives grew rapidly, and Denmark prospered. As a Social Democratic party was formed and added its voice to the clamor for constitutional reform after 1880, a "change of system" was prepared and executed in 1901. The Liberals came to power, passed a free-trade law, and replaced the state church by local ecclesiastical administration. The Radical Left broke away from the Liberals in 1905 and from 1913 to 1920, supported by the Social Democrats, controlled the government. Thus the long-awaited constitutional revision finally occurred in 1915: suffrage was granted to all men over twenty-five and most women, the appointive seats in the Landsting were abolished, and full ministerial responsibility to the Folketing was enacted.

Denmark was neutral in World War I, and afterward a series of shifting coalitions headed the government. Struck hard by the Great Depression, the country underwent economic recovery in the late 1930s. The Nazis overran the Danes in 1940, but left a government in place until 1943. In 1945 a restoration occurred, and in 1953 the constitution was revised, producing a single-house parliament (Folketing). As many as twelve parties won seats in it, and minority coalitions were common. Socialist rule was frequent during the postwar period—though in 1968, 1981, and 1988, non-socialists won elections. Denmark enjoyed the highest standard of living in the European Community, but it also had the highest foreign debt and thus continuing economic problems.

In the post–World War I period the Scandinavian Social Democrats achieved "prodigious democratic continuity,"[42] aside from the period of wartime exile; they were in power for much of the time in Sweden and in Norway and were dominant throughout the period in Denmark and Finland. When non-socialists won majorities and formed governments, they accepted much of the welfare state that had been constructed. The powerless monarchs were scarcely controversial; they served as relatively inexpensive symbols of national unity. The resultant social and political stability enabled Scandinavia to make a striking contribution, in relation to its numbers, to the world economy. If, in 1990, the limitations of social democracy seemed to have been reached, the countries concerned were an ornament to freedom still.

CHAPTER 9

The Coming of Democracy, 1800–1990: Part Two

Britain

If the seventeenth century was characterized by torture and killing for political reasons, attended by conspiracy and conflict, then the eighteenth century, writes J. H. Plumb, in its political structure "possesses adamantine strength and profound inertia."[1] Muller puts it that throughout the eighteenth century "England remained the freest country in Europe, with the most vigorous press, the most open public debate, the most influential public opinion."[2] But much of the population did not participate in all this. In the nineteenth century, however, Britain, emerging from the Napoleonic Wars victorious and more nearly master of the whole world than any power had ever been before, was thrown into a vortex of political change lasting into the twentieth century, from which it emerged with liberty and democracy. And those things it kept after it lost its world power and its economic preeminence.

William Pitt resigned in 1801, was called upon to form a new cabinet in 1803, saw it falter and fail, and died in 1806. After a brief Whig interval, the Tories resumed their headship of the government, and the man of mediocre gifts who became prime minister in 1812, Lord Liverpool, kept that office until 1827. He had to deal with the post-1815 economic crisis: British manufacturers were overstocked; agriculture suffered; the unemployed multiplied.

The radicals, with such able spokesmen as the journalist William Cobbett, held mass meetings and submitted petitions. Each wave of violence into which radical agitation erupted prompted a new wave of repression: depredations by a crowd at Spa Fields in 1816 provoked the Coercion Acts, suspending *habeas corpus* and providing punishments for sedition. A large crowd that had gathered in Manchester to hear a speech on behalf of reform was attacked by soldiers; the affair was termed the "Peterloo massacre." It led to the Six Acts, which tightened repression, and public opinion seemed to disapprove. However, violent radicalism now turned the tide in favor of harsh measures. The discovery of the so-called Cato Street conspiracy (intended to blow up the whole cabinet by dynamite) was accepted by many as justification of the Six Acts.

Tories during the period were repressive and reactionary, but not only so. Robert Peel led the passage of laws greatly reducing the number of capital offenses; William Huskisson pushed through the reduction of import duties, beginning to move Britain toward free trade; Francis Place campaigned successfully for the repeal of the Combination Acts that had been passed in 1799 and 1800 to obstruct any kind of unionization of workers. The repeal was at once followed by a series of destructive strikes, the result being that some restrictions were restored.

The climax of Tory reform came in 1828–29. The Irish leader Daniel O'Connell was elected to Parliament, but by the Test Act no Catholic (or Nonconformist Protestant) could hold public office. Reluctantly, to head off civil war in Ireland, the Tories repealed the Test Act and enacted Catholic Emancipation. It gave Catholics the vote and the right to hold any office except lord chancellor of England and lord lieutenant of Ireland, though requiring that any prospective officeholder take an oath in effect promising to accept the Protestant monarchy and the establishment of the Anglican church. The Lords removed a provision that would have done the same for Jews—whose emancipation came only in 1858.

Reform was in the air. Contributors to its force included John Wesley (d. 1791), Methodism, and Protestant Nonconformity generally, which persistently raised the question of what was right and righteous, and Jeremy Bentham (d. 1832) and Utilitarianism, whose calculus of pleasure and pain was frankly monetary. (In Bentham's *Principle of Morals and Legislation,* he admitted, he was to be found "valuing everything in money,"[3] but in those terms he sought to promote the greatest happiness of the greatest number.) Many of the working class followed Methodism, many of the rising middle class became Utilitarian. Though neither Wesley nor Bentham was a democrat or anything like one, the logic of the reform they helped stimulate drove the country in a democratic direction.

The accession of William IV compelled an election to be held (a requirement abolished only in 1867), which went to the Whigs. They were now committed to parliamentary reform. The electoral system for the House of Commons was a patchwork of varying sizes of constituencies, qualifications for voting, and habits of honesty and dishonesty. The cabinet headed by Earl Grey proposed to increase the degree of equality in the electoral process by piecemeal change. A bill doing so failed; Grey dissolved Parliament and held a new election. Commons passed the bill, but Lords rejected it. A revised bill was again passed by Commons, but Lords demanded unacceptable amendments. Grey requested the king to appoint enough new peers to pass the bill; he refused, and the cabinet resigned. The king could not manage to arrange a replacement for it, recalled Grey, promised to appoint the peers—and then persuaded the stubborn Tories to abstain in the final triumphant vote, so that peers did not have to be created after all.

This remarkable episode, which dragged on from March 1831 to June 1832, was crucial in British constitutional history. It set permanent limits on the ability of the House of Lords to act in a way contrary to public opinion, and took a clear step toward a more representative House of Commons. The First Reform Bill actually was modest in the provisions by which it added and subtracted members for specified constituencies and extended the franchise to all those who paid a certain rental or occupied a house or shop yielding a certain rental. A freeholder of a plot that produced a profit of forty shillings annually kept the franchise that he had since 1430; the value of that amount of money had changed some in the ensuing four centuries but not a great deal. The other details need not detain us, for they held only for forty years. The important thing was that once the gesture was made in the direction of equal constituencies and broadened suffrage, it was probably unavoidable that voices should be raised demanding to go the rest of the way. For the time being the middle class obtained much greater weight in elections, and the era of seats in Commons as the property of the gentry was over for good. Finally, elections were made direct (previously the municipal corporations did the electing in most boroughs) but not yet secret.

The First Reform Bill was followed by significant social legislation, indicating a readiness to abridge the principles of *laisser faire* to a considerable degree. The Factory Act (1833) prohibited the labor of children under nine and limited that of older children and women; moreover, it established a system of inspectors that could not be evaded as earlier laws had been. Slavery in the colonies was abolished. The Poor Law was reformed; the government of the towns was reorganized, and standards of honesty and efficiency were greatly raised thereby.

But grave problems remained. The domination of Protestants in Ireland, an almost wholly Catholic country, rankled even though in 1838 the collection of tithes for the (Anglican) Church of Ireland was modified. In England, radicals believed that the people's miseries would be remedied by enactment of a People's Charter that would inaugurate universal manhood suffrage, equal constituencies, and annual parliaments. Chartism culminated in a monster petition, but when presented to Parliament (1848) it proved to have many bogus signatures, and the consequent ridicule buried the movement.

An organization that did achieve success was the Anti-Corn Law League, which united a number of local groups advocating free trade in 1839. Most duties on grain, other foodstuffs, and manufactured goods were abolished or reduced by measures passed by Commons and then, after a tug of war lasting only two months this time (in 1846), by Lords as well. The repeal of the Corn Laws was carried through by the Tory (now usually called "Conservative," as "Whig" became "Liberal") prime minister, Sir Robert Peel. It was he who was responsible for establishing the admirable Metropolitan Police force in London and then throughout England. He had an argument with the new queen, the eighteen-year-old Victoria (1837–1901), but was reconciled with her as he began his second ministry, which lasted from 1841 to 1846.

Peel's government ended in tragedy not of his making: the Irish potato famine that began in 1846 and lasted until 1850. Ireland, then the most densely populated but far from the richest of European countries, depended heavily on the potato. A blight struck, nearly one million died, and afterward more than a million emigrated. By 1911 the Irish population had fallen to half of what it was in 1841.[4] The Irish famine triggered Peel's conversion to free trade and his initiative in repealing the Corn Laws. But the critics of Peel in the Conservative party, led by Benjamin Disraeli, brought him down.

For twenty years both parties were divided, and few important domestic changes took place. An exception, in 1853, was a measure bringing substantial improvement to government. Entry by examination, previously used for the employees of the East India Company, was introduced for what came to be called the "civil service." The British bureaucracy thereupon received a uniformity it had not had, but also a reputation for probity and devotion to the public weal that was to last a long time.

In the circumstances of domestic dullness and drabness, Lord Palmerston's flamboyant policy as foreign minister became popular, and he was prime minister twice. But the figure taking the next important step in the reform process was Benjamin Disraeli, the central figure in a ministry of Lord Derby. It was Disraeli who, correctly sensing the return of popular agitation for parliamentary reform, decided to "dish the Whigs" by supporting a Second Reform Bill (1867). The principle was retained that suffrage should be related to property or, as an alternative, contribution through taxes to the finances of the realm, but the level of requirements was reduced, so that the electorate rose from about one million to two million. There was also some equalization of constituencies. A Scottish Reform Bill and an Irish Reform Bill, passed on the same day a few months later, extended the same general scheme of change to the rest of the United Kingdom.

Although Derby called the Second (English) Reform Bill a "leap in the dark," as it brought most of the urban working class into the electorate, it served to restore stability to the body politic. The two decades of divided parties came to an end. Each party was now headed by a brilliant leader, and the two parties alternated during the subsequent period in what might be called the classic model of the two-party system. Derby yielded to Benjamin Disraeli, the Conservative, while William Ewart Gladstone became prime minister after the Liberals swept the 1868 elections.

Gladstone tried his best to conciliate Ireland by disestablishing the (Anglican) Church of Ireland and improving the position of Irish tenant farmers, though neither then nor later did he succeed. His achievements in his first ministry (1868–74) lay rather in the Education Bill, seeking to make English elementary education catch up with Prussian and American standards, and the Judicature Act of 1873, which put the English higher courts in order in a way that lasted into the 1990s.

When Disraeli became prime minister in 1874, he did so in considerable part through espousing a program of "Tory democracy" domestically and of imperial consolidation abroad. Gladstone and the Liberals returned in 1880, and in the Third Reform Bill (1884) they enfranchised rural laborers and virtually legislated universal male suffrage, leaving without the vote only domestic servants, bachelors living with their families, and men with no fixed residence. The electorate was doubled again. Another measure redistributed seats in Commons so that boroughs and counties ceased to be the basis of the lower house, single-member districts became almost universal, and those districts were determined more or less by size of population.

Disraeli died in 1881. Gladstone and the Liberals continued to alternate with the Conservatives under other leaders. "Home Rule" for Ireland, by way of a separate Irish legislature, was proposed by Gladstone but failed of passage in 1886 and again in 1893. On the earlier occasion a group of Liberals led by Joseph Chamberlain refused to follow Gladstone in this respect, called themselves "Liberal Unionists," and in effect broke off from the party. In 1888 Lord Salisbury, the Conservative prime minister, carried through an important reform of local government by replacing the appointed justices of the peace with elected county councils, the justices of the peace retaining judicial functions only. In Salisbury's third cabinet, organized in 1895, the Liberal Unionists allied themselves with the Conservatives, strengthening the elements wedded to "Tory democracy." The Workmen's Compensation Act of 1897 and a new codification of factory laws in 1901 were the chief consequences.

Chamberlain, who was a vigorous supporter of such domestic reform, became increasingly identified with the cause of the empire, which had become steadily more popular. Its achievements were celebrated in Queen Victoria's Diamond Jubilee (the sixtieth anniversary, 1897, of her accession to the throne); its weaknesses were exposed in the Boer War (1899–1902). The old queen died in 1901, having finally succeeded in making the monarchy popular. Soon after the war Chamberlain espoused an imperial preferential tariff, and the Conservatives divided so deeply on the matter that the cabinet had to resign.

The Liberals now swept into power under Sir Henry Campbell-Bannerman, being confirmed by a landslide in the 1906 elections. They were not the only victors. The Labour Representation Committee had been formed in 1900 from the three-year-old Independent Labour party and the Trades Union Congress. Its reception by organized labor was cool. However, the Taff Vale decision by the House of Lords (the supreme judicial body), declaring unions to be legal entities capable of being sued, changed the situation. The new Labour party won twenty-nine seats, allying itself with the Liberals in power.

The new Lib-Lab alliance, as it was dubbed, pushed through the Trade Disputes Bill, the Old-Age Pension Law, free meals for schoolchildren, the eight-hour workday for miners, and other measures. Beginning in 1906, however, the government and its majority in Commons clashed with Lords and its Conservative majority. First the issue was religious tests in state-supported schools; after two or three other tussles, the crisis came with the "People's Budget" of 1909, introduced by the man who had become the prime mover of reform, David Lloyd George. In the election of January 1910 the Liberals saw their strength fall to the level of the Conservatives', but with Labour and Irish Nationalist support pressed on to the confrontation with Lords.

The death of Edward VII, Victoria's son, and the accession of George V postponed the showdown, for both sides wished to give the new king breathing space. Commons passed resolutions to the effect that Lords should have no right to veto a money bill, that any other bill should become law after being passed in three successive sessions of Commons (if two years had elapsed), and that a parliament should last no longer than five years. A bill with those provisions was introduced and passed the House of Commons in the autumn of 1910. After Lords rejected it and another election had been held that did not materially change the balance of political forces, the Parliament Bill was passed again by Commons but in effect rejected by Lords. Prime Minister Asquith announced that the king stood ready to create new peers; several hundred would have been needed. Lords yielded, and since then the upper house has been able only to delay legislation. Other welfare measures now followed, including health and unemployment insurance and a minimum-wage law. A substantial strike movement occurred in 1911–12, despite all the legal benefits that workers had gained.

One other change had long been sought by Liberals and reformers of various kinds: payment of members of the House of Commons. A chancery judge ruled that a certain labor union, in Walthamstow, could not be compelled to subscribe in order to pay one of the Labor members, most of whom supported themselves in such manner. Sixteen members of parliament lost their salaries; attempts at voluntary replacement of the compulsory contributions failed; and Commons voted £400 per year to each member. Clark comments:

> The proportion of members of parliament who owed their importance not to eminence in business, or in society, or in thought, but to sitting in parliament at the will of some paymaster, was growing. There were such members in all parties, and the modern parties themselves were among the paymasters.[5]

It was an additional bit of evidence about the difficulty in assuring democracy, or more broadly freedom, by specific political devices. Without payment, some able people could not afford to stand, and those who could might still be tempted by corruption in all its forms; with payment of a tolerable salary, there were still unavoidable additional costs, such as campaign expenses, and more money would assure a pleasant or luxurious life. Finances could not assure either wisdom or responsiveness to the public weal. But such matters eluded all but the subtlest observers.

On the eve of World War I the chief domestic crisis was over Ireland. Home Rule had been Gladstone's solution to the Irish question and the reason for his failure. From 1893 to 1912 it was an idea in abeyance. Protestant hostility and fear of Catholic rule over Ulster were added to the opposition of Conservatives. For Liberals, Home Rule had been a promise to their Irish Nationalist allies that had to be kept, rather than a deep concern of their own.

The Parliament Act was now tested. Home Rule passed the Commons three times, and despite rejection by Lords was signed by the king and became law. However, a simultaneous act postponed its coming into effect until after the war, which had broken out some weeks before. The ministry also promised that an amendment regarding Ulster would be introduced at that time. But the postwar situation overtook all these arrangements. An almost exactly identical legislative history attended the bill disestablishing the Anglican church in Wales, but the danger of civil strife there was insignificant compared with Ireland.

World War I had effects of all kinds, not least on the constitutional history of Britain and other powers. It killed and maimed many of the actual and potential leaders from all walks of life; no one can begin to assess how different things might have been if those sacrifices had not been made. It also destroyed the common people by the million in several countries. Nevertheless, in one respect it furthered the growth of free societies. In Clark's words, "before the war was over, and in consequence of the activity of the whole population in national work, the idea that the British constitution was democratic became firmly fixed."[6]

Partly it was a question of broadening participation in government. That process began in May 1915, when the Liberal cabinet under Herbert Asquith (prime minister since 1908) gave way to a coalition cabinet under the prospect of criticism of the conduct of the war. Increased criticism nonetheless led to Lloyd George's replacing Asquith in December 1916. For the time being the extension of war powers subjected the liberties of the citizen to sweeping invasion and private industry and commerce to unprecedented interference. The public accepted or even demanded such action; they regarded it as needed to bring about victory. Meanwhile, however, two measures served to move the British polity in a democratic direction: the act that brought all children into full-time schooling from the ages of five to fourteen, and the reform that gave the vote to almost all males (six months' residence was the minimum requirement) and most females.

At the end of World War I the party alignment changed. The Liberals split as Lloyd George actually supported some Conservative candidates to keep promises he had made for the sake of coalition. The coalition won the election of 1918; the dissident wing of the Liberals, led by Asquith, now refused to support the government, but Labour outpolled them and, with fifty-nine seats, became the official opposition.

In Britain, as in other Western countries, there was an amazingly swift return of prewar conditions in many respects, but ending government controls of industry could not be carried out quite so easily as demobilization of the armed forces. State control of the mines and railroads was terminated in 1921, but the government continued to regulate and intervene. The previously operative principle of unanimity in the cabinet was given up in 1932, when ministers dissenting from the position just taken on import duties were given the right to speak their minds on the subject without resigning. In 1928 the suffrage for women was given to those between twenty-one and thirty (the previous age requirement).

Ireland was lost, except for the north. The Sinn Fein party led the so-called Easter Rebellion of April 1916, organized a parliament of their own, and declared Irish independence. The British Parliament passed Government of Ireland Act, which set up two legislatures, one for the south and one for the north. The latter began to function in May 1921; the Sinn Feiners, having won almost all seats in the elections in the south, formed their own legislative body. The British accepted Dominion status for an Irish Free State, which was in effect independent from the time the constitution passed by the Dail Eireann went into effect in December 1922. Most of Ulster refused to go along and retained its links with Britain.

In October 1922 Lloyd George was deserted over the Greco-Turkish War by Conservative supporters of the coalition, and an election brought in a Conservative ministry under Stanley Baldwin. His decision to plump for a protective tariff lost the party seats, and the Labour party was propelled into power for the first time under Ramsay MacDonald. But in less than a year the possibly (but not certainly) forged "Zinoviev letter," in which the Comintern urged revolution on Britain, led to their defeat in another election, and the return of Baldwin for the period 1924 to 1929.

In May 1929 Labour won a plurality of seats in Commons for the first time, 287 as against the Conservatives' 261 and the Liberals' 59. Ramsay MacDonald returned as prime minister for two years and then, when the cabinet fell as a result of the Great Depression, headed a coalition ministry of the three parties. However, this gambit split Labour; MacDonald had to yield to Baldwin as head of the coalition in 1935, then Baldwin to Neville Chamberlain in 1937, Chamberlain to Winston Churchill in 1940. The coalition lasted to 1945.

During the interwar period the internal organization of Britain was little affected with regard to political machinery, but one important change occurred outside it. In the words of Paul Johnson, Britain had no constitutional bill of rights, but

had instead the Common Law tradition, arbitrated by the judges, which effectively upheld rights of liberty and property and was, indeed, the legal framework within which the British created the first modern industrial society. This continued to function throughout the nineteenth century as an effective legal setting for industrial enterprise.[7]

The labor unions, however, by creating the Labour party acquired sufficient power to make a sizable dent in the Common Law balance. The Trade Disputes Act of 1906 had given unions complete immunity from civil action for damages; "such immunity existed nowhere else in the West." The legal scholar A. V. Dicey declared, "It makes a trade union a privileged body exempted from the ordinary law of the land." Thereafter there were efforts to abridge the special statutory status of unions, but the latter struck heavy blows at Conservative and Labour governments alike right up to 1979.

The British fought World War II with something like the same state controls as in the first War, but afterward did not dismantle them in the same manner, since Labour won the 1945 election and proceeded to nationalize several industries and modes of transportation. The prewar liberties of speech, press, and assembly, however, returned, and elections remained free. The welfare state was introduced, chiefly by Labour. Free medical care was extended to the entire population (indeed for many years to foreigners however briefly present in the country); in 1944 free secondary education was provided, with the raising by stages of the age of compulsory school attendance to sixteen. Successive Labour and Conservative governments nationalized and denationalized industries and enterprises. The economy deteriorated as the Empire disintegrated, whether or not as a result, and the immediate postwar years were grim ones. Immigration, especially from the West Indies and south Asia, raised the nonwhite population to two million; many filled jobs whites were reluctant to take.

What seemed an abortive attempt at party realignment occurred in the 1980s. A group disgruntled at Labour leftism left to form a Social Democratic party. In mid-1987 it merged with the remnant of the once-powerful Liberal party to form the Social and Liberal Democrats, but a faction following Dr. David Owen opposed the merger and remained outside it. Thus instead of the hoped-for strong third party there were, in early 1990, two weak ones.

The elections of 1951 returned to power the Conservatives under Churchill, now seventy-seven. He resigned and was succeeded in turn by Anthony Eden, Harold Macmillan, and Sir Alec Douglas-Home (who gave up his peerage to become prime minister). In 1964 Harold Wilson became head of the first Labour cabinet since 1951; in 1970 the Conservatives were back under Edward Heath. After a period of Labour prime ministers from 1974 to 1979, Margaret Thatcher, the first British woman to head the government, took office.

Thatcher soon became the most unpopular prime minister in the history of British polling, but, after sending armed forces to defeat Argentina in its attempt to seize the Falkland Islands, she rocketed to a peak of popularity. She took a hard-line free-market position on several issues, though retaining the welfare state. She did much to restore industrial productivity and competitiveness, and the arrival by 1977 of enough North Sea oil to satisfy half of Britain's needs helped to improve the economic situation substantially, beginning in the south of England. Thatcher won the elections of 1983 and 1987. The reign of Elizabeth II, beginning in 1952, deepened popular approval for the monarchy while leaving it without significant power.

The consensus of the British people seemed before 1979 to "have joined Tory paternalism with Labour commitment to the regulatory state,"[8] to have settled on a mixed economy (with both private and state-owned sectors, the former outweighing the latter) in a free polity, with universal suffrage determining, through the decisive power vested in the House of Commons, the making of laws for the nation. Thatcher challenged that consensus to the extent that she strove to reduce sharply the government's role in the economy. How far she would succeed remained uncertain. In any case British freedom appeared firm and secure.

Steps toward European Unity

The postwar movement toward the unity of Western Europe began with the formation in 1951 of the Coal and Steel Community—composed of France, West Germany, Italy, Belgium, the Netherlands, and Luxembourg. After the plan for a European Defense Community (linked with one for a European Political Community) had been rejected by the French parliament in August 1954, a different approach was taken. In 1957 the Treaty of Rome, signed by the same six nations as belonged to Coal and Steel, formed the European Economic Community (EEC). It envisaged a common market for both industry and agriculture as well as free movement of people, capital, and goods. In 1973 Britain, Ireland, and Denmark joined; in 1981, Greece; in 1985, Portugal and Spain. Others, it was rumored, were getting ready to apply.

The EEC has remained intergovernmental, with a Council of Ministers and a Permanent Commission, except for a European Parliament, directly elected first in 1979. The goal of removal of all barriers to free trade and free movement of capital and people was proclaimed for 1992. After the European Atomic Energy Community (Euratom) was also formed in 1958, the three (Coal and Steel, EEC, and Euratom) were referred to as simply the European Communities (EC). Their leading figures clearly hoped that they were precursors of a political union that would include the West European countries and eventually some from the East as well.

The United States of America.   Washington had been elected and (in 1792) re-elected by unanimous vote of the Electoral College, but in the latter year John Adams was challenged as vice-president, and his margin was only seventy-seven to fifty. The division of the politically interested into two parties that had taken shape at the time of the ratification of the Constitution continued with changes in the election of 1796, the first time a clear-cut contest between two parties occurred for the presidency.

The Federalists, whose ablest leader was now Alexander Hamilton, nevertheless nominated John Adams, and their opponents, rallying round Thomas Jefferson, called themselves Republicans and nominated him as their candidate. As representatives of the commercial Northeast, the Federalists leaned in the direction of a stronger central government and a conciliatory attitude toward Britain; the Republicans, representing the agricultural South and West, defended states' rights and showed sympathy for France and its Revolution. The electors were required by the Constitution to vote for two persons for president, the one receiving the highest number becoming president and the runner-up vice-president. Thus, since Adams received seventy-one votes and Jefferson sixty-eight, Jefferson became Adams's vice-president, and the two opposing parties shared the highest offices. Sixteen states voted: in six, the popular vote chose the electors; in the other ten the legislatures made the selection.

During the undeclared war of 1798 with France the Federalists pushed through Congress three measures called the Alien and Sedition Acts, aimed at a number of newly arrived Frenchmen and their Republican supporters alike. Many were indicted, few brought to trial and convicted. Republicans probably benefited from public disapproval of infringement—even though in few cases—of free speech by the dominant Federalists. Moreover, the so-called Kentucky and Virginia Resolutions, brought forward by Jefferson and his collaborator James Madison, were passed by the two states' legislatures concerned: they denounced the three acts and affirmed it as a prerogative of the states to decide when a Congressional enactment violated the Constitution.

The Federalists went down to defeat in 1800, sixty-five to seventy-three. Half of the states, eight out of sixteen, now chose electors by popular vote, half by legislatures. Republicans captured both houses of Congress. However, the presidency was decided only after a curious minuet. Jefferson and his running mate, Aaron Burr, received an equal number of votes, so the House of Representatives, strongly Federalist, had to decide between them. After thirty-five ballots Hamilton urged the choice of Jefferson; he disagreed with Jefferson but suspected Burr's ethics—justifiably, as it turned out. Jefferson became president. The Republicans hastened to amend the Constitution so that the electors should vote separately for president and vice-president.

The Federalists, up to the very night before Jefferson was inaugurated, strove to fix their dominance in the courts by the Judiciary Act of 1801, creating new courts and new judgeships and filling them with men sympathetic to their party. The act was modified both in letter and spirit by the Republicans, and many of the judges who had been given "midnight appointments" were left without salary or duties.

However, one of them, named William Marbury, had failed to receive his commission and went to the Supreme Court to get it. Chief Justice Marshall declared that Congress in granting the Court the authority to issue such writs as Marbury sought had passed a law violating the Constitution. Thus in Marbury v. Madison (1803), the Court established the doctrine of judicial review. It held that the Court had the power to declare laws unconstitutional, and proceeded to do just that in the case of the law in question. There were precedents for such action; still, this rule "placed in the hands of the Supreme Courts of the United States a degree of authority not then enjoyed by any similar body of men anywhere else on earth."[9] Few judicial bodies have matched this power since then.

The Republicans then sought a remedy for application of the new doctrine of judicial review (even though it had in the 1803 case operated to frustrate their Federalist enemies). They sought to impeach an associate justice for partisanship, and then unwisely added other charges. The Senate refused to convict him, and the precedent was established that a man could not be impeached for anything for which he could not also be indicted.

The purchase of Louisiana in 1803, for a paltry $15 million approximately, yielded to the United States something like a fourth of what came to be its continental area. The territory had been French, Spanish, and again French. At the outset, therefore, Jefferson appointed the officials as the European monarchs had done before, but that practice lasted only a short time. Aaron Burr switched parties to become a Federalist, becoming involved with a succession of schemes to break off part of the country in the North or West; his plot to become head of an independent Louisiana led to his trial before Chief Justice Marshall on circuit duty. He was acquitted, after an action that saw an affirmation of both the executive's and the judiciary's prerogatives.

Jefferson won reelection by a landslide in 1804 against Federalists discredited by one of Burr's plots, but he declined to run for a third term and was succeeded by James Madison. Britain continually interfered with America's seaborne trade during the Napoleonic Wars, and two groups of militants aspired to expand into territories in European possession: Canada, owned by Britain, and Florida, owned by Spain. In the War of 1812 Madison took the side of the "War Hawks" and was reelected by a combination of the West and South against the North.

The expansionists failed to annex Canada or Florida, but the war had important economic and social consequences: commerce was greatly damaged before and during the fighting, importation of foreign goods declined dramatically, and manufacturing benefited by transfer of capital, in New England and the Middle Atlantic states especially. Correspondingly the invention of the cotton gin made cotton growing profitable, leading to the plantation system in the South and a great increase in the number of black slaves who made it run. Growth of the woolen industry led to more sheep raising in the back country of the North. In general greater American economic self-sufficiency caused diminished contact with Europe and heightened concern with the West.

Madison now led Congress to establish a reliable army and navy, a new national bank and currency, a national system of roads and canals, and a protective tariff. Thus the Republicans seemed to shift toward the Federalist doctrines Jefferson had once opposed; the Federalists themselves dwindled to a shadow of their old strength. The Republican James Monroe swept the election of 1816 but remained uneasy at the progress of the new nationalistic sentiments.

Chief Justice Marshall, who had been the lonely Federalist (though he managed to sway his fellow justices by his magnetism and learning) during several Republican presidencies, now found himself closer to the mainstream as it (so to speak) veered his way. The Court came to be recognized as an institution of fundamental importance, able to override not only lower federal courts but also state courts and to declare invalid the actions of state governors and legislatures. The base assumption, stated explicitly in McCulloch v. Maryland (1819), was that the government of the United States "is emphatically, and truly, a government of the people," emanating from the people and not from the states.

The government was indeed one of laws and not of men, in theory and more often than not in practice; and by the Court's decisions the laws protecting private property were construed broadly and firmly, in days when private property was much more widely distributed than later on. Suffrage was extended to all adult males in the new western states as they were admitted to the Union, and soon the older seaboard states followed suit—a dramatic example of the influence of the frontier. In all these respects Americans might justifiably claim that "the political system of the allied powers is essentially different . . . from that of America," a fact adduced in the Monroe Doctrine (that is, the message of the president of December 1823 that acquired that name) as the reason for opposing any extension of European rule in the New World.

The Northwest Ordinance of 1787 had established procedures by which newly settled lands could become states. From then until 1812 only five states were added to the original thirteen: Vermont, Kentucky, Tennessee, Ohio, and Louisiana. However, admission then speeded up: from 1816 to 1821 Indiana, Mississippi, Illinois, Alabama, Maine, and Missouri followed. There was no longer serious danger from the Indians; the economy, the population, and the self-confidence of American whites all grew rapidly. Part of the economic expansion was of the cotton-growing plantation system, which carried slavery along with it.

The slave trade had been ended by law in 1808. All northern states abolished slavery or took measures designed to terminate it, and southern states seemed poised to do the same when cotton growing was revolutionized through the cotton gin. When the admission of Missouri was requested, there were eleven free states and eleven slave states and therefore an equal number of senators from each group. The balance of population was different and was widening: in 1820 the free states had 123 members of the House of Representatives while the slave states had only 89, partly because the original Constitution in a curious compromise had provided that five slaves counted as only three men in apportioning seats.

The problem of Missouri occasioned a constitutional crisis. After prolonged debate and consideration of several different solutions, the upshot was that Maine and Missouri were admitted, the former as a free and the latter as a slave state, keeping the balance even. However, all the territory in the Louisiana Purchase north of 36°30' other than Missouri was to be forever free. In the same year Florida, in most of which law and order had virtually broken down as a result of the weakness of Spanish rule, passed to the United States by agreement with Madrid, following an expedition in pursuit of warring Indians under General Andrew Jackson.

In 1820 Monroe won reelection with the votes of all electors but one, and in 1824 the Federalist party had ceased to be a factor in American politics. In that year four Republicans stood for the presidency: the so-called "Virginia dynasty" from which all presidents but one had come was represented by William H. Crawford; John Quincy Adams, Henry Clay, and Andrew Jackson were perceived as candidates of the Northeast and (the latter two) West respectively. Adams, the brilliant and cosmopolitan aristocrat, won after Clay, forced out of the race by coming in fourth, threw his support to the New Englander. The Republicans now split. Supporters of the Adams administration came to be called National Republicans; adherents of Jackson took the name Democrats.

In 1828 Jackson tried again and won, partly because the suffrage had broadened in the old states and was universal from the first in the new ones, partly because more of the ordinary men were exercising their right to vote, and Jackson was a man of the "people" quite ignorant of public affairs. In most states constitutional conventions held in the three decades following 1820 extended democracy by making more officials elective but placing limits on the powers of legislatures. Though Virginia and North Carolina abandoned a franchise based on ownership of property only in the 1850s, universal suffrage prevailed in all other states much earlier (the states prescribed conditions for voting, not the federal government). As for the presidency, by 1828 only Delaware and South Carolina entrusted the choice of electors to the legislatures; all others used popular vote.

The election of Jackson was the doing of the West, the South, and substantial anti-Adams sentiment in the Northeast. It looked as if the day of the common man had arrived: a "noisy and disorderly rabble" celebrated the inauguration in unrestrained fashion, and Jackson's appointments to the cabinet and other offices drew on men deservedly unknown to the educated and politically concerned public. Moreover, he introduced the "spoils system" in the sense that he took the previous practice of occasional appointment of men who were politically congenial and had rendered significant favors in the electoral campaigns, and elevated it into a broadly applied principle.

Jackson used the fact that he had an unprecedented popular mandate to support his extension of the powers of the presidency. He cast many vetoes and was the first to employ the "pocket veto," which was provided by the Constitution and enabled a president to kill a bill passed in the closing days of a session of Congress by declining to sign it.

He also worked for the passage of laws he desired and threw his weight effectively onto one side of the growing sectional conflict. This tangle pitted John C. Calhoun and the doctrine of nullification (that any state could declare any federal law of no effect within its borders) against Daniel Webster, spokesman of the Northeast and nationalism. Jackson, and indeed the West, came down on the latter side. A confrontation in 1832–33 between a convention called by the South Carolina legislature, which announced nullification of two tariff laws, and the presidency was settled by a compromise piloted through by Henry Clay, but the issue would recur.

Jackson also came into conflict with the Bank of the United States, the second institution of the sort, chartered in 1816. In 1832 Jackson was overwhelmingly reelected. The election was of special interest because it was the first in which national nominating conventions chose the presidential and vice-presidential candidates. In this regard the two major parties followed the lead, oddly enough, of the first organized third party in American history, the Anti-Masonic party. Jackson now returned to the assault on the bank. Together with overexpansion and reckless borrowing on the part of the West, Jackson's mishandling of public finance is often cited as the cause of a boom as well as the bust that became known as the Panic of 1837.

The opposition to Jackson took the name of "Whigs," but were unable to organize a united party. Six men received electoral votes, but the majority went to Jackson's chosen successor, Martin Van Buren. His administration suffered from the depression that began before he was inaugurated, and the Whigs made the most of their opportunity. With their candidate, the war hero General William Henry Harrison, they swept the Electoral College. He died after one month in office, and the Southerner John Tyler succeeded him. Whig disunity finally led to Tyler's being read out of the party at the instance of Henry Clay. But recovery had set in; the panic had undermined the labor unions that had just begun to flourish, and they did not regain their strength for some time.

Free public schools spread from the 1830s on, so that by the 1860s they existed in most of the North though not in the South. Free was not the same as universal; it is estimated that one-fourth of the white children of the North were in such schools by the time of the Civil War and only one-tenth or so in the South. The churches retained their predominant influence on education, both higher and lower. At that stage of the history of the United States, Christianity and free political institutions seemed to be closely linked to each other. De Tocqueville observed:

Liberty regards religion as its companion in all its battles and its triumphs, —as the cradle of its infancy, and the divine source of its claims. It considers religion as the safeguard of morality, and morality as the best security of law, and the surest pledge of the duration of freedom. . . .[10]

The observation reflected his general views but also what he saw in America at that time. In the Jacksonian era, when equality had abruptly approached realization, he was fearful lest the liberty and also the democracy that he found in the United States degenerate into an autocratic system. He warned of his belief "that it is easier to establish an absolute and despotic government amongst a people in which the conditions of society are equal, than amongst any other. . . ."[11]

In the middle of the nineteenth century a crisis supervened in American history that seemed to threaten the end of freedom. However, the danger appeared to have little to do with an excess of equality; rather, a crucial factor was the gross inequality to be found in the institution of slavery. Moral, legal, and political arguments were mobilized on both sides. The economic factor was and is in dispute. To this day it is unclear whether slavery was economically profitable, or at any rate more so than the use of free labor; it is not even clear that most Southerners believed it to be so. To be sure, the South's virtual monopoly of the world's cotton market produced great prosperity, and it seemed economically risky to change the organization of the production of King Cotton, as it came to be called. Nevertheless, even greater profits might be accessible if there was change —or so some thought.

In 1844 former President Van Buren was passed over; instead the Democrats chose James K. Polk. His opponent was Henry Clay, the Whig choice. Polk won on a platform favoring annexation—of Texas, which had been independent of Mexico since 1836, and by extension and implication the whole region west to the Pacific. It now consisted of two parts: first was the Oregon country, north of the forty-second parallel, conceded to the United States by the 1819 treaty with Spain, and south of 54°40′, conceded to Britain by agreement with Russia (the owner of Alaska from the time of Bering's voyage of 1741). The entire area was under joint occupation of Britain and the United States. By treaty it was now divided, in 1846; the 49° boundary was extended to the Pacific Ocean, but Britain received all of Vancouver Island. The second part was the (Mexican) Southwest. In 1846 war broke out with Mexico, and by the Treaty of Guadalupe Hidalgo in 1848 the Rio Grande became the boundary.

The "manifest destiny," as one statesman would have it, of the United States was accomplished in the sense that (with the trifling exception of a bit of land in Arizona) the 1990s boundaries of the contiguous territory of the United States had been reached. The realization of that "destiny" at Mexico's expense did not please some Americans, and the treatment of the Indians who inhabited the plains of the interior troubled many. Repentance of those deeds was considerably delayed, and often announced by men other than those who originally committed or legitimized them.

Influenced by British moves toward free trade, Polk led the lowering of tariffs. Finally, he and Congress faced the question of how the enormous new annexations would affect slavery. A substantial body of opinion wished to ban slavery throughout the new territories, but did not prevail. The balance of North and South in the Senate, which had existed since 1820, would be tipped the moment a free state was newly admitted (the inhabitants of a territory were still assumed to have the right to decide between slavery and its prohibition).

In 1848 a hero of the Mexican War, General Zachary Taylor, as the Whig candidate faced the Democrat Lewis Cass—and then also the antislavery group that organized as the Free Soil party with Van Buren as their candidate. The split among the Democrats threw the election to Taylor, but the Free Soilers had won impressive victories too. Now the question of admitting new states could be postponed no longer. California and New Mexico clamored for entrance as free states.

In the lengthy and intricate process that produced the so-called Compromise of 1850, California was admitted as a free state; a strict fugitive-slave law was passed to conciliate the South; the slave trade, but not slavery, was abolished in the District of Columbia. President Taylor, who inexplicably opposed the Compromise, died and his successor, former Vice-President Millard Fillmore, signed the five bills that made it up. For the moment both North and South, despite some strong opposition, accepted it. The aged Henry Clay may deserve the most credit.

In the election of 1852 the Democratic candidate, Franklin Pierce, carried twenty-seven states to four for the Whig candidate, General Winfield Scott. Pierce supported the Compromise wholeheartedly; Scott's position was ambiguous. But the nation's verdict was clear, and the Whig party fell apart as a result.

The dislocations and ills of the Industrial Revolution, the Irish potato famine, and the Revolutions of 1848 sent masses of Irishmen, Germans, and others across the Atlantic; and antiforeign feeling produced a new political party called the Know-Nothings, from the stock answer given by one of them to queries how he would vote. But the issue of slavery elbowed antiforeignism aside. The man who did most to precipitate a showdown was Senator Stephen A. Douglas. He authored the Kansas-Nebraska Act in 1854, which would have created new territories with those two names from which states could be formed as either slave or free, depending on the wishes of the inhabitants.

The result was dramatic. In the North all three parties—Democrats, Whigs, and Know-Nothings—divided sharply over the Act, while in the South all three united solidly in its favor. Out of the total disarray among the old parties was born a new Republican party, using an old and honored name in the changed context. The Whigs disappeared; in the South many of them became Democrats, but the Northern Whigs with few exceptions went into the new party. In the election of 1856 the Democrats, abandoning Pierce for James Buchanan, minister to England, defeated the overconfident Republicans who had named John C. Fremont.

The country was plainly sliding toward a crisis. The Supreme Court delivered a dubious decision in the Dred Scott case, thus strengthening the cause of slavery. Buchanan attempted to bring clearly antislavery Kansas into the Union as a slave state. The so-called Panic of 1857 deepened popular dissatisfaction with the federal government, which seemed powerless to restore amity. A new leader emerged in Illinois, Abraham Lincoln, who won the Republican nomination and in 1860 defeated three opponents: Stephen A. Douglas, who had beaten him in a Senate race in 1858; John C. Breckenridge, candidate of the "fire-eaters"; and John Bell, whose supporters were the remnants of the Whigs and Know-Nothings.

When Lincoln's election became known, the Southern states seceded, beginning with South Carolina. They also united, to become the Confederate States of America, instead of becoming individually independent. A British writer observes: "It seemed wiser to federate, as it had seemed wise to those earlier Founding Fathers of 1776: in adopting this course the Southerners showed how, in spite of everything, they were still intensely American."[12] The constitution they adopted was closely modeled on the Constitution of the United States. It was submitted in March 1861 and in April was ratified by all seven states that had seceded: South Carolina, Mississippi, Florida, Alabama, Georgia, Louisiana, and Texas (in order of secession).

The North hesitated, at first incredulous and conciliatory; Lincoln at his inauguration urged Southern return to the Union. But an incident on 12 April 1861, at Fort Sumter, South Carolina, just off Charleston, came when opinion was hardening on both sides. The result was the outbreak of the Civil War. Secession followed in Virginia (whose capital, Richmond, now became also the Confederate capital), Arkansas, North Carolina, and Tennessee. The North held the other states, and during the war admitted Kansas (1861), West Virginia (forty-six western counties of Virginia that broke away, 1863), and Nevada (1864).

Despite the greater population and resources of the North, the South held on for four years, for several reasons: it had a great general in Robert E. Lee, while Lincoln sought in vain for a comparable commander; the South needed only to defend, the North to try to put down what it regarded as a rebellion and conquer largely hostile territory; the Confederacy was trying something new, and many rallied to its cause with enthusiasm.

But the South also had weaknesses. The Northern blockage by cutting cotton exports gravely injured the Southern economy, while northern manufacturing boomed. President Jefferson Davis was less than a charismatic leader. The Confederacy had no political parties, which played a crucial role in government in the United States. The doctrine of states' rights, which had helped to precipitate the break in 1861, also hindered the efforts to weld the Confederacy into a nation.

The Civil War was the most important event in American history since the federal union was created. It left Abraham Lincoln, assassinated only days after Lee's surrender at Appomattox, as the preeminent national hero and martyr, though he was often ridiculed and denigrated by his contemporaries and was only narrowly reelected in 1864. It was he who in the Emancipation Proclamation freed the slaves of the Confederacy and began a series of actions by other states and the Congress that forbade slavery throughout the country.

The war gave the industrial interests of the Northeast new power and prosperity. The Homestead Act (1862) was designed to make the public lands of the central and western regions available at negligible cost to those who were prepared to farm, and farmers indeed took up the offer fast, though land speculators figured out how, as middlemen, to make fortunes at their expense. The acceleration of westward expansion that followed the Civil War brought new affluence and new freedom to millions who had either failed in the East or successfully sought opportunity in the new West, or both.

In 1865 the immediate issue was restoration of normal civilian government in the defeated states. Lincoln's vice-president and successor, Andrew Johnson, was a southern Democrat (having run on a two-party ticket). He was a conciliator as Lincoln had declared himself to be in his Second Inaugural Address ("with malice toward none"), but Johnson was no diplomat. He undertook to follow the line initiated by Lincoln in making the process of restoring normal government relatively easy and in supervising it as president with no consultation with Congress.

The Radical Republicans, led by Thaddeus Stevens, worked out their own program of "reconstruction" and advanced to direct confrontation with the president, climaxed by impeachment proceedings—the only ones in American history —in which Johnson kept his office by a single vote in the Senate. The Radicals were furious and proceeded to start "reconstruction" all over again. Many whites were disenfranchised, and the vote was given to most Negroes (as they were then called; "black" was not regarded as a flattering term, and "African American" was unknown). "Carpetbaggers" (white northerners newly arrived with Radical views) and "scalawags" (southern whites or northerners long resident in the South) led Negroes to the polls, and new state governments were set up. From 1868 to 1870, the former Confederate states, having now undergone "thorough" reconstruction, were readmitted to the Union.

In the election of 1868 the Republicans nominated Ulysses S. Grant, the last

Union commander in the Civil War. He won against the Democrats' Horatio Seymour, but only by a narrow margin of the popular vote owing to Negro support; he was defeated in the white vote. Now the president was subservient to Congress, and the South was subservient to the federal government as a result of the Union troops that occupied it. Corruption was rife in the carpetbagger-scalawag governments of the southern states and also in the North; the Grant administration was involved in one gigantic scandal after another, often reflecting bribery by business of government officials.

In 1872 Grant was reelected, defeating Horace Greeley, candidate of the forces appalled by the excesses of Radical reconstruction in the South. They comprised a combination of Democrats with a new faction calling itself Liberal Republican; the candidate, Greeley, had many weaknesses, and it was an easy triumph for Grant.

However, the scandals of his administration now began to surface; the Panic of 1873 laid low the economy. In consequence the Democrats swept the House of Representatives in the midterm elections of 1874. Thus in 1876 the Radicals pulled back, and the Republicans nominated Rutherford B. Hayes of Ohio. He was defeated in the popular vote by Samuel J. Tilden, the Democratic candidate. Highly questionable procedure was followed by the Republicans. Double returns from the three states that Union troops still occupied—South Carolina, Louisiana, and Florida—were jimmied to produce a one-vote Electoral College margin, followed by a one-vote margin in a new Electoral Commission, for Hayes.

The real bargain behind this apparent reversal of the voters' wishes[13] was between Democratic leaders, who were promised federal appropriations for public works and patronage, and Republican leaders ready, as Hayes was, to withdraw Union troops from the remaining southern states. They were indeed withdrawn, and "reconstruction" came to an end. Negro suffrage was also terminated, and the Fourteenth and Fifteenth amendments passed into the shadows for many decades.

The Negroes were no longer property, but they were not prepared for freedom. Their owners had provided for them as slaves, and they had little notion of how to provide food, housing, and protection for themselves. Some, indeed, ignored "emancipation" and continued to work as before; many now ceased to work. The Freedmen's Bureau (officially bearing a longer name) had from 1865 saved many Negroes as well as whites from starvation by distributing supplies; a measure termed the "Southern Homestead Act" operated for a decade to permit some Negroes (and whites) to occupy eighty-acre tracts and farm them.

In general, however, the grant of freedom via Emancipation, since it was not followed by any effective measures to set the freed slaves on a viable economic footing, produced frustration in the freedmen and no basis for a challenge to the white supremacy that the post-1877 South proceeded to institutionalize. In 1883 the Supreme Court ruled in the Civil Rights cases that the prohibition of discrimination and guarantees of equal treatment contained in the Fourteenth Amendment applied only to the states and not to individuals or organizations. "Jim Crow," the system of legal and customary separation of the races and the relegation of the Negro to second-class citizenship (or, in effect, no citizenship at all), was thereupon fixed on the South and was in full force by 1900.

It was expansion westward that had upset the precarious balance between slave and free territory and therefore precipitated the Civil War. Expansion resumed in the postwar period. The Senate refused to ratify a treaty annexing the Dominican Republic, but the House, on the distribution of sufficient Russian bribes, appropriated the money necessary to buy Alaska. In the same year, 1867, Midway Island was annexed—to acquire renown seventy-odd years later as the site (more or less) of a crucial naval battle of World War II.

On the North American mainland, the area between California and Oregon in the West and Texas and Minnesota in the East remained short of population and therefore lacked states. The admission of Nebraska in 1867 completed the unfinished business of the debate over the Kansas-Nebraska Act. A gold rush precipitated Colorado into statehood in 1876. From the 1860s on the migration of the Mormons into Utah first created a theocracy as pure as ever existed in America, but as other migrants enveloped it the sect gave up polygamy (in 1890) and Utah became a state in 1896. North Dakota and South Dakota, Washington, and Montana had gained admission in 1889, Wyoming and Idaho in 1890.

In that year the federal Bureau of the Census announced that the continuous frontier line had disappeared, leading the historian Frederick Jackson Turner to develop his thesis that the search for free land in the westward movement explained America's free institutions. And indeed the more dramatic phase of westward expansion was at an end. As the miners and cattlemen had joined the farmers in settling and populating the Great Plains, the grimmest phases of white-Indian relations accompanied the process.

There had been blood shed and bad faith shown in earlier relations between the two, and the worse record is that of the whites. The Indians of the Northwest (that is, north of the Ohio River) were greatly reduced in number and stripped of much of their land by trickery before the War of 1812. Tecumseh, a Shawnee, managed to unite several of the tribes in a confederacy but was defeated at Tippecanoe (1811) and killed two years later. Deceit produced a treaty with the Creeks, a more advanced tribe than many, under the presidency of John Quincy Adams, and Adams tried to defend them, in vain. In the 1830s the "five civilized Indian Nations" (the Creeks, Cherokees, Choctaws, Chickasaws, and Seminoles) were forcibly removed to "Indian Territory" in Oklahoma; the result was death and poverty. The halfbreed Sequoya had striven to bring the trappings of civilization to his Cherokees—with a written language, a Bible translation, a constitution for the Cherokee nation, and an elected legislature; he was convinced that that effort would save his people. He was wrong.

Many of these Indians were agricultural and sedentary. But the Plains Indian was different: he, "by habit and heredity, was a hunter rather than a cultivator; . . . his ideas of land ownership were communal, not individual; . . . the last thing he wanted was to become a homesteader."[14] As Morison puts it:

> In contrast to the blacks who were denied their ambition to participate on equal terms in American civilization, the Indians, who desired above all to continue their own way of life, were deprived of hunting grounds which would have made that possible, and were pressured to "settle down" and become "good" farmers and citizens.[15]

Many of the Plains tribes resisted the white incursions into their hunting grounds and destruction of the great buffalo herds that sustained them. The federal government sometimes killed them, sometimes put them on reservations and tried to take care of them, often wrote treaties with them that were broken or ignored but after a time stopped that farcical practice. In 1887 the Dawes Act sought to break up reservations into individual homesteads. Not only was the Indian of the West not a farmer, but he also had no Protestant ethic, no idea of deferred gratification, no means of preventing speculators from reducing him to instant squalor and degradation. In summary, many Indians went to the cities, many remained on reservations, few managed to find a way of living happy lives even when sizable financial settlements were awarded them by later-day courts.

Indians were a factor in the admission of the last three of the contiguous forty-eight states to the Union. The Five Civilized Nations, or those who survived, were made American citizens in 1901, and Oklahoma became a state in 1907. Not long after the final defeat of the Apaches and the surrender of Geronimo (later to become a Christian convert and a respected celebrity) in 1886, New Mexico and Arizona settled down to become states (1912), with substantial Indian and Mexican (that is, mixed Indian and Spanish) population.

The ethnic make-up of the United States was by this time almost entirely white, since not many Indians (or Native Americans) were left, virtually no Asians had yet immigrated, and the percentage of Negroes was small. Since by the 1890s the latter were mainly disenfranchised, almost all voters were Caucasian.

However, there was a good deal of heterogeneity among the whites. In the seventeenth century most arrivals were English (with a few Dutch and Swedes thrown in). In the eighteenth and early nineteenth centuries, millions of Scotch-Irish, Irish, and Germans came in; later, many from southern and eastern

Europe. A large number of Jews were included—the first sizable non-Christian group—but the Italians, Poles, Irish, and other Roman Catholics created a greater religious problem, for America had been mostly Protestant up to that time. From 1820 to 1920 38 million Europeans arrived, the heaviest decade being 1900–1909, when 8.7 million came.

Assimilation was the lot of a large share of immigrants or at least their children, who learned English quickly and declined to speak the parents' tongue, but there was resistance from the nascent labor unions and fear from those who saw the newcomers successfully mobilized by big-city political machines. Nevertheless, the greatest transoceanic migration in history and the greatest migration of any sort in modern times had transported a vast horde of people to the United States, attracted by the promise of freedom—to improve themselves, to give their families what they themselves had not had, to vote, to do as they please. What is astonishing is how often the promise was fulfilled.

By the so-called Compromise of 1877 the sectional conflict was set aside, and the conflict of the two parties came to replace it. Small third parties sprang up but did not grow: the Greenback party, founded in 1876, the Prohibitionist party (1872), the People's Party or Populists (1891), which developed out of the farmers' Alliances of the previous decade. In 1880 the Republicans nominated James A. Garfield and elected him over the Democratic candidate, General Winfield S. Hancock, and the Greenback candidate, who polled enough votes to deny Garfield a majority. (The Electoral College, of course, was not dependent on the popular vote in any event.) A disappointed office seeker shot Garfield within a few months of his inauguration, and Vice-president Chester A. Arthur replaced him.

Arthur well administered the Pendleton Act (1883), which established a new civil-service system to make federal offices open only to those who were most successful in examinations testing the fitness—measured in rather limited terms —of the applicants. The specified, or "classified," lists of offices could be expanded by the president. The fortuitous fact that the party in the White House changed every four years from 1880 through 1900 led each prospective retiree from the presidency to try to protect his own appointees. By 1914 over half the federal employees were on civil service.

In 1884 the heart and soul of the Republican party, James G. Blaine, was nominated but defeated by Governor Grover Cleveland of New York, despite the characterization of the Democratic party by a Protestant minister as linked with "rum, Romanism, and rebellion." This time either the Greenback or the Prohibitionist vote would have been enough to deny Cleveland a majority of the popular vote. The Democratic president had trouble with his party, but both plumped for a lower tariff. On that issue Benjamin Harrison, a lesser light of the Republicans, recaptured the White House for his party in 1888. They raised the tariff to its highest point to date; they protected the burgeoning industries, including even hitherto nonexistent ones, of both the North and the "New South" (though the former overshadowed the latter by far); and they made a gesture to farmers by placing duties on many agricultural products to boot, though few eggs and little butter would enter on ocean-going ships. The result was to cut drastically the federal revenues and to raise substantially consumer prices. Since Congress also appropriated large sums for domestic improvements, the result was a deficit.

The Republicans lost heavily in the elections of 1890, and in 1892 Harrison was defeated by Cleveland. The third-party candidate was James B. Weaver of the Populists, who polled over one million votes, while each of the two major-party candidates polled over five million, though Cleveland had a heavy electoral-vote majority. Weaver's party battened on the frustration of the farmers but failed to attract support from the chief labor organization, the American Federation of Labor (founded 1881). The Populists demanded an increase of the money supply, on the basis of dubious and naive economics, but also a series of other reforms that were later adopted, such as the income tax and election of U.S. senators by popular vote. Their leaders were ill-educated and quirky, such as Ignatius Donnelly, whose writings were designed to prove that civilization arose in Atlantis and that the works of Shakespeare were written by Bacon. (Unfortunately it seems that America has been unusually prolific in amiable eccentrics—or, some would say, nuts—and that Americans have been especially easy marks for tales of conspiracies in high places and wondrous scientific discoveries.) On the other hand it must be said that better educated people had less excuse for failing to understand the disastrous consequences of high tariffs.

The decline of revenues produced by the 1890 tariff helped to precipitate the Panic of 1893. Many businesses failed, and the gold standard that many thought sacrosanct appeared about to topple. Silver purchase was discontinued, and purchases of gold from abroad helped to restore confidence. The post–Civil War growth of industry had brought with it labor troubles as well as organization, and strikes over a two-decade period reached their climax in the Pullman strike of 1894. The elections of that year reflected voter determination to blame the depressed economy on somebody, and the somebody was the Democratic party, since Cleveland was in office. The Republicans made large gains, and the Populists through increasing their vote by 40 percent over 1892 began to cherish hopes of doing as the Republicans did in 1860.

"Free silver" more and more appealed to the electorate as a panacea, and to steal the Populists' thunder the Democrats adopted the slogan. In the campaign of 1896 some Gold Democrats deserted party ranks and refused to support William Jennings Bryan, the "boy orator" who assailed the gold standard. But

William McKinley, the Republican candidate, held firm for gold, and he won an election following as hard-fought a campaign as any thus far. It had seen a reshaping of American politics: Bryan was the candidate of the farmers of the South and West and to some extent of labor as well; McKinley, of the industry of the Northeast.

Populism was mortally wounded, though it lingered on until 1912. As one survey puts it, the party died but some of its ideas were taken over and were adopted by the nation: "the third party, almost certainly, would be absorbed into one or the other or both of the older parties, but such of its ideas as had merit would survive, and win eventual acceptance."[16] In the Populist case, such ideas included the Australian secret ballot, the initiative and referendum, and the direct election of U.S. senators. If their monetary ideas were half-baked, the attention they drew to the banking and currency system served to lead to the Federal Reserve Act—which Bryan himself helped to draft.

The decades after the Civil War saw an America mainly concerned with its own affairs, including its expansion across the continent. By the 1890s it began to look across the water in several directions. The United States acquired ascendancy in Hawaii and, obviously needing a mid-Pacific base, annexed it in 1898. The following year the islands of Samoa were divided between the United States and Germany.

McKinley intervened in Cuba to prevent Spain from putting down a rising in its colony; in the ensuing Spanish-American War the adversary yielded all her holdings in the hemisphere—Puerto Rico as well as Cuba, and also Guam and the Philippines. The United States annexed all such territories except Cuba, though it kept legally buttressed influence over that newly independent state until the 1930s. Filipino rebels against Spain were almost victorious when American annexation took place, and they turned swiftly against the newcomers from whose hands they had expected independence. It took about three years for the revolt to be put down. Americans had clearly arrived in Asia, and Secretary of State John Hay made the country's presence felt by the "Open Door" notes of 1899, in which each power was invited to observe principles of fairness to all others in trade, but with little perceptible result. The United States reluctantly joined in the multinational force that put down the Boxer Rebellion in the spring of 1900, but remitted much of the indemnity awarded to it. China, in gratitude, decided to use the funds in question to educate Chinese students in the United States and to promote education and science in China.

Imperialism was the Democratic choice for the chief issue of the election of 1900. However, McKinley won reelection, running against Bryan again, but within months after his inauguration he was assassinated by an anarchist and succeeded by Theodore Roosevelt.

T.R. was the hero of the war in Cuba and the standard-bearer of American expansionism. He proceeded to manage a revolution against Colombia of the isthmus of Panama, which promptly formed an independent state willing to permit the United States to build the canal Roosevelt desired. His active policy with regard to other Latin American countries led him to formulate a "Roosevelt corollary" to the Monroe Doctrine, which set forth two warnings: one to European nations not to try to intervene in the hemisphere henceforth, and another to Latin American nations to avoid "chronic wrongdoing" or "impotence" threatening "civilized society"—or risk American intervention. Roosevelt turned the Dominican Republic into something like a protectorate, and his successors took similar steps in Central American countries.

In the early years of the century the defunct Populist party, based in the rural areas, was replaced as the spearhead of reformism by the new Progressive movement, drawing on the urban middle classes and in particular small business, threatened by the power of the great corporations on the one hand and the specter of labor organization possibly leading to socialism on the other. It made headway in promoting new methods of city government, such as the city-manager system that seemed less prone to corruption and more efficient than two-party election of mayors.

Even more, on the state level reform governors defeated entrenched party machines, as happened in Wisconsin (Robert LaFollette), Missouri (Joseph Folk), New York (Charles Evans Hughes), and California (Hiram Johnson). Oregon led the way to adoption of several new devices, popularized and defended by a nonofficial from that state, William S. U'Ren, from 1891 to 1910: the Australian (secret) ballot, voter registration, the initiative, referendum, and recall, the direct primary (which Wisconsin actually pioneered in 1903), and a measure combating corrupt practices.

They were the devices that became the latest political fashion, touted in the schools as the way to make democracy work, or at any rate work much better, to frustrate the machine politicos, and to secure able representatives who would be genuinely responsible to the electorate. The results did not always justify the hopes of the reformers, but adoption of such measures acquired an impressive momentum and pushed the federal government in the same direction. Direct election of U.S. senators was proposed by constitutional amendment, and one passed the House four times between 1894 and 1902. The Senate finally yielded in 1912, after more than half the states adopted preferential primaries that produced senators chosen by the people. Many senators had had close ties with large corporations or political machines, but the Senate had gathered together a great many gifted men. Fortunately, the Seventeenth Amendment, which became law in 1913, did not significantly depress the intellectual level of that body though it probably did not raise it either.

The political changes of the early years of the century helped lead to social legislation. The individual states followed Maryland (1902) in legislating workmen's compensation, or employer's liability, thereby setting aside the common-law rule that in order to obtain any damages the injured worker had to prove employer negligence that partook of no contributory negligence by himself or any other worker. By 1921 only six states held out. Child labor was limited in certain states, and compulsory school-attendance laws had the same effect. Conditions of labor for women were somewhat improved. But in respect to social legislation the United States was far behind European countries, where unemployment insurance and old-age pensions were common.

The reformers also attacked the production and consumption of alcohol. Prohibitionists formed an Anti-Saloon League in 1893, which became an outstanding example of a single-issue political group: if "wet," the candidate was opposed; if "dry," supported. First localities, then states passed laws prohibiting liquor; in 1919 the Eighteenth Amendment made prohibition part of the Constitution. It was soon to be regarded as a disastrous mistake, which created the industries of bootlegging (illegal sale), moonshining (illegal production), and, worst of all, organized crime, which owed its rise in America to prohibition.

Curiously, woman suffrage went hand in hand with prohibition. The antialcohol crusaders assumed that women would take their side if they were given the vote. But the suffragettes, as they were called, also were inspired by their British sisters who had nothing to do with the liquor issue. America's first women voters were given that status in Wyoming Territory in 1869; by 1911 six states in the West, including Wyoming, had so acted. The Nineteenth Amendment took effect in 1920, giving the suffrage to women nationwide.

In this process the individual states had been in the vanguard; the country as a whole had lagged behind. As Muller puts it:

Feminists were able to make . . . converts because of different views that still confuse the status of women, some holding that women were just as good as men in every respect except physical strength, and should therefore have equal opportunity in all occupations except those requiring such strength; others granting that women were essentially different from men, perhaps mostly unsuited for some vocations, and in any case obliged to consider their natural role as housewives and mothers, but holding that they should nevertheless be granted the same civil and political rights. All were agreed on these rights, however, and by the dawn of our century political equality was in sight.[17]

Finland was the first to give full citizenship to women; Norway and Denmark soon followed. But the larger nations, including the United States, did so only after World War I.

Under Theodore Roosevelt, then, the United States seemed to move in the direction of democracy *par excellence,* imposing its will and sometimes its institutions—in some cases, an unintentional parody of them masking a quite different sort of polity—on the rest of the hemisphere, inviting imitation from countries of the Old World, perhaps, but generally avoiding involvements there.

With respect to the domestic scene, Roosevelt groped toward the stance of a reformer. He supported the regulation of certain types and aspects of business. The Sherman Antitrust Act, passed in 1890 and soon having proved unenforceable, was the object of an attempt to revive it selectively. The similarly moribund Interstate Commerce Commission, created by an act of 1887, was actually given new life by the Hepburn Act of 1906. Federal meat inspection and the Pure Food and Drug Act (1906) began protection for the consumer but left untrue advertising alone. The ill-treatment of natural resources at the hands of big business was combated by a variety of conservation measures, which Robert LaFollette, having become senator, considered Roosevelt's supreme achievement.

In 1904 Roosevelt's swelling popularity enabled him to smash his Democratic opponent, Judge Alton B. Parker. The president was blamed, perhaps unfairly, for the Panic of 1907; at any rate the panic revealed defects in the nation's system of banking, investigation of which led to the Federal Reserve System a few years later (1913). Declining to run for a third term (already it was common to think of a limitation to two terms for a president), Roosevelt chose as Republican candidate William Howard Taft, the physically gigantic Secretary of War. Taft faced William Jennings Bryan, who did little better than Parker in 1904, and became president.

The new occupant of the White House lacked Roosevelt's charisma but also had a higher regard for the proper role of Congress. On issues involving the tariff, conservation, and regulation of business, Taft was charged with allowing opponents of Roosevelt's policies to carry the day. The charges were at least partly unfair: he was responsible for sponsoring jurisdiction over the telephone and telegraph communication for the Interstate Commerce Commission and other reform measures. Nevertheless the militant progressives in the Republican party had lost confidence in Taft. At the 1912 national convention he was renominated, turning back a challenge from Roosevelt himself, who was returning with gusto to the political wars.

But Roosevelt was determined to run, and was chosen by a new Progressive party as its candidate. Licking their chops at the Republican split, the Democrats nominated Governor Woodrow Wilson of New Jersey. Two slogans as well as two candidates confronted each other: Roosevelt's "New Nationalism" faced Wilson's "New Freedom." Taft had no slogan and could muster little enthusiastic support. Wilson won 435 electoral votes, Roosevelt 88, and Taft 8. The Democrats also swept the elections to Congress. Eugene V. Debs, running as before on the

Socialist party ticket, won no electoral votes but nearly nine hundred thousand popular votes.

Socialism in America never achieved the successes it registered on the European continent, Australasia, or later in the so-called Third World. It produced the militant, orthodox Marxist, and tiny Socialist Labor party of Daniel De Leon, which dates from 1877. The Socialist party of America (SPA), which first nominated Debs for the presidency in 1900, was formally organized under that name a year later, having broken away from the SLP previously as the Social Democratic party. (The Communists, and the Socialist Workers party, consisting of Trotskyists, which broke off from the former, were to take form only after the Russian Revolution of 1917.)

The SPA aspired to the same uncompromising ideals for the future that the Marxists did, but concentrated their attention on measures they considered realizable in the near future, such as public ownership of utilities and railroads, public works for relief of the unemployed and needy, heavier taxation of the rich, and political reforms on the lines of the Oregon system. Like the Populists and Progressives, the Socialists managed to further the adoption of such reforms without ever winning power in any unit larger than cities or chalking up the votes necessary to become a major party.

In 1914 Congress added two pieces of legislation to those restricting unfair business practice: the Clayton Antitrust Act and the act creating the Federal Trade Commission. Labor unions were apparently exempted by several provisions of the Clayton Act from action often taken earlier against strikes and boycotts; Samuel Gompers, founder of the American Federation of Labor, termed such exemptions labor's Magna Carta.

What evaluation should be placed on measures restricting the freedom of businessmen and labor leaders—or corporations and unions—to act is constantly in dispute. The unrestricted or only mildly restricted freedom of both could and did do harm to the well-being and the rights of others; the public perception of how much restriction was wise changed over the years. At the stage of development the United States had reached in 1914, it seemed to the most thoughtful people that what was needed was greater governmental control of industry, less control of labor.

The federal government also embarked, during the Wilson administration, on a course of matching dollars with state appropriations in the cause of agricultural and other sorts of vocational education, as well as in building highways. The revenues produced by the new federal income tax supplied most of the money and served thus indirectly to begin a seemingly inexorable process of shifting the power of government from the states to the nation. The Federal Reserve System now in operation proved far more effective and certainly longer lasting than any previous attempt at a national banking system. In the words of one assessment, the result of all this was: "by infringing a little on freedom the Wilsonians hoped to strengthen equality of opportunity."[18] To a certain extent they may claim to have done so.

Further trial and error in such directions was prevented by the outbreak of World War I. The United States maintained neutrality for close to three years. However, after the sinking of the British liner *Lusitania* in May 1915 public opinion was moving quite rapidly in a pro-Allied direction, and the peril that seemed to threaten British control of the seas after the battle of Jutland a year later drove the United States into greatly enlarging the navy and strengthening the army.

In the election of 1916 Wilson narrowly defeated Charles Evans Hughes, who resigned as justice of the Supreme Court to become the Republican candidate. Wilson had extorted from Germany a promise to observe the rules of war (giving warning of imminent hostile action and providing care for noncombatant passengers) with its U-boats. After his reelection he tried to mediate peace. But Germany now withdrew its promise on the ground that America had failed to stop illegal actions by the Allies. Wilson broke relations; German submarines sank three ships; Congress declared war on 6 April 1917. Wilson declared, "The world must be made safe for democracy," and doubtless meant it, despite the factors of national security and power that also figured in the nation's entrance into the conflict.

The war had striking effects on the American polity. The federal government raised unheard-of sums, taxes increased, price rose, fortunes were made. Much popular opinion supported such actions, but not all of it, and legislation was enacted to punish "disloyal" deeds and words. Some fifteen hundred people were arrested for violating those laws, chiefly Socialists and pacifists (some were both), along with a few who sympathized with the German cause. In an opinion written by Oliver Wendell Holmes, a unanimous Supreme Court declared that a "clear and present danger" might require limitations of civil liberty: "When a nation is at war, many things that might be said in time of peace are such a hindrance to its effort that their utterance will not be endured so long as men fight, and . . . no court could regard them as protected by constitutional right."[19]

As for the organizations and functions of the federal government, they greatly expanded. Six large agencies were set up to build ships, furnish food and fuel, regulate foreign trade, operate the railroads, and plan industrial production. It seemed that the government had taken over the economy—except that many of the members of the war boards were in fact businessmen taking time from their permanent jobs. Most important, the productive capacity and output of all sectors of the economy immensely increased. In the fighting, American sacrifices, though modest in comparison to those of their European allies, tipped the balance to assure victory.

However, the diplomatic outcome was a bitter disappointment to Wilson and many others. At Paris the United States helped redraw the map of Europe, but the Treaty of Versailles was rejected by the Senate because some wanted no League of Nations at all, while others wanted the treaty as drawn and a League without the "reservations" the Republicans had attached to it. A grotesque drama was thus played out in which a treaty favored by the overwhelming majority of senators (some, with the reservations, some, without) was rejected by the Senate, because neither Wilson nor Senator Henry Cabot Lodge was willing to compromise.

Thereupon Wilson called for a "solemn referendum" on the Treaty, and the election of 1920 provided one of sorts. More accurately, the victory of the conspicuously untalented Warren G. Harding, Republican, over the Democrat James M. Cox, governor of Ohio (also Harding's state), bespoke the electorate's reaction against the war, against the party held responsible for the economic depression that had set in and for the numerous and serious strikes of the period, and against the length and tediousness of the debate over the treaty. Harding's victory was crushing in its size.

The United States negotiated a separate peace with Germany, Austria, and Hungary, and seemed to turn its back on the troublesome Old World. The federal government, under Republican leadership, withdrew from competition with private business or interference with it that had occurred in wartime and imposed substantial restraints on the activities of labor unions. Harding proceeded to appoint a few good people and many bad ones, who became involved in bribery, corruption, and scandals reminiscent of the administration of what some called the other failure as president, Ulysses S. Grant.[20]

Harding collapsed and died in August 1923 and was succeeded by Calvin Coolidge, the vice-president. In 1924 a new law regulated immigration, limiting the newcomers from outside northern Europe. The background to this act was fear: of Communist expansion outside Russia after the October Revolution of 1917 and of native radicalism, held responsible for several bombing outrages in 1919–20 and associated, not very plausibly, with the new American Communist party. All this had culminated in the "Red Scare" of 1919–20, in which both governmental and nongovernmental measures were taken against Communists but also against Socialists and pacifists.

By 1923 prosperity had returned for several social groups, farmers being the chief exception, but many workers did not benefit either. One result was the attempt to put together a working-class, or "farmer-labor," group to function as a third party. Stemming from earlier efforts, such a party was formed under the Progressive name and ran Robert LaFollette as its candidate in the election of 1924. Coolidge, symbol of economic revival, defeated a "dark horse" who had captured the Democratic nomination, John W. Davis, by an enormous margin; but a sign of trouble manifested itself in the fact that LaFollette polled almost five million votes.

Coolidge declared that he did not "choose to run" again, and so in 1928 his Secretary of Commerce, Herbert Hoover, was the Republican candidate who confronted Alfred E. Smith, the Catholic governor of New York. Again the Republicans had a landslide victory: this time there was no Progressive candidate, and Norman Thomas, who was to become the perennial Socialist candidate, whom everyone respected and few voted for, obtained only about 250,000 votes.

If women's rights and prohibition of alcohol had gone hand in hand in wartime and earlier, during the 1920s they seemed to part company. Women won in their assaults on many masculine strongholds. Thousands became secretaries and secured other jobs in the business world. Nellie Tayloe Ross was elected governor of Wyoming in 1924, the first woman ever to be so chosen, and "Ma" Ferguson of Texas soon followed her. Divorces multiplied, sexual double standards long familiar in America (and elsewhere) tottered, and women secured admittance to the "speakeasy" where there was served the liquor that was banned by constitutional amendment.

Prohibition was ineffective in its aim, but it was all too effective in providing the demand to which the new industry of organized crime in America responded. Bootlegging of illegal (all) and poisonous (some) alcohol flourished on a wave of bribery and corruption. In 1933 the Eighteenth Amendment was repealed, and the "noble experiment" came to an end. However, organized crime did not and turned to bank robbery, kidnapping, and "protection" rackets—later to be succeeded by the sale of drugs on a large scale.

The Hoover administration was led by a man who had been a distinguished administrator and effective humanitarian on several continents but had scant ability as a politician. In October 1929, only a few months after his inaugural, the New York stock market crashed. Prices and wages fell, unemployment spread, and the nation confronted the Great Depression and helped (especially from spring 1931) to spread it to the rest of the world. Industry and agriculture nearly collapsed.

Congress responded with the Hawley-Smoot tariff, signed by the president in June 1930. The measure provoked retaliation from Britain, which now fully jettisoned the free trade from which it had benefited for almost a century, and also from several other countries, and helped to drive the levels of world trade downward when the opposite was sorely needed. The legislative and executive branches combined to create a Reconstruction Finance Corporation (RFC) which loaned money to both public and private outfits of many kinds, sparing many from bankruptcy, and Federal Home Loan Banks, which saved numbers of families from foreclosure. As expenditures to combat depression rose and revenues fell, the Treasury began the practice of borrowing money, or "deficit financing," which has never ceased since.

In the election of 1932 Franklin D. Roosevelt, Assistant Secretary of the Navy under Wilson and later governor of New York, challenged Hoover. He promised a "New Deal," though it was then far from clear what that exactly was to mean. The electorate wanted change, and voted for FDR by a 472-to-59 margin in the Electoral College, 22.8 million to 15.7 million in the popular vote. Almost 900,000 voted for Norman Thomas and well over 100,000 for the Communist candidate, William Z. Foster. It is a wonder that a country with perhaps seventeen million unemployed did not produce more radical voters or any revolutionary action at all. Still, the banking system had virtually fallen apart by the time Roosevelt was inaugurated in March 1933, and he faced an emergency indeed. He declared, "the only thing we have to fear is fear itself," and then proceeded to close all banks for eight days.

The New Deal was on its way, the president leading the Congress to pass a series of measures based roughly on the assumption that private enterprise was to continue but under regulation by government designed not only to end the Great Depression but to prevent the boom-and-bust cycle from doing further damage. Roosevelt sought "the three R's": relief (some dole, or direct relief payments, and some federally conducted public works), recovery (expanded loans), and reform (crop reduction; support for labor-union organizing; regulation of banking, transportation, utilities, and the stock market; tariff reduction; federally supported housing; and "social security"). The government itself developed power sources through the Tennessee Valley Authority, but for the most part did not try to compete directly with private business.

In 1936 the Republican challenger, Alfred M. Landon, was overwhelmed by a 523-to-8 electoral count and a popular-vote margin of 27.7 million to 16.7 million, the far Left doing much less well than in 1932. The depression was not over, but the improvement in the economy was noteworthy. A coalition had been forged that consisted of the Solid South, the non–Anglo-Saxon ethnic groups that had been mobilized by the big-city machines of the North, the midwestern farmers saved by New Deal assistance, the labor unions that thrived under FDR, and the liberal intellectuals—and also a few businessmen, whose Democratic numbers were to grow.

The New Deal coalition, confronting rich Anglo-Saxons who seemed dominant in the shambles that 1936 left the Republican party in, marked a sharp reorganization of American political life. "All income groups had been well represented in both major parties [in the nineteenth century]," declares one authoritative work;[21] now the two parties moved much closer to division by social class. The division was to last a quarter-century at least.

Armed with the confidence produced by his great victory, Roosevelt proceeded to take on the Supreme Court, which had declared unconstitutional some of his favorite measures. His "court-packing" bill aroused fear and hostility in even some of his supporters, but it failed—or in a sense succeeded, for the Court seemed to respond to the threat by a new willingness to approve New Deal legislation brought before it. In the midterm elections of 1938 the pendulum swung against FDR, sufficiently so that Republicans made gains in Congress and, acting with southern Democrats, were in a position to prevent any further movement to the left.

But the New Deal was not repealed, it was merely contained. It had reduced the power of the states and increased that of Washington, D.C., along with the capital's payrolls of federal employees and the cost of the federal government and its programs. It interfered with the property rights of the rich and assumed as a permanent obligation aspects of the welfare of the poor. However, it also gave millions a stake in society and probably staved off a crisis that might have shaken the foundations of the entire nation.

During the later 1930s the rise of Nazi Germany, its junior partner Fascist Italy, and militarist Japan drew increasing American attention. The prevailing reaction was to try to insulate the United States against foreign troubles by way of the neutrality laws of 1935 and 1937. Even after World War II broke out in September 1939 the country was reluctant to help Britain and France against Hitler or even to strengthen American defenses. It was after France and the Low Countries had been overrun and while German armies were fast advancing into the USSR, in August 1941, that the House of Representatives came within one vote of refusing to extend the draft law for the army. In the campaign of 1940 FDR, facing the Indiana businessman Wendell Willkie as his Republican opponent, promised not to send "your boys" into any foreign war. True, by way of "Lend-Lease," Congress authorized aid to Britain of military equipment in March 1941, and after Hitler attacked the Soviet Union in June aid was extended to that country as well.

In December the Japanese attack on Pearl Harbor brought America into the war, and from then on every nerve was strained to gain victory. "Under the stress of a war that required intelligent foresight if it were to be won, planning ceased to be a dirty word and became a necessity in modern administration," writes Samuel Eliot Morison.[22] The federal government created new agencies, the whole nation was mobilized for war production, the armed forces were immensely increased in manpower (and women, too, took part) and quality of equipment. Black units were organized and fought well, though integration of fighting units had to await the Truman administration; an unsurpassed military record was made by the Japanese-American units from Hawaii and the mainland. The United States sustained over one million casualties, and more than a third of those died. The cost in money was immense, though the country emerged with an expanded and improved industrial plant and suffered no postwar depression.

In 1944 there was held the first wartime presidential election since 1864; Roosevelt was elected to a fourth term with a 432-to-99 majority in the Electoral College, but the popular vote went to him more narrowly. He was already a sick man, and he died in April 1945. He was succeeded by Harry S. Truman, whose presidency surprised many who at the start scorned him as ordinary. He led the country into the United Nations, organized at a conference held in San Francisco in late April, whose Charter was approved by overwhelming vote of the Senate. The change from the end of World War I was striking.

America was indeed thrust into the international arena by the war and then the peace, and at the same time the nation faced new challenges and difficulties. The puzzlingly intransigent and often hostile attitude of the USSR and the spread of Communist rule into Eastern Europe and East Asia led to the so-called Cold War (the phrase was credited to Walter Lippmann), but domestically there was an enthusiastic return to normalcy, as Harding once put it.

To almost everyone's surprise except his own, Truman won the election of 1948 with 303 electoral votes to 189 for Governor Thomas E. Dewey of New York, 39 for Governor J. Strom Thurmond of South Carolina (candidate of the short-lived States' Rights Democrat or "Dixiecrat" ticket), and zero for Henry A. Wallace, candidate of a Communist-dominated leftist coalition using the name Progressive. The New Deal had shown unexpected durability. Nevertheless Truman's program for further extension of welfare measures and civil-rights reform, labeled the "Fair Deal," mainly failed of passage in Congress.

An effort by international Communist forces to extend their sway beyond China (a People's Republic was proclaimed in Peking in October 1949) to adjoining areas extending from India all the way to the Korean peninsula was climaxed by an attack by North Korea in June 1950 across the thirty-eighth parallel southward. Truman sent American forces to help South Korea. The Korean War, as most people termed what Truman branded "a police action, not a war," ended in stalemate and roughly the *status quo ante*. It was concluded by an armistice reached under President Dwight D. Eisenhower (1953–61), who defeated the brilliant and articulate Adlai E. Stevenson twice to preside over a tranquilly uneventful administration. In 1954, in the case of *Brown v. Board of Education*, the Supreme Court ordered an end to segregation in U.S. schools. In 1959 Alaska and Hawaii became the forty-ninth and fiftieth states.

From 1961 to 1969 moderate Democrats held the presidency: John F. Kennedy, who became the darling of intellectuals and whose assassination in November 1963 shook the whole nation, and Lyndon B. Johnson (1963–69), who sought to run both a war in South Vietnam designed to stop a Communist takeover and ambitious domestic programs under the slogan of a "Great Society"—with unhappy results for the treasury. The civil-rights movement, led by Dr. Martin Luther King, Jr. (assassinated in 1968), by nonviolent direct action achieved desegregation of many private and public facilities before a period of rioting erupted. Forces espousing feminism, gay liberation, environmentalism, and leftist politics focusing on the Vietnam War made their appearance; and the last-named had much to do with pushing Richard Nixon, elected in 1968 (after narrowly losing to Kennedy in 1960) and Secretary of State Henry Kissinger into arranging with the USSR and PRC a purported settlement in January 1973 that collapsed in 1975, resulting in a complete Communist victory. In the meantime a convoluted scandal beginning with a break-in to the Democratic National Committee headquarters in the Watergate complex in Washington, D.C., drove Nixon to resign in 1974, although he had won a one-sided victory in 1972. Paul Johnson calls all this "America's suicide attempt." [23] Certainly the sixties were a period of often hysterical public demonstrations, paralysis of government, and the sexual, racial, and other revolutions that occurred with dizzying speed.

Nixon, a Republican, was replaced by Republican Vice-President Gerald Ford, who lost the presidency to Democratic Governor Jimmy Carter of Georgia in 1976, in turn replaced by Ronald Reagan (1981–89), a former film actor and governor of California. Reagan did much to rehabilitate the presidency as a respected office but left the heritage of a ferocious federal deficit. In January 1989 Vice-President George Bush succeeded him. A pattern of Republican presidents and Democratic Congresses, in sometimes uneasy coexistence, had developed. In the turbulent two decades following the Kennedy presidency, the American system had showed that it could survive a great many shocks. Some would argue that the limits of liberty had been extended too far, but the popular consensus did not seem to agree.

CHAPTER 10

The Coming of Democracy, 1800–1990: Part Three

Poland

The Constitution of 1791 had converted the elective monarchy into a hereditary one (note that an elective monarchy has seldom if ever been an example of a free polity), created a two-chamber legislature, and abolished the liberum veto—a noteworthy instance of how taking away the powers of a national assembly may under certain circumstances advance the cause of freedom. But the constitution did not last: it led to Russian manipulation that created the Confederation of Targowice, subsequent Russian and Prussian invasion, and the Second Partition, in turn provoking a revolution in 1794 that was put down and followed up by the Third Partition in 1795. It wiped Poland off the map. A Poland of sorts was restored as the Duchy of Warsaw by the Treaty of Tilsit between Alexander I of Russia and Napoleon, and lasted from 1807 to 1815.

The Congress of Vienna in effect partitioned the country once again. There were five parts of the new settlement: under Prussia, West Prussia and the Grand Duchy of Posen (Poznan); under Austria, Galicia; the Free City of Cracow; the Kingdom of Poland, united with the Russian crown; and the former Polish provinces of the Russian Empire. The Poles strove to extend the autonomy permitted them in Prussia and to obtain something comparable from Austria (in vain for decades, later with much success), but what seemed to promise most for the future freedom of the nation was the Kingdom set up by the Congress of Vienna (therefore "Congress Poland"). The Polish nobility retained its economic and social ascendancy in all five parts without being granted significant political power in any. Emancipation of serfs occurred in different ways in the different units. In Prussia, the peasants had to yield from one-seventh to one-third of their land to their lords as the price of personal liberty, and/or agree to substantial payments in money or services (1821–23). In Cracow during the 1820s the peasants retained all the land they had tilled but became rent-paying farmers not owners. For the time being the serfs in Austria and Prussia were little affected.

The Constitutional Charter of the Kingdom of Poland (1815) provided for Polish frontiers, passports, and citizenship. It was not so different from the Constitution of 1791—it provided for a hereditary monarchy and a two-chamber legislature—but the monarch was now the Russian tsar. The document contained "an impressive sounding section on civil liberties"; however, people said that the constitution of the Duchy of Warsaw had no guarantees of civil liberties but nobody noticed it, whereas the kingdom's did have but nobody noticed it either.[1]

The tsar, Alexander I, took the constitutional experiment of Poland seriously; the fact that he retained Finland's constitutional arrangements when he conquered it, extended something of the sort to Bessarabia, and was crucial in forcing constitutions on several West European monarchs if they were to be restored to their thrones argues that this was not mere sham. Out of his knowledge of Alexander as the friend of his youth, Prince Adam Czartoryski began with high hopes for the new system.

Clouds soon appeared in the blue sky. Alexander made his brother Constantine commander-in-chief of the Polish army; the grand duke was unstable and unpredictable, arriving in Warsaw hating the country (through he came to be fond of it later). The first viceroy was General Józef Zajaczek, but both before and after his death Constantine and Nicholas Novosiltsev, the extraconstitutional representative of the tsar, ruled instead.

Alexander I had "reveled for a while in the part of a constitutional monarch,"[2] and had told the Polish Diet in March 1818 that he was so pleased with the new constitution that he planned to extend the benefits of "free institutions" to other parts of the empire—presumably Russia itself. However, his enthusiasm cooled as Polish secret societies spread, provoking censorship, which in turn led to criticism in the Diet. After an acrimonious session of 1820 the Diet was not reconvened until a few months before the tsar's death in 1825, during which interval the leaders of a secret society were arrested and tried. More arrests of Poles occurred after the Decembrist revolt in Russia itself.

Nicholas I was now tsar. In 1828 he visited Warsaw, was crowned king of Poland, and swore to uphold the constitution. But his degree of toleration of constitutions was strictly limited, and when the French and Belgian revolutions of 1830 occurred he proposed to send a Russian army including Polish troops to suppress them. The mere proposal led to a Polish revolution.

It began on November 29 with an uprising taken over by conservatives who wished to retain the system of 1815. The Grand Duke Constantine played an almost wholly conciliatory role; Nicholas I instead demanded surrender. The Sejm proclaimed the dethronement of the tsar. The Polish army fought the Russian army; at length, in September 1831, the new Russian commander, Ivan Paskevich, took Warsaw, and the mopping up was soon complete. Paskevich became Prince of Warsaw, viceroy (1832), and effective ruler of the country until his death in 1856. The constitution of 1815 was more or less set aside (lawyers argued about exactly what had happened to it) by the Organic Statute of February 14/26, 1832.

Now Poland was "an indivisible part" of the Russian empire. She was assured civil liberties, use of the Polish language in administration and the courts, and her own legal codes, but those assurances were mostly empty. Centralization and Russification proceeded little by little during the Paskevich era. Some nine thousand emigrated; others were punished, exiled, or sent to serve in Russian Asia. The Congress Kingdom "lingered on in name only" for nearly thirty years; "one by one, the surviving Polish institutions were dismantled."[3]

In the meantime the Republic of Cracow continued, for a time prospering; its institutions of self-government were limited by the three Residents of Austria, Prussia, and Russia, who had to approve all executive decisions of the President. In 1836 Austrian and Russian troops occupied the city as a result of the killing of a police agent, and remained there for four years. What was intended as a nationwide rising in 1846 miscarried, and the Republic (or Free City) was occupied and then, via an Austro-Russian treaty, annexed by Austria.

As Davies puts it, "most historians would agree that the risings were launched and supported by the nobility but that they failed, among other reasons, because the mass of the peasantry remained apathetic towards them." Poland's overlords noticed the fact, and acted. In April 1848 the governor of Galicia, on behalf of the Habsburg emperor, announced the emancipation of the serfs in Austrian Poland, several months before the rest of the Austrian peasants were freed; in 1850 earlier steps toward emancipation were completed in Prussia.

As for Russia, the gauntlet was laid down by the events that followed. The defeat of 1831 was not accepted by either the conservatives around the Hôtel Lambert in Paris, home of Prince Adam Czartoryski, or the radicals of the Polish Democratic Society in London, known as Whites and Reds respectively. In 1856 the new emperor, Alexander II, and the new viceroy, Prince Michael Gorchakov, seemed to offer hope of change, starting with an amnesty to Polish émigrés and exiles. Concessions followed that virtually restored the regime of 1832 before it was in effect set aside, with the Marquis Alexander Wielopolski as the central figure. But the radicals and he were far apart, and when he tried to draft the extremist leaders into the army, revolution broke out in January 1863.

This time there was no Polish army, and the insurgents were overwhelmed by regular Russian forces. However, it was not until May 1864 that General Fedor Berg could report (a bit prematurely even then) the end of the campaign. By a decree of February Polish peasants in the Russian empire were emancipated under conditions more beneficial to them than the Russian emancipation of 1861. Their land allotments were bigger, no redemption payments were required, and the new Polish administrative unit on the local level in the countryside, the gmina, gave the peasants a favorable position. (But the Polish peasants did not come to love Russia; the religious issue, stemming from discrimination against Catholics and on behalf of Orthodox, remained.)

An Administrative Committee headed by Nicholas Miliutin (who played an important part in several of the Great Reforms of the 1860s and 1870s in Russia) had worked out the February 1864 emancipation. The Kingdom of Poland ceased to exist; Warsaw became the capital of Vistula Land. By 1871 its only administrative peculiarity was the continued use of the Napoleonic Code; for the rest, the ten Polish *gubernias* were ordinary parts of the Russian empire.[4] Thousands were exiled, and this time there was no amnesty. It also seemed that there was no hope—for independence of the nation or freedom for its people.

For the next forty years there could be little or no political life in Russian Poland, but the so-called positivists supported a direction of energies toward education, technology, and "organic work," against a background of anticlerical and antiaristocratic attitudes common to much of European liberalism.

In contrast, to Austrian Poland—that is, Galicia—the *Ausgleich* of 1867 yielded virtual autonomy by 1871. There was a Sejm, from which Polish peasants were excluded until 1889, and all Ruthenians (Ukrainians) were much underrepresented. Jews had full equality of rights after 1867, and there was some assimilation. Polish Catholic nobles were dominant. Education made significant progress, industry less, and agriculture next to none at all.

Prussian Poland became German Poland as well in 1867–71. That meant, in the following decade or so, pressure on Polish Catholics along with German ones as a result of Bismarck's *Kulturkampf* and then Germanization with less religious content. But agriculture prospered as did food-related industries. The Prussian Pole "was better educated; he was disciplined, hard-working, and enjoyed a higher standard of living [than the Pole living under Austria or Russia]; he could compete on nearly equal terms with the Germans."[5]

Nevertheless it was in Austrian Poland that the closest thing to a Polish national revival on Polish soil took place, and also where the nascent Ukrainian national movement, suppressed and expelled from the Russian empire, found refuge. The Shevchenko Society, named for the great poet who did much to give form to the Ukrainian language, was founded in 1873; a chair of Ukrainian history was established at Lemberg University in 1894 and to it was appointed Mykhailo Hrushevsky from Kiev. A Lithuanian revival, challenging with difficulty a centuries-old partly Polonized heritage, was also roughly treated in Russia, but its supporters found something of a haven in East Prussia.

There were Polish deputies in the Austrian parliament, after 1895 ranging from Socialists to conservatives, and Galicia increasingly became a safe harbor for Poles from the Congress Kingdom and the hope that it could serve as a future Piedmont for a united Poland. In Prussian Poland, after 1890 Caprivi granted some concessions to the Poles that were soon drowned in a wave of German nationalism. In Warsaw, Polish nationalism found a voice in Roman Dmowski, who in 1893 pushed through a revamping of a group called the Polish League, from which the National Democratic movement developed. A Populist party followed in Galicia.

Socialists from all three parts of the divided country and the emigration united to form a single delegation at the Brussels congress (1891) of the Second International. The section chiefly concerned with national independence formed the Polish Socialist party (PPS) at a secret conference near Vilna in 1893; Józef Pilsudski became the leader. The internationalists, whose chief theorist was Rosa Luxemburg, formed the Social Democracy of the Kingdom of Poland (SDKP) the following year, but it fell apart and had to be revived in 1900 under the leadership of Feliks Dzierzynski as the Social Democracy of the Kingdom of Poland and Lithuania (SDKPiL). In 1897 the new Jewish Bund (League of Jewish Workingmen of Poland, Lithuania, and Russia) had added to the complexity of the picture.

In 1904–5, the Russo-Japanese War gave hope to the enemies of tsarism everywhere, precipitated the Revolution of 1905 throughout the Russian empire, and led to the creation of a representative assembly. In the First Duma, the Polish Circle (*Kolo,* a word used in several parliamentary or semiparliamentary contexts) was made up of fifty-five National Democrats, or Endeks; in the Second Duma it was forty-six, led by Dmowski himself; in the Third Duma (each of the first two lasting but a few months) elected under an altered suffrage, the Polish-Lithuanian-Belorussian contingent was reduced to 18.[6]

The aftermath of the Revolution of 1905 was a time of regrouping of Polish political forces. PPS split in two in 1906; Pilsudski took out a minority that included most of the Fighting Organization (*Organizacja Bojowa*), which conducted robberies to finance the party and some terrorism; the majority called itself the PPS Left. But soon Pilsudski's party overshadowed it. In both Russian and German Poland school strikes sought Polonization of instruction. In Austrian Poland party conferences were held openly, the press examined alternative political programs, and Polish Socialist participation in a general strike led by Austrian Social Democrats helped to extort from the emperor consent to universal manhood suffrage in Austria.

In Congress Poland a spectrum of views now took shape that ranged from Dmowski's Neoslavism (equality of all Slavs, Polish-Russian reconciliation, reorientation of Austria-Hungary through achieving predominance of the Slav majority) through Progressive Democratic, Socialist, and Peasant positions. Dmowski became increasingly anti-Semitic, and also declared that Prussia was the greatest threat to the Poles. But the National Democrats in Galicia, feeling themselves unable to take up a pro-Russian line, criticized Austria's alliance with Germany and attacked Ukrainians as Poland's chief enemy.

In 1914 Prussian Poland had a per capita income of $113, Russian Poland $63, Austrian Poland $38[7]—but Galicia was the freest of the three. By September 1915 the Central Powers had driven the Russians entirely out of ethnic Poland; Germans permitted local elections and the functioning of political parties —an improvement over Russian rule—but carried economic exploitation very far; Austrians were milder in economic matters but slower to permit local self-government.

In 1918 all three governments of the foreign rulers of Poland collapsed. On November 7 radicals in Lublin proclaimed a Polish People's Republic, but it lasted only a few days. On November 14 the Regency Council, formed by the Germans and Austrians in accordance with the Two Emperors' Declaration of November 1916 promising to restore the Kingdom of Poland, handed over power to Pilsudski.

Pilsudski ruled in fact (not in law) a state that regained independence after 123 years (but would keep it for only 21 more). The question was now what boundaries the new Poland would have. Small wars with the West Ukrainian Republic, Germany, Lithuania, and Czechoslovakia ensued over the next four years; and one big one, with the Russian Soviet Republic, erupted from a border skirmish in February 1919. The front swayed from a point near Kiev to the suburbs of Warsaw. General Mikhail Tukhachevsky, all of twenty-seven years old, issued an order of the day: "To the West! Over the corpse of White Poland lies the road to world-wide conflagration."[8] On 31 August 1920, what was said to be the last great cavalry battle of European and perhaps world history was fought, but the Soviets had been defeated two weeks earlier. A Polish-Soviet treaty established the frontier in March 1921.

The Poland established by the Constitution of 17 March 1921 set up a bicameral Sejm elected by universal suffrage, guaranteed civil liberties, and made the president (elected by the Sejm for a seven-year term) responsible to the legislature. The so-called parliamentary or constitutional period (1921–26) had its achievements. "Starting with the core of institutions left by the Germans' Polish Kingdom, a modern state had to be built in haste in the most adverse conditions of war and economic disruption"[9]: an army, a legal system, a civil service, and a functioning communications system were created; compulsory free education was introduced in 1922.

But the problems were deep. The heterogeneous ethnic make-up of the country was one: in 1931 Poles were 68.9% of the population, Ukrainians 13.9%, Yiddish-speaking Jews 8.7%, Belorussians and Germans below 4%, but these minorities were majorities in certain areas. The political system did not work well. After a period of confusion and turmoil, Pilsudski carried out a coup in 1926 and became the real ruler, presiding in effect over what came to be called the regime of the "colonels," or the *Sanacja* (a slogan meaning "return to health"). Its "vague, if forceful, ideology . . . imagined that the evil in men's souls could be scrubbed clean by military spit and polish."[10] It was not Fascist; the only Fascist sympathizers in Poland opposed Pilsudski. The parliamentary façade was retained, and the opposition continued to function.

First the regime tried to win an election fairly, then it intimidated the opposition, and in 1935 a new constitution made elections less important. A few weeks after it was adopted, Pilsudski died, but his successors carried on as before. As Davies writes, "the arbitrary acts of the Sanacja regime were no more edifying than the political squabbles which preceded them."[11]

In the late 1930s economic conditions were harsh, Ukrainians were ill-treated, Jews still suffered from anti-Semitism, peasants were only marginally better off, workers unhappy. Yet artists and scientists flourished, and in contrast to Nazi Germany and Soviet Russia, Poland was not in such bad shape. In 1939 the two totalitarian powers signed an agreement, invaded Poland from both west and east, and inflicted unprecedented suffering on the country. Six million of the former population of Poland died, in fighting, executions, pacifications, the camps. Almost three million were Jews. Over eleven million died in occupied Poland, of which over five million were Jews.[12]

The Polish government went into exile, first in France, then in England; from July 1941 to April 1943 it had relations with the USSR. When the Germans discovered the graves of forty-five hundred Polish soldiers at Katyn and the exiled Polish government demanded that the International Red Cross investigate, the Soviets severed relations.[13] The Polish resistance was slow to form, but by the end of 1942 the Home Army (Armia Krajowa, or AK) had come to head a network of trained soldiers numbering about four hundred thousand.

The Jews of Poland had been crammed into ghettos soon after Nazi conquest. In an uprising in the Warsaw ghetto in April 1943 a handful of young Jewish men and women held off an SS brigade for three weeks before being exterminated. In July 1944 the Home Army led a revolt against the Nazis, expecting that the Poles would liberate their capital before the Soviets arrived. Stalin denounced the Home Army, which fought on until October before surrendering while the Soviets watched from across the Vistula. In Davies's words, "it was the end of the old order in Poland. . . . The Nazis had done the Soviets' work for them."[14]

When the Soviet Army crossed the Bug River in July 1944, entering what Moscow was ready to recognize as postwar Poland, the Soviets created at Lublin a Polish Committee of National Liberation. It became the nucleus of the postwar government, with only the temporary addition of one genuine non-Communist, Stanislaw Mikolajczyk (June 1945 to October 1947). Just over half of its prewar territory was taken into the new Poland, which with the addition of the lands east of the Oder-Neisse line emerged as four-fifths the total area of 1939, with only two-thirds of the population of that time.[15] The people were now almost entirely ethnically Polish and religiously Roman Catholic—homogeneous to a degree unprecedented in Polish history.

The Polish Communist party, destroyed by Stalin,[16] had been replaced in 1942 by the Polish Workers' party, led by a scruffy handful of unknowns. From 1944 on it imposed on the nation a government ordered by Stalin, detested by most of the people. Yet the man who became its leader, Wladyslaw Gomulka, with a few others, "believed that hard-line Polish communism offered the one sure guarantee for Poland against Soviet imperialism." Declares Davies:

They would have concurred wholeheartedly with Stalin's dictum that communism in Poland resembled "a saddle on a cow." Unlike Stalin, however, they would have preferred to trim the saddle to fit the cow, instead of hacking the cow to fit the saddle.[17]

And for the first few years it was Soviet puppets who headed the Polish regime. Collectivization of agriculture, billed as the center of Communist policy, made headway; collective farms more than doubled in size in the early 1950s.

After the death of Stalin came the virtual abandonment of collectivization in Poland, and mounting levels of protest leading to the crisis of October 1956, in which the Polish people held back from revolution Hungarian style but danger of a mass uprising seemed real enough. Gomulka was named First Secretary of the party and faced down Nikita Khrushchev to survive as head of what was billed as a reformist, national-Communist regime but soon reverted to repression. In 1970 riots led to his replacement by Edward Gierek, leader of the party in Silesia; in 1980 strikes spread from the Gdansk shipyard to bring down Gierek and spawn the voluntary trade union Solidarity, led by Lech Walesa. Soon General Wojciech

Jaruzelski, having been shifted from premier to party secretary, imposed martial law. An uneasy calm was broken after Mikhail Gorbachev visited Warsaw in July 1989. A strike became a virtual uprising; the party yielded to a compromise by which Jaruzelski was elected president, but a non-Communist cabinet took over with approval of Walesa and Solidarity.

Poland—through a series of drastically changing geographical permutations—developed many of the prerequisites of a free society and once or twice seemed on the verge of establishing one: in the Constitution of 1791 and in the state created by the initiative of the Polish people in 1918. A bitter irony of the whole story is how the Nazi attack on Poland, which triggered World War II, led ultimately to the destruction of the Nazis and the partitioning of Germany. From those events however emerged not freedom for the Poles but in effect colonial subjection. Nevertheless in early 1990 it appeared that after half a century freedom was in the process of returning to Poland, though the miserable economic situation imperiled the political, legal, and other gains that had been made.

The Balkans, 1804–1914

In the eighteenth century the peoples of what would become Romania, Bulgaria, Greece, and eastern Yugoslavia were living under Ottoman rule. They were mainly Christian, peasant, rural, and were generally healthier than their Muslim fellow subjects of the sultan, for not quite clear reasons. They suffered from heavy taxation and a variety of minor discriminatory regulations, but under the millet system the Orthodox, Armenian (Gregorian),[18] Roman Catholic, and Jewish populations had their own religious authorities who were simultaneously given governmental powers and obligations.

The head of all Orthodox, by the end of the eighteenth century, was the patriarch of Constantinople, a church official who was Greek by custom. He had acted in conjunction with the government of the sultan (often called the "Porte" or "Sublime Porte" from the chief governmental building in the capital) in suppressing the Serbian patriarchate at Pech and the Bulgarian archbishopric at Ohrid in 1766 and 1767 respectively.

Next to the Greeks in order of influence within the Ottoman Empire were the Romanians, who enjoyed autonomy limited by the Turkish power of appointment of the *hospodars* (or ruling princes). After certain Romanian nobles assisted Peter the Great's invasion in 1709, the Porte ceased to appoint Romanians and named instead Phanariot Greeks (so called from the section of Constantinople, the Phanar, in which most of those concerned lived). Serbs and Bulgars, who were mainly peasant peoples, occupied the lowest place on the ethnic ladder—aside from the Montenegrins, who had kept near-independence throughout the centuries of Ottoman rule in the Balkans and had won the sultan's recognition of full independence in 1799, and the Albanians, whose separate identity was scarcely understood.

In 1804 a former soldier and livestock merchant named Karadjordje Petrović led a Serbian rising directed chiefly against the Janissaries, a group of Ottoman soldiery long composed of Christian boy-conscripts compelled to convert to Islam but by now Muslim born, unruly and undisciplined. The immediate provocation was a massacre of a hundred or more Serbian notables; the aim was to get rid of Janissary cruelty and to get back the limited autonomy Serbs had possessed earlier —at the local level, not in Serbia as a whole. The revolt simmered. At length, in 1808, Karadjordje proclaimed himself hereditary ruler of Serbia, to act with a governing council that would also function as supreme court.

The European powers played shifting roles in this and the other Balkan revolts. Russia in particular caused disappointment by first seeming to support Serbian independence (a goal not originally sought by the Serbs) and then, by the Treaty of Bucharest of 1812, leaving the Serbs to fend for themselves against Ottoman vengeance. The sultan's armies reentered Belgrade in 1813. But two years later another Serbian leader, Miloš Obrenović, led a revolt provoked by another massacre (this time of men who had actually rebelled), and by 1816 a settlement was reached granting partial autonomy to Serbia under Miloš. The following year Karadjordje returned from Austrian territory in which he had found refuge, was murdered at Miloš's order, and was beheaded; his head was sent to the Ottoman governor who had it stuffed and sent to the sultan.

The Greeks caught the germ of revolution soon after the Serbs stumbled into armed struggle. Greek merchants in Odessa founded a revolutionary organization called Philike Hetairia (Society of Friends) in 1814, and hopes were placed in Russian help. The aim was a general Balkan revolt, and it was in order to arouse one that Karadjordje returned to meet death in 1817. In Moldavia and Wallachia, the Danubian Principalities (the future Romania), Tudor Vladimirescu joined the Hetairia and soon was leader of many peasants and smallholders. In 1821 an abortive uprising was launched in Moldavia under Alexander Ypsilanti, a Greek who had been aide-de-camp to Tsar Alexander I. Before it failed, Ypsilanti seized Vladimirescu and executed him for having tried to save himself from the wreck of the revolt by talks with the Porte.

As the Moldavian uprising was collapsing, one occurred in the Peloponnesus. There the individual Greek villages had something of the same kind of self-government the Serbs had before and after the revolts of 1804–13 and 1815–16; a difference was that there also were elective provincial bodies and a Senate for the whole Peloponnesus, and two Greeks were elected to sit on a council of the Ottoman vezir along with two Muslims. Large landowners and part of the clergy,

ful, using for the most part Serbs educated in Austria, in an area where there had been only local government. Also Austrian educated was Peter Jovanović, who became metropolitan of a Serbian Orthodox church newly recognized by the sultan and by the patriarch of Constantinople (ecclesiastically supreme over the Serbs since 1766) and remained in that post from 1833 to 1859. Serbs took the place of Turks, Greeks, and Jews in commerce. Miloš had issued a law in 1836 to protect the peasant family from having all its property seized by creditors, though it was unevenly enforced. Miloš would not, however, accept the new position of the prince, defined in the "Turkish Constitution"; he abdicated, and after fleeting reigns of two sons of his, Alexander Karadjordjević was elected by an assembly.

Alexander's reign was a tranquil one (1842–58), in which an important legal code was adopted and steps were taken to give Serbia a decent educational system; but he was forced out and the Obrenovići returned—first old Miloš and then his son Michael, who had earlier been prince for three years. The position of the assembly was regularized, but the ruler and council were more important. Michael's aim was to unify all Serbian territories, and to that end he built up the army to be the best in the Balkans. He was assassinated in 1868, and his chief adviser, Iliya Garashanin, frustrated the pro-Karadjordjević conspirators to place his grandnephew Milan on the throne.

A new constitution provided new guarantees of civil rights (though not of free assembly or association) and strengthened the assembly as it weakened the council. The assembly would now be made up of three-quarters elected and one-quarter prince-appointed members and received the right to approve all laws, which was in fact restricted in various ways. Prince Milan was brought to declare war on the Ottoman Empire following the revolt in Bosnia-Hercegovina in 1876. His army was soundly defeated but Russia crushed the Turks. By the Treaty of Berlin (1878) Serbia was recognized as independent and gained a smallish chunk of territory around Nish. In 1882 Milan proclaimed himself king.

The kingdom of Greece was off to a poor start under young King Othon. Bavarian advisers ran the government for the first decade, but the French, British, and Russian "parties," each composed of Greeks relying on the patron power concerned, came to be the decisive political factions. The Turks forced the patriarch of Constantinople to excommunicate the church in the new kingdom, which became the separate Church of Greece, under a synod appointed by the Catholic king; Constantinople accepted the new arrangement in 1850. The previous year the sharply controverted step had been taken to make the artificial literary language *(katharevousa)* the official language for government, education, and the press, whereas the popular spoken language *(demotiki)* was something quite different.

In 1843 economic, military, and political problems combined to produce a revolt that forced the calling of a constituent assembly. The British and French parties helped to introduce a constitution prescribing a two-house legislature (the lower elected by universal male suffrage) and an absolute veto for the king, who also appointed and dismissed ministers. The new government was reasonably popular, especially when its leaders gave voice to the *Megale Idea* (Great Idea) of bringing everything from Crete to Trebizond under a single Greek flag. Such hopes, expressed during the Crimean War, were temporarily dashed by the defeat of Russia in 1856.

In 1862 occurred another military coup. Othon and his queen returned to Bavaria, while an eighteen-year-old Danish prince was chosen to become George I of Greece. He reigned until 1913, and in that half-century won great popularity. He was the British candidate, and Britain yielded the Ionian Islands to him as a sort of coronation gift. He also received a new constitution (1864), with a unicameral legislature elected by universal male suffrage, secret and direct, to which the ministry was to be responsible though the king could appoint and dismiss it and had other powers George was chary about using.

Romania had a native aristocracy, the large landlords or boyars, and a Christian government, the Phanariot Greeks. Beginning with the Treaty of Küçük Kajnarci (1774), which marked the permanent tipping of the military balance in Russo-Turkish relations against the Porte, Russia gradually acquired a kind of protectorate over the two Danubian principalities, Moldavia and Wallachia. After the Treaty of Adrianople, Russia was able to appoint an administrator, Count Paul Kiselev. He oversaw the preparation of Organic Statutes for Wallachia (1831) and Moldavia (1832), which provided for election for life, from among the boyars, of the hospodar, or prince, of each principality. He was to be assisted by a council, and a legislature was to have boyar predominance. Boyars were exempt from taxation and were also given full ownership of the land they had held— which enabled them to use the new position they had attained to create a stronger and more prosperous agriculture, especially in the second half of the century. This limited constitutional system, based on boyar ascendancy, was at any rate not the sort of autocracy that Russia, the foreign power with decisive influence, remained in that period.

The two principalities remained separate for the time being. However, in 1847 a customs union was established between them, and sentiment for unification grew as resentment of Russian interference increased and Romanian young men studying in Paris gained therefrom the determination to build their own free nation. In 1848 a petition in that sense was submitted to the hospodar of Moldavia, and in Wallachia a revolution occurred. In the city of Islaz, a manifesto for a nonclass system was issued.

A provisional revolutionary government was set up in Bucharest, controlled by Ion Bratianu, whose Liberal party was to shape much of Romanian political history for close to a century. It tried in vain to achieve acceptance from the Porte. Russian troops invaded the principalities and put the revolutionaries to flight. Russia together with Turkey agreed that they would jointly name the hospodars, for seven-year terms. Russian forces stayed until 1851 but were back in 1853. The Crimean War followed, culminating in a shattering defeat for Russia.

By this time Romanian refugees and others in France had managed to win the sympathy of Napoleon III, one of the victors in the 1854–56 war. The upshot was that in 1858 the powers met in Paris and replaced the Organic Statutes of 1831–32 with an agreement to establish the United Principalities of Moldavia and Wallachia, with a Central Commission made up of members of the two assemblies and a common court of appeal.

Almost at once, however, the new arrangement was infringed. Colonel Alexander Cuza, a rather obscure officer, was elected hospodar in Moldavia and then also in Wallachia; the powers (the neighbor, Austria, was engaged in war with France) consented to the personal union, but only as an exception. Then the sultan agreed to unification of the principalities, nominally for Cuza's lifetime only; however, in December 1861 the hospodar declared that Romanian "union is accomplished."

Cuza presided over a period of limited but real reform. The lands of the monasteries were expropriated. Next came what was in effect a coup d'état by which the prince broke the power of the conservative coalition blocking further land reform, securing via a plebiscite approval of an increase in his own power and broadening of the franchise. He then was able to push through an Agrarian Law (1858). It compelled the boyar to give up not more than two-thirds of his land, and the peasant was made full owner of an allotment based on the number of cattle owned. A hastily formulated measure poorly administered, it failed in its aim of turning the peasantry into a class of free, independent farmers, and much of the land remained great estates producing for export. Educational measures and the adoption of legal codes were more successful.

But dissatisfaction with Cuza's policies and personal life led to his overthrow in 1866 and replacement by a foreign prince: Charles of Hohenzollern-Sigmaringen, from the Catholic southern branch of the Prussian ruling family. Carol (the Romanian spelling) was technically still a vassal of the sultan, but actually the ruler of a united and virtually independent country.

The practice of importing surplus German princes to become monarchs of newly independent Balkan countries risked bringing in men initially and clumsily ignorant of their new domains but might eventually—given the ethic of noblesse oblige transmitted in many royal families—produce good results. It was so in Charles's case. At first, and for several years, he was involved in disputes with the political parties, which, as Charles and Barbara Jelavich point out, "represented only a fraction of the Romanian people," and other embarrassments.[20] A constitution (July 1866) was proclaimed by the provisional government, based on the Belgian constitution of 1831: A two-house legislature could pass laws, but the prince possessed an absolute veto power; the boyars retained their dominance as before.

Neither in Serbia nor Greece nor Romania was there democracy, but there was a framework for a truly representative system—which was, after all, just coming into being in England and France. In 1877 Romania entered the war that erupted after a peasant rising in the Ottoman provinces of Bosnia and Hercegovina on the side of Serbia, Montenegro, and Russia. By the Treaty of Berlin (1878) that ended the war, Romania was recognized as fully independent and acquired the Dobrudja, replacing with a greater area the Black Sea coast that she simultaneously lost to Russia.[21] And King Carol (as he was proclaimed in 1881) lived to become a popular and successful monarch.

The last of the Balkan states to achieve independence was Bulgaria, partly as a result of the chronic banditry that created disorder for a century or more and partly because of the geography that placed the country near Constantinople and athwart the paths of several different armies in the nineteenth century. Bulgaria was an agrarian country like its neighbors in contrast to Romania, for example, the smallholding peasantry was growing in strength at the expense of the landowners. Secular education began spottily in the 1830s, and the Bulgarian clerics took the first bold steps to obtain ecclesiastical leaders from among their own conationals. In 1866, led by Bishop Ilarion, they expelled the Greek bishops who had long controlled the church there. Four years later the sultan legalized the situation by issuing a firman creating a Bulgarian exarchate.

In 1876 a coalition of revolutionary groups launched a revolt. Bulgarian rebels massacred some Turks who lived among them; Ottoman irregular troops (regulars were needed elsewhere) killed many in reprisal—hence the "Bulgarian horrors" that agitated Gladstone and others in western Europe. Soon it was a Russo-Turkish War that was being fought—and won, after embarrassing difficulties, by Russia.

Bulgaria, was, at first, the greatest beneficiary. In the Treaty of San Stefano (near Constantinople, today Istanbul's airport) a large Bulgarian state was established that included much of Macedonia. Vienna and London were furious, and demanded the reconsideration out of which came the scrapping of San Stefano and the new Treaty of Berlin: a thin, autonomous Bulgaria stretched along the Danube, with an elected prince "confirmed by the Sublime Porte with the consent of the Powers," was separated from a modest-sized semiautonomous province called "Eastern Rumelia" south of the Balkan range. Montenegro, Serbia, and Romania were recognized as fully independent; but Montenegro's gains were reduced and she retained only a narrow bit of Adriatic shore, while Romania (as indicated above) had to hand over southern Bessarabia to Russia, receiving the Dobrudja as compensation. Greece gained nothing tangible, Serbia a bit of territory around Nish, while Bosnia and Hercegovina (which the Serbs desired) went instead to Austrian "administration." It was to be a fateful decision.

A few months after the Congress of Berlin the Russians helped adopt a constitution for Bulgaria (1879) and find a prince, Alexander of Battenberg, for the new state, truncated as it was. There were two assemblies (not two houses of one assembly), an ordinary one and an extraordinary one (to handle constitutional amendments and elections of rulers); the former was elected by universal manhood suffrage and alone could impose new taxes. The prince had the power to appoint the cabinet, and his signature was required for a measure to become law. There was also elective self-government, down to the village level. As in the neighboring states, civil liberties were guaranteed and a court system provided for. Alexander promptly quarreled with the new Bulgarian Liberal and Conservative party leaders and also with the Russians—among other grievances, Bulgarians objected to the fact that all army ranks from captain on up were reserved for Russians. The government of the province of Eastern Rumelia was based on a new Organic Statute that was a kind of legal stew, into which each of five powers threw in some articles for a total of 495. The sultan appointed as governor a Christian, Aleko Pasha. The new regime accomplished one thing only: it intimidated or taxed away the Muslim landlord class, and in the south as well as in the north a chiefly peasant Bulgaria emerged.

In September 1885 a revolt in Philippopolis (Plovdiv) removed Aleko Pasha's compliant successor and demanded that Alexander become monarch of a united Bulgaria; he reluctantly did so. The king of Serbia at once declared war, and the Bulgarians smashed his army. The union was now accepted on all sides, but the prince was not. Alexander III of Russia engineered the overthrow and abdication of Prince Alexander, and he was at length replaced by Ferdinand of Saxe-Coburg. The strong leader Stefan Stambolov defied Russia and helped achieve some stability. Stambolov was dismissed in 1894; not long afterward Ferdinand (whose infant son was proclaimed a convert to Orthodoxy, the predominant religion of Russia as well as of Bulgaria) and Nicholas II, the new tsar of Russia, effected a reconciliation. The one outstanding territorial issue, Macedonia, was resolved for the time being when a chaotic and lawless area was pacified in 1903 by the so-called Mürzsteg reform program.

Ferdinand declared the full independence of Bulgaria in 1908 and took the title tsar. He seemed to be riding high as Bulgaria allied itself with Serbia and Greece, and together the three states, along with Montenegro which had the role of beginning hostilities, crushed the Turkish forces. But then Serbia and Bulgaria clashed over Macedonia, and the hitherto superior Bulgarian army was defeated. Sofia lost the southern Dobrudja to Romania. Most of Macedonia went to Serbia; a tiny strip reaching to the Aegean was given to Bulgaria.

In Greece the barren land generated a passionate nationalism that managed in 1881 to acquire fertile Thessaly and southern Epirus, annexed as part of the settlement reached at the Congress of Berlin, but the country remained poor. In these regions Muslim landowners were driven out, as in Bulgaria, but were replaced not by Greek peasants but by Greek landowners. A kind of two-party system developed after George I in 1875 decided that the ministry would be formed by the parliamentary majority. One party sought internal development, the other expansion. Repeated efforts to annex Crete failed, but there emerged on the island a politician with such evident skills that he was finally brought to Athens in 1910; his name was Eleutherios Venizelos.

Supported by the king, Venizelos convened a national assembly that improved the constitution of 1864 somewhat. Compulsory elementary education was provided for, and the quorum in the assembly was reduced to avoid paralyzing the legislative process. Other than constitutional amendments, laws were passed that regulated factory labor and authorized distribution of some of the Thessaly estates. Venizelos's backers swept the March 1912 elections. In December 1913 Crete was finally annexed. But the improving economic and political picture was at once clouded by World War I.

In post-1878 Romania the position of Jews, who continued to stream in to avoid discrimination or worse in Russia, was supposed to be made legally equal to that of ethnic Romanians by provisions of the Treaty of Berlin. Only a few gestures were made in that direction. Jews still could not own land, and only after 1879 were a very few able to become naturalized citizens. In March 1881 Prince Charles was crowned king. In 1884 all male taxpayers received the vote, but it was exercised through a system of curias dependent on the amount of property owned. The system was introduced by the Liberals, but the king learned to manipulate it with great success. The Liberals, who had led the establishment of independent Romania, yielded to a group of Conservatives in 1888, who lasted until 1895; the two parties alternated from then until 1914.

The great estates of largely absentee landlords produced a socially unhealthy situation. Three quarters of the estates were leased to tenants (27% of whom were Jews), who in turn managed the peasants on a sharecropping or rental basis. Population increase pressed on a land area with backward agriculture and no significant attempts to modernize it. As a result in 1907 a large-scale insurrection by the peasants of Moldavia spread southward and was not put down until eleven thousand were killed. Only now was some legislation directed to protecting the peasantry, but it had only very modest results. King Carol died a few months after the outbreak of World War I. He had made an alliance in 1883 with Austria which the government set aside, to his great disappointment. His nephew Ferdinand I took over and led Romania into war on the Allied side in 1916.

Like Carol of Romania frightened and angered by Russia's conduct in the peace following the Russo-Turkish War, Milan of Serbia accepted an even closer relationship with Austria that approached protectorate status. Milan and the Progressive party enacted measures of a liberal kind: freedom of the press, compulsory elementary education, independence of the judiciary, a national bank. They were challenged on the left by the new Radical party headed by Nikola Pašić, which supported universal manhood suffrage and sought to bring the peasantry into political life. By both violence and electoral victory the Radicals undermined the king's position and led him to abdicate in 1889. A new and more liberal constitution had just been drawn up, but it did not last.

Milan's successor, Alexander, governed with the Radicals, restoring the constitution of 1869 and achieving a strong political position. A series of scandals in the Obrenović family, however, culminated in the overthrow and murder of Alexander in June 1903 by young officers embarrassed by the king's behavior. The dynasty was extinct, and Peter Karadjordjević was elected king. The constitution of 1889 was restored with minor changes; Serbia now had a two-house legislature, three-fifths of whose members were appointees of the king. The Radicals, by now not behaving very radically, were in power from 1906 to 1918.

The great cataclysm of World War I was precipitated by the problems of the South Slavs, or Yugoslavs, of whom the Serbs were the only independent people outside of tiny Montenegro. Within the Habsburg Empire—somewhat similarly to the case of the Poles—plans were hatched for a united Yugoslav state.

From the 1860s two rival currents had appeared among the Croats, who were akin to the Serbs ethnically and linguistically but differed in religion and therefore alphabet: the Roman Catholic Croats used Latin letters and the Orthodox Serbs used Cyrillic. Ante Starčević visualized a greater Croatia that would include both Slovenes to the north and Serbs to the east; Bishop Josip Strossmayer transformed the old idea of a restored "Illyria" (the ancient term) into a new Yugoslavism, the difference being that the old Illyrianism (before 1848) had sought to unite South Slavs within Austria-Hungary, while the new Yugoslavism sought to cross the border to the east. A Croatian-Serbian coalition, formed in 1905 within the Habsburg Empire, sought to move in the latter direction.

In 1908 the Austrians annexed Bosnia-Hercegovina, which they had occupied since 1878; the result was to infuriate Serbia, whose foreign policy had shifted sharply away from Vienna and toward St. Petersburg as the Karadjordjevići returned to the throne and which regarded the region as ethnically akin to itself (in fact 43% were Orthodox Serbs, 20% Roman Catholic Croatian, the last third Muslim). A group of young Bosnians assassinated the Archduke Franz Ferdinand in Sarajevo on 28 June 1914; the motive seems to have been fear that he would "become an oppressor of the Serbs"[22] when he succeeded his then eighty-four-year-old father as emperor. The ensuing diplomatic dance off to the most unspeakable military horrors in man's history to date will not be summarized here.

East Central Europe, 1918–1990

The peace, motivated in considerable part (where the Balkans were concerned) by the notions of self-determination based on nationalism held by Woodrow Wilson, produced in eastern Europe the two new states of Yugoslavia and Czechoslovakia, carved out of Habsburg territory; one state much enlarged, Romania, which obtained Transylvania from Hungary and Bessarabia from Russia; one state, Greece, which sought extensive new territories and was prevented from gaining them; Bulgaria, which fought on the wrong side, lost its Aegean coast to Greece and a few bits of territory to Yugoslavia. In fact, Czechoslovakia was proclaimed independent by Czechs and Slovaks abroad in October 1918. The Kingdom of the Serbs, Croats, and Slovenes was proclaimed on December 1, and on the same day an assembly of Romanians from Transylvania and the Banat declared their union with Romania. These actions were in effect ratified by the peace conference at Paris in 1919.

In Czechoslovakia, which "inherited the most valuable part of the old Austro-Hungarian Monarchy, with most of the industrial areas,"[23] land reform was enacted in April 1919, before the constitution was adopted the following February. The great estates were expropriated, with compensation, and divided among the peasantry.

The constitution, borrowing heavily from that of France, established a functioning democracy. Thomas Masaryk was elected president and reelected in 1927 and 1934; Eduard Beneš was in effect permanent foreign minister until he succeeded Masaryk on the latter's resignation at the age of eighty-five in 1935. Beneš belonged to the National Socialist party (no connection with the Nazis of Germany), centrist in its views. On its right were the National Democrats led by Karel Kramář, who succeeded the Young Czechs of the Habsburg Empire; on its left, the Social Democrats, which in 1920 split, the majority forming a Czechoslovak Communist party under Bohumír Šmeral, an active antinationalist in prewar Social Democratic ranks. Finally there was the Agrarian party, based on a sturdily independent Czech and Slovak peasantry, led by Antonín Švehla, which was "the dominant party in the history of independent Czechoslovakia," leading coalition after coalition.[24]

The system worked quite well; the problem was not the suffrage or distribution of powers within the government but ethnic diversity. The Czechs had been part of Austria and were much more advanced than the Slovaks, who had been part of Hungary and had little education, industry, or political consciousness. Then there were the Ruthenians of the eastern tip. Czechs were at least nominally— Slovaks fervently—Catholic. The Ruthenians were Orthodox. They were Ukrainian in speech and totally peasant. There were also German and Hungarian minorities, the most significant being the Sudeten Germans of the western fringe of the Czech lands.

The Slovaks had their own parties: the National party under Milan Hodža, supporting Czechoslovak unity but seeking greater autonomy for Slovaks; Father Andrew Hlinka's Slovak People's party, which has been compared with clerical Fascist groups in Austria and Spain; and Communists, again stronger than their brethren of the Left, the Social Democrats.

Resentment at better-educated and superior-acting Czech officials was a problem in Slovakia and Ruthenia; Czechs were in turn looked down on by the Germans, who rallied to the banner of the new Sudeten German party in 1935 and overnight made it the second strongest party in parliament. But despite political and ethnic tensions, Czechoslovak democracy nevertheless lasted until Hitler destroyed it with the consent of Britain and France.

Why did it, alone in Eastern Europe, succeed in lasting? Hugh Seton-Watson credits its social balance among bourgeoisie, workers, and newly landed peasantry (social pluralism, in other words); the weakness of Catholic political influence, even Hlinka's extremism being restrained as long as Czechoslovakia remained united; the relative prosperity of the Czech lands in particular; and the tradition of humane and tolerant behavior preached by earlier Czech figures and Masaryk in the period of independence. Seton-Watson notes that Austria had the same sort of social structure, but the other factors were peculiar to Czechoslovakia.

Czechoslovakia had much military as well as economic and political strength, as well as fortifications that might have given the Nazis a run for their money, and they had, they (wrongly) thought, powerful allies. In September 1938 Hitler summoned Neville Chamberlain three times to Germany. The third time, joined by Edouard Daladier of France and Benito Mussolini of Italy, they decided at Munich to dismember Czechoslovakia; the Sudetenland went to Germany. The Poles took the opportunity to annex Teschen. Hungary, by Italo-German arbitration, was awarded a broad strip of southern Slovakia; in March Budapest seized the Carpatho-Ukraine. A few days earlier Hitler had marched into Prague;

Bohemia-Moravia became a protectorate, Slovakia was proclaimed nominally independent but was controlled by Nazi Germany.

It was now that Britain and France guaranteed Poland and Romania against aggression. In September it nevertheless occurred without any effective opposition, though war was declared, eventually fought, and finally won.

In 1945 Czechoslovakia was liberated by Soviet and American troops—actually, Prague was freed by the anti-Soviet Russian forces led by General Andrei Vlasov, a fact that has remained a rather well-kept secret. The hope for a democratic government cherished by Beneš, who returned from exile to become president, was dashed by the Communist coup of February 1948. Czechoslovak democracy was destroyed, and the shock felt in the West was much greater than the news that the shaky or sham democracies in the rest of Eastern Europe had been Sovietized.

For two decades Prague was subservient to Moscow. Quiet during the crisis of late 1956, Czechoslovakia enjoyed the modest hope of "socialism with a human face" for several months under the Slovak Alexander Dubček before it was dashed by the Soviet invasion of August 1968. For the following twenty-one years the Czechoslovak intelligentsia were made into taxi drivers and street sweepers; political and cultural repression was unrelieved, domestic tranquillity being secured by a reasonable supply of food and consumer goods. Suddenly, however, in November–December 1989, following the East German reform movement, mass protest reached a crescendo that toppled the hard-line regime. The opposition made its leader, the playwright Václav Havel, president and democracy seemed to have returned to Czechoslovakia almost overnight.

The preparation for democracy that the Czechs and (to a lesser extent) Slovaks had received under the Habsburgs had produced results surpassing anything European democrats had managed south of Scandinavia and east of France during the interwar period and clearly accounted for the smoothness of the changes of 1989–90.

Yugoslavia's story had ups and downs but was in general less happy. The Kingdom of the Serbs, Croats, and Slovenes combined Slovenia, Croatia, Bosnia-Hercegovina, and the Vojvodina from the Habsburg Empire with independent Serbia and Montenegro. This meant a largely Roman Catholic west and north, with a good deal of industry, schools, and roads, mixed with a largely Serbian Orthodox east and south, lacking much of any of those things—with a Muslim minority of over one million (out of twelve million total), largely in Bosnia. Most important, however, was probably the fact that the more advanced Croats looked down on the Serbs who were politically dominant—the opposite of the situation in Czechoslovakia. The political parties were: the old Serbian Radicals under the aged Nikola Pašić; the group that had broken off from the Radicals in 1901 and called itself Democratic, but allied itself with the Radicals for a time after 1919; the Croatian Peasant party led by Stjepan Radić, who carried his stance of opposition to the Hungarian and German landlords over into boycott and abstention vis-à-vis the Serb politicos; the Slovenian Populists; the Yugoslav Muslim Organization; and the Communists, which became the third strongest party in the elections of 1920.

A Constituent Assembly, finally elected in November 1920, adopted a basic law called the Vidovdan Constitution (so named from the day of St. Vitus on which it was adopted, 28 June 1921 — also the anniversary of the battle of Kossovo in 1389 and the assassination of the Archduke Franz Ferdinand in 1914). It created a Skupština, or unicameral National Assembly of 315 deputies elected for four years by universal, direct, secret suffrage of all males over twenty-one, with something like proportional representation, no royal veto, and civil liberties. But there was no legal provision for reflection of ethnic diversity, and the administrative law of 28 April 1922 divided the state into thirty-three departments controlled by the center — Belgrade, in the hands of the so-called *srbijanci* Serbs (from the old kingdom, as against the *prečani* Serbs from the Habsburg lands).

The chief antagonism was between Serbs and Croats. At the start it led to polarization over adoption of a constitution. The verdict seems to be that Premier Pašić was too clever by half in achieving a Pyrrhic victory by pushing it through, while the Croat leader Radić was self-defeatingly intransigent in his boycottism, and thus from very early on the kingdom was set on a path of tension.[25] Radić was actually jailed for a few months but, having agreed to accept the constitution, was freed and became a cabinet minister for a time; however, he was assassinated in parliament in 1928. Pašić had died in 1926.

Radić's successor as leader of the Croats, Dr. Vladko Maček, was invited by the king to negotiate. Maček proposed an ethnic federation, in which each of seven units would have even its own army. Alexander felt unable to accept, and in January 1929 inaugurated a royal dictatorship. His motives were patriotic, his understanding of the political problems meager.[26] He wished to avoid Serbian nationalism; he succumbed to advisers who ate and drank it. Introducing a constitution in 1931 to supersede the "Vidovdan" document, he decided to dismantle the dictatorship, but there was not time for him to do so. He was assassinated in Marseille along with the French foreign minister in October 1934 by Macedonian and Croatian terrorists backed by Italy and Hungary.

Alexander was succeeded by Prince Paul, his cousin, regent for eleven-year-old Peter II. Forces on all sides sought ethnic conciliation. In Seton-Watson's words:

The height of Serbo-Crotian friendship was reached in August 1938, when Dr. Maček came to Belgrade to confer with the Serbian leaders, and was met at the railway station by a crowd of some 50,000, of which the majority were Serbian peasants who had walked miles or had spent their few pennies on transport, to come and cheer the Croatian leader.[27]

However, it seems they cheered him not merely as a token of their willingness to accept Croats as brothers but because he was seen as the most prominent fighter for democracy. Maček made common cause with the Serbs opposing the ministers of Prince Paul, then in August 1939, on the very eve of the outbreak of World War II, reached agreement (the *Sporazum*) with the Serbs in power. Croatia was awarded a remarkable degree of autonomy. However, the Slovenes and Bosnian Muslims demanded something similar; the *prečani* Serbs were unhappy with their new minority status in autonomous Croatia; and the fanatical and terrorist *Ustasa* (Insurgent) Croatian movement (founded in 1929) demanded full independence. The *Sporazum* was a failure.

Prince Paul yielded to Nazi demands to join the Tripartite Pact on 25 March 1941. A military coup promptly overthrew him; the Nazis as once invaded and crushed the Yugoslav army, whose Croats fought poorly or not at all or even mutinied and whose Serbs did not distinguish themselves.

Yugoslav freedom, never having reached fruition, flickered and died, and postwar Communism did not revive it. It seems a case when opportunities existed and were lost. As Joseph Rothschild puts it, "while the elites of all of interwar Yugoslavia's ethic communities were culpable, the srbijanci Serbian politicians and bureaucrats, who were as consistently dominant in the authoritarian 1930s as in the parliamentary 1920s, bear major responsibility for her political fragility."[28]

Hitler dismembered Yugoslavia into a nominally independent Croatia run by the Ustaša under Ante Pavelić and a tiny rump Serbia; the remainder was annexed by Axis satellites. Yugoslav resistance became polarized between the heavily Serbian forces of General Drazha Mikhailovich and the Communists led by Josip Broz Tito, who gained support from the British and other allies. At the end of the war it was Tito who emerged in power. His government had one merit questioned by few: it did its best to bridle the ethnic antagonisms that truncated freedom between the wars and counted many victims during World War II. And after Stalin denounced Tito in 1948, the system preserved Yugoslav independence. In the 1960s, modest political and economic liberalization took place, and the republics were given greater power. After Tito died in 1980, leaving as his legacy a weak rotating executive, much discontent and national tensions surfaced. In early 1990 pessimists believed the country to be on the verge of break-up into several parts.

National or ethnic feelings had contributed to the destruction of the Czechoslovak Republic in 1938, threatened Communist Yugoslavia with the very fate from which Tito could claim to have rescued the former kingdom in 1945, and elsewhere in Eastern Europe imperiled national unity. (To be sure, such antagonisms, in the 1990s, were dangerous to autocratic regimes as well as to democracies in every corner of the world.)

Romania had a smaller minority problem. There had never been either a Czechoslovakia or Yugoslavia before 1918, but there had been a Romania for over half a century. She now more than doubled both area and population. The gains were Transylvania (Iuliu Maniu was the leader), Bessarabia (annexed by Russia in 1812 and retained except for 1856–78), southern Dobrudja, and the Bukovina. The Liberal party under Ionel Bratianu regained its former ascendancy; he himself had been prime minister from 1909 and resumed that office in December 1918. There were also the Socialists, who led worker discontent culminating in the general strike of October 1920. However, repressive measures left the party, and the Communists who split off, insignificant in interwar politics.

The party that came to represent the majority was a product of fusion (carried out in October 1926) of Maniu's (Transylvania) National People's party with the Peasant party of the Old Kingdom, founded at war's end. The successes of the resulting National Peasant party were owing to the land reform that was first promised in March 1917, was enacted in July, and much of which was carried out in 1921. The boyars' influence was finally undermined, though peasant agriculture still had many weaknesses that grew worse as peasants continued to subdivide small holdings. Still, Rothschild points out, "the Romanian land reform was undoubtedly the most extensive one in interwar Europe (excluding the Soviet Union)."[29]

In 1928 occurred the only fully free election Romania has ever enjoyed (as was true of the election to the Constituent Assembly in Russia in late 1917). The National Peasants carried off 349 out of 387 seats; the resulting reform government abolished censorship, curbed the police, moved toward decentralization, and repealed export duties. Unfortunately the moment did not last. King Ferdinand died in late 1927; his son had been forced to renounce the throne and go into exile, but in June 1930 returned to claim the kingship and was accepted even by Maniu. However, Carol II's importation of his mistress, Magda Lupescu, led Maniu to resign.

There ensued a wretched decade of royal corruption, the rise of the quasi-Fascist Iron Guard, misery, and misrule. In 1938 Carol imposed royal dictatorship but had Corneliu Codreanu, leader of the Iron Guard, and thirteen followers "shot while trying to escape." The king tried in vain to conciliate Hitler; instead in 1940 he had to give up Bessarabia and Bukovina to Hitler's temporary partner —Stalin—northern Transylvania to Hungary, and southern Dobrudja to Bulgaria.

Next came Romania's enthusiastic participation in war against the USSR; again her withdrawal to join the Allies; and finally the doomed attempt of Romania's democrats, headed by Maniu, to establish a free polity. With nothing but the weakest Communist party in eastern Europe to build on, the Soviet government imposed a Communist regime under Gheorghe Gheorghiu-Dej. At length the government in Bucharest, after 1965 headed by Nicolae Ceausescu, managed to achieve a degree of independence in foreign policy. However, Ceausescu kept a rein on domestic change comparable to Stalin's rule in Russia and in the late 1980s led the country inexorably into an economic cul-de-sac of unbelievable wretchedness unparalleled in Europe. In December 1989 he was overthrown by a popular revolution, and Romania began to move shakily toward democracy.

Romania made a pass at freedom in the 1920s, enjoyed a fleeting moment of it in 1928–30, was frustrated in its hope to recover it in the 1940s. An indigenous lament of the gap between reality and the pretense of several politicians during the period put it thus in 1937: "The greatest and most fruitful revolution which could be accomplished in Romania would be simply to apply the existing laws." [30] After a searing indictment of the privileged class in that unhappy country, Hugh Seton-Watson once forecast a (not very near) future in which the Romanian people, "perhaps the most naturally talented in all Eastern Europe," would carry the country to a position of honor. [31]

Bulgaria and Greece—the one defeated and the other victorious—saw minor frontier changes at the end of World War I. Bulgaria lost a few small bits of territory but also a significant grain-producing area in the southern Dobrudja and her Aegean sea coast in western Thrace. (The southern Dobrudja was regained in September 1940 and kept at the end of World War II; the Aegean coast was not.)

Filled with refugees, reparation obligations, and resentment, the country experienced much turmoil from which came the abdication of Tsar Ferdinand and, in October 1919, the victory at the polls of Aleksandur Stamboliiski and his Peasant party. Stamboliiski, who had suffered imprisonment for opposing war against Russia, headed a government that carried out a thoroughgoing land reform. Socially the country enjoyed surprising health: it had the best social-security and insurance system in the Balkans, high literacy, accessible education, a thriving cooperative movement, and a year's compulsory labor service (military service was forbidden by the peace treaty) for the youth.

Politically the picture was darker. Stamboliiski moved in the direction of dictatorship, organizing an "Orange Guard" of ruffians to do his bidding. In June

1923 army units, aided by Macedonian terrorists of the dreaded IMRO, over-threw Stamboliiski and murdered him and many of his followers. The Communists, who had been the second strongest party, were indifferent to his fall. They were soon destroyed by his successor, Aleksandur Tsankov, after they tried an uprising in September in obedience to Moscow's orders (the Soviets having declared their past attitude to Stamboliiski erroneous).

Several elections to the Subranie (the unicameral legislature) followed over the next several years, without establishing political order. In May 1934 a group of young officers and technocrats carried out another coup; this time the constitution of 1879 was suspended and remained so. In less than a year, in January 1935, Tsar Boris removed them and established a royal dictatorship. It lasted until his death, which followed closely on a stormy interview with Adolf Hitler in August 1943. A year later Bulgaria deserted the alliance with the Nazis into which Boris had led it and began to fight alongside the Soviets.

After two rigged elections at war's end, the longtime Communist leader Gheorghe Dimitrov became prime minister. The chief opponent of the new Communist regime, Nikola Petkov, the peasant leader, was arrested and executed in September 1947, and no further resistance was offered to the coming of communism there. For decades Bulgaria seemed the very model of a Soviet satellite and then ally. Perhaps it was the habit of emulation that began the sudden reform movement in late 1989, but it proceeded rapidly, toppling from power Todor Zhivkov (first secretary of the party from 1954 and president from 1971) and introducing an uncertain future of free choice.

In Greece there was determination, led by Eleutherios Venizelos, to use the collapse of the Ottoman Empire to realize the full majesty of the *Megale Idea* (for a greater Greece). He obtained Allied consent to landing Greek troops in Smyrna in Asia Minor in May 1919, and by the peace Treaty of Sèvres in August 1920 Greece was to administer the area for five years. But the Greek army advanced into the interior, and, owing to domestic opposition to this adventure, in November 1920 the Venizelos party experienced a resounding defeat at the polls. Venizelos resigned and left Greece; his adversary, former king Constantine, returned in triumph to Athens.

The Greek army, however, continued to advance into Anatolia, until the Turkish nationalist leader Mustafa Kemal held it and drove it back. Greece was humiliated, the king was forced to abdicate in favor of his son George II, and as the Jelaviches put it, "land that had been inhabited by Greeks for 2,500 years [in Anatolia] were evacuated."[32] The commander-in-chief of the army and four ministers were shot.

As Mustafa Kemal skillfully completed by diplomacy and force the extension of his rule over Asia Minor, Eastern Thrace, and the islands of Tenedos and

Imbros, a new peace treaty was concluded at Lausanne (July 1923) providing for population exchange. A million and a half Greeks left what was now the Turkish Republic (the sultan having fled), most for Macedonia; almost half a million Muslims, mostly but not all Turkish, left Greece. It was the first of several large-scale exchanges of population in modern times, all attended by suffering and impoverishment of innocent people powerless against the political leaders responsible for their misery.

The next decades saw rapid political change. Venizelos's followers swept the December 1923 elections, but the military junta that controlled the royal government had other plans—proclamation of a republic, which Venizelos opposed. A succession of military governments ruled in Athens from 1924 until 1928, when Venizelos returned again to form a government lasting four years. His rivals, and the royalists, followed him in power, and George II was recalled again in 1935.

With royal consent, General Ioannis Metaxas became dictator in 1936, and the "regime of August 4" that he headed was stable and efficient over the next five years. It was Metaxas who rejected Italian demands pursuant to her annexation of Albania in October 1940 with a sharp "Oxi!" (no!) and promptly sent Greek forces that repelled and drove far back into Albania the Italian invaders.

But Hitler bailed out Mussolini in April 1941 when he overran both Yugoslavia and Greece (Crete held out another month), and until October 1944 Greeks endured Nazi occupation with very little collaboration. Civil war between Communist partisans and others began while Germans were still there, and it was not until 1949 that the Communists were defeated. Reconstruction of a country that had lost one-tenth of its population through war and starvation then took place. Some stability was restored under the government of General Alexandros Papagos in 1952. In subsequent decades the republic was restored (1973) as was the constitution of 1952 (1974). Greece's first Socialist government took over in 1981 and was thrown out of office by the elections of 1989. Plagued by terrorism, a shaky police system, and a sluggish economy, in early 1990 democracy was wobbly in the country, but it had survived.

Independent Albania was created only in 1913, and no sort of stable government was established before or during World War I. The country was scarcely a unit; mountain clans were more significant than whoever was in Tirana. Italy, Greece, Serbia, and Montenegro claimed or sought parts of Albania; they were all brought to withdraw by 1922, and for three short years there was a stab at creating a constitutional monarchy in which the chief religious groups—Muslim, Orthodox, and Catholic—would be satisfied. By 1925 it had failed, and an Italian protectorate operating through Ahmet Zogu as president (he had been premier from 1922 and in 1928 was proclaimed king) was established.[33] In April 1939 an Italian army invaded, and there was proclaimed a "personal union" by which

King Victor Emmanuel of Italy became king of Albania as well. At the end of the war Albania was a kind of Communist offshoot of Yugoslavia, though it soon broke with Belgrade, Moscow, and Peking in that order. In early 1990 the country had the distinction of being one of the last remaining Stalinist states in the world.

An interesting, even ironic, result of the collapse of the Ottoman Empire and the war with Greece was the emergence of Turkey as a prime candidate for what has been called "crossing the institutional divide" that separates the heritage of oriental despotism from the category of constitutional and democratic states. The empire had experienced many reforms before: military reforms designed to preserve the Sublime Porte, especially from Selim III (1789–1807) onward; the Tanzimat reforms of the mid-century, culminating in the first Ottoman constitution in 1876 (the sultan had full executive power, assisted by a two-chamber parliament, the lower indirectly elected and the upper nominated by the ruler). But the system lasted only a year, and from 1878 to 1908 there was no further movement in the body politic.

In the latter year occurred the Young Turk revolt, which forced the sultan to restore the constitution, now amended to give the power to the Parliament. But the army was the arbiter, and after the Ottoman Empire was defeated and the sultanate collapsed it was the war hero Mustafa Kemal (a nickname meaning "perfection" bestowed by a teacher) who led the establishment of the republic in October 1923 and became the first president. According to Yapp, he attempted to apply six principles:

(1) the republic
(2) nationalism, fostered by schools and propaganda
(3) populism, designed to involve the populace as a whole through "People's Houses" in towns and village institutes in the countryside
(4) statism. Since in 1914 Greeks and Armenians controlled 80% of the money economy, the state was given the task of spearheading economic development
(5) secularism—religious courts and schools were abolished in 1924, women were given the right to vote and sit in parliament (1924); the Latin alphabet replaced the Arabic, the Gregorian calendar replaced the Muslim; important as a visual symbol was the abolition of the fez in 1925
(6) revolution, which had no particular meaning but an important general one as embracing the five foregoing points and the overall goal of what came to be called "modernization."[34]

The constitution of April 1924 codified the new polity, including a clause retaining Islam as the state religion (one that was removed in April 1928). Kemal, now with the surname Atatürk ("Father of the Turks"—chosen in 1934 when all Turks were required to select surnames), died in 1938. His alter ego Ismet Inönü became president.

An abortive attempt at establishing an opposition party had been made in 1930, but while Atatürk lived benevolent dictatorship was the best description of the government. He operated through a single Republican People's party. In 1946, after the war (which Turkey joined on the Allied side only in the last few months), the party split, and a new Democrat party appeared. Inönü restrained army men who wanted to destroy it, and he made an extraordinary public statement: the logic of the multiparty system (now at least for the time being accepted) implied the possibility of a change in government. The new popularity of democracy and the spread of education have been credited with related events: the abandonment of certain restrictions on freedom of speech and press, the legalization of trade unions (1947, though the right to strike was granted only in 1963), and so forth.

Thus groundwork was laid for the victory of the Democrat party (DP) at the polls in 1950 and a shifting of the political underpinnings, so that the prime minister became more important than the president—the office that Kemal had held so long. The DP relaxed secularism a bit, though it still restricted the activities of the religiously zealot dervish orders. Even slight movement in such a direction, however, led the army to carry out a coup jailing DP leaders and to introduce a new constitution the following year (1961).

Out of the wreck of the old DP there now emerged a new Justice party (along with two other parties), which won elections in 1965 under Suleyman Demirel, a former engineer. The army moved again in 1971, imposing martial law in much of the country that was lifted only two years later. But left-wing terrorism grew to such a point that another coup in 1980 brought back military rule and still another constitution (November 1982). Many friends of Turkish democracy accepted the need for strong measures to bring terrorism—which can destroy the possibility of law and order at any level—under control. However, a fully functioning system of political and economic freedom seemed still a difficult and elusive goal.

Russia and the USSR, 1801–1990

Under the Empress Elizabeth (1741–61), there had been a few feeble echoes of nascent West European liberalism, and they may have had a role in the first important step toward breaking down Russia's monocentered society: the emancipation of the gentry, 1762 and 1785 (introduced by Peter III, confirmed and codified by his widow Catherine II).

Catherine (called the Great) had other plans for bringing Russia—her adopted country, as she was born princess of Anhalt-Zerbst—closer to the West and herself into the good graces of the liberal publicists of the day, Voltaire and the

other *philosophes* of France. Those plans yielded some halting educational improvements, an abortive reform of municipal government, and a more or less
effective corporate organization of the gentry now freed from compulsory state
service and, in greater numbers than before, apt to live on their estates in the
provinces and to take a greater role in provincial affairs. After a brief reign by her
son Paul, who tried to undo almost everything his mother had accomplished,
Paul's son Alexander I became tsar in 1801.

He too had plans, similar to his grandmother's in spirit but broader in scope.
He gathered a group of young reformer friends around him who discussed constitutional possibilities and actually began to institute parts of a projected constitutional reform for the country—chiefly the creation of a State Council (1810) that
would prepare legislation (not in any way that went outside the emperor's will
and direction) for enactment and the replacement of the so-called "colleges"
created by Peter I with modern ministries discharging the responsibilities of the
central administration. Michael Speransky, son of a priest, and one of the ablest
of prerevolutionary Russian statesmen, was the tsar's chief assistant counseling
constitutional reform up to March 1812, when he was abruptly dismissed—
though near the end of the reign he was entrusted with significant powers as
governor of Siberia and introduced reforms there.

Alexander, however, became embroiled in the diplomacy and wars of the
Napoleonic period, culminating in the French invasion of Russia (with an army
including many non-Frenchmen) in 1812. The tsar led the coalition that defeated
Napoleon and had much to do with the peace worked out at Vienna in 1815; he
compelled several West European sovereigns to adopt constitutions they were less
than eager to accept, notably in the case of Louis XVIII and the Constitutional
Charter under which the Bourbons were restored in France. He also granted a
constitution to Poland, retained constitutional arrangements for Finland, and
introduced measures of the sort in Bessarabia.

But though he continued to weigh proposals for a Russian constitution, he did
nothing further with them. In the later years of his reign he became aware that
young officers who had ridden with him to Paris in 1814 were plotting in secret
societies to introduce a constitution, but did nothing to stop them. After his death
in December 1825 the young men attempted a revolt; these "Decembrists" believed—quite wrongly—that Alexander's brother Constantine, who had renounced the throne, would be amenable to their aims. The successor, Nicholas
I, suppressed the revolt with a few executions but carefully studied the details of
what the hundreds of people investigated for participation had in mind.

Nicholas, "the gendarme of Europe," put down the Polish revolution of 1830
and the Hungarian revolution in 1849, but helped secure the victory of the Greek
rebellion. Despite his conservative or reactionary domestic stance, often charac-

however, found these arrangements more or less satisfactory; they at first kept aloof from the revolt.

Both Greeks and Muslims killed one another and committed atrocities; it was Ottoman massacres that were reported in the press of the European powers, not least the hanging of the patriarch of Constantinople and some bishops of his in front of their church by Janissaries on Easter eve 1821. The uprising spread to the rest of Greece. In January 1822 a Greek assembly, meeting at Epidaurus, announced a new constitution for an independent Greece that was based on the government of the French Directory, the executive to consist of five men. It never took effect.

Philhellenism, Europeans' fascination with the modern Greeks (perhaps too easily equated with fifth-century B.C. Athenians), settled the issue. The entire Ottoman fleet was sunk by a joint British-French-Russian squadron in the bay of Navarino in October 1827, by a strange accident rather than plan; the upshot was war between Turkey and Russia.

The three allied powers were now able to impose their will on the Porte: an independent Greek kingdom under a seventeen-year-old Bavarian prince was set up, and the new king, Othon, arrived in 1833 to rule roughly the southern half of Greek-inhabited territory. But three-quarters of the Greek population remained under the Ottomans, and the formerly favored position of Greeks in the imperial government and economy was drastically altered. Serbia benefited by the intervention of the powers in Balkan affairs; the sultan recognized the full autonomy of the state in 1830 and in 1833 gave up an additional strip of land south of it.

However, Serbian notables were dissatisfied with the autocratic rule of Miloš Obrenović, who was said to run the country like a Turkish pasha. Serbia had no continuing political or legal tradition. There was an ancient custom of assembling the armed males to decide issues called the *skupština,* but at least in recent times such bodies were called to ratify, not debate, decisions of the leaders. Knowing that neither Turkey, Austria, nor Russia wished for fully constitutional systems to be established in the area, Miloš fended off oppositional demands for a genuinely representative assembly and council.

But Russia backed the movement for a council of notables (provided for in the sultan's rescript of 1830 but not implemented), and as a result the sultan issued the so-called Turkish Constitution, which was the basis of Serbian government from 1838 until 1869.[19] A council of seventeen, appointed for life by the prince, shared power with him; they had to approve all laws and taxes, though he possessed an absolute veto. The ministers, after an amendment, had to be appointed from council members and were already responsible to the council.

Miloš had created a nation in that he made the central government meaning-

local self-government, the zemstvo, established in 1864 at the county and province levels, in which to exercise their new citizenship; a reformed judiciary (1864) benefited them, but also the entire population now given trial by jury, irremovable judges, and a trained bar. There was also a new system of municipal self-government (1870) and an immensely important reform of the army: the normal term of service was reduced from twenty-five to six years with further reduction for breadwinners, only sons, and graduates of different levels of schooling; the worst sorts of brutality in army discipline were ended; the introduction of elementary education for the peasant recruits did a great deal to create popular literacy.[35] Many officials helped in all this, notably the brothers Nicholas and Count Dmitry Miliutin. The restoration of university autonomy (abolished in 1835) in 1863 and the extension of secondary education may also be considered part of the Great Reforms.

Progressives begged Alexander II to pursue the principle of reform further: they petitioned him to "crown the edifice," which meant creating a national zemstvo—that is, parliament—and in general to do for Russians "what he had done for the Bulgarians"—that is, grant a constitution. The revolutionaries, whose first underground circle (that of Durov) dated to 1848, during the 1860s had formed several such groups and tried terrorism; in the 1870s they undertook the killing of several officials and in 1881 assassinated the Tsar-Liberator himself. The result was to give all reform a bad name (a consummation the revolutionaries were not averse to having brought about) under the reign of Alexander III (1881–94) and the first half of the reign of Nicholas II (1894–1917), since he vowed to continue the policies of his father.

It now proved possible to harness some of the worker dissatisfaction with conditions of nascent capitalism to the socialism of a section of the intellectuals, in the Social Democratic party. It was formed nominally in 1898, in fact in 1903, when it at once split into Bolshevik and Menshevik (Majority and Minority—misnomers for many of the following prerevolutionary years) factions and later parties. The Socialist Revolutionary part tried also to mobilize the workers but placed great hopes in the peasantry, and the Western-liberal Constitutional Democrats sought to rise above class divisions. In the Revolution of 1905, unintentionally triggered by the government that courted a disastrous war with Japan, mutinies and strikes compelled the tsar to grant a legislative assembly (Duma) and revamp the State Council into a partly nominated upper house of a kind of parliament, as well as promise civil liberties.

Under the prime ministry of Peter Stolypin, the government (with help from the new Duma) carried out an all-embracing land reform, undermining the village communes to establish an agriculture based on self-sufficient peasant farms, and adopted a number of important measures relating to labor and education. Stolypin was assassinated by a double agent in 1911, and his successors were increasingly briefly in office and successively less able. By the time World War I broke out, strikes were mounting again in intensity.

At the outset the war united the nation, made patriotism popular, and enabled nongovernmental bodies, such as the national zemstvo organization and war industry committees, to play significant roles. But the long strain of war, which stretched the staying power of western European governments to the limit, was too much for the state over which Nicholas II presided. He was disheartened by the murder of Rasputin, the "elder" (holy man, not a monk) who had seemed to be able to keep the tsar's hemophiliac son alive; he was unable to handle the political whirlwinds that enveloped him.

In February 1917 (by the old calendar) a crisis in food supply for the capital, Petrograd, precipitated a political crisis. Out of it came abdication of the tsar and his dynasty, formation of a Provisional Government headed by liberals that was committed to postponing important decisions until a Constituent Assembly could be properly elected, and resurrection of a device used briefly in 1905, the Soviets (Councils) of Workers' Deputies led by Mensheviks and Socialist Revolutionaries, soon to include Soldiers' Deputies as well and to be flanked by Soviets of Peasant Deputies.

The ineffective leadership of the Provisional Government; the return from abroad of Vladimir Ilich Lenin, who demanded of his fellow revolutionaries action not speeches; the impasse on the German-Austrian front—these and other things led to a series of crises for the Provisional Government and, on 25 October/7 November 1917, seizure of power by the Bolsheviks in Petrograd and within a few days in the rest of the country as well.

The imperial family were often charged with the things royalty often are suspected of: waste of money, needless luxury, indifference to the sufferings of the lower classes. They were not the right charges for the last Romanovs: Nicholas and Alexandra hated court life and loved the common people. But the tsar could not handle the power he retained. The liberals who headed the Provisional Government were reluctant to wield what power they possessed. One party, the Bolsheviks, and one man (better, two men, Lenin and Leon Trotsky) were prepared to seize power and use it. And they did.

The new masters of the country were challenged with words by the Mensheviks, with arms by others; within a few months civil war broke out. A coalition was forged by some of the Socialist Revolutionaries and Constitutional Democrats; the leaders of the army; and the leaders of the ethnic minorities, who made up about half of the population—the other half being Great Russian. Or, more accurately, it was not forged. The three groups fought separately more often than together, and although the White armies were in the outskirts of Petrograd and within striking distance of Moscow from the south in October 1919, that was their last gasp, militarily speaking.

By March 1921 the Reds were victorious almost everywhere (not before 1926 in Central Asia) against their enemies in uniform; but a deep domestic crisis, beginning with peasant revolt on the Volga and culminating in the revolt of Red sailors in the great Kronstadt base near Petrograd, provided a new threat. Lenin introduced the New Economic Policy, permitting virtual peasant ownership of land, small-scale private enterprise in the towns, and foreign investment (of which there was in fact not much). All this enabled Russia to recover, by 1927, to the approximate economic level of 1913. Lenin's successor, Joseph Stalin, thereupon launched a so-called Second Revolution, collectivizing the land, nationalizing industry, severing all contact with foreign countries, and plunging the country into an abyss of terror and poverty. The hatred of the regime provoked by the savage treatment he had meted out to the people, his destruction of the army leadership in the purges of 1936–38, and his refusal to prepare for Nazi attack in 1941 despite clear signs that it was imminent, led to the USSR's narrowly escaping defeat by Hitler, after unimaginable death and destruction. While planning new purges of real or imagined enemies, Stalin died in 1953.

In subsequent decades his successors wrestled with his heritage—Nikita Khrushchev by ending most of the terrible concentration camps but breaking his nails on the economic problem, Leonid Brezhnev by seeking foreign technology and large agricultural investments, Yuri Andropov, with new work discipline, and, after the strange interlude of Konstantin Chernenko, the more dramatic efforts of Mikhail Gorbachev. At the beginning of 1990 the balance sheet stood as follows: there was an amazing change for the better in journalism, history writing, and the publication of critical belles-lettres of past and present; the political system had changed, so that genuine elections had been held, law given new meaning, and a parliamentary life of sorts had come into existence; but the economy, after partial and gingerly experimentation with the market and free enterprise, had actually slid backward.

Alexander Solzhenitsyn argued that Russia in the 1970s and 1980s was less ready for democracy than it was in 1917. There is no way of proving such an assertion, but it is plausible. At the time of the Revolution the prerequisites for democracy were being created: some experience, lasting half a century, with local self-government in both urban and rural settings; the rule of law as practiced in some of the best courts of continental Europe, although political cases were often tried in special conditions after Vera Zasulich was acquitted in 1878 for the attempted assassination everyone had seen her perform; the spread of private property among the peasantry and the success some landlords and more entrepreneurs were having in creating capitalism in both agriculture and industry; the astonishing rise in popular literacy, the development of the universities, the attainment of both high quality and broad popularity among practitioners of the fine arts—literature, painting, and music especially. Some of those prerequisites disappeared or were forgotten under Lenin and Stalin; since then there have been stirrings of life in some of them that were thought dead. The capacity of Russians and other peoples of the USSR for democracy need not be doubted; the difficulty of ridding the country of the institutional heritage of the past seventy-odd years remained great.

CHAPTER 11

India, China, and Japan

India

City life arose around 2000 B.C. in the Indus valley and during the first millennium B.C. in the valley of the Ganges, as the inhabitants learned how to control the great rivers sufficiently to begin irrigation agriculture. The Indus valley civilization disappeared; the reasons may be several but are certainly mysterious. Some time after 2000 B.C. the Aryans entered India from the northwest—it is not known where they began their migration. They came with cattle and "were first and foremost cattle-breeders and beef-eaters"; they raised some grain. Aryan society was comparable to Homeric Greece or the Celtic West, one of "a warrior aristocracy, interested in feeding and fighting but little concerned with its humbler foot-slogging peasantry."[1] From the time the Aryans appeared, the Indians were deeply preoccupied with religion. Perhaps their only equals in that respect have been the Jews and the Egyptians. The Jews made the written record of what they believed to be their long colloquy with God the foundation for their life both sacred and secular; the Egyptians had no record comparable to that of the Jews and a conception of the conjoining of deity with kingship that was shared by neither of the other two peoples. Only the Indians, of the three peoples, managed to carry their long experience of a religious culture into a large continuous territorial entity of today, for much of their history seemingly little concerned about political unity—in contrast, say, to the Chinese—or about the tension between indigenous and foreign influences—as were, for example, the Russians.

The Aryans called the indigenes they conquered "*dasyus* ('dark-skinned,' later meaning slaves), in which are seen the origins of the caste system"[2]—that is, the higher the caste the lighter the skin. The mass of the population of the subcontinent continued to live in dispersed villages. The village "as an administrative and social unit remained constant,"[3] but the political structures built on it were diverse and changing. Tribal assemblies existed for a time, and then had superimposed on them the governments of kingdoms large and small. Some smaller states were nonmonarchical and have been called republican, since their chief or president was elected and was assisted by a council of elders selected, it seems, from families of the Kshatriya caste—landowning and military aristocrats. But the most important institution in the republics was the general assembly, or *parishad*, which had prescribed organization and procedures. More prevalent were kingdoms, several of which contested in the sixth century B.C. for control of the Ganges valley.

The Aryans had a complex, sometimes fierce and sometimes erotic pantheon. In the sixth century, there were several new sects, and two lasted: Jainism (the teachings of the *Jina*, or Conqueror, Mahavira) and Buddhism (from *bodhi*, the "enlightenment" Siddharta received at Bodh-Gaya). However, Buddhism "perished in the land of its birth,"[4] and Jainism remained the faith of a small minority.

The evolved Hindu worldview that became dominant was one that perceived reality in the predicament of the individual, who must suffer countless rebirths as a result of good and bad behavior in past incarnations, one's *karma* (literally "work" or "deed") or "the unseen ripening of past actions." The ancient Hindu conception of freedom or liberation *(moksha)* involved the gaining of insight into the cosmos that would enable the individual to escape from further births and to embrace extinction. Like other apparently fatalist and anti-individualist teachings (Islam, Calvinism, Marxism), however, this one need not paralyze the will. In Basham's words, "we cannot escape the law of karma any more than we can escape the law of gravity or the passage of time, but by judgment and forethought we can utilize the law of karma to our own advantage."[5] One way to do so was to accept the duties dictated by one's station in life—family, caste, and religion (recognizing that religion might dictate the rest).

From the start, then, Indian political life was characterized by a tension between the fact of power vested in the emperor or prince (the subcontinent rarely enjoyed, or suffered from, political unity) and the theory that judged the ruler on the basis of his defense of Hindu values and placed little emphasis on his role on earth or in the cosmos (in contrast to, say, Confucianism). It may well be true that "autocracy is substantially the only form of government with which the historian of India is concerned. . . . the nature of a despotic government remains much the same at all times and in all places, whether the ruler be a saint or a tyrant."[6] However, there still may be alternatives to autocracy potentially present in the Indian past—for example, in the extent to which there was self-government in the Indian villages and in the very indifference to government consequent upon the fact that the Hindu attention is focused elsewhere.

The single unified and centralized empire in ancient Indian history, the Mauryan empire, was founded in about 325 B.C. by Chandragupta Maurya (the "Sandrocottos" who had just met Alexander the Great in the Punjab?). His grandson, Ashoka, presided over a bureaucracy that he did his best to supervise and make responsible for the welfare of the people. He was a Buddhist, but the later Buddhist attempt to portray him as a tireless proponent of a missionary Buddhism is now regarded as exaggerated; in his numerous edicts he laid down a set of principles based on Hinduism[7] but not specifically Buddhism, supporting a common ethic of peaceful civic virtue for a very diverse society.

The empire soon declined and fell apart. Nevertheless, the ideals that antedated Ashoka but which he strengthened—*dharma,* the "social order" and chiefly the caste system—survived in such a manner that loyalty to them came to take clear precedence over loyalty to the state. The result may have been, as already suggested, to impede the growth of political institutions for many centuries.

In the decades after 300 B.C., there was compiled *Arthashastra,* a guide for princes, in which maximizing power is set forth as an end justifying deception, assassination, and "disinformation," and virtuous rule is recommended as a way of persuading a conquered people to accept their lot. However, the text was forgotten for a long period and only rediscovered about a century ago, and this Indian Machiavelli did little to shape the statecraft of the intervening centuries.

The Seleucids (heirs in the east to Alexander the Great) allowed Bactria and Parthia (present-day Afghanistan and northwest Pakistan) to slip out of their grasp, and so-called Indo-Greek monarchies existed there. Further east there were other kingdoms, as well as republics, ruled by Central Asian invaders or indigenous royalty. The original inhabitants of the peninsula, speaking Dravidian languages, had been driven to the south by Aryan invasion and then largely Aryanized; from the third century A.D. or thereabouts we know of small kingdoms there as well.

During the so-called Gupta period, beginning in A.D. 320, a large state came to control much of northern India, and there is evidence of some decentralization. It was the age of classical Sanskrit literature in the north and a flourishing Tamil literature in the south, including plays, epic poetry, and the *Kamasutra,* a famed treatise on the art of love. However, by the sixth century the Gupta kingdom had lost much territory, partly as a result of the invasion of Huns (*Hunas* in Indian sources) from the northwest, and the dynasty came to an end.

In the late seventh century came from the west a new religion in the train of new conquerors, the Muslim Arabs, who annexed Sind. The kingdoms of north central India, however, kept the Muslims at bay until the time of Sebüktigin, a Turkish slave converted to Islam who was appointed governor of Ghazna in 977. The Ghaznavid dynasty conquered much of northwestern India. Meanwhile the Cholas, "by far the most important dynasty in the subcontinent at this time,"[8] had emerged in the south, ruling much of the peninsula and northern Ceylon, and, uniquely, conducting maritime warfare to expand control of various ports and islands of Southeast Asia.

So-called feudatories (singular, *samanta*) had by now come into existence. The term designated "either a conquered ruler or, more often, a secular official . . . who had been given a grant of land in lieu of a salary" but who thereafter asserted the right to rule the area concerned.[9] In other words, it was service or office land that the feudatory occupied; India's *samanta* class "had no fortresses and experienced no age of chivalry and feudal warfare. Instead, it has always been a nobility of service."[10] and therefore was not feudal. There was, however, a trend toward decentralization, accompanied by an apparent decline in trade, and certain technological changes (such as introduction of the wheel into the villages, which helped to make them self-sufficient), which contributed to the prevalence of the village and rustic values in medieval India.

The Ghaznavids paved the way for the permanent Muslim conquest of northern India. Delhi was occupied in 1193, and a few years later there was proclaimed the Turkish Mamluk (Slave) dynasty, the first of six dynasties to rule there up to 1526. To be a slave was not dishonorable—it was said that "a slave was a better investment than a son, whose claim was not based upon proved efficiency"[11]— and was a convenient route to power for those lacking royal blood. The sultanate of Delhi became the dominant power in most of the peninsula, but from the 1330s on it lost the south and Bengal. At length the invasion of Timur, the great Barlas Turk conqueror, defeated the army of the sultan (1398) and reduced Delhi to one of several northern states.

A century later the Portuguese reached India; in 1498 Vasco da Gama landed at Calicut on the Malabar coast, and Portugal's headquarters for Asia was soon established at Goa. For the time being, however, less attention was paid to the arrival of Europeans than to the conquests of Babur. A Chagatai Turk, descended directly from both Timur and Genghis Khan, after being forced out of central Asia he seized Delhi in 1526 and founded the Mughal empire. The new dynasty was Muslim, but the third emperor, Akbar the Great (d. 1605), laid stress on alliance with Hindu warriors, ended discrimination against Hindus, and tried to limit the influence of the *ulama* (Muslim clergy) on the affairs of state. Akbar studied Christianity, Zoroastrianism, and Jainism in addition to the two major religions of the country, Islam and Hinduism. He was remembered as wise, tolerant, and noble.

His grandson Shah Jahan—known in the West for erecting the Taj Mahal, arguably the most beautiful building ever constructed, as tomb for his empress—was also tolerant and a patron of literature, but he raised the state's share of the gross agricultural output from one-third to one-half. He was put in prison (and there died) by his son Aurangzeb, who imposed a severely puritanical Islamic dictatorship. After his death in 1707, the empire rapidly fell apart.

An imposing state arose in the form of the Maratha empire in west-central India. Founded by a gifted leader named Sivaji in 1653, the state was made the major power in India by Baji Rao (d. 1740), the chief minister of the time. It was a highly decentralized state, in which the *jagirdars* (tax farmers) "claimed virtual ownership of the territory [they] controlled."[12] The Maratha king owned allegiance to the Mughal emperor, but it was a tie without real meaning.

During the previous three centuries the far south had been controlled by "the last great medieval Hindu kingdom," Vijayanagar. Roughly half the produce went to taxes, though "various layers of local landowners" reduced that fraction before it reached the central government. The Vijayanagar empire was conquered by Muslim princes by 1652.

In the early seventeenth century several European nationalities made their appearance in India. To the previous Portuguese settlements were added those of the Dutch (from 1609, near Madras), the Danes (from 1620, at Tranquebar on the east coast), and the English (1612 at Surat near Bombay); the French (Pondichéry, acquired 1674) came later. Portugal was soon squeezed out as a result of corruption in her Indian affairs, overextension of commitments from Brazil to southern Africa to Macau on the part of a small and none too populous country, and superior British sea power. The Dutch—also a not numerous people—concentrated profitably on the East Indies; the Danes never did become real competitors; the French did not make a serious effort, though for a time it appeared that they might.

The British were the winners, in a prolonged competition in which their navy was decisive. When Aurangzeb died in 1707, Britain had only a few square miles of territory at Bombay, Madras, Calcutta (founded by an Englishman in 1690), and two or three other spots. Half a century later, "when rich Bengal was acquired, nothing, not even an Act of Parliament, could stop the masters of the sea and the Gangetic valley from becoming rulers of India."[13] The argument is related to the witticism that the British acquired their empire in a fit of absent-mindedness.

Into the crumbling Mughal empire came the Persian invaders under Nadir Shah in 1739. He took Delhi, massacred thousands, and annexed the province of Kabul to Iran; he then withdrew, carrying off immense booty. But the Great Mughals learned nothing therefrom. Nadir Shah's successors, who were Afghans, mounted repeated incursions, and one, Ahmad Shah 'Abdali, at Panipat in 1761 smashed the army of the Marathas, who had come to dominate the Delhi court. Though the Mughal empire nominally survived until 1857, it was reduced to Delhi city and environs, in a manner reminiscent of the Byzantine Empire in its last years, when it was little more than Constantinople. The 1761 battle also dealt a heavy blow to the Maratha state.

A few years earlier the intermittent Anglo-French conflict (it has been called the Second Hundred Years' War, dated at 1689–1783 or even 1666–1815) found a flash point in India—along with Europe (War of the Austrian Succession, 1740–48) and America (King George's War). The English lost Madras and then regained it at the peace of 1748. Successful French political interference in the affairs of the eastern Indian states provoked one Robert Clive, a former accountant who had taken up soldiering, to seize Arcot with 210 men in 1751, which in turn led to humiliation of France. A new phase of the conflict (the Seven Years' War/French and Indian War, 1756–63) led to Clive's victory in 1757 at Plassey over Siraj-ud-Dawlah, *nawab* (virtually ruler) of Bengal; British defeat of his successor, Mir Qasim, at Buxar, in 1763; and the effective end of French efforts at ascendancy in the peninsula.

Clive returned in 1765 from a period in England. He was master of Bengal and, if he had wished, all of south Asia. However, he chose to work out a system of "dual government," whereby an Indian prince was left as nominal administrator but the East India Company named his deputy, who was also deputy *dewan* (who had the tax-collecting power, with consent of the Mughal emperor). First applied to Bengal and Bihar—the deputy was a Persian, Muhammad Riza Khan, a company officer—this system was continued for a century, and indeed came to be the model for the entire portion of the British Empire that was not composed mainly of British colonists: the indigenous ruler was retained, but a Britisher (or other person in British employ) held the power. To be sure, the supreme authority in India in the eighteenth century was not the Crown but the East India Company (the popular title was the Company Bahadur—the Valiant, or Honourable, Company).

Warren Hastings was appointed governor of Bengal in 1772, and by the Regulating Act of 1773 became governor general of Fort William in Bengal with supervisory powers over Madras and Bombay. The language of administration and judicial proceedings remained Persian, and the British who did not know the language were often at the mercy of their Indian subordinates who did. The resultant anomalies led to the impeachment of Hastings (he was acquitted but retired). Lord Cornwallis, the recently vanquished commander in America, became governor general in 1786–93. He substituted Britishers for Indians in the higher government posts, and began the deprivation of Indian opportunity for public service and social separation of the two races that would cause trouble later on. The British Parliament now undertook to set India's financial affairs in order. Feeling "an affinity with the zamindars [tax collectors of the Mughals] . . . they too easily assumed them to be tropical replicas of themselves."[14] Thus the Permanent Settlement of 1793 turned the *zamindars* of Bengal into landowners, while a stratum of lesser landholders were turned into tenants.

But the new assessment was too high, the *zamindar* class experienced a large-scale turnover, and a new group took their place. They were much more remote from the *ryot* (peasant) than before, psychologically and physically; an absentee landlord system, dependent upon the foreign rulers, was created; it replaced "the organic ties between the two classes of rural society by an impersonal cash-nexus."[15] Cornwallis also relieved the *zamindars* of their police functions and created a new police force; at the same time he introduced a new Code, retaining customary civil law and the Islamic criminal law, from which he deleted such penalties as mutilation and impalement.

Other territories were acquired through a series of wars, either intentionally acquisitive in motive or reluctantly pacifying of irregular bands, so that by 1818 the East India Company controlled the whole subcontinent up to the Sutlej River in the Punjab[16]—about half of it remaining under Indian princes, totaling over 360 political units, reminiscent of the Holy Roman Empire. The deep cleavages among castes and classes in Indian society "rendered it unusually willing to call in unwelcome outsiders to defeat the still more unwelcome neighbor," and in any case politics and government were far from the first consideration for either Hindu or Muslim.[17]

Thus the British administrators of the early nineteenth century were able to reorganize government and society in the new areas almost single-handedly: this was true of Mountstuart Elphinstone in Bombay, Sir Thomas Munro in Madras, and Sir Charles Metcalfe in Delhi. Elphinstone recognized the holders of office land, or *jagirdars,* as full landowners; Munro tried to eliminate the middleman from land assessment, but often left the peasant unprotected against local officials; Metcalfe tried to preserve the communal village. However, in no case was the indigenous society of India revolutionized,[18] and in the main the changes could be summed up by the fact that the governor general, the Company Bahadur's representative, in effect replaced the Mughal emperor.

As governor general (1828–35), Lord William Bentinck did his best to suppress *suttee* (the burning of widows on the funeral pyres of their husbands), infanticide, and *thuggee* (ritual murder and robbery in the name of the goddess Kali)— bringing down on his own head reproaches for interfering with local religious practices but defending what he regarded as the universal moral law. He also substituted English for Persian as the language of government and supported it as a medium of instruction—eloquently seconded by Thomas B. Macaulay before Parliament.

All of this marked a replacement of the notion that the British were "wardens of a stationary society"—the East India Company acting for the Mughals—by one that had them "trustees of an evolving one"—a Westernizing society on its way to Indian self-government[19] that Indians educated in the English language and curricula were bound to demand at some point regardless of whether the British declared them ready. However, a complex British debate continued about what policy toward India should be. On the other end of the cultural interchange, some Indians accepted Western influences fully; some rejected them entirely; a few, following Rammohan Roy, from 1815 on sought to combine Western and Hindu values.

A series of small wars led to the annexation of Sind in 1843, the great Sikh state of the Punjab in 1849, and the princely state of Oudh in 1856. By the year 1857—a century after the British had first established themselves in India—the East India Company dominated the subcontinent, though about two-fifths remained nominally under princely rule.

In 1857 a mutiny broke out in the Bengal army and soon became a revolt. It began by a rescue at Meerut of soldiers who had refused to accept new cartridges for Enfield rifles and had been placed in irons. The·cartridges, which had to be bitten off, were supplied with a fat of mixed beef (which Hindus would not eat) and pork (which Muslims would not eat). As soon as the British discovered the mistake, it was reversed—too late. Muslim and Hindu units together captured Delhi, as well as much of the north.

A lengthy British campaign followed, with excesses on both sides. After victory, the army was reorganized as an efficient, professional body largely made up of northwesterners, and the Government of India Act (1858) was passed. The act transferred power from the East India Company to the crown (Queen Victoria was proclaimed Empress of India in 1876), governing through viceroys from 1858 to 1947. Britain promised nonintervention in religious matters, a commitment she kept to a large extent, and equality of the races in recruiting civil servants, which she did not. In consequence both separation and hostility between Britishers and Indians deepened.

Lord Ripon (viceroy in 1880–84) sought to create institutions of elective local government but was frustrated by organized white groups—who by their successful campaign against Ripon "inadvertently demonstrated to a generation of young Indian nationalists the tactics of political agitation and protest." In 1885 the result was the founding of the Indian National Congress.[20] During its first twenty years, the Congress was almost entirely the spokesman for the small, English-educated middle class that was mainly urban, Hindu, and loyal to the Crown but sought a share in governing the country.

At length, in 1905, Viceroy Lord Curzon's order dividing Bengal into two provinces[21] triggered a nationwide protest, accompanied by a boycott of British goods with consequent benefit to indigenous industry. Shortly afterward the Muslim League was organized. The Liberal victory in the British elections of 1906 led to the fashioning of a reform by John Morley, head of the India Office in London: the Indian Councils Act of 1909 (the Morley-Minto reforms). A tiny Indian electorate eligible through property and education was able to elect members of legislative councils (which had existed in some provinces since 1861) throughout the country.

G. K. Gokhale, acknowledged as his political mentor by Mohandas K. Gandhi, at once introduced into the Supreme Legislative Council a bill for free compulsory education, and though it failed repeatedly it helped to establish a platform for Indian nationalism to state its aims. At his Coronation *durbar* (ceremonial celebration) held in 1911 George V announced the reunification of Bengal (to please Hindus), and the capital was moved from Calcutta to Delhi (to please Muslims, since it was the old Mughal capital). But such measures were tardy.

During World War I, despite the way Indian soldiers distinguished themselves fighting for Britain (and were rewarded by being finally admitted to the officer corps), anti-British feeling grew. The Amritsar massacre of 13 April 1919 resulted in the killing of four hundred Indians and the wounding of twelve hundred more. It radicalized millions, and helped provide the broad support for Gandhi that from August 1920 on made his *satyagraha* (clinging to the truth) movement the spearhead of the growing national demand for *swaraj* (self-rule). Gandhi (later called "Mahatma" or "Great Soul") was a Gujarati barrister who studied in South Africa and returned to India shortly after the outbreak of World War I. He now called for nonviolent boycott of all British goods and institutions.

By the Government of India Act (the Montagu-Chelmsford reforms) in 1919 Britain transformed the Supreme Legislative Council into a bicameral legislature (Council of State and Legislative Assembly). The majority of the members of both would be elected, but the franchise would be limited though enlarged: one million for Assembly, only seventeen thousand for the Council. "Dyarchy" (dual government) was installed at the provincial level, at which both appointed and elected ministers would exist—the former in "reserved" departments (such as justice and police), the latter in education, public health, and so forth. Once again a measure that would have been enthusiastically welcomed a few years earlier was denounced as insufficient when enacted. However, despite Gandhi's best efforts Hindu-Muslim unity, a fragile form of which had been achieved in the Lucknow

Pact of 1916, could not be maintained, and the two movements went their separate ways from 1921 on.

Gandhi advocated boycott of the elections for dyarchy, and at first the Congress followed him. However, by the time of the 1924 election Motilal Nehru and others who wished to participate won out, and the Congress made impressive gains. Liberals (a breakaway group from Congress), Unionists (mainly Muslim with some Hindus and Sikhs in the Punjab), and the Justice party among Tamils in the south were also active. The British soon recognized that dyarchy would not last long. In 1928 an All-Parties Conference at Bombay appointed a committee chaired by Motilal Nehru; it submitted a report favoring dominion status. By 1930, however, Congress took a stand for independence.

In 1935 London produced another Government of India Act: this one expanded the franchise to forty thousand. (Compare the "leap in the dark" of 1867, when the electorate was increased from one million to two million; the British had certainly become more accustomed to large numbers of voters.) The act also provided for a federation including both British Indian provinces and princely states, if half of the latter acceded; they never did, and the federation did not come into effect. Since 1929 the Congress's president had been Jawaharlal Nehru, son of Motilal, who had spent years at Harrow, Cambridge, and London, "a Bloomsbury figure, a politicized Lytton Strachey, transplanted to an exotic clime."[22] Nehru stood for a socialist republic; nevertheless, other leaders of the Congress entered the elections and won a stunning victory. It then proceeded to form ministries in several provinces and to work with the British in doing so.

At the outbreak of World War II the viceroy, the Marquess of Linlithgow, declared India at war without consulting nationalist leaders; Congress's provincial ministers (not all immediately or with enthusiasm) resigned in protest. The leader of the Muslim League, Mohammed Ali Jinnah, led his colleagues to adopt an ambiguous resolution promptly interpreted as calling for an independent Pakistan (Land of the Pure). When the Japanese neared the Indian border, Gandhi called for British withdrawal, threatening nonviolent struggle; he was jailed, and violence erupted, which was soon put down.

The postwar Labour government in 1947 proceeded to grant independence, but it proved impossible to avoid partition between Pakistan and the remaining territory, which kept the name India. More important, no one could either prevent or stop communal rioting that killed from two hundred thousand to six hundred thousand.[23] The adjoining states of Burma and Ceylon (Sri Lanka) received independence in 1948.

Independence did not bring lasting peace or democracy to the whole subcontinent. In 1946 a Constituent Assembly for British India was elected, and in the light of British Labour party plans an interim government was formed with Jawaharlal Nehru as prime minister. Those who favored a separate Muslim state maintained a stance of opposition to the majority until August 1947, and eventually became a separate Constituent Assembly for Pakistan. It was entrusted with preparing and at length (1956) produced a constitution. It was suspended two years later, and martial law was proclaimed. In 1962 another constitution followed, in 1973 a third; it was suspended in 1977, and martial law was reinstituted by Mohammad Zia-ul-Haq.

In June 1988 a decree of President Zia proclaimed enactment of the (Islamic) Shari'ah and repealed all secular civil law; in August he was killed in an unexplained plane crash. In November an election gave the Pakistan People's party the largest number of seats, and its leader, Benazir Bhutto, became the first woman prime minister of any Muslim country. What her government would do about Zia's decree and in general what the fortunes of democracy would be under her leadership remained uncertain; so far Pakistan has not managed to establish firmly a free society either in theory or practice.

All princely states were absorbed by either India or Pakistan. The Nizam of Hyderabad had a plan to make his state independent, but it failed and the state fell to India. An undeclared Indo-Pakistani war at the time of partition left Kashmir with a cease-fire line but no legally recognized boundary dividing it; in another such war in 1971 East Pakistan seceded from the West and became an independent state as Bangladesh. Other geographical changes involved Indian invasion or annexation of the remaining European colonial enclaves on the coast and the semi-independent state of Sikkim in the north.

As for democracy, India was more fortunate than Pakistan or Bangladesh—to say nothing of Burma. Jawaharlal Nehru pushed a resolution through the Constituent Assembly proclaiming India a republic. Partition was decided by the new viceroy appointed by the Labor government, Admiral Lord Louis Mountbatten, soon after he arrived in India in March 1947. The line was to be drawn by a mixed committee with a British chairman; in fact the latter, Sir Cyril Radcliffe, had to do the job by himself. The British officially withdrew on 15 August 1947, and India and Pakistan became independent. Gandhi, who had fought in vain for Indian unity and less than successfully for the equality of all men—Brahmins and *harijans* (untouchables), Hindus and Muslims, and held this principle to be true Hinduism—was hailed as Father of the Nation but was assassinated by a Hindu fanatic in January 1948.

The Constituent Assembly served both to draw up a constitution—which was adopted in November 1949 and took effect in January 1950—and to function as a legislature in the meantime. One writer declares that free voting and asserting the will of the majority have deep roots in Indian history, but he acknowledges that "in its institutional form as it is understood and practised in India today, democracy is a legacy of the British."[24]

A "federal constitution with unitary features," the basic document provides for a two-house legislature: the Rajya Sabha or Council of States, and the Lok Sabha or Lower House) elected by universal suffrage. The upper house is elected by the state legislatures on the basis of population. An apparent American borrowing is judicial supremacy; there is a Supreme Court appointed by the president of the republic—whose substantial constitutional powers are exercised usually with advice or consent of the ministry.

Nehru, leader of the Congress, was prime minister from the time of independence until his death in 1964. He had been the pilot of the vehicle carrying India into the world of postcolonial, independent nations. During the period from 1947 to 1964 he and other political leaders constantly voiced a commitment to "socialism," but in fact presided over a mixed economy (not unlike certain Scandinavian statesmen. They attempted to root out social evils and promote economic reforms, but they had also to deal with the emergence of tradition-minded peasant castes and other rural interests that took a newly prominent role in state and local politics.

Nehru was succeeded by another Congress leader, Lal Bahadur Shastri, who died in 1966. At that point Nehru's daughter, Indira Gandhi (no relation to the Mahatma), became prime minister. Her declaration of a state of emergency in 1975 contributed to her fall in the 1977 election, in which a coalition of opposing groups called the Janata party won overwhelmingly. Morarji Desai was prime minister for two years, but in January 1980 Mrs. Gandhi was returned to office, as the coalition proved united only in their opposition to her.

One of the most important political currents of the era of independence was the drive for ethnolinguistic unity, which led to extensive redrawing of internal borders and renaming of states. The determination of the Sikhs to have their own state led to prolonged confrontation with the central government and, ultimately, to the assassination of Mrs. Gandhi in 1984. She was succeeded by her son Rajiv, but the Nehru dynasty fell in the election of 1989, when V. P. Singh became prime minister for a five-party National Front coalition.

D. P. Singhal wrote in 1983: "while it is possible to say that democracy is safe in India, much will depend on its future growth."[25] A similar evaluation was made by Robert L. Hardgrave, Jr.: "India, the world's largest democracy, sustains a fragile stability and confronts an indeterminate political future."[26] That is the optimistic view. Police brutality, corruption, and bureaucratic abuses are endemic in a country of seven hundred million, where the shadow of caste overrides legal right, and the misery, unsurpassed elsewhere, of countless poor defies governmental attempts to provide a bare minimum of modern services.

Nevertheless, two or three institutions have escaped corruption and remained above politics: the armed forces, the electoral commission, and to a lesser extent the courts. India clings to democratic ideals and aspirations, and has demonstrated the vitality of its democracy by turning out a prime minister who had nearly established herself as dictator and by then justifiably getting rid of the government that replaced her.

There is much to be said for the optimistic view. If India cannot securely boast the achievement of democratic government, it is very near to being able to do so. Marx was wrong, or at any rate was guilty of exaggeration, when he wrote in 1853 that Britain had produced in India "the greatest, and, to speak the truth, the only social revolution ever heard of in Asia." Yet he was close to the truth of what would happen almost a century hence. Britain took an oriental empire and, after nearly two centuries of colonial rule, withdrew, leaving behind it a democracy. In the early twentieth century, an Indian nationalist criticized the viceroy for his autocratic ways: "Lord Curzon is not acting like an Englishman; he's acting like an Asian despot."[27] Indians built a political system on Western models and reinterpreted their own tradition to justify doing so. Despite severe and searing problems that remain, from any standpoint it is a success story.

China

Karl August Wittfogel declares, "in China the legendary trial blazer of governmental water control, the Great Yü, is said to have risen from the rank of a supreme hydraulic functionary to that of king, becoming, according to protohistorical records, the founder of the first hereditary dynasty, Hsia."[28] Yü and the Hsia dynasty (traditional dates: 2205–1776 B.C.) are not accepted by modern scholars as historical, and the harnessing of the rivers may not have been achieved until the First Emperor, but they may still serve as a symbolic prefiguring of much of Chinese history.

In the Shang or Yin dynasty, we encounter already a highly developed city life and civilization that were "both brilliant and barbaric."[29] It left behind the first historical records, incised in bone and carapace rather than consigned to paper. In that form survives the first Chinese written language, which ever since has been the basis for cultural unity among people speaking different and sometimes mutually unintelligible dialects.

The next dynasty, Chou (traditional dates: 1122–221 B.C.) seems to have been less a unity than a congeries of states that have been called feudal. The lords, however, were different from those of Western feudalism in several respects: there were ministerial lords, serving at the court of the king; subinfeudation was rare, and, most important, when it did occur, the lords assigned lands "not in a contractual way" to organized knights and barons but to "office holders and persons permitted to enjoy sinecures. They were not fiefs but office lands."[30]

Whatever the precise character of the "feudal-familial system," it weakened during the Ch'un-ch'iu period ("Spring and Autumn" from the "Annals" bearing that designation, 770–476 B.C.)[31] and subsequently disappeared. Beginning with Duke Huan of the state of Ch'i in the mid-seventh century, a new interstate position developed—that of hegemon (*pa*)—which effectively replaced the Chou monarch. At the same time, quite separate states took shape and fought each other, while "barbarians" on the periphery both gained in strength and were absorbed into the Chinese cultural area.

During the Chan-kuo ("Warring States," 475–221 B.C.) period, one state after another succumbed to stronger neighbors, until Chou itself was overcome and, in 221 B.C., the state of Ch'in emerged as the victor and sole survivor of the prolonged wars. Despite the political chaos of the later Chou, in the words of Edwin O. Reischauer, "this was an age of dynamic growth, bursting energy, and tremendous creativeness, unparalleled by any later stage in Chinese history. Possibly the multiplicity of states and their rivalries served as stimuli."[32] The comparison with ancient Greece comes to mind. The possibility of a continuing political pluralism, instead of the intermittently centralized, unitary empire, seemed to impend.

However, a closer look reveals a new, different trend: a "replacement of the old feudal structure by systems of incipient bureaucracy under monarchy."[33] Duke Wen of Chin[34] in the seventh century reduced the influence of Chou royalty in his state and appointed his own men, on the basis of merit and seniority, in a hierarchical structure like that of a military command. Local governors (prefects) were appointed; all officials were paid, in cash or kind. Armies changed character: nobles, following a fixed code of behavior, shooting from war chariots, were replaced by conscript soldiers and mercenaries fighting on foot, in large units of several thousand men, with some cavalry but few or no chariots. Other states followed suit or developed variations on the same theme.

In 221 B.C, the king of Ch'in, taking the title of First Emperor (Shih Huang-ti), divided China into forty commanderies subdivided into counties, connected and extended existing walls into a Great Wall, dug canals, and on what became the "traditional territory of China [proper]"[35] created an empire that lasted 2,132 years, the longest-lived political institution on the planet. It was an oppressive government from the first. Millions were conscripted to construct giant public works, and thousands died en route to or from or on the site of the task; hundreds of intellectuals were killed for criticizing the emperor, and books were burned (many of them were later reconstructed, reportedly from memory). The process of intellectuals' shaping the writings of Confucianism and Taoism to imperial needs and uses began.

The Ch'in dynasty did not last; it provoked an uprising that placed on the throne Liu Pang, founder of the milder Han dynasty. It lasted—except for the brief usurpation of Wang Mang (A.D. 9–25)—for some four hundred years, leaving behind "a practical example of imperial government and an ideal of dynastic authority" that influenced all succeeding regimes. Modern writers insist, justifiably, that strong and stable government in fact obtained during only a few short periods of those four centuries.[36]

Nevertheless Han China gave us something near an ideal type, to use Max Weber's phrase, of what nineteenth- and twentieth-century writers called oriental despotism: it had a developed bureaucracy, post, census, conscription for both military and civil service, law that the monarch could easily circumvent, eunuchs (who could not think in terms of inheritance of wealth or power),[37] systematized taxation, public works, and warfare (in Marx's words, two major functions: plunder of the interior and plunder of the exterior). In order to staff officialdom with educated men, beginning around 200 B.C. the practice was instituted of awarding posts to those who passed written examinations. In the reign of Wu Ti and subsequently the Confucian classics came to be the basis for an imperial examination system. In T'ang times it assumed the form that, with interruptions, served as the route to most official positions until 1905.[38] The remarkable thing about this complex of governmental institutions was how it could last, reconstitute itself when apparently smashed, and resist change except when enough force was applied from without.

When the Han dynasty declined and fell (A.D. 220), a period of disunion ensued in which barbarians occupied the north and Chinese (the Six Dynasties) ruled in the south. Protofeudal tendencies appeared—by widespread consensus, the only time in Chinese history such a phenomenon is to be found subsequent to the Chou dynasty. A variety of doctrines and religions (in China the line between them is easily crossed) competed for the allegiance of elites with Confucianism: Taoism, Legalism,[39] but above all Buddhism, which rapidly expanded after 300. Those and other doctrines mixed with local cults to form "an amorphous mass of creeds and practices collectively known as Chinese popular religion."[40]

China regained its lost unity under the brief Sui (581–618) and the long-lasting and brilliant T'ang (618–906) dynasties. A rebel army took the capital Ch'ang-an in 881 and destroyed it; it was never the capital again. After a brief interlude of disunity in the tenth century, the Northern Sung (960–1127) consolidated itself, with capital at K'ai-feng. A chief councilor, Wang An-shih (in office, 1069–76), of an early emperor carried out a series of sweeping financial, educational, and military reforms that led him in recent times to be praised or blamed as a Socialist—quite inaccurately.

The nomadic and pastoral peoples of the north organized temporarily imposing states: the (Mongol) Khitan (whose name was reported by Marco Polo to Europe as "Cathay" and as "Kitai" became the Russian word for China) established the Liao empire (907–1125); the (Tibetan) Tanguts formed the Hsi-hsia kingdom in 1038. The Liao, who had made Yen-ching (today's Peking) a Chinese capital for the first time, were overthrown by another pastoral people, the (Tungusic) Juchen. The latter, who called their dynasty Chin (1115–1234), then destroyed the Northern Sung.

South of the Yangtze, where the northern nomads found it uncomfortable to try to stay, a Southern Sung dynasty (1127–1279) was founded, with capital at present-day Hangchow. The Chin and Southern Sung empires lived in peace for some time, both professing to be animated by the same Confucian principles. In the Sung increasing abuses among officials helped to evoke a reaffirmation of ethical norms called Neo-Confucianism (*li-hsüeh* or "school of universal principles"), led by Chu Hsi (1130–1200). The school, which "might be described as transcendental moralists in Confucianism," dedicated themselves to the rebuilding of a moral society.[41]

Philosophical and political conflicts led to the banning of the Chu Hsi school for a time, but it then regained freedom and finally recognition as orthodoxy. The Neo-Confucians urged that the well-field (*ching-t'ien*) and the feudal system (*feng-chien*) be restored. As K. C. Hsiao puts it, "the well-field system was expected to overcome the fault of inequality in poverty and wealth, and the feudal system . . . would correct the fault of overcentralization of authority" that had occurred in the Sung.[42] Freedom receded still further under the dynasty; but Sung culture in the broadest sense, from the fine arts to the art of living, reached a new level of development that placed China "far ahead of the rest of the world at the time."[43]

Militarily the Sung were also impressive; but they made the stupid mistake of allying themselves with the Mongols against the Chin, and when they had to confront the Mongols alone they fought stubbornly but ultimately in vain. The first conquest dynasty to overwhelm all of China proper, the Mongols founded the Yüan dynasty, which lasted from 1279 to 1368. They took over from the Chin the practice of ranking ethnic groups hierarchically, with the southern Chinese on the very bottom. Religious toleration was practiced, but the Confucian examinations were now offered only intermittently, and thus the so-called *ju*, or Confucian scholars, suffered a blow.

The fact that China had become part of an empire that extended all the way to Russia, and even the arrival of the Polos and Franciscan missionaries in the

terized by the slogan "Orthodoxy, autocracy, and nationality "(*narodnost'*, a Russian translation of the German term *Volkstum*), he was responsible for certain reforms: the first effective codification of Russian laws, carried out in 1832 under the supervision of Michael Speransky (made a count a month before he died); improvement of the lot of the "state peasants" (over half of the 80-odd% of the population who were peasants; those living on state lands, as contrasted with the "serfs" who lived on gentry estates), the work of Count Paul Kiselev; a statute for the city government of St. Petersburg (1846). But though he tightened the censorship, the great flowering of Russian literature—beginning with the greatest of all Russian writers, Alexander Pushkin—began to be visible during his reign, and the growth of the Russian universities started to gather momentum, despite the tsar's distrust of the young men who were forming literary circles and would soon organize politically radical or revolutionary groups.

They identified the two fundamental evils of Russian life as autocracy and serfdom. Nicholas did his best to preserve and strengthen autocracy, although he once objected, in response to a committee proposal to create new supervisory bodies at the local level, that the five hundred reliable officials needed to staff them could not be found in the entire empire. He did recognize the evil of serfdom; he believed, however, that it was too soon to enact emancipation. There were several small steps taken during his reign, nevertheless, to prepare the way: the most significant was probably the introduction of "inventories" in the western provinces, which sought to determine and record the mutual rights and obligations of landowners and serfs, chiefly in 1847–48 and subsequently.

The Crimean War, ending in Russian defeat and humiliation, provided the impetus needed to bring about the most sweeping set of reforms in prerevolutionary Russian history. Nicholas I died in a mood of despair, and Alexander II acceded amid widespread conviction that not only must the war be ended but it also must be followed by change.

Emancipation of the serfs (1861) was the first and most fundamental step. The peasants on the large estates were freed and given "allotments" of the lands they had previously been permitted to work for their own benefit (less a varying slice, called the "cut-offs" reverting to the landlords); the allotments were to be redeemed by payments extending over forty-nine years. At least it was not a landless emancipation, as a few earlier laws had projected, and though the freed serfs themselves and many intellectuals argued that the quantity of land given the peasants was insufficient, that was not the main problem: it was the arrangement of land in scattered strips, the wasteful three-course system of tillage, the dependence of the peasant family on the village commune, and altogether the way the land was cultivated, sown, and used.

The emancipated peasants were presently given a role in the new system of

Mongols' capital (Ta-tu, then known in Europe as Cambaluc, modern Peking), did not lead to a breakdown of the Sinocentric outlook that had deepened during the Sung. Under the Mongols certain privileges were granted to religious groups and merchant and craft guilds, and laws and punishments were relatively lenient —and yet there was "brutalization, i.e., a destruction of the sources of humanism and refinement, and their replacement by crudeness and force."[44]

The inability of the Mongols to master Chinese government led to rebellion and civil conflict from which there emerged a new indigenous dynasty, the Ming (1368–1644). The founder, T'ai Tsu, was a strong and colorful personality who created "a system of highly centralized power and fragmented government structure," which later emperors found "inefficient and inconvenient."[45] He abolished the central secretariat and with it the office of prime minister; he also strengthened the censorate.

"These changes," Mote writes, "brought the form of despotism to the peak of its development, and made the Ming monarch the strongest ruler in China's long history."[46] Civilian officials, recruited via the increasingly formalized examination system, did the will of the emperor or might be subjected to the most inhuman tortures, such as the death of 3,357 cuts of a knife, with a pause after every ten strokes to permit the victim to regain feeling.

Despite Ming political oppressiveness, there was cultural ferment, especially in its last century of the dynasty. The scholar-statesman Wang Yang-ming (d. 1529) introduced Buddhist-derived elements of meditation into Confucianism and preached religio-philosophical relativism. Against such views, in the early 1600s, the scholars of the Tung-lin Academy (near Suchou) protested, seeking to revive neo-Confucian morals and accomplish ethical reform in government. Popular novels (such as *The Water Margin,* known in translation as *All Men Are Brothers*) and drama (dating from Yüan times) flourished; scholarship achieved prodigies.

In 1644 a Chinese rebellion overthrew the Mings' government in Peking; a Ming general then called on the Manchus (descendants of the Juchens of the Chin dynasty) for help, and they proceeded to seize the capital and proclaim a new (Ch'ing) dynasty (1644–1911).

The Ch'ing proved to be the last of the dynasties. In some respects it seemed to exhibit decay—its poetry and painting could not match those of earlier eras. In other respects it demonstrated new possibilities—agriculture leaped forward with new crops, such as American-introduced maize, sweet potatoes, and peanuts, and new areas for old crops, such as Szechuan, Kwangsi, and Taiwan for rice; the population climbed from perhaps 150 million in 1700 to 430 million in 1850, and in the later nineteenth century migrants streamed into the Manchurian north and the west of China proper.[47] The class structure was affected; though peasant farming remained standard in the north, in the center and south large landlords came to be ever more common. The Ch'ien-lung emperor sponsored the compilation (1772–82) of an amazing thirty-six-thousand-odd volume set of Chinese writings (though suppressing anti-Ch'ing works); such popular novels as the *Hung lou meng (Dream of the Red Chamber)* appeared; the new school of Empirical Research and Han Learning developed methods new to Chinese scholarship.

There was a new element with which the Manchus had to contend: not merely, as earlier, a few Western visitors prepared to accept the China they found (except in the religious sphere), but a seaborne, wealthy, and powerfully armed West challenging the Chinese order of things in myriad ways. The empire was forced to cede Hong Kong and grant trading privileges. An indigenous revolution employing the ideology of Protestant pietist Christianity seemed to be near succeeding in the 1850s; the T'ai-p'ing rebellion was not crushed until 1864. Other revolts multiplied the dangers to the dynasty, whose chief officials, such as Li Hung-chang, undertook a variety of military and technological adaptations to the confrontation with the West but resisted any significant political reform. The Western powers and Japan extorted further concessions, and Japan defeated China in a short war in 1894–95.

In this atmosphere of humiliation two leading thinkers, K'ang Yu-wei and Liang Ch'i-ch'ao, argued that the Chinese classics implied a need for reform, and the Kuang-hsü emperor was won over to their views. In 1898 he reached his majority and thus power passed from his reactionary aunt and adoptive mother, Tz'u-hsi, to him for three months. The "One Hundred Days" were terminated by her countercoup, and the antiforeign and antireform current led to the Boxer Rebellion (of the "Righteous and Harmonious Fists") in 1900.

When foreign troops seized Peking, Tz'u-hsi fled. Li Hung-chang, Chang Chih-tung, and other officials made peace. The empress made half-hearted gestures of reform, such as abolition of the ancient examination system and the dispatch of students abroad, but the prestige of the Manchus was at an end. On 10 October 1911, troops in Hupeh mutinied and occupied the city of Wuhan; it is remembered as the crucial day of the Revolution that toppled the alien dynasty and the empire itself. A republic was proclaimed.

For decades it was simply a sham. The leader of a nationalist group, Sun Yat-sen, was elected provisional president and then resigned in favor of Yüan Shih-k'ai, the head of the single agency that had been successfully modernized—the Peiyang army. Yüan soon turned the presidency into a dictatorship and even attempted to make himself emperor, provoking a revolt; while it was in progress, he died. Other generals followed, but regional "warlords" became as powerful as those in the capital.

A movement starting among students in the new universities led to the May

Fourth incident of 1919, in which the Versailles conference's decision to turn Germany's holdings in Shantung over to Japan was the immediate target of protest —the broader target being the ills of the abortive republic. Sun Yat-sen now returned to Canton; he established a new government there but concentrated on rebuilding his Nationalist party (Kuomintang) with aid from Soviet advisers and on the model of the Soviet Communist party. A Communist-Nationalist alliance was concluded that enabled Sun to plan a march to the north. He died in March 1925. The commander of the Nationalist army, Chiang K'ai-shek, fought his way to the political leadership as well. Chiang limited the Communists' influence in March 1926 and broke with them in April 1927. The Northern Expedition, launched in July 1926, was resumed in spring 1928 and completed by fall. On 10 October 1928, a National Government was proclaimed with capital at Nanking.

The Nationalist government brought China closer to a free society than, probably, at any time since Ch'in Shih Huang-ti ended the Chou dynasty—but it was not very close. Unification of sorts was achieved, by dint of Chiang's strong financial backing from the coastal regions and the West. The government was modernized, transportation and communication improved, industry encouraged; "Western ideas found expression in education, in the rising position of women, and in a relatively free press."[48] A Chinese middle class began to grow in numbers and strength. Unhappily, the rural majority benefited very little from Nationalist rule, and the Communists exploited their grievances. Chiang drove the Communists out of their Kiangsi base, and via a Long March to northern Shensi Mao Tse-tung and other leaders established a new center around Yenan by mid-1936.

Japan was steadily encroaching on China's attempts at self-government. Beginning in 1931, she conquered Manchuria and set up a puppet government there under the last Ch'ing emperor, P'u-yi. In July 1937 a minor clash between Japanese and Chinese troops led to a war that was ended only by Allied (chiefly American) victory in August 1945. The war weakened the Chinese middle class. The Nationalists, by being forced inland—their wartime capital came to be Chungking—were thrown increasingly into the arms of the rural gentry. The Communists had husbanded their strength and learned how to mobilize the peasantry. In the civil War the weary and poorly led Nationalists were forced back and finally driven from the mainland to find refuge in Taiwan. The Communists proclaimed the People's Republic of China (PRC) in Peking on 1 October 1949.

On the mainland there ensued periods of virtually unrelieved horror and costly economic blunders, with some offsetting developments in the areas of public health and education; on Taiwan, after a slow start, unprecedented economic growth and prosperity were achieved. In the PRC there followed, from 1978, belated economic moves pointed in similar directions but from a very much inferior starting point. Nevertheless, the standard of living was significantly raised, and hopes for political freedom rose high with the demonstrations of spring 1989. Such hopes were dashed by the brutal massacre of students in Tienanmen Square in Peking on 4 June, which began a many-sided retreat from economic as well as political reform and sent the country marching backward at double time. In the meantime free elections held in the Republic of China on Taiwan yielded strength to a legal opposition and provided evidence that a certain amount of political liberty was appearing along with the spectacular economic successes the Chinese there had achieved.

The story of freedom in China has been a tortuous one indeed. The variant of feudalism[49] that prevailed during the Chou period, under which cultural pluralism of a dazzling kind developed, in general undergirded a polity that was much freer than obtained during the entire two-millennia duration of the empire, and during that time the oppressiveness of government probably grew greater, not less, up until the lengthy crisis of the nineteenth century.

Attempts to produce a modernized Chinese political and social system on the part of high Ch'ing officials—Sun Yat-sen, Yüan Shih-k'ai, Chiang K'ai-shek, and others—were not noted for their emphasis on liberty, and democracy long remained a distant goal for those few who voiced concern about achieving it.

However, the million people who filled Tienanmen Square in support of the movement for democracy in May–June 1989 and raised their own Statue of Liberty as symbol of their aims, as well as the people on Taiwan, from both the Kuomintang and the opposition, who in recent years talked democracy and have begun to act it too, demonstrate that the few of the past have become the many of the present and, perhaps, the future.

The unexcelled achievements of Chinese culture through the ages have in many cases been the work of artists and thinkers who learned to shut out the world of politics from their own private visions and artistic creations. The achievements of the central government, or despotism, were also great in terms of producing the longest-lasting political institution—the Chinese Empire—on the planet. The Chinese have had to learn patience, and no people has done better in retaining goals while deferring hope for their realization. In 1990 democracy and liberty are on the wish-list for many, and a setback or two will not remove them.

Japan

In a Han history Japan first makes its appearance in Chinese chronicles (at some point after 108 B.C.) as the land of Wo, which is "divided into more than 100 states."[50] Some kind of unification was probably achieved by A.D. 350, and soon afterward Japan was strong enough to gain influence over much of southern Korea. In the later fifth century, however, the young Japanese state declined markedly in power.

The court was located in the Yamato district, perhaps near present-day Osaka. There was a hereditary emperor, whose highest officials were drawn from two groups: *muraji* (vassals from ancient times) and *omi* (who had sworn allegiance during unification); but intrigues within the court helped to weaken it. Japan was divided into semiautonomous units called *uji,* perhaps derived from the old Wo states.

Probably during the early sixth century, Buddhism was introduced to the Yamato court, but it seems to have already been known to many ordinary people. The primitive nature worship of the Japanese came to be called *Shinto* to distinguish it from the newly imported Buddhism. The ideals of the new religion inspired the policies (or policies at any rate attributed to him) of Prince Shotoku, regent for his empress aunt, but his "17 Article Constitution" (604), in which he sets forth rights and duties for ruler, ministers, and people, is even more strongly influenced by Confucianism and the notion of a centralized political system that he admired in China. He is also known for establishing relations with (Sui) China on an equal basis for the first time.

A few years later the borrowing from China became very extensive. In an attempt to imitate the political and social system of the T'ang, Nakatomi no Kamatari and the prince who became the emperor Tenchi carried through the *Taika* (the name of the current era) reforms. They centered in an edict of 646 that may be said to begin the more or less reliable record of Japanese history. The Taika reforms abolished the great private holdings of land and agricultural workers and instituted the allotment of land to peasants in accordance with a census, an imperial post, and imperial appointment of provincial governors. The program could not be carried out all at once, but was implemented over the next few decades. A new imperial court, at Nara, attracted many from the old *uji* elite who moved there, casting aside the habits of what John Hall calls "primitive feudalism" and "divesting themselves of their former localized and warlike qualities."[51] T'ang law codes were introduced with some amendments to fit the Japanese situation.

The *ritsu-ryo* system (*ritsu* = criminal code, *ryo* = civil and administrative codes) thereby established on the basis of borrowing from China was in theory a highly centralized autocracy, operating through a bureaucracy recruited from students having passed certain examinations. In fact men of noble descent and rank could be favored, so that in reality there was a "compromise between the new principles of the ritsu-ryo system and the old spirit of respect for birth."[52] By the new system, in principle all land was state property. However, in 723 land newly cultivated could be retained by the family of the first tiller for three generations, and in 743 that land became its permanent possession. As both nobles and monks hastened to sow crops, the principle of public ownership of land began to give way.

The period of Sinicized government lasted from 710 to 784, with capital at Nara, and for a century or two following 794 in the Heian period with capital at Kyoto—both cities being laid out in rectangular, checkerboard fashion in imitation of Ch'ang-an. During those centuries the influence of Buddhism deepened, and the new religion permanently transformed Japanese life. The emperor Shomu, like the semilegendary Shotoku, was inspired by Buddhist ideals, and moreover was zealous in spreading the faith. In 741 he ordered the building of Buddhist monasteries for men and nunneries for women in each province, assigning lands to support each institution in the T'ang fashion. The result was that the monks accumulated riches and aspired to power. The Chinese borrowings were thus manifold, extending from government to law to city planning to religion; nevertheless, they often proved superficial, and with the passage of time gave way in several areas. This was notably the case in the political realm. By the ninth century the *ritsu-ryo* system had greatly weakened, though forms and titles continued for a time, and the borrowing from China was reduced to a shadow. Instead of direct rule by the emperor, a system developed whereby an official named *sessho* (regent) or *kampaku* (chief councilor) acted as the real ruler. From 884 the holder of either office (often both together) needed to be a member of the Fujiwara family (descended from Kamatari) and the emperor's maternal grandfather or father-in-law.[53] It was the beginning of the system by which the emperor reigned but an official ruled; the duality has been compared with the relation of the Merovingian king and the Carolingian mayor of the palace in France.[54]

During the Heian period private estates grew apace. Younger members of the imperial family and aristocrats frustrated by Fujiwara control of the highest officialdom were obtaining lower official posts in the provinces, securing lands, and building up armed forces of their own. The aristocracy that came to own these estates became rich and powerful, though the court aristocracy also kept their position for the time being, and the great eleventh-century novel *The Tale of Genji* records the life of the Heian court in its ripest phase.

To private ownership were added tax immunities, and the result was the *shoen* form of proprietorship, wherein the owner "assumed most of the duties of governance as well as all of the fiscal rights which had once belonged to the central government."[55] Thus was formed a provincial military aristocracy, the warrior or samurai[56] class, ready for battle with local or central forces at any time. Monastic and priestly armies also were organized and repeatedly descended on Kyoto to enforce some demand. In the same period, invention of the two *kana* syllabaries made possible for the first time an effective Japanese writing system (previously only Chinese characters, for a totally different kind of language, were available), and Buddhism was subjected to extensive Japanese adaptation. In the eleventh century a series of emperors who had already abdicated and become Buddhist priests for a time supplanted the *sessho* and *kampaku* system to wield considerable power; they were known as the "cloistered emperors" *(insei)*.

A period of confused civil conflict ended in 1192 with the establishment by Minamoto Yoritomo of the *bakufu* ("tent government," from the headquarters of a warrior engaged in fighting) or shogunate at Kamakura. It would last there until 1333, and elsewhere until 1868. During the Kamakura period "the military leadership and feudal practice existed in equilibrium with those of the Kyoto court."[57] However, it was a balance that was shifting in the direction of the Kamakura shogunate. Yoritomo relied on "the customs and institutions of the warrior class," including the rite of audience with himself in which a vassal would pledge royal service—a tie unlike European homage in that it was one-sided, not contractual, and without legal support;[58] nevertheless, it had a rather similar effect. This was also a time when the feudal, military clique was integrated with the manorial system to form a "single feudal structure."[59]

In 1274 and 1281 attempted Mongol invasions were defeated. The Japanese attributed a crucial role to the sudden typhoons that both times destroyed most of the invaders' fleets; they were regarded as "divine winds" *(kamikaze)*—a term that would be given to suicide flights by Japanese aviators in 1945. Despite the great pride the Japanese had in their successful defense of the country, the families of the Kyushu vassals who had fought and died needed compensation that the shogunate had no means of supplying.

In 1333 the emperor Go-Daigo attempted to restore the imperial power. He failed when Ashikaga Takauji led an army that expelled him from Kyoto. There Takauji founded a new shogunate nominally under a different branch of the imperial family, while Go-Daigo established a court in Yoshino to the south; the division lasted for sixty years. The Ashikaga never did achieve control over the whole samurai class or the whole country; "during the Ashikaga period [1338–1573] it was not the shoguns but the local lords (later to be known as daimyo) who were the key figures."[60] In Halls' words, during the period the samurai, or *bushi*, "took over the remnants of the imperial system of government and eliminated most of the court proprietorships."[61] They did so in the persons of the *shugo*, or military governors, that were becoming "the real masters of the countryside."[62]

There was continual feudal warfare, but not total chaos. From the reunification of the two imperial courts in 1392 until 1467 (a period often termed the

Muromachi shogunate, after the district of Kyoto where the shoguns lived), the Ashikaga were able to keep a degree of peace and order in the region of the capital. Moreover, despite the amount of military disruption, the economy grew steadily; barter was replaced by the use of money. Though borders between feudal domains were often tax barriers as well, the so-called *za* system enabled craftsmen and merchants to obtain exemption from frontier duties and important privileges in localities; they have been compared to the guilds of medieval Europe. At the same time commercial towns developed around trade centers, including Buddhist temples and feudal castles; Sakai came to rival the free cities of the contemporary West.

Culturally the Ashikaga period was brilliant; it saw the flourishing of Zen (seeking individual "enlightenment" through rigorous discipline) and other varieties of Buddhism, the tea ceremony, the "cultivation of the little" in esthetics and life-style, painting, gardening, the No drama (interspersed by short comic pieces called *Kyogen*).[63]

Beginning with the struggle centering in Kyoto called the Onin War (1467–77), the Ashikaga shogunate weakened and, after a century of intermittent warfare known as the *Sengoku* (Warring States), finally collapsed. The Onin War, "a major break-point in Japanese political history," began "the fully decentralized phase of Japanese feudalism."[64] The military governors were superseded by the new local lords, known as *daimyo;* the old *shoen* holdings, yielded to the fief, and "the true daimyo domain was simply a composite of separate fiefs" over which the *daimyo* was overlord.[65]

Both emperor and shogun remained in Kyoto, but without political power. Old feudal families disintegrated and new ones took their place, esconced in castles. The *bushi* became an officer class commanding foot soldiers. All class distinctions became less marked. The peasants of the newly more important villages were much freer than the quasi-serfs of the earlier estates, and self-governance by the villagers in many respects came to be a reality.

In the sixteenth century for the first time Europeans arrived in Japan. A band of Portuguese were shipwrecked on a small island off southern Kyushu in 1543 and promptly taught the Japanese how to make muskets. In 1549 Francis Xavier landed and spent over two years in Japan, launching the Jesuit mission that was to make several hundred thousand converts to Christianity. In Reischauer's words, "the sudden appearance of European trader and missionaries" doubtless contributed to the reunification of the country.[66]

One *daimyo* and the first of the "three unifiers," Oda Nobunaga, made an attempt to restore unity. He tried to break the power of the Buddhist monasteries, a task completed in 1590 by his general Hideyoshi (so lowborn as to have no surname). Both leaders conducted "sword hunts" by which arms were taken away from farmers and townsmen, and thereby strict class distinctions were to be restored. After Hideyoshi unwisely launched two expeditions against Korea that failed, he died. In 1603, three years after winning the decisive battle of Sekigahara, Tokugawa Ieyasu founded a shogunate with headquarters at Edo.

Rejecting the label "centralized feudalism" that some Western historians have applied to the Tokugawa shogunate, Duus terms it "a hybrid state held together by feudal bonds at the top and by bureaucratic means at the bottom."[67] The *daimyo* swore loyalty to the shogun and were invested with their lands; land tenure was expected to be hereditary but often was not. The lords were required annually to pay ceremonial visits to Edo and their wives and children to live there; they were required to furnish military and economic help.

The shogun established a complex hierarchy of loyalties for the *daimyo*. Three families bore the Tokugawa surname; another 20 collateral houses *(shimpan)* came next; house *daimyo (fudai)* followed—145 in the eighteenth century—having been given *daimyo* status by Ieyasu or his successors. The outer *daimyo (tozama)* numbered 97 in the eighteenth century, less honored than the previously listed categories but treated generously and with caution, since they had not been allies so long. After Sekigahara the shogun had managed to triple his own holdings (to almost seven times those of the largest *daimyo*); he seized lands when lords died without heirs and confiscated many more, reassigning them to allies.

During the seventeenth century, as a result of Confucian ideas and, increasingly, of the real situation, the shogun came to be regarded as the official to whom the emperor had delegated the authority to keep the peace and the *daimyo* as the shogun's officials. At the bottom of the social pyramid, the villagers were organized into neighborhood associations to assume joint responsibility for paying the land tax and for local peace and order.[68] But above the village and town level, in the Tokugawa period the powers of civil government lay entirely in the hands of the samurai, the military class whose commander-in-chief was the shogun.

The shoguns were annoyed at the quarrels among traders and missionaries from different European countries. They also feared that the Spanish conquest of the Philippines might be followed by similar efforts farther north. They therefore determined to stamp out Christianity even at the expense of trade, which Ieyasu (d. 1616)[69] was eager to continue and expand. From 1587 there were anti-Christian edicts, but only after 1612 was persecution keenly felt, and only after the Shimabara rebellion was put down in 1638 was Christianity crushed. Virtually total seclusion was imposed on Japan with modest exceptions: the Dutch could trade through Nagasaki, and some trade with the Chinese and Koreans continued. Moreover, a good deal of information from abroad managed to reach Japanese authorities.

However, from 1639 to 1853 Japanese isolation was very great; Japanese society was nearly frozen in place, and one result was prolonged domestic peace. To this kind of situation Confucianism (of the Chu Hsi school) seemed especially relevant, and it was vigorously promoted by the Tokugawa. Buddhism became less influential at the governmental level, and the shoguns were watchful lest the monasteries recover their power. However, as part of the anti-Christian policy, the government in 1640 required everyone to register at a (Buddhist) temple, with the exception of a few families allowed to register at Shinto shrines, and thereby nearly the whole people was in effect blanketed into the category of Buddhist believers.

The warrior code of the samurai was somewhat reformulated in Tokugawa times as *Bushido* (The Way of the Warrior), and under governmentally induced infusion of Confucian ideas and terms was turned into a prescription for loyal, disciplined public service. The incident of the forty-seven *ronin* (1703) had elements of both old and new: a *daimyo* was forced to commit suicide for a technical offense, and forty-seven of his now masterless samurai, or *ronin*, after long and clever preparation, assassinated the official responsible for the death of their master—and despite public sympathy were then forced to kill themselves.[70]

Periodic efforts were made by shoguns and their entourage to institute reforms, which usually meant efforts to recapture the real or imagined feudal virtues of the past. For the most part they failed, but economic change was occurring. Commercialized agriculture and village industries were growing, as were cities and towns. The consolidation of *daimyo* realms led to the end of the guilds (*za*) and the multitudinous domestic tax barriers.

In a word, capitalism was growing out of feudalism: in Japan "wealthy commoners felt sufficiently protected by the class distinctions and prejudices of feudalism to venture into long-range investments in manufacturing and trade"— unlike the nonfeudal countries of mainland Asia.[71] As merchants rising from the lower classes acquired wealth and invested it, economic developments had cultural consequences. An urban commoner culture took form; for example, full development of both the *Kabuki* and the puppet theater dates from Tokugawa times.

Domestic change and gradually increasing foreign pressure were taking effect when Admiral Matthew C. Perry led a squadron of American warships into Uraga Harbor in 1853 and demanded that Japan open itself to commercial and diplomatic relations with the outside world. A national crisis ensued, out of which came a coup d'état led by the two *tozama daimyo*s of Satsuma and Choshu in 1868. The "restoration" of the young Meiji emperor (who had acceded the previous year) was proclaimed, the capital was moved to Edo, the last shogun fled, and Japan began rapidly to enter the modern world. All subjects were made equal before the law, peasants given the right to own land, the samurai were deprived of their former status and replaced by a conscript army, and the *daimyo* domains were replaced by prefectures governed by appointed imperial officials. Writes Duus, "in the space of a decade, the Japanese experienced a political change that had taken centuries in some parts of the West."[72] There were uprisings, but most were minor except for the Satsuma revolt of 1877.

Abolishing feudalism proved easier than constructing a new order. Private industries, often owned by persons close to the government, were expanded to serve as a basis of national strength. National loyalties were fostered by a determined attempt to support Shinto religion and Confucian ethics in preference to Buddhism. In seeking the best kind of political system for Japan, a series of missions to Europe led the authorities to choose as their model Germany. A peerage was instituted in 1884, a cabinet system in 1885, and a privy council to protect the constitution in 1888. The constitution was finished in 1889. Elections were held for the lower house of the new Diet, which could initiate legislation and had to approve the budget; if it did not, the previous year's budget might be followed. Only about five hundred thousand were eligible to vote, but the number increased as the tax qualification was lowered (in 1900 and 1920), and in 1925 universal manhood suffrage was adopted. The House of Peers completed the Diet.[73]

Japan defeated China in the war of 1894–95 and Russia in the war of 1904–5; annexing Korea, which it already controlled, in 1910. By the time the Meiji emperor died in 1912, Japan had "achieved equality with the West and had, in fact, become the strongest military and imperialist power in Asia."[74] After limited participation in World War I, Japan succeeded in gaining much influence in China.

Two major political parties were organized in 1881–82: Itagaki Taisuke's Liberal party and Okuma Shigenobu's urban-oriented Progressives. In the early years of the constitution the oligarchs who survived from the restoration generally had the emperor's ear and ran the government. However, the parties gained in strength and the oligarchs weakened and died; a party cabinet was chosen in 1918 and then again in 1924 (which introduced universal male suffrage). But they tended to find their leaders among officials. The Left produced a small Communist party consisting of intellectuals in 1922, as Socialists attempted to organize a labor movement.

Militarist leaders worried about the danger from the Left, the doubling of population (from thirty to almost sixty-five million from 1868 to 1930), and the refusal of numerous countries to permit immigration of the surplus. They also distrusted the parties' ability to handle such problems and were angry at their unwillingness to support the conquest of new territories to relieve population pressures and obtain food and other raw materials. Extremist officers launched a revolt in February 1936, which was put down; however, the more moderate Tosei-ha (Control) faction in effect took power. The elections of spring 1937 indicated strong support for the parliamentary system. However, in July the army struck at the Marco Polo Bridge near Peking, and the full-scale Sino-Japanese War that ensued enabled the military to dominate for eight years.

Wartime Japan had a cautious collaboration with Germany and less close ties with her allies Italy and the USSR. There was national mobilization and an attempt to centralize political groupings in an Imperial Rule Assistance Association, but the Meiji Constitution was not abrogated. After the sneak attack on Pearl Harbor on 7 December 1941 brought the United States into the war, Japan made extensive conquests and was then driven back from them until the country was reduced to economic and, for most of the cities, physical ruin. The dropping of two nuclear bombs and Soviet entry into the war in August helped precipitate the end on 14 August 1945.

General Douglas MacArthur as Supreme Commander, Allied Powers, pushed through a new constitution after an initial draft produced by a Japanese committee was judged unsatisfactory. In April 1946 a Diet was elected, women as well as men voting. In May 1947 the new constitution took effect. It retained the emperor as symbol of the nation but declared that "sovereign power" resided in the people; a House of Representatives, with four-year terms, had more power than the new House of Councilors, which replaced the House of Peers (the old peerage was abolished) and served for six-year terms. The Diet chose the prime minister, and an independent judiciary exercised judicial review. A lengthy bill of rights was included, and Article 9 renounced war and forbade armed forces (though "Self-Defense Forces" were created in the 1950s). The constitution came to be both popular and successful. An extensive land reform laid a foundation for a prosperous independent peasantry that has been called the foundation stone for Japanese democracy.

The U.S. occupation having completed its work to general American satisfaction, a peace treaty effective April 1952 restored national sovereignty. The document was not signed by the USSR or either China; but relations with Taipei were soon established and, though Peking was recognized in 1972 and diplomatic relations with the Republic of China on Taiwan ended, other ties with the latter were maintained. Relations with the USSR were restored in 1956.

Japanese postwar politics were not more turbulent than those of Western Europe. The Communist vote reached a peak in 1949 with 10 percent; the party was in effect banned during the Korean War but reappeared, no stronger, after 1952. The Japan Socialist party, close to Peking, became the chief opposition to the Liberal Democratic party, which has dominated Japanese politics since two parties united in 1955 to form it. One Liberal Democrat after the other held the prime ministership with more or less skill and effectiveness, presiding over an unprecedented economic upsurge, a prosperity by the 1990s not significantly exceeded elsewhere in the world, and what seemed to be a firmly rooted democratic system. A series of scandals tarnished the Liberal Democrats and led to the fall of more than one premier; as a result the Socialists increased their vote, but seemed still some distance from being able to win a national election. No doubt the almost total ethnic homogeneity of the population resulted in financial and social advantages that the Western democracies did not share.

Conclusion

By the last decade of the twentieth century democracy had appeared to have established itself solidly in Japan, somewhat shakily in India, to be an uncertainly voiced goal for the future in the official policy of the People's Republic of China, and an aspiration much closer to being realized by both people and government in the Republic of China on Taiwan. If the analysis central to this book is valid, Japanese democracy was predictable, India's a more remarkable achievement in that the "institutional divide" may have been crossed. Despite the stunning economic achievements of South Korea, Taiwan, Hong Kong (which faced annexation by the PRC and probable economic ruin by 1997), Singapore, and (in initial stages) Thailand, and certain steps toward democracy in South Korea and Taiwan, free political systems remained an elusive objective for mainland Asia east of Turkey and Israel.

CHAPTER 12

Latin America

Before Columbus

The pre-Columbian civilizations of the Western Hemisphere had no more free institutions than the empires of the ancient Orient.[1] As in the case of the latter, that did not mean an absence of cultural achievement. The Mayas, who before Christ were settled in the region from southern Mexico to Honduras, developed possibly the highest of the civilizations preceding Columbus's voyages. Their mathematics and astronomy, as well as applications thereof in engineering, were impressive indeed. Pedro Carrasco writes that when the Mayan inscriptions are fully deciphered, the pictographs may come to be understood as a form of writing.[2] Nevertheless no true writing system is known to have existed anywhere in pre-Columbian America. In the later fifteenth century the great Mayan cities were abandoned and the civilization was in full decay, for reasons not fully known.

To the northwest and south there were currently more vigorous states, especially those of the Aztecs and Incas. They had much in common from the standpoint of social and economic organization. In the simpler Inca state, there was state control of agriculture, craft production, and trade; in the semi-complex Aztec state, there was state control of agriculture but some degree of independence in craft production and trade.[3] All civilized areas of the Andean region had been brought under the rule of the Incas, whose empire was "a thoroughly organized absolute, paternal, socialistic, and theocratic despotism."[4] All power derived from the Inca, ruler and representative of the sun god.

The Mesoamerican region was more heterogeneous politically. During the

1430s a coalition of the Aztecs (with capital at Tenochtitlán), Texcoco, and Tlacopan was formed, but the Aztecs were dominant in this "triple alliance" for only about fifteen years before Cortés landed at Veracruz in 1519. In the Aztec polity there was somewhat less centralization than among the Incas, but the difference did not matter very much for the individual. The principal Aztec deity was the god of war and was propitiated by a system of human sacrifice unsurpassed in extent anywhere, any time. The Incas developed a device of knotted ropes called the *quipu,* and the Mesoamericans used pictographs—these were the only means of communication or preservation of tradition other than word of mouth. In the pre-Columbian empires there were notable cultural achievements, in particular in mathematics and astronomy among the Mayas and Aztecs, oral literature among Incas and Aztecs, pottery and textiles among all three.

The size of the (entirely Indian) population of pre-Columbian Latin America is the subject of debate resulting from widely divergent estimates by demographers. Central Mexico may have had twenty-five million, or half that, or many fewer people; Peru, from two or three to twelve to fifteen million; Brazil possibly about eleven million; the Caribbean islands and coast perhaps several million more.[5] No scholarly consensus is in sight. Regarding their behavior one fact is clear: they did not all live in peace with one another, and such peoples as the Incas and Aztecs were successfully imperialistic with regard to the ethnic groups they ruled, taxed, or exterminated.[6]

Colonial Spanish America

The conquest began in 1492 with the landfall on one of the Bahamas (which one is still disputed) of the Spanish ships led by Christopher Columbus, a Genoese born Colombo and called Colón by the Spaniards whom he served. By 1515, with the founding of Havana, the Caribbean had been explored and the major islands settled. The coasts had been touched, and the Pacific had been reached over Panama, when Hernán Cortés with six hundred men was ordered only to trade and explore in Mexico. His men founded the town of Veracruz, which new town promptly authorized Cortés to conquer and colonize; he proceeded to do so.[7] After a campaign characterized by deceit on Cortés's part and delusion on the part of the Aztecs (who believed Cortés to be the returning god Quetzalcóatl), he took the capital in 1521 and his forces fanned out as far as Baja California in the north and Nicaragua in the south, where they clashed with Spaniards from Panama.

The conquest of Peru followed. In 1530 Francisco Pizarro launched an expedition that destroyed the Inca empire. His subchiefs conquered Chile and western Argentina in the south and Ecuador and southern Columbia in the north. An abortive attempt to colonize eastern Argentina was made in 1535; those settlers found refuge in Asunción to the north. In 1580 Buenos Aires was refounded to serve as a seaport for Paraguay. During the next century the territories thus far staked out were filled in.

The government of the Spanish colonies lay with the Council of the Indies, established in 1524. The overseas officials it nominated to the king included the viceroy of New Spain (1529) in Mexico City, governing all Spanish territory north of Panama, and the viceroy of Peru (1544) in Lima, governing all other Spanish-held territory on the continent. From Peru the viceroyalty of New Granada was removed in 1717 (then dissolved in 1723 but restored in 1739); with seat at Bogotá, it governed today's Venezuela, Colombia, Panama, and Ecuador. In 1776 the viceroyalty of the Río de la Plata was taken from Peru and established in Buenos Aires.[8] The viceroys, and the captains-general who usually became their nominal subordinates, had in each case an *audiencia,* or court that gave him advice. Initially the town council, or *cabildo,* had some autonomy and was locally chosen, but soon came to consist of councilmen who had been the highest bidders for the positions.

Beginning with arrangements made by Columbus, Indians were distributed among Spanish colonists to provide them with tribute and labor, while the colonists were to protect the Indians. In practice this *encomienda* system became one of slaveholding. Bartolomé de Las Casas, a Dominican priest who had been an *ecomendero,* espoused the cause of the Indians with a sweeping series of proposals partly adopted in Charles I's New Laws of the Indies in 1542.[9]

The laws did not achieve their objective, but the *encomienda* died anyway. The main reason was a horrendous decline in the Indian population, from twenty-five million to one million in the period from 1519 to 1605, according to a recent estimate. European and African diseases, compounded by psychosocial factors, were responsible.[10] A new system, the *repartimiento,* provided for compulsory Indian labor for minuscule wages through part of the year only, on public works and on Spanish ranches, mines, and so forth. This system did not work well either, and wage labor came to supplant it on the mainland, while large numbers of black slaves were imported to replace the dead Indians of the Caribbean.

The Aztec and Inca rulers were initially friendly to the foreigners. The Spaniards exhibited both cruelty and treachery. Nevertheless their program, as conceived by crown and clergy, was a relatively moderate program designed to implant Christianity, to harness the Indians to the service of the Spanish, and to cement Spanish rule beyond the possibility of reversing the conquest. But the changes, once initiated, set in process a revolution in native society that went far beyond what the royal bureaucracy and the clergy had contemplated.[11]

That was the dilemma of European imperialism for several centuries. Should the conquerors restrict themselves to ruling through indigenous authorities, leaving the societies concerned essentially alone, or should they seek to remake them, imposing European notions of law, property, government, morality, and religion? There was never any easy answer. Equally difficult to resolve is the dispute about whether—for any given country or countries concerned, metropolitan or colonial—the result of imperialism was net benefit or harm. (Of course there were among men coming from all European countries to colonies those who wished only profit for themselves at any cost to the indigenes, but their numbers or motives do not necessarily answer the question just posed.)[12]

In Spanish America, the interaction between "the dominant Spanish culture —which tried to impose its values and customs—and the dominated native culture—which insisted on preserving its own values and customs" took various forms over the centuries of the colonial period, depending on "the pre-Columbian inheritance and on the strength of the opposing parties." Those forms were "syncretism, resistance, interbreeding, hispanicization."[13]

Before long there was in Spanish America a quite clearly delimited hierarchy of social groups partly determined by ethnic background, ranging from Spaniard officials, Creoles (born in the New World), and elite immigrants to the mass of the Indians and, at the very bottom, Negro slaves. At first there were governors (*gobernadores*), often also entitled captains-general (*adelantados*), who had royal warrants for conquest of areas on their funds and consequently received power and privilege. This variant of feudalism was quashed after the first decades, and viceroys, who were direct agents of the Spanish kings, took its place.[14]

A number of Castilian institutions were taken over into the New World, especially at first in the area of municipal self-government. But the subjugation and oppression of the Indians by way of the *encomienda* system in the towns, as well as forced labor in the mines, the rural *haciendas,* and the *mita,* or corvée, for public works, excluded the mass of the population from participating in or benefiting from anything like free institutions. By 1600 there were no longer any really effective institutions of self-government in Spanish America, and there had been none in Portuguese America up to that time.

It was the aim of Charles I, and the monarchs who preceded and succeeded him, to Christianize the Indians. Clergy accompanied Columbus on his second voyage and on every expedition thereafter. The friars, Franciscans and Dominicans, "frequently combined with missionary zeal a sensitive social conscience and love of learning."[15] The Franciscans penetrated the area north of the Rio Grande first and continued to dominate the mission field there up until Mexican independence.

Jesuits arrived last, in 1572 (in Brazil they were first, from 1549), and were the most influential of all the orders. They achieved their most notable success in

Paraguay, where they maintained thousands of Guaraní Indians in their pre-Hispanic social forms, isolated from slave hunters and planters, until they were expelled by royal order in 1767. In 1569, by the action of Philip II, the Spanish Inquisition was established in Mexico City and Lima (and briefly in Cartagena) but not elsewhere in the hemisphere.[16] After a short time Indians were exempted from its jurisdiction because they were regarded as recent converts with limited understanding of the faith.

The result of all the mission activity was that the Indians (except in the remoter areas) of Spanish (and Portuguese) America became Christians and intermarried extensively with white Iberians. Unfortunately, the majority of nonsedentary and semisedentary Indians, though converted, died, as a result of maltreatment, malnutrition, and disease. However, there were soon many more brown-skinned people in the south of the hemisphere than in the north; in Brazil there was also extensive intermixture with the Negroes being brought in from Africa.

Following the War of Spanish Succession (1702–13), the new Bourbon kings, especially Philip V and his two immediate successors, undertook a program of reform in both Spain and the colonies. The main effect on the colonies lay in the improved quality of officialdom and heightened efficiency. Trade restrictions were decreased, and the bureaucracy in Madrid with functions affecting America was scaled down. Agricultural output rose, mining revived, and industry expanded despite Spanish mercantilist legislation.

In the 1780s intendants (governors) were placed in provincial capitals to improve administration, with reasonably good results. Less successful was the replacement of the officials with the titles *corregidor* and *alcalde mayor* (who were notorious for mistreatment of the Indians) by new *subdelegados,* who soon came to behave quite as badly as their predecessors.

In general Indians and *mestizos* benefited little from eighteenth-century economic growth, while Creole (American-born Spaniards) landowners, merchants, and mine owners grew rich. In consequence there were popular revolts. The worst in the whole colonial period was that in Peru in 1780–83 of José Gabriel Condorcanqui, a descendant of Tupac Amaru, the last Inca, who took his ancestor's name.

Spain suffered defeats in the Seven Years' War that impelled her to fortify colonial ports and strengthen American armies. For officers it drew on upper-class Creoles, offering privileges and exemptions from most civil law as inducements to take up that career. The result was to give rise to an officer class that was to have all too successful a subsequent history in many Spanish American countries.

The Revolutions in Spanish America

By the later eighteenth century, life was comfortable for many Creoles in the cities, but they chafed under mercantilist restrictions on colonial commerce and exclusion (with few exceptions) from the highest levels of both ecclesiastical and governmental authority. The ideas of the French and British Enlightenment combined with the examples of United States independence and French Revolutionary success to stimulate a movement for independence of the colonies from Spain and other European countries. Many of Latin America's leaders who fought for independence also wished to establish constitutional governments, democracies, and free societies. Those four goals were not identical, but that fact became clear only gradually and painfully. Often the assumption was made that independence from the mother country would be automatically, or at any rate easily, followed by self-government and internal freedom. It was not to be so.

The first uprising was that led by Toussaint-Louverture in Haiti, which by January 1804 had produced a black republic—not, by the way, an achievement the Ibero-American Creoles admired. Many North Americans were skeptical of the whole revolutionary movement, though it owed so much to their own: John Adams declared that the notion of forming free governments in South America was as absurd as trying "to establish democracies among the birds, beasts and fishes."[17] Numerous South Americans have thought otherwise, but their struggle has been long and difficult.

When Napoleon occupied Spain, a liberal constitution was proclaimed in Cádiz by a Cortes that made clear no concessions were to be expected. Purporting to be loyal to King Ferdinand VII,[18] the Creole leaders prepared to act. Three foci of revolutionary action appeared. In the first—Caracas—Simón Bolívar, educated in Europe, a Freemason and liberal, cooperated with Francisco Miranda, an old revolutionary whom he persuaded to return from England. They managed to summon a congress, elected by town councils, which proclaimed Venezuelan independence—the first such act in South America—and adopted a liberal constitution.

But royalist and clerical resistance, fortified by fear that a great earthquake in March 1812 indicated divine disapproval, was strong. Indians and blacks generally stood aside from involvement with either side. Miranda was accused of betrayal and turned over to the Spaniards; he died in a Spanish prison, while Bolívar was allowed to leave for Colombia. There he raised an army and returned to capture Caracas, but in 1814 the fall of Napoleon gave a fillip to the royalist cause, and Bolívar was driven out once more. However, he rallied forces that liberated first Colombia (1819) and then Venezuela and Ecuador.

For a short time all three were united into a single state, the Republic of

Colombia (termed Gran Colombia by historians). At Cúcuta (in Colombia near the Venezuelan border) in 1821 a constitutional convention adopted a Constitution superseding a temporary document of 1819 based on Bolívar's ideas. It created executive (Bolívar was elected president), judicial, and legislative branches— the last-named elected by a small group of property holders (as was the "liberal" standard in western Europe at the time). It did not contain the "Areopagus," or moral power, Bolívar had advocated that would "act in the realms of education and civic purity, seeking to eliminate sloth and other social ills."[19] The Cúcuta convention also declared the children of black slaves free at birth and abolished Indian tribute.

The second focus of revolution was Mexico. It began with the uprising led by Father Miguel Hidalgo in the Querétaro region, prematurely disclosed and launched in 1810. The priest roused the Indians to take part by the "Grito [Call] de Dolores [the name of his parish]," declaring the Virgin of Guadalupe[20] the patron of revolt, and proclaimed both the abolition of slavery and of Indian tribute. That day, 16 September is celebrated as Mexico's independence day.

But Hidalgo reaped a fearful whirlwind. In Guanajuato in September an Indian mob, reinforced by others, broke into the granary and hacked to death five hundred Creole adults and children.[21] The Creoles first hesitated, then opposed the movement. By summer 1811 Hidalgo had been executed. His revolt, writes a sober scholar, "lasted only three months and its impact upon the struggle for independence was largely counter-productive [because of] its lack of clear objectives and the terror it provoked among creoles who might have supported a less destructive movement for political reform."[22]

However, revolt continued to smolder. A former student of Hidalgo's, the *mestizo* priest José María Morelos, took over the leadership of the movement until he too was captured and shot in 1815. Guerrilla fighting continued until the Spanish revolution of 1820 produced Creole determination to produce an independent but conservative Mexico. Consequently the officer Agustín de Iturbide made peace with the revolutionary leader he had just been fighting, and together their forces won a quick victory. On 28 September 1821, Iturbide declared Mexican independence, which lasted, and soon afterward had himself proclaimed emperor, in which position he did not last. His short-lived empire included not only Mexico but also the region from present-day Guatemala to Costa Rica. When Iturbide abdicated in March 1823, that region declared itself independent as the United Provinces of Central America; the state was to dissolve into fragments in 1837–38.

In Mexico a constituent Congress assembled in November 1823 and drew up a constitution (enacted 1824) that "bore a striking resemblance to that of the United States."[23] It provided for a federal union of nineteen sovereign states, which would choose their own governors and legislatures, and four territories. There would also be a national Congress composed of a Senate elected by state legislatures and a Chamber of Deputies chosen from electoral districts. The president and vice-president were to be elected by a majority of the state legislatures, all with an equal vote. There was no "full-scale bill of rights . . . no guarantee of equal treatment under the law."[24] Roman Catholic Christianity was the state religion, and no others were permitted.

Ironically, for the first several years of independence much of Mexican politics was managed by Freemasons, who were traditionally anti-Catholic. They came from two different lodges, York Rite (the charter brought by the American minister, Joel R. Poinsett) and Scottish Rite (the charter furnished by the British minister). The Mexican government abolished slavery in 1829, chiefly to make Texas less attractive to the Anglos flooding into that part of Mexican territory. In the same year, in a country struggling to establish economic and political stability, almost all native Spaniards were expelled—the motive being to deprive an anticipated Spanish invasion of collaborators, but the actual result was a severe loss of human capital. Mexican independence was not off to a good start.

The third focus of revolution was Buenos Aires. The Creoles there had repelled two British invasions in 1806–7. On 25 May 1810, a *cabildo abierto*[25] followed the lead of Mariano Moreno, a Creole leader, deposed the viceroy, and created a junta to rule in the name of Ferdinand VII (who, as noted, had been forced to abdicate). Moreno seems to have been impelled by Rousseauan notions of a social contract under which legitimate authority, having lapsed in Spain, reverted to the people—in this case, of Argentina, or, to use the name adopted in 1813, the United Provinces of the Rio de la Plata. Today 25 May is celebrated as Independence Day (though independence was formally declared only in 1816). As in the case of the north, the viceroyalty fell to pieces. Upper Peru eluded Buenos Aires's control and became Bolivia (1820), the territory around Asunción became Paraguay (1813), and the so-called Banda Oriental after a lengthy conflict was recognized as independent Uruguay (1828).

In Chile a *cabildo abierto*, summoned by a reluctant captain-general, in 1810 had established a Creole junta nominally loyal to Ferdinand VII; but a royalist counteroffensive, launched by the viceroy of Peru, overthrew the junta and a prolonged civil conflict ensued. Buenos Aires sent Colonel José de San Martín to support the patriotic forces, by now under the political and military leadership of Bernardo O'Higgins. An illegitimate son of an intendant who refused to have anything to do with him, O'Higgins had become a liberal in European exile. The new Chilean state declared its independence in February 1818. Initially its armies suffered defeats. However, San Martín's and O'Higgins's armies won a decisive victory over the royalists at Maipú in May 1818, and the Chilean republic was restored.

In August 1820 San Martín sailed north for Peru. He landed south of Lima and bluffed the Spanish army into evacuating the city. He then entered Lima and proclaimed Peruvian independence. However, at once intrigues and political squabbles erupted, and San Martín, convinced that only monarchy could restore order to Spanish America, sent emissaries to Europe to hunt for a prince.

He met in secret with Bolívar in Guayaquil; exactly what was said is unclear, but Bolívar was now left in a position of leadership that he skillfully manipulated until a united force under his long-time lieutenant, José Antonio Sucre, defeated the Spanish army in the last major battle of the Wars of Independence at Ayacucho on 9 December 1824.

Colonial Portuguese America

In the train of a rather different sort of history, Brazil gained independence without fighting. Before 1492 the Portuguese had received from the papacy a grant of pagan lands in Africa. After Columbus's first voyage Spain asked the same for the newly discovered territories. Papal grants were accordingly made, but Portugal objected and the line of demarcation was moved by the Treaty of Tordesillas (1494) to 370 leagues west of the Cape Verde Islands.

In 1500 the fleet of the Portuguese Pedro Alvares Cabral, bound for India, was driven off course to the west, and he discovered that Brazil was on his nation's side of the line. Tiny and poor Portugal, concentrating on Asia and Africa, had little time for the new land. However, a valuable dyewood dubbed brazilwood brought a few traders and settlers. In 1533 French harassment induced João III to establish a new administrative system whereby the coastline was divided into fifteen parallel strips extending to the Tordesillas line and made hereditary captaincies. The captain *(donatário)* was at the same time a feudal vassal of the king and an entrepreneur who hoped for profit from his own estates and from taxes levied on colonists to whom he gave land.[26] Actually only two captaincies, Pernambuco and São Vincente, succeeded; but solid colonization of the coast had at least begun. In 1549 a central administration was founded at Bahia, and the first Jesuits arrived at that time. By 1630 the donatarial system had been superseded by royally appointed officials in almost all the captaincies.[27]

The economic development of Brazil was now under way. Sugar (first cultivated in 1521) soon became the chief crop, and, in order to provide employees for the plantations, Indians were enslaved, despite continual Jesuit efforts to stop the practice and also to improve Portuguese treatment of them. In the seventeenth century Caribbean sugar provided unwelcome competition for Brazilian sugar, and the industry suffered as a result. The discovery of gold in Minas Gerais (northeast of Rio de Janeiro) in the 1690s and subsequently in several other regions led to a notable shift in the political and economic center of gravity. Along with mining, cattle raising grew to satisfy increasing urban demand.

The ethnic composition of the new country changed rapidly. Indians as slaves seldom lived long. Especially after 1550 Africans were imported in sizable numbers as a substitute. By 1585 black slaves were about one-fourth of the total "settled" population of Brazil. In 1798 black slaves made up 42% of the total; by 1819 31%.[28] There was much mixing of races, perhaps more in Brazil than in any other country.

During the period that Portugal fell under the rule of Spain (1580–1640), the country was allowed a good deal of autonomy and the two empires were kept separate. A Council of Portugal sat in Madrid, and one of the three Secretaries of State belonging to the Council was for "India and the Conquered Territories." In Lisbon there was a Council of State, and the Spanish kings kept as before two Secretaries of State, one for Portugal and the other for its empire. After Portugal regained its independence, the Overseas Council (Conselho Ultramarino) was the agency managing the empire, from 1642 to 1750. The line of Tordesillas (1494) was gradually forgotten and formally abandoned with the Treaty of Madrid between Portugal and Spain in 1750, producing approximately the boundaries of today.[29]

In 1759 the Marquês de Pombal, minister of José I, expelled the Jesuits from all Portuguese territory. As they wished, he forbade enslavement of Indians; but, as they did not wish, he ended the *aldeas* policy (by which the Jesuits had separated the Indians from the whites) and consequently made the Indians accessible as paid workers to be exploited by the colonists. The order had become "Brazil's largest landowner and greatest slave-master" (that is, of blacks not Indians). The Jesuits' disappearance removed the most influential of the orders, and in the next few decades the other orders were also destroyed or weakened; the consequence was the "enfeeblement of the Catholic church" in nineteenth-century Brazil.[30]

The administration of the vast area of Brazil, rapidly being penetrated though as yet far from settled, was confusing. Officials and clerics had overlapping and ill-defined jurisdictions, with few cartographers available to clarify boundaries. In 1763 the governor of Rio de Janeiro was substituted for the governor of Bahia as chief official with the title of viceroy, but other governors mainly ignored him. In the localities there were municipal councils appointed by the crown or elected by a small group of property holders. However, royal judges and, above all, the district militia officers (*capitães môres*) found it easy to interfere even with this limited form of self-government, and the militia officers "became a symbol of despotism and oppression."[31]

When Napoleon invaded Portugal in 1808, the Portuguese court escaped to Rio de Janeiro. The prince-regent replaced the previous mercantilist policy pursued by Lisbon by opening Brazilian ports to foreign trade, founding a Bank of Brazil, and encouraging local industry. The Creoles (Brazilian whites) welcomed such steps but resented the Portuguese newcomers who came with the court to compete for opportunities.

In 1820 a liberal revolution occurred in Portugal, and the leaders demanded that the king (as the prince-regent had become in 1816) return. He did, leaving his eldest son Dom Pedro as regent. But as the Lisbon regime sought to reverse the post-1808 concessions to Brazil, in December 1822 Dom Pedro rejected its demand that he too return home and was proclaimed emperor of Brazil. Thus, as an empire not a republic, the country became independent, with only minor protests at what had occurred. The first nation to recognize Brazilian independence was the United States; others, including Portugal, followed suit.

Independent Latin America, 1825–1914

Independence brought few immediate improvements. Blacks remained slaves or only nominally emancipated persons. Indians showed a preference for isolation and took little part in the political process even when permitted to do so. Mulattoes (half-black, half-white) and *mestizos* (half-Indian, half-white), "more aggressive than the Indians but distrusted by the Creoles," showed themselves ready— in the person of the *gauchos* and *llaneros,* the cowboys of Argentina and Venezuela respectively—for violence in redress of their grievances.[32]

As for the mainly Spanish (or Portuguese, for Brazil) whites, in most of the territory south of the Rio Grande[33] they were a minority consisting of landowners, clergy, and intellectuals. They were apt to be fiercely individualistic defenders of their privileges, unwilling to subject their liberties to the laws they enacted for the lower orders. Altogether the constitutions they wrote for the new states were honored as often in the breach as in the observance. And yet people from the ethnically and socially less-fortunate groups did on occasion break out and rise to positions of economic and political power.

For decades after Independence, throughout most of Latin America *hacendados* (owners of large landholdings or *haciendas*), clergy, and the military, often allied with merchants, supported local bosses *(caudillos)*—"violent men of destiny who broke all the bonds of national and social order"—but still kept up the pretense of republicanism and free elections. Their power base resided not in genuine political parties but shifting groupings based on the ties of *personalismo.*

Mexico and Central America

At the time of independence, Mexico was "Spain's most productive colony" and in 1800 may have had a per capita income about half that of the United States.[34] At Independence it also had the largest population of any Latin American nation — 5.8 million.[35] The central government did not control much of the country: *caudillos* ruled in many localities; Indian revolts disrupted order in the far north-west and far southeast; and regionalist pressures in Jalisco (around Guadalajara) led to tension, in Yucatán to civil war. Shafer sums up: "the chief features of government were instability, irresponsibility, and lack of funds. In its first half century the Mexican republic averaged more than one chief executive a year."[36]

The shaky northern boundary was threatened by what was happening in Texas, then Mexican territory. From the 1820s North Americans began entering Texas, at first with Spain's encouragement. But a few years later Mexico City tried to slow down North American migration and to increase Mexican migration, in vain. In 1836 a Texan constitutional convention declared independence from Mexico, and it first seemed as if Mexico and the United States would accept this as a lasting solution. However, events outran it: in 1845 Texas was admitted to the Union, and war was the result. In the Mexican War, concluded by the 1848 Treaty of Guadalupe Hidalgo, Mexico lost everything north of the Rio Grande.

A prolonged competition between Liberals and Conservatives erupted into civil conflict, from which eventuated Liberal ascendancy: its features included the Constitution of 1857, the presidency of the Zapotec Indian Benito Juárez, and the Reform Laws (1859–60) that confiscated all ecclesiastical property except the churches themselves (although much of it had already disappeared) and separated church and state.

However, the ambitions of Napoleon III of France and the concentration of the United States on its Civil War combined to permit a French invasion in 1862 that, two years later, installed Maximilian von Habsburg as emperor and his wife, the Belgian princess Carlotta, as empress. After the Union won its victory, American bolstering of Juarista forces and pressure on the French led them to withdraw their army, and in 1867 Maximilian was captured and shot.

In the period of Restoration (of the republic), Juárez reduced the size of the Mexican army from sixty thousand to twenty thousand and acted in a conciliatory way toward many French sympathizers despite liberal calls for revenge. He pushed through completion of the Mexico City–Veracruz railroad and appointed a commission that strove to reform education: primary schooling was proclaimed to be free and obligatory (unfortunately reality was recalcitrant), and favor was shown the positivist philosophy of Auguste Comte, which became official state doctrine in the 1880s. Juárez died in office in 1872.[37]

Four years later his successor was overthrown by a revolt led by Porfirio Díaz; he became president and soon effective dictator of Mexico until 1911. There were several regional *caudillos,* each with his own army, but Díaz was in charge. Under the Portfiriato, there was no political change but considerable economic development, spurred by the positivist intellectuals (termed the *cientificos*) who were apostles of "progress" rather than of democracy. Díaz managed to hire a British firm to drain Mexico City successfully, solving a long-standing and hitherto insoluble problem. His *cientifico* secretary of the treasury, José Limantour, brought order into governmental finances and greatly improved Mexico's image abroad. The result was an increase both in private investment and the importation of foreign capital. The economy grew, but popular income and consumption actually declined. On the surface Mexico "never had seemed more stable and prosperous." [38] And yet the Mexican Revolution was at hand.

As for Central America, the attempt at union of 1823 did not last long. A Liberal dictator, Francisco Morazán, presided over disestablishment of the Roman Catholic church, and Congress passed other anticlerical legislation. In the late 1830s the union fell apart. Guatemala, the capital of the colonial captaincy-general, tended to take the lead, but neither economic nor political success was achieved except for Costa Rica. There the intense educational effort of a minister (named in 1885), Mauro Fernández, paved the way for the later emergence of a functioning democracy.

The Andean Republics, 1815–1914

In 1830 Bolívar's creation, "Gran Colombia," [39] disintegrated into Colombia (then called New Granada and including Panama), Ecuador, and Venezuela; Bolívar himself resigned from office and died in bitter disappointment when about to sail for European exile. New Granada was composed of sharply differing geographical regions among which movement was difficult, and strict racial distinctions prevailed, separating the white elite from the Indian, African, and mixed lower classes. The elite valued intellectual achievement and produced some impressive talent; it took its politics very seriously, but the result was not a functioning system.

In the 1840s a revolution was put down by a coalition of moderates and former followers of Bolívar that became the Conservative party; the opposition took the name Liberal. But the Conservatives were also vaguely and romantically liberal. Under Bolívar's vice-president, Francisco de Paula Santander, much educational emphasis had been placed on the utilitarian writings of Jeremy Bentham, and his ideas continued to be influential. Conservative leaders hailed the "second French Revolution" in 1830. The Jesuits were welcomed back to New Granada in 1844 but chiefly for educational reasons; they were to be expelled, to return, and to be expelled again in the near future.

In the 1860s a sterner, more practically oriented view, positivism, reared its head. As in Mexico and other parts of Latin America, the technocratic bent of the followers of Auguste Comte mingled with the enthusiasm for free enterprise of the social Darwinian Herbert Spencer. The Liberals enacted the Colombian Constitution of 1863 (which officially abandoned the name "New Granada"). It carried federalism to an astonishing extreme—the states could even issue their own postage stamps—and confirmed or broadened freedoms. The Liberals also enacted anticlerical measures.

However, President Rafael Núñez, a Liberal who came to prefer order to liberalism, introduced a new constitution in 1886, which lasted with many amendments to 1936. It instituted a highly centralized system, by which the president appointed the governors and the governors named the mayors, and a concordat with the papacy was accompanied by a restoration of the church to a commanding position.

Núñez inaugurated a period of conservatism or even reaction that lasted until 1930; although he tried to found a new party, he and his successors allied themselves with the Conservatives. But both earlier and during that near half-century, political chicanery and violence, including civil war, were endemic. The worst episode took place in 1899–1902.

This disaster was followed by the loss of Panama in 1903. (Theodore Roosevelt may or may not have said "I took Panama," but it was approximately true in any case.) The consequence was construction of the Panama Canal and the cession —for all practical purposes—of a Canal Zone to the United States (until the administration of Jimmy Carter agreed in effect to retrocession). The Colombian electorate remained very small, although a law of 1909 resulted in minority representation in the Congress and cabinet, thus reducing political turbulence somewhat.

Ecuador, with a mostly Indian and *mestizo* population of fewer than one million (at Independence), was one of the poorer nations economically. In the fifteen years after the dissolution of Gran Colombia its political scene was dominated by General Juan José Flores—a Venezuelan of low birth and a military man, as in the case of other figures assuming leadership in independent Latin America, but who by marriage was able to enter the Quito nobility. In 1860 Gabriel García Moreno, a conservative Catholic, seized power. He raised the Roman Catholic church to an exalted position indeed; in 1873 the Congress dedicated Ecuador to the Sacred Heart of Jesus.

García was able to stimulate some economic growth and kept order for some years; but after he was assassinated in 1875, Liberals and Conservatives squabbled. General Eloy Alfaro, a charismatic figure who has been compared to Giuseppe Garibaldi, in 1895 led a liberal army into Quito and established a military government that severely restricted the privileges of the church. After he died in 1912 the Liberals and clergy managed to compromise. In 1916 "the debt-peonage of the sierra" linked to the law on imprisonment for debt was ended, and the life of the upland Indians benefited thereby.[40]

At Independence Venezuela also had fewer than one million people. Its first president was José Antonio Páez. A cowboy *(llanero)* who had become a general, he was "a typical lower-class caudillo" in whose leadership, writes Shafer, "Venezuela was on the whole fortunate" during most of 1830–46.[41] For example, in 1834 Venezuela was one of the first Latin American countries to legislate religious toleration. The country was less fortunate during the remainder of the one hundred years that followed Independence. After Páez, General José Tadeo Monagas and his brother alternated holding the power for fifteen years; from 1870 on, Antonio Guzmán Blanco for nearly twenty; General Joaquín Crespo in the 1890s, during which period the administration of Grover Cleveland insisted on an arbitration between Venezuela and Britain because "the United States is practically sovereign on this continent, and its fiat is law," but Crespo was otherwise not memorable. In 1909 Juan Vicente Gómez took power; he lasted, a repulsive despot, to 1935.

Thus in the half-century or so following Independence the Andean republics into which Gran Colombia had dissolved experienced an era of political turbulence, sometimes armed conflict, marked in each case by the strife between two parties bearing the names Liberal and Conservative, often decided by generals, with scant participation in the real politics of the period even by the small group that had the vote. some economic development occurred; the gulf between the white elite and the brown and black masses was bridged in the case of a few individuals only; corruption was widespread. In sum, democracy was no accurate term to describe the political system of Colombia, Ecuador, or Venezuela.

The most optimistic evaluation of change in the third quarter of the nineteenth century is that liberal reformers, despite the fact that their concerns were with the middle and upper social strata, "largely completed the job of clearing away the legal structure of individual and corporate special privileges inherited from the colonial regime and abolishing the most glaring restrictions—political, religious, and economic—on individual liberty." In six Spanish American countries, the final abolition of slavery took place from 1851 to 1854: Venezuela, Colombia, Ecuador, Peru, Argentina, and Uruguay, which had all adopted laws of free birth before or at Independence, now freed "the slaves born too soon to benefit from the free-birth principle."[42]

Farther down the Andes, the former empire of the Incas was beset by serious problems. Peru and Bolivia each had a small, mainly Creole minority that controlled politics, an Indian majority (foremost among the tribes: Quechua and Aymara) that had no vote, and an intermediate *mestizo* group growing in size. However, grave conflicts and tensions existed between and within both.

Bolivia had begun with Antonio José Sucre, Bolívar's favorite lieutenant, as effective and then formal president, but with the best of intentions he achieved little result. Andrés Santa Cruz became president in 1829 and created a confederation of Peru and Bolivia (originally Upper Peru), but it lasted only a short time (1835–36) and was broken up by Chile. Bolivia lost its seacoast to Chile in the War of the Pacific (1879–84), after which two parties, Conservatives and Liberals, emerged that were not very sharply opposed. Conservatives, among whom silver-mining magnates were strong, dominated from 1884 to 1899; thereafter tin replaced silver as the chief export and Liberals replaced Conservatives in the government—via a revolt. In this fight Liberals turned to Indians for help, but after victory disarmed the Indian troops and executed their leaders; politics returned to the hands of the 13 percent of the population that was white. The Liberals lost some eastern territory to Brazil in 1903 and split in two in 1914; the Republicans, as the breakaway party called itself, overthrew the Liberals in 1920 by force.[43]

As for Peru, it started with military aggression against neighbors north and south, which was generally unsuccessful. After the confederation with Bolivia collapsed, there was a period of civil war in the 1840s after which Ramón Castilla, a *mestizo* (in Peru the word used was *cholo*), emerged as *caudillo* from 1845 to 1862. It was then that the "guano era" began. Peru had discovered a bonanza in the form of bird droppings used for fertilizer that required merely to be shoveled onto ships bound for Europe in order to yield immense revenues. The money was mismanaged, however, and neither the economy nor the polity was stabilized.

In 1872 Manuel Pardo founded the Civilista party, the first "organized political party with a coherent program" in Peruvian history.[44] A year later Pardo was the first civilian president to take office. He tried without success to reduce the size and influence of the military. The army was unable to save Peru (which fought alongside Bolivia) from much suffering and the loss of some territory to Chile in the War of the Pacific, but retained most of its own power. A new elite emerged "whose political expression was the Civilist party," consisting of *hacendados* and bankers.[45] The *civilistas* startled Peru by backing their former enemy Nicolás Piérola, who was elected in 1895. He presided over what has been called the "Aristocratic Republic" (1895–1919), a period of unparalleled "political stability and economic progress."[46] He tamed the military by first reducing its size and then expanding it as a vehicle of social mobility for middle and even lower classes. As peasants migrated to the cities, a modern labor movement took shape. World War I brought further social change, and amidst mounting unrest twenty-five years of *civilista* rule ended in 1919 with the election of José Leguía, who promised reform.

The last of the Andean republics, Chile, had little more than half a million people. Despite the fact that it had been poverty-stricken before Independence, in many respects it "became the principal success story among the former Spanish colonies."[47] Its long, narrow shape was unique in the world; the smaller size of its "effective national territory" (a central valley of six hundred kilometers by eighty kilometers or less) manageable. Creole landowners held about eighty percent of the good land, the chiefly *mestizo* peasants being either their tenants or hired laborers.

The first government after Independence was headed by the father of independent Chile, Bernardo O'Higgins, who did much to open the country to British and other foreign trade and to encourage the development of the port of Valparaiso. He decreed prohibition of entail—by which a landowner could will transmission of his property from eldest son to eldest son in perpetuity—but the Senate he himself had appointed suspended the measure. He was driven into exile in 1823. O'Higgins's liberalism had been sometimes tactless, but his liberal ideas were shared by others. Later the same year Chile became the first Latin American country to abolish slavery; it also again prohibited entail, a measure reversed and reenacted until the practice was finally ended by law in 1857.

In the later 1820s there was a period of disorder from which the businessman Diego Portales rescued the country. Following a confused revolt of 1829, he became the chief figure in a government that accomplished the feat of subordinating the military to civil authority. Liberals, at first his targets and hostile to his policy, were won over. Taming the military, an action all Latin America needed, was achieved in Chile alone. Portales established a conservative political system, by way of the Constitution of 1833, which lasted almost a century—until 1925. It provided for a small electorate qualifying through literacy and property holding, an indirectly elected presidency, and Roman Catholicism as the state religion. Other Latin American constitutions of the period were similar; the difference was that this one was "functioning and viable" by European or North American standards, earning for Chile the reputation of being "the England of South America."[48] From 1831 to 1861 three elected presidents served ten years (two terms) each. Portales broke up the confederation of Peru and Bolivia by aggressive war, and he was killed by one army faction in 1837.

The Portalian state, as it came to be called, was a politically conservative system though a good deal of economic development occurred during the time it lasted. Parliament took an increasingly active role in governing; the presidency grew weaker. Both parties collaborated in furthering such change. Liberals managed to enact what amounted to religious toleration (long in de facto operation for Protestant foreigners) from the 1860s to the 1880s. Conservatives took the initiative in eliminating property (though not literacy) qualifications for voting in 1874. A Radical party, founded in 1861, was surpassed in its radicalism by the Democratic party (1887), which announced support for political democracy, labor legislation, and compulsory free education.

President José Balmaceda, elected by a reform of the early 1880s that awarded the vote to all literate males over twenty-five, tried to reverse the diminution of executive power, which had reached a point that a ministry needed support from a majority in Congress to stay in office (though the constitution provided for no such thing). However, he failed, only provoking a brief civil war during which his forces were overcome, and he committed suicide in 1891.

The victory of Congressionals did not mean governmental stability: From 1891 to 1915 there were no fewer than sixty cabinets, with an average life of just over four months.[49] During the 1890s the number of major parties increased from four to seven. Given the domination of the parliamentary leaders, "few of the eligible literate males thought voting worthwhile."[50] But signs of impending change appeared; industrial mining strikes increased during the 1890s and subsequently. Luis Recabarren led the growth of Marxism among workers, organizing the Socialist Workers party in 1912 and the Communist party in 1920. Congress responded by passing some labor legislation, beginning with workmen's compensation in 1916.

The River Plate Republics, 1825–1914

Independent Argentina was a country where the tensions between the provinces and Buenos Aires prevented real unity from emerging. Provincial leaders desired to annex Paraguay and Uruguay. Argentine troops were driven back from Paraguay. In a two-state war involving Argentina, Brazil, and Uruguayan armies, Brazil first managed to annex Uruguay, then lost it again. As a result of British mediation (and London's policy of fragmentation), Uruguay became an independent state in 1828.

Buenos Aires saw a struggle between federalists and centralizers. In 1819 a constituent congress adopted a centralist constitution that met with prompt rejection by the provinces. In what Argentines call "the terrible year twenty," the country fell apart politically. A government of the province of Buenos Aires began to put things back together. Later in 1820 landlords and military men called on the merchant and lawyer Bernardino de Rivadavia to head a liberal regime, and he responded.

The government in which he was the dominant figure sought to reduce the size of the army, created a new university, limited the role of the church, legislated freedom of worship (1825), and above all attempted to promote economic development. Rivadavia had a dream of making Argentina a part of the European world he knew and loved. It is often said that he appeared too soon. In any case he became president in 1825 but was ousted two years later.

Soon thereafter the federalists found a leader in Juan Manuel de Rosas, born in the upper class, who had become a sort of lord of the southern frontier.[51] Having earlier served as governor of Buenos Aires province, in 1835 he became dictator and ruled until 1852. His equally clever wife, Doña Encarnación, organized a kind of secret police called the Mazorca (Ear of Corn) that beat or killed the persons of the opposition and seized their properties. However, Rosas treated blacks and mulattoes with respect, espoused simple virtues and rejected complex foreign ideas as well as their supporters, and altogether achieved widespread popularity among the masses unaware that "his policies were not improving the life of the ordinary person but [were] inexorably concentrating landed property in a few hands."[52] He blamed the country's troubles on the Unitarios, the group seeking a more closely united country (though he had other enemies as well). The slogan "Death to the Unitarios" was printed on all official correspondence and laws and was required to appear on all newspaper mastheads.[53]

All of this, however, applied only to Buenos Aires province; the government was national only in name. Rosas joined with the other provinces to form an Argentine Confederation, which lacked a president, congress, or administrative apparatus but simply authorized Buenos Aires to handle defense and foreign relations for the country. However, Rosas gradually and cautiously extended his influence. His accumulated foreign and domestic enemies finally had enough. A coalition headed by his former ally, the governor of Entre Ríos, Justo José de Urquiza, in 1852 defeated Rosas in battle, from which the loser fled into exile in a British ship.

Urquiza summoned a convention that produced the Constitution of 1853— which lasted until the present (though it was replaced during the Perón years). It was federalist in substance, but set up a national government with a president, Congress, Supreme Court, and administrative apparatus. The constitution did not prescribe suffrage, but restrictions on universal male suffrage were judged to be excluded by implication—even though for decades longer in practice things were different. The best feature of the document was freedom of speech, which was actually put into effect.

Buenos Aires held out for a decade against acceptance of the new constitution. Urquiza served as president from Paraná, his modest (five thousand population) upriver capital. Then, after two brief civil wars, Buenos Aires rejoined the rest of the country under the governor Bartolomé Mitre, who then became president.

In 1868 he yielded the office to "the greatest of all Argentina's nineteenth-century liberals," Domingo Sarmiento.[54] Born of poor Creole parents, he early became a *unitario,* wishing to combat "barbarism" by means of education and economic development—both of which he hoped immigration would further. He declared, "an ignorant people will always elect a Rosas"; and he left Argentina with "clearly the best school system in Latin America."[55] He promoted the election of his minister of education, Nicolás Avellaneda, as his successor. One feature of his term as president was the "conquest of the desert," by which the Indians of the south, who had occupied much territory without using its resources, suffered severe casualties, and the survivors were confined to reservations (much as in the United States in the same period).

From the 1880s until World War I, the Argentine economy grew at a rate that left the rest of Latin America far behind. Railroad building was producing real national unity. Wool became the leading export, but live cattle and refrigerated beef, as well as wheat, were also important. The hopes of Sarmiento for a solid small farmer class built up by immigrants that would undermine the "barbarism" of the *gaucho* culture were disappointed—from 1810 to 1914 three million immigrated, especially from Spain and Italy, but many became tenant farmers or laborers. The white influx did much to eliminate blacks and Indians as recognizable groups. As for the *gauchos,* they virtually disappeared, though their ghost remained in the form of a growing cult of the no-longer-existent cowboy.

The oligarchic polity produced economic wonders but was thoroughly corrupt. Under General Julio Roca (president in 1880–86 and 1898–1904), the "conqueror of the desert," free compulsory public education (1884) was introduced; by 1914 60 percent of the population was literate. Buenos Aires was made a federal district, and the province had to build a new capital of its own—the result being to contribute to national unity in place of a favored but detached capital-province.

In the 1890s new political parties challenged the oligarchy: the Radicals, whose leader Hipólito Yrigoyen became, and the Socialists, led by Juan B. Justo. In 1905 Yrigoyen attempted an armed revolt, which was crushed, and after a short jail term led his party in boycotting elections. The oligarchy introduced a new electoral law providing for a free, obligatory, and secret vote for all males over eighteen. In addition, the party winning the largest vote would receive two-thirds of the seats in the Chamber of Deputies; the party with the second largest total would receive the other one-third.

Skepticism was replaced by astonishment; the reform worked. The Radicals elected Yrigoyen, who became president in 1916. Argentina was advancing economically at a rapid rate; politically there were hopeful developments. There was a disadvantage: "by 1914 Argentina was an economic colony of Great Britain." One Englishman cried, "Take Canada from us, but not Argentina."[56] There were, however, worse fates that had befallen nations at that point in history, and Britain did not at any rate control Argentine politics; some thought things might have been better if it had.

As for Paraguay, Creoles there managed to throw off domination of Buenos Aires, declaring independence in 1811. The population was for the most part Guaraní Indians, once having been reputed to enjoy the benefits of a Jesuit-led Utopia, by now poor subsistence farmers. For most of the time from 1811 until 1840 Dr. José Gaspar Rodríguez de Francia was dictator; he "largely sealed the country off from the outside world."[57] At his death Carlos Antonio López managed to end isolation and begin modernization. His son Francisco Solano López led the country into the Paraguayan War (1865–70) against Argentina, Brazil, and Uruguay, in which 50% of the population of half a million perished and Paraguay lost much territory. The impoverished country suffered from political turbulence thereafter. Edward Schaerer, elected president in 1912, encouraged economic growth, and World War I, by increasing foreign demand for Paraguayan foodstuffs, especially meat, brought temporary prosperity.

At Independence (1828) Uruguay had only sixty thousand people. Soon two parties formed: the conservative Blancos, or Nationalists, supported by Rosas, the Argentine dictator, and the liberal Colorados, representing the middle classes of the miniature (sixteen thousand-person) capital, Montevideo. In 1872, following a civil war, an agreement between the two parties granted domination over four out of the fifteen departments (provinces) to the landowner-clerical Blancos; in 1897 a Blanco rising resulted in increasing the number to six out of the then nineteen political units. Immigration made Uruguay a largely white country of over one million by 1908, and educational expenditures raised literacy to nearly 50% by the turn of the century.

In 1903 a Colorado journalist, José Batlle y Ordóñez, was narrowly elected president by the Congress and proceeded to end the curious political division of the country by appointing Colorados to posts in Blanco departments. The Blancos revolted; in a civil war with heavy casualties, Batlle won. He "dominated the political life of Uruguay" from 1903 until his death in 1929.[58] In the government now truly national in its geographical outreach, "elections were fair, the press free, and the army apolitical"[59] Since Batlle left undisturbed the economic domination of rural Uruguay by the owners of great estates, they tolerated him, and an era of relative prosperity and stability was ushered in.

Brazil, 1822–1914

Independent Brazil was an empire from 1822 to 1889. A Constituent Assembly drew up a constitution, adopted in 1824, that created a centralized government of four branches: executive, legislative, judicial, and "moderating."[60] The Parliament had a Chamber of Deputies elected for four years and a Senate whose members had life tenure. Indirect elections were provided for, the vote being confined to free adult males with an annual income of one hundred dollars or more.

The emperor in effect had both executive and "moderating" powers. He appointed a cabinet (responsible to him and removable by him), the presidents of provinces, and bishops; he could veto legislation; he could dissolve the Chamber of Deputies and hold new elections at any time; he was, however, required to consult the ten-man Council of State before exercising the "moderating" power. The constitution lacked a provision Dom Pedro much wished to insert but sacrificed for the sake of speedy approval of the document: abolition of slavery. The centralizing character of the constitution led the five northeastern provinces promptly to revolt and to declare themselves the independent Confederation of the Equator, but the rebellion was soon put down.

At the moment of Independence Brazil's economy was shifting from the production of gold, silver, sugar, and ships to coffee. With few Indians, Brazil imported many Africans as slaves; in 1822 there were more than one million. Seldom did a slave survive more than seven years' hard labor on a plantation or in a mine, and thus the slave trade was indispensable to maintain the labor force for the economy as then constituted.

The emperor, Pedro I, and his chief advisers were abolitionists. They placed their hopes on European immigrants not simply to replace slaves but also to raise the economic level of the whole country, and specifically to furnish soldiers for new elite units. The war for Uruguay in 1825–28 wrecked this hope. German and Irish soldiers and their families were attacked by the indigenous population; they replied by violence, the mutiny was bloodily suppressed, and Brazil was compelled to accept the independence of Uruguay. The slaveowners and their spokesmen were in the saddle. A treaty with Britain (1826) to stop the slave trade should have taken effect in 1830, but Parliament refused to furnish the means to enforce it.

Abandoned even by the army, Pedro fled in 1831. He left behind his five-year-old son, who acceded as Pedro II under a regency and was crowned at the age of fifteen. In the late 1830s Conservative and Liberal parties took shape; and the Liberals, identifying themselves with the majority of Pedro, were elbowed aside but then returned to power in 1844. The young emperor believed in the desirability of rotating the two parties in power and used his "moderating" power to bring that about. Brazilian participation in the Paraguayan War (1865–70) cost the country much in men and money and had the unpleasant result of inducing the army to interfere in politics. Pedro II, himself a Mason, refused to approve a papal encyclical forbidding Catholics to be Masons.

A struggle between the high clergy and government ensued; certain priests combined Masonry and abolitionism. In 1860 about half the population consisted of black slaves, and many Brazilians were aware that slavery had been abolished in Spanish America and would soon be in the United States. Finally, in 1871, the Rio Branco Law of the Free Womb enacted that every child henceforth born of a slave was free at birth. When he or she reached the age of eight, the former master could choose between commanding the child's labor until the age of twenty-one or a payment from the government; almost all slaveowners chose the former.

In 1881 Liberals pushed through the Saraiva Law, which substituted direct elections for the indirect system of choosing electors who then chose the deputies, and broadened the suffrage a bit—but still only 142,000 voters decided things for fourteen million.[61] Slavery was the burning issue; in the 1880s provinces and municipalities began individually to abolish it, and opinion turned increasingly against recapture of runaways. In 1888 emancipation without compensation was enacted by Parliament. In consequence many slaveowners deserted the empire.

Republicanism was growing, and a Republican party was founded in Rio de Janeiro in 1870. In São Paulo many Republicans were plantation owners; in Rio they were apt to be students and professionals; in the rural areas monarchists held sway. The Paulistas were underrepresented in government and leaned to federalism as a principal plank of a Republican platform. From 1887 some Republicans were thinking of making common cause with the army, where dissatisfaction was growing.

In 1889 a military coup d'état decided the course of events; the empire was overthrown, and "no one rose to defend [it]."[62] What came to be called the Old Republic was proclaimed; it would last from 1889 to 1930. But 1889 "did not mark a significant break in Brazilian history"; the economy rested as before on export of farm products and foreign investment; the oligarchy dominated. A new constitution (1891) created a federal system, in which the states possessed extensive powers, but the central government could intervene in the states. Suffrage was made "universal" but was conditioned on literacy, which meant that the electorate did not grow by much.[63] Tenure for senators, the Council of State, and the "moderating" power were abolished; separation of church from state was enacted. None of these reforms wrought the hoped-for "miraculous effects." "The main accomplishment of the Republic was to bring into power a new oligarchy of coffee planters and their clients."[64]

At first military men dominated the government and put down local rebellions, especially one of 1893, but the following year the civilian former governor of São Paulo, Prudente de Morais, was elected president and "government thus returned to the great [coffee-producing] estate owners" who remained in control until 1930.[65] Other Paulistas followed in the presidency: a notable example was Francisco de Paula Rodrigues Alves, "generally regarded as Brazil's ablest civilian president" (his term was 1902–6).[66] In the 1910 election the oligarchy was challenged by a new Civilista party, which was strong enough to hold "the first democratically elected nominating convention in the country's history."[67] Its candidate, Riu Barbosa, conducted an American-style campaign, unprecedented in Brazil, but was defeated in a far from free election.

The population remained largely rural and impoverished; the small contingent of industrial workers were poorly paid and enjoyed the protection of almost no labor legislation. But the real political power lay in the states, which could impose tariffs and export duties, raise militias, control public lands, regulate immigration, and contract loans from abroad. The *coronéis* (colonels of militia, often simply local bosses who had acquired that rank) were left alone by the state political machines "to fight out their rivalries at the level of the munipio," but the winners were expected to support the state bosses. The literacy required for voting limited those casting ballots to 4% or fewer up to 1930, and the caudilhos who ran the municipalities exercised effective control undisturbed by the people's will. As for the national scene, the machines of the two states of Minas Gerais and São Paulo, first covertly and then, from 1919, explicitly, alternated the presidency between them.

Mexico and Central America since 1910

During the first years of the century the long-lived Díaz regime began to accumulate effective enemies: Francisco Madero, who was wealthy but democratic in his views; Pancho Villa, chief of the northern cowboys; Emiliano Zapata, leader of land seizure by peasants. In 1911 followers of Madero drove Díaz to resign, and Madero was elected president. However, he soon faced dissatisfied Zapata men on the left and, on the right, Victoriano Huerta and other army officers and reactionaries, who murdered Madero in February 1913.

A period of violent confusion ensued. Huerta seized power but could not keep it. By now President Woodrow Wilson was determined to intervene on behalf of "decent government" but was unsure how to do so. Venustiano Carranza, honest but limited, cooperated with Alvaro Obregón in taking the capital; Huerta was overthrown. Wilson's forces were in Veracruz with no notion of what to do with it (they evacuated it months later).

At Aguascalientes a Revolutionary Convention assembled in October 1914. Pancho Villa temporarily became master of the situation. Obregón, recognizing Villa's political instability, fought and defeated him in April 1915 and drove him back north to Chihuahua. The weak Carranza government survived to summon a constitutional convention at Querétaro (November 1916 to January 1917), and it produced a basic document.

The Constitution of 1917 was strongly anticlerical: the church could not even own property; antihacendado: estates were to be broken up and village lands restored; antiforeign: aliens could not own land in certain areas and must promise not to appeal to home governments for support. The church was removed from all education except that it could operate private colleges. Other provisions legalized labor unions, regulated industrial work, and upheld the right to strike. With the adoption of a radical constitution, the Mexican Revolution was over.

Carranza was elected president without opposition and held the post from 1917 to 1920. Zapata was assassinated by Carranza's troops in 1919. Carranza threatened Obregón, but from the latter's base province, Sonora, came a determination to clean up the political scene. Carranza, forced to flee, was murdered. Obregón was elected president and managed to ride out his term by putting down a revolt in 1923–24.

General Plutarco Elías Calles won the election of 1924. His reforms designed to consolidate the revolution, like Obregón's, were not swift or numerous, but he took decisive action to implement the anticlerical provisions of the constitution. In 1926 the church proclaimed an imminent interdict,[68] but it had become an ineffective weapon; many Catholics then resorted to arms. The rebellion of the Cristeros smoldered for some time, was mediated by U.S. Ambassador Dwight Morrow, and by mid-1929 religious peace returned.

Obregón was assassinated when about to resume the presidency. Calles announced that there would be no more *caudillos* in Mexico, but still continued to rule as boss (*jefe máximo*) until 1934. In 1930 he halted land distribution, which had transferred twenty million acres to four thousand villages in the form of *ejidos*, or communal farms. They had not been a success; the peasants on them had no incentive to work. But in other respects the revolution had produced substantial changes in Mexican society without destroying the upper classes or private ownership. The Indian was finally honored, the pre-Columbian heritage highly valued. José Vasconcelos as minister of education under Obregón encouraged such attitudes by supporting the great radical muralists Diego Rivera, José Clemente Orozco, and David Alfaro Siquieros. Vasconcelos also helped build a new federal school system, and the national university became autonomous (1934).

In that year Lázaro Cárdenas, who has been compared with Franklin D. Roosevelt, was elected president. Adroitly he removed Calles's supporters and in 1936 sent Calles himself into exile. In 1938 he remade a loose governmental party into the Party of the Mexican Revolution (PRM), most of whose million members belonged to Vincente Lombardo Toledano's labor confederation (CTM) or a new peasant confederation (CNC), or both.[69] He doubled the number of *ejido* peasants, distributing forty-four million acres. (His successor, General Manuel Avila Camacho, distributed eleven million acres, but chiefly to peasant families rather than the dubiously successful *ejidos*.)[70] In March 1938 Cárdenas expropriated foreign-owned oil holdings, a sensational step that yielded greater benefit to national pride than to economic growth.

During World War II Mexican light industry developed, and, paradoxically, the military became a less important factor in politics. Beginning with the election of Miguel Alemán in 1946, all presidents have been civilians. Under Alemán Mexico prospered and built—highways, dams, and, most spectacular of all, the new University City to house the National University of Mexico. Alemán changed the name of the ruling party to Partido Revolucionario Institucional (Institutional Revolutionary party) without changing its character, and both corruption and waste were rife.

President Adolfo Ruíz Cortines was honest but had to deal with a problem not of his making. The population was increasing at a fantastic rate: from 1934 to 1958 it grew from about sixteen million to over thirty-two million.[71] In 1958 Adolfo López Mateos was the first president to be elected by women as well as men voters—it proved that the PRI's margin of victory was scarcely affected though the total number of ballots cast was increased.[72] López Mateos, "the most fondly remembered president of the postwar era," distributed some thirty million acres of land to both families and *ejidos* and embarked in 1960 on an unprecedented program of governmental construction of low-cost housing, much needed as the urban passed the rural population.[73]

Strenuous governmental efforts in rural education finally produced results: the percentage of illiterates fell from 28 (1970) to 17.1 (1980). But the extended prosperity of the period was ended by a sharp downturn in the economy in 1982; intellectual and some broader public opinion was troubled. In 1988 the single-party system was challenged by election results that left in doubt the position of the PRI. The country had rid itself of some chronic political ills, such as *caudillismo,* military ascendancy, and domination by the upper classes. However, Mexico was still seeking an orderly polity and economic stability.

In Central America the picture was mixed. In Costa Rica social reforms piloted through by Rafael Calderón Guardia in the 1940s and others by José Figueres in the 1950s did not remove substantial economic problems but produced a democracy that has survived into the 1990s, unlike her neighbors—amid much scholarly debate about how this remarkable situation came about. Herculean efforts to create democracy in Guatemala, El Salvador, and Honduras remained inconclusive in their effects.

A new element was introduced into the hemisphere with the victory of Communism on an island in the Caribbean. Cuba and Puerto Rico were the last remnants of the Spanish empire in the Americas. By 1817 Cuba had come to be the chief Spanish-American importer of black slaves, who made up about 39% of the population, the whites 42%, free blacks and mulattoes 20%. The importation of slaves continued.[74] In succeeding decades the economy boomed: by 1860 Cuba produced one-fourth of the world's sugar; the railroad built after 1834 in an arc south and east of Havana was the first in all Latin America and one of the first in the world.[75] A ten-year revolutionary war from 1868 to 1878 failed to win independence but helped induce the Spanish Cortes to pass in 1869 a free-birth law; slavery was completely abolished in 1886.

In 1898, as a result of the Spanish-American War, the United States acquired both Cuba and Puerto Rico. The latter became a territory and later a "commonwealth" of the United States. Cuba received nominal independence qualified by the Platt Amendment (1901), which provided for U.S. intervention in certain circumstances, until repealed in 1934. From 1933 to the end of 1958 Fulgencio Batista was effective dictator of Cuba. He was overthrown by a revolution led by Fidel Castro, who proclaimed the regime to be Communist in 1961. Thereafter Cuba belonged to the Soviet camp, though Castro made no secret of his disapproval of the reformist policies of Gorbachev.

Aside from the statelet of Grenada, there have been at least two unsuccessful attempts to spread Communism: in Chile under the Marxist president, Salvador Allende (1970–73), and in El Salvador by way of a prolonged guerrilla war, as well as a third apparently unsuccessful attempt, in Nicaragua under Daniel Ortega Saavedra from 1979 until his defeat at the polls in 1990. In the wake of Castro's victory new groups sprang up more or less ready to use violence in furthering their revolutionary aims, such as the Tupamaros in Uruguay and the guerrillas in Venezuela and Peru; Che Guevara, a close associate of Castro, was killed when trying to foment revolution in Bolivia. However, although Latin American leaders often used visits to or from Castro or Ortega to demonstrate their independence (or antipathy) in regard to the United States, they have been quite ready to suppress armed Communist rebels within their own borders.

The Andean Republics since 1910

Venezuela suffered from the long and brutal dictatorship of Juan Vicente Gómez from 1909 to 1935, but already from the 1920s oil began to yield enormous revenues. After Gómez died in 1935, two military men served as president for the next decade. The second was overthrown by a coup of younger officers who gave the leader of an oppositional coalition, Rómulo Betancourt, the provisional presidency. A new electoral law granted the vote to everyone over twenty-one, and other reforms were rapidly—too rapidly, as Betancourt later declared—enacted or seemed to impend. The dominant party, Acción Democrática, elected its candidate, Rómulo Gallegos, in 1947, but he was overthrown not long after inauguration.

Another military regime was installed, moving during the period 1948–58 "from the merely deplorable to the despicable."[76] A formidable coalition took shape and overthrew the regime. Betancourt was elected president once again, and from the time of his inauguration in February 1959 Venezuela, despite its "dreadful political history, installed open competition and free elections."[77]

Betancourt's party had aided Castro to come to power in Cuba, but leftists at first criticized his government and then resorted to guerrilla action and terrorism. He and his successors fought back, and deprivation of university autonomy in 1970 resulted in loss of important leftist bases (though many moderate students did not approve of the endemic violence). Poor agricultural methods and a rural scene dominated by large estates were combated by a law of 1960 expropriating holdings over 370 acres with compensation, a measure that had mixed results. Oil was a dangerously exclusive pivot of the rest of the economy, but the government did its best to diversify industry and exploit new mineral resources, especially in Guayana in the east.

Nevertheless in 1990 it could be argued that oil brought "deep social change" to Venezuela, and as a result "a combination of powerful mass organizations and strong, skilled leadership" produced "the oldest and most stable mass democracy in South America." In six consecutive national elections power was transferred peacefully, "the opposition replacing the government on each of the last four occasions (1968, 1973, 1978, 1983)."[78] In December 1988 another orderly election brought Carlos Andrés Pérez to power.

Colombia continued under the same sort of conservative governments that ruled in Bogotá from 1884 until 1930. Modest economic growth took place, based on the export of bananas and coffee and some industry. The Liberal party recaptured the presidency in 1930 with promises of state action to remedy social ills. Peaceful elections followed through 1946. President Alfonso López (1934–38 and 1942–45) led the elimination in 1936 of qualifications to vote based on literacy and property, introduced certain economic and social reforms, and removed mention of the church from the constitution. Liberals seemed to have achieved a lasting majority.

However, the apparent political tranquillity was shattered. In the election of 1946 the Liberals split their vote between two men, and the Conservative won with a minority of ballots cast. One of the two Liberal candidates, José Eliécer Gaitán, was assassinated in April 1948; his supporters turned to violence. The Conservative president, Mariano Ospina Pérez, killed, beat, and intimidated Liberals to a point where they withdrew their candidate. Thereupon, in November 1949, the pro-Fascist and pro-Falangist Laureano Gómez, newly returned from Franco's Spain, chalked up almost 100% of the vote. Soon, however, he turned to repression, and Ospina supporters were among his victims. In 1953 Gómez was overthrown, and his military replacement was in turn removed from office four years later.

From 1948 to the late 1950s "La Violencia" (the violence) as Colombians came to call it, involved guerrilla action undertaken or supported by the two parties— Liberal and Conservative—rather than class struggle and a mixture of motives that defy easy characterization. Certainly, "La Violencia" brought about the deaths of many—at least one hundred thousand—and destroyed much property.[79] In 1957 a curious agreement—the Declaration of Sitges—was reached between the two parties under which they would alternate in the presidency and share offices, and which would establish a system in which a two-thirds vote in Congress would be required on all matters of substance. This agreement was then approved by plebiscite.

On this basis the Liberal Alberto Lleras Camargo became the first president, and the agreement on the presidency was kept until it expired in 1974. Colombia enjoyed a talented elite, skilled at recruiting from the growing middle class, and able to avoid military dominance. She continued to suffer from some of the same economic ills that beset neighboring countries, such as *latifundios* little touched by land reform and *minifundios* in which farming methods were inefficient beyond belief. However, she was afflicted with a level of violence peculiar to herself; in the 1960s "La Violencia" of earlier times was joined by a new phenomenon— urban terrorism. By the 1980s, drug traffickers had become strong enough in scale to assassinate officials with impunity and drench much of society in corruption. The election of Liberal Virgilio Barco Vargas in 1986 brought into being a single-party government after prolonged coalition rule, headed by a man determined to break the power of the drug lords.

Ecuador lost territory to Brazil in 1904 and to Colombia in 1916, and yielded a large chunk to Peru by treaty in 1942 though its leaders subsequently and repeatedly denounced it. Its economy was very weak, its political history bizarre.

For years José María Velasco Ibarra was the central figure. "The archetype of the demagogue," he was expert at manipulating nationalist slogans. He was elected president in 1933, 1952, 1960, and 1968 and seized power in 1944, but only finished one of those terms.

Between 1948 and 1960 three civilian administrations managed completion, and many hoped the influence of the military had receded; it was not to be so. In Shafer's words, "when the junta of 1966 was ousted, that was the twelfth unscheduled change in administration since 1931."[80] A land-reform law took effect in 1965 and within a decade had begun to have palpable results. However, continued military ascendancy and political instability left the immediate prospects cloudy.

The turn of the century found Peru in the throes of trying to contend with nascent labor problems. In 1915–19 President José Pardo managed to get some laws enacted regarding child and female labor, but enforcement proved difficult. Students at the University of Lima joined workers in a general strike in January 1919, which failed.

In 1924 Victor Raúl Haya de la Torre founded the Alianza Popular Revolucionaria Americana (APRA); the announcement was made in Mexico and was intended to create a movement embracing the whole continent—a hope never realized. In Peru, however, this semi-Marxist (but not Communist) group attracted a considerable following. In the election of 1931, the first under a new law enabling all literate males over twenty-one to vote and to do so by secret ballot, APRA came in a respectable second to Colonel Luís Sánchez Cerro. Apristas now openly advocated rebellion and, responding to governmental repression, resorted to violence. Haya was imprisoned and then exiled.

Sánchez Cerro was assassinated in 1933, but his successor Oscar Benavides continued his policies. Banned from 1931 to 1945, APRA in a "fairly free election" won a majority in the lower house and half of the Senate; "understanding that it would not be allowed to elect Haya de la Torre," it used a cover name for itself and joined in a coalition behind José Bustamante.[81] However, the military overthrew him in 1948. APRA remained illegal under a regime that promoted economic development and even granted women the vote in 1955.

Thereafter APRA had political ups and downs. Haya topped the poll for the presidency in 1956, but Congress, exercising its prerogative to choose between the two leading candidates if none received one-third of the votes, elected Fernando Belaúnde Terry, a charismatic figure new to politics. He pushed through Congress a mild land-reform law in 1964 but a year later loosed the army on leftist guerrillas, which largely dispersed them. But he did not satisfy the military, which seized control in 1968.

The Peruvian military, considered "bourgeois" by the Left and leftist by the

Right, held sway for a generation.[82] The junta declared the aim of a "national revolution." It proceeded to distribute eleven million acres of land—a partially successful measure that broke the back of the ancient *latifundio* but left many small farmers in poverty—and pursued a program of economic nationalism, seizing foreign interests and insisting on Peruvian holding of a majority of stock in foreign companies.

General Juan Velasco Alvarado headed the military regime from 1968 to 1975, when a coup replaced him by General Francisco Morales Bermúdez, a man more supportive of private enterprise. A Constituent Assembly successfully produced a new constitution in July 1979, and the sophisticated civilian Belaúnde was returned to the presidency in the 1980 elections. In 1985 APRA's dynamic young candidate, Alan García Pérez (Haya had died in 1979), brought that party to the presidency for the first time. He had to contend with the mindless violence of the Maoist guerrilla group Sendero Luminoso (shining path) and grave economic problems.

In Chile the 1918 congressional elections swung the country somewhat to the left, followed by the 1920 election as president of Arturo Alessandri, an Italian immigrant's son who had transformed himself from a conservative lawyer into a spokesman for the lower classes. The Liberal Alliance for three parties (Radicals, Liberals, and Democrats) had a majority in the Chamber of Deputies but not in the Senate, which blocked much of Alessandri's reformist program. He was forced out of office in 1924 by a military coup; the following year he was recalled by Major Carlos Ibáñez, leader of another coup; he acceded after being promised a new constitution.

One was adopted: it separated church and state, provided for direct election of the president, and made the cabinet responsible to the president. But Alessandri was compelled to resign once again. Ibáñez became dictator-president and spent a great deal of money on modernization, which earned him the title of the first Latin American practitioner of authoritarian reformism, or "democratic Caesarism."[83] The Great Depression brought him down; he was forced in turn to resign in 1931.

Alessandri was soon elected once more and from 1932 to 1938 played a more centrist part than before. Leftists, responding to the Moscow Comintern's call for Communist collaboration with other leftists against the Nazis, produced a Chilean Popular Front, combining five parties with the new workers' confederation. It narrowly won the elections of 1938, electing the right-wing Radical Pedro Aguirre Cerda, but Congress was in the hands of the opposition. The Popular Front accomplished little and fell apart when Aguirre resigned for reasons of health in 1941.

Women were granted suffrage in 1949. Literacy and age qualifications limited the electorate, though literacy reached 80% in 1960 (and stayed there). Chile faced severe economic problems, and the post-1941 presidents were unable to make headway in dealing with them. New political groups sought voter support: FRAP (a leftist formation dating from 1956) and a Christian Democratic party (PDC) with roots reaching back to the 1930s but newly renamed and reorganized.

In 1958 Arturo's son Jorge Alessandri narrowly won the presidency, wishing to apply free-enterprise solutions but failing to resist pressures that frustrated them. In the "quiet and fair" election of 1964 the PDC leader, Eduardo Frei, received a majority of the vote.[84] He strove for "Chileanization" as a remedy for the country's economic ills, meaning not necessarily nationalization but more extensive indigenous ownership. He achieved only modest successes and was accused of subservience to the United States.

In 1970 a Chilean election shook the whole hemisphere. Salvador Allende, a Socialist[85] running on behalf of a coalition called popular Unity (UP: Communists, Socialists, Radicals), won 36.3% of the vote, the center-right Alessandri 34.9%, the PDC Radomir Tomic (Frei was barred by the constitution from running again) 27.8%. Allende believed in socialization of the economy by stages, and declared that "neither socialism nor communism was a creed for despotism —which raised doubts about either his candor or his understanding of the nature of communist regimes."[86] During his presidency, land reform attained breakneck speed; most farms of more than two hundred acres were expropriated and converted into state-controlled cooperatives; many land seizures by radical groups also took place. The result was rapid decline in agricultural output. Nationalization of mining, industry, and publishing proceeded rapidly, with some support from the traditional elites.

However, problems began to multiply. Inflation leaped upward to exceed 300 percent; the national debt rose sharply. Mounting turbulence climaxed in September 1973 when the Chilean military, previously proud of its apolitical reputation, intervened. It overthrew Allende, reported him a suicide, and installed a new government headed by General Augusto Pinochet Ugarte, "probably with the support of a majority of Chileans."[87] Chile soon was in the grip of "one of the harshest dictatorships of the contemporary world," though spartan policies effected a shift "from a state-supported, import-substituting industrialization model to an export-oriented economy with low tariff barriers and few government subsidies"[88]—and low inflation. In 1988 Pinochet attempted a plebiscite and lost. In December 1989 the Christian Democrat, Patricio Aylwin, was elected president, and Chilean democracy seemed to have been restored.

Argentina, Paraguay, and Uruguay since 1910

Yrigoyen's happy inauguration in 1916 began a fourteen-year period of Radical power. The Argentine president first reached some degree of accommodation with organized labor and then, after a general strike in January 1919 (when the army had to intervene), pulled back. The army became increasingly professionalized and the officer corps better educated. Yrigoyen, superb as a candidate for office but very poor as an administrator, returned, after an interval, for a second term in 1928. The Great Depression made his incompetence intolerable, and a coup led by General José Uriburu removed him in 1930. It was "the end of the constitutional continuity that had lasted for 68 years and also the end of the long period of economic expansion based on the export of raw materials."[89]

The conservatives now held power for thirteen years, until 1943. Uriburu aspired to head a corporative of Fascist regime. He won little support, and General Agustín Justo was elected—narrowly, even though the Radical candidate had been disqualified—as candidate of the coalition of National Democrats (conservatives), Antipersonalist Radicals, and Independent Socialists, termed the Concordancia. Justo's successors had to contend with World War II. There was support for the Axis among officers and outside pressure from the Allies; Argentina remained neutral. In June 1943 the army overthrew President Ramón Castillo.

After a confused period of transition, Colonel Juan Domingo Perón rose to power. Athlete, scholar, middle-class graduate of the military academy, he had admired Nazi and Fascist achievements while serving in Europe and was willing to imitate particular methods of theirs without seeking to duplicate their systems. As Secretary of Labor, he shrewdly built up worker support by promise and performance, resulting in an enormous increase in organized labor—from 10% of the labor force in 1943 to 60% in 1951—and a great number of new supporters of the government. Identifying himself with the so-called shirtless (*descamisados*), he declared that Argentina was (in 1946) "a country of fat bulls and undernourished peons."[90]

Perón achieved immense popularity. He fixed wages, prices, and rents by decree, expanded the welfare system, mobilized small gangs of toughs in some circumstances and large mobs in others to frighten opponents. In a complicated series of maneuvers, he rose to a position from which he could win the presidency as candidate of a new Labor party in February 1946. As El Líder he and his gifted mistress, Eva (often called Evita), whom he married just after the crisis of October 1945, rode on a wave of nationalism to great power.

In 1949 a new constitution was introduced; it provided for woman suffrage, an enhanced role for government, and immediate reelection of the president. Perón in fact received a second term, 1952–58, during which his policies became more conservative, partly as a result of Eva's death in 1952. His regime was authoritarian rather than totalitarian. He used intimidation against the opposition, but it could still operate openly in Congress and elsewhere; he purged the Supreme Court after a vote in the Chamber approving such action; he used a heavy hand on the press and the universities. Nevertheless opposition deputies, professors, and students continued to criticize his government.

Argentina had the most advanced economy in Latin America, but governmental costs rose high. Taxes were raised that were hardest on the poor (despite Perón's populism), and the agricultural sector was badly exploited. The damage Perón did to the economy helped lead to his downfall, but the precipitating factor was his anticlerical policy, which offended part of the military. They removed him from office in September 1955.

Argentina had a population more than 90 percent literate, the highest standard of living in Latin America, and the clear lead in modernization south of the Rio Grande. But the two decades that followed Perón's overthrow brought neither resumed economic growth nor restored political order. A series of military dictatorships ensued, several of which sought to reestablish constitutional government. In 1973 Peronistas gathered strength and at length managed to elect Perón himself president once more; he lasted only a few months and died in July 1974, leaving his wife to succeed him from the vice-presidency.

Isabel (so called, though her name was María Estela) Martínez de Perón tried to master the political turbulence and failed; a group of officers overthrew her in March 1976. In 1982 the military regime blundered into a war over the Falklands/Malvinas by seizing the islands and then were humiliated by suffering expulsion at British hands. In the wake of this needless disaster, the lawyer Raúl Alfonsín was elected president in October 1983, and the Radicals won a majority in Congress. He did his best to wrestle with the many economic and political problems he inherited but left behind an economy in disarray. The Peronista candidate, Carlos Saul Menem, surprised no one by being elected in May 1989 but surprised almost everyone by inaugurating a tough economic policy of the sort that had yielded spectacular success in Chile and Bolivia.

Paraguay remained poor and obscure. The Chaco region was the subject of a dispute with Bolivia that erupted into war in 1932–35, ending in a treaty by which Paraguay gained much of the contested territory, but the war had imposed heavy burdens on an already poor population. One dictator succeeded another. For thirty-five years beginning in 1954, General Alfredo Stroessner held power in "a country that in many ways remained in the nineteenth-century Age of the

Caudillos."[91] However, in February 1989 General Andres Rodriguez overthrew him in a military coup and in May was overwhelmingly elected to a four-year term as president, promising a transition to democracy.

In the twentieth century Uruguay started better than Paraguay but seemed to be finishing worse. José Batlle y Ordóñez was president for two terms but had a decisive influence whether he was in office or not. He finally pushed through a constitutional reform in 1917 creating a modified collegiate executive (since he admired the Swiss system) but one directly elected by the voters rather than the Congress. The reform introduced proportional representation (the party coming in first was to receive two-thirds, that in second place one-third of seats in Congress and a National Council of Administration) and sharply separated church (which had very little influence in Uruguay anyway) and state. Batlle nationalized utilities, much industry, and many banks. He began to nationalize railroads (completed in 1948). A welfare system, which included an eight-hour workday and accident and old-age insurance, made the country unusual indeed on the continent, though Montevideo benefited much more than the countryside from such measures.

To head off a Blanco coup, President Gabriel Terra with aid from the military carried out a coup that resulted in the constitution of 1934. Women had received the vote in 1932; voting was now compulsory for both sexes. The administrative council was abolished. A fully collective executive was created in 1951. It had nine members, six from the party winning the most votes and three from the runner-up, the chairmanship ("president") rotating among the majority group. The population stabilized, life expectancy was high, literacy exceeded 90% and embraced even the *campesinos*.

But the Colorados could not rule forever. Economic stresses multiplied; the export of wool and meat could not pay for everything. In 1958 a Blanco president was elected; some headway was made against inflation. In 1962 the party won by a much reduced margin; in 1966 Colorados regained power, and the voters ended the collegiate executive so that General Oscar Gestido was a real president.

However, problems multiplied. The economy remained in poor shape. The revolutionary group called Tupamaros (named after Tupac Amaru, the last Inca) carried out terrorist actions deliberately intended to destroy the system—even by provoking foreign intervention. Leftists formed a Broad Front that frightened the military, and others, by the size of the vote it gained in 1971. The military virtually suppressed the Tupamaros, took an increasingly active role in politics, and from 1973 were operating an authoritarian government. Uruguay was an immense disappointment to those who saw in it a model welfare state that others ought to emulate.

Brazil since 1914

The Brazilian military played a prominent role from the time the republic was established in 1889, and the dominant political elements were the *fazendeiros,* the owners of great coffee plantations. However, other forces gathered some strength around the time of World War I. In 1916 several groups merged to form a Brazilian Socialist party, and from 1919 on some modest labor legislation was pressed. In the 1920s São Paulo overtook Rio de Janeiro as the center of industrial growth, but Rio had more of its children in school. The national literacy rate, however, was only 30% in 1920. Religious miracles and prophets complicated the political scene; dissatisfaction with the oligarchy and nationalist idealism came to affect many of the younger officers of the military.

In 1930 the demands for reform came to a head, finding their center in the state of Rio Grande do Sul and its governor, Getúlio Vargas. He became the candidate of a Liberal Alliance and won 1.1 million votes, though the incumbent's chosen candidate was declared the winner with 1.9 million. A rebellion took place in October among the officers (and the enlisted men who followed them) of several provinces, and in consequence the military in general deserted the regime. A three-man junta replaced it, but Vargas made his way slowly north to Rio de Janeiro and became president. He held the post for a total of fifteen years.

Much of that time he ruled as a dictator; however, "he did not establish a police state, and his forgiveness of enemies was legendary."[92] During the years 1930–45 he made the federal government decisively superior to the states and promoted economic nationalism and industrial growth. He demonstrated consummate political skill, using the younger officers extensively but listening to everyone. Within weeks he dispensed with Congress, the state legislatures, and governors—whom he replaced, in most states, by interventors. The big planters and industrialists of São Paulo conspired to overthrow Vargas, launching a revolt in July 1932; Vargas crushed it but treated the vanquished very gently. He then had a Constituent Assembly elected that prepared a new constitution, hewing rather closely to the system of the 1891 document. The Constituent Assembly turned itself into Chamber of Deputies.

A Communist party, led by Luís Carlos Prestes, made itself heard on the left, while a new Integralista party emerged on the right. In 1935 Vargas replied to a Communist call for revolution by outlawing the party. A new Constitution of 1937, bearing little resemblance to a real constitution, established an Estado Novo (New State), in which the president was to rule by decree. All legislative bodies were dissolved, the political parties and states ceased to exist, the state militias were incorporated into the national army, and interventors responsible to the president permanently replaced state governors.[93] In 1938 the Integralistas attempted a coup against Vargas; they failed and were largely suppressed. Vargas had dealt with both political extremes, and World War II soon gave further reason for government by decree.

Under Vargas Brazil made progress, but more striking was the growth of bureaucracy and the assumption of government responsibility in the social and economic fields. Illiteracy was reduced, but in 1970 it was still not much under 40%. In 1945 three-quarters of employed Brazilians were still in agricultural or pastoral sectors of the economy, and the country remained extremely dependent on export. Nevertheless, industry made considerable headway in the Vargas period.

In 1945 Vargas announced elections. His followers organized not one party but two: the Brazilian Labor party (PTB) and the Social Democratic party (PSD). An anti-Vargas Democratic National Union (UDN) also took shape. There were now nearly six million voters, literate women having been added to literate men. General Eurico Dutra was elected, Vargas retired, and a Constitution of 1946 restored the parties, states, state legislatures, and state flags that the so-called Constitution of 1937 had abolished. The Communist party, the largest in the hemisphere, having announced that it would fight for the USSR in the event of a war with Brazil, was suppressed as the result of a decision by the Supreme Court, pressured by an embarrassed Dutra.

In general, however, a new period of political participation and activity ensued. Vargas now reappeared in politics as a friend of representative government and the poor, and was elected president again in 1950. Inflation and other economic problems bedeviled the new Vargas government. Finally, in 1965, a murder of an air force major was traced to Vargas's bodyguard; in August high officers took the evidence to Vargas and demanded his resignation. Instead he committed suicide.

After a brief period of confusion, the governor of Minas Gerais, Juscelino Kubitschek, was elected president (with only 36% of the vote). For five years he spent money freely to encourage economic development, a policy symbolized by the building of a new capital, Brasília, in the interior. But he ignored inflation and corruption. In 1960 the revulsion at both these chronic ills led to the election of Jânio Quadros, governor of São Paulo. As president he was honest but incompetent, and the astonishing achievement of electoral victory by anti-Vargas forces after thirty years of being out of office ebbed away to nothing; Quadros resigned in 1961.

The vice-president, João Goulart, who had been Vargas's protégé and presumed successor, was allowed to return from abroad and succeed Quadros only on accepting a constitutional amendment establishing a parliamentary system, under which the president had little power and the prime minister much. Nevertheless, within a year Goulart had regained the former powers of the presidency via plebiscite, but he rapidly alienated the military and the propertied elite by turning to the left, proposing radical division of the great estates and other measures, such as suffrage for illiterates and enlisted men. In April 1964 the military overthrew him.

Marshal Humberto Castello Branco, former army chief of staff, became president and instituted indirect election of the president and reduction of political parties to two. Several military leaders followed him, none for long. Under military rule, economic growth to a point some were calling an "economic miracle" took place, but the regime was repressive and brutal with the opposition.

In 1985 the electoral college chose the governor of Minas Gerais and candidate of the opposition party, Tancredo de Almeida Neves, as the first civilian president since 1964. However, he fell ill and died before he could assume office. Vice-President José Sarney, leader of a dissident faction of the ruling party that had joined with the opposition to support Neves, took over. His government restored direct presidential elections and gave the vote to illiterates. However, Brazil was afflicted by mountainous economic problems: a gigantic foreign debt, high inflation, much increased unemployment, and a stagnant gross national product. Much of the population had not yet been drawn into the politically concerned or active citizenry. The *fazendeiros* and military had not been decisively replaced as arbiters of the national destiny. In October 1988 a new constitution was promulgated. In December 1989, a conservative candidate, Fernando Collor de Mello, edged out a radical; he plunged ahead with needed reform. In Brazil freedom flickered like a candle—now bright, now dim.

Conclusion

Robert Shafer, writing in 1977, discerned five kinds of political groups in Latin America: those who preferred evolution to revolution as the way of progress; those concerned only for lessened "dependency"[94] on the United States and other outside forces; those intent on economic development by whatever methods attained; those interested in social justice alone; those who "think the ultimate test is whether Latin America has open or closed societies, democracy or autocracy."[95] Those five groups overlap, and it is not necessary to confine one's preoccupations to a single value—political, legal, economic (or intellectual or spiritual, a congeries of values Shafer does not mention). What one can affirm with confidence is that unless freedom in all the realms is reasonably well secured in any given country of Latin America, the prospects for prosperity, economic growth, human rights, and happiness will remain clouded.

The economies of Latin America have suffered from several ills: runaway inflation (recently nearing 2,000% in Brazil), the heavy burden of foreign debt (for which reckless American banker-lenders must share the blame with Latin American borrowers), and population growth so rapid that it overtakes efforts at social welfare. The continent has placed much faith in industrialization, and government intervention to hasten it has not always been successful. It has recognized the desirability of land reform, seldom with the strength to accomplish it on any significant scale or the skill to carry it out wisely, though Mexico, Bolivia, and Cuba have done so roughly and without compensation and Venezuela is doing so with the money to repay estate owners. For the rest, the great *hacendados/fazendeiros* remain in the saddle, while the Indian and other peasants continue to be outside the modern world—leaving aside the question whether they prefer to remain so.

As for politics, the picture is mixed. Governmental centralization has broken down the rule of local and regional despots under various names and titles and immensely strengthened the national executives. The suffrage has been extended, with elimination of property, literacy, and gender qualifications. Political parties have taken various forms but in general have become a settled feature of the political landscape. The depressing phenomenon has repeatedly surfaced of the good candidate who is a bad president: for example, Yrigoyen in Argentina or Velasco Ibarra in Ecuador. Even the good president, when he or she appears, has grave difficulty in uniting the citizenry or imparting to it any shared vision of the nation's future.

The weight of the military in Latin American history since independence has been enormous. Otherwise it might have been possible to avoid or shorten such prolonged, devastating, and ultimately inconclusive conflicts as the War of Paraguay against Argentina, Uruguay, and Brazil (1865–70), the War of the Pacific (1879–84) between Chile, Peru, and Bolivia, and the Chaco War (1932–35) between Bolivia and Paraguay; and, at least as important, to prevent the military coups that made a mockery of constitutional and democratic processes so often and in so many countries—despite the fact that military rule was not always worse than civilian rule and that generals were sometimes also effective reformers. The preponderant Roman Catholic church retains its hold on the great majority and politically has retreated from quite unequivocal support of traditional orders to an apolitical stance, encouragement of liberal reform, or, with increasing frequency, an astonishing leftist radicalism.

Many attempts have been made to cast a balance sheet regarding which political trends are in the ascendant: in recent decades several military coups have displaced civilian governments, and certain countries have seen long, painful histories of struggle for democracy seemingly reversed and at least temporarily forgotten. Nevertheless, at the turn of the last decade of the twentieth century, the advance of democracy in Latin America was clearly the prevailing current, whether or not it was to be long-lasting. A recent assessment was that "it was evident that the long-range trend in Latin America was toward more government by law and by the people."[96] For a continent and a half that has faced immensely difficult problems of multiethnic populations, colonial and foreign oppression (along with benefits), and delayed or attenuated development of national consciousness—through which alone so many problems of the modern world appear capable of being addressed—that statement might occasion some satisfaction with the present or even optimism for the future.

Conclusion

Freedom—or pluralistic society, constitutional government, or democracy—is, to be sure, not the only value in the social or political context. It has not protected the societies of the West and Japan from the suffering and destruction of war, the misery and want of economic depression, the discrimination or oppression that has afflicted minorities—racial, ethnic, religious, or other—the miscarriage of justice for individuals or groups, the unjust deprivation of property or unreasonable restrictions on its use, the inefficiency and incompetence of bureaucracies, the lack of courage of public officials.

Free societies have not eliminated individual or group fears and hatreds. They have failed to inculcate in all their inhabitants respect for their fellow citizens, a readiness to compromise or to accept defeat in legally conducted political struggle, to bear private burdens for the public good, the habit of gratitude or praise when long-denied justice is finally done, the acceptance of civility as the standard governing all public discourse no matter with how despised an enemy. Many citizens of a democracy fit the following description:

He enjoys the liberties hard won over centuries by the alliance of philosophic genius and political heroism, consecrated by the blood of martyrs; he is provided with comfort and leisure by the most productive economy ever known to mankind; science has penetrated the secrets of nature in order to provide him [with the rock music he is listening to; and yet much of the teen-aged and twenties generation is entirely absorbed in this subculture of the subnormal.][1]

The passage refers to an adolescent, but its substance may apply to any adult who may have ceased to listen to rock (if he or she ever did) but is unaware of his or her blessings, political and economic, and how they came about. Our educational system needs to be better; at present any survey, no matter how superficial, yields examples of absurd misconceptions and horrifying ignorance—partly because the subjects surveyed are currently taught only very poorly or not at all. But even if our schools were improved, it would remain true that the young do not understand the travails and sacrifices of previous generations—of course they never do, although it is possible that American youth did respect them more, say, a half-century ago.

Part of what scandalizes the educated person about all this applies chiefly to the United States, but part is common to all democratic countries and results from a surfeit of prosperity, technological wonders, and labor saving. The best that can be said of them is, to paraphrase Winston Churchill, that they are the worst possible societies except for all the others; or, from another angle, they provide the instruments to be preferred over all others known to humans for correcting ills, offering hope for economic betterment, and living in peace.

The view of history set forth in this book is based on the recognition that there are all sorts of societies and a variety of paths of development that a society may follow. A few examples may help. Both Russia and China began with protopluralistic societies and became monist for centuries before moving in the direction of pluralism again, fell back into total monism, in the last years showing renewed shoots of pluralism. As for Italy, it enjoyed republican institutions, next an autocratic empire took over then gradually disintegrated, then semifeudal institutions existed for some time and yielded to a gradual process of unification and democratization—from rough pluralism to monism to complete pluralism. Beginning much later, France and England marched from pluralistic feudalism almost straight, even if painfully and slowly, to pluralistic freedom. Japan tried to copy Chinese monism, failed, but then developed its own variety of feudalistic pluralism from which it could leap spectacularly and swiftly to freedom. (Important ethnic changes occurred in several of these countries while there were occurring the institutional changes in question, but it seems very difficult to find any connection between ethnic and institutional change.)

The conclusion that follows from these examples of sequential development is that there is no inexorable series of phases of history, bearing the names "modes of production" or something else, through which mankind has had to pass or need to be expected to pass in the future. "Modernization," a popular category for explaining world history during the past few decades, certainly has affected every part of the planet to some degree, but the incontrovertible kernel of modernization is technology—which has, to be sure, affected men's lives in a breathtaking number of respects, ranging from air travel to television to flush toilets to immunization to refrigeration to plastics to computers. The borrowing of Western technology has neither secured freedom nor prevented tyranny and acts as no determinant of institutions. Far from assuring liberty, it may greatly ease the task of oppression for the tyrant, as Evgeni Zamiatin forecast in his novel *We*.[2]

If the Marxist sequence—slavery, feudalism, capitalism, and socialism, with the possibility of substituting the Asiatic mode[3] for the first two—cannot be depended upon to bring about human liberation[4] and modernization cannot be relied upon either, what can one say of the future?

This author and probably most of his readers will assume that freedom is a positive value, and that a free, pluralistic society, founded on the rule of law and strong property, is the likeliest to produce a happy and prosperous population, and the best thing to do is to try to create one where none exists. Unfortunately many believe that the way to success is to use the time-honored Western devices for obtaining reform—writing pamphlets, signing petitions, holding mass meetings, passing resolutions, marching in the streets, and shouting slogans or displaying them on signs. The assumption has often been that evil men, either in non-Western countries or in Western capitals, are responsible for nonfree systems, and if they can only be driven out (or worse) all will be well, or at any rate very much better.

Those methods are likely to work only in societies that already have a heritage of partial freedom. Instances are easy to find in which driving out the allegedly tyrannical incumbent has been followed by something as bad or even worse—Park Chung-hee by Chun Doo-hwan, the Shah of Iran by Ayatollah Khomeini, Idi Amin by Milton Obote (granted, not quite as bad). There are institutional prerequisites for democracy, and without them demonstrations or even elections may be unable to produce the system desired.

"Crossing the institutional divide" (a phrase that seems to be Karl A. Wittfogel's invention)[5] is the great unrecognized issue of our time. Much public discourse about the Third World proceeds from the assumption that the course of development for mankind has been and will be unilinear; the categories specified for past, present, and future may be rough or primitive, but the assumption is very widely made. Thus one is told that Bangladesh, for example, is "two hundred years behind" the United States or (unwittingly adopting the Marxian category for an area for which Marx himself would never have been so foolish as to use the term) that Saudi Arabia, say, is "still feudal" because it demands women be veiled.[6]

The Marxist-Leninist unilinear scheme (though it was not the view of Marx himself, as pointed out earlier) in which slavery, feudalism, and capitalism are to be found everywhere as a prelude to the inevitable socialism is professed and often acted upon by the USSR. However, there are other unilinearisms. Foreign-aid programs and foreign-policy pronouncements are drawn up in Washington, D.C., but also in other Western capitals on the assumption that what is needed, or possible, is for the United States, or Britain, or Sweden to push, drag, or nudge the Third World along the same path they themselves have traveled hitherto. Raymond Aron is one of those who have questioned the unilinear view of history: "if the truth of the Asiatic [mode] of production is admitted, two types of society, fundamentally different, and two kinds of evolution must be recognized."[7] There may be more than two, if we look hard enough. In any case a single path for civilization, in the past or future, cannot be assumed.

Another assumption is that Americans (or others) may expect to remake economic institutions, the environment, or health care in Third World countries independently of politics, avoiding governmental interference with the foreigners trying to help and being rewarded by official gratitude because of the obvious selflessness of the efforts concerned. (A recent horrifying instance is the attempt of Westerners to carry famine relief to Ethiopia, where the problem was partly created and the solution partly impeded by the policy of Mengisthu.) It may at times be prudent to pretend that the economy or medical care are separate from politics—but they are not.

Bangladesh or Saudi Arabia or some other such country may indeed cross the institutional divide. But it may not be the choice of the people—in the country concerned—even to try, or to persist if it proves difficult, costly, or painful to do so. The safest course for a foreign observer is to urge that the attempt be made only if the governing group (with, one would hope, the consent of the people even if democracy is still impossible) is fully conscious of the goal, committed to work toward it, can find some real or alleged domestic roots for the tree they wish to grow, and can hope for some support or encouragement abroad.

There can be undue and suicidal haste in the search for democracy. The late Andrei Sakharov declared, in his 1975 Nobel lecture: "We need reform, not revolution. We need a flexible, pluralist, tolerant society"—not, we need instant democracy, which he knew to be out of the question.

It would then be desirable to explain two things to different audiences: To the conservatives and traditionalists: that the past, even if it lays heavy burdens on the present, does not exclude trying to create a different society that can preserve much of what is good in tradition. To radical student leaders and journalist-critics: one election does not create democracy, a second party does not necessarily mean a responsible or viable opposition, and the best place to chart the future course of a distant land is *not* the streets or campuses of the United States where howling mobs with signs cavort by day but are able to go home at night without fear of suffering the consequences of their simplistic nostrums (usually formulated more with their domestic opponents in mind than inhabitants of the remote places whose names appear on their placards).[8]

One of the most astute of our political scientists, Hannah Arendt, and the first to offer an extended analysis of totalitarianism, argued in 1968 that "the crisis of the present world is primarily political" and that the decline of the "Roman trinity of religion, tradition, and authority," along with the undermining of Roman political foundations, is at the root of our troubles. She argues that "new political bodies" may be needed to restore to "the affairs of men . . . some measure of dignity and greatness."[9] For Arendt, "to be human and to be free are one and the same."[10]

If Arendt had lived to early 1990, she would have seen political freedom, which she placed ahead of philosophical freedom,[11] come to be valued throughout the earth as never before—to the astonishment and delight of millions, though some on the extreme right doubt the depth and durability of recent changes, and some on the extreme left are afraid that capitalism may flourish along with freedom.

This long journey might end with a couple of straightforward, simple definitions (or evocations) of freedom from England and Russia respectively. The first comes from William Pitt the Elder, defender of the unruly American colonists, debating the excise bill of 1763:

> The poorest man may in his cottage
> bid defiance to all the force of the Crown.
> It may be frail;
> The roof may shake;
> the wind may blow through it;
> the storms may enter,
> the rain may enter, —
> but the King of England cannot enter.[12]

The other was composed by Russian revolutionaries, possibly by Nicholas Chernyshevsky, for dissemination among peasants, but might indeed strike near the level of peasant comprehension: "Now here's just what real freedom is on this earth: the people are everyone's leader and every official is obedient to the popular assembly.[13] Courts are just, and courts treat everyone the same, and no one dare treat the peasant improperly. The [internal] passport does not exist, nor does the head tax. Military conscription does not exist. Now that's freedom like freedom really is."[14]

Freedom is essentially simple; it is based on the natural wish of the human being not to be interfered with or, in the complex world of the late twentieth century, to suffer no more interference from higher authority than necessary to assure the "general welfare"—as the Founding Fathers put it—to protect the country and the human race from the consequences of their willed or unintentional folly in myriad directions, to lessen pain and increase happiness.

But attaining freedom—that is, creating and maintaining a free society—is extremely difficult and has eluded the best efforts of many a would-be liberator or liberating army or party or group. For those who would undertake the task, study and reflection on the past ought to be the bedrock on which the edifice rises. In the words of T. S. Eliot:

> And the end of all our exploring
> Will be to arrive where we started
> And know the place for the first time.
> Through the unknown, remembered gate
> When the last of earth left to discover
> Is that which was the beginning . . .[15]

This is of course not the end of history.[16] However, owing to the devoted labors of scholars in recent times especially, one can traverse the whole path from the beginning to the present and understand the chief lines of the story in a way that a century or two ago could not be done in anything like the depth now possible.

Free societies embrace much more of the planet than in the time of Pericles or the Hebrew prophets and have cast aside many institutional constraints to which the ancient world clung. Nevertheless one may discover that man is the same now as then; the state of being free is not significantly different for the modern American or Japanese as compared with the ancient Greek (the freeman, not the slave) or Hebrew. Raymond Aron cites as hypothesis "that freedom is the strongest and most enduring desire of all mankind" in the context of discussing, in 1965, the future of Soviet Communism,[17] a proposition that might have served as a prediction of the remarkable events of 1989–90 throughout Eastern Europe in particular. But under whatever institutions man lives, the human spirit has been and remains everlastingly free.

Notes

Introduction

1. George Shultz, "National Success and International Stability in a Time of Change," in *Thinking about America: The United States in the 1990s,* ed. Annelise Anderson and Dennis L. Bark. Stanford, 1989, 519.
2. Francis Fukuyama, "The End of History?" *The National Interest* (Summer 1989):3, 4.
3. Herbert J. Muller, *Freedom in the Western World: From the Dark Ages to the Rise of Democracy.* New York, 1963, xiv.
4. Herbert J. Muller, *Freedom in the Modern World.* New York, 1966, ix.
5. Other volumes with apparently similar titles have quite different contents. For example, Benedetto Croce's *History as the Story of Liberty* (translated from Italian), New York, 1941, is a meditation on the issue, not a history of it. To be sure, the original Italian title is quite different: *La storia come pensiero e come azione* (History as thought and action).
6. Gertrude Himmelfarb, address in *Our Country and Our Culture: A Conference of the Committee for the Free World.* New York, 1983, 50.
7. In a demonstration on the Stanford University campus, the mob's shouted slogan was "Hey, hey, ho, ho, Western culture's got to go."
8. Herbert Butterfield, *The Whig Interpretation of History.* 1931; reprint, London, 1959, v, 3–4.
9. Ibid., 109.
10. What I mean here is "Greek freedom" rather than "Jewish freedom." The two phrases are explained more fully in the chapters that follow, but in brief: Greek freedom is a relatively rare phenomenon in history, based on free or partly free institutions; Jewish freedom is existential and is the possession of all human beings past and present.
11. Herbert J. Muller, *Freedom in the Ancient World.* New York, 1961, 192.
12. James A. Michener, *Poland.* New York, 1983, 189–90.

417

13. Shultz, *Thinking about America*. Continues without a break the passage cited in note
    1 above.
14. Donald W. Treadgold, *The West in Russia and China*, vol. 1, *Russia: 1472–1917*.
    1973; reprint, Boulder, Colo., 1985, xxi.
15. John E. E. D. Acton, 1st Baron Acton, *The History of Freedom and other Essays*,
    London, 1907, 39.
16. There were, of course, minor conflicts in Europe, brief in duration and limited in
    territory affected. Outside Europe, there was bloodshed enough in the American Civil
    War and the T'ai-p'ing rebellion in China.

Chapter 1

1. William Foxwell Albright, *From the Stone Age to Christianity: Monotheism and the
   Historical Process*. 1940; reprint, Baltimore, 1957, 198.
2. John Bright, *A History of Israel*, 3d ed. Philadelphia, 1981, 36.
3. Thorkild Jacobsen, "Mesopotamia," in *The Intellectual Adventure of Ancient Man: An
   Essay on Speculative Thought in the Ancient Near East*, ed. H. and H. A. Frankfort et
   al. Chicago, 1946, 202–4.
4. Thorkild Jacobsen, "Primitive Democracy in Ancient Mesopotamia," first published
   in *Journal of Near Eastern Studies* 2 (1943); and Geoffrey Evans, "Ancient Mesopotamian Assemblies," first published in *Journal of the American Oriental Society* 78 (1958),
   both reprinted in *Problems in Ancient History*, vol. 1, *The Ancient Near East and Greece*,
   2d ed., ed. Donald Kagan. New York, 1975. Evans refines Jacobsen's original argument.
5. George E. Mendenhall, "Law and Covenant in Israel and the Ancient Near East."
   Reprinted from *The Biblical Archeologist*, Pittsburgh, 1955, 10.
6. Dietz O. Edzard, "Mesopotamia and Iraq, History of, 1 and 2," *Encyclopaedia Britan-
   nica* (hereafter cited as *EB*), 1974, 11:980.
7. T. G. H. James, "Egypt, History of, 1," *EB*, 1974, 6:460.
8. Ibid., 462.
9. See the remarks in Muller, *Freedom in the Ancient World*, 96 and 98.
10. Wolfram Th. von Soden, "Mesopotamia and Iraq, History of, 2," *EB*, 1974, 11:980.
11. One unresolved problem is the role of the Hurrians; they apparently came to be the
    foremost ethnic component of the Mitanni population and founded some smaller states
    to the west. Their racial or linguistic character is uncertain, but leading elements
    were evidently Indo-Iranian.
12. This masquerade had its parallels elsewhere in history. Ivan the Terrible established
    a shadow monarchy in half of Muscovy over which he pretended not to rule; Peter the
    Great delighted in a plethora of mock ceremonies in which he pretended not to be tsar
    at all and paid homage to others assigned to act in that capacity.
13. Karl A. Wittfogel, *Oriental Despotism*. New Haven, 1959, 90.
14. Bright, *History of Israel*, 74.
15. Peter J. Parr, "Syria and Palestine, History of," *EB*, 1974, 17:940, gives this interpre-
    tation. I find it more convincing than others.
16. Harry Thomas Frank, *Discovering the Biblical World*. New York, 1975, 66.
17. Yehezkel Kaufmann, *The Religion of Israel: From Its Beginnings to the Babylonian Exile*.
    Translated and abridged by Moshe Greenberg. Chicago, 1960, 2. This volume is an

abridged translation of seven volumes out of the eight published under this title up to 1956.

18. William A. Irwin, "The Hebrews," in *Intellectual Adventure of Ancient Man,* ed. H. and H. A. Frankfort et al., 227.
19. Quoted in ibid.
20. Martin Noth, *The History of Israel,* 2d ed. New York, 1960, 88.
21. Bright, *History of Israel,* 163.
22. See "Israel: 3. History of Israel," in *New Catholic Encyclopaedia.*
23. Mendenhall, "Law and Covenant in Israel and the Ancient Near East," 18.
24. Ibid., 19.
25. Albright, *From the Stone Age to Christianity,* 285.
26. See the treatment in Bright, *History of Israel,* of the period of Judges and Kings.
27. Ibid., 204.
28. Seymour Cain, "Biblical Literature, 3 and 4a," *EB,* 1974, 2:897.
29. Bright, *History of Israel,* 265.
30. Ibid., 2695
31. Frank, *Discovering the Biblical World,* 130–31.
32. L. H. Silberman, "Judaism," *EB,* 1974, 10:290.
33. Irwin, "Hebrews," 352.
34. Ibid., 359.

Chapter 2

1. See the interesting three-part article entitled "Urban Revolution" (to which the reader is referred who tries to look up the term "Civilization") in the *International Encyclopaedia of Social Sciences,* vol. 16. New York, 1968. V. Gordon Childe, a leading Marxist anthropologist, is cited as advancing two criteria as marking "the first achievement of a civilized way of life": the formation of cities and the invention of writing; the earliest instance is given as the lower plain of the Tigris and Euphrates, in which irrigation was used to supplement rainfall for agriculture. The concept of civilization is traced much further back, but special weight is given to the part played by Lewis Henry Morgan, who in turn much influenced Marx and Engels, in formulating the concept.
2. John Chadwick, *The decipherment of Linear B.,* 2d ed. London, 1970. This is the detective story, as it were, for the layman; specialists are referred to other works of his.
3. W. H. McNeill, *The Rise of the West.* Chicago, 1963, 193.
4. B. Raphael Sealey, "Greek Civilization, Ancient, 2," *EB,* 1974, 8:335.
5. McNeill, in *Rise of the West,* 198–99, writes eloquently and persuasively about the ethos of equality and civic-mindedness that he believes attended the invention of the phalanx, but some authorities do not accept such arguments.
6. Sealey, "Greek Civilization," 8:338.
7. Ibid., 343.
8. Ibid., 344.
9. Raphael Sealey, *A History of the Greek City-States, 700–338 B.C.* Berkeley and Los Angeles, 1976, 164–66.
10. Albright, *From the Stone Age to Christianity,* 336.
11. McNeill, *Rise of the West,* 203.

12. Herodotus, *History,* Rawlinson trans. New York, 1947, 188–89.
13. Karl A. Wittfogel, *Oriental Despotism.* 1957; reprint, New York, 1981, 355.
14. Herodotus, *History,* bk. 7, 396.
15. Russell Meiggs, "Greek Civilization, Ancient, 3," *EB,* 1974, 8:356.
16. T. Cuyler Young, Jr., "Iran, History of, 1," *EB,* 1974, 9:835.
17. Richard McKeon, ed., *The Basic Works of Aristotle.* New York, 1968. *Politics,* bk. 2.
18. Ibid., bk. 3, chap. 7.
19. Ibid., bk. 7, chap. 7.
20. Ibid., bk. 3, chap. 14.
21. F. E. Peters, *The Harvest of Hellenism: A History of the Near East from Alexander the Great to the Triumph of Christianity.* New York, 1970, 59.

Chapter 3

1. Peters, *Harvest of Hellenism,* 170.
2. Ibid., 183–84.
3. Ibid., 187.
4. I have relied on Lily Ross Taylor, *Roman Voting Assemblies from the Hannibalic War to the Dictatorship of Caesar.* Ann Arbor, 1966.
5. Ibid., 5.
6. M. Cary and H. H. Scullard, *A History of Rome,* 3d ed. New York, 1975, 67.
7. Ibid., 174.
8. Muller, *Freedom in the Ancient World,* 256, 264.
9. Paraphrased by John P. V. Dacre Balsdon, "Rome, Ancient, 2," *EB,* 15:1096.
10. Cary and Scullard, *History,* 197.
11. E. Badian, "Rome, Ancient, 3," *EB,* 1974, 15:1100.
12. Peters, *Harvest of Hellenism,* 332–33.
13. Badian, "Rome, Ancient," 236.
14. Carry and Scullard, *History,* 236.
15. Ibid., 237–38.
16. Edward Togo Salmon, "Rome, Ancient, 4," *EB,* 1974, 15:1107.
17. Muller, *Freedom in the Ancient World,* 250–51.
18. Peters, *Harvest of Hellenism,* 387.
19. Salmon, "Rome, Ancient," 1107–8.
20. Peters, *Harvest of Hellenism,* 392.
21. Cary and Scullard, *History,* 450.
22. Peters, *Harvest of Hellenism,* 392.
23. Salmon, "Rome, Ancient," 1111.
24. Ibid.
25. Cary and Scullard, *History,* 450.
26. Mason Hammond, contribution to *Encyclopedia of World History,* rev. 3d ed., 117.
27. Peters, *Harvest of Hellenism,* 610.
28. Cary and Scullard, *History,* 530.
29. Fergus Millar, *The Emperor in the Roman World (31 B.C.–A.D. 337).* Ithaca, 1977, 619.
30. Margaret Deanesly, *A History of Early Medieval Europe from 476 to 911,* 2d ed. London, 1960, 150.

31. Kurt Raaflaub, "Freiheit in Athen und Rom: ein Beispiel divergierender politischer Begriffsentwicklung in der Antike," *Historische Zeitschrift*, 238 (1984):565–66.
32. Malcolm Todd, "Germanic Peoples," *Encyclopedia Americana*, 1988, 12:583–84; Courtenay Edward Stevens, "Germany" (in part), *EB*, 1986, 20:44–46. Tacitus, in his *Germania*, distinguished sharply between the Germanic invaders and the indigenous Celts, but modern scholars see little cultural difference.
33. Henry Bradley, *The Goths*. New York, 1903, 13.

Chapter 4

1. L. A. Siedentop, "Liberalism: The Christian Connection," *TLS*, 24–30 March 1989, 308.
2. John E. E. D. Acton, *The History of Freedom and Other Essays*. London, 1909, 25–26.
3. Ibid., 34.
4. Lynn White, Jr., in *The Pirenne Thesis*, ed. Alfred F. Havighurst. Boston, 1958, 83
5. Under the three-field (or three-course) system, the common land was divided into three parts of which one or two (but usually one) in rotation lay fallow each year, the rest being cultivated. Thus one-third rather than one-half (as in the two-field system) went to fallow.
6. Lynn White, Jr., 82–83. The three inventions are singled out by Lefebvre des Noëttes, whom White cites, and then he adds the observations on fuel.
7. Louis Bréhier, *Le monde byzantin*, vol. 2, *Les institutions de l'empire byzantin*. Paris, 1949, 182.
8. Ibid., 582–83.
9. Alan Cameron, *Circus Factions: Blues and Greens at Rome and Byzantium*. Oxford, 1976, 308–11.
10. Bréhier, *Les institutions*, 582.
11. George Ostrogorsky, *History of the Byzantine State*, rev. ed. Translated by Joan Hussey. New Brunswick, 1969, 106.
12. Chapter 11 deals with the relation of freedom to India, China, and Japan.
13. The similarities are analyzed in a provocative, controversial, and illuminating manner in Wittfogel, *Oriental Despotism*. Recent Soviet historians have offered as alternative terms "state mode of production" and "politarism," but the meanings greatly overlap if they are not the same. See Donald W. Treadgold, "Soviet Historians' Views on the 'Asiatic Mode of Production,' " *Acta Slavica Japonica* 5 (1987); Chinese translation in *Shixuelilun* (Beijing) 2 (June 1987).
14. Philip Curtin, Steven Feierman, Leonard Thompson, and Jan Vansina, *African History*. Boston, 1978, 30–36, 81–84, 157–61.
15. Marc Bloch, *Feudal Society*. Translated by L. A. Manyon. Chicago, 1961, chap. 28.
16. The Christian church used two adjectives to distinguish itself from bodies of heretics: catholic, meaning universal, and orthodox, meaning correct in doctrine. The former term came to be most often used in the West, the latter term in the East.
17. The Merovingian dynasty was named after Clovis's grandfather, Merovech, who led a Frankish force against the Huns at the decisive battle of the Catalaunian Fields in 451.
18. However, Arabs remained north of the Pyrenees for some time. About 890 they established a robbers' nest at Le Freinet (near Fréjus on the Riviera) and from there

raided north up the Rhone valley and into Switzerland until the count of Provence captured Le Freinet in 972.

19. Avant-propos of Henri Berr in Bréhier, *Les institutions*, viii.
20. Muller, *Freedom in the Western World*, 40.
21. Joseph F. O'Callaghan, "Spain, History of, 2," *EB*, 1974, 17:406.
22. Quoted in Bloch, *Feudal Society*, 160.
23. Ibid., 116.
24. Ibid., 171–72.
25. Maurice Keen, *The Pelican History of Medieval Europe*. Harmondsworth, Middlesex, England, 1969, 49.
26. Bloch, *Feudal Society*, 445–46.
27. Ibid., 382.
28. Ibid., 389.
29. Quoted in ibid., 451.
30. Ibid., 452.
31. Ostrogorsky, *History*, 106–7.
32. Deanesly, *History of Early Medieval Europe*, 409.
33. Dmitri Obolensky, *The Byzantine Commonwealth*. New York, 1971, chap. 2.
34. Warren T. Treadgold, "The Revival of Byzantine Learning and the Revival of the Byzantine State," *American Historical Review* 84 (1979):1245–66.
35. Cyril Mango, *Byzantium: The Empire of New Rome*. New York, 1980, 136.
36. Imre Boba has persuasively argued that the Moravia to which Cyril and Methodius went was not present-day central Czechoslovakia but the region around Sirmium, present-day Sremska Mitrovica in Serbia. See Boba, *Moravia's History Reconsidered: A Reinterpretation of Medieval Sources*. The Hague, 1971.
37. Bréhier, *Les institutions*, 20–22.
38. Obolensky, *Byzantine Commonwealth*, 117.
39. Ibid.
40. Ibid., 308.
41. Marshall G. S. Hodgson, *The Venture of Islam*, 3 vols. Chicago, 1974, 1:206–8.
42. F. E. Peters, *Allah's Commonwealth: A History of Islam in the Near East*, A.D. 600–1100. New York, 1973, 84–85.
43. Hodgson, *Venture*, 2:120.
44. Peters, *Allah's Commonwealth*, 576.
45. Ibid., 104. An interesting parallel is to be found in the Russian notion of "Moscow the Third Rome," expounded by a monk of Pskov around 1500, and other aspects of the ideological stance adopted by Ivan III, who simultaneously anathematized the Byzantines and took them as his model for how to rule.
46. Peters, *Allah's Commonwealth*, 140.
47. Ibid., 159. The institutional consequences of the invention of paper on the growth of bureaucracies worldwide deserve study and reflection.
48. Ibid., 267–68.
49. Fazlur Rahman, "Islam," *EB*, 1974, 9:920.
50. Peters, *Allah's Commonwealth*, 515.
51. Rahman, "Islam," 921.
52. Hodgson, *Venture*, 2:119–20.
53. Ibid., 916.

54. Ibid.
55. Peters, *Allah's Commonwealth*, 588.
56. Wittfogel, *Oriental Despotism*, 85.
57. Peters, *Allah's Commonwealth*, 745.
58. Hodgson, *Venture*, 2:346.
59. Ibid., 2:434.
60. Ibid., 3:439.

Chapter 5

1. Donald MacGillivray Nicol, "Byzantine Empire," *EB*, 1974, 3:564.
2. See chapter 11 of this volume.
3. See the illuminating essay by F. W. Mote, "The Growth of Chinese Despotism," *Oriens Extremus* 8 (August 1961):1–41, in which Hsiao is quoted.
4. Edwin O. Reischauer and John K. Fairbank, *East Asia: The Great Tradition*. Boston, 1960, 524.
5. Quoted in Z. N. Brooke, *A History of Europe from 911 to 1198*. London, 1960, 177.
6. Bloch, *Feudal Society*, 380–82.
7. The "phantom emperors" held the title when the empire had lapsed in fact; from 924 to 962 the title itself disappeared.
8. *Hamlet*, act 4, sc. 5.
9. William L. Langer, ed., *New Illustrated Encyclopedia of World History*. 2 vols., New York, 1975 (hereafter cited as *NIEWH*), 1:227.
10. See page 87.
11. Quoted in Brooke, *911 to 1198*, 172.
12. Langer, *NIEWH*, 1:239.
13. Brooke, *911 to 1198*, 505.
14. Langer, *NIEWH*, 1:213–14.
15. F. W. Maitland, *The Constitutional History of England*. Cambridge, 1948, 91.
16. C. H. Haskins, "England and Sicily in the Twelfth Century," *English Historical Review* 27 (July–October 1911):664–65. He writes that we must bear in mind "the possibility of a connexion between [the] Domesday Book and the fiscal registers which the south had inherited from its Byzantine and Saracen rulers." But he clearly has in mind more than a possibility.
17. Wittfogel, *Oriental Despotism*, 214.
18. Langer, *NIEWH*, 1:219–20.
19. Henrik Enander, "Scandinavia, History of, 1," *EB*, 1974, 16:307.
20. Obolensky, *Byzantine Commonwealth*, 163.
21. Ostrogorsky, *History of the Byzantine State*, 371.
22. Ibid., 375.
23. See ibid., long footnote on 404.
24. See the lengthy account with a critical examination of the sources in Obolensky, *Byzantine Commonwealth*, chap. 6.
25. Ibid., 235.
26. Hodgson, *Venture*, 2:42.
27. Langer, *NIEWH*, 1:283.
28. Carl Brockelmann, *History of the Islamic Peoples*, trans. New York, 1947, 195.

29. Ibid., 240.
30. Langer, *NIEWH*, 1:222.
31. J. G. Edwards, "Edward I's Castle-Building in Wales," *Proceedings of the British Academy* 32 (1946).
32. Colin Platt, *Medieval England: A Social History and Archeology from the Conquest to AD 1600*. London, 1978, 102.
33. Previté-Orton, *A History of Europe from 1198 to 1378*, 3d ed. London, 1951, 119.
34. Ibid., 264.
35. O'Callaghan, "Spain, History of," 411.
36. *Hansa* meant a group or association. The term came to be applied to a group of largely North German towns in the Baltic that was important from the thirteenth century to the fifteenth century. The league was formally dissolved much later.
37. Obolensky, *Byzantine Commonwealth*, 249.
38. Ibid., 252.
39. Ostrogorsky, *History of the Byzantine State*, 514.
40. Hodgson, *Venture*, 2:416.
41. Previté-Orton, *1198 to 1378*, 136.
42. Muller, *Freedom in the Western World*, 14.
43. Barnette Miller, *The Palace School of Muhammad the Conqueror*. Cambridge, Mass., 1941, 71.
44. Steven Runciman, *Byzantine Civilization*. New York, 1956, 163. He notes that there is no evidence that the characters of eunuchs were warped by their physical impairment. Over the long expanse of Byzantine history, he declares, they were no more corrupt or less patriotic than "their completer fellows."
45. Wittfogel, *Oriental Despotism*, 357.
46. Muller, *Freedom in the Western World*, 68.
47. George H. Sabine, *A History of Political Theory*. New York, 1946, 218–19.
48. Bloch, *Feudal Society*, xviii. The earliest example Bloch could find of the use of the terms *féodal* and *féodalité* to cover society as a whole was in a book published posthumously in 1727 entitled *Lettres historiques sur les Parlemens*, written by Boulainvilliers, but it was Montesquieu who gave the term currency in the sense mentioned.
49. Bloch, *Feudal Society*, chaps. 21, 26.
50. Sabine, *History of Political Theory*, 220.
51. John Dickinson's preface to *The Statesman's Book of John of Salisbury*. New York, 1927, xxv.
52. Ibid. (Policratus), 65.
53. Sabine, *History of Political Theory*, 255.
54. Ibid., 258. See page 102.
55. Ibid., 307.
56. Dante Alighieri, quoted in Muller, *Freedom in the Western World*, 64–65.

Chapter 6

1. The name was taken from *Jacque*, the "by-name of a peasant," in turn derived from the word for a peasant's short tunic.
2. W. T. Waugh, *A History of Europe from 1378 to 1494*. London, 1949, 19.
3. Ibid., 37.

4. Ibid., 97.
5. Paul Cram, in *NIEWH*, 1:322.
6. Waugh, *1378 to 1494*, 404.
7. Norman Davies, *Heart of Europe: A Short History of Poland*. Oxford, Eng., 1984, 292.
8. Hans Roos, "Poland" (in part), *EB*, 1986, 25:924.
9. Waugh, *1378 to 1494*, 409.
10. C. A. Macartney, "Eastern Europe," in the *New Cambridge Modern History*, vol 1. Cambridge, Eng., 1957, 382–83.
11. Waugh, *1378 to 1494*, 380.
12. Ibid., 387.
13. Such is the finding of Ralph E. Giesey, *If Not, Not: The Oath of the Aragonese and the Legendary Laws of Sobrarde*. Princeton, 1968. The book is a fascinating piece of detective work.
14. H. G. Koenigsberger, "Spain, History of, 4," *EB*, 1974, 17:421.
15. Henrik Enander, "Scandinavia, History of, 1," *EB*, 1974, 16:312.
16. Obolensky, *Byzantine Commonwealth*, 258.
17. Waugh, *1378 to 1494*, 437.
18. Obolensky, *Byzantine Commonwealth*, 319.
19. J. L. I. Fennell, *The Emergence of Moscow, 1304–1359*. Berkeley, 1968, 14.
20. Muller, *Freedom in the Western World*, 282.
21. Quoted in ibid., 284.
22. W. E. Lunt, *History of England*. New York, 1946, 372–73.
23. Ibid., 375.
24. Ibid., 380–83.
25. J. Russell Major, *Representative Government in Early Modern France*. New Haven, 1980, quotes the whole statement, 183–84.
26. Waugh, *1378 to 1494*, 264.
27. Muller, in *Freedom in the Western World*, suggests the mixed blessing that this event brought when he writes that Savonarola "had delusions as a prophet, and so had helped to bring upon the city the French King Charles VIII, a dwarfish half-wit in whom he saw the Lord's instrument for the salvation of Italy" (127).
28. Ibid., 292.
29. A. J. Grant, *A History of Europe from 1494 to 1610*. London, 1954, 342.
30. It was still Capetian, by descent through a second son, Charles of Valois, brother of Philip IV, when the Salic Law excluded royal descent through a woman in the succession of 1328.
31. Grant, *1494 to 1610*, 488.
32. W. F. Reddaway, *A History of Europe from 1610 to 1715*. London, 1959, 101.
33. Crane Brinton, in *NIEWH*, 1:465.
34. Grant, *1494 to 1610*, 20.
35. Koenigsberger, "Spain, History of, 4," 17:423.
36. Paul Cram, in *NIEWH*, 1:301.
37. Reddaway, *1610 to 1715*, 24.
38. Waugh, *1378 to 1494*, 325.
39. Grant, *1494 to 1610*, 86.
40. Ibid., 114.
41. Ibid., 493.

42. Reddaway, *1610 to 1715*, 39.
43. The name of a region not a city, since negotiations took place between the emperor and representatives of Sweden at Osnabrück and between him and representatives of France at Münster (thirty miles separated the two towns).
44. Reddaway, *1610 to 1715*, 199.
45. Ibid., 168.
46. Norman Davies, *God's Playground: A History of Poland*, 2 vols. New York, 1982, 1:323. See the fine diagram on 324–25.
47. James Bryce, *The Holy Roman Empire*. London, 1913, 250.
48. Davies, *God's Playground*, 334.
49. Ibid., 212.
50. Oscar Halecki, *Borderlands of Western Civilization*, New York, 1952, 168–72.
51. Ibid., 339. The Confederation of Warsaw in 1573 had included the entire Sejm.
52. C. A. Macartney, "Hungary, History of," *EB*, 1974, 9:33.
53. Grant, *1494 to 1610*, 11.
54. Langer, *NIEWH*, 1:439.
55. Obolensky, *Byzantine Commonwealth*, 369.
56. Carl Brockelmann, *History of the Islamic Peoples*. New York, 1947, 295.
57. Bernard Lewis, *The Arabs in History*. New York, 1967, 165.
58. Obolensky, *Byzantine Commonwealth*, 365.
59. The terms boyars *(boiare)* and gentry *(dvorianstvo)* changed their meaning considerably over the centuries. See the articles in the *Modern Encyclopedia of Russian and Soviet History:* Joseph T. Fuhrmann, "Absolutism"; Paul Dukes, "Nobility of Russia"; Richard Hellie, "Dvoriane"; Robert O. Crummey, "Boiar."
60. I am aware of the substantial scholarship that shows how far Peter fell short of doing all he wished to do.
61. George H. Sabine, *A History of Political Theory*. New York, 1946, 333.
62. Muller, *Freedom in the Western World*, 208.
63. James A. Michener, *Poland*. New York, 1983, 189–90.
64. Muller, *Freedom in the Western World*, 160–69.
65. An authoritative recent examination of the question of who the author was concludes that he was Philippe du Plessis-Mornay (1549–1623), a diplomat, soldier, and later adviser to Henri de Navarre (Henry IV). Julian H. Franklin, *Constitutionalism and Resistance in the Sixteenth Century*. New York, 1969, 139.
66. Abbreviated text of the *Vindiciae*, found in ibid., 149.
67. Sabine, *History of Political Theory*, 475.
68. Muller, *Freedom in the Western World*, 224–25.
69. Grant, *1494 to 1610*, 381.
70. This takes Switzerland to be a medieval phenomenon dating to the League of Three Forest Cantons in 1291, but "federal government" is not the best description of the resulting association for some centuries thereafter.
71. Quoted in Grant, *1494 to 1610*, 424.

Chapter 7

1. Muller, *Freedom in the Western World*, 290.
2. See chapter 11 of this volume.

3. So J. A. Sharpe argues in *Early Modern England: A Social History, 1550–1760*. London, 1987, 30–39.
4. Ibid., 304.
5. Ibid., 306.
6. Crane Brinton, in *NIEWH*, 1:454.
7. Muller, *Freedom in the Western World*, 307.
8. Lung, *History of England*, 468.
9. Muller, *Freedom in the Western World*, 308.
10. Sir George Clark, *English History: A Survey*. Oxford, 1971, 356–57.
11. Lunt, *History of England*, 483–86; Clark, *English History*, 351.
12. Clark, *English History*, 352.
13. France and England would once again be pitted against each other in war during most of the period, from 1793 to 1815.
14. Modern medicine has suggested that George III actually suffered from porphyria rather than insanity.
15. Muller, *Freedom in the Western World*, 352.
16. R. R. Palmer, *The Age of the Democratic Revolution: A Political History of Europe and America, 1760–1800*, 2 vols. Princeton, 1959, 1:41.
17. Ibid.
18. Major, *Representative Government in France*, 667.
19. Ibid., 630.
20. Ibid., 672.
21. Montesquieu, *Esprit des Lois*, Book 11, 6, translated by Thomas Nugent.
22. Palmer, *Democratic Revolution*, 1:94.
23. It is true that consent of the medieval States General and local estates had been assumed to be necessary for a time, especially from about 1350 to 1450, but no right to do so had reached the level of law or political theory.
24. Emile, as quoted in John Morley, *Rousseau*, 2 vols. London, 1873, 2:224–25.
25. Muller, *Freedom in the Western World*, 389.
26. M. Reinhard, *Religion, révolution et contre-révolution*. Paris, 1985, 173. The *culte décadaire* related to the replacement of the seven-day week by the ten-day week, or *décade*, another innovation that did not last.
27. Quoted in Sabine, *History of Political Theory*, 593.
28. John D. Hicks, George E. Mowry, and Robert E. Burke, *The Federal Union*. Boston, 1970, 203.
29. Palmer, *Democratic Revolution*, 1:223–24.
30. Ibid., 1:235.
31. W. F. Reddaway, *A History of Europe from 1715 to 1814*. London, 1959, 105.
32. William Harvey Maehl, *Germany in Western Civilization*. University, Ala., 1979, 208.
33. Editors, "Germany, History of," *EB* 1974, 8:94.
34. Maehl, *Germany*, 251.
35. Ibid., 252.
36. "Carolingian" here is an adjective derived from Carolus, Latin for Charles; it has nothing to do with the dynasty of Charlemagne, which has the same etymology.
37. Gudmund Sandvik, "Scandinavia, History of," *EB*, 1974, 16:317.
38. Quoted in Davies, *God's Playground*, 1:367.
39. Reddaway, *1715 to 1814*, 272.

40. Davies, *God's Playground*, 2:143.
41. C. A. Macartney, "Hungary, History of," *EB*, 1974, 9:35.
42. Brockelmann, *History of the Islamic Peoples*, 335.
43. Palmer, *Democratic Revolution*, 2:572.

Chapter 8

1. Reddaway, *1715 to 1814*, 174.
2. Ibid., 479.
3. Maehl, *Germany*, 312.
4. R. R. Palmer, *A History of the Modern World*, 2d ed. New York, 1956, 502.
5. Ibid., 579.
6. Joel Colton in "France," *EA*, 1988, 11:804.
7. Technically there was no such city as Budapest. Buda and Pest were separate, and indeed Pest was the only one of the two to be active in the March days of 1848.
8. Hajo Holborn, *A History of Modern Germany, 1840–1945*. Princeton, 1982, 148.
9. Gordon A. Craig, *Germany, 1866–1945*. New York, 1978, 29.
10. Fritz Fellner, "Austria," *EB*, 1986, 14:515.
11. Robert A. Kann, *A History of the Habsburg Empire, 1526–1918*. Berkeley, 1977, 454.
12. C. A. Macartney and George Barany, "Hungary," *EB*, 1986, 20:765.
13. Hungary's ability to vault from postfeudal monarchy through communism toward democracy was arrestingly indicated by the invitation extended in late 1989 to Otto von Habsburg, who would be king-emperor if Austria-Hungary still existed, to stand for the presidency of the new Hungary. (He declined.)
14. The writer was Friedrich Nietzsche; the quotation here is a paraphrase of Nietzsche by Craig, in *Germany*, 35.
15. Quoted in ibid., 45.
16. Ibid., 273.
17. Ibid., 292.
18. In the Alsatian town of Zabern (Saverne), a young Prussian lieutenant made insulting references to the people of Alsace; in the ensuing hullabaloo, a succession of governmental blunders led to a refusal to answer an interpellation, hence the vote.
19. Craig, *Germany*, 390.
20. Quoted in ibid., 415.
21. Ralph Flenley, *Modern German History*. London, 1968, 369.
22. Holborn, *History of Modern Germany*, 700.
23. Craig, *Germany*, 543.
24. Ibid., 763–64.
25. Richard C. Eichenberg, "The Federal Republic of Germany," in *Politics in Western Europe*. Stanford, 1988, 161.
26. Walter Dirks writing in *Frankfurter Hefte*, August 1953, as quoted in Richard Hiscocks, *Democracy in Western Germany*. London, 1957, 52.
27. Stanley G. Payne, *A History of Spain and Portugal*, 2 vols. Madison, 1973, 2:422.
28. Ibid., 428.
29. Ibid., 446.
30. Ibid., 456.

31. Ibid., 467.
32. Ibid., 640.
33. Ibid., 661.
34. Payne writes, "Even the Republican constitution of 1911 was less democratic, because of its sectarian anticlerical provisions" (ibid., 518).
35. Ibid., 572.
36. Quote, without attribution, is from Sir J. A. R. Marriott, A *History of Europe, 1815–1939.* London, 1960, 103.
37. Marino Berengo, "Italy" (in part), *EB*, 1986, 22:224.
38. George Martin, *The Red Shirt and the Cross of Savoy.* New York, 1969, 659.
39. See Paul Johnson, *Modern Times.* New York, 1985, 56–58.
40. Ibid., 100, quoting Ivone Kirkpatrick, *Mussolini: A Study of a Demagogue.* London, 1965, 144.
41. Jorgen Weibull, "Denmark," *EB*, 1986, 17:239.
42. Johnson, *Modern Times*, 604.

Chapter 9

1. Quoted in J. A. Sharpe, *Early Modern England: A Social History, 1550–17760.* London, 1987, 350.
2. Muller, *Freedom in the Western World*, 313.
3. Quoted in R. J. White, *Europe in the Eighteenth Century.* New York, 1965, 277.
4. Clark, *English History*, 430.
5. Ibid., 492.
6. Ibid., 514.
7. Johnson, *Modern Times*, 601.
8. Gerald A. Dorfman, "Great Britain," in Dorfman and Peter J. Duignan, *Politics in Western Europe.* Stanford, 1988, 47.
9. John D. Hicks, George E. Mowry, and Robert E. Burke, *The Federal Union*, 5th ed. Boston, 1970, 306.
10. Alexis de Tocqueville, *Democracy in America.* pt. 1, 1. It was first published in 1835 and 1840.
11. Ibid., bk. 4, pt. 2.
12. Hugh Brogan, *Longman's History of the American People.* London, 1985, 320.
13. "Apparent," because the so-called "Redeemers," by practicing widespread intimidation and persuasion backed with money, kept many Negroes from voting for Tilden.
14. Samuel Eliot Morison, *The Oxford History of the American People*, vol. 3 (1869–1963). New York, 1972, 62.
15. Ibid., 58–59.
16. John D. Hicks, George E. Mowry, and Robert E. Burke, *The American Nation*, 4th ed. New York, 1965, 209.
17. Muller, *Freedom in the Modern World*, 77.
18. Hicks, Mowry, and Burke, *American Nation*, 375.
19. In Schenk v. the United States.
20. A 1962 poll of seventy-five leading American scholars by the *New York Times Magazine* yielded the judgment that there had been only two presidential failures: Grant and Harding. Ibid., 441.

21. Ibid., 601.
22. Morison, *Oxford History of the American People,* vol. 3, 340.
23. Johnson, *Modern Times;* the title of chapter 18.

Chapter 10

1. Piotr S. Wandycz, *The Lands of Partitioned Poland, 1795–1918.* Seattle, 1974, 76.
2. Michael T. Florinsky, *Russia: A History and An Interpretation,* 2 vols. New York, 1970, 2:706.
3. Davis, *God's Playground,* 2:332–33.
4. Ibid., 64.
5. Wandycz, *Partitioned Poland,* 229.
6. Ibid., 317–18.
7. Ibid., 330.
8. Davies, *God's Playground,* 2:396.
9. Norman Davies, *Heart of Europe: A Short History of Poland.* Oxford, 1984, 123.
10. Ibid., 125.
11. Ibid., 425.
12. Ibid., 463.
13. Davies, *Heart of Europe,* 67. The dead of Katyn Forest (near Smolensk) were but part of a total of over fifteen thousand Polish prisoners who disappeared from Soviet captivity in spring 1940. Few doubt that the Soviets killed them all.
14. Ibid., 78.
15. Ibid., 489.
16. From 1938 on, some five thousand, "practically the entire active membership of the party," were killed. Ibid., 545.
17. Ibid., 548, 553.
18. The Armenian church was named for Saint Gregory the Illuminator, reputedly responsible for conversion of the country to Christianity about A.D. 300. It became Monophysite after the Council of Chalcedon (451) and nominally remains so.
19. Charles and Barbara Jelavich, *The Establishment of the Balkan National States.* Seattle, 1977, 58.
20. Ibid., 124.
21. The Bessarabian coast became Romanian in 1856; it was given to Russia again in 1878.
22. Kann, *History of the Habsburg Empire,* 418.
23. Penfield Roberts, in *NIEWH,* 2:944.
24. Hugh Seton-Watson, *Eastern Europe between the Wars, 1918–1941,* 3d ed. Hamden, Conn., 1962, 174.
25. Joseph Rothschild, *East Central Europe between the Two World Wars.* Seattle, 1974, 216.
26. Seton-Watson, *Eastern Europe,* 224.
27. Ibid., 236.
28. Rothschild, *East Central Europe,* 278.
29. Ibid., 291. It needs to be remembered that the Soviet "land reform" (or rather spontaneous seizure and distribution of land in 1917) was reversed with a vengeance after 1928 when collectivization began.

30. *Adevarul* (The truth) of 25 February 1937, as quoted in ibid., 322.
31. Seton-Watson, *Eastern Europe,* 216.
32. C. and B. Jelavich, *Balkan National States,* 315.
33. Ibid., 319.
34. Malcolm Edward Yapp, "Turkey and Ancient Anatolia," *EB,* 28:931ff.
35. See Jeffrey Brooks, *When Russia Learned to Read: Literacy and Popular Literature, 1861–1917.* Princeton, 1985.

Chapter 11

1. *Oxford History of India,* 3d ed. 1961, 33.
2. D. P. Singhal, *A History of the Indian People.* London, 1983, 28.
3. Romila Thapar, "India" (in part), *EB,* 1986, 21:30.
4. Author uncertain. One might note that two of the other great world religions may be similarly described: Judaism and Christianity, both of which originated in Palestine but were virtually nonexistent there for many centuries. Buddhism proceeded to spread to China, Korea, Japan, Southeast Asia, Tibet, and Mongolia.
5. A. L. Basham, *The Wonder That Was India,* 3d rev. ed. New York, 1968, 324–25.
6. *Oxford History of India,* 8.
7. Hinduism is a term coined by Westerners to describe the ancient religious system of India, out of which a complex pantheon and the theory and practice of the caste system emerged. Its main thread comes from the Aryans who entered the peninsula in the second millennium B.C., and in the sixth century B.C. it was challenged by two new major sects: Jainism and Buddhism.
8. Thapar, "India," 48.
9. Ibid., 49.
10. August von Haxthausen, *Studies on the Interior of Russia.* Chicago, 1972, 250. Adapted by S. Frederick Starr from *Studien über die inneren Zustände . . . Russlands,* 3 vols. Hanover and Berlin, 1847–52. He was referring to Russia, but in India the situation was similar. Karl Marx and others noted the similarities between Indian and Russian society; the differences of course were great and obvious.
11. Philip B. Calkins, "India" (in part), *EB,* 21:51.
12. Shanti Prasad Varma, "India" (in part), 74.
13. *Oxford History of India,* 335. The tone is triumphal, but the facts are correct.
14. Cornwallis's aim, to cite a recent study, was "to stabilise a hereditary landed aristocracy," a notion according both with Whig ideas of the sanctity of property and French Physiocratic doctrine that land was the source of all wealth (propagated in India by Philip Francis of the Calcutta Council). C. A. Bayly, in *New Cambridge History of India,* vol. 2, pt. 1 (1988):65.
15. *Oxford History of India,* 535–36. This was the central act of the British policy praised by Karl Marx as "blowing up" the economic basis of the Indian village community, thus producing "the greatest, and, to speak the truth, the only *social* revolution ever heard of in Asia" (New York *Tribune,* 22 June 1853).
16. Curiously paralleling to a considerable extent the geography of the post-1947 division of the subcontinent between India and Pakistan.
17. T. G. Percival Spear, "India" (in part), *EB,* 21:86.
18. Karl Marx (see n. 10) therefore exaggerated the extent of British-introduced change.

19. Ibid., 88.
20. Spear, "India," 95.
21. One with a Muslim majority, the other with a Bihari- and Oriya-speaking Hindu majority, thus neither with a majority of Bengali Hindus—who led the movement nationwide.
22. Johnson, *Modern Times*, 472.
23. Ibid., 474, 770. Four different recent estimates over that range are cited. This was one instance when estimates made at the time were greater (one to two million) than proved to be the reality, but the suffering was on a gigantic scale: "a procession of terrified Hindus and Sikhs, for instance, stretched for fifty-seven miles [eastward] from the West Punjab."
24. Singhal, *History of the Indian People*, 408.
25. Ibid., 413.
26. Robert L. Hardgrave, Jr., and Stanley A. Kochanek, *India: Government and Politics in a Developing Nation*, 4th ed. New York, 1986 (but the sentence was evidently in the 3d ed., written by Hardgrave alone), 1.
27. Quoted by Ainslee Embree in "Human Rights in South Asia: The Conflict of Value Systems," in *Cross-Cultural Aspects of Human Rights: Asia*, ed. Linda Lum. Washington, D.C., 1988, 18.
28. Karl A. Wittfogel, *Oriental Despotism*, rev. ed. New Haven, 1959, 27.
29. L. Carrington Goodrich, "China" (in part), *EB*, 1986, 16:66.
30. Wittfogel, *Oriental Despotism*, 33.
31. Cho-yun Hsu, "China" (in part), *EB*, 1986, 16:68.
32. Edwin O. Reischauer and John K. Fairbank, eds., *East Asia: The Great Tradition*. Boston, 1960, 54.
33. Hsu, "China," 69.
34. Not to be confused with Ch'in.
35. Hsu, "China," 72.
36. Ed., "China," 72.
37. Nevertheless, in the Later Han period eunuchs were permitted to adopt sons who could inherit their noble titles.
38. In Reischauer and Fairbank, *East Asia*, Reischauer writes: China was "already beginning to develop a modern type of civil service based on merit. It was almost two thousand years before the West adopted a system similar to, and perhaps inspired by, that of the Chinese" (107).
39. Confucianism (from K'ung-fu-tzu, traditional dates: 551–479 B.C.) began as a teaching of ethics carried into the political realm; in the Han period, with Legalist borrowings, it was given an authoritarian tinge original Confucian teaching lacked. Taoism was a congeries of religious, philosophical, and protoscientific ideas traced to Lao-tzu and Chuang-tzu of Chou times. Legalism was a school associated with the Ch'in that stressed law but as the fiat of the ruler, not a restraint on him or a protection of the citizen.
40. Erik Zürcher, "China" (in part), 83.
41. James T. C. Liu, "China" (in part), 102.
42. Both systems were thought to have existed in the Chou period. (The "well-field system" was so named from the fact that the Chinese character for "well," somewhat like #, yielded a pattern of eight [peasant, purportedly communal] fields around a

central [lord's] field.) K. C. Hsiao, *Chung-kuo cheng-chih ssu-hsiang shih*. Taipei, 1954, 503, as quoted in F. W. Mote, "The Growth of Chinese Despotism," *Oriens Extremus* (August 1961):13. But the Neo-Confucians and other Sung thinkers nevertheless reacted to the problems of their time by advocating greater power for the sovereign: "from the statesmen there came a force tending toward greater real power, and from the philosophers a force providing philosophical justification of that power. . . . [T]he Sung marked a turning point in the growth of despotism" (Mote, "Growth," 14, 16).

43. Liu, "China," 104.
44. Mote, "Growth," 18. See also Herbert Franke, "China" (in part), *EB,* 109.
45. Charles O. Hucker, "China" (in part), *EB,* 111.
46. Mote, "Growth," 26.
47. Chusei Suzuki, "China" (in part), *EB,* 118–19.
48. Wittfogel, *Oriental Despotism,* 435.
49. An attempt was made by Derk Bodde to evaluate Chou (and other) feudalism in China in a comparative context and with examination of differing theoretical views of Westerners in "Feudalism in China," in *Feudalism in History,* ed. Rushton Coulborn. Hamden, Conn., 1965, 49–92. However, it was based on a 1950 conference, and an updating would be highly desirable.
50. Taro Sakamoto, "Japan" (in part), *EB,* 1986, 22:305.
51. John Whitney Hall, *Japan: From Prehistory to Modern Times,* New York, 1970, 50, 46.
52. Sakamoto, "Japan," 306.
53. Ibid., 308.
54. Coulborn, *Feudalism in History,* pt. 3, 204–5. He makes the comparison with the later Kamakura shogunate, but the duality began earlier.
55. Hall, *Japan,* 69.
56. On the changing use of the term, see Peter Duus, *Feudalism in Japan.* New York, 1969, 45.
57. Hall, *Japan,* 78.
58. Duus, *Feudalism in Japan,* 49.
59. Edwin O. Reischauer, "Japanese Feudalism," in *Fedualism in History,* 31–32.
60. Reischauer, in *East Asia,* 555.
61. Hall, *Japan,* 78.
62. Ibid., 110.
63. Reischauer, in *East Asia,* 565.
64. Hall, *Japan,* 127.
65. Ibid., 129.
66. Reischauer, in *East Asia,* 581.
67. Duus, *Feudalism in Japan,* 81–82.
68. Kitajima Masamoto, "Japan" (in part), *EB,* 318.
69. He resigned the shogunate in 1605 but continued to rule behind the scenes.
70. Reischauer comments, "one can see how great was the Tokugawa peace if the Incident of the Forty-Seven Ronin was the most renowned event during a period of two centuries" (*East Asia,* 621).
71. Ibid., 642.
72. Duus, *Feudalism in Japan,* 106.
73. Marius B. Jansen, "Japan" (in part), *EB,* 326.
74. Ibid., 327.

Chapter 12

1. See Miguel León-Portilla, "Mesoamerica before 1519," in *Cambridge History of Latin America* (hereafter cited as *CHLA*), ed. Leslie Bethell, 7 vols., 1984, 1:19.
2. Pedro Carrasco, "The Political Economy of the Aztec and Inca States," in *The Inca and Aztec States, 1400–1800: Anthropology and History,* ed. George A. Collier, Renato I. Rosaldo, and John D. Wirth. New York, 1982, 27.
3. Ibid., 38.
4. Robert S. Chamberlain, in *NIEWH,* 1:382.
5. Leslie Bethell, "A Note on the Native American Population on the Eve of the European Invasions," in *CHLA,* 1:145–46.
6. Robert Jones Shafer writes that the conquest produced "a few hundred thousand Spaniards, about a million blacks carried from Africa in chains, and 30 to 50 million conquered Indians" (*A History of Latin America.* Lexington, Mass., 1978, 123).
7. Writes Benjamin Keen: "Cortés thus drew on Spanish medieval traditions of municipal autonomy to vest his disobedience with a cloak of legality" ("Latin America," *EB,* 22:817).
8. Shafer, *History of Latin America,* 85.
9. Charles I, the king of Spain, was also Charles V as Holy Roman Emperor.
10. Keen, "Latin America" (in part), 822.
11. Woodrow Borah, "The Spanish and Indian Law: New Spain," in Collier, Rosaldo, and Wirth, *Inca and Aztec States,* 270.
12. The literature bearing on both questions is immense and need not be cited here, but a titillating passage appears in Johnson's *Modern Times,* 148–62. One lineal descendant of the Hobson-Lenin school, which indicted imperialism for the ills of the Third World and credited it with no less than the postponement of the doom of world capitalism for decades by its profit to the metropolitan nations, is "dependency theory." It has had great influence on the study of Latin America in the United States (see n. 94 below).
13. Nathan Wachtel, "The Indian and the Spanish Conquest," in *CHLA,* 1:248.
14. J. H. Elliott, "Spain and America in the Sixteenth and Seventeenth Centuries," in *CHLA,* 1:292ff.
15. Keen, "Latin America," 824.
16. No formal tribunals existed in Brazil, though several lengthy inquisitorial investigations were conducted during the colonial period.
17. Quoted by David Bushnell, "The Independence of Spanish South America," in *CHLA,* 3:108.
18. Ferdinand assumed the Spanish throne briefly in 1808 but was almost at once forced by Napoleon to abdicate; he was restored to the throne only in March 1814 after Wellington liberated Spain.
19. Shafer, *History of Latin America,* 333.
20. In 1531 the Indian peasant Juan Diego reported an appearance of a brown-skinned Virgin Mary to him at Guadalupe Hidalgo, near Mexico City.
21. Shafer, *History of Latin America,* 311.
22. Timothy Anna, "The Independence of Mexico and Central America," in *CHLA,* 3:65.

23. David Bushnell and Neill Macaulay, *The Emergence of Latin America in the Nineteenth Century*. New York, 1988, 65.
24. Ibid.
25. In colonial Spanish America the *cabildo* was the town council, usually composed of Creoles, who had little power in government otherwise, and might have a dozen members. A *cabildo abierto* was not a continuing institution but a special meeting, called by the council or the governor, that assembled a few score of the local elite to deal with an emergency.
26. Keen, "Latin America," 825.
27. James Lockhart and Stuart B. Schwartz, *Early Latin America*. New York, 1983, 243.
28. Maria Luiza Marcílio, "The Population of Colonial Brazil," in *CHLA*, 1:54.
29. Frédéric Mauro, "Portugal and Brazil: Political and Economic Structures of Empire," in *CHLA*, 1:467.
30. Dauril Alden, "Late Colonial Brazil, 1750–1808," in *CHLA*, 2:613.
31. Keen, "Latin America," 826.
32. John J. Johnson and editor, "Latin America" (in part), *EB*, 832.
33. With the exceptions of British Honduras and Guiana, Dutch Surinam, French Guiana, not to mention the entire West Indies.
34. Bushnell and Macaulay, *Emergence*, 45.
35. Shafer, *History of Latin America*, 377.
36. Ibid., 434.
37. The importance of the restoration period is stressed by Michael C. Meyer and William L. Sherman, *The Course of Mexican History*, 2d ed. New York, 1983, 414.
38. Shafer, *History of Latin America*, 551.
39. The *Gran* is an addition by later historians to the name it bore in its time, to distinguish it from what became today's Colombia.
40. Malcolm Deas, "Colombia, Ecuador and Venezuela, c. 1880–1930," in *CHLA*, 5:663–70.
41. Shafer, *History of Latin America*, 480.
42. Bushnell and Macaulay, *Emergence*, 190.
43. Herbert S. Klein, "Bolivia from the War of the Pacific to the Chaco War, 1880–1932," in *CHLA*, 5:563–73.
44. Bushnell and Macaulay, *Emergence*, 245.
45. Peter F. Klarén, "The Origins of Modern Peru, 1880–1930, in *CHLA*, 5:587.
46. Ibid., 602.
47. Bushnell and Macaulay, *Emergence*, 108.
48. Harold Blakemore, "Chile from the War of the Pacific to the World Depression, 1880–1930," in *CHLA*, 5:500.
49. Ibid., 534.
50. Shafer, *History of Latin America*, 576.
51. John Lynch, "The River Plate Republics from Independence to the Paraguayan War," in *CHLA*, 3:617–18.
52. Shafer, *History of Latin America*, 388.
53. Bushnell and Macaulay, *Emergence*, 129. The slogan was gradually lengthened until it read "Death to the Vile, Filthy, Savage Unitarios."
54. Ibid., 228.
55. Ibid.

56. Johnson and editor, "Latin America," 834.
57. Paul H. Lewis, "Paraguay from the War of the Triple Alliance to the Chaco War, 1870–1932," in *CHLA*, 5:475.
58. Juan A. Oddone, "The Formation of Modern Uruguay, c. 1870–1930," in *CHLA*, 5:464.
59. Shafer, *History of Latin America*, 582.
60. The "moderating power" was "an invention of the French publicist Benjamin Constant." Emília Víotti da Costa, "Brazil: The Age of Reform, 1870–1889," in *CHLA*, 5:735. There was also a Brazilian positivist named Benjamin Constant; he was one of those who helped push the military to end the monarchy in 1889.
61. Shafer, *History of Latin America*, 422.
62. Víotti da Costa, "Brazil," 767–77.
63. The electorate quadrupled and still remained less than five hundred thousand in a population of over thirteen million. Boris Fausto, "Brazil: The Social and Political Structure of the First Republic, 1889–1930," in *CHLA*, 5:800.
64. Víotti da Costa, "Brazil," 777.
65. Shafer, *History of Latin America*, 528.
66. Lewis W. Bealer, Arthur S. Gelston, Jr., George I. Blanksten, and Rollie E. Poppino, "Brazil" (in part), *EB*, 15:207.
67. Shafer, *History of Latin America*, 537.
68. The term *interdict* meant suspension of the sacraments, a punishment used a number of times in medieval times to compel a ruler to submit to papal authority.
69. Shafer, *History of Latin America*, 695.
70. Thomas E. Skidmore and Peter H. Smith, *Modern Latin America*. New York, 1984, 242.
71. Meyer and Sherman, *Course of Mexican History*, 647.
72. Ibid., 651.
73. Ibid., 661.
74. Bushnell and Macaulay, *Emergence*, 264.
75. Ibid., 267.
76. Shafer, *History of Latin America*, 753.
77. Ibid.
78. Daniel H. Levine, "Venezuela: The Nature, Sources, and Prospects of Democracy," in *Democracy in Developing Countries*, vol. 4, *Latin America*, ed. Larry Diamond, Juan J. Linz, and Seymour Martin Lipset. Boulder, Colo., 1989, 247.
79. Ibid., 748.
80. Ibid., 787.
81. Ibid., 759.
82. Ibid., 764.
83. Ibid., 578.
84. Ibid., 722.
85. Shafer comments that "the Socialist party in Chile was different from those in many countries in including Trotskyite and Maoist communists and being more in favor of violence than the Chilean Communist party" (ibid., 724).
86. Ibid.
87. Ibid., 714. Shafer notes the charges that the United States was responsible and mentions the fact that anti-Allende officers thought the United States might sympa-

thize with a coup. He concludes, "no evidence has been found, however, that the United States played a direct role in the 1973 coup" (ibid., 728–29).
88. Arturo Valenzuela, "Chile: Origins, Consolidation, and Breakdown of a Democratic Regime," in Diamond, Linz, and Lipset, *Democracy in Developing Countries,* 159, 194.
89. Tulio Halperin Donghi, "Argentina" (in part), *EB,* 14:55.
90. Quoted in Skidmore and Smith, *Modern Latin America,* 91.
91. Shafer, *History of Latin America,* 801.
92. Ibid., 662.
93. Ibid., 666–67.
94. For a seminal statement of dependency theory, see Fernando Henrique Cardoso and Enzo Faletto, *Dependency and Development in Latin America.* Berkeley, 1979. It is clearly indebted to Marxian analytic assumptions and socialist political goals, though it would take us afield to assess exactly the extent of the debt. A related intellectual development is "liberation theology," for which the Peruvian Fr. Gustavo Gutiérrez is a central figure.
95. Shafer, *History of Latin America,* 805.
96. Johnson and editor, "Latin America" (in part), 842.

Conclusion

1. Allan Bloom, *The Closing of the American Mind.* New York, 1987, 75. I apologize to Bloom for ending this passage with my own, carefully bracketed, paraphrase of what he is getting at. I have reservations about the book but not about this passage.
2. *We* was written during the Russian civil war (1917–21) but could only be published much later. The book in turn may have had antecedents; Elizabeth Stenbock-Fermor suggests Jerome K. Jerome, but Zamiatin deserves credit enough.
3. This is a Marxian category present-day Marxist-Leninists either refuse to acknowledge, attempt to explain away, or strive to treat in a gingerly manner keeping it distant from any possibility that it can be equated or compared with socialism. See my article, "Soviet Historians and the 'Asiatic Mode of Production,'" *Acta Slavica Japonica* (Sapporo, Japan) 5 (1987); Chinese translation in *Shixuelilun* (Beijing, China), 1988. Non-Marxists need not be similarly embarrassed in dealing with it.
4. This goes also for dependency theory, world-systems analysis, "liberation theology," and other offshoots of Marxism.
5. See Wittfogel, *Oriental Despotism,* 204 and passim.
6. Veiled—as they never were in any feudal area!
7. Raymond Aron, *Democracy and Totalitarianism.* Translated by Valence Ionescu. New York, 1965, 213.
8. This might be a suitable point at which to pay tribute to Raymond Gastil's long-continuing periodic assessment of freedom country by country on a quantitative basis in the periodical *Freedom at Issue.* There is no pretense of analyzing the history of each country or the direction of change, if any; the assessment merely applies to the way things are at the moment, but by so doing provides us all with valuable service.
9. Hannah Arendt, *Between Past and Present.* New York, 1968, 140.
10. Ibid., 167.
11. Gabriel Masooane Tlaba so argues in his interesting though flawed *Politics and Freedom: Human Will and Action in the Thought of Hannah Arendt.* New York, 1965,

181. I myself do not place political freedom ahead; it is simply the chief subject of this book.

12. Quoted in C. A. Goodrich, *Select British Eloquence.* New York, 1963, 65.

13. The original reads "the mir," which means the village commune, but clearly the context suggests lifting the village institution to the national level.

14. N. G. Chernyshevskii in "Barskim krest'ianam ot ikh dobrozhelatelei poklon," *Polnoe sobranie sochinenii* 16:946–53. I am indebted to Alan Kimball, a leading specialist on Russian populism, for calling this passage to my attention.

15. T. S. Eliot, "Little Gidding," from *Four Quartets.*

16. Apologies go to Francis Fukuyama, whose article is referred to in the Introduction, when he says that it is the end—in a good sense, to be sure.

17. Aron, *Democracy and Totalitarianism,* 229. Aron declares the word "freedom" to be "so equivocal that it calls for a further study," but the meaning of the sentence quoted seems clear enough.

Index

About the Author

DONALD W. TREADGOLD, Professor of History, Jackson School of International Studies, University of Washington, is author of *The West in Russia and China*. Professor Treadgold has been both editor of the *Slavic Review* and President of the American Association for the Advancement of Slavic Studies.